Acclaim for *The Tombstone Tourist*

"Stanton's writing is infused with the passion and enthusiasm of a fan of both pop music and road tripping, and he buoys the project with eclectic anecdotes of the departed and incredible attention to detail."
—*Minneapolis Star Tribune*

"The world, it seems, is Stanton's memorial park, and he's chosen to share many years of painstaking work just locating and seeking out the burial of literally hundreds of musicians. . . . Stanton manages to keep from moralizing or sensationalizing; this is neither *Hollywood Babylon* nor *Tales from the Crypt*."
—*Blues Access*

"A lively and informative guide to the life, death, and resting places of a great many American musical legends. Stanton doesn't criticize anyone's musical taste in this book. He gives enthusiastic and honest accounts of the lives of the musicians and the facts about their deaths."
—*Statesman Journal* (Oregon)

May you find some joy and enlightenment as you browse your way through this book. Enjoy it as you remember these great contributors to our sense of fun and adventure. Happy Birthday Woldy & Carly December 2, 2009

THE TOMBSTONE TOURIST

MUSICIANS

2nd Edition
2003

SCOTT STANTON

POCKET BOOKS

New York   London   Toronto   Sydney   Singapore

POCKET BOOKS, a division of Simon & Schuster Inc.
1230 Avenue of the Americas, New York, NY 10020

ISBN: 0-7434-6330-7

First Pocket Books trade paperback edition August 2003

10   9   8   7   6   5   4   3   2

POCKET and colophon are registered trademarks of
Simon & Schuster Inc.

Book designed by Helene Berinsky

Manufactured in the United States of America

For information regarding special discounts for bulk purchases,
please contact Simon & Schuster Special Sales at 1-800-456-6798
or business@simonandschuster.com

To Robin:
My wife, my friend, and my reluctant editor.
Now that this project is finished, I promise to play more Enya.

To Taylor:
My daughter and treasure.
I pray every night that as you grow older, your proper upbringing
will eventually lead you away from Aaron Carter and 'NSync and to
something sophisticated, say like Cheap Trick or Jimmy Buffett.

To My Donor Family:
Without you, none of this would be possible. Thank you.

Any day above ground is a good day.

BOB DYLAN

You're hot, up-and-coming in your twenties, then in your late twenties you're not so cute anymore. From twenty-eight to forty-two you're in the toilet, then at forty-five they say, "God, he survived the alcohol, there must be something good about him." You play until fifty-five when you become the grand master, go to Europe, come back at sixty, drink the rest of your life away, and then die at about sixty-seven, onstage, or immediately thereafter.

JOHN MAZZOCCO, bass player for John Lee Hooker

The music business is a cruel and shallow money trench, a long plastic hallway where thieves and pimps run free, and good men die like dogs. There's also a negative side.

HUNTER S. THOMPSON

I'd be sitting in the car and something would come on the radio and I'd say, "What's that crap? Nirvana?" Well, change the station. You know, got any Otis Redding? Somebody who died doing his job, not some pissy little spoiled kid.

KEITH RICHARDS, the Rolling Stones

ACKNOWLEDGMENTS

FOR THOSE ABOUT TO ROCK, WE SALUTE YOU!

To my parents, Joanne and Dale Stanton of Anaheim, California, who thought nothing of driving to New York and back just to get a few more headstones between the covers. Also, I firmly believe if you don't thank your mom and dad for something along the way, you will burn in hell.

To Robin, my wife, friend, and traveling partner of sixteen years who was the first to understand what I was trying to do.

Oftentimes we go through life without stopping to show our appreciation to those who truly made a difference in our lives. So I would be remiss if I did not take a moment for my doctor and friend (not necessarily in that order), Ranae Ratkovec, M.D., medical director of the Heart Failure and Transplant Program at Providence Portland Medical Center in Portland, Oregon. I could not have asked for a kinder, more compassionate, and forthright individual during my time of need, and for that I thank you.

To the doctors and staff at the Providence Portland Medical Center Heart Failure and Transplant Program—Gary Ott, M.D. (who now knows me inside and out!), Rae Sullivan, R.N., Wayne Beckett, Kim Rusch, R.N., and Surena Vukovich—who all put the "fun" in congestive heart failure. A very heartfelt thank you for everything you have done for my family and myself.

To the remaining doctors and staff who made living in the hospital a life changing experience—Dr. Handy, Dr. Reinhardt, the entire second floor Telemetry and CICU units (the best!), pharmacist Danielle Benz, Dr. Joe Sullivan and his wonderful associate Nurse Sue, Allison McColl, and Debbie Dorst and all those at the Oregon Clinic.

Upholding that fine tradition of bloodsucking, bottom-dwelling parasites that feed off the talent and sweat of struggling artists is my agent Dave Dunton of Harvey Klinger, Inc. in New York City (okay, I'm joking—I have no talent to feed from!). Thank you for your guidance, humor, and ability to take abuse without the slightest provocation. Besides, you're the only agent I know who understands why I have the "brown M&M" rider in my contract.

To my editor, Lauren McKenna of Pocket Books in New York City, the patron saint of patience. Even if your friends never thought living next to Joey Ramone was cool, I stand in total awe and amazement. And though they don't live next to anyone famous, I stand in awe of the talents of Kate and Doug Bandos of KSB Promotions who put the "fun" in six feet under.

To these fine folks from around the world (most of whom I have yet to meet!) who went from being fans of the website to contributing photographers: Derek Adams of London, England, Brett Bonner of Oxford, Mississippi, Joe Baird from Japan (but his head's in Mississippi), Eddie Wood (whose head and the rest of his body is firmly in Mississippi), Bert Dros of the Netherlands, Ed Naratil and Sheila Stanford from New York, Cindy and Jim Funk of Michigan, Paul Kozar, John Wing of Bristol, England, Marina Gundorova from St. Petersburg, Russia, W. A. Williams of Texas, Michael P. Smith of New

Orleans, Louisiana, Dick Waterman of Oxford, Mississippi, Tim Murphy and Duane Crosson of Portland, Oregon, and Julie Blattberg from NYC.

To my best man and good friend Randy Farrar, whom I could count on to answer the occasional jazz-oriented stupid question of the week ("Hey, Randy, think I should include Duke Ellington under 'Legends'?"). And thank you to Cheryl Farrar for the five-minute lecture on "how to write a successful Hollywood treatment and become famous without really trying." I think it's working!

Speaking of famous, hey, NIKKI! You $%# rock! (and no, I still won't get a tattoo). Oh, and thank you for staying alive long enough to read this.

To my good friends and family Jeff and Jena Lougee, Steve Orr, Suzanne Gratton, James and Denise Fritze, Kim and Doug Rusch, Pam and Mike Burback, Sergei Gundorov, Darren Chesin, Tim Murphy, Mark and Monica Wiechmann, and Marilyne and Nelson Wiechmann, who were all more than willing to let me know when my fifteen minutes of fame were over.

To Sandra Doyle of Philadelphia, Pennsylvania, and Padraic Ansbro for their work on the first edition, and to Derrik Ollar of Photos Today in West Linn, Oregon, for developing most of the pictures you see between the covers (and if they look a little fuzzy, that's because I still can't take a decent photo). Finding graves is hard work, so a special thanks goes out to Mary O'Donnell and Caryn Watsky for the artists buried in Florida, David Bourgeois for Eddie "Guitar" Jones, Denise Fritze for the new Otis statue, Loren Rhoads for a great magazine (*Morbid Curiosity*), Harlan and Lao McCanne for Pigpen and Belushi ("Damn, it's cold out here!"), Bill Dohn for Macon, Georgia, lore, Michael Carroll for anything and everything in this book about the Bay Area, Wade Donaldson for the Waylon picture, and Sabrina Feldman for the last-minute Canned Heat photo.

When you write about dead musicians, you naturally get to meet a lot of interesting people with great stories of the past. Special thanks to Michael McConnell for the Foghat pictures and stories, and blues enthusiast Roger and Jennifer Stolle at Cat Head Delta Blues & Folk Art in Clarksdale, Mississippi, who were a great resource for anything south of the Mason-Dixon line (and who helped me realize that a white guy in Oregon cannot really have the blues, but rather it was probably just a simple case of clinical depression). A tip of the hat to Lisa Benton and Taunia DeMosley (the Ready Girls) for all the info on the Pretenders, Sean Gordon for a few last-minute Doug Sahm photos, Rob Humphreys for the Eddie Cochran memorial plaque, Roy Morales for a great Gene Clark grave photo and location, the fine folks at the Judy Garland House and Museum (so that's what a Winkie sword is!), Jeff Varner of Left Bank in Los Angeles for a few Spinal Tap moments, Eric Predoehl for everything "Louie Louie," and Tim McCormick of Green Tree Publishing for moving this project into the big leagues! To Thomas Bethune of New York who made my second visit to Jamaica a pleasure (a picture of whom can be found in the Peter Tosh chapter), Kevin Dorsey for all things Jimmy and Tommy Dorsey, Jonas Crudup (son of Big Boy Crudup), and a nod of recognition to Patrick Price for updates on Buddy Holly and company.

And finally thanks to Barry Bilicki for the Karen Carpenter promo shots, Albert Haim for answering a few questions about the late, great Bix (wait, aren't all these artists "late" and "great"?), Kim Kelly for working on the original layout, Justin Borucki for supporting the project via *Guitar World* magazine, Ingrid Croce for the thoughtful note regarding her husband, Judy Freed for a wonderful afternoon bringing me up-to-date on her father-in-law, and Susan Olsen and the Friends of Woodlawn Cemetery. And of course I cannot fail to mention John Perrella and Tone "Flubis" Latzer who, as "Scott Stanton," did a better job at being me than me on *To Tell the Truth*. And to the hundreds of fans of the website who e-mailed me questions and comments only to never receive a reply—I'm sorry, but now that this is done and over, it looks like I finally have some free time on my hands.

CONTENTS

⬤➞ HAS BEENS, SHOULD-HAVE BEENS, ONE-HIT WONDERS, AND A FEW REALLY GREAT ARTISTS

FOREWORD

by Nikki Sixx

Say I got trouble, trouble in my eyes,
I'm just looking for another good time,
My heart, my heart, kickstart my heart!
> "Kickstart My Heart,"
> Mötley Crüe

That night in Hollywood, California, is still a bit of a haze to me. I had just come home from a sold-out tour in Japan (where I had been arrested for throwing a bottle of Jack Daniel's on the bullet train during a drunken rage). The world tour was finally over, but I had nobody to go home to—no girlfriend, family, or friends. So I hopped a flight to Hong Kong to binge while the band members and road crew went to their homes in L.A. I managed to finally get home to L.A., and went clubbing directly from the airport. When I finally scored some drug I craved (90 percent of my time was spent looking for drugs), I was already so drunk and pilled out I couldn't even focus. Then I did something I never did—I had the dealer shoot me up with heroin.

What do we have here?
Male, Caucasian. Approximate age twenty-five. Possible drug overdose.
Now, anyone who knows anything about junkies knows we're too proud to let anyone else fix us, but considering I couldn't even find a vein for my fix, I let the bastard do the deed. He didn't know how much to give me, so he gave it all to me. It was a fatal mistake. I turned blue and collapsed. Dr. Feelgood overdosed me.

Heroin? Do we know if he's taken anything else?
What I do remember is hotel doors racing past me as paramedics wheeled me down the hotel corridor on a gurney. Lights were spinning above me out of control and sirens were screaming in the distance (not really aware that they were probably for me). I remember hearing waves of people coming in and out of audio focus.

He's stopped breathing. I don't have a pulse.
We're losing him! WE'RE LOSING HIM!!
So there you have it. On December 23, 1988, Nikki Sixx overdosed in room 312 of the

Franklin Plaza Hotel and was pronounced dead on arrival at Cedars Sinai Hospital at 1:38 A.M. This should be the end of the story, but God has played an evil trick on me. He made me stick around a while and work through my bullshit.

I've always loved music. I've been head-over-heels infatuated with it for as long as I can remember. It just always seemed to speak to me, whether it was Alvin and the Chipmunks or some country music blaring from the radio in the kitchen at my grandma's house. It hypnotized me. I began making up my own nursery rhymes as a kid and would get all my cousins and friends to sing them. That's a scary thought considering it's the same mind that wrote "Shout At the Devil." I was meant to do this and I really don't think I had a choice. It controlled me from the beginning like I was possessed. It is all I could think about. I had no choice but to be a rock 'n' roll star.

As the years rolled by two things probably pointed me toward that eventful night at the Franklin Plaza Hotel—a completely bleak and utterly confusing childhood and the dream of a better life. It was a life where I wasn't left behind like a used bag whenever my mom met a new man. It was the life where roots would grow and I wouldn't be yanked from my friends every time my grandfather and grandmother needed to move on to make a living (I don't blame them). My only friend through those years was music. It never lied to me. It never hit me. It never laughed at me. It was just there for me.

You always hear stories about bands and their climb to the top. The funny thing is, it's just a simple dream and you either have the magic or you don't. Hank Williams, Kurt Cobain, Jimi Hendrix, Nikki Sixx, Johnny Thunders—what's the difference? Just that I'm alive and they're not! Why? I don't know, but to me it's ironic that I died and yet I sit here to write the foreword to this book. Hell, I did as many drugs as Johnny, drank as much alcohol as Hank, and even had a shotgun in my mouth like Kurt. Like I said, there must be a master plan for us, I just haven't seen the blueprints. So why ask why?

You know, once you're at the top it's not all glitter and gold. You'll be on the road for eighteen months straight—city after city, hotel after hotel, your excesses night after night are just a way to fight off the boredom. You wake up with a hangover just to roll out of bed and do it again—it can get fucking redundant. You know it's not all that glamorous puking up your guts every day (even in a five-star hotel). Hey, but what about the girls? They're just another toy to help the clock tick faster till you're back onstage. For the most part they're just a place to dump your load until the drug dealer shows up (you don't even wanna know their names). In one of my diaries the entry read, "I've decided to start mixing Coke with my whiskey in hopes that I'll stop throwing up blood." Yes, I would try to clean up from time to time, but then some fan would flip a bindle of smack into my jacket pocket and I'd be strung out again. And what about my collision course with authority? You try getting harassed or thrown in jail night after night on false or outdated charges. It really burns your ass when you're a target. But in the end, I knew I was gonna make people uncomfortable with their conservative, mundane, underdosed lives.

I gotta tell you, I have no regrets in life. I loved every minute of it. In fact, I've loved it to death. Aahhh, to be a rock 'n' roll star.

But you ask, wasn't that all part of the package, Mr. Sixx? Oh yeah, it's not just the music, man—it's a fuckin' lifestyle. A way of life that you either survive or end up as a footnote in this book. All said and done, it's not the drugs, the alcohol, or even the plane crashes that get you—it's the lifestyle that will ultimately kill you.

Most people have one of two choices—you either read this book or end up in it. I chose both.

P.S. To the young bands out there, here is my advice:

Don't be afraid of the fire, run right through it!
Some of you will die,
Some of you will get burned,
And some of you just might make it.

See you
in Hell

Nikki Sixx

Nikki Sixx is the songwriter, bass guitarist, and founding member of Mötley Crüe.

INTRODUCTION

I've never aspired to become a writer, photographer, archivist, or rock 'n' roll's unofficial undertaker. All I really wanted to accomplish was take a few pictures of some graves, throw them together, and print a few copies for my musician friends and bandmates. But that's not how it really worked out. Next thing you know I've got a webpage, and e-mails from dead-musician devotees in England, Finland, Australia—hell, I even get e-mail from a fan in Newfoundland. Then I have to hire a publicist, publishing attorney, researchers, and distributors, attend book conventions, and record a few (hundred) radio interviews. My god, I was even on Howard Stern, CNN, and *To Tell the Truth!* So, great—I've got a book, I've sold a few copies, and now it's over. My fifteen minutes of Warhol Fame are over.

Then I get a call.

"Good afternoon, this is David Dunton calling from the Harvey Klinger Agency in New York City. May I speak with Scott Stanton?"

My answer was direct and to the point—I hung up.

The phone rings again. "I'm sorry, I think we got cut off. As I was saying, this is David Dunton and I'm a literary agent representing hundreds of authors worldwide. I got a copy of your book and would like to see if we can work together."

As easy as it would be to hang up the phone, a response was required at this point. "Look Dave, I don't mean to be rude, but I have no illusions of fame, fortune, and book signings with Gore Vidal. So don't tell me that you can book me on the *Today Show* with that perky Katie Couric, or that Jerry Hall is on line two. Besides, I am a journalist [okay, that's a stretch, even for me] damnit. And as a journalist I have to uphold the ethics and integrity of my brethren. I cannot, and I will not compromise my personal ethics so you can parade my life's work like some cheap, tawdry . . ."

"I can get you a check for your efforts."

Ouch, cheap shot. He immediately locates my weak spot and exploits it to its fullest potential. Nonetheless, I gave Mr. Dunton the time to hit me with his best shot, trade a couple of rock 'n' roll stories, a few musician jokes, ask for the same publishing deal that Hillary Clinton got, and in general yank his chain. But as with every deal, there are always conditions.

"I'll be honest with you, Dave. I am basically living in the hospital waiting for a new heart. Is that going to be a problem?"

Without missing a beat, he replied, "Only if you die."

You have to respect a man who can make a dead man walking laugh. I signed that week.

But I'm getting ahead of myself.

The genesis of the idea for a directory of the dearly departed began in 1991 with the simple desire to create a webpage with something other than pictures of the family cat or a list of one's favorite movies (remember, this was way before "You've got mail!"). At first I created the Dead Pool, but that only lasted a couple of months (seems that people were dying every day and I had to keep updating the damn site). After toying with a few ideas of a more sedate nature, I stumbled upon an idea while on business in Macon, Georgia. I was walking through Rose Hills Cemetery when I came upon two matching guitar-etched marble tombstones with a dozen cards, letters, and simple flower arrangements. So I got to thinking—if the final resting place of Duane Allman and Berry Oakley is honored by fans around the world nearly every day of the year (even some thirty years after their passing), what about all the other great musicians (and I'm thinking beyond just Jimi, Janis, and the Lizard King)? What ever happened to Karen Carpenter, Muddy Waters, Frank Zappa, and Steve Clark from Def Leppard? But imagine my surprise when I found out there was not a single source for the final resting places of anyone outside of Hollywood, California. If you want Humphrey Bogart or Marilyn Monroe, piece of cake. But if you want Miles Davis, well, that's another story.

So really, how hard could this be? I've got carte blanche to fly pretty much anywhere I need to go, take a couple photos, talk to a few groundskeepers and gravediggers, and there you have it—an instant bestseller. Unfortunately it didn't exactly work out that way. First, as it turns out, most cemetery managers are not exactly all warm and fuzzy when you want to run through their park for the musically inclined members of the six feet under club. Unless you are dying (or a family member is looking a little peaked) they really don't want to turn their sacred acreage into some funky tourist attraction.

Second, I wasn't really a photographer, and despite the fact that my subject material didn't move, I still couldn't take a decent picture. And finally (and most importantly), I wasn't by any stretch of the imagination a good speller, much less a writer of any significance. Nonetheless that didn't stop me from a planes, trains, and automobile tour of America, Canada, Mexico, Jamaica, and a good chunk of Europe. And what I estimated would take six months has now dragged on well past ten years. During all this time I logged well past one million miles, catalogued close to a thousand musicians, have taken over five thousand pictures, have enough magazines, newspaper articles, and general paper crap to fill four file cabinets, and got a daughter and a new heart in the process. So you might ask, what have I learned from all this? I've learned that Louis Prima (not David Lee Roth) is just a gigolo, that Michael Jackson stole all of Jackie Wilson's moves, that Willie Dixon wrote pretty much the first two Led Zeppelin albums, that Mama Cass Elliot's cause of death was not sandwich-related (and that she hated being called "Mama"), that there is no conspiracy covering up the deaths of Jim Morrison, Johnny Ace, or Kurt Cobain (regardless of how many internet sites claim the contrary), that when Diana Ross dies she'll be lucky if someone other than the funeral home representative shows up at her funeral, that the drummer from Toto did not die from spraying his fruit trees, that alcohol, cocaine, or heroin never did anyone any good, that death was a good career move for Elvis, and after walking in well over two thousand cemeteries past row after row of the dearly departed, life is too short to do something that you don't want to do. And I'm truly ecstatic that I was able to finish this book.

Enjoy!

THE LEGENDS

ROY ACUFF

BORN September 14, 1903
Maynardville, Tennessee

DIED November 23, 1992
Nashville, Tennessee

CAUSE OF DEATH Congestive Heart Failure
Age 89

Known as the King of the Hillbillies, the Backwoods Sinatra, the Caruso of Mountain Music, and finally as the King of Country Music, Roy Acuff sold more records in the 1930s and forties than any other country star. But the roles of musician and performer were only a small part of the legacy of Roy Acuff. Through his fifty-year association with the Grand Ole Opry, in addition to performing, he was responsible for establishing country music publishing and was the founder of the entire Nashville music industry as we know it today.

In the Beginning . . .

Born Roy Claxton Acuff in Maynardville, Tennessee, Roy was one of five children born to Neill and Ida Acuff. They were a musical bunch; Dad played the fiddle, Mom the piano and guitar, and young Roy demonstrated an affinity for the harmonica. In high school, he even sang in the glee club.

Roy also enjoyed sports and excelled in basketball and baseball. In 1929, when the Acuffs moved to Arlington, Tennessee, Roy found a place for himself on a semiprofessional baseball team. He was reportedly set to join the New York Yankees when he suffered severe sunstroke and collapsed; this was followed by a nervous breakdown, leaving Roy bedridden for most of 1930. This turned out to be (for us) more a blessing than a curse; it was during this bleak period that Roy realized he would never have a baseball career, and turned to the fiddle for solace.

Roy first found success in front of an audience in 1932, when he toured with Dr. Hauer's Medicine Show, playing the fiddle and performing in skits (often in blackface). The ensuing years found him performing around Knoxville and on radio with various permutations of musicians. He made his first recordings in 1936 with his string band the Crazy Tennesseans at American Record Corporation of Chicago. By 1937, Roy was dissatisfied with ARC, and stopped recording with them; however, in 1938, ARC was taken over by Columbia, and Roy was persuaded to re-sign with them.

By this time, Roy had made a couple of appearances at the Grand Ole Opry, and was a big hit with songs such as "The Bird" and "Wabash Cannonball" (which became one of the most popular songs that year). He toured all over the United States in 1940 with his band the Smoky Mountain Boys. He and the band also appeared in the Republic Pictures film *Grand Ole Opry* that year. They would go on to perform for the U.S. Armed Forces throughout the world during World War II.

The Roy Acuff Museum has one of the largest and most impressive displays of Gibson, National, and Dobro guitars and mandolins—all from Roy's personal collection. Located on the grounds of Opryland in Nashville, this collection boasts over 200 instruments, including some 1930s Dobros, a rare Epiphone Recording guitar from the late 1920s, several Vivi-Tone solid-body electric guitars, and a rare custom HG-24 Hawaiian guitar.

The next professional move by Roy Acuff was to be a momentous one for the country music world. In 1943, he cofounded Acuff-Rose Publishing Company, which was the first country music publishing house in the U.S. The company played an integral role in the growth of country music, providing protection to songwriters and performers (including Hank Williams and Marty Robbins). It was this development, more than any other, that led to the birth of Nashville as the country music hub of the world. And it was Roy's unique style as a performer that led to the transformation of country music from a field dominated by bands to one dominated by individual singers.

In the End . . .

By 1962, Acuff had sold more than twenty-five million records. That same year, he was elected the first living member of the Country Music Hall of Fame (on the plaque, he was identified as the King of Country Music, and the moniker stuck). In the ensuing years, Acuff cut back on his touring, but remained a powerful presence at the Opry throughout the 1980s. In fact, he was the only member to have his own dressing room at the Opry. In 1987, he received the Grammy Lifetime Achievement Award, and it couldn't have been a more fitting honor.

The Grand Old Man of the Grand Ole Opry died at the age of eighty-nine at Baptist Hospital in Nashville of congestive heart failure. At Acuff's request, exclusive private services were held just hours after his passing—he wanted to go out with class and dignity, surrounded by his dearest friends and family. He was buried in a family plot in Spring Hill Cemetery in Madison, near Nashville. A largely attended memorial service was held the following month at the Opry.

Spring Hill Cemetery
Madison, Tennessee

Driving north on Briley Parkway, turn right onto Gallatin Avenue. Drive past the light and

go to the second entrance to the cemetery on your right. Drive about fifty feet and turn right at the first road and park. Walk up to the Hill Crest section and you will see the large Acuff memorial. Facing the Acuff monument, walk two hundred feet to the left to the Monroe Family monument where everyone except Bill Monroe lies.

Elvis Presley was a country boy to start with and he just kinda put a swivel in his hip and did country music. I like to swing out, but I swing it from the heart. Presley swings it from the hip.

Roy Acuff

THE ALLMAN BROTHERS BAND

Butch, Dickie, Berry,
Duane, Gregg, and Jai

DUANE ALLMAN

BORN November 20, 1946
Nashville, Tennessee

DIED October 29, 1971
Macon, Georgia

CAUSE OF DEATH
Motorcycle Accident
Age 24

BERRY OAKLEY

BORN April 4, 1948
Chicago, Illinois

DIED November 11, 1972
Macon, Georgia

CAUSE OF DEATH
Motorcycle Accident
Age 24

Formed in 1969 with Gregg and Duane Allman, Berry Oakley, Dickey Betts, Jai Johanny Johanson, and Butch Trucks, the Allman Brothers's mixture of rock, R&B, jazz, and western swing was the basis of the "Southern sound" that tore the lid off rock 'n' roll. And though the band has been around for over thirty years, they are most identified with the early lineup featuring Duane on slide and Berry on bass. A lineup that lasted only three years.

In the Beginning . . .

Raised by their mother from an early age (their father was murdered the day after Christmas when they were children), Duane and Gregg showed all the promise of their future legacy. Bored with the beach music of the area surrounding Daytona Beach, Florida, the brothers immersed themselves into the "classics"—Jackie Wilson, Otis Redding, B. B. King, and the up-and-coming Beatles. With a taste for R&B and the blues, it wasn't long before the brothers began starting their own groups. During Gregg's senior year, their classes were all but forgotten as they pursued their music full-time.

One of the first groups the brothers formed together was the Allman Joys. With the family station wagon loaded with gear, the band hit the road playing roadhouses, bars, and dives—six sets a night, seven nights a week—from Jacksonville to Mobile, Alabama, and everywhere in between. After the original Allman Joys fell apart in '67, they reformed with a new drummer and keyboardist and moved to the West Coast in search of a recording contract. Duane recalled, "They'd send in a box of demos and say, 'Okay, pick out your next LP.' We tried to tell them that wasn't where we were at, but then they got tough. We figured maybe we could squeeze an ounce or two out of this crap." Renamed Hour Glass by the studio executives, the result was a disappointing, overproduced pop album. Disappointed and disgusted with the West Coast studio system, the band returned to the South but soon drifted apart. In 1968 Gregg returned to L.A. to fulfill their contract with Liberty Records, while Duane made his way through a couple of bands, and then finally down to Alabama as a member of the famous Muscle Shoals rhythm section.

While the Rock and Roll Hall of Fame in Cleveland has Duane's famed gold-top Les Paul guitar, the "world's largest" collection of ABB memorabilia can be found at the band's former residence at 2321 Vineville Avenue in Macon, Georgia. Known as the Big House, owner and ABB road manager Kirk West has amassed an impressive collection of ABB memorabilia (and stories!) through his twenty-five-plus years associated with the band. For reservations and hours of operation please call (but not before 10:00 A.M.!) 478-742-0503.

Down the street from the Big House sits the Georgia Music Hall of Fame that not only honors Duane and Berry, but also houses an impressive collection of Georgia greats from the B-52's to Otis Redding and beyond.

Two guitars that you and I will never see in our lifetimes include Duane's arch-top Gibson acoustic, which hangs in Gregg's home. Dickey has Duane's National in his living room.

During his year with Muscle Shoals, Duane recorded an incredible selection of blues, funk, rock, and R&B, playing on classic tracks as Aretha Franklin's "This Girl's in Love with You," Wilson Pickett's smash hit "Hey Jude," and a number of Boz Scaggs's early recordings. However, Duane became disenchanted with studio life and longed to record as a front man. On one of his many road trips back to Jacksonville, he jammed with Dickey Betts, Berry Oakley, Butch Trucks, and Jai Johanny Johanson. After a blistering two-plus hours of nonstop jam session, Duane called for his brother to join them back home and "round this thing out and send it somewhere." So on March 26, 1969, Gregg hung up the phone, packed his bags, and the Allman Brothers Band was formed.

First ABB rehearsal home on College Street in Macon, Georgia.

With Gregg back with his brother, the six members pooled their money (which wasn't much) and rented a house at 309 College Street in Macon, Georgia (just down the street from Rose Hill Cemetery). Six months later the band traveled to New York City to record their first album. While garnering solid reviews, the album only sold moderately well, so the band took to the road. Over the next two years the band performed over five hundred dates all across the U.S.—aided only by five roadies and one Ford Econoline van. During that short time, the ABB mixture of rock, jazz, blues, and western swing developed the basis for the "Southern sound."

In the End . . .

In the last year of his life, Duane recorded some of his most important work. He had just finished his last of three albums of incendiary electric slide with Delancy and Bonnie, a number of groundbreaking studio sessions, and a short tour with Derek and the Dominoes with Eric Clapton (which produced the rock classic "Layla"). In March of '71 the ABB played two nights at the Fillmore East, which was later released as *At Fillmore East*. In addition to the live album, Duane completed three songs for the next ABB release *Eat a Peach*— "Stand Back," "Blue Sky," and the only original tune that Duane ever recorded with the ABB, "Little Martha."

At the end of October the band took a rare break from touring and recording, and returned to Macon, Georgia. After stopping by the band's Big House to offer birthday wishes to Berry's wife, Duane took off on his motorcycle. As Duane traveled west on Hillcrest, a pipe truck driven by Charles Wertz entered the intersection of Hillcrest and Bartlett. To avoid a collision, Duane laid his bike down and skidded ninety feet across the intersection's centerline. Hearing the crash, Wertz walked over to the unconscious rider and turned off the still-racing engine of the motorcycle. The impact tore the helmet from Allman's head and caused severe liver, chest, and head injuries. Although revived twice, Howard Duane Allman died after three hours in the operating room, in what is now Middle Georgia Hospital, one month shy of his twenty-fifth birthday.

They were a pain in the neck. They used to practice at home with their electric guitars up full blast. The noises that came out of that house sounded like they were killing a couple of cats in there.

A former neighbor of the Allman brothers

The following Monday over three hundred people attended services in Macon's Memorial Chapel. With Duane's guitar case placed in front of the flower-adorned casket, the band took their places, and Gregg sang out the old blues classic "The Sky Is Crying." Making it clear that the band's tribute lay in the music, they continued with Stormy Monday, In Memory of Elizabeth Reed, and Statesboro Blues.

The ABB immediately went back on the road, later adding Chuck Leavell on keyboards. Berry also began to pull out of the grief that enveloped him following Duane's death. Taking an active role in the recording of the *Brothers and Sisters* album, Berry was becoming the unofficial leader and visionary of the band. Creatively, the band was at their peak.

On a Saturday afternoon, almost one year later to the day, three blocks from Duane's accident, Berry was riding his motorcycle and failed to make the curve on Napier Avenue near Inverness Street and struck the left side of a city bus. Bleeding and visibly shaken, he refused medical treatment. One hour later friends carried him back to the same hospital. However, Oakley died moments later of head injuries and internal bleeding.

Due to legal and financial disputes, Duane's remains were still in cold storage, awaiting final instructions from family members. It wasn't until after Berry's death that they were buried side by side, with matching tombstones, in the Civil War section of the historic Rose Hill Cemetery in Macon.

Rose Hill Cemetery
Macon, Georgia

Duane and Berry are buried in the historic Rose Hill Cemetery in Macon, Georgia. Located ninety miles south of Atlanta, take I-15 south to the second Riverside Drive exit outside Macon. Turn left off the exit and drive past the Riverside Memorial Cemetery, through the College Street light, and turn left into the main entrance of the cemetery. Park at the entrance of the cemetery (the roads are very narrow and uneven throughout the cemetery), and look for the map on the outside of the cemetery office. They are buried at Carnation Ridge above Soldiers Square. Once through the gates, veer right and look for the six hundred Confederate gravesites down toward the railroad tracks. From here you will see a flagpole. Standing at the flagpole facing the river, look to your left, and down in the ravine you will see their two long, matching stones. Except for a brief period in 1999, the site has been maintained by the Georgia Allman Brothers Band Association (GABBA).

H & H Restaurant
807 Forsyth Street
Macon, Georgia

Located just down the street from the original Capricorn recording studio, owner Mama Louise serves some of the best soul food in the region. Her association with the band began when the group recorded their first album. Story has it that the band was so poor they

could only afford one lunch plate for the whole band. When Mama Louise saw the boys eating off the same plate, she promptly went back and brought out enough food for the whole group. Ever since then, she has been considered a member of the ABB family. Two whole walls of the restaurant are devoted to the band, including gold records and backstage photos along with photos of related bands like Gov't Mule and the Outlaws. Naturally there's a juke-box loaded with Allman Brothers, Otis Redding, and lots of great R&B. Oh yeah, leave room for dessert!

THE ALLMAN BROTHERS' OTHER SIDEMEN

LAMAR WILLIAMS
January 14, 1949—January 19, 1983
When Berry Oakley passed away in 1973 during the making of the *Brothers and Sisters* album, Lamar was asked by Jaimoe to audition. So in 1972 he teamed up with the ABB and played on *Brothers and Sisters*, *Win, Lose, or Draw*, and the live double-LP *Wipe the Windows, Check the Oil, Dollar Gas*. During his tenure with the Brothers, Lamar became friends with keyboardist Chuck Leavell. When the Brothers broke up in the late seventies, Lamar, Chuck, and Jaimoe formed Sea Level. Lamar succumbed to cancer and was buried in Mississippi at the Biloxi National Cemetery (Section 13b, Row 1, Plot 5).

DOUGLAS ALLEN WOODY
October 2, 1956—August 26, 2000
Allen Woody was the third bass player the Allman Brothers have lost over the years. Known for his commanding stage presence and powerful riffs, Allen began playing bass during his teens. In the early 1980s he worked with former Lynyrd Skynyrd drummer Artimus Pyle before joining with the ABB in 1988. Woody, along with new guitarist Warren Haynes, provided the ABB with a much-needed revitalized sound that proved to be the band's most creative period since the heydays of the 1970s. Woody and Haynes broke off in 1994 to form Gov't Mule. Just days before the Gov't Mule tour to support *Life Before Insanity*, Woody was found dead in a Marriott Courtyard hotel room in Queens, New York City, from natural causes. He was buried at Hermitage Memorial Gardens near Nashville, Tennessee.

Many have written to me and asked about the fence that, for a very brief period, surrounded the matching headstones. The story goes that back in 1998 Candace Oakley (Berry's sister, but not the heir to the estate) took it upon herself to erecte a ten-foot-high fence topped with razor wire. She claims that the fence was needed to keep fans from desecrating the gravesite. In fact, the only damage that the graves have seen in the last twenty years is from the installation (and subsequent court-ordered removal) of the fence. Since then, she has taken it upon herself (along with her husband, Buford) to yell, scream, and threaten anyone who attempts to pay their last respects.

Disappointed fans at the gravesite in 1998, just days after Candace Oakley erected the fence to keep fans out. The fence has since been removed.

LOUIS ARMSTRONG

BORN August 4, 1901
New Orleans, Louisiana

DIED July 6, 1971
Corona, Queens, New York City

CAUSE OF DEATH Kidney Failure
Age 69

With a distinctive, gravelly singing style and a stage personality grounded in the vaudeville and minstrel eras, Louis Armstrong's genius for improvisation and technical skill on the cornet make him the single greatest American musical icon. He was first and foremost a jazz trumpet player without peer—a virtuoso soloist who was one of the most colorful and influential forces in the development of American music. Throughout his lifetime and after, he has elevated jazz to an art form far larger than the self-appointed aficionados of the genre.

In the Beginning . . .

Greatness is often born of humble beginnings. The story of Louis Armstrong is no exception. Born in New Orleans on Perdido Street in the notorious Storyville section of town (long since torn down), Armstrong had to fend for himself at an early age. Abandoned by his father, Willie (and there is some doubt if he was really Louis's father) and raised by his grandmother until the age of ten, Armstrong developed strategies for dealing with the brutal poverty he knew, which included scheming and stealing. When his mother, Mary Ann, took Louis and his older sister back, he had already developed an inner toughness disguised by the outward charm and sentimentality, the combination of which became a lifelong trademark.

A pivotal event occurred in his life when, while ringing in the new year of 1913, Armstrong fired a borrowed .38-caliber pistol into the air. Promptly arrested, he was sentenced to an indefinite stay in the New Orleans Home for Colored Waifs. A military-style school for juvenile delinquents, the boys were taught reading, writing, and arithmetic in an environment of regular meals and good hygiene. In addition, there was also a school band that gave concerts on special occasions to raise money for the school. The musicians were dressed to the nines in sharp uniforms and performed "Home, Sweet Home" and "The Swanee River (Old Folks at Home)" in classic New Orleans style. Armstrong was intrigued and quickly was moved to bugle.

After two years at the school, Armstrong was returned to the chaotic care of his mother, where he began work delivering coal via a mule cart. However, the taste of music he received at the boys' home would not go away. He scraped up enough nickels and dimes to purchase

Upon his death in 1971, Armstrong willed his entire estate to Queens College in New York City (Armstrong had no children or close relatives). Upon his wife's passing in 1983, the Louis Armstrong Archives became trustees of his home and personal possessions. This immense collection includes five trumpets with fourteen mouthpieces, 650 reel-to-reel tapes with boxes hand-decorated by Armstrong himself, eighty-six scrapbooks, 1,500 albums dating back to the 1930s, 5,000 photographs, and 270 sets of band arrangements. The archives is open to the public Monday through Saturday in the Rosenthal Library, while home tours are scheduled to begin in Fall 2003. For hours of operation and an appointment, please call 718-997-3670. As for Satchmo's first cornet, that is now on display at the American Museum of Natural History in Washington, D.C.

an old used cornet. By age seventeen Armstrong was sitting in with numerous bands and playing honky-tonks and bars all though the city. Within four years after his release from the home, a shy Armstrong was taken under the wings of Joe "King" Oliver. Their relationship proved to be one of the key elements in the early development of jazz.

By 1918 musicians were leaving the city by the busload. With Storyville gone (or, should we say, bulldozed), the cotton crop decimated by the boll weevil, and the rise to power of Chicago, Los Angeles, and Kansas City as economic trade centers, Armstrong traveled outside of the city playing to tourists and businessmen on the riverboats of the great Mississippi River. Upon his return to New Orleans he mar-

Although he had no children of his own, he took an instant liking to the children around his home in Corona, Queens. When he returned from the road, children would race to be the first to carry his bags into the house. He would return the favor by teaching the neighborhood kids how to play the trumpet.

ried a prostitute, but was relieved when he received a telegram from King Oliver asking him to join Oliver in Chicago as second cornet in the Creole Jazz Band. Armed only with his cornet and what few clothes he owned, Armstrong joined what is now considered the finest improvisational jazz ensemble ever to record. Playing for both black and white audiences at the Lincoln Gardens ballroom, Armstrong and Oliver developed a unique dueling cornet style that was featured prominently in their 1922-'23 recordings. His muted solo on "Dippermouth Blues" alone was considered the first great jazz solo to be recorded.

Offstage, Armstrong was receiving the attention of Lillian "Lil" Hardin, an educated and refined woman who was also the band's piano player. She took a romantic as well as professional liking to this scruffy, provincial musician. She relished the challenge and soon became his wife and de facto business partner. She eventually convinced Armstrong to leave the tall shadows of King Oliver for a bigger piece of the pie as a solo artist. For the next two years, Armstrong recorded in New York with Fletcher Henderson, blues giant Bessie Smith, and Sidney Bechet. He returned to Chicago in late 1925 and went into the studio for a series of recording sessions known as the Hot Fives and Hot Sevens. For the next four years he recorded over sixty sides with Lil, Kid Ory, Johnny Dodds, and later Earl "Fatha" Hines (who replaced the now-divorced Lil on piano). Armstrong was now billed on radio and in live performances as "the world's greatest trumpet player."

In the End . . .

The impact of the Depression forced a move back to New York City. The 1930s saw Armstrong transitioning from a great musician into a great entertainer. For the next fifteen years he fronted a series of big bands and toured America with an occasional visit to Europe. After 1935 his career came under the control of Joe Glaser, who ensured a steady diet of concert dates, recording sessions, and movie appearances.

It's been hard goddamn work, man. I feel like I spent twenty thousand years on planes and railroads, like I blowed my chops off. Sure, pops, I liked the ovation, but when I'm low, beat down, I wonder if maybe I hadn't been better off staying home in New Orleans.

Louis Armstrong, 1969

In 1947, his music considered primitive compared with the bebop style emanating from Kansas City, Armstrong formed Louis Armstrong's All Stars with Jack Teagarden, Barney Bigard, and Hines. With equal amounts of jazz and entertainment, the All Stars became the highest-paid jazz combo on tour. With the occasional personnel change, the All Stars' fourteen-year run took them to all parts of the world, including a forty-five-date trip to Africa (hardly a nation known for its jazz clubs). During this time, Armstrong was featured in over twenty films, including his most famous roles in *Hello Dolly* with Barbra Streisand and *High Society* with Grace Kelly and Bing Crosby. In May of 1964 the single "Hello Dolly" knocked the Beatles' "Can't Buy Me Love" off the #1 spot on *Billboard*'s chart.

For the remaining ten years of his life, Louis suffered from heart and kidney problems. While they never stopped him from performing (though his doctors wished he would), his health was in steady decline. Just two weeks before his last engagement, gasping for breath, Louis told his doctor, "Doc, you don't understand. My whole soul, my whole spirit is to blow that horn. People are waiting for me. I've got to do it, I just have to do it."

He made his last engagement at the Empire Room of the Waldorf-Astoria Hotel in New York City. He played each night for two weeks with just enough energy to come down from his room to blow for an hour. Then he went right back to his room to rest until the next show. Immediately after the engagement, he checked back into the hospital for observation.

Released several weeks later, Louis relaxed at home, hoping to get his strength up for the next show. There was none. Late in the evening of July 5th, 1971, Armstrong made a call to his manager to secure rehearsal dates for the band. Early the next morning he died quietly at his home of kidney failure.

Twenty-five thousand mourners paid their respects as his body laid in state at the National Guard Armory on Park Avenue on direct orders of the president of the United States. The following day a simple ceremony was held at the modest Corona Congregational Center. No music other than the Lord's Prayer was played with Frank Sinatra, Ella Fitzgerald, Pearl Bailey, and Dizzy Gillespie acting as honorary pallbearers.

Flushing Cemetery
Queens, New York
From the entrance at 16306 Forty-sixth Avenue there are three paths from the office. Take the left road until you come to Section 9. His black marker is twenty feet from the corner of the section (next to "Barto"). Buried next to his wife, Lucille, he shares the cemetery with Johnny Hodges from the Duke Ellington Band (Section 11, Subsection D on the road) and Dizzy Gillespie (Section 31, Plot 1252-31).

Located at 34-56 107th Street in Corona, Queens, the Louis Armstrong House was purchased by Armstrong and his third wife, Lucille, in 1943 and it is here that they lived out the rest of their lives. Built in 1910, the house was originally a two-story, clapboard-sided house designed as a two-family residence. Today the Armstrong House remains exactly the way it was at Lucille Armstrong's death in 1983.

Now owned by the Louis Armstrong Archives at Queens College, they have been working for a number of years to open the Louis Armstrong House as a public museum, educational center, and major tourist attraction in New York City.

LILLIAN "LIL" HARDIN ARMSTRONG
February 3, 1898—August 27, 1971

Although relegated to a mere footnote in the history of jazz, it is safe to say that, but for the dedication, insight, and influence of Lil Hardin Armstrong, there would be no Louis Armstrong as we remember him today.

Born in Memphis, Tennessee, and educated at Fisk College, Lil moved to Chicago to study at the Chicago College of Music in 1917. She began to perform with such artists as Freddie Keppard and Johnny Dodds before moving to New Orleans to work with King Oliver's Creole Jazz Band. It was during this time that she met King Oliver's young, shy cornet player Louis Armstrong. They married on February 5, 1924.

Immediately she became a major influence in his musical life. She taught the young musician how to read music, wrote the music for a majority of his compositions, and transcribed many of his songs with her talent for arranging. She finally convinced Louis of his great talent and persuaded him to move to Chicago and go solo. After a brief stint with Fletcher Henderson, they teamed up as part of Louis Armstrong's historic Hot Five and Hot Seven bands in 1927. They later moved to New York where Lil earned a postdoctorate in 1929 at the New York College of Music. In 1931 the marriage was over and they divorced in 1938.

During the 1940s up until her death in the early 1970s, Lil was considered a fixture in the developing Chicago club scene. She performed solo and with ensembles in such Chicago locations as the Tin Pan Alley Club, the Mark Twain Lounge, and the Garrick Stage Bar. She toured Europe occasionally but always returned home to Chicago.

Lil Hardin with King Oliver (left), circa 1920.

After her separation and divorce from Louis, Lil continued to live at the home they shared at 421 East Forty-fourth Street in Chicago. She never remarried and some claim she loved Louis all her life. She never took off the rings he gave her and saved every letter, photograph, and even one of his old cornets. She died suddenly just two months after the passing of Louis. In what must be one of the saddest ironies in jazz history, while playing "St. Louis Blues" at a Louis Armstrong memorial concert, in the middle of her solo she simply slumped over and died. She was buried at Lincoln Cemetery on Kedzie Road on Chicago's South Side.

From the main office, cross the street to the south annex and veer right and park at the Garden of Peace Mausoleum near the entrance. Lil is at rest on the top row of Wall G, Crypt 63, Tier 5.

GENE AUTRY

BORN September 29, 1907
Tiago, Texas

DIED October 2, 1998
Los Angeles, California

CAUSE OF DEATH Natural Causes
Age 91

Orvon Gene Autry's career spanned over six decades as an entertainer and cultural icon. As a recording artist, movie and television star, rodeo and concert performer, and later a broadcast executive and major league baseball owner, Autry is the only person to have five stars on Hollywood's Walk of Fame. Held in little regard by country music artists and film critics, the sheer output and success of his movie and recording career guarantee that Gene Autry will remain the quintessential image of America's Singing Cowboy.

In the Beginning . . .

Born in Texas and raised in the small town of Ravia, Oklahoma, young Orvon Gene Autry learned to play the guitar from his mother. The Oklahoma farm boy (despite legend otherwise, Gene was not a cowboy) modeled his soft, nasal voice after the popular country yodeler Jimmie Rodgers. As a teenager, he was talented enough to travel with the Fields Brothers Marvelous Medicine Show. It was during this time that Autry paired with songwriter Jimmy Long and the two started their long and successful partnership.

In 1928 Autry was working as a telegrapher for the railroad in Oklahoma. With the transmissions done for the day and little to do, Autry was sitting in the office alone when the legendary cowboy humorist Will Rogers walked through the doors. Rogers advised the young singer to give radio a try. Autry wasted no time and traveled to New York to began his radio career. The following year he made his first recordings for the American Record Corporation. In 1931, just three years after the chance meeting with Will Rogers, Autry recorded the first record to ever sell one million units—a certified gold record. "That Silver-Haired Daddy of Mine" (cowritten by Jimmy Long) made Gene Autry a household name.

Autry continued his radio show (now with the Sears-sponsored WLS Barn Dance in Chicago) until 1934, when he starred in the first of many in a series of westerns. Autry's acting debut in the film *In Old Santa Fe* continued the following year in his first starring appearance in the science-fiction western serial *The Phantom Empire*. All told, Autry and his trusty steed Champion made ninety-three movies and was continually ranked as either the number one or two Top Western Star at the box office. Despite the fact that he retired

The Autry Museum of Western Heritage (4700 Western Heritage Way in Griffith Park, adjacent to the L.A. Zoo) in Los Angeles holds a remarkable collection documenting western heritage and culture, as well as the personal collection of America's Favorite Singing Cowboy. Only open on the weekends, a smaller collection of Autry memorabilia can be found closer to his birthplace in Gene Autry, Oklahoma. His final home at 10985 Bluffside Drive in Studio City, California, is just around the corner from the Western Heritage Museum.

from the big screen in 1953, he is still the only western star on the list of Top 10 box office moneymakers.

Autry's recording output did not suffer despite the heavy film schedule. Up until 1956, he made 635 recordings, including more than two hundred of his own compositions. During his active recording and performing period he sold over 40 million records, including "Back in the Saddle Again" (1941), "South of the Border" (1939), and "The Last Roundup" (1947). In 1941 "Be Honest with Me" was nominated for an Academy Award and in 1949 he recorded his biggest seller "Rudolph the Red-Nosed Reindeer" with sales exceeding thirty million copies.

In the End . . .

In 1956 Autry retired from active performing in films, radio, rodeos, and recordings to concentrate on his vast real estate and radio station holdings. For several years he was ranked in *Forbes* magazine's list of wealthiest Americans before he fell below the Top 400 in 1995, when his estimated wealth was a mere $320 million.

The remaining years of his life were filled with honors, including induction into the Country Music Hall of Fame, the Nashville Songwriter's Hall of Fame, and the National Cowboy Hall of Fame. In 1988 his longtime dream was achieved with the grand opening of the fifty-four-million-dollar Autry Museum of Western Heritage. He passed away quietly in his sleep at the grand age of ninety-one, just three months after friend and fellow singing cowboy Roy Rogers.

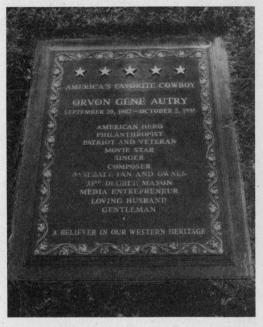

Forest Lawn Hollywood Hills
Los Angeles, California

As you enter through the gates drive about a hundred feet and park to the right. Look for the statue about a hundred feet off the road. Walk toward the statue in the Sheltering Hills section and look to your right for Space 1048. America's Favorite Singing Cowboy shares the cemetery with Liberace, Andy Gibb, Bobby Fuller, Rick(y) Nelson, Jeff Porcaro (Toto), Melvin Franklin (Temptations), Bobby Troup, Jack Teagarden, two of the Mills Brothers, and a whole host of Hollywood film and television stars.

A lot of that is true. I got better as I went along. I couldn't get any worse.
Gene Autry, responding to critics regarding his acting ability.

COUNT BASIE

BORN August 21, 1904
Red Bank, New Jersey

DIED April 26, 1984
Hollywood, Florida

CAUSE OF DEATH Cancer
Age 79

The 1940s and '50s saw a lot of bandleaders come and go. One of the preeminent bandleaders at the time was William "Count" Basie, whose sparse, economic keyboard style and supple rhythmic drive was the epitome of swing. While other renowned jazz orchestra leaders garnered praise and fame as soloists or composers, Basie spent the better part of forty-five years perfecting the art of being a bandleader itself. A generous yet underrated pianist, he was not afraid to share the stage with the likes of Jimmy Rushing, Billie Holiday, Lester Young, and Big Joe Williams.

In the Beginning . . .

William Basie started his musical life in Red Bank, New Jersey, as an only child. After a brief try at the drums, he switched to piano at the urging of Duke Ellington's drummer, Sonny Greer. While still in his late teens, he gravitated to Harlem, where he encountered Fats Waller. Awed by Waller, he sat behind him at the old Lincoln Theater, hanging on every note. After a couple of weeks, Waller asked if he knew how to play. When Basie replied no, Waller offered to teach him.

Through Waller, Basie was offered the job as an accompanist for various blues singers and vaudeville acts. It was pure fate when a roadshow he was performing with was left stranded in Kansas City. It was in Kansas City that Basie would meet and work with several jazz musicians who would later be key members of his band. He first joined Bennie Moten's band in 1929, where he played and recorded for the next six years. When Bennie died, Basie recruited most of the band, which would serve as the nucleus of his famed band. Scale for the musicians at a typical nightclub was fifteen dollars a week for playing from 8:00 P.M. to 4:00 A.M., except Saturdays (when it was 8:00 P.M. to 8:00 A.M.) Beer was a nickel, whiskey was fifteen cents, and they played seven days a week.

One night at the Reno Club in Kansas City, the announcer called Bill over to the microphone for the usual few words of introduction. He commented that "Bill" was rather an ordinary name (as compared to Earl "Fatha" Hines or Duke Ellington). He said he was going to start calling him by the more royal title of "Count." Bill thought the announcer was kidding, but from that point forward he was always known as Count Basie.

The band enlarged from nine to thirteen players as they moved from Kansas City to Chicago, and then finally to New York City. The big break came at the Famous Door club on Fifty-second Street. In addition to being one of the hippest places to be seen, the Famous

---

While the American Jazz Museum in Kansas City, Missouri, promotes a display on the Count, the fact of the matter is that they only have a couple of photographs of Basie and his big band during the golden years of swing. Visits to the Library of Congress and Smithsonian also yielded nothing of value. As it turns out, the Basie estate still has 99 percent of all Basie memorabilia in their possession and there are no plans for any type of public display in the near future.

Door also had national and local radio wires. The whole country was now able to hear the wall of sound created by the Count Basie Orchestra.

By then a series of legendary recordings by the Basie band had begun appearing in stores under the Decca label. Those early hits included "Swingin' the Blues," "Jumpin' at the Woodside," and his theme song "One O'Clock Jump." At one of his recording sessions, Count Basie was paid the grand sum of $750 for twenty-four singles with no royalties. He later remarked that it was the most expensive lesson of life.

In the End . . .

During the late forties and early fifties, many great jazz musicians passed through the Count Basie Orchestra. Harry Edison, Walter Page, and Eddie "Lockjaw" Davis were just a few of the greats to swing with the Count. By the early 1950s he was forced to cut his band back to eight players due to the decline in the popularity of the big band sound. Nonetheless, there was no noticeable change in his simple "stride" style that flowed with intensity.

The early 1960s saw Basie playing President Kennedy's inaugural ball. In 1965 he did a tour with Frank Sinatra. It wasn't until 1976 that Basie was forced to slow down when he suffered a near-fatal heart attack. But after only six months, he was back at the piano, leading the band through full sets of jazz standards.

His final year saw a short, stocky, witty man who sported a yachting cap offstage enjoying the good life at his home in Freeport, the Bahamas. He died in 1984 after a brief battle with cancer.

Pinelawn Cemetery
Farmingdale, New York

As you approach the cemetery, the park is divided by the roadway. Turn into the park opposite the main office and take the right fork, parking next to the outdoor mausoleum. The Count and his wife are buried in the South Gallery of the Forsythia Court, Row 57, Tier D. Guy Lombardo is located on the same wall to the left, second row from the bottom. He shares the cemetery with jazz great John Coltrane (Garden of Sanctuary, Section 60, Grave 49, Plot Q, Range 46, Block 1) and "Yakety Yak" sax master Curtis "King Curtis" Ousley (Forsythia Court, Row 15, Tier D, West End).

If you play a tune and a person don't tap their feet, don't play the tune.

Count Basie

THE BEACH BOYS

DENNIS WILSON

BORN December 4, 1944
Hawthorne, California

DIED December 28, 1983
Santa Monica, California

CAUSE OF DEATH Drowning
Age 39

CARL WILSON

BORN December 21, 1946
Hawthorne, California

DIED February 6, 1998
Los Angeles, California

CAUSE OF DEATH Cancer
Age 51

Carl, Mike Love, Brian, Dennis, and Al Jardine.

In the tradition of the Beatles and the Rolling Stones, the Beach Boys were America's greatest rock band. The epitome of the original California surf sound, the Beach Boys combined the close harmonies of the Four Freshman with their love of Chuck Berry-style rock 'n' roll with cars, girls, high school, and surfing. The result was a veritable hit factory chronicling the angst and excitement of adolescence in the 1960s—"Surfin' Safari," "Little Deuce Coupe," "I Get Around," to name but a few. But drugs, mental illness, and internal strife diminished the band's creativity by the early 1970s.

In the Beginning . . .

Raised in a middle-class suburb of Los Angeles, California, brothers Brian Wilson (songwriter, bass, piano, vocals), Dennis Wilson (drums, vocals), and Carl Wilson (guitar, vocals) formed a band with cousin Mike Love (vocals) and friend Al Jardine (guitar, vocals) in 1961. They performed live previously as Kenny and the Cadets, the Pendletones (in homage to the popular shirt worn by surfers), and as Carl and the Passions (later to become an album title) until Dennis suggested they record "Surfin' " as the Beach Boys. The song charted and with the help of the brother's father, Murray Wilson (who became their first manager), they were signed to Capitol Records in 1962.

The Beach Boys' first Top 40 hit came quickly with "Surfin' Safari." The following year the band released their first album and hit gold with "Surfin' U.S.A.," "Surfer Girl," "Little Deuce Coupe," and "Be True to Your School." By now Brian was handling all the producing duties, as well, and most of the songwriting and lyrical content, too. Brian also lent his considerable talents to other projects, including Jan and Dean's number one hit "Surf City" as cowriter and backing vocalist.

By the second year after signing with Capitol, the Beach Boys were a bona fide hit. But the constant touring, recording, promotion, and touring again began to take their toll. The pace was so frenzied that Capitol released the band's fourth album, *Little Deuce Coupe*, one month after *Surfer Girl*.

The Beach Boys dominated the charts up through 1963, and with the release of "Fun, Fun, Fun" at the start of 1964, it looked like a repeat of the previous year. However, the British Invasion changed pop culture before the year end and the Beach Boys felt the pres-

---

One of the "newer" releases, the fifty-seven-track *Hawthorne, California, Birthplace of a Musical Legacy* opens with an introduction of the Beach Boys' first hit "Surfin'," followed by a 1961 rehearsal recorded where it all began: at 3701 West 119th Street, Hawthorne, home of brothers Brian, Carl, and Dennis Wilson. Included on the album are rehearsals of such Beach Boys classics as the #1 hit "Good Vibrations," a demo of "Surfin' U.S.A.," radio promos, a guest appearance by Jan and Dean's Dean Torrence on "Barbara Ann," a live recording of "Shut Down," and an unreleased Dennis Wilson track, "A Time to Live in Dreams." Talk about your original garage band! Unfortunately, the house has since been demolished. As far as any real memorabilia or collections, most of the Beach Boys' equipment and collectables are still in the hands of the surviving members of the band.

sure from the Beatles, the Kinks, the Yardbirds, and the Rolling Stones. But oddly enough, 1964 was a banner year with their first number one single, "I Get Around," and three gold albums including their first number one LP, *Beach Boys in Concert*. However, the schedule was too much for Brian and after almost losing his hearing, he quit touring with the group and devoted all his energies to writing and studio recording.

By the time the band released *The Beach Boys Today* and *Summer Days (and Summer Nights)* Brian's songwriting approach was scattershot, schizophrenic, and sadly romantic. Unlike the early teen hits, Brian and the group were taking longer between records, experimenting with complex, layered vocals and sophisticated recording techniques. The climax of this phase (and the cornerstone of their career) was *Pet Sounds*. Hailed universally as one of the greatest albums ever recorded, the album was recorded virtually single-handedly by Brian with lyricist Tony Asher. Despite the hits "Wouldn't It Be Nice" and "Sloop John B," initial sales were disappointing.

In the End . . .

By the opening of 1967, Brian was hailed in the press and in music circles as a genius and true music visionary. That label wasn't entirely without merit with the release of the number one single "Good Vibrations." However, Brian was slowly falling into a cycle of drugs and mental illness. He attempted to produce a new album tentatively entitled *Smile*. Aside from a single released in 1967, the album would become a "masterpiece" by legend only. Adding to his personal and professional problems the continuing internal conflicts (especially with Mike Love), Brian ceded leadership of the Beach Boys.

Oddly enough, the only Beach Boy who knew how to surf was Dennis (on the far left).

Not surprisingly, the Beach Boys suffered critically and commercially in Brian's absence, and record sales declined. In the next six years they released seven albums and numerous singles—none of which matched their previous run on the charts. In 1974, just when most of the record companies and fans alike lost patience, the group released a compilation of early material called *Endless Summer*. Not only was it the first "oldies" album to top the American charts, but it also sold better than the original recordings! By now the Beach Boys, guided by Carl Wilson, were a solid mainstay on the concert trail and oldies airplay.

The 1980s began much like the 1970s—a new record company and a lackluster release. And while an accident in the mid-seventies forced Dennis to move over to the keyboards for a couple tours, he was back behind the drums in the late seventies. Unfortunately, by now divorce(s), drugs, and alcohol began to take their toll and chances are if you saw the Beach Boys in concert after 1979, someone else was on drums while Dennis aimlessly roamed the stage, pretending to sing. Truth be told, Dennis had ceased to be a creative force in the band since the early seventies. While he was pictured on *Keeping the Summer Alive* (1980), Dennis did not have anything to do with the album. The fact of the matter is that most drum parts on the Beach Boys' records were played by Hal Blaine, Ricky Fataar, and others. So those closest to Dennis were shocked, but not surprised, when

I haven't talked to Brian in a while. I don't even know his phone number.

Carl Wilson, at a 1993 record release party.

in 1983, three days after Christmas, Dennis drowned in Marina Del Ray while diving at the location where his boat *Harmony* had been docked. Friends report he was drinking heavily when he dived into the marina off a friend's boat, bringing up personal items that he had previously thrown overboard. The following day the Beach Boys announced that they would continue to record and tour without Dennis.

While Carl grew tired of the infighting and lack of musical growth (he left the group in 1981 but rejoined shortly after releasing a solo album), he continued through most of the decade with the group, including their induction into the Rock and Roll Hall of Fame (1988), and the release of the hit "Kokomo" from the movie *Cocktail*. Blessed with perfect pitch, Carl was lead singer on such classics as "God Only Knows" and "Good Vibrations," and was the acknowledged leader and stabilizing presence over the last two decades. So it came as quite a shock when he was diagnosed with both lung and brain cancer in the mid 1990s. But as sick as he was, he performed with the group for their annual summer tour in 1997 as both singer and guitarist. Even in the fall members were expecting a full recovery, but it was not to be. He died in February of the following year at home with his family by his side. Upon his death, the Beach Boys officially disbanded only to "re-form" again sans Brian Wilson.

When the movie *Cocktail* (starring Tom Cruise) was released in 1988, it was considered just your basic run-of-the-mill teen summer flick with no real redeeming value. However, travel agents from around the country began getting calls from would-be vacationers requesting to spend the week on the beach in Kokomo. Insisting that Kokomo was a little island "in the Florida Keys," travel agents were at a loss. There is no island paradise called "Kokomo"—it doesn't exist! The only place called Kokomo exists in Indiana, 750 miles from the nearest beach.

Westwood Memorial Park
Los Angeles, California

As you enter the cemetery (on Glendon, one block off Wilshire Boulevard), drive straight ahead to the office. Turn left at the office and drive to the end of the lawn section on your left. Carl is buried near the corner of the lawn section opposite the entry gate, next to Minnie Riperton.

Dennis was granted a burial at sea and his body was released in the Pacific Ocean at 33-53.9° N, 118-38.8° W. The boat slip at 13929 Bellagio Way, Basin C-1100 in Marina Del Rey, California, is the site of impromptu memorials every year just after Christmas.

The Heart and Voice of an Angel

♥ CARL DEAN WILSON ♥

DEC. 21, 1946 – FEB. 6, 1998

The World is a Far Lesser Place Without You

PIERCE BROS. WESTWOOD MEMORIAL PARK

1218 Glendon Avenue
Westwood, California

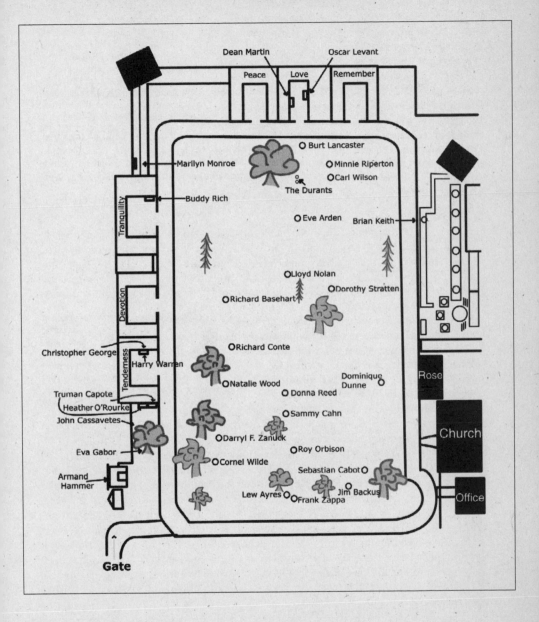

THE BEATLES

JOHN LENNON
BORN October 9, 1940
Liverpool, England

DIED December 8, 1980
New York, New York

CAUSE OF DEATH Murdered
Age 40

GEORGE HARRISON
BORN February 25, 1943
Liverpool, England

DIED November 30, 2001
Los Angeles, California

CAUSE OF DEATH Cancer
Age 58

The most endearing, influential, and popular band of the twentieth century, the Beatles reshaped rock 'n' roll music by emphasizing the group as a whole, emphazising albums over singles, and affecting fashion and culture worldwide. John, Paul, George, and Ringo were more than just a band, they were a musical phenomenon.

In the Beginning . . .

Inspired by the British skiffle craze in the mid-1950s, John Lennon formed the Quarrymen in 1957. A huge fan of American rock 'n' roll, John began to incorporate music by Gene Vincent, Buddy Holly, the Coasters, and Elvis Presley into the band's repertoire. That same year one of the members invited a fifteen-year-old Paul McCartney to one of their performances. Later that same year, the group added Paul and George Harrison to the group. As members came and went, the nucleus of John, Paul, and George remained constant. But just as gigs were getting few and far between and the band was about to break up, the manager of the club the Casbah, Mrs. Mona Best, called to see if the Quarrymen were available. They played as a trio as Johnny and the Moondogs until early 1960.

While valued by collectors at $7,500, the initial pressing of *Yesterday . . . and Today* (1966) with the original butcher cover is not the most expensive LP in the Beatles' catalog. That honor goes to the test pressing on pink vinyl of *A Hard Day's Night* on the United Artists label. If in excellent condition, this album will set you back about $12,000.

From the summer of 1960 the band continually changed their name, but soon started calling themselves the Silver Beetles (in homage to Holly's Crickets), later shortening it to just the Beatles. Mona's son Pete Best joined on drums, as did John's friend Stuart Sutcliffe. In 1961 the Beatles really started to become a huge sensation as they toured heavily in the U.K. When Stuart left the Beatles to pursue his art career (he died in 1962 of a brain hemorrhage), the band was just John, Paul, George, and Pete. Although they only wrote a handful of songs together, the songwriting team of Lennon and McCartney began adding original songs between cover songs at their gigs. In May of 1962 they auditioned for producer George Martin, who would sign the group only if they got a new drummer. Pete was asked to leave the band and Ringo Starkey (later Starr) was brought in to round out the fabulous foursome. Within the year, with the release of their 1963 hit song, "Please Please Me," the group shot to number one in Britain and sold over 2.5 million albums in the U.K. alone.

⬤—▶ Believe it or not, there is no one central museum that is dedicated to the Beatles, most likely because Paul McCartney, Yoko Ono, Olivia Harrison, and Ringo Starr have never loaned any of their collections/possessions to any of the usual sources. Naturally, the Rock and Roll Hall of Fame has several of their stage costumes, instruments, and a selection of memorabilia; however, the Hard Rock Casino in Las Vegas, Nevada, has a huge, sealed case of Beatles collectables that barely scratches the surface. Fortunately, the Beatles Story, a modest collection of memorabilia, has recently opened in Liverpool, England, and looks to become a permanent collection.

In 1964 Capitol released their first U.S. album *Meet the Beatles*, featuring a remix of previously released material. After over 70 million people tuned in to watch the Beatles on *The Ed Sullivan Show*, Beatlemania official took hold on both sides of the Atlantic. Following the release of their first film, *A Hard Day's Night*, the group performed at twenty-five stadiums in their first-ever tour of North America.

In the End . . .

Following the release of *Revolver*, the Beatles embarked on their final concert tour, playing their last concert on August 29, 1966 in San Francisco. Upon their return, they spent much of the time recording the groundbreaking opus *Sgt. Pepper's Lonely Hearts Club Band*. The following year their manager, Brian Epstein, died from a self-administered drug overdose. Rather than hire another manager, the Beatles took the reins of management themselves and continued to insist that no breakup was imminent. Still, discontent among the members was increasing as the sessions for the next album, *The Beatles* (aka the White Album), were filled with tension. Feeling left out of the creative process, Ringo walked out of the sessions, returning a short time later. The recording session continued; however, most of the album was created by the members recording separately. At the beginning of 1969, the group reluctantly began preparing for the new album *Let It Be*. But major business and personal changes took place, with Paul marrying Linda Eastman, John formally marrying Yoko Ono, and Allen Klein was made business manager. In December of 1970, Paul filed a lawsuit against Klein to disband the Beatles.

In 1975 Lennon retired from music to concentrate on raising his son with Yoko. Five years later he resurfaced to record his first album, *Imagine*, in six years. On December 8, 1980, John and Yoko were returning from a late-night recording session when John was walking toward his apartment at the Dakota in New York City and was shot by a deranged fan. He died at the scene.

After a successful post-Beatle career as a filmmaker, solo artist, and a member of the Traveling Wilburys, George announced in 1998 that he was being treated for throat cancer. The following year he was attacked and stabbed several times at his home in England. In the fall of 2001, he lost his fight with cancer, which had spread throughout his body.

When Lennon and Harrison passed away, the press reported that they were both cremated. When George Harrison passed away at a private residence in Los Angeles, his body was taken to Hollywood Forever in Los Angeles. His family then took possession of the cremains and have plans to release his ashes into the Ganges River in India.

As for Lennon, his remains are still unconfirmed. Though reported cremated, the funeral home that provided the service has not been confirmed, and indeed in 1992 Yoko Ono did admit that Lennon has been interred in a cemetery. However, that cemetery still remains a mystery.

STUART SUTCLIFFE
June 23, 1940—April 10, 1962

History dictates that at one time the Fab Four might have been John, Paul, Pete, and Stu. But as fate would have it, Pete Best was fired and Stu Sutcliffe quit the band to pursue his real passion—art. In fact, it was Sutcliffe's passion for art and literature that made a deep impression on John, imparting a stronger enthusiasm toward his own studies. Paul McCartney and

> When we first came to town, these guys like Dean Martin and Frank Sinatra and all these people wanted to come over and hang around with us. We don't want to meet those people. The only person that we wanted to meet in the United States was Elvis Presley.
>
> John Lennon

George Harrison were soon joining John in the intellectual discussions with Sutcliffe and his college buddies. Eventually John convinced Sutcliffe to join the band as bass guitarist.

In the summer of 1960, the band was attacked after a gig in North Liverpool. During the fight, Sutcliffe was knocked to the ground and kicked in the head. In November of that year while in Hamburg with the Beatles, Sutcliffe met and fell in love with Astrid Kirchherr, a German photographer. By the end of the year, Sutcliffe began exhibiting angry and passionate outbursts that resembled mild seizures, with symptoms so intense that he often suffered from sudden and violent headaches. Eventually Sutcliffe left the Beatles, returning to Germany to be with Astrid, and continued his art education. By Christmas of 1961, Sutcliffe's headaches had evolved into violent fits and blackouts. His personality had become morose and his features were pale and haunted. Yet he refused to believe that his headaches were the result of anything worse than overwork, and examinations by numerous doctors resulted in nothing definite. By March of 1962, Sutcliffe's

headaches grew to include temporary blindness and pain so violent that he had to be held down lest he hurt himself. On April 10, Astrid found Sutcliffe unconscious in his room and called for an ambulance, where he died in her arms en route to the hospital. The cause of his death was reported as "cerebral paralysis due to bleeding into the right ventricle of the brain." X-rays taken after his death showed a small brain tumor beneath a depressed area of the skull, where he had been kicked three years earlier. Sutcliffe was buried at the Huyton Parish Church Cemetery in the town of Huyton, England, in Section 1939, Number 552.

BRIAN EPSTEIN
September 13, 1934—August 27, 1967

Remembered primarily for discovering the Beatles and with mishandling their career, Epstein never realized the full potential of the group's marketing value and literally gave away millions of dollars' worth of licensing rights. As a result of his naiveté, the Beatles received little or no money for their initial recordings, concerts, a myriad of novelties produced that bore their names and likenesses, nor the copyrights to most of their music.

Epstein was introduced to the Beatles when a customer came into his family's Liverpool music shop to purchase their record. Epstein sought out the band and eventually convinced them to hire him as their manager. He worked hard to promote the band, but had difficulty signing them to a label, eventually getting a demo in the hands of producer George Martin, who signed the aspiring group. Firing Pete Best, Epstein then brought in Ringo Starr on drums, and by 1963 they were the biggest-selling band in Britian's history. Three years later, with impending loss of control over management of the group and various lawsuits regarding royalties, Epstein suffered from severe bouts of depression. After two unsuccessful attempts at suicide, he took an overdose of sleeping pills and locked himself in his bathroom. The following day he was discovered by his secretary. And while there was speculation as to whether his overdose was accidental or intentional, the coroner ruled that his death was ruled accidental due to the "incautious self-overdose" of the drug Carbitrol. Epstein was buried in Section A, Grave H12 in the Liverpool Jewish Cemetery in the Fazakerley area with none of the members of the Beatles present. In 1999 his grave was desecrated when the marble monument was broken off.

HELP!

A few selected Beatle sites in Liverpool and London, England

Eleanor Rigby Gravesite

Yes, Eleanor Rigby truly does exist and is not just a fictional character from one of the Beatles' most famous songs. The inspiration for the song of the same title had its roots in 1957 when Paul first met John at a gig that John was playing at St. Peter's Parish Church in Woolton (a Liverpool suburb) and John asked Paul to join the band two weeks later. Eleanor Rigby is buried in the center of the small cemetery just behind the church.

John Lennon's Homes

While his mother lived at 1 Blomfield Road, John lived at 9 Newcastle Road until the age of five. John then moved in with his Aunt Mimi at 251 Menlove Avenue until he was twenty. During his teen years John began to develop a relationship with his mother, until she was run over by a car driven by a drunk, off-duty policeman in front of the Menlove Avenue home and killed. Julia Stanley was buried in the nearby Allerton Cemetery in what is now an unmarked grave.

George Harrison's Homes

Born at home at 12 Arnold Grove, George lived in this modest home until the age of seven. The family then moved to 25 Upton Green were George lived until he was nineteen years of age and was the site of most of the early Beatle rehearsals. The family then moved to 174 Macket's Lane, but lived here less than two years due to the constant intrusion of fans outside the home once Beatlemania broke loose. His last home was a simple one-hundred-plus-room mansion located on Friar Park Road in Henley-on-Thames, Oxfordshire, England. Visitors can only see the guard shack at the gated entrance (see photo above).

Brian Epstein's Final Residence

The home at 24 Chapel Street in the exclusive Belgravia district in London was not only the site of the record release party for *Sgt. Pepper's Lonely Hearts Club Band*, but it is also the site of Epstein's third and final suicide attempt.

The Beatles' Home

The Beatles only lived together in one home once in their brief career. John, Paul, George, and Ringo all lived at 57 Green Street in London near Hyde Park. Three months later John, wife Cynthia, and son Julian moved into a place of their own.

Abbey Road/EMI Recording Studios

Made famous by the Fab Four, the studio continues to draw fans and musicians alike as a successful, fully functioning recording studio and tourist site. Tours are available to Studio One and Studio Two (the Beatles' primary recording studio), and the street crossing depicted on the cover of Abbey Road is to the right of the entrance and remains one of the most popular tourist attractions in London today.

BIX BEIDERBECKE

BORN March 10, 1903
Davenport, Iowa

DIED August 7, 1931
New York, New York

CAUSE OF DEATH Pneumonia
Age 28

Publicity photo, circa 1932.

One night on Chicago's South Side at a small club called the Plantation Inn, both Bix and Louis Armstrong were playing with their respective bands. As the evening progressed the concert turned into a battle of the bands. That evening after the show, one of the band members saw Louis crying in the corner. He was crying because he "could never play as good as Bix."

In the Beginning . . .

Unlike many of the musicians born at the turn of the century, Bix was born into the financially and culturally wealthy Beiderbecke family, who made their fortune in the lumber trade. Bix's early life was filled with strong family ties and a good education. Having never taken a cornet lesson, Beiderbecke's unusual sound can be attributed to a well-rounded education of classical music mixed with the then-hot sounds emanating from New Orleans. Many stories have been told of how Beiderbecke would take a rowboat out on the Mississippi River to listen to the riverboat bands. He would then race home and, purely by ear and memory, copy the songs note for note, phrase for phrase, and beat for beat. While Beiderbecke loved the open style of the New Orleans Negro bands, he never played in a band in Davenport. Practicing to the phonograph, Beiderbecke developed an off-tonality sound that made him famous. He first started playing professionally at the Lake Forest Academy in Chicago, where he enrolled in every open musical organization. His first band was the college prep band the Wolverines. The band was so good that in the spring of 1924, Hoagy Carmichael booked them for a fraternity dance party on the Indiana University campus. The students thought he was so great that he was booked on the campus for the next ten weeks.

 For the true collector an original copy of the third side of the Chicago Loopers (which was inadvertently released under the name "Willard Robison and His Orchestra") is an extremely rare find, valued at over five hundred dollars.

These were some of the best days for Beiderbecke—hot music, girls, and Prohibition booze—but there was no money for those who wanted to play hot jazz. Even after accept-

The Louisiana State Museum Jazz Collection in New Orleans has the largest collection in the world of instruments owned and played by jazz musicians. On display is the piano used by Bix to compose "Candlelights and Flashes," a pair of cufflinks and a handkerchief (donated by friend Hoagy Carmichael), and one of his cornets. At the Davenport, Iowa, Putnam Museum of History and Natural Science, they have in their possession his Golden Bach Stradivarius cornet (with "Bix" engraved in the bell) and his piano. However, until the museum is able to fund a permanent exhibit, the Bix display is usually only open to the public during the Bix Beiderbecke Memorial Jazz Festival held each July, a major event for Bixophiles. There is also the Tribute to Bix Beiderbecke, which takes place in Kenosha, Wisconsin, on the weekend nearest March 10 (Bix's birthday). And finally, those visiting historical jazz sites in Queens often stop at the apartment house at 43-30 Forty-sixth Street, Sunnyside, Queens, where Bix passed away.

ing an offer to play in Frank Trumbauer's band for a hundred dollars a week, he left sizable bar bills all around Chicago. By the time he left Chicago in 1925, Beiderbecke was wearing the pants of one friend and the coat of another—both garments threadbare.

In the End . . .

Rather than go on the road to make ends meet, Bix hung out in Chicago playing with Charlie Straight and a few other bands. With money tight and tired of jobbin' on one-night stands, Beiderbecke joined the nationally known Jean Goldkette Orchestra with Joe Venuti (violin) and Jimmy Dorsey (clarinet) in 1926. The following year he teamed up with the Paul Whiteman Band, where he was the featured soloist.

In 1929 the downward spiral continued. Tired of the commercial music that was required by most of the bands at the time, Beiderbecke played less and less frequently and continued the careless lifestyle that started during his Wolverine years. His apartment in New York resembled more of a fraternity house than a home. Babe Ruth and others came by often because Beiderbecke was a big fan and both were big drinkers. Great fun—but not much music was being made.

His final days were passed too quickly. With little money left and suffering from a bad cold, Beiderbecke was forced to take a club date in Princeton, New Jersey. That night pneumonia set in and in two days Bix Beiderbecke was dead—after only four years at his prime.

Oakdale Cemetery
Davenport, Iowa

Located on Eastern Avenue, drive through the cemetery gates and take the road on the left. Stay to the right of the administration building. Go up the hill past the Davenport Monument and stay to the right as the road forks. Continue down the hill, staying to the right, and straight ahead on the left you will see the eight-foot Beiderbecke granite monument. His individual plot marker can be found to the right of the family monument.

If you didn't spend so much money on fancy clothes, you would have more money to buy gin.
Bix Beiderbecke, commenting on a fellow musician's sense of priorities.

LEONARD BERNSTEIN

BORN August 25, 1919
Lawrence, Massachusetts

DIED October 14, 1990
New York, New York

CAUSE OF DEATH Cancer
Age 71

Considered the Renaissance Man of Modern Music, Leonard Bernstein's life and work existed entirely in the superlative. Described in his early career as "hopelessly fated for success," Bernstein fulfilled and exceeded everyone's expectations. A dynamic figure both on and off the stage, he reveled in having his hands in multiple projects at any one time. Constantly on the move, creating, performing, producing, touring the world with the New York Philharmonic, or guest-conducting throughout the U.S. and Europe, Bernstein poured all his creative energies into every effort.

In the Beginning . . .

Conductor and composer Leonard Bernstein was born in Lawrence, Massachusetts, to Jennie and Samuel Bernstein. For a musician, he began rather later in life than most: At the age of ten, he fell in love with his aunt's piano and insisted that his parents provide lessons. At sixteen, he saw his first live symphony concert and gave his own first recital at his high school. During summer camp, Bernstein produced his version of *Carmen*, and sang the title role himself! He entered Harvard in 1934, and began a radio series in Boston called *Leonard Bernstein at the Piano*. At age nineteen, he met his idol Aaron Copland, and the two became fast friends. By age twenty-two, he had already performed several piano recitals, appeared on TV, and made his first solo recording. On the advice of friends, he decided to study conducting under Fritz Reiner at the Curtis Institute of Music in Philadelphia.

In 1943 he was invited by Arthur Rodzinski to be the assistant conductor of the Philharmonic Symphony Society of New York (known as the New York Philharmonic). Four months later on November 14, fate's habit of smiling on Bernstein presented him with the opportunity to debut with the NYP when the guest conductor, Bruno Walter, fell ill and Rodzinski could not return to New York in time to take over. Of course, Bernstein gave fate a hand by vigorously studying the program when he noticed that Walter seemed ill. Confidently leading the orchestra, Bernstein received warmer and warmer applause after each successive number. At the end of the concert, the applause was deafening. Since the concert was broadcast nationally, Bernstein became an overnight sensation.

Bernstein conducted the New York City Center orchestra from 1945-47 and appeared as a guest conductor in the U.S., Europe, and Israel. In 1953, he became the first American

Over a forty-four year span, from 1953 to 1967, Leonard Bernstein gave many of his most significant music manuscripts to the Leonard Bernstein Collection at the U.S. Library of Congress. *West Side Story, Wonderful Town, The Age of Anxiety,* and the film score *On the Waterfront* are just a few of the manuscripts in the library's possession. The collection also makes available upon request thousands of photographs, correspondence, writings of all kinds, commercial and noncommercial recordings, business papers, fan mail, programs, and family scrapbooks. Considered one of the largest single collections in the library's possession, nearly ten years after his passing they are still cataloging all the inventory and don't expect to be finished soon. A small selection of memorabilia is on display in the Performing Arts Reading Room at the Library of Congress in Washington, D.C.

to conduct at La Scala in Milan, Italy. From 1958 to 1969 he was conductor and musical director of the NYP, sometimes conducting from the piano. He made several tours with the NYP to Latin America, Europe, the Soviet Union, Japan, and Canada. After 1969, he continued to write music and appeared as guest conductor throughout the world.

Bernstein is most remembered, perhaps, for his flamboyant conducting style. Not satisfied with the prescribed textbook techniques, Bernstein would often completely fly off the podium, flinging his arms like some great bird in a triumphant climax. His passionate style caused problems. Along with the occasional injury from a fall, he tended to intimidate some orchestras with his aggressive movements when guest-conducting. Bernstein was also well known for his love of diversity, writing symphonies inspired by his Jewish heritage (*Jeremiah* and *Kaddish*), and from his deep respect of Catholicism (*Mass*). He was equally at home with other musical styles, such as jazz and boogie-woogie, and wrote for ballet (*Fancy Free*), Broadway musicals (*Candide* and *West Side Story*), and film scores (*On the Waterfront*).

In the End . . .

Age did little to slow Bernstein's pace. Rather, he seemed to accelerate. Between 1985 and 1990, he conducted no less than fifteen concerts and made at least three foreign tours, including an appearance in Japan, where he collapsed from exhaustion. On October 9, 1990, at the age of seventy-two, Bernstein announced his plans to retire from public performances due to failing health. Five days later, on October 14, Leonard Bernstein died at his home from cardiac arrest brought on by mesothelioma. A private funeral was held at Bernstein's home on October 16, followed by internment at Green Wood Cemetery in Brooklyn, New York.

Green Wood Cemetery
Brooklyn, New York

At the front gate, you can ask for a cemetery map and list of other prominent permanent residents. Enter the park from the Twenty-fifth Street and Fifth Avenue main entrance, turn left onto Battle Avenue, and drive around the twisting road to Border Avenue. Turn left onto Border, then turn right at Garland Avenue and stop about fifty feet up from Garland (you will see the beginning of a small foot path on

your right). Follow the footpath into Section G/H, turning left in the middle of the section at the intersection of the two paths. Walk about fifty feet and on your right you will see the "Bernstein" bench.

I'm not interested in having an orchestra sound like itself. I want it to sound like the composer.
Leonard Bernstein

RICHARD BERRY

BORN April 11, 1935
Extension, Louisiana

DIED January 24, 1997
Los Angeles, California

CAUSE OF DEATH Aneurysm
Age 61

Richard Berry's contribution to the world of music does not include a discussion of tonality or form; he did not conduct the Boston Symphony Orchestra, he didn't invent a new form of music, and he never had a #1 hit record. Rather, Richard Berry wrote and recorded a simple but indelible three-chord, famously slurred song that encourages even the tone deaf to sing at parties. Richard Berry wrote what has become the cornerstone of rock 'n' roll. Richard Berry wrote "Louie Louie."

In the Beginning . . .

Born in Extension, Louisiana, Berry taught himself piano as a teenager growing up in Los Angeles. He attended Jefferson High School, where he sang in the choir. Following in the footsteps of fellow alumni doo-wop singer Jesse Belvin, Berry once said, "If you could sing like Jesse, you had the girls."

As a member of the local doo-wop music community that included Belvin, Cornell Gunter, and Young Jesse (to name a few), Berry first joined the Flairs, later recording with the Flamingos. Modest success came to the group with the occasional regional hit. In 1954, the songwriting team of Leiber and Stoller were working with the Robins on "Riot in Cell Block No. 9" when they asked Berry to sing the bass line. He was not given credit on the record, even when the song became a major hit. He also contributed his vocals for Etta James's recording of "Roll with Me, Henry."

Prized among collectors is a mint-condition 1957 release of "Louie Louie" by Richard Berry and the Pharaohs on Flip Records. Note that there are three versions—one with "Rock Rock Rock" on the B-side (rare), one with "You Are My Sunshine" (rarer, both worth about fifty dollars), and the 78 version (really rare at one hundred dollars).

In the summer of 1955, Berry was backstage when he heard a local dance band play a dance tune with a distinctive introduction. The five-note "duh duh duh—duh duh" pattern became the basis for Berry's "Louie Louie." For the lyrics, Berry borrowed the story line of a lovelorn Caribbean sailor talking to the bartender Louie from Frank Sinatra's song "One for My Baby" and Chuck Berry's "Havana Moon." The song was recorded by Berry's group, the Pharaohs, as a calypso-tinged B-side, but "Louie Louie" became the hit. However, attempts for a follow-up hit were unsuccessful and Berry sold the song for $750 to pay for his wedding.

Not much memorabilia is left from a man who wrote a handful of doo-wop hits and one monster party classic. Fortunately, Eric Predoehl is the editor of the quarterly *Louie Louie* newsletter (PO Box 2430, Santa Clara, CA 95055), for all the latest "Louie Louie" releases, video specials, as well as your very own copy of the complete and final 120-page report from the FBI that confirms our belief that the two-plus-year investigation was a good use of our tax dollars (not!). As for the birthplace of "Louie Louie," that would be backstage at the Harmony Park Ballroom in Anaheim, California.

The song made its way up the West Coast as a classic bar-band rocker. In 1963, both the Kingsmen and Paul Revere and the Raiders recorded "Louie Louie" in the same week. The Kingsmen's version—sloppy and energetic with slurred lyrics—became a hit after a Boston DJ declared the song the worst record of the week. It went on to sell millions of copies.

As the song was heard in every bar with a jukebox, the FBI began a thirty-month-long investigation into rumors that the song was obscene. Although the Kingsmen's lead singer, Jack Ely, was never questioned, the FBI determined that the lyrics were unintelligible at any speed.

In the End . . .

For the next twenty years Berry played the local club and lounge circuit, performing Top 40 numbers for the audience. Despite the success of "Louie Louie," Berry never enjoyed the financial remuneration that thousands of recordings of the hit had offered.

In 1983 radio station KFJC-FM in Los Altos Hills, California, broadcasted a show called *Maximum Louie Louie* and invited Berry on the show. Expecting about ten or fifteen cover versions of his song, Berry was astonished when the station offered over eight hundred versions over a sixty-hour period—from the original version to reggae, disco, heavy metal, punk, and high school marching bands. An added bonus for Berry was the appearance of Jack Ely, the original vocalist for the Kingsmen (this was the first time that Berry had met anyone from the group that made his song famous). Shortly afterward, with the help of an artists' rights group, Berry secured 25 percent of the publishing rights to the song, acquiring over two million dollars in royalty payments during his last ten years.

Never the picture of perfect health (he had suffered from polio as a child and a lifetime of nightclub gigs had taken their toll), Richard Berry passed away in his sleep from complications of an aneurysm.

Inglewood Park Cemetery
Inglewood, California

A private ceremony was held at Inglewood Park Cemetery, where he was laid to rest in the Sunset Mission mausoleum. The cemetery is about ten minutes from the L.A. Airport—take I-105 to West Century Boulevard. Turn left on Aviation Boulevard, and continue on Florence Avenue to the main gate. From the main entrance of the cemetery, turn right at the first road (away from the office) and park in front of the new, windowless mausoleum. Take the left entrance and turn left at the first hallway through the doorway. Walk about halfway to Plot 222, on the right, third row from the bottom. If you walk back toward the opposite side of the mausoleum and upstairs to the Sanctuary of Bells, you will find the final resting places of blues greats Charles Brown (926) and Lowell Fulson (927), as well as the legendary Ella Fitzgerald (1059).

A fine little girl she wait for me,
Me catch the ship for cross the sea,
Me sail the ship all alone,
Me never think me make it home.

The original first verse to "Louie Louie."

JOHN BONHAM

BORN May 31, 1948
Redditch, Worcestershire, England

DIED September 25, 1980
Windsor, England

CAUSE OF DEATH Choked on Vomit
Age 32

Bonham with Jimmy Page (left) for one last publicity shot.

The most successful and influential rock quartet of the seventies, Led Zeppelin grew out of the British blues scene and defined a generation of heavy metal and progressive rock. The primary foundation upon which Led Zeppelin was built was the massive low-end thunder of drummer John Henry "Bonzo" Bonham. While Bonham's insatiable appetite for booze, carnage, hotel destruction, and wild orgies have been well documented since his passing, nobody can deny the thunderous power behind his drum kit. His legendary heavy right foot on the bass and lightning-fast triplets were his trademark, earning him the distinction as one of rock 'n' roll's greatest drummers.

In the Beginning . . .

Receiving his first full drum kit at the age of fifteen, John Henry Bonham quickly developed a reputation as a talented musician. Working in and around the Birmingham area with the likes of Terry and the Spiders and A Way of Life, he was also known as the only drummer in the area banned from many of the nightclubs due to his thunderous and violent playing style.

Bonham first played with future Led Zeppelin frontman Robert Plant in the band the Crawling King Snakes. After going their separate ways in other bands, the two came back together in The Band of Joy, which lasted two years and released three singles. When that band broke up, Bonham toured with Tim Rose. By 1968 his fame was such that he was sought out by both Joe Cocker and Chris Farlowe. At the same time studio musician and former Yardbird Jimmy Page, along with John Paul Jones, were seeking a singer and drummer to complete contractual obligations from the old Yardbird lineup. Within three weeks of their first rehearsal, the New Yardbirds were en route to their first date in Copenhagen at the start of their two-week tour.

By the end of their first couple of gigs, their new name had already been decided. When friend Keith Moon heard about the New Yardbirds, he commented that the new group would "go over like a lead zeppelin." Manager Peter Grant changed the spelling to avoid mispronunciation and thus Led Zeppelin was born. Once back in England they recorded their first album in thirty hours for a total sum of £1,800 (including the cover artwork).

Initially ignored in England, Led Zeppelin began their first tour of the States in late 1968. When their first album was released in 1969, the floodgates of fans and record sales opened to the maximum. Over the next six years the band's reputation as a live act continued to grow, filling huge arenas and breaking attendance records once set by the Beatles. Despite the band's refusal to issue "hit" singles, their albums sold in the tens of millions.

Other than part of a drum kit and some signed drumsticks at the Hard Rock Cafe in Washington, D.C., there is no permanent display of LZ memorabilia. Bonham's widow, Pat and son, Jason (an excellent drummer in his own right), still have 99 percent of Bonham's equipment and memorabilia in their private possession.

By 1975, Led Zeppelin tours often made news not just for the music but from the mystique surrounding the band. Classic stories about trashed hotel rooms, motorcycles ridden in hotel corridors, and groupies galore (including the notorious GTOs) only added to the legend. Unfortunately, by 1977 the band's live appearances began to suffer. Bonham's addictions and drinking binges, Jimmy Page's deteriorating health, and the death of Robert Plant's young son and Plant's near-fatal auto accident only added fuel to the rumor that the famed Zeppelin was breaking up.

In the End . . .

After falling off his stool during the third song of one of the last gigs, it became readily apparent to all that Bonham's heavy drinking was beginning to take its toll. The band played their final show on the Tour Over Europe on July 7, 1980. After taking a brief hiatus, they began rehearsals for the full-scale North American tour called Led Zeppelin: The Eighties—Part I. Unfortunately, the days of Led Zeppelin were numbered.

On September 24th, Bonham departed from his Old Hyde Farm for Bray Studios. Along the way he had his driver pull over at a pub for two ham rolls and four quadruple vodkas. During the first day of rehearsal, Bonham downed four more sizable drinks, along with his anxiety medication to help cope with his withdrawal from heroin addiction. According to Jones, the rehearsal went well and the band retired to Page's nearby home. During the course of the evening, Bonham continued to down one or two drinks every hour. All told, he consumed more than forty measures of vodka. After midnight Page's assistant, Rick Hobbs, helped Bonham up to a guest bedroom where he laid the drummer on his side, propped up with pillows.

The following day, as the band was getting ready to leave for the studio, Plant sent his assistant to check on Bonzo. There he found the drummer on his back in a pool of vomit. Jones called for an ambulance; however, resuscitation was futile—Bonham had been dead for several hours.

St. Michael's Church
Rushock, England

Located thirty minutes from Birmingham between Kidderminster and Bromsgrove, St. Michael's Church and adjoining cemetery are located in the small town of Rushock. As you enter the churchyard, follow the path around to the left side of the church. The grave and monument are located about twenty-five feet from the church building.

The tensions of traveling on the road are a fucking nightmare. If you're arguing with the wife at home or she's moaning about how you're away, a television will go out the window. And a lot of time, Bonham didn't want to be away from home.

road manager Richard Cole

KAREN CARPENTER

BORN March 2, 1950
New Haven, Connecticut

DIED February 4, 1983
Los Angeles, California

CAUSE OF DEATH Heart Failure Brought on by Anorexia Nervosa
Age 32

In the twenty-five years since they first entered the music world, the Carpenters have gone from being called a bland, sugar-coated, homey pop band to a timeless classic. They have outlasted the same burned-out musicians who openly showed nothing but contempt for their brand of music. Their repertoire of love songs are rich with Richard's arrangements and Karen's vocals. Her haunting, somewhat sad vocals carry such a distinctive tone that many of her fellow singers regard her as one of the great ones. Yet fate has decreed that the Carpenters' name will forever be remembered with an undercurrent of sadness.

In the Beginning . . .

Karen was born in New Haven, Connecticut. The Carpenter family moved west while Richard and Karen were in their teens. Considered a child prodigy, Richard always had the ear for music and was content to practice every day while Karen was more of a tomboy. It was only later in her teens that Karen followed in Richard's footsteps, not as a vocalist, but rather as the drummer.

Their first big break came as they performed and reached the finals of the prestigious Battle of the Bands at the Hollywood Bowl in 1966. Signed by RCA records, the Richard Carpenter Trio (with Karen on drums and Wes Jacobs on bass and tuba) cut eleven tracks, but all were turned down. Their contract was quietly bought out and no songs were released from the sessions.

After this initial disappointment, Richard and new songwriting partner John Bettis landed an unusual residency as a duo playing the Coke Corner on Main Street in Disneyland. After five months of faking banjo and standard Americana tunes (and throwing in a few Beatles songs), they were summarily fired for being too radical. In the meantime, Karen tried out for Kenny Rogers's First Edition, but was turned down. Finally, in the spring of 1969, their demo taped landed on the desk of Herb Alpert (of Herb Alpert and the Tijuana Brass), and they were instantly signed to a recording contract with A&M Records. Since Karen was only nineteen at the time and legally still a minor, her parents had to sign for her.

Soon after the Richard and Karen Carpenter Performing Arts Center opened in 1994, the staff began receiving requests from visitors for information about the Carpenters. Richard was ultimately persuaded to lend some of the Carpenters memorabilia for display. Visitors now can find the group's original instruments and original scores of some of their greatest hits. The center now showcases Richard's Wurlitzer 140-B electronic piano, as well as Karen's 1965 Ludwig Super Classic drum set. The Carpenter Center is located on the campus of the California State University at Long Beach at 6200 Atherton Street.

The first ten years were a mixture of recording and touring. Openly mocked by record executives and artists alike, the laughter stopped when the first four albums went gold and all their concerts were sold out. The antithesis of the Rolling Stones, Frank Zappa and the Mothers of Invention, and a host of psychedelic bands out of San Francisco, this brother-sister act offered a unique, chaste sound of blended harmonies and solid pop hits. Though the financial and creative rewards were abundant, Karen wanted more. She confided in her good friend, Olivia Newton-John, that she wished for a home with a white picket fence, a happy marriage, and beautiful children. Sadly, she would never achieve these in her lifetime.

In the End . . .

As their touring and recording schedule continued into the eighties, Karen began to tire easily. The band noticed that her appetite had diminished considerably and her weight had dropped below one hundred pounds. Richard was also battling demons of his own. Strung out on Quaaludes and methamphetamines, Richard was unable to sleep or concentrate. Finally in the fall of 1978, at a Las Vegas performance at the MGM Grand, Richard announced the end of the live shows. This was their last professional live engagement. It was a sad, anticlimactic finale to an illustrious stage career.

As Richard took a year off to assess his personal and professional obligations, Karen sunk further into the self-denial and psychotic disorganization that is common to all sufferers of anorexia nervosa. Her weight had dropped below eighty pounds and she was literally starving herself to death. The recovery rate for anorexics after five years of the disease is very low. Karen was in her sixth year of this insidious disease when she sought the help of a New York psychologist.

After spending the next year living alone in New York and attending daily outpatient counseling sessions, Karen returned to her luxurious Century City condominium near the studios. After a dismal solo album recorded with famed producer Phil Ramone, she looked forward to reuniting the Carpenters. She was also in the process of dissolving a

The Carpenters' home at 9828 Newville Avenue in Downey, California, where both Richard and Karen lived for a time with their parents, Agnes and Harold (Karen's bedroom, where she collapsed, is the top-floor left room). The childhood home at 55 Hall Street in New Haven, Connecticut, is also a popular stop for fans.

failed marriage to real estate developer Tom Burris. With these failures behind her, recording with Richard again would be a welcome change for the better.

On the afternoon of Thursday, February 3, 1983, a distraught Karen got off the phone with her mother. Karen wanted to spend the weekend with Olivia Newton-John, but Agnes Carpenter felt that Karen was in no physical shape to be gal-paling around with her socialite friends. Once again, her mother's dominating personality dispensed the guilt that had worked so effectively in the past, which had Karen driving to Downey to spend the weekend at her parents' house. For dinner that night they drove to Bob's Big Boy and Karen enthusiastically ate a large portion of shrimp salad and then stopped next door for a takeout order of tacos. As they returned home Karen complained of being tired and moved to the living room couch. Although she had gained fifteen pounds and was proudly telling everyone that she was cured of her anorexia, her dark, sunken eyes told another story.

Friday morning Agnes woke at 8:45 for her ritualistic visit to the hairdresser. She went down to the kitchen only to discover the coffeemaker had yet to be turned on. Agnes then heard the rumble of the closet door in the room where Karen was sleeping. While preparing breakfast, Agnes called for Karen twice but heard no reply. She went upstairs only to discover Karen lying straight ahead in the closet, eyes rolled back and not breathing. Agnes phoned the paramedics and her son Richard (who lived around the corner), but it was of no use. Karen Carpenter had died instantly of heart failure.

Four days later, over five hundred people filed into the Downey Methodist Church for funeral services, with another five hundred waiting outside. After a tearful embrace of Richard, Herb Alpert led the six pallbearers to Karen's marble crypt. The day before the service, Tom Burris threw his wedding ring into the coffin and has not been heard from since.

An autopsy report released later in the year indicated that Karen died of pulmonary edema (heart failure), anorexia, and cachexia (a condition of abnormally low weight). The report further ascribed that Karen was taking ipecac syrup to induce vomiting. She had also been taking a powerful thyroid medication to increase her heart rate and metabolism (thus burning more calories). Her mother also found more than five different prescription drugs in her purse.

Forest Lawn Memorial Park
Cypress, California

Located thirty miles from Los Angeles, take Interstate 91 south toward the Carmenita exit, and turn right. Drive to Lincoln Avenue and turn right. Continue down about one mile. The cemetery is at 4471 Lincoln Avenue and will be on the right. Turn into the entrance of the cemetery and drive through the iron gates past the information booth. Turn right onto the first road, past the booth, and continue until it ends. Walk toward the Ascension Mausoleum with the large (two-story) glass mosaic recreation of *The Ascension*. Enter the left portal, through the glass doors, and walk to the first hall on the left to the Sanctuary of Compassion. Look up and you will see perhaps the most beautiful and exquisite tomb in America. She shares this sarcophagus with her mother and father.

KAREN CARPENTER
1950-1983
A STAR ON EARTH—A STAR IN HEAVEN

I just want to tell you, love, that I think you've got a fabulous voice.

John Lennon to Karen Carpenter

SORRY, NO CHILDREN ALLOWED
Artists who left without the benefit of an heir apparent

Karen Carpenter
Married and subsequently divorced, when she died at the age of thirty-two, she was survived by her brother and both of her parents. Today only Richard survives.

Buddy Holly and Richie Valens
Both Buddy and the Big Bopper were married. However, shortly after the plane crash, Buddy's widow Maria Elena suffered a miscarriage. Richie was not married at the time of the accident.

Louis Armstrong
Three marriages and a 50-plus-year career produced no offspring.

Robert Johnson
Please don't bother writing to correct the author. While the Mississippi courts have declared that the legendary bluesman fathered a child in the thirties, based on the testimony of a ninety-year-old witness to the actual moment of conception, I don't give a flying rat's behind. No DNA evidence, conflicting statements, and the fact that the man doesn't look anything like the great bluesman pretty much discounts this ruling.

Jim Morrison
Not that the Lizard King didn't try. While several women have come forth to make the claim, none have taken the required DNA testing to prove their misguided claim to fame.

Jimi Hendrix
See the Jim Morrison explanation above.

Janis Joplin
Unlike Morrison and Hendrix, I'd think we would know if an heir apparent was in the wings. However, no husband, no boyfriend, and persistent rumors of lesbian affairs pretty much discounts any pregnancy theories.

Andy Gibb
And who wouldn't want to give fatherhood a try with Victoria Principal as your girlfriend? Unfortunately, Andy was too busy with a drug addiction, depression, and bankruptcy to father a child.

Stevie Ray Vaughan
Married briefly to Lenora Bailey, they divorced without the benefit of children. SRV often stated that his only true love was his guitar, making the prospect of offspring a biological impossibility.

John Belushi
Although married to his longtime sweetheart, Judy, drugs, alcohol, and a hectic schedule for most of his professional life made the idea of fatherhood impossible.

HARRY CHAPIN

BORN December 7, 1942
New York, New York

DIED July 16, 1981
Jericho, New York

CAUSE OF DEATH Heart Attack During a Car Accident
Age 38

Ignoring ever-changing tastes and trendy styles of the day, Harry Chapin remained dedicated to folk music in an electrified rock age that prized flamboyant arrangements, elaborate stage productions, and pounding dance beats. His principle contribution as a troubadour of the modern times was to weave the tale of the common man—tales of lost opportunities, cruel ironies, and life's hypocrisies.

In the Beginning . . .

The son of a swing band drummer for Tommy Dorsey and Woody Herman, Harry began his musical odyssey on the trumpet before taking up the guitar in his teens. Despite being on the road during much of Harry's childhood, the family of six was very closely knit. One of Harry's early musical pursuits was singing in the Brooklyn Heights Boys' Choir after the family moved to the Brooklyn Heights section of New York City when Harry was in his teens. Among his acquaintances in the choir was Robert Lamm, later of the rock group Chicago. At age fifteen, he formed his own group with his other brothers. When the eldest dropped out of the group, the father took his place.

Harry put music on hold when he studied architecture at the Air Force Academy and later philosophy at Cornell University. With the rise of folk music in Greenwich Village, Harry drifted back to his first love. In 1964, he reteamed with his brothers and father and recorded his first album, *Chapin Music*. Completely ignored by industry insiders, Harry and his brother Steve reformed another band. Rather than looking for paying gigs, the two rented the Village Gate in New York City and played to fans and record executives alike. Their strategy worked and they received a record contract with Elektra.

In 1972 he released his first hit single, "Taxi," followed by a string of commercially successful albums. His follow-up single, "Cat's in the Cradle," secured his legacy musically and financially. Rather than rest on his good fortune and a couple of hit records, he began a series of benefit concerts for a variety of causes. Spiritual security, not financial security, is what he sought, for Harry Chapin was not only a troubadour of modern times but also a social reformer.

In the End . . .

Of the estimated two hundred-plus concerts a year Chapin did, over half were benefit concerts. In addition to supporting homeless causes and victims of drought and famine, he founded the World Hunger Year (WHY) organization and was often seen greeting fans in their cars as they waited to attend his fund-raisers, thanking them for their contributions.

Harry began his final day like most

other days—returning calls, organizing benefits, and driving into Manhattan to take care of business appointments. He drove back to his Huntington Bay, Long Island, home to prepare for the evening concert. He was scheduled to perform at a free outdoor music festival at the Lakeside Theater. It was an appointment that he would fail to keep.

Not long after he entered the Long Island Expressway, he suffered a heart attack at the Jericho Turnpike. He slowed his blue Volkswagen Rabbit to fifteen mph and attempted to pull off the expressway from the fast lane. With emergency blinkers on, he swerved to the right, only to sideswipe another car. As he attempted again to turn off, he was struck from behind by a large tractor-trailer rig that crushed the back end of his car. Due to the impact speed, he continued traveling down the expressway, and sparks from the Rabbit ignited the fuel tank. The truck driver, Robert Eggleton, suffered extensive burns as he cut Chapin from the car and dragged him from the flaming wreckage. But it was too late, as Harry Chapin had died from the heart attack.

Huntington Rural Cemetery
Huntington, New York

Harry's wife, five children, three brothers, mother, father, and a few close friends accompanied the singer/songwriter/ humanitarian to his final home. From New York City drive twenty miles east on the Long Island Expressway. Take the 49 north off-ramp and drive 5.5 miles north from the expressway. As you enter the cemetery on your left, take the road to the right at the office. Drive around to the top of the cemetery. Just behind the top of the cemetery lies three sec-

tions. His rock monument is in the center section (Section 6L) about forty feet from the gravel road.

> *This one is scaring fathers from coast to coast. I suspect wives are buying it [the record] as zingers for their husbands.*
>
> Harry Chapin, remarking on the lyrics to his hit "Cat's in the Cradle."

CLIFTON CHENIER

BORN June 25, 1925
Opelousas, Louisiana

DIED December 12, 1987
Lafayette, Louisiana

CAUSE OF DEATH Long-term effects of diabetes
Age 62

What Bob Marley did for reggae and Muddy Waters did for Chicago blues, accordionist Clifton Chenier did for zydeco; he dominated the zydeco music scene of Cajun Louisiana for over thirty years. By mixing generous helpings of blues, R&B, and rock 'n' roll with traditional Cajun-laced, French-Louisiana music, he was responsible almost single-handedly for zydeco's international recognition.

In the Beginning . . .

Born and raised in south Louisiana to sharecropper parents, Clifton was taught as a youth to play the accordion by his father, Joseph Chenier. At an early age Clifton was inspired by the records of Amade Ardoin (the first Negro to record blues records with an accordion) and regularly attended neighborhood dances to watch his dad play a healthy mix of blues and Cajun songs. By age twenty-two, Clifton and his brother, Cleveland, moved to Lake Charles, Louisiana, and for the next ten years the brothers led weekend bands at clubs and honky-tonks in south Texas and Louisiana,

While his first hit single with Specialty is worth only fifteen dollars, the harder-to-find Post and Elko singles including "Country Bred," "Tell Me," and "Louisiana Stomp" are worth about thirty-five to forty dollars each. He also appeared in two very hard-to-find documentary films: *Dry Wood and Hot Pepper* (1973) and *Dedans la Sud de la Louisiana* (1974).

with an occasional trip to California. It was during this time that they released their first record, "Ay Tee Fee," a national hit that established him as a "name" artist.

Following their regional success and recording of several popular jukebox records, they began to tour more widely. Known primarily as a rhythm and blues singer, he returned to

In an effort to get Clifton off the road, his wife, Margaret, and Clifton opened Clifton's Club near New Iberia in the late 1970s. (To get to the club, take the same route as the cemetery, but before coming to the cemetery turn right onto Ferdinand Crochet Road. Drive one mile to Barquet Road, and the club is the large, nondescript building on the corner. Unfortunately, as Margaret's health began to decline, she closed the club for good in 1996.)

As far as memorabilia goes, there remains a woeful lack of zydeco relics displayed to the public. While the Old U.S. Mint in the French Quarter of New Orleans houses the state's largest collection of music memorabilia (including Louis Armstrong's first cornet), it contains very little with respect to zydeco. For the last ten years, talk of a zydeco museum has been just that—talk.

his south Louisiana roots in the early 1960s, recording zydeco music. After several false starts on the Specialty, Chess, and Argo record labels, Clifton paired with Chris Strachwitz of Arhoolic Records. His association with Chris in 1964 would last over twenty years and propel Clifton into an international recording star.

In the End . . .

From the time he met Strachwitz, Clifton began a nonstop touring schedule that included festival appearances and dates in the U.S., Canada, and Europe. Always the showman, Clifton would take the stage wearing a cape and crown (he was, after all, the King of Zydeco) with his natty gold tooth reflecting the stage lights. Backed by the flawless Red Hot Louisiana Band (featuring his son C. J. Chenier on washboard, the great Blind John Hart on saxophone, and Paul Senegal on guitar), Clifton would tear through a repertoire of rock 'n' roll, blues, waltzes, and two-step in the purest Acadian tradition.

By the late 1970s Clifton began to tire easily. Diagnosed with diabetes, his touring schedule was slowed considerably. But try as he might, he was in demand. In 1984 he won the first ever Grammy Award for a zydeco recording. That same year he was invited to perform at the White House for President Reagan. Unfortunately, as his illness grew more serious, his potent live shows became a fond memory. He died quietly at his home in the winter of 1987.

All Saints Cemetery
outside Loreauville, Louisiana

From New Iberia (about forty minutes from Lafayette), take Route 86 to Loreauville. Drive past the Patio restaurant on the left and turn right onto LA 3242 (the sign will say Lake Dautcrive). Drive 1.5 miles and turn left on Harold Laundry Road. Drive 1.5 miles and the cemetery will be on your right.

Pull into the second driveway and drive halfway up toward the mausoleum. Clifton's unmarked grave on the right (in the main center section) is made of a simple white, above-ground cement slab. His grave is in the same row as Broussard and Veret, and his plot is the one closest to the road. Naturally, as the undisputed King of Zydeco, Clifton Chenier was buried wearing his crown.

> I started as a sugar cane cutter in the fields of Loreauville, Louisiana. I remember people used to laugh at me for playing the accordion, and now today everybody wants to play the accordion and zydeco music like Clifton!
>
> Clifton Chenier

PATSY CLINE

BORN September 8, 1932
Winchester, Virginia

DIED March 5, 1963
Camden, Tennessee

CAUSE OF DEATH Plane Crash
Age 30

Despite a career that only lasted a short six years, Virginia Hensley "Patsy Cline" Dick has assumed the legendary status as Queen of Country Music, a status that all women of country will be measured against. Upon her sudden passing in 1963, she had eight albums to her credit. Since then there have been over forty additional releases of her timeless material. Possessing a dynamic voice and an extended vocal range, she injected so much emotion into her songs that she was often moved to tears while performing.

In the Beginning . . .

Because of her poverty-stricken upbringing, Virginia Hensley sought refuge from her grim reality by performing anywhere, anytime she could. Regardless of whether she was dancing, singing, or performing, her single-minded goal was to become a member of the Grand Ole Opry.

After years of appearing locally in Winchester, Virginia, in school plays, church choirs, and small clubs, Virginia took her first step toward the big time. When Opry star Wally Fowler and his Oak Ridge Quartet performed locally, Virginia bluffed her way backstage for an audition. You can imagine the look in Virginia's mom's eyes when her daughter brought Wally Fowler back to their modest home after the show with an invitation to audition for the Grand Ole Opry. Although she received an offer from Roy Acuff to perform, money was tight and she returned to Winchester and her clerk's job at Gaunt's drugstore.

By age sixteen, Virginia entered Winchester's Handley High School. In extreme poverty, she lived with her mom, Hilda, and her sister, Sylvia Mae, in a two-room home at 608 South Kent Street. Poor as church mice, Virginia dropped out of high school in her sophomore year, telling her mother, "It's more important for us to eat than for me to get an education."

Until funds are secured for a Patsy Cline Museum in Winchester, Virginia, fans can see the bulk of memorabilia in either Nashville, Tennessee, or Winchester. In Nashville the Grand Ole Opry has an extensive collection, including stage costumes (see right), hand-tooled boots, personal letters, and a re-creation of the living room from Patsy and Charlie's Nashville home (including the custom hand-tooled leather bar). Down the road at the Country Music Hall of Fame and Museum, the one piece of memorabilia guaranteed to stop any fan in their tracks is the travel clock owned by Patsy, stopped at the precious moment of her passing—6:20.

In Winchester, stop by the Visitors' Center for a map of the city. In old downtown, you will find her home at 608 South Kent Street, Gaunt's drugstore on Valley Avenue (where they keep a section of the store just as when she worked there), G&M Music at 38 West Boscawen Street (where she first recorded), and Kurtz Cultural Center, which has a nice display including one of her mink coats.

Virginia continued to develop her talent at the local beer joints, fraternal clubs, and racetracks. After a quick spell with Gene Shiner's Metronomes, Virginia joined local boys Bill Peer and the Melody Boys. After a marriage to Gerald Cline (which she deeply regretted), Bill changed her name to Patsy (Virginia sounded "too proper"). Some months later Hilda took Patsy back to Nashville, where she sang with Roy Acuff and his Smoky Mountain Boys at a local amusement park.

In 1954 Patsy was asked to sing on the *Town and Country* radio show. Patsy earned fifty dollars and over one million new fans. From the show she cut her first single, "It Wasn't God Who Made Honky-Tonk Angels." The following month she signed a record contract with Bill McCall and his 4 Star Music Sales (a contract that was about as good as her first marriage). In addition to releasing some forgettable pop tunes, she auditioned and won a spot on Arthur Godfrey's *Talent Scout* TV show on CBS. Persuaded to drop the cowgirl outfits for cocktail dresses, she sang "Walkin' After Midnight" on the first show and subsequently sold 750,000 copies. With another hit single she released her first album, *Patsy Cline*.

In the End . . .

In 1957, Cline married local Winchester native Charlie Dick and moved to Nashville, Tennessee. She toured extensively with Faron Young and Ferlin Husky to make money while she waited for her 4 Star contract to expire.

By the end of 1962, Patsy added two more albums to her name, several hit singles, a new home, and two beautiful children. Her increasingly sophisticated image was reinforced when she played the Hollywood Bowl in Los Angeles with country legend Johnny Cash. She followed that concert with an engagement for a week at the Las Vegas Mint Casino. She also performed landmark concerts in Hawaii and Carnegie Hall with the Jordanaires (backup singers to Elvis Presley).

Patsy and Charlie's home at 608 South Kent Street in Winchester, Virginia. Up until her passing in 1998, Hilda Hensley (Patsy's mom) lived directly across the street.

In February of 1963, she cut her final recordings for a March release on the Decca label. With her current single, "Leavin' on My Mind," Patsy, along with Hawkshaw Hawkins, Cowboy Copas, and other Opry stars, played a Kansas City benefit for the family of country DJ Cactus Jack Call (whom Patsy did not know). She topped the bill on what was fated to be her final performance.

After the concert they were delayed by bad weather and a heavy fog. Dottie West offered to drive them back to Nashville. With her bags packed and waiting in the lobby, Patsy and Hawkshaw backed out at the last minute. They finally left Kansas City two days later after manager and pilot Randy Hughes called his wife and she reported clear skies in Nashville. Unfortunately, she was viewing the sky through the eye of the storm. Randy left Kansas City and stopped in Dyersburg, Tennessee—just behind the storm front. Although Hughes was not rated for instrument flying and several commercial airlines canceled their flights, Randy, Patsy, Hawkshaw, and

How can an artist nearly forty years gone keep releasing new material? Well, it all depends on where the tapes are misplaced. In the case of her latest release, *Patsy Cline: Birth of a Star*, one just has to look in the attic of her former Nashville home. After she died in 1963, her husband Charlie Dick sold the house at 1305 Bell Grimes Lane to country singer Wilma Burgess. When she sold the house in 1998, the new owners discovered the lost tapes—performances culled from her 1957-58 appearances on Arthur Godfrey's *Talent Scouts*.

Cowboy Copas left Dyersburg at 6:00 P.M. They flew just a short time when witnesses saw the plane flying erratically. No doubt panicking along with his passengers, Randy revved the plane to climb, then slowed down to find a place to land the plane in the darkness of night. The plane, now flying upside down, clipped tree tops before plunging straight into the ground.

Reported overdue at 9:00 P.M., the bodies of all four passengers were found at daybreak the following morning by friend and country singer Roger Miller. Surrounded by broken guitars, boots, and Patsy's handmade dresses, Patsy's travel clock lay next to her, stopped at 6:20—the precise moment of impact.

Shenandoah Memorial Park
Winchester, Virginia

From Highway 50, take 522 south and drive approximately two miles. Before you reach the light, turn right into the first entrance into the cemetery. Drive through the gates and turn right at the first road. Drive fifty feet to the first bench on your left. Patsy's grave is just off the road next to the bench.

She liked to come to Tootsie's with Charlie. We'd have a few beers, laugh, and play music. She loved to laugh. She told dirty jokes. She liked to howl and laugh. She had a good heart. She was a really good person, a person you wanted to have in your corner.

Roger Miller

THE DAY COUNTRY MUSIC DIED

OTHER MUSICIANS WHO DIED ON THAT FATEFUL FLIGHT OF MARCH 5, 1963

Lloyd "Cowboy" Copas
July 15, 1913—March 5, 1963

Cowboy Copas emerged as one of the great post-World War II coun-try singers, becoming a regular at the Grand Ole Opry. A skillful gui-tarist and honky-tonk-style singer, Cope built his career in the Midwest through a string of one-nighters, only to find his memory forever associated with Patsy Cline. He replaced Eddy Arnold as lead vocalist for Pee Wee King and His Golden West Cowboys at leg-endary radio station WSM and the Grand Ole Opry. From 1944 until 1951 he had a string of hits including "Signed, Sealed, and Delivered," "Tennessee Waltz," "Breeze," and "Candy Kisses." At the time he was such a major star that Hank

Williams opened for him. However, with rock 'n' roll beginning to emerge, Cope found that his straight honky-tonk whiskey-soaked style did not lend itself to rockabilly-type numbers. He spent nine years in obscuri-ty before he hit it big in 1960 with "Alabam." He then delivered hit after hit to his record company, returned to the Opry, and was enjoying his return to the big time at the time of his death.

Hawkshaw Hawkins
December 22, 1921—March 5, 1963

He possessed the good looks and personality of a hillbilly heart-throb and the talent to mix honky-tonk with classic country. The result was membership into the Grand Ole Opry before he took that fateful plane ride. He had just returned to the charts with "Lonesome 7-7203" when he passed away.

Cowboy Copas and Hawkshaw Hawkins were buried near each other at the other Music Row—Forest Lawn Memorial Park

north of Nashville. As you turn into the cemetery located on South Dickerson Road in Goodlettsville, with the office on your right, turn left at the first intersection and park. On the right is a long, narrow strip known as Music Row. Look for Hawkshaw Hawkins (next to Lefty Frizzell) in the narrow section. Directly across the street from Hawkshaw you will find Lloyd "Cowboy" Copas. Randy Hughes, Patsy Cline's manager and son-in-law to Cowboy Copas, is also buried next to Cope across from Music Row.

Patsy Cline Crash Site Memorial
Camden, Tennessee

Located eighty-five miles west of Nashville, from Highway 40 take exit 126 and travel north on Highway 641 for fifteen miles. At the intersection of Highway 641 and Highway 70 in Camden, drive through the intersection and take the first left onto Mt. Carmel Road in front of the McDonald's restaurant. Drive three miles and park on the right. Walk down the dirt path approximately three hundred feet to the stone memorial.

KURT COBAIN

BORN **February 20, 1967**
Aberdeen, Washington

DIED **April 5, 1994**
Seattle, Washington

CAUSE OF DEATH **Suicide**
Age 27

Kurt Cobain never wanted to be the spokesman for his generation. He never wanted to be a rock star. Unfortunately, it's not a role you campaign for. It is thrust upon you, and you live with it. Or you don't.

In the Beginning . . .

Kurt was remembered by family and friends as a happy, inquisitive, and energetic child. At age eight, his world changed drastically when his mother filed for divorce. Sullen and withdrawn, Kurt lived with his mother for one year before moving in with his father. Diagnosed with chronic bronchitis and scoliosis, this once energetic child grew into a sickly teen. To compound matters, in 1979 a great-uncle, and later another uncle, committed suicide. Life in the Cobain family was not easy.

When his father remarried, their relationship deteriorated and Kurt was thrown out of the house. He bounced around, living with different relatives and his mother, but nothing ever lasted more than a year. One day, Kurt's mother took all the guns out of the house and threw them into the Wishkah River during a fit of rage. The next day Kurt fished the guns out and pawned them for his first amplifier.

Meanwhile, punk was thriving and music sounded like Kurt felt—raw, desperate, and angry. He dropped out of high school, never held a job, and was booted from one friend's couch to another, eventually living under a bridge in Aberdeen, Washington. He finally persuaded his friend, Kris (later Krist) Novoselic, to form a band. After a couple name changes, from Fecal Matter and Skid Row, Nirvana was formed.

They moved to Olympia and by 1988, Nirvana had recorded a batch of demo tapes. They released their first single, "Love Buzz"/"Big Cheese," and the following year released their first album, *Bleach* (total cost to produce the album: $606.17). They dropped original drummer Chad Channing and guitarist Jason Everman and brought Dave Grohl in on drums. That's when everything clicked. *Nevermind* was released in 1991 and by Christmas it was the number one selling album of the year.

Unless you were among the five thousand mourners at the candlelight vigil held at the Seattle Center the evening of his memorial service, then chances are you didn't get one of the numerous articles of clothing and personal effects that his widow, Courtney Love, handed out to the crowd. The addition to his home where his body was found was torn down by the new owners within days after Courtney sold the home. And while Courtney still has in her possession the bulk of Kurt's Nirvana memorabilia, Seattle's Experience Music Project has a few lyric sheets and guitars in their collection.

Kurt Cobain's troubled last days

Drugs, guns and threats; and then he disappeared

Once *Nevermind* was released, Cobain battled to make sense of his new circumstances and to find a way to create rock 'n' roll for the masses, and still uphold his own integrity. The pressure of that effort and a struggle with drug addition led to an attempted suicide in Rome and two aborted efforts to detox. Sometime in April 1994, he wrote the following letter:

To Boddah

Speaking from the tongue of an experienced simpleton who obviously would rather be an emasculated, infantile complain-ee. This note should be pretty easy to understand. All the warnings from the Punk Rock 101 courses over the years, since my first introduction to the, shall we say, ethics involved with independence and the embracement of your community has proven to be very true. I haven't felt the excitement of listening to as well as creating music along with reading and writing for too many years now. I feel guilty beyond words about these things. For example when we're backstage and the lights go out and the manic roar of the crowd begins, it doesn't affect me the way in which it did for

He's probably going to turn up dead and join that stupid club.
Wendy O'Connor (mother of Kurt Cobain), to Courtney Love two hours before Kurt was found dead.

Freddy Mercury, who seemed to love, relish in the love and adoration from the crowd which is something I totally admire and envy. The fact is, I can't fool you, any one of you. It simply isn't fair to you or me. The worst crime I can think of would be to rip people off by faking it and pretending as if I'm having 100% fun. Sometimes I feel as if I should have a punch-in time clock before I walk on stage. I've tried everything within my power to appreciate it (and I do, God, believe me I do, but it's not enough). I appreciate the fact that I and we have affected things when they're gone. I'm too sensitive. I need to be slightly numb in order to regain the enthusiasm I once had as a child. On our last 3 tours, I've had a much better appreciation for all the people I've known personally and as fans of our music, but I still can't get over the frustration, the guilt and empathy I have for everyone. There's good in all of us and I think I simply love people too much, so much that it makes me feel too fucking sad. The sad little, sensitive, unappreciative, Pisces, Jesus man! Why don't you just enjoy it? I don't know! I have a goddess of a wife who sweats ambition and empathy and a daughter who reminds me too much of what I used to be, full of love and joy, kissing every person she meets because everyone is good and will do her no harm. And that terrifies me to the point to where I can barely function. I can't stand the thought of Frances becoming the miserable, self-destructive, death rocker that I've become. I have it good, very good, and I'm grateful, but since the age of seven, I've become hateful towards all humans in general. Only because it seems so easy for people to get along and have empathy. Only because I love and feel sorry for people too much I guess. Thank you all from the pit of my burning, nauseous stomach for your letters and concern during the past years. I'm too much of an erratic, moody baby! I don't have the passion anymore, and so remember, it's better to burn out than to fade away. Peace, love, Empathy Kurt Cobain.

> Frances and Courtney, I'll be at your altar.
> Please keep going Courtney / for Frances
> for her life which will be so much happier without me.
> I LOVE YOU. I LOVE YOU

Cobain was cremated, his ashes allegedly spread in the Wishkah River in Washington. Shortly after his memorial services, Courtney Love began to shop around the ashes to various cemeteries in the Seattle area. Cemeteries were very reluctant to house the final remains of rock's angry prophet-of-the-week. Several cemeteries quoted her amounts close to $100,000 just for the security alone. At Lake View Cemetery in Seattle, known as the final resting place for both Bruce and Brandon Lee, she was politely told, "I'm sorry, but one cultural icon is enough for this cemetery." Within the year Courtney released a statement to the press indicating that she had spread Kurt's ashes in the Ganges River in India. Interesting choice, since neither Kurt nor Courtney had been to India. She also claims that she scattered Kurt under the weeping willow at their former home, in a living room altar, and beneath a Buddha in her bedroom (wow, that rocker really gets around!). Given that bit of misinformation, some are skeptical of her reports through friends that she released his ashes in the Wishkah River. It is generally believed that she still has some or all of Kurt's remains in her possession.

 "Where the hell is the extra song?!" screamed Kurt to Howie Weinberg, who mastered the album *Nevermind.* What was one man's mistake is another man's treasure. The first pressing of the CD omitted the last "hidden" track "Endless, Nameless." A number of fans returned the CD in exchange for the more common release. The only way to tell if you have the more valuable first pressing is to look at the total time registered on the CD—42:39 for the first pressing versus 59:23 for the later release. The first pressing is now worth about twenty-five dollars to collectors.

BETTER TO BURN OUT THAN FADE AWAY
ARTISTS WHO OPTED OUT VIA THE PERMANENT SOLUTION

Danny Gatton—age 49
Known as the Greatest Guitarist You've Never Heard, Gatton was a legend in the Washington, D.C., area and a musician's musician to Chet Atkins, Les Paul, and Buddy Emmons (to name a few). Why, after a brief argument with his wife, he chose to end his life with a self-inflicted gunshot wound is a mystery to his family and friends to this day.

Ian Curtis—age 33
Formed in the aftermath of the punk explosion in England, Joy Division was known for the band's dynamic, manic live shows (in part due to lead singer Curtis's ill health). An epilepsy sufferer, he was prone to breakdowns and seizures while on stage. Soon it became difficult to discern the seizures from his usual onstage jerkiness. As time went by, Curtis grew weaker and more prone to seizures. In May 1980, two days before beginning the group's first U.S. tour, Curtis was found hanged in his home, with a note that read "I just can't cope anymore."

Donny Hathaway—age 33
Best remembered for his duets with Roberta Flack ("Where Is the Love" [1972] and "The Closer I Get to You" [1978]), his compositions were recorded by such luminaries as Aretha Franklin and Jerry Butler. Why he chose to jump from his fifteenth-floor room at New York's Essex House hotel remains a mystery to all who knew this talented man.

Phil Ochs—age 35
Favorably compared with Woody Guthrie, Ochs was considered one of the finest topical folksingers of his generation. However, after the liberal climate that spawned his success ebbed and an attempted strangulation that permanently impaired his singing voice, Ochs succumbed to his schizophrenia and was found hanged at his sister's home in New York.

Danny Rapp—age 41
Known as the lead singer for the doo-wop group Danny and the Juniors, who had a #1 hit with "At the Hop." After a reissue in 1976 returned the hit to the U.K. Top 40, Danny led a quiet life in Arizona before turning a gun on himself in 1983.

Susannah McCorkle—age 55
With a repertoire of three thousand songs, McCorkle was a direct stylistic descendant of the great Billie Holiday. With her warm, sultry voice she lingered just far enough behind the beat to offer the listener a unique interpretation of old, familiar pop-jazz standards. In 2001, after writing a suicide note and will, she jumped from her apartment at 41 West Eighty-sixth Street in New York City.

Don't forget **Paul Williams** of the Temptations, **Screamin' Lord Sutch** (who worked with Jeff Beck, Jimmy Page, and Keith Moon), jazz trombonist **Frank Rosolino** (after killing his two children), **Del Shannon** (of "Runaway" fame), **Chris Acland** of Lush, songwriter **Tommy Boyce** (who wrote many of the Monkees' hits), **Pete Ham** and **Tom Evan** of Badfinger, **Michael Hutchence** of INXS (and later his girlfriend Paula Yates), **Doug Hopkins** from the Gin Blossoms, jazz singer **Phyllis Hyman**, **Richard Manuel** from The Band, and lastly the musically forgettable **Wendy O. Williams**, lead singer of the Plasmatics.

EDDIE COCHRAN

BORN October 3, 1938
Albert Lea, Minnesota

DIED April 17, 1960
Chippenham, Wiltshire, England

CAUSE OF DEATH Auto Accident
Age 21

To many, fifties rock 'n' roll went out of fashion with hula hoops and poodle skirts. But Eddie Cochran's twangy guitar riffs, the defiant attitude of his songs, and his dynamic performances made him an icon to then-newcomers the Rolling Stones, the Beatles, and the Who. To each generation of teenagers who hear it, "Summertime Blues" is more than a song—it has become the universally accepted anthem of teenage angst and rebellion.

In the Beginning . . .

Born in Minnesota and raised in Oklahoma City, this future guitar hero's first entry into music was with the school band on the clarinet. He had tried out as a drummer and as a trombonist and had been rejected for both. While listening to country and western music on the radio, he fell in love with the guitar. He taught himself to play and began to develop the sound that laid the groundwork for West Coast power-chord rock. The family moved to Southern California in 1953. Like many teenage rockers, Cochran started playing in a local group at parties but made the leap to professional when he made his first recording with country songwriter Hank Cochran (no relation) in 1955. But after about a year Hank left the liaison to pursue what would become a career as successful country singer, songwriter, and performer (he cowrote Patsy Cline's "I Fall to Pieces").

Cochran met Jerry Capehart, an aspiring songwriter, and the two formed a partnership. Cochran's first national hit came about in an unusual way. In mid 1956, Cochran and Jerry Capehart were recording music for some low-budget films. Cochran appeared in the *The Girl Can't Help It* where he sang "Twenty-Flight Rock" and "Sitting In the Balcony," which became a Top 20 hit in early 1957. He became a national teen idol but did not like the limelight and promotional work of stardom. So instead of capitalizing on this success while

This memorial marker was placed at the site of Eddie's birthplace at the corner of Frank Avenue and East Front Street in Albert Lea, Minnesota. Eddie's original home was torn down to make way for a park several years ago.

While Eddie's prized sunburst Gretsch electric guitar is in the possession of Cleveland's Rock and Roll Hall of Fame and Museum, the bulk of his material can be found at the Freeborn Country Historical Museum in Albert Lea, Minnesota. On display visitors can find family photos, original recordings, and many of his stage outfits (including those from his last tour with Gene Vincent).

Elvis was in the army, Cochran began writing a song about the summer hassles of teenagers, "Summertime Blues." The witty and impassioned lyrics of teenage angst quickly made the song a Top 10 hit in both America and England. Cochran's next hit about the hassles of having a party, "C'mon Everybody," made the Top 40 in 1959. All told, Cochran appeared in three movies *(The Girl Can't Help It, Untamed Youth,* and *Go, Johnny Go!)* and had three major hits in the U.S. and nine in the U.K. before the decade was out.

In the End . . .

Even though Cochran preferred production and songwriting, in the spring of 1960 he planned one last major tour with Gene Vincent. The U.K. was in the grips of rock 'n' roll mania and the tour was so successful that it was extended from five to fifteen weeks. It was the first tour of an American rock 'n' roll star. Cochran became an instant star in Britain and was followed from town to town by kids like George Harrison. In fact, the song that Paul McCartney used to impress John Lennon when they first met in 1957 was "Twenty-Flight Rock."

Ironically, since the tour was such a success, Cochran decided to fly back to the States for a break. Although the tour was getting the receptions reserved for Elvis, Cochran was homesick and he wanted to get married and work with production and songwriting. On the early, wet morning of April 17, 1960, the taxi Cochran was in en route to Heathrow Airport blew a tire and crashed into a lamppost on the A4 near Bath. Cochran's girlfriend and songwriter, Sharon Sheeley, and teen rocker Gene Vincent both survived the accident, but Cochran later died in the hospital on Easter Sunday. Cochran left behind his two rock standards, "Summertime Blues" and "C'mon Everybody," and for teens he became their second rock 'n' roll martyr. Cochran's short but brilliant career ended at the unbelievably young age of twenty-one.

Forest Lawn Memorial Park
Cypress, California

Located thirty miles from Los Angeles, take Interstate 91 south toward the Carmenita exit. Turning right, drive to Lincoln Avenue and turn right, continuing down about one mile. The cemetery is at 4471 Lincoln Avenue and will be on the right. Turn into the cemetery entrance and drive through the iron gates past the information booth. Drive straight ahead about three hundred feet and stop at the first statue you come to on the left side. From the road even with the statue, walk fifteen rows toward the wall, then walk sixteen plots over to the left. His flat, double-sized bronze marker is five rows from the wall in the Tender Promise section in Plot 104/105.

He could play anything—jazz, country, blues, rock 'n' roll. I was just completely amazed. I used to watch his hands; they were very delicate looking and flexible, as if they didn't have any bones. He could stretch his fingers all over that fingerboard.

friend Dave Schrieber of the Kelly Fours

Monument at the Eddie Cochran Crash Site
Rowden Hill on the A4 Road
Chippenham, England

As you head down the hill toward Chippenham on Rowden Hill (toward the bridge), the crash site is on the right side, about two miles from the town center. As the car was heading down the hill it hit the curb, causing the tire to blow. The car spun around and hit the post. The plaque below is not at the exact spot of the crash. The actual crash site is about another ten feet down the hill.

Eddie Cochran Tour Program
Finsbury Park, England (April 1960)

This is the actual program that both Eddie and Gene headlined in the last weeks of the tour.

FINSBURY PARK

LARRY PARNES
presents

A Fast Moving Beat Show

MONDAY APRIL 4th   ONE WEEK ONLY

1	OVERTURE	The Empire Orchestra	6	GEORGIE FAME ... New Singing-Pianist
2	BILLY RAYMOND	Your host and compere		
3	TONY SHERIDAN TRIO	From TV's "Oh Boy"	7	DEAN WEBB ... of TV's "Oh Boy" Recording fame
4	PETER WYNNE	The New Golden Voice	8	BILLY RAYMOND ... Star of H.M.V. Records

5 BILLY RAYMOND introduces
For the first time in England
EDDIE COCHRAN
Hit Recorder of "C'mon Everybody"
and "Summertime Blues"

9 The Rock 'n' Roll Idol of Millions
GENE VINCENT
Backed by the fabulous Wildcats
(by kind permission of Marty Wilde)

INTERMISSION
THE EMPIRE ORCHESTRA

FULLY LICENSED BARS IN ALL PARTS OF THE THEATRE

BABY, YOU CAN DRIVE MY CAR
ARTISTS WHO MET THEIR FATE ON THE HIGHWAY

Jesse Belvin—age 26

A major influence in the development of West Coast black vocal music, Belvin is best known as the author of the doo-wop classic "Earth Angel." The single sold over two million records in 1954 for the Penguins. His fatal car crash came less than four hours after Belvin had performed the first integrated concert in Little Rock, Arkansas. During the performance white supremacists managed to halt the show twice, shouting racial epithets and urging the white teenagers in attendance to leave at once. As Jesse and his wife, JoAnn, and their driver were driving down the highway, the horrific single-car crash instantly took the lives of Jesse and his driver. JoAnn died later from her injuries at Hope Hospital. One of the first state troopers on the accident scene stated that both of the rear tires on Belvin's black Cadillac had been "obviously tampered with," however, no investigation was ever done. Belvin's two children were left orphans with their paternal grandmother agreeing to assume legal custody.

Marc Bolan—age 30

A singer and performer who influenced artists as diverse as the Damned, Gary Glitter, and the Sex Pistols, Marc Bolan was best remembered for his 1972 hit "Bang a Gong." While his popularity waned after his only American hit, he continued to stay busy up until his final days. On the night of September 16, 1977, Marc had dinner with his common-law wife, Gloria Jones. At approximately 4:00 A.M., with Jones at the wheel, the purple Mini left the road as it crossed a bridge, shot through a fence, and crashed into a sycamore tree. Bolan's side took the impact and he was killed instantly.

Keith Godchaux—age 32

As Grateful Dead founding member Pigpen's health began to decline (he died in 1973), he was replaced by Keith Godchaux from Dave Mason's band (along with his wife, Donna, on vocals). Asked to leave the Dead at the end of 1979, Godchaux rebounded into a band called Ghosts, which later reformed as the Heart of Gold Band. After a sensational first gig, they went into the Dead's Front Street Studio for rehearsal. Afterward Godchaux and a friend had just left a toll booth when their car drove into the back of a flatbed truck, fatally injuring Godchaux.

Johnny Horton—age 35

Country singer and songwriter Johnny Horton was killed by a drunk driver on November 5, 1960 in a head-on accident on a Milano, Texas, bridge following an appearance at the Skyliner in Austin. His wife, former widow to Hank Williams, became a country star's widow for the second time in seven years. Oddly enough, the Skyliner was the last club Hank Williams had played before his untimely death in 1953.

Jack Anglin—age 46

In 1940, country artists Jack Anglin and Johnnie Wright became the popular vocal duo Johnnie and Jack. Success came to a sudden end in 1963. Driving alone to attend a memorial service for Patsy Cline, Anglin rounded a bend on New Due West Avenue in Madison, Tennessee, at high speed, crashed down an embankment, and was pronounced dead at the scene.

Add to the list **Chris Bell** of Big Star, **D. Boon** of the Minutemen, jazz trumpeter **Clifford Brown**, **Cliff Burton** of Metallica, **Tommy Caldwell**, **Harry Chapin**, **Bessie Smith**, **Razzle** of Hanoi Rocks, **Rushton Moreve** of Steppenwolf, **Red Sovine**, **Dottie West**, **Clarence White** of the Byrds, and **Michael Hedges**.

NAT "KING" COLE

BORN March 17, 1919
Montgomery, Alabama

DIED February 15, 1965
Santa Monica, California

CAUSE OF DEATH Cancer
Age 45

Considered by many as one of the finest crooners in the vein of Sinatra or Crosby, Nat "King" Cole is recognized by the jazz elite as one of the finest jazz pianists and jazz vocal stylists ever. His warm, smooth, romantic baritone and relaxed singing style sold over 21 million records over his lifetime. His songs "Mona Lisa," "When I Fall in Love," and the holiday season classic "The Christmas Song" are permanent fixtures on late-night radio forty-plus years after they were recorded.

In the Beginning . . .

Born Nathaniel Adams Coles in rural Alabama on St. Patrick's Day in 1919, Cole was only one of five children that lived past infancy of the thirteen born to Perlina Adams Coles. Moving from Montgomery, Alabama, to Chicago in the early 1920s, Cole grew up in the ghetto on Chicago's South Side. Living in a modest flat off Forty-fifth Street, the Coles household was filled with the music of Earl "Fatha" Hines, Jimmie Noone, and Art Tatum. By age twelve, Cole was steeped in classical piano techniques and learned to read and write music. Three years later, Cole had formed the quintet Nat Coles and His Royal Dukes where they played for a dollar a night.

By 1935, Nat Coles was well known in and around the Chicago jazz club scene. Working and jammin' with Art Tatum, Les Paul, and Louis Armstrong, Nat was considered a versatile and up-and-coming standout. However, it wasn't his singing he was best known for, but rather his skills as a jazz pianist. Playing in the style of Hines, Cole worked primarily in the black nightclubs making about sixteen dollars a week.

His first recording date was with the Solid Swingers led by his brother, Eddie. Considered an uninspired but solid first effort, the record allowed them to book the group down south through Texas and Mississippi. Shortly after, both Eddie and Cole joined the Chicago cast of a successful Broadway show. It was in the show that Cole met his first wife, Nadine. As the showed traveled throughout the U.S., Nat and Nadine were married in Michigan. Two months later the show came to a sudden halt due to limited audience appeal. Stranded in Los Angeles, California without a dime to his name, Cole made a few dollars playing solo in small clubs around town. He never left.

The early days were hard. Club owners only wanted to hire well-known dance bands. For two years Cole played constantly, sometimes making five dollars a night, sometimes nothing at all. Through it all he caught the interest of Count Basie, Johnny Mercer, and other musicians on the developing Los Angeles scene. In 1938 he formed the Nat "King" Cole Trio with Wesley Prince on bass, the great Oscar

Nat's home at 401 South Muirfield Road in L.A.'s fashionable Hancock Park area.

Moore on guitar, and Cole on piano. The timing could not have been more perfect. The big-band sound was passé and expensive (sixteen musicians and road crew), and the drumless sound was perfect for the smaller clubs. Working almost every night for the next two years, the trio was growing stronger and gaining in popularity. With each member making only twenty-five dollars a week, Nat took other gigs to make ends meet. The result was a greater appreciation by the jazz community for Cole's keyboard talents.

The string of hits began in 1944 when "Straighten Up and Fly Right" sold a half million copies. Touring with the trio nationwide, getting heavy rotation on the radio, and appearing in movies and radio specials, Cole and the boys were earning more money in a week of engagements than in their first two years of playing combined.

In August of 1946, Cole flew to Chicago to record Mel Tormé and Bob Well's composition "The Christmas Song." Full of holiday symbolism and sentimental images, "The Christmas Song," with a full arrangement of strings, along with being a hit record, changed the focus of his music for the rest of his life.

In the End . . .

The next fifteen years of his life showed a meteoric rise to the top. Now married to Maria, Cole continued a routine of recording (over seven hundred songs in his lifetime) and concert engagements in the U.S., England, France, and the rest of Europe. Combined with his impeccable dress, style, and manners, he was considered one of the most successful artists of his time, both artistically and financially.

The final days of Nat "King" Cole came quickly. A lifetime smoker, a tumor was discovered in his lung during an engagement in Las Vegas at the close of 1964. Riding the success of "Ramblin' Rose" and "Those Lazy Hazy Crazy Days of Summer," Cole continued to work for several weeks until, finally too weak to walk, he was admitted to St. John's Hospital in Santa Monica, California. Despite treatment for cancer and the upbeat prognosis as reported in the trade papers, Nat's health quickly deteriorated. After a ride to the beach with Maria, Cole died quietly in his sleep.

Forest Lawn Memorial Park
Glendale, California

Drive through the gates straight ahead on the main road going up the hill and stay toward the right on Cathedral Drive. Turn right on Freedom Drive and continue straight to the end. With the Freedom Mausoleum on your left, park in front of the staircase leading to the entrance. Walk up the steps and turn right upon entering the mausoleum. Walk down the hallway and look to

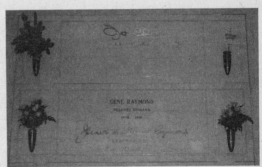

your left until you see the bust of actor Alan Ladd in the Sanctuary of Heritage. Look to the top row where he shares this quiet sanctuary with Ladd, just above Jeanette McDonald.

First time I laid eyes on Nat, he looked like a real mean guy—his eyes almost closed, glintin' out at you, diggin' what was goin' on. After I met him I found out how wrong I was.

guitarist Oscar Moore

JOHN COLTRANE   GIANT STEPS

JOHN COLTRANE

BORN September 23, 1926
Hamlet, North Carolina

DIED July 17, 1967
Long Island, New York

CAUSE OF DEATH Liver Cancer
Age 40

Whether on the soaring tenor saxophone solo on "Milestones" (with Miles Davis), the majestic soprano recordings on "My Favorite Things," or his delicate work on "Expressions," John Coltrane at his best made some of the finest jazz ever recorded. A performer and composer, Coltrane is arguably the most influential innovator in the development of modern jazz. His encouragement and patience with lesser-known musicians set a new and exemplary standard of diversity and selflessness.

In the Beginning . . .

John Coltrane was born a tailor's son in Hamlet, North Carolina, and raised during the roaring twenties and thirties in Philadelphia. His close location to New York City (which at the time was fast emerging as the center for a new American art form called "jazz"), only urged John further to develop a strong interest in music. First playing clarinet, he later switched to alto saxophone.

With the onset of World War II, Coltrane was drafted into the navy. Stationed in Hawaii, he made the best of his situation by playing clarinet in the U.S. Navy Band. Upon his release he returned to Philadelphia, determined to make his mark as a serious jazz musician.

It didn't take long for his first big break to happen—playing in the road band for blues

Both "Giant Steps" and "My Favorite Things" are considered required inventory of any music library. His collaboration with Miles Davis on *Milestones* and *Kind of Blue* are both excellent additions. His collaboration with Thelonious Monk on the song "Well, You Needn't" is recommended not only for the great solo, but also for the story behind the recording. During the session, Coltrane was so loaded that he began to doze off in the studio during the taping. Just as Monk reached the end of his solo he looked over to Coltrane and shouted, "Coltrane! Coltrane!" Coltrane jumped up and played a perfectly articulated solo, sat down, and fell back to sleep again. The desperate cries of the band leader can be heard on the recording.

singer Eddie "Cleanhead" Vinson in 1947. Less than a year later he joined Dizzy Gillespie's big band—the same band that provided invaluable training for Charlie Parker, Earl "Fatha" Hines, and Billy Eckstine. When the economics of eighteen musi-

Every Sunday, her long dreadlocks gathered under a white habit, Sister Mary Deborah along with Bishop King preach the gospel of jazz beneath a portrait of patron saint and jazz legend John Coltrane. The church, founded in 1971 by Bishop King, praises God through the music of Coltrane and is located on the corner of Gough Street and Turk in San Francisco, California. The church has a small membership with new people coming in each week to witness the house band Ohnedaruth. In addition to musical services the church welcomes the community by providing free meals and housing assistance for the poor. And Sister Deborah hosts the popular radio show *Uplift* on KPOO-FM, which plays four hours of the master every week.

SAINT JOHN COLTRANE
AFRICAN ORTHODOX CHURCH

cians on the road became unworkable, Dizzy formed a quintet with Coltrane, moving to the tenor sax.

After the Gillespie experience, Coltrane hit an artistically slow period in the early 1950s. He joined and quit a host of uninspiring jazz and blues groups. Even a switch of style to cool jazz with ex-Duke Ellington sideman Johnny Hodges was lacking in warmth and conviction. It was during this time that Hodges released Coltrane from the band due to an increasing dependence on heroin, a habit that would follow Coltrane for the next five years.

In the End . . .

When Miles Davis lost Sonny Rollins, he did not hesitate to knock on Coltrane's door. In their first year together they made five albums for the Prestige label. At the time, the band was often referred to as the "J & B (Junk and Booze) Band" by insiders, due to the individual members' self-medicating habits. Despite their various addictions, Coltrane pushed the music to the limits of conventional jazz. Miles, considered an enlightened bandleader, gave Coltrane the freedom to develop his "sheets of sound." But his continuing drug problem forced Miles to ask Coltrane to leave.

After a brief stint with brilliant pianist Thelonious Monk in 1957, Coltrane took the cure and a new bride. Naima, a Muslim from Philadelphia, added a quiet yet deep spirituality to Coltrane through their marriage. He then rejoined Miles Davis to record the jazz classic "Milestones." By the beginning of the 1960s, he formed his legendary quartet with McCoy Tyner and Elvin Jones, and released what is considered not only his finest work to date, but also some of the greatest jazz classics ever recorded. Even today Jones has remarked that the musical rapport was such that the group never had to rehearse.

By 1966, in the closing days of his life, Coltrane replaced Tyner and Jones with his wife and religious associate Rashied Ali. Spiritually correct but musically disappointing, he released a couple avant-garde Buddhist-inspired recordings. During this time he was suffering from serious liver problems. He died quietly at home at the age of forty.

Pinelawn Memorial Park
Farmingdale, New York

Ornette Coleman played "Holiday for a Graveyard" as seven hundred mourners filled New York's St. Peter's Lutheran Church. People from all over the world came to say good-bye to the dashiki-draped body of John Coltrane.

From the Southern Parkway east, take exit 33 to Farmingdale Road and turn right. Go to Wellwood Avenue and turn left; Pinelawn Cemetery will be on the right. Drive through the entrance past the office, turning left on Walt Whitman Drive. Turn right on Oak Drive, drive about two hundred feet, and park. Walk toward the center of the Garden of Sanctuary. Turn at the first right on the concrete path before reaching the center. He is located nine rows off the path and four rows from the path leading to the center of Section 60, in Grave 49, Plot Q, Range 46, Block 1 in the Garden of Sanctuary.

> *My goal is to live the truly religious life, and express it in my music. If you live it, when you play there's no problem because the music is part of the whole thing. To be a musician is really something. It goes very, very deep.*
>
> John Coltrane

SAM COOKE

BORN January 22, 1931
Clarksdale, Mississippi

DIED December 11, 1964
Los Angeles, California

CAUSE OF DEATH Murdered
Age 33

His intonation was exquisitely exact. His command of pitch and texture were flawless. His skills as a vocalist were—and remain nearly forty years since his untimely death—unsurpassed by the vocal royalty of his days. Neither Otis Redding, Aretha Franklin, Ray Charles, or Clyde McPhatter could reach his status as a stylist and vocalist of widespread, enduring influence. Yet Sam Cooke—SAR label owner, producer, songwriter, performer, and supreme architect of gospel-pop crossover—will forever be remembered with a tinge of sadness and mystery.

In the Beginning . . .

Sam Cook was born in the heart of the northern Delta in Clarksdale, Mississippi, in 1931. Like Robert Johnson and Charley Patton's family before him, the Cook family were drawn to Clarksdale because of the relative prosperity the area had to offer. At the end of every week, they would come from the surrounding plantations and head for the colored part of town. Exhausted from picking cotton, okra, and corn, the sharecroppers would take what little money they had and head to the bars and juke joints for blues and booze—hence the beginning of the Delta blues.

But Sam Cook Sr. had no time for the juke joints and whorehouses that lined Issaquenna Street in Clarksdale. As a member of the Baptist church, the Reverend Cook (a fine singer in his own right) and family spent their free time in the Lord's service. Between the gospel choir of the church and the street musicians of the marketplace, it comes as no surprise where Sam's musical heritage derived.

> *Them sisters fell like dominoes when Sam took the lead. Bang! Flat-out. Piled three-deep in the aisles.*
>
> **Wilson Pickett**

With the coming of the Great Depression, the Cook family moved to Chicago, where the Reverend Cook continued his work with the church, and Sam, with his brothers and sisters, went to school. Living in Chicago during the Depression left little money for anything outside basic necessities. For spare pocket change, Sam would perform for commuters at the streetcar stop, having dragged a washtub from home in which he would climb atop. Rather than sing the hymns from his father's church service, he would perform many of the pop hits of the day. Across town, two brothers named Phil and Leonard Chess began distributing the electrified Delta blues of Muddy Waters, Howlin' Wolf, and Little Walter. The same music that Cook had grown up with had followed him to Chicago.

The Hacienda Motel, where Sam Cooke was gunned down, is now known as the Polaris. Located at 9137 South Figueroa Street in seedy South Central Los Angeles, it still caters to the same clientele as when Sam stayed there.

Upon graduation from high school, Cooke (he added the "e") founded the Highway QC's. A cross between the Ink Spots and the gospel songs of his childhood, the QC's hit the quartet circuit within a year. Although they didn't make any money, the fact that they were having fun, still young and out on the road made it all worth it. It was very heady stuff for a sixteen-year-old from the wrong side of the tracks when the group started singing live for Chicago's WIND radio.

Within two years Cooke began his tenure with the famous Soul Stirrers. Replacing thirteen-year veteran R. H. Harris as lead was no small feat. Being a youthful nineteen didn't help the transition, either. But after a one-day rehearsal, the Soul Stirrers, with Sam Cooke as lead, debuted at Wendell Phillips High School (admission was twenty-five cents) and brought the house down. Sam had hit the big time at last.

While Sam stayed on the road with the Soul Stirrers as the nation's top gospel group, another music phenomenon was sweeping the country. White artists began covering classic R&B tunes and selling thousands of records. In addition to releases by the Crew Cuts, Patti Page, and an unknown Southerner named Elvis, a single show by Alan Freed in New York would gross more than the Soul Stirrers made in a year. Sam saw an opportunity and recorded "Loveable," "I Don't Want to Cry," and "That's All I Need to Know" under his pseudonym Dale Cook (so as not to offend his gospel audience). The songs were mild hits but record producers knew they had a star in the wings.

In the End . . .

When Cooke became the first successful gospel-to-popular music crossover artist, many from the church warned him of an unspeakable evil that would result from mixing gospel and nonsecular music. Others tried to change his mind, but Cooke was undeterred, more determined than ever to become a mainstream artist. His first big hit, "You Send Me," stayed on the charts for four months in 1957. But as the hits came and the touring increased, his personal life was falling apart.

After "You Send Me" was released, his first wife committed suicide. Later, close friend Jesse Belvin ("Earth Angel") and his wife were killed in a car accident in which their tires were cut by redneck segregationists. However, the event that changed his life and personality was the drowning death of his infant son, Vincent. Cooke was so grief-stricken that he had to be assisted from the funeral. Afterward, his relationship with his friends and second wife, Barbara, became turbulent.

Bertha Franklin, the motel manager who shot and killed Sam Cooke.

Cooke's final night began innocently enough at Martoni's Italian restaurant in Los Angeles. Cooke was sitting at the bar drinking martinis (and plenty of them) when Lisa Boyer was introduced to the singer. They had been talking for a while when Sam went to pay the bill—he had $2,000 cash in his wallet, a fact not lost on Boyer.

As his party moved to a table, Cooke went back to the bar and continued his conversation with Boyer in a separate booth. After the party broke up, most of the group went to a local nightclub to catch a new act in town. Sam said he would meet them for the 1:00 A.M. show. That was the last time they would see Sam alive.

Boyer and Cooke left Martoni's about 2:00 A.M. as it was closing, and drove in Cooke's Ferrari to the Hacienda Motel off Figueroa—a notorious hooker's hotel in the wrong part

> As far as the story behind his death, the family has information that leads us to believe a set-up and cover-up were involved. The media is not always correct.
>
> nephew David Cook Jr.

Sam Cooke as he lies in the office of the Hacienda Motel.

of town. What happened next is unknown to everyone but Cooke and his date. Boyer testified that Cooke had taken her into the room against her will and proceeded to rape her. She claimed she tricked Cooke into letting her go to the bathroom, where she gathered her clothes (along with Cooke's) and ran down the street to call police. Cooke then emerged from the room, dressed only in an overcoat and one shoe, and went down to the manager's office. "Is the girl there?" he asked. "I didn't see no girl," Bertha Franklin, the hotel manager, replied. When Franklin refused entrance to the locked office, Cooke broke down the door and searched the small one-bedroom apartment. Cooke grabbed Bertha's wrists, demanding to know where the girl was, when a struggle ensued. She grabbed a gun off the TV and shot at Cooke three times. One of the bullets entered the left armpit, tore through both lungs, and pierced his heart. The author of "Twistin' the Night Away," "Chain Gang," and "Wonderful World" was dead, sitting upright against the blood-splattered wall, his Ferrari still idling outside the office.

Six hours after the shooting, the police had no idea just who was at the morgue. They never did an initial investigation of the crime scene and simply took the statements of Boyer and Franklin at face value. However, the hotel was a mob scene by noon the next day, with rioting happening in different parts of Los Angeles. The two funerals in Chicago and Los Angeles were awash in a sea of fans, friends, and family. At the Los Angeles funeral the widow didn't arrive with the funeral party, but instead arrived in Cooke's Rolls-Royce with his banker and her new boyfriend, Bobby Womack, by her side. To add insult to injury, Womack was dressed in Cooke's clothes.

After a hearing was held the following year, conflicting eyewitness testimony surfaced regarding the facts. Despite Boyer's and Franklin's testimony to the contrary, Cooke registered under his own name (with Boyer standing next to him). That night no one had heard any yelling or Cooke breaking down the manager's door, and it was determined that Cooke was beaten on the head and arms and shot from a downward angle (not with Cooke hunkered over the manager). Boyer also testified that she had never been to the Hacienda Motel, yet police records have shown that she was a regular customer, using the motel on an hourly basis to service her clients. So in the end, the questions remain: Was Cooke set up by Boyer and Franklin? Did Boyer steal Cooke's wallet with the missing $2,000? Did Barbara Cooke refuse to hire investigators because she didn't want to risk a drop in sales? Nearly forty years after the fact, we'll probably never know.

Forest Lawn Memorial Park
Glendale, California

The five-thousand-dollar, glass-topped bronze casket was lowered into the ground in the locked, walled south Garden of Honor. The garden is so small you will find Cooke (and Sammy Davis Jr.) in a matter of minutes. The only problem is that you will have to jump the twelve-foot wall (an offense that will get you arrested if caught), because the door is always locked from the outside as well as the inside. Good luck!

HAPPINESS IS NOT A WARM GUN
OTHER MUSICIANS WHO WERE MURDERED

Marvin Gaye—age 44

A product of his father's church's solid gospel-inspired upbringing, Marvin Gaye hit the big time with the R&B standard "I Heard It Through the Grapevine." In the 1980s he returned from Europe with an intense cocaine addiction and was living at his parents' home when he quarreled with his father a day before his forty-fifth birthday. The senior Gaye ended the argument with two bullets to his son's chest.

Al Jackson—age 39

A session drummer and member of the renowned Booker T. and the MGs, he is best remembered for his work with Otis Redding, the Ventures, Al Green, and the hit song "Green Onions." He was shot and killed by an intruder into his home. The case remains a mystery to this day.

Little Walter—age 37

Best known as Muddy Waters's greatest harpist, Little Walter Jacobs defined the Chicago blues sound for much of the 1950s. He enjoyed a successful solo career after leaving Muddy with the hit singles "Juke," "Old Mean World," and Willie Dixon's "My Babe." A short man with a quick temper and a reputation as a drinker, he died in his sleep after injuries received in a bar fight.

Lee Morgan—age 33

A jazz trumpet player with exemplary talent, Lee Morgan started his career with Dizzy Gillespie, later to join Art Blakey's Jazz Messengers before going solo. Shortly after his best-selling album *The Sidewinder* was released, he was shot and killed by his girlfriend onstage at Slug's Club in New York City.

Tupac Shakur—age 25

Well known for his albums and run-ins with police, Tupac was gunned down on the Las Vegas strip as a passenger in the car driven by Death Row Records owner Suge Knight. Many believed that his murder would end rap's East Coast/West Coast rivalry; however, six months later the Notorious B.I.G. was gunned down in a similar fashion. Despite suspects in both murders, no charges have been filed.

Felix Pappalardi—age 43

Felix Pappalardi was a member of the seventies rock group Mountain, who, with Leslie West and Corky Laing, hit the charts with the FM radio classic "Mississippi Queen." He was shot to death by his wife in their New York home. After a well-publicized trial, Gail Pappalardi was found guilty of the lesser charge of criminally negligent homicide. However, the sentencing judge, dumbfounded by the jury's verdict, offered no leniency and sentenced her to the maximum allowed—four years in prison.

Add to this list **Bobby Fuller** ("I Fought The Law and the Law Won"); **Stacy Sutherland** of the 13th Floor Elevators (who was shot by his wife); **Peter Tosh, Junior Braithwaite,** and **Carlton Barrett,** who all met violent gun deaths in Kingston, Jamaica; Tejano singer **Selena,** who was gunned down by the president of her fan club in a Days Inn Motel; rapper **Freaky Tah** of the Lost Boyz by a still unidentified gunman; **Mia Zapata** of Seattle's the Gits was brutally raped and murdered in the streets of Seattle in a highly publicized murder; **John Lennon** of the Beatles; the world's greatest bass player **Jaco Pastorius,** and blues legend **Sonny Boy Williamson I.**

JIM CROCE

BORN January 10, 1943
Philadelphia, Pennsylvania

DIED September 20, 1973
Natchitoches, Louisiana

CAUSE OF DEATH Small Plane Crash
Age 30

Even in death, Jim Croce's voice could not be silenced. Four of his songs became hit singles posthumously. His music remains fresh, as if he did somehow manage to save time in a bottle. When listening to his music, one cannot help wondering what direction his work might have taken had he survived.

In the Beginning . . .

Born to James and Flora Croce, James Joseph Croce began his music career at the age of four when he sang at family get-togethers. Jim did not think much about music again until he was sixteen. Working at a summer job, he met two older black gentlemen who played guitar. Jim asked them for lessons and they agreed to teach him some chords. Needing an instrument, Jim "borrowed" his brother's neglected clarinet and traded it for a guitar at a Center City pawn shop.

In 1963, Jim attended Villanova University in Pennsylvania, where he met and befriended Tommy West. It was here that he was introduced to the talents of Lenny Bruce, Oscar Brand, Jack Kerouac, Bob Dylan, Woody Guthrie, Leadbelly, and Ramblin' Jack Elliott. Absorbing their works, he molded their influence into his own personality and performing style. It was also while a student at Villanova that he met his wife, Ingrid. They soon became singing partners, writing songs and working local clubs together. Jim was also doing solo gigs at small clubs and coffeehouses in New York's Greenwich Village during this time.

His first long-term gig was in a Lima, Pennsylvania, bar called the Riddle Paddock. The Paddock was known for its tough crowd of construction workers, rednecks, and hippies. Here, Jim practiced his humorous stories between songs to help keep fights to a minimum. He often joked about being able to get out of the way of a fight by removing his guitar faster than anyone else could. "That's why I don't use a guitar strap anymore," he would chuckle.

Jim and Ingrid married in 1966. For the next two years Jim worked two jobs, selling air time and writing commercials for a black radio station in West Philadelphia and teaching special education at Pulaski Junior High in Chester, Pennsylvania. They both continued singing at the Paddock and writing songs together.

In 1968, Tommy West persuaded Jim to move to New York, promising to get him enough publishing money and gigs to make it worth the trouble. Jim and Ingrid became the first act to sign with Tommy's new production company: Cashman, Pistille and West. Their first album, *Ingrid and Jim Croce: Another Day, Another Time*, produced in 1969, was a flop. Throughout the year, Jim spent many exhausting hours on the road between college

---

The bulk of Croce memorabilia, including lead sheets, guitars, and the like, can be found at Croce's, a restaurant and nightclub owned and operated by Jim's widow, Ingrid, in San Diego, California. The Hard Rock Cafe in New York City and in San Diego also have small collections. A Hall of Fame-style museum in New Jersey will be setting up an exhibition of photos, a jacket, and lead sheets of Jim's in the near future.

gigs. When not on the road, Jim and Ingrid spent their time broke, living in a tiny Bronx apartment, waiting for something to happen.

In 1970, Jim had enough of New York and of doing college tours (the experiences of which he recorded in the song "New York's Not My Home"). Feeling that he'd given it his best shot, he decided to leave New York. He and Ingrid escaped to the small town of Lyndel, Pennsylvania, where life was much calmer. Jim went back to driving a truck and doing bar gigs. It was here that Jim met guitarist Maury Muehleisen. Jim worked with Maury, occasionally doing backup for his local concerts. Maury's own solo album failed, so Jim invited him to move in with them, and the two men began a close personal and professional friendship.

In February 1971, Jim learned that Ingrid was pregnant. "I decided I was going to put every energy I had into getting back to music," he recalled. Jim felt strongly about the work he'd done during his retreat to the country. He sent a tape to Tommy West that contained the songs "Time In a Bottle," "You Don't Mess Around with Jim," and "Operator (That's Not the Way It Feels)."

In the End . . .

In September 1971, only a few weeks after his son, Adrian James, was born, Jim went back to New York to record his first solo album *You Don't Mess Around with Jim*. The album was an instant success, with the single "You Don't Mess Around with Jim" giving Jim his first Top 10 hit. There followed two more albums (which yielded four hit singles posthumously). Jim soon became a popular headliner at clubs and concerts such as the Philadelphia Folk Festival and made appearances on national television as the host of several *Midnight Special* talent shows.

Croce hated taking commercial jets, as they were always losing his luggage and instruments. He preferred smaller planes. "I'd rather travel on a small plane," he once said. "At least you have everything with you." On September 20, 1973, he and his band had just finished a concert for two thousand students at Northwestern State University in Louisiana. At the peak of his career with "Bad, Bad Leroy Brown" at the top of the national charts, Croce was killed when his chartered twin-engine plane crashed on take-off at Natchitoches, Louisiana. Four members of his band, including Maury Muehleisen and the pilot, were killed when the plane hit a tree and went down two hundred yards from the runway.

Haym Salomon Memorial Park
Frazer, Pennsylvania

Upon entering the grounds make a right turn and go up the hill toward the large white office. At the office, turn right and go about thirty feet. On your right will be an oak tree and a sign indicating Section B/B. About twenty feet behind the oak tree you will see a pine tree, and beneath that is Croce's grave.

I'd worked construction crews, and I'd been a welder while I was in college. But I'd rather do other things than get burned.

Jim Croce, on why he got into music.

BING CROSBY

BORN May 3, 1903
Tacoma, Washington

DIED October 14, 1977
Madrid, Spain

CAUSE OF DEATH Heart Attack
Age 73

His voice was unmistakable; that mellow, velvety smoothness belonged to only one man. Ironically, that unique voice was the result of a medical oddity. Just before his first radio show in 1931, Bing developed nodules on his vocal cords. He lost his voice as a result, and upon returning, it had changed to what Bing called "the effect of a lad singing into a rain barrel."

In the Beginning . . .

Born in Tacoma, Washington, Harry Lillis "Bing" Crosby got his childhood nickname from his favorite character, Bingo from the comic strip Bingville Bugle.

In 1920, Bing entered Gonzaga University in Spokane to study law, but found more pleasure and money in playing drums for a local band called the Musicaladers. He later joined Al Rinker, whose sister, jazz singer Mildred Bailey, helped them break into show business. In October of 1926, Bing and Al recorded their first song, "I've Got the Girl," with Don Clark's orchestra in Los Angeles. Paul Whiteman heard them in L.A. and hired them to play in Chicago in December of 1926. Bing's first records with Whiteman were "Wistful and Blue" and "Pretty Lips." While in Chicago, Bing studied music with the Dorsey brothers, Bix Beiderbecke, and Eddie Lang. Bing and Al achieved modest success with Whiteman's Rhythm Boys, before Bing's drinking and carousing caused Whiteman to fire him for not taking his work seriously.

In 1931, Mack Sennet was impressed with Bing's performance and signed him to do a short musical comedy film titled *I Surrender, Dear,* which led to five more films with Sennet. His famous series of seven "road" films with Bob Hope and Dorothy Lamour began in 1940 with *Road to Singapore.* However, his acting milestone occurred in 1944 with his starring role as a priest in *Going My Way,* for which Bing won an Academy Award for Best Actor.

Depending on whom you wish to believe, second wife, Kathryn, or eldest son, Gary, Bing was either lovable, charming, and romantic, or hypocritical, overbearing, and abusive. In *Going My Own Way* (Doubleday), Gary Crosby paints a very gruesome image of his father. Gary described Bing as a strict authoritarian and child abuser who beat his four sons (by his first marriage) with a studded belt, humiliated them in public, and cheated on

---

The largest collection of Bing memorabilia is housed at Gonzaga University in Spokane, Washington. Items on display include his Oscar, gold and platinum records, photos, books, personal correspondence, trophies, and awards. The collection holds well over 150 items, with many more as yet to be cataloged, including several of Bing's toupees and master transcription discs of his broadcasts of the World War II Kraft Music Hall. The collection is located in the Crosbiana Room at the Crosby Student Center, Gonzaga University, East 502 Boone Ave, Spokane, Washington, 99202 (509-328-4220, ext. 4297). But to be brutally honest, it wasn't worth the drive up there. The home that his father built and where Crosby was born at 1112 North J Street in Tacoma is still standing today. However, his residence in Hollywood, California, at 594 South Mapleton Drive has been demolished to make way for producer Aaron Spelling's 123-room mansion.

his alcoholic wife, Dixie Lee. All the while, he maintained a sparkling image as the all-American father and husband. Kathryn Crosby's portrait of Bing is another image entirely. She remembers him in her book *My Life with Bing* (Collage) as a charmingly irresponsible man who couldn't bear to be around when the going got tough. Bing would take off with his pals for fishing or golf whenever his first four sons were having mental or marital difficulties, or problems with alcohol and drugs. Kathryn's Bing was the man whose eyes twinkled with mirth and mischief.

In the End . . .

After fifty years of working on stage, in radio, film, and television, Bing's work diminished from 1969 through 1974, during which time he recorded only two albums. Early in 1974, Bing fell ill and both he and Kathryn feared that he had lung cancer. On January 13, a large, but benign, tumor was removed from his left lung. Bing recovered, albeit slowly, but managed to record ten albums in three years and began doing live concerts again. In March of 1977, during a televised celebration of his fiftieth anniversary in show business, Bing fell from the stage into the orchestra pit twenty-five feet below, rupturing a disc in his back. After several months in the hospital, he resumed his hectic schedule, flying to Norway for a concert in August and then to England to tape his Christmas special with David Bowie. After appearing at the London Palladium and on the BBC's *Dance Band Days*, Alan Dell's radio show, Bing flew to Spain to play golf.

On October 14, 1977, at the La Moraleja golf course near Madrid, Spain, a happy and singing Bing showed no sign of fatigue as he and his partner finished eighteen holes of golf, defeating two Spanish golf pros. Bing carded an 85, saying, "It was a great game" as he

bowed to the applause of several fans after making his last putt. As the four golfers walked back to the clubhouse, Bing suddenly collapsed from a massive heart attack. His companions carried him to the clubhouse where a physician administered oxygen and adrenaline, but to no avail.

Holy Cross Cemetery
Culver City, California
As you enter the cemetery off Slauson Avenue, turn left and drive past the former office up the hill. You will see the grotto cave on your left. He is buried four rows from the cave, six spaces to the left of Bela Lugosi, and shares the section with Kid Ory, Rita Hayworth, and Sharon Tate. This cemetery is also home to Lawrence Welk, Mario Lanza, and Spike Jones.

I think popular music in this country is one of the few things in the twentieth century that have made giant strides in reverse.

Bing Crosby

ARTHUR CRUDUP

BORN August 24, 1905
Forest, Mississippi

DIED March 28, 1974
Franktown, Virginia

CAUSE OF DEATH Stroke
Age 68

Few contemporaries disputed that Arthur "Big Boy" Crudup was the Father of rock 'n' roll, least of all Elvis Presley. Elvis admitted as much to interviewers: "Down in Tupelo, Mississippi, I used to hear old Arthur Crudup bang his box the way I do now, and said if I ever got to the place I could feel what old Arthur felt, I'd be a music man like nobody ever saw." That song Elvis first recorded in 1954 was Crudup's "That's All Right, Mama." The song launched Presley's career, but did nothing for Arthur, which unfortunately was the story of his life.

In the Beginning . . .

Arthur Crudup was born and raised in the Mississippi Delta to a typical sharecropper family. Dubbed "Big Boy" for all the usual reasons, he continued as a sharecropper through much of his early life. It wasn't until his early thirties that he even began to consider a career in music. Drawn to the church, he taught himself the basics on guitar and started playing church socials, house parties, and singing in local choirs around Forest, Mississippi. Like many blacks from the South, he moved to Chicago in 1939 as a member of the Harmonizing Four gospel quartet. After working the gospel circuit for a year, his girlfriend's aunt threw him out of the house. Selling his blues on the South Side of Chicago by day, Crudup lived in a cardboard box by night.

One day while playing on the streets, a producer's assistant dropped a couple coins into Crudup's hat and told him not to move. A few minutes later he came back with Lester Melrose for an audition. Melrose agreed to record Crudup if he came up with some original material—not the same old standards that all the other street singers performed. Crudup quickly developed the ability to construct basic pop tunes using simple hooks, standard boy-meets-girl themes, and lots of repetition. In 1942, Melrose began a ten-year on-again-off-again relationship with Crudup, recording most of his music during that period. Behind Crudup's simple country vocals, Melrose added electric guitar, bass, and drums to record his classics "That's All Right," "My Baby Left Me," and "If I Get Lucky."

All during the forties and fifties, musicians were often denied payments for their publishing rights by unscrupulous producers. They tolerated this arrangement because a

---

As to be expected, not much memorabilia was left after Arthur "Big Boy" Crudup's passing. With all of his homes torn down, the Key guitar (see photo on the right) is the only one of two of the legend's guitars to survive him. That guitar remains in the family. The other guitar belongs to the estate of the late C. C. Humbles (a close friend of Crudup's). As for the unpaid royalty payments that were never made during his lifetime, the family is happy to report that shortly after Crudup's passing, the family put a lien on the record company and when they tried to sell it, they ran into a legal roadblock which forced them to compensate Crudup's heirs.

hit record would bring more people to their live performances, thus securing them a livable income. Unfortunately for Crudup, he suffered from horrible stage fright. Though he toured occasionally with Elmore James and Sonny Boy Williamson II, he was not able to make a living from the record sales or session dates. Even when Elvis recorded his songs, Crudup wouldn't see a dime of royalty payments from the publisher. In 1952, he quit in disgust and went back to farming and a successful moonshine operation in Mississippi.

In the End . . .

In the late 1960s, Dick Waterman took over Crudup's management in an effort to secure his financial shortcomings and book him into smaller venues and festivals. By now, Arthur Crudup was credited on records by Creedence Clearwater Revival, Rod Stewart, Elton John, Canned Heat, and B. B. King, but still never saw a dollar of royalty payments from his publishing company.

His stage fright gone, he resumed his music career and began appearing at blues and folk festivals on the East Coast. At the end of the sixties, he released his final album, toured Britain in 1970, and two years later played to enthusiastic audiences in Australia.

Starting in 1968, Waterman began an aggressive campaign to get Arthur his back royalties. He negotiated with the publishers and three years later secured a deal to pay Crudup over $750,000 in royalty payments. After driving his family to New York to sign the papers and receive the first check, the publishers reneged on the deal, and refused all payments to the aging legend.

Near the end of his life, the documentary *Arthur Crudup: Born in the Blues* was released. A year later he suffered a stroke and died at the Northampton-Accomac Memorial Hospital in Nassawadox, Virginia.

Local Cemetery
Near Franktown, Virginia

From the easternmost shoreline of Virginia, take Highway 13 south about seventeen miles past the Accomac town turnoff to Hare Valley Road (no light, but there is a McDonald's on the right side). Turn right and drive to the end of the road. Turn left on Bayside and drive past the Methodist church on your right. When you come to Wellington Neck Road, turn right (if you see Bethel Baptist Church, you went too far!). Turn right on Wellington and drive past the cemetery on your left. The next cemetery on your right (around the sharp curve) is his. With the first marker stolen, the family put up a much larger monument that is easy to see from the road.

It keeps me going to have played with those guys—like Arthur Crudup, Sonny Boy Williamson and even Lonnie Johnson the day before he died.

bluesman Buddy Guy

MILES DAVIS

BORN May 25, 1926
Alton, Illinois

DIED September 28, 1991
Santa Monica, California

CAUSE OF DEATH Stroke
Age 65

Better than any of his contemporaries, Miles Dewey Davis III knew how to make music, money, women, and headlines. Fortunately, his legacy as a musician and composer has endured the strongest since his passing. From a style of music that has known more great players than great bands, the list of musicians that broke into the front ranks through Davis's bands reads like a who's who of jazz musicians—John Coltrane, Sonny Rollins, Gerry Mulligan, Bill Evans, Cannonball Adderley, Chick Corea, Herbie Hancock, John Scofield (to name but a few). But great players don't always make great bands. Davis knew the difference and insisted on having both.

In the Beginning . . .

Born and raised on the east side of St. Louis, Davis first started playing the trumpet at age thirteen. Within three short years, Miles was already playing professionally when he was asked to replace a sick horn player in the Billy Eckstine band. For two weeks the young Miles played alongside Dizzy Gillespie and Charlie "Bird" Parker. His parents, reluctant to allow Miles on the road at such a young age, instead agreed to allow him to attend the Juilliard School of Music in New York City. After a semester of skipping classes and practicing ten to twelve hours a day, Miles moved in with Charlie Parker and later became a member of his quintet. For the next several years Miles performed and recorded with Benny Carter, Coleman Hawkins, and again with Billy Eckstine.

In the spring of 1945, Davis made his first recording with blues singer Rubberlegs Williams. Shortly after he recorded "Now's the Time" and "Ko-Ko" with the Charlie Parker Quintet. In 1948, Miles collaborated with Gil Evans and Gerry Mulligan for a nine-piece orchestra, but for most of the next decade Davis primarily recorded with smaller groups. Working with Evans, John Coltrane, Cannonball Adderley, and other jazz giants, Davis perfected his sparse trumpet style, culminating in the classic jazz albums *Miles Ahead* and *Sketches of Spain*. Now a commanding figure in contemporary jazz, Davis was also the leader of the "Birth of Cool" movement.

Miles's career might have continued in high fashion if not for the obstacles that a serious drug habit would deliver. Often found in the streets or at a friend's apartment, Miles found himself locked into a heroin habit for over four years. He finally broke free cold turkey, only to find himself plagued by a series of illnesses. One illness reduced his voice to his often-imitated whisper, which would became chronic.

For an artist of his talent and stature, there is no single display of Davis-related memorabilia on exhibit today. The first (and currently the only) museum show of Davis memorabilia was held in late 2001 through early 2002 at the Missouri History Museum in St. Louis. Entitled *A Miles Davis Restropective*, the museum pulled together from private collections and the Davis estate an incredible exhibit via images, text, and sound recordings that showcased the creative journey of one of the greatest jazz innovators of the twentieth century. Unfortunately, there are no plans for another Davis exhibit, permanent or otherwise, in the future.

Despite his ongoing health problems, Miles continued to create his musical vision with such jazz luminaries as Herbie Hancock, Wayne Shorter, Quincy Jones, and Tony Williams. His musical tastes moved from soft, cool jazz to harder-edged funk and rock. From his variety of recorded material, no two albums featured the same lineup, and no two concerts were ever the same. Adding electric keyboards and even plugging his horn into an amplifier, Davis continued to defy his fans and contemporaries to satisfy his own musical needs.

In the End . . .

By 1970, Miles Davis's music was less of a concern to the press as they focused attention more often on his contradictory platitudes regarding race, women, and other musicians. Often described as bitter, hostile, and arrogant, he nonetheless enjoyed the fruits of his labors by acquiring many of the materialistic trappings he would so resoundingly criticize only moments before. In most interviews he seemed obsessed with analyzing everything in terms of race—oftentimes to his detriment.

Throughout the eighties Davis searched for new avenues of expression, recording with such varied artists as John Scofield and Prince. Davis also returned to his roots, working with Quincy Jones to re-create some of his early Gil Evans pieces. In his final year of life (in which his strength slowly evaporated from his already emaciated frame), Davis continued to tour and record. He performed at the Montreux Jazz Festival in July 1991, which was followed by honors from the French minister of culture two days later. He continued to astonish audiences by again performing some of his great (and lengthy) works from the 1950s—despite his obviously frail appearance. His final concerts were performed back in the States at the Hollywood Bowl. Two weeks later he was admitted to a hospital in Santa Monica, California, where he died of complications from pneumonia and a stroke.

Woodlawn Cemetery
The Bronx, New York

Davis was laid to rest in a private ceremony at historic Woodlawn Cemetery. Located in the Bronx, New York, take the Bronx River Parkway north and exit at 233rd Street. Turn left and Woodlawn Cemetery is on the left. His rather large, above-ground monument and crypt is located at the intersection of Heather, Fir, and Knollwood avenues.

Stop at the office at the entrance and ask for a cemetery map. This large, beautifully landscaped cemetery is home to literally hundreds of historical figures, including Duke Ellington, who is buried directly across the street from Davis.

Never take Seconals and play chromatics.

Charlie Parker, giving advice to his young sideman Miles Davis.

WILLIE DIXON

BORN July 1, 1915
Vicksburg, Mississippi

DIED January 29, 1992
Los Angeles, California

CAUSE OF DEATH Heart Failure
Age 76

Willie Dixon with Leonard
"Baby Doo" Caston, circa 1940.

No single blues songwriter can boast a body of work as prolific and influential as that of Willie Dixon. As a singer, songwriter, producer, and musician, Dixon contributed to literally hundreds of blues standards. Dixon's five hundred-plus song catalog includes such classics as "Backdoor Man," "My Babe," "Wang Dang Doodle," "I'm Ready," "Little Red Rooster," and "You Need Love" (aka "Whole Lotta Love"), and is only rivaled by the artists who have covered his music—Howlin' Wolf, Sonny Boy Williamson, Little Walter, Eric Clapton, The Doors, Otis Rush, Led Zeppelin, and Muddy Waters (to name a few). Without Willie Dixon, Chicago may never have become the Blues Capital of the World.

In the Beginning . . .

Born one of fourteen children in the heart of the Mississippi Delta, Willie Dixon began his musical saga as a gospel singer. After a short stint on a southern prison work farm, he moved to Chicago at the age of seventeen. A big man, Dixon spent a year boxing and under the name James Dixon was a Golden Gloves heavyweight champ in 1937 before he began his illustrious career in the blues.

After another quick trip to jail again (as a conscientious objector during World War II), he segued into music playing stand-up bass and vocals for the Five Breezes and later in the Big Three Trio. The Trio signed with Columbia in 1947 and they enjoyed a solid five-year ride on the road and in the studio. From Chicago, down through Alabama and Mississippi, up through Kansas and over to the East Coast, they played everywhere. After a year or so they were such a star attraction that the blues circuit couldn't afford them anymore—not at four hundred dollars a week.

Having recorded for Leonard Chess's label since the late forties, Dixon became chief house producer, arranger, A&R man, and house legend in '52. For the next twenty years

2120 South Michigan Avenue in Chicago is one of the most famous addresses in all of music history. The home of the legendary Chess Records label from 1957-'67 housed the studio and the record company that begat historic recordings by Muddy Waters, Chuck Berry, Howlin' Wolf, Bo Diddley, John Lee Hooker, Buddy Guy, and dozens of others. The Rolling Stones immortalized the address in the 1960s blues instrumental entitled "2120 South Michigan Avenue" on the *12 X 5* album (much of which was recorded at the studio). The building was purchased by Maria Dixon and donated to Willie Dixon's Blues Heaven Foundation. After a full renovation, the grand opening took place in late 1997. Unfortunately the ten-dollar admission gets you but a handful of photos on plain white walls. The foundation does not have any memorabilia nor do they have any of the original Chess recording equipment. Your best bet is to take your picture in front of the building, look inside at the few tourist trinkets for sale, then move down to Buddy Guy's Legends for blues, booze, and tons of blues memorabilia all throughout the club.

he produced, accompanied, and wrote dozens of hits for Muddy Waters, Howlin' Wolf, Magic Sam, Little Walter, Koko Taylor, and many other artists.

In the late sixties Dixon continued to work at Chess while capitalizing on the new enthusiasm for the blues overseas. He continued working clubs in the U.S. and touring with Memphis Slim in Europe. He later joined several American folk-blues festivals in Europe and played a major role in starting the Chicago Blues Festival.

In the End . . .

By the beginning of the seventies, Willie Dixon's legacy was secure. Although he wrote music for the black audiences of the fifties, Dixon's songs proved adaptable to other contexts, most prominently with English groups such as the Rolling Stones, Eric Clapton, Jeff Beck with Rod Stewart, and Led Zeppelin.

In fact, in 1987 after a lengthy and protracted legal dispute with Led Zeppelin over the band's refusal to credit Dixon on its 1969 smash hit "Whole Lotta Love" (which the band lifted note for note), Dixon settled for a large settlement, which funded the Blues Heaven Foundation. Funny thing, when you listen to Led Zeppelin's first two albums, you are listening to a chunk of Dixon's catalog.

In 1988, MCA (which bought the Chess recordings) released a box set of thirty-six songs from his fifty-plus years in the blues. Two years later he released his biography *I Am the Blues*. Now retired from performing, he lived quietly in Southern California until his passing in 1992.

Burr Oak Cemetery
Alsip, Illinois

Upon Dixon's passing he was shipped home to Chicago to join Otis Spann and Dinah Washington at Burr Oak Cemetery. Upon entering the cemetery, park your car at the office and walk up the center road directly across from the office entrance. Walk about two hundred feet and look to your left as you approach the first fork in the road. When they lowered his

casket into the Acacia Lawn section, Lot 18, Grave 1, there was a crowd of over five hundred that sang and danced to a live band next to his grave well past midnight.

> There wasn't a blues recording made by Leonard or Phil Chess where Will wasn't present in the studio or in the control room. In spite of whoever is credited as producer, when you get right down to it, Willie was the guy.
>
> **Chess Records executive Dick LaPalm**

THE DORSEY BROTHERS

JIMMY DORSEY
BORN February 29, 1904
Shenandoah, Pennsylvania

DIED June 12, 1957
New York, New York

CAUSE OF DEATH Cancer
Age 53

TOMMY DORSEY
BORN November 19, 1905
Shenandoah, Pennsylvania

DIED November 26, 1956
Greenwich, Connecticut

CAUSE OF DEATH Choking
Age 51

The Dorsey Brothers, circa 1935: Jimmy (left) and Tommy (right).

With an elegant, compelling tone and superior phrasing, Tommy Dorsey, the Sentimental Gentleman of Swing, was rarely surpassed as a player of ballads. Frank Sinatra has often said, "Everything I know about phrasing, I learned from Tommy."

In the Beginning . . .

Determined to escape the poverty of a coalminer's salary, the elder Dorsey took it upon himself to teach Jimmy and Tommy the fundamentals of music. As a teenager, Tommy formed Dorsey's Novelty Six, and later Dorsey's Wild Canaries (both with his brother Jimmy). By the late 1920s, Tommy was in big demand by such prominent dance orchestras as those led by Jean Goldkette and Paul Whiteman. He then moved from his Pennsylvania hometown to New York, where he was in demand both in the studio and in pit orchestras. Although his trombone was recorded heavily in the 1920s with Bix Beiderbecke and other major jazz stars, he was not considered a notable soloist. He was mostly admired by his contemporaries, however, for his technical skill, his pure tone, and his simple yet elegant phrasing.

After moving to New York, Tommy again teamed with his brother Jimmy to form the Dorsey Brothers Orchestra. The union proved highly successful but short-lived. In a highly publicized row at the Astor Hotel, after Tommy's last set was done, Jimmy and Tommy exchanged a few snide remarks. Then, in a blink of an eye, Tommy whacked Jimmy in the face and deposited Jimmy on his backside. Jimmy immediately jumped up, chairs went flying, and the two world-famous millionaire bandleaders mixed it up like schoolboy rivals. The only difference was that the room was filled with reporters, and the fallout between the two big band giants was front page news.

It is hard to believe that after dozens of Top 10 hits and millions of records sold, that the only piece of memorabilia that exists of the two brothers is a modest plaque in downtown Shenandoah, Pennsylvania. Their homes long torn down, this is all (other than Jimmy's grave up on the hill) that remains in their hometown. As far as their instruments, lead sheets, autographed photos, or collectable records—they do not exist in any collection of notice. Having checked with the Smithsonian, the Library of Congress, the Dorsey family, and twenty other jazz museums, the location of their memorabilia remains a mystery.

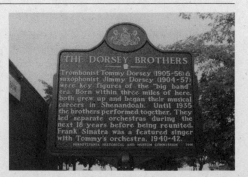

In the End . . .

Tommy continued with his own orchestra and spin-off groups such as the Clambake Seven. The well-crafted arrangements were augmented by the excellent jazz solos of Bunny Berigan, Buddy Rich, and Charlie Spivak. During the 1940s, the band was best known for taking a standard ballad and playing it at a dance tempo. The band found a new legion of fans when a young Frank Sinatra fronted the orchestra, much to the delight of the young girls in the front row.

Upon the death of their father some fifteen years after the Astor incident, Jimmy and Tommy finally started talking again. In the early 1950s, with the popularity of big bands dropping, they reformed the Dorsey Brothers Orchestra, which was particularly successful in television performances. Between 1935 and 1953, Tommy had scored almost two hundred hits with his various orchestras.

In November of 1956, Tommy returned to his Greenwich, Connecticut, estate on Flagler Drive after a concert at the Statler Hotel. After playing with his children, Stephen and Susan, the bandleader had dinner with his wife and her mother. Later that night, he took several sleeping tablets and fell into a deep sleep. The following morning his manager discovered his body. He had drowned in his own vomit, failing to awaken after he became ill. The following year the elder Dorsey succumbed to cancer.

Kensico Cemetery
Valhalla, New York

Tommy's funeral was a big event, with pallbearers including Jackie Gleason, Tex Benecke, Guy Lombardo, and Joe Venuti. From the Taconic State Parkway, just after the hamlet of Valhalla, turn left onto Lakeview Avenue and drive into the cemetery. Turn left onto Tecumseh Avenue, drive past the lake, and turn left onto Cherokee Avenue. Park just past the intersection of Ossipee and Cherokee. On the right about fifty feet from the road is the large marble Dorsey monument.

Annunciation Cemetery
Shenandoah, Pennsylvania

From Main Street in the small town; drive up the hill to the town's only cemetery. As you drive up the hill, do not turn right to go through the entrance, but rather drive through the exit and park on the left. Jimmy's monument is ten spaces from the road and six rows from the fence line.

The whole band hated Tommy Dorsey because he was such a tough leader. But we used to clap for him after he played because he played so beautifully. He had a beautiful tone and amazing breath control.
Buddy DeFranco

DUKE ELLINGTON

BORN April 29, 1899
Washington, D.C.

DIED April 24, 1974
New York, New York

CAUSE OF DEATH Lung Cancer and Pneumonia
Age 74

The New York Times obituary headline read "A Master of Music." There are very few artists who would merit such a title. However, for Edward "Duke" Ellington, it was an understatement. Although he was a gifted piano player, he considered himself a composer and arranger with the orchestra as his primary instrument. It was as composer and bandleader that Ellington led one of the most remarkable and self-defined orchestras in jazz for fifty years. He wrote literally thousands of compositions, always with individual musicians in mind—some who stayed with the legend for twenty years. To quote arranger Billy Strayhorn, "Ellington plays the piano, but his real instrument is his band."

In the Beginning . . .

Born in Washington, D.C., to Daisy and James Ellington . . . the elders served as ideal role models for their only child. His father was a respected butler who ran his own catering business and occasionally served at the White House. Solid, middle-class, the Ellington family was able to afford a comfortable rowhouse in LeDroit Park just off of U Street. Hence they taught young Edward everything that we now associate with the great artist—a distinct sense of style and an abundance of class.

Although he took piano lessons as a boy, Duke's first love was baseball (eventually becoming a peanut vendor at Washington Senators' games). It wasn't until his teen years, hanging out at a billiard parlor next to the Howard Theater, that Ellington began to focus on a career in music. He became entranced with the rolling style of the itinerant piano players at the theater. Seeking out the best of ragtime and hot jazz pianists, he came under the wings of Oliver "Doc" Perry and Louis Brown. The two pianists taught Duke how to

Dating approximately from the time Duke Ellington permanently moved to New York City in 1923 to the time the material was transferred to the Smithsonian National Museum of American History in Washington, D.C., in 1988, the bulk of the material in the Duke Ellington Collection is dated from 1934 to 1974 and comprises sound recordings, original music manuscripts and published sheet music, hand-written notes, correspondence, business records, photographs, scrapbooks, news clippings, concert programs, posters, pamphlets, books, and live video performances. In addition, the collection also contains music manuscripts of William Grant Still, Eubie Blake, Mary Lou Williams, and other friends of the Duke.

In 1997 sculptor Robert Graham's Duke Ellington memorial was unveiled. The black-patinated, bronze twenty-five-foot-tall memorial features Ellington standing next to an open grand piano supported by three ten-foot-tall minimalist columns. The impressive memorial can be found in New York City's Central Park at Fifth Avenue and 110th Street.

In Washington, D.C., directly above the U Street/Cardoza metro stop at Thirteenth and U streets, is an impressive twenty-four by thirty-two-foot painting of Duke overlooking the historic Shaw District.

read music and improved his overall technique. Although poor music reading skills led to his dismissal from several large ensembles, he was able to play with small groups and eventually started booking jobs under the name of Duke Ellington's Serenaders. By 1920, at the age of twenty-one, he earned enough as a musician to support his new wife, Edna, and son, Mercer.

In 1923, Ellington left the security of Washington and moved to New York City. He quickly made a name for himself via live radio from such clubs as Connie's Inn, the Exclusive Club, Ciro's, the Plantation Club, and most importantly, Harlem's the Cotton Club. In 1927, Ellington's band, The Washingtonians, landed a permanent spot at the Cotton Club. Their popularity grew with the increased sales of radio players as people tuned into NBC across the country. The eleven-piece orchestra featuring Johnny Hodges, Barney Bigard, and Harry Carney is now considered Ellington's first great period during his four-year residency at the club.

During this time Ellington signed with Irving Mills to produce and publish Ellington's music. After the run at the Cotton Club, Mills had the band traveling the country in two private Pullman coaches, avoiding the growing problems of racial segregation and allowing Duke to write on the road. The band also traveled abroad, playing in London and Paris. Ellington also began to compose music for Hollywood, including the Marx Brothers' *A Day At the Races*, as well as the tunes "Sophisticated Lady," "Caravan," and "Reminiscing in Tempo." In 1940 Billy Strayhorn joined the Ellington Orchestra and coauthored many of the band's signature numbers including "Chelsea Bridge" and "Take the 'A' Train."

In the End . . .

In the 1950s (known to Ellington aficionados as the Newport Era), drummer Sonny Greer was replaced by Louis Bellson and the band played with a renewed sense of rhythmic urgency and vitality. Bellson stayed on for three years. Soon after, Johnny Hodges rejoined the band (after a four-year absence) with Ellington reinvigorated and ready to charge forward.

With big bands in less demand, Ellington began to focus his talents on ballet, Broadway shows, film scores, and he continued to write longer works for concert performances. Ellington and his band became the most sought after band in the world—performing in New

Clockwise: Freddie Jenkins, Cootie Williams, Sonny Greer, Arthur Whetsol, Juan Tizol, Wellman Braud, Harry Carney, Fred Guy, Barney Bigard, Joe Nanton, Johnny Hodges, and Duke Ellington at the piano.

York, Chicago, Cairo, New Delhi, Los Angeles, and most every country in Europe. His band played with such greats as Louis Armstrong, Billie Holiday, Cab Calloway, the Mills Brothers, Dizzy Gillespie, Miles Davis, Ella Fitzgerald, and dozens of other legendary artists. Unfazed by the advent of bebop in the 1940s and progressive jazz of the 1950s, Ellington continued to outcompose and outperform them all—going on to compose two thousand pieces of music during his lifetime.

Ellington continued his productive output during the 1960s with the film score for *Paris Blues* and followed with the composition "Suite Thursday." As the sixties progressed, a increasingly central aspect of Ellington's work were religious themes. He regularly gave concerts in cathedrals and churches and recorded musical portraits of gospel legend Mahalia Jackson, as well as jazz greats Louis Armstrong and Sidney Bechet. Age did nothing to diminish his punishing tour schedule, which included an African concert tour in 1966, where he performed at the World Festival of Negro Arts in Senegal. Ellington the pianist also found time to record with the Count Basie Orchestra, an aging Louis Armstrong, John Coltrane, Coleman Hawkins, and a trio featuring Max Roach and Charlie Mingus.

By 1970 many of Duke's gifted sidemen—Cat Anderson, Shorty Baker, Barney Bigard, Johnny Hodges, Quentin Jackson, Wallace Jones, Oscar Pettiford, Billy Strayhorn—had passed away. During the final years, advanced age and cancer began to take their toll on the legend. In the final months of his life he finished his autobiography, *Music Is My Mistress*. He died of cancer and pneumonia in New York City.

Woodlawn Cemetery
The Bronx, New York

Duke Ellington was laid to rest in a private ceremony at historic Woodlawn Cemetery. Located in the Bronx, New York, take the Bronx River Parkway north and exit at 233rd Street. Turn left and Woodlawn Cemetery is on the left. His impressive crosses at the intersection of Heather, Fir, and Knollwood avenues frame the Ellington family plot (Section II, Subsection D).

Stop at the office at the entrance and ask for a cemetery map. Directly across the road you can see Miles Davis's black marble headstone. This large, beautifully landscaped cemetery is home to hundreds of historical figures, including Coleman Hawkins, Cootie Williams, W. C. Handy, Irving Berlin, and George M. Cohan.

In our years of recording together, I've known Duke to arrive an hour early, two hours late, and at every point between these two extremes. I have never known him to arrive anywhere at the wrong moment.
Irving Townsend

THE DUKE ELLINGTON ORCHESTRA
THE FINAL RESTING PLACES OF A FEW OF THE GREAT SIDEMEN

Johnny Hodges
July 25, 1907—May 11, 1970

This gloriously talented saxophonist is best known as Duke Ellington's premier sideman. He led all of Ellington's creations from 1928 to 1951. Afterward he led his small band for four years, but later rejoined Duke for the remainder of his career. Despite the warnings of doctors and three hospital stays in his last year, he continued Ellington's punishing tour schedule, only to die of heart failure in the dentist chair. Buried near Louis Armstrong and Dizzy Gillespie in Flushing Cemetery in Flushing, Queens, drive past Armstrong's monument toward the back gate. His upright monument and bench are on the road in Section 11, Subsection D, next to the large tree.

Billy Strayhorn
November 29, 1915—May 31, 1967

Aside from a few arrangements for Lena Horne and Carmen McRae and playing piano for Mercer Ellington's first group, Strayhorn will always be remembered for his association with the Duke as composer, arranger, and pianist. Upon his death from cancer in 1967, he was cremated and his ashes scattered at the Seventy-ninth Street boat basin at New York City's Riverside Park.

Ben Webster
March 27, 1909—September 20, 1973

The rough and sometimes unpredictable saxophonist played with Fletcher Henderson, Cab Calloway, Teddy Wilson, and a host of other great big bands before joining Ellington in 1940. Often thought of as a poor man's Coleman Hawkins, his true style emerged during his years with the Duke. He left in 1944 when he took the piano one night and stayed a little too long for Ellington's taste. Ben retaliated by cutting one of Ellington's best suits into small pieces. He rejoined Ellington in 1948 for a couple more years before moving toward solo and small group performances. He moved to Copenhagen in the 1960s and created a large body of work that made him a legend in Europe.

Upon his death he was buried at Assistens Cemetery in Copenhagen, Denmark, in Afdeling R on the road. The area is also know as Jazz Island, with jazz pianist Kenny Drew buried nearby. Don't be surprised by fans smoking a "respectful" joint on the grass next his grave, but please bear in mind that nude sunbathing is no longer allowed in the middle area of the cemetery grounds (bummer!).

Charles "Cootie" Williams
July 24, 1910—September 14, 1985

Cootie Williams is probably best remembered for "Concerto for Cootie," specially written for the talented trumpet player by Ellington. After eleven years, Cootie moved over to the Benny Goodman Orchestra. When he tried to come back after a year, Ellington convinced him to go solo. Cootie's recordings included the likes of Charlie Parker, Eddie "Lockjaw" Davis, and Bud Powell. He returned to Ellington in 1962 and stayed for another twelve years.

He is buried just down the road from Ellington at Woodlawn Cemetery in the Bronx, New York, in the Alpine Section near the corner of Heather and Park behind the Keith monument.

ELLA FITZGERALD

BORN April 25, 1918
Newport News, Virginia

DIED June 15, 1996
Los Angeles, California

CAUSE OF DEATH Complications from Diabetes
Age 78

A singer who could satisfy the most discriminating jazz aficionado, Ella Fitzgerald's talent lay in her ability to embellish any popular song with her own inimitable style without destroying the song's identity. Listening to Fitzgerald's pureness of tone, acute rhythmic sense, and the gift of swing, it was easy to understand why she was known throughout the world as the First Lady of Swing.

In the Beginning . . .

Ella's early years in Harlem were filled with pain and suffering. Born in Virginia, she never knew her father (he left shortly after birth), and her mother died during her teens. When Ella went to live with her aunt in Harlem, her stepfather abused her and she was forced to fend for herself. To earn money she ran numbers and helped prostitutes hide from the law. Sent to reform school, Ella spent much of her teens at the New York State Training School for Girls. Like many of the other girls, Ella was crowded into the school's decaying cottages and dark basements.

At age sixteen, she entered an amateur talent contest on a dare at the infamous Apollo Theatre. She originally was scheduled to dance; however, the glare of the lights and the audience frightened her so that she froze onstage. Instead, she opened her mouth and sang "The Object of My Affection," and won first prize and the admiration of a sideman who worked with bandleader Chick Webb. They became fast friends and three years later in 1938 she delivered her first hit, "A-Tisket, A-Tasket." That song established Ella as a nationally known artist.

After Chick's death, she appeared in major clubs and theaters in the U.S. and Canada. She learned to sing bop and developed her improvisational scat style by traveling with Dizzy Gillespie, but it wasn't until the 1950s that manager Norman Granz put her on the road to wider acceptance with the songbook album series. She played Carnegie Hall in 1957 and toured Europe the following year with Duke Ellington. She also recorded with Oscar Peterson, Louis Armstrong, Joe Pass, and Count Basie. All told, by 1980 she had

On April 24, 1997, the Ella Fitzgerald Collection was officially donated to the Library of Congress after being on loan since 1996. The collection consists of Fitzgerald's entire music library, including photographs, recordings, and videotapes. Her music consists of more than ten thousand pages of scores, lead sheets, and individual musicians' parts for more than one thousand ensemble and symphony orchestra arrangements. The display is open to the public during normal hours of operation.

recorded over 180 albums of classic American music and received numerous awards and honors, including the Kennedy Center for the Performing Arts' Medal of Honor Award, thirteen Grammy Awards, the National Academy of Recording Arts and Sciences' Lifetime Achievement Award, more than a dozen honorary doctorates, and the first Society of Singers Lifetime Achievement Award, named "Ella" in her honor.

In the End . . .

Unlike so many of her notable contemporaries, Ella sang in a voice that did not confess pain. On the contrary, Ella's joy was born from her refusal to succumb to all the degradation of her childhood. She did not live the life that made headlines; rather, she purged personal demons from her singing in favor of exalting the purity of melodic composition. Swing, bop, bossa nova, soul, or American standards all came together under her pure vocal talent.

Ella remained in the jazz spotlight for more than a half century when her health began to deteriorate. First her eyes suffered from the glare of stagelights, then her breathing became labored. The beginning of the end occurred after a concert in Niagara Falls, New York, when she was hospitalized and diagnosed with congestive heart failure in 1989. Four years later diabetes forced the amputation of both legs below the knees. Cataract surgery was performed several times to save her failing eyesight.

The final curtain came to the First Lady of Swing on a summer Saturday morning. Surrounded by family and friends, she died at 2:30 A.M. in her Beverly Hills home.

Inglewood Park Cemetery
Inglewood, California

A private ceremony was held at Inglewood Park Cemetery, where she was laid to rest in the Sunset Mission mausoleum Sanctuary of Bells. From the main entrance of the cemetery (about ten minutes from the L.A. Airport), turn left at the first road (away from the office) and park in front of the new, windowless mausoleum. Take the righthand entrance and stay to the right as you walk through the doorway. Walk to the end of the hall and take the stairs to the second floor. As you finish the climb up the stairs, you will see her eye-level nameplate on Crypt 1063. To the left, you will see the name of blues great Charles Brown (Crypt 926).

She encompassed the kind of singing that dealt with jazz, that dealt with singing the popular song as only she could, and I felt that, male or female, she was it. She was the best singer on the planet.

Mel Tormé

ALAN FREED

BORN December 21, 1921
Johnstown, Pennsylvania

DIED January 20, 1965
Palm Springs, California

CAUSE OF DEATH Bleeding Esophageal Varices and
Cirrhosis of the Liver
Age 43

Using the phrase "rock 'n' roll" on his popular radio programs, Alan Freed was credited with coining the term that has come to symbolize a generation. Although there is much speculation as to whether or not he created the term, he did act as a catalyst in exposing rock 'n' roll to the mainstream music world.

In the Beginning . . .

Born Aldon James Freed, Freed's love for music and penchant for hustling came to him early in life. Upon entering college in Ohio, Freed abandoned his journalism major to pursue broadcasting. His first job in radio came in 1942 when he was hired by WKST, a small, one-man station in New Castle, Pennsylvania, where he did everything from sweeping to announcing on an evening classical music program.

Between 1943 and 1951, Freed moved from one radio station to another, in an almost desperate effort to gain a wider audience. In February 1951, after a one-year absence from radio due to a contract dispute, Freed met record store owner Leo Mintz in Cleveland. A regular sponsor of radio programs, Mintz told Freed that a growing number of white teenagers were coming into his store to buy "race" records by Charles Brown, Fats Domino, and Ruth Brown. He told Freed he would buy him a radio show if he'd play nothing but rhythm and blues. After initially balking at the idea, Freed realized that America's teenagers were "starved for entertainment" and had no music with which to identify or dance. He also realized that R&B was regarded by whites as music for blacks only, and it would require a white champion for the music to gain acceptance in American society. Freed became a genuine fan of R&B and succeeded in building a large white audience for the music that had previously been considered lewd, its sexually suggestive rhythms fit only for lower-class blacks.

Freed's R&B program began on the evening of July 11, 1951. He adopted the nickname Moondog after the station received positive reaction from Freed's joking

━━●━ While there is no "official" Alan Freed museum, there are two large collections of photos, programs, concert posters, and the like. The first collection can be found at Cleveland's Rock and Roll Hall of Fame Museum. Highlights of this collection include videotapes of *The Big Beat* and the Christmas Jubilee show, along with personal footage of Freed on the air. The second collection belongs to the Freed estate. The Rock and Roll Hall of Fame Museum is open to the public seven days a week. The Freed estate can be viewed online at www.alanfreed.com.

antics during a song called "Moondog Symphony." Quick to take advantage and expand on every opportunity, Freed began to interject comments and noise during songs. He would scream over the music, "Hey, hey, hey! Go, go, go! Let's rock 'n' roll!" He then began pounding out the beat on a phonebook and periodically rang a cowbell. Freed's program was not directed at any one audience, and as a result the boundaries that isolated R&B began to fall. In March of 1952, Freed put on the first of several stage shows to promote R&B music, its artists, and to make himself some extra money. His first "concert" exceeded expectations and had to be canceled when the audience overflowed and small riots ensued. Still, by 1953, R&B was not yet accepted widely by trade papers such as *Billboard* and *Variety*, who were not ready to let go of the traditional black-white boundaries of popular music. However, by 1957 Freed had gone through numerous successful stage shows, a syndicated radio program, managed two R&B groups, appeared in five music-oriented movies, and changed jobs twice before taking a position at WABC in New York. But after one of his last stage shows in Boston that year ended in a violent altercation, things seemed to grow progressively worse for the DJ and his career.

In the End . . .

In 1957, ABC, which aired Dick Clark's *American Bandstand,* as well as Freed's radio program and TV show, *The Big Beat,* required all its DJs to sign an affidavit to the effect that they were in no way involved in the exchange of cash for play time. Freed refused to sign the affidavit as it was worded, pointing out that Dick Clark had been allowed to write and sign his own statement, while Freed had not been given that opportunity. Freed was fired from WABC and shortly after his television show *Rock 'n' Roll Dance Party* was canceled when the camera showed singer Frankie Lymon dancing with a white girl.

Late in 1959, Freed was subpoenaed to testify and claimed payments he'd received from record companies were for "consultation," not as an inducement to play their records. The payola controversy resulted; Freed was fired from his radio and television programs. In December 1962, Freed pleaded guilty on two of the twenty-nine counts of commercial bribery against him. He was fined and his sentence was suspended. He never recovered from this blow to his life and career. The legal fees forced him into bankruptcy, and chain-smoking, heavy drinking, unemployment, tax evasion charges, and internal injuries suffered in a 1953 car accident all took their toll on Freed. Moving to Palm Springs, California, Freed died alone in January 1965. His few remaining friends claim his death was the result of a broken heart, forsaken by those he had helped during his career.

Rock and Roll Hall of Fame
Cleveland, Ohio

When Freed passed away in 1965, his ashes were interred in the basement of the main mausoleum at Ferncliff Cemetery in Hartsdale, New York (Unit 8, Alcove S-T, Column B, Niche 2 in the photo to the right). Unfortunately, this was not Freed's choice for a final resting place. To rectify the situation in 2002 his family decided to place his ashes in an undisclosed location within the walls of the museum.

Live fast, die young, and make a good-looking corpse.

Alan Freed

LEFTY FRIZZELL

BORN March 31, 1928
Corsicana, Texas

DIED July 19, 1975
Nashville, Tennessee

CAUSE OF DEATH Stroke
Age 47

The recorded history of country great Lefty Frizzell gives little indication of the enormous stylistic impact he has had on country music since 1950. Had Lefty died the way Hank Williams died—hard, fast, and young—he'd probably be remembered with the same respect Williams commands today. But as it was, Lefty fought through a twenty-five-year career to keep his personal life together and his soul intact, only to eventually succumb to his own worst habits.

In the Beginning . . .

Molded by the styles of Jimmie Rodgers and Ernest Tubb, William "Lefty" Frizzell began performing in his early teens. His first professional singing job was on the Sunday afternoon variety program on radio station KPLT in Paris, Texas. While the show didn't have the most stringent audition requirements ("If you were breathing, you got on the air," the station manager later recalled), the station gave Frizzell the confidence and a fifty-mile-radius listening audience. After two years, at age seventeen with a new bride and a child on the way, a two-seater Model-A with bad brakes, and a hundred-dollar red-and-white embroidered cowboy singer's suit, Frizzell felt he was ready for the big time.

In 1947, at the age of nineteen, Frizzell made it to the big time, but not in the way he would have liked. During one of his nightly shows at the Cactus Garden near Roswell, New Mexico, a fourteen-year-old "honky-tonk Lolita" had eyes for the local singer. Since Frizzell never took the affections of the girl seriously, she turned him in (along with four other local musicians) on a charge of statutory rape. The prosecuting attorney, sensing a media storm of publicity, refused to drop the charges, despite the lack of evidence. Fortunately, for Frizzell, the radio station that carried his show live also owned the local newspaper, so his name never made the front pages. Unfortunately, the judge found all the youths guilty and sentenced them to two to three years in prison, suspended to six months. Wracked with guilt and grief, Frizzell penned the honky-tonk classic, "I Love You a Thousand Ways," as a message to his wife. During the same six-month stretch he also wrote the barroom classic, "If You've Got the Money, I've Got the Time," along with a dozen other songs. Upon his release, once recorded, both songs reached number one on the country charts, becoming the first of thirteen Top 10 records Frizzell would score between 1950 and 1951. By April of 1951, he was the hottest young singer in country music and was touring with Hank Williams on equal billing.

Frizzell's career spanned more than a quarter century. In 1959 he released "Long Black Veil" followed by "Saginaw, Michigan" five years later. In between he saw a nonstop routine of recording, concerts, Grand Ole Opry performances, and personal appearances.

Located at 912 West Park Avenue in Corsicana, Texas, The Lefty Frizzell Country Music Museum pays tribute to the man with a display of sheet music, photos, records, and outfits. Near the museum is a lifesize statue of Frizzell in Beauford Jester Park. Naturally, the new Country Music Hall of Fame in Nashville has an impressive display of the legend's memorabilia that was donated by his family. He was inducted into the Country Music Hall of Fame in 1982.

As much as the Living Legend designation bothered Frizzell, the admiration of the young ladies was the least of his troubles now. With his drinking steadily increased, his attitude toward his career turned more ambivalent. He was simply getting tired of one hotel after another. The road no longer held any romance for him—just another night at another nightclub, with a different pickup band that didn't know the songs.

In the End . . .

Disinterested in music and unnerved by the echoes of his own style in every song played on the radio, Frizzell reacted by withdrawing from the Nashville scene. This had a predictable impact on his recording work, as he ventured into the studio only a handful of times after 1965. In 1972, he recorded *The Legendary Lefty Frizzell* on ABC Records. In hindsight, critical acclaim and subsequent sales have shown this to be one of his best albums. Unfortunately, the trade press and radio stations chose to ignore the release. Afterward, every gig and every appearance seemed to be a lesson in time.

On July 8th, Frizzell was preparing to leave on a short tour of Delaware honky-tonks when he turned to his wife and her friend and said, "I've done more than I even wanted to do. And I'm so tired, I can't even stand it." Several hours later, Frizzell woke up next to his bed in a pool of vomit. When he tried to get up, he realized he couldn't move his left side. After dialing a friend, an ambulance arrived at the house on Cline Court. However, on the way to the hospital, Frizzell suffered another stroke—this time a massive cerebral hemorrhage. Lefty lapsed into a coma from which he never awoke.

Forest Lawn Memorial Garden
Goodlettsville, Tennessee

Known as Nashville's other Music Row, the cemetery is located north of downtown Nashville on South Dickerson Road. As you turn into the cemetery, the office will be on your right. Turn left at the first intersection and park. On the right is a long, narrow strip known as Music Row. Lefty can be found in the middle-left part of the row near Hawkshaw Hawkins and David "Stringbean" Ackerman. Directly across the street you will find Lloyd "Cowboy" Copas.

Hank Williams and I did some shows together and one day he said, "You need to join the Opry." I looked at him and said, "Look, I got the number one song, the number two song, the number six song, and the number eight song on the charts, and you tell me I need to join the Opry?"

Lefty Frizzell

BOBBY FULLER

BORN October 22, 1942
Goose Creek, Texas

DIED July 18, 1966
Hollywood, California

CAUSE OF DEATH Murdered
Age 23

"I fought the law—and the law won." These words became an anthem for a generation of disaffected American youth during the turbulent 1960s. The words, in their most popular incarnation, were sung by Bobby Fuller, fronting the Bobby Fuller Four. Bobby, like so many young talents of those unsettling times, was destined to die a tragic and untimely death—a death that is a source of controversy and speculation to this day.

In the Beginning . . .

Bobby Fuller's career began in the family garage in his hometown of El Paso, Texas. He, along with his brother, Randy, and two friends, honed their musical skills after school. Their greatest musical inspiration came from fellow Texan Buddy Holly. After graduating from Ysleta High School in 1960, Bobby and the boys moved on to the El Paso club scene, where they were hugely popular as the Bobby Fuller Four. From there, they were spotted by a music promoter, who recommended they take their act to Los Angeles, where they could more effectively advance their rockabilly-infused sound. It was solid advice.

By 1965, Hollywood's Sunset Strip was teeming with a wide variety of musical talent. The Byrds, the Doors, Frank Zappa, Love, and the Bobby Fuller Four were just some of the bands that were fighting the onslaught of the British Invasion led by the Beatles. But it was the BF4 that producer Bob Keene selected and dropped into his Del-Fi recording studio. The first big single released by the group was "Let Her Dance," followed by the whirling guitars and sonic vocals

Just because you have the original release of "I Fought the Law" doesn't make you a rich man. The Mustang label release is only worth twenty dollars—and that's in perfect condition! The really rare seven-inch single can be found on either the Eastwood or Exeter labels, released in 1962-64. These rare BF4 recordings go for two to three hundred dollars a record.

of "I Fought the Law." The band followed the national Top 10 hit with "Love's Made a Fool of You." By January 1966, their skyrocketing popularity enabled them to tour the States on their own, as well as with bigger-name bands such as the Grateful Dead.

Bobby was found in his mother's car next to his apartment just off the Sunset Strip at 1776 North Sycamore Avenue in Hollywood, California.

Like one of the A-Bone dragsters from his songs, success came hard and fast. Within two years of landing in Los Angeles, the BF4 landed three hit records, appeared on TV's *Hullabaloo, Where the Action Is, Hollywood A Go Go, Shebang*, and the awful teensploitation movie *The Ghost in the Invisible Bikini* (starring Nancy Sinatra, Boris Karloff, and Basil Rathbone). Despite the success, the band was falling apart. Less than a month before the BF4 were to tour Europe, the tour was canceled.

Recording sessions for the latest album had been so difficult that the brothers were not even on speaking terms and drummer Dalton Powell was quitting the band. Bobby was going to schedule a meeting with the band to officially disband and concentrate on a solo career. The meeting never took place.

In the End . . .

Fuller's brief glimmer of a career came to an end on a Hollywood street in 1966. His body was found by his mother, Loraine Fuller, in the front seat of her Oldsmobile in a vacant field next to his apartment building. Mysteriously, the car appeared late in the afternoon—fourteen hours after Bobby was last seen alive. There was blood on his shirt, abrasions on his lifeless twenty-three-year-old body, and, curiously, gasoline in the car. The coroner initially ruled the death a suicide by inhalation of gasoline. Despite the gruesome crime scene, they later changed it to accidental asphyxiation with the note, "There was no evidence of foul play."

Stories as to what really happened abound. Was it a murder for the purpose of collecting insurance money, or a professional hit related to Bobby's alleged affair with a club owner's ex-girl? What is known is that Bobby was found in full rigor mortis with excessive bruising about his face, chest, and shoulders, drenched with a toxic fluid. No traces of drugs, alcohol, or ingestion of gasoline were found during the autopsy. To add insult to injury, a Hollywood division policeman on the scene destroyed crucial evidence by throwing the gas can in the dumpster and refusing to impound the car. No prints were ever taken, making it seem to the family that the case was closed before it was even opened. Even thirty-five years since his tragic passing, brother Randy remarked during an interview, "Now how can a man that's dead, in rigor mortis, drive a car and pour gasoline on himself?"

Forest Lawn Hollywood Hills
Los Angeles, California

As you drive through the entry gates, the first section on your right is the Sheltering Hills section. Turn right at the first opportunity and drive about halfway up the section (for landmarks, look for a drainage grate in the street, near a tree stump/trash receptacle) and park. In this vicinity, look for
the grave of Ernest Rosecrans Sr. (one of the gravesites nearest the street). Follow this row in approximately thirty-six graves and you will find Robert G. Fuller in Plot 362.

> What we play is Texas rock 'n' roll. And it's nothing new. It's the same thing the Beatles have been trying to play but can't. They come close but they're not from west Texas.
>
> Bobby Fuller

JUDY GARLAND

MGM publicity photo, circa 1942.

BORN June 10, 1922
Grand Rapids, Minnesota

DIED June 22, 1969
London, England

CAUSE OF DEATH Accidental Overdose
Age 47

Judy's parents the Gumms were hoping for a boy, since they already had two daughters—the child who would have been Frank Jr. was named Frances instead. It was a prophetic beginning for someone who would be plagued her whole life with feelings of inadequacy, and with the sense that she was a disappointment to all who knew her.

In the Beginning . . .

At 5:30 A.M. on the tenth day of June 1922, Frances Ethel Gumm was born in Grand Rapids, Minnesota. Her proud parents, Frank and Ethel Gumm, were local entertainers. By the time she was two years old, little Frances Gumm was already fascinated with the world of entertainment. Her two older sisters, Mary Jane and Virginia, were already singing together between shows at their parents' theater. "Baby," as she was then known, couldn't wait to join her sisters onstage. In December of 1924, she did just that—and stole the show. A star was born.

By the early 1930s, the Gumm Sisters were an established act. In 1934, they became the Garland Sisters, at the suggestion of George Jessel, for whom they were opening at the time. Frances, who was always the standout among the three girls, would be signed by Metro Goldwyn Mayer as "Judy Garland" before the end of 1935. In the first major tragedy of her life, Judy's father died two months later.

Garland's film career spanned from 1936 to 1963, but she was always best loved, revered, and respected as a vocalist. In fact, by all accounts it was her singing that got her the contract with MGM—without a screen test! She made her first professional recording in 1936 with "Swing, Mister Charlie" and "Stompin' at the Savoy" on Decca Records. At fourteen, she was one of the youngest recording artists ever.

Garland brought more to a song than a beautiful voice. She skillfully employed vocal techniques such as vibrato and tremolo in order to influence the mood of a song. These techniques, coupled with her rich, textured voice, gave her a distinctive style through which she masterfully conveyed emotions and intensity in a way few other performers could. When Judy Garland sang a song, people not only listened to it, they felt it.

During her years at MGM (1935 to 1950), Judy's voice matured and her vocal style developed greater polish. The studio experimented with different types of musical arrange-

The largest collection of Judy Garland memorabilia can be found at Garland's birthplace in Grand Rapids, Minnesota. Located in the home she lived in until 1927, the Judy Garland Museum has been fully restored and houses numerous items from the film *The Wizard of Oz*, the carriage used in the Emerald City scene, and Winkie swords used to guard the Wicked Witch's castle. Around the corner at the old school is another fine collection from the Itasca County Historical Society. However, of the five pairs of red ruby slippers in existence, only one is on public display at the Smithsonian in Washington, D.C.

ments, testing Garland's technical skill in the process. She met and surmounted each musical challenge, but it was a double-edged sword. The main purpose of Garland's studio-controlled singing career was to amplify and enhance her screen image. Ultimately, her gift was both nourished and strangled by the studio.

When Judy was fired by MGM in 1950, she opted to break away from her studio-created image. She began performing live, reinterpreting her standard songs with a new power. Garland virtually reinvented herself for the concert stage, and in so doing, acquired a whole new legion of fans and admirers. Her concert years were marked by intense, evocative performances that commanded the attention and respect of audiences.

While at Metro, Garland developed more than her vocal style. She also developed a studio-supported drug habit that began when she was in her teens. Studio head Louis B. Mayer was so concerned about Judy's weight with her propensity to carry around an extra twenty pounds that he had her put on diet pills, under the direction of a studio doctor. These diet pills, containing amphetamines, killed her desire for food, but made it difficult for her to sleep. Sleeping pills were the prescribed remedy. She was treated like a studio commodity, not a child, all done with her mother's knowledge and approval.

Before long, Garland was a fifteen-year-old drug addict. By the time she reached her early twenties, the monster had taken hold, and the real Judy had almost completely disappeared. During this time, she was renowned for her starkly unprofessional behavior, including frequent tardiness, absenteeism, and fits of uncontrollable weeping. Drug addiction would ultimately contribute to the end of her career with Metro, make her an unreliable stage performer in later life, and push her toward a premature death.

Drug addiction was not the only tragedy in Judy's life. Her personal relationships, particularly with men, were marked by disappointment. At seventeen, she became romantically involved with bandleader Artie Shaw, who cared for Judy but never took their romance seriously. He broke her heart when he eloped with Lana Turner. (This also reinforced Judy's notion that she was ugly compared to the other starlets on the lot.) This disappointment led to Judy's first marriage to David Rose, a musician friend of Shaw's who helped Judy through the breakup. They married in 1941 and separated less than two years later.

Late in 1944 Judy became engaged to director Vincente Minnelli. (By all accounts, she was in love with married screenwriter Joseph L. Mankiewicz at the time—he is believed to have been her only true love.) Minnelli and Garland were married from 1945 through 1951, and had one now-famous daughter. In 1952, Judy wed her business manager, Sid Luft. Luft was said to be one of the few people who could control Judy. During their years together, Judy's addiction, although ever present, was kept at bay. They had two children, Lorna and Joey, and were divorced in 1965. From 1965 through 1967, Judy was married to bit actor Mark Herron in an ill-advised union and in 1969 she was married to discotheque manager Mickey Deans, an Englishman eleven years her junior.

In the End . . .

By 1968, Judy's problems with drugs had taken over. In addition, she was having horrible financial problems, brought on by years of mismanagement. She was unable to perform, since by this time she was well known both for forgetting lyrics and not showing up for performances. In 1969, she married Mickey Deans, to the bewilderment of friends and family. Their relationship was tempestuous. They had yet another argument on the

She just plain wore out.

Ray Bolger, the Scarecrow in *The Wizard of Oz.*

night of June 21, after which Garland left their home. Several versions have transpired since her passing; however, the fact remains that Deans went to bed alone. When he awoke the next morning for a call for Garland, he did not find his wife next to him. Discovering the bathroom door locked, Deans had to crawl through the bathroom window to find his wife dead.

The coroner attributed the death to an accidental overdose of sleeping pills with alcoholism as a contributing factor. Depsite rumors of a suicide, the official coroner's report stated the cause of death as "incautious self-overdose of her medication." Upon hearing of her death, many in the entertainment community expressed surprise that she had lived that long.

Garland's body was flown to New York for burial. There was a public viewing at a funeral home, which drew more than 21,000 people. Deans selected a $37,000 crypt for Garland, for which he could not pay. Her estate couldn't pay for it, either, since she died thousands of dollars in debt (despite all of the sold-out concert dates). All expenses associated with Judy Garland's funeral and burial were paid by Liza Minnelli. The chosen crypt was not yet built at the time of her death, so Judy wasn't interred until November 4, 1970.

Ferncliff Cemetery
Hartsdale, New York

From New York City take Interstate 87 north until it crosses Route 7. Take Route 7 north two miles to Secor Road and turn right onto Secor. Drive up the road and the cemetery is on your left. Park in front of the "old" mausoleum and office. As you walk through the doors, you will find yourself on the second floor. Turn right, then left, then right again as you weave your way through the halls. Cross over into the "new" mausoleum and take the stairs up to the top level. Looking at the bottom row, she can be found in Unit 9, Alcove HH, Crypt 31. Much like at Marilyn Monroe's crypt, there are always flowers present.

HOUSES OF THE HOLY
MUSICIANS AND THEIR "FINAL" RESIDENCES

Judy Garland
4 Cadogan Lane
London, England

When Garland went "Over the Rainbow," there was no mistaking the innocent Dorothy from *The Wizard of Oz* with Judy Garland, sporadic performer and habitual drinker and pill popper. Married to her fifth husband, night club promoter Mickey Deans, for only six months, the honeymoon was over on the evening of June 21, 1969. Witnesses reported seeing Garland run screaming from the home they shared. After retiring for the evening, Deans found Garland the next morning dead on the toilet in full rigor mortis. From the Knightsbridge underground station, take the Sloane Street exit. Walking along Sloane Street, turn right into Pont Street and the second street down is Cadogan Lane.

Del Shannon
15519 Saddleback Road
Canyon Country, California

Amide several gold records and expensive musical instruments sat Del Shannon, slouched over a wooden chair dressed only in his bathrobe (minus his toupee) with a single bullet wound to the head. An obvious suicide, his widow sold the home shortly after his death. Today the new owners reportedly throw a "Del Shannon" party in his honor on the anniversery of his early demise. However, they report that the late rocker known for his hit single "Runaway" has yet to make an appearance.

Kurt Cobain
171 East Lake Washington Boulevard
Seattle, Washington

Cobain, with a practice (but failed) run at suicide in Rome the previous year, was discovered in the greenhouse above the garage adjacent to the house one morning in 1994. Discovered by an electrician who noticed the body lying on the floor days after the actual suicide, Cobain put an end to his miserable, dope-plagued, multiplatinum life with a single shot to the head with a Remington M-11 twenty-gauge shotgun. Found with the shotgun resting on his chest, Cobain died instantly from a blast that entered the roof of his mouth and lodged in his skull. The first thing the new owners of the Cobain Death House did was bulldoze the auxiliary garage and greenhouse next to the main house (they must not have been fond of gardening). But that didn't stop fans from driving by and being, well, a general nuisance during the first year of his passing. Now, despite being one of the most publicized addresses in rock 'n' roll, the house doesn't really seem to be all that important anymore as the curious just don't seem to come around.

MARVIN GAYE

BORN April 2, 1939
Washington, D.C.

DIED April 1, 1984
Queens, New York

CAUSE OF DEATH Murdered
Age 44

The marvel that was Marvin Gaye's voice, the voice that made for an extraordinary career, was only matched by his turbulent lifestyle. A product of Berry Gordy's Motown record label, Gaye, alongside the Temptations, the Supremes, and Smokey Robinson, epitomized the Motown sound of the 1960s and later went on to produce one of the most influential and powerful bodies of popular music through the 1980s. Unfortunately, a steady diet of drugs, touring, and questionable business and lifestyle choices have clouded a once-brilliant legacy.

In the Beginning . . .

The son of a failed Pentecostal minister, Marvin Pentz Gay (he added the "e" when he recorded for Motown) was schooled in the finer points of gospel in Washington, D.C., in the late forties. After being discharged from the U.S. Air Force, Gaye worked with rock 'n' roll pioneer Bo Diddley briefly before joining the vocal group the Moonglows. Formed during the golden age of doo-wop, the lush melodies and melodic harmonies produced by the Moonglows would become the cornerstone of Gaye's musical career. When the Moonglows broke up, leader Harvey Fuqua enticed the young singer to audition with a new label in Detroit run by Berry Gordy, called Motown Records.

With a recording contract and through marriage to Gordy's daughter Anna Gordy, Gaye was now part of the Motown family. Initially signed as a session singer and drummer, Gaye played on a number of early Motown singles including most of Smokey Robinson's Miracles hits. Ambitious but shy, Gaye saw himself developing into a crooner much like Frank Sinatra or Nat "King" Cole. Indeed Gaye's first recording in 1962, *The Soulful Mood of Marvin Gaye*, saw the young vocalist singing standards such as "Mr. Sandman" without much chart success. Success finally came later that same year when Gaye recorded the infectious dance hit "A Stubborn Kind of Fellow" followed by the equally rhythmic "Hitch Hike." As Gaye began his successful climb up the charts, Gordy began to utilize Gaye's "soulful and sexy" image, pairing him with Mary Wells ("What's the Matter with You, Baby"), Kim Weston ("It Takes Two"), and for a number of hits with his most famous partner, Tammi Terrell. Between 1967 and 1969 the sweeping lyricism of the songwriting team Ashford and Simpson brought a new meaning to love ballads with "Ain't No Mountain

---

The unfortunate thing about singers is that, compared to groups, they leave very little in the way of memorabilia. Very few of them save their original lyrical doodles and I have yet to see a musician's museum with a wall full of microphones. And in the case of Marvin Gaye, his legacy as a businessman was disappointing as he left his estate with virtually nothing. Upon his death he left a trail of personal debts, back taxes to the IRS, alimony to former wives, and child support payments so large that his estate (settled twelve years after his passing) was left penniless. His royalty payments and personal possessions have been sold or payments diverted to pay off the enormous liens and taxes owed by the estate. The only potential memorabilia item of value that Gaye kept was the white military-style uniform that the singer wore on his last tour. It was the same stage outfit he was wearing at his funeral and subsequent cremation.

High Enough," "Your Precious Love," and "Ain't Nothin' Like the Real Thing"—all Top 10 hits for Gaye and Terrell. With sixty hits during his tenure with Motown, Gaye's high point had to have been in 1967 with the release of the international hit "I Heard It Through the Grapevine."

With Curtis Mayfield and Isaac Hayes recording albums with intense themes in the early 1970s, Gaye responded with a dim portrait of America with his 1971 release *What's Going On*. His first record since his seclusion after Terrell's death from a brain tumor, Motown only halfheartedly promoted the concept album. Despite the lack of marketing, the release spawned two hit singles and Gaye's first hit in the album market.

In the end . . .

Selecting his own songs, writing his own material, and producing his records were Gaye's declaration for the 1970s. With the success of *What's Going On*, Gaye surprised critics and fans by turning to his new favorite obsession—sex. In 1973 he released the ultimate late-night seduction album *Let's Get It On*. Though the record was a success, his personal life was unraveling. His bitter divorce from Anna resulted in the album *Here, My Dear* in compliance with the court order to turn over all proceeds from his next album in lieu of alimony and child support. By the late 1970s, undependable in the studio and on the road, he moved to Europe to leave his problems and Motown behind.

This Los Angeles Police Department crime scene photo shows Marvin Gaye's bedroom as it appeared just after the shooting. Marvin was sitting on the right side of the bed before being shot two times by his father.

On the comeback trail in the early 1980s, Gaye returned to the States in 1982. But with his judgment so completely clouded by his heavy cocaine use, he failed his friends, musicians, and business associates at every turn. When he moved into his parents' house in Hollywood, California, in 1983, things went from bad to worse. Never a warm relationship to begin with, Gaye junior berated and insulted the senior Gay to the point of breaking. After Gaye beat his father around the back and forearms, the senior Gay simply walked back to his room to retrieve the gun Gaye gave him four months earlier for protection. Gay walked into his son's room and shot him as he sat on his bed. He then walked over to his son and shot Gaye again at point-blank range. Gaye was pronounced dead thirty minutes later at the hospital. Marvin Gay senior was sentenced to probation.

Gaye was cremated, his ashes scattered in the Pacific Ocean from the deck of a yacht.

Gaye's first wife, Anna Gordy Gaye, held back a small amount of the remains, which she keeps in her home today.

He had always done a lot of cocaine but no one can handle freebasing. I guess Marvin thought that he had been taking cocaine for so long that he could do it, but he couldn't. It took him out. That's what messed up Marvin.

band member Nolan Smith

GEORGE GERSHWIN

BORN September 26, 1898
Washington, D.C.

DIED July 11, 1937
Los Angeles, California

CAUSE OF DEATH Brain Tumor
Age 38

The truly great songwriters of the twentieth century can be counted on one hand—Jerome Kern, Rodgers and Hammerstein, Irving Berlin, and George Gershwin. Along with brother and lyricist Ira, George's presence on the musical scene from 1920 until his premature death in 1937 was nothing short of pure genius. Whether popular show tunes, musical scores, concertos, or opera, Gershwin's music embodied the true American experience.

In the Beginning . . .

Phonographs were still wax-coated cylinders and phones were still a novelty when Jacob Gershvin was born in Brooklyn, New York. When he turned twelve, a piano was hauled up the side of the Second Avenue apartment block where the Gershvins lived. However, the piano and the lessons were originally for Ira, not George. George was thoroughly relieved to continue his typically adolescent activities while Ira was busy practicing his scales. But Ira eventually went back to his books and, in time, George took to the piano with enthusiasm.

George studied the piano along with composition, music theory, and harmony through much of his early teens. Working evenings in his father's restaurant for less than a dollar a day, he was ecstatic when he was offered twenty-five dollars a week playing popular songs at a mountain resort. If his mother, Rose, was displeased with her son becoming a musician, she was even more unhappy when George dropped out of high school altogether to pursue his first love—music.

George began working for music publisher Jerome H. Renick and Company as a song plugger. He worked for four years in Tin Pan Alley as one of the pianists who played new tunes in hopes of selling the sheet music to those in show business. George finally quit when he realized he could write better songs than what he was selling.

His first taste of success as a songwriter came shortly after he played piano for Victor Herbert and Jerome Kern's *Miss 1917*. In the same theater Gershwin also had two of his songs performed by Vivienne Segal. Writing songs at a feverish pace, he asked Ira to put words to his music. It turned out to be a lifelong partnership not since matched in musical circles.

In 1918, the Gershwins provided the music for their first musical, *Half Past Eight*, followed by the more successful *La La Lucille. Music for Scandals, Blue Monday Blues,* and *For Goodness Sakes* continued to showcase the brothers' talents. In 1924 popular bandleader Paul Whiteman had heard a brief operetta that Gershwin had written entitled *Blue Monday*. Whiteman commissioned a symphonic jazz piece with Gershwin to debut later

---

When Ira Gershwin retired in the 1960s, he established the Gershwin Archive to oversee the publishing arm of the Gershwin songwriting team. Upon his passing at the age of eighty-five, the entire Gershwin collection was turned over to the Library of Congress in Washington D.C., where their manuscripts and personal papers are now on permanent display.

that year. When Gershwin read about the premiere of this "exciting new composition" in the newspaper, he realized that he had completely forgotten about the agreement. With less than three weeks before the debut, Gershwin worked feverishly to finish the piece on time. *Rhapsody in Blue*, the ambitious jazz symphony, debuted as part of a series of compositions performed by Paul Whiteman's band. When it was over, Gershwin was hailed the next day by critics as "an extraordinary talent."

In the End . . .

George was not content to write just popular music. He traveled to Europe with Ira to visit with Stravinsky, Prokofiev, Ravel, and other masters of the concert hall. Upon his return to New York, he put the finishing touches on *An American in Paris*. After the debut at Carnegie Hall with its bluesy themes and scoring for taxi horns, this piece left no doubt among his fans and critics about his status as a musical icon.

For millions of Americans, the 1930s were a time of unemployment and financial ruin. For the Gershwins, it was a time of personal prosperity. They were commissioned to write music for a Hollywood movie for $100,000. Between film scores, musicals, concerts, and the demands of high society, George never had an idle moment.

George and Ira's final success as a songwriting team was not really a success at all—at least not at first. Based on a novel by DuBose Heyward, the story of a disabled black man and the inhabitants of Catfish Row was initially a box office failure and closed after just 124 performances. However, when *Porgy and Bess* was revived in 1953 with Cab Calloway, the play became a long-running Broadway success with productions appearing in over twenty countries.

On their second trip to Hollywood, in 1937, they discovered that RKO was looking for a hit score for the next Fred Astaire–Ginger Rogers musical. Moving into lavish settings in Beverly Hills, the brothers continued to work, welcomed Stravinsky and Schoenberg for afternoon socials, and threw lavish parties in the evenings. So it came as a surprise to everyone when George began complaining of headaches and dizziness that spring. When he began to forget portions of his own compositions during performances, worried friends urged Gershwin to see a physician. While several visits to doctors and specialists found nothing, in a very short time the normally tanned and healthy George began to deteriorate.

On Friday, July 9th, after spending the morning at the piano, he decided to lie down for a nap. He never woke up. That evening he was rushed to Cedars of Lebanon Hospital in Los Angeles. Arriving in a coma, it was found that George was suffering from the effects of a brain tumor. After waiting over a day for a famous neurosurgeon to arrive from the East Coast, George was operated on to remove the tumor. But it was hopeless. At 10:35 on the morning of Sunday, July 11, 1937, America's musical genius was gone. When George's body returned home to New York, over three thousand people (including Berlin, Kern, and other great patrons of the performing arts) attended the funeral. Gershwin was first laid to rest at Mt. Hope Cemetery in Hastings-on-Hudson, north of New York City.

Any party with George Gershwin was a Gershwin party. When he left the room, the party was over, that was clear.

Oscar Levant

Westchester Hills Cemetery
Ardsley, New York

In the early 1940s Gershwin was moved to a permanent family mausoleum at Westchester Hills Cemetery. Located north of New York City, take 87 north, exiting at 9A in Ardsley. Turn left (south) and drive about one mile past the Ardsley office park. Turn left into the cemetery and the Gershwin mausoleum is the fourth monument on the right, across from the office. Please note that this is a Jewish cemetery and is closed on Saturdays.

Ira Gershwin
December 6, 1896—August 17, 1983

After his brother's death in 1937, Ira Gershwin worked alongside Vernon Duke, who finished *The Goldwyn Follies*, which the brothers had been working on before George's death. Gershwin continued with his Hollywood connections and collaborated with Jerome Kern on *Cover Girl*, which included the song "Long Ago and Far Away" (a hit for Bing Crosby and also covered by Perry Como and Guy Lombardo). He also collaborated with Kurt Weill for both the stage musical and film adaptation of *Lady in the Dark* and with Harry Warren on *The Barkleys of Broadway* starring Fred Astaire and Ginger Rogers. His biggest success during his post-George years would be his collaboration with Harold Arlen in 1954 for *A Star Is Born*, which featured Judy Garland on "The Man That Got Away" (which Frank Sinatra remade into "The Gal That Got Away"). During the 1960s, Gershwin retired from active songwriting to oversee the Gershwin Archives at the Library of Congress. Upon his passing at his home in Beverly Hills, California, Ira was brought together with his brother George one last time and is resting comfortably at the Gershwin Family mausoleum at Westchester Hills Cemetery, Ardsley, New York, along with several other Gershwin relatives.

I WRITE THE SONGS
OTHER GREAT SONGWRITERS FROM THE TIN PAN ALLEY DAYS

Jerome Kern
January 27, 1885—November 11, 1945

If he had only written the score for *Showboat*, Jerome Kern's position as a musical genius would be secure. Instead, he also wrote "Smoke Gets In Your Eyes," "The Way You Look Tonight," and countless other songs for movies and Broadway musicals. A master of the American musical comedy in the Roaring Twenties, Kern collaborated with Otto Harbach and Oscar Hammerstein (later of Rodgers and Hammerstein) to create Kern's finest work in *Showboat*. Later in life he worked in Hollywood with Dorothy Fields and Johnny Mercer, creating Oscar-winning works with the films *Swingtime* and *Lady Be Good*. Kern also wrote hit songs for Dinah Shore, Glenn Miller, Peggy Lee, and Bing Crosby. He was laid to rest (actually placed into the wall) at Ferncliff Cemetery in Hartsdale, New York. As you enter the gold doors to the main mausoleum, turn right at the first hallway, then left, then right again. Walk down the hall two niches and turn right. Kern's marble wall unit is at eye level at Unit 4, Alcove C, Private Niche 1.

Irving Berlin
May 11, 1888—September 22, 1989

The author of "White Christmas," "Alexander's Ragtime Band," "God Bless America," "Cheek to Cheek," "Anything You Can Do (I Can Do Better)," "There's No Business Like Show Business," and hundreds of other American classics was the most successful songwriter during the first half of the twentieth century. Once a singing waiter at New York's Pelham Cafe, Berlin's songs were covered by no less than Bing Crosby, Ethel Waters, Billie Holiday, Bessie Smith, Frank Sinatra, and Louis Armstrong. An astute businessman, he bought back all his copyrights in the 1920s and built his own theater, the Music Box, where Berlin staged his own shows. His greatest Broadway success, however, came in 1946 with *Annie Get Your Gun*. Producers of the landmark musical originally asked Jerome Kern to write the music; however, when he passed away, Berlin stepped in. Berlin retired in 1966 to run his various publishing concerns and became a virtual recluse for the last thirty years of his life. And unlike his songwriting peers, the Berlin estate refuses all requests to use Berlin's songs in commercials. Berlin is buried at New York's Woodlawn Cemetery in the Columbine section on Heather Avenue, next to the James Hill monument.

George M. Cohan
July 3, 1878—November 4, 1942

A prolific songwriter with over five hundred songs to his name—"The Yankee Doodle," "Give My Regards to Broadway," "Over There"—Cohan also directed forty plays on Broadway. From 1905 until 1920 he ruled New York's theater district, eventually opening his own theater. However, Cohan's influence diminished when he took the side of the theater owners and producers during the actors' strike in 1919. In 1939 he was awarded the Congressional Medal of Honor and seventeen years after his passing a statue of the songwriter, producer, and occasional actor was unveiled on Broadway. His impressive mausoleum is located on the road in the Butternut section of Woodlawn Cemetery in the Bronx, New York.

DIZZY GILLESPIE

BORN October 21, 1917
Cheraw, South Carolina

DIED January 6, 1993
Englewood, New Jersey

CAUSE OF DEATH Cancer
Age 75

Together with Charlie Parker and Thelonious Monk, Dizzy Gillespie introduced radical and harmonic changes to traditional swing, which became the foundation for modern jazz. A leading bebop trumpeter and composer, as well as early developer of an inimitable mode of scat singing, Dizzy also originated the hipsters uniform of beret, goatee, and dark glasses.

In the Beginning . . .

The son of a bricklayer and part-time bandleader, John Birks "Dizzy" Gillespie (the surname was born from his youthful antics and expressive personality) gained a working knowledge of several instruments during his youth. Gillespie first began on the trombone; however, his arms were too short to reach the seventh position. He switched to trumpet and taught himself to play. Without proper training, Gillespie acquired the habit of puffing out his cheeks when blowing—a style that would become Gillespie's trademark. In his teens he won a music scholarship to the Laurinburg Institute in North Carolina; however, his family moved to Philadelphia in 1935 before his schooling was completed. Gillespie's first major professional association was with traditional swing group the Frank Fairfax Band. By 1937 Dizzy was an accomplished soloist when he replaced his idol, Roy Eldridge, in the Teddy Hill Band. Two years later Dizzy was a featured soloist with Cab Calloway (the "Hi-Di-Hi-Di-Ho" man), where his playing style began exhibiting some of the elements of modern jazz.

Dismissed by Calloway (he called Gillespie's experimental sounds "Chinese music"), Gillespie floated between bands playing with Earl "Fatha" Hines, Ella Fitzgerald, Benny Carter, and Fletcher Henderson before joining Billy Eckstine in 1944. Working with Charlie Parker, the group allowed Gillespie the opportunity to explore a new style of music—bebop. Later that year, Gillespie, along with Parker, performed with the first bebop combo at New York's Onyx Club. Although critical acclaim was lacking, the quality of the recordings offered by Parker and Gillespie, including "Dizzy Atmsophere" and "Shaw 'Nuff," was astounding. Gillespie and Parker made an ill-fated trip to Los Angeles to introduce bebop to the West Coast, but the new music and Parker's drug addiction made for a bad combination.

Continuing with the small group format, Gillespie sat in after hours with other musical experimentalists like Thelonious Monk at Minton's Playhouse in Harlem as the foundation for bebop began to take form. During the mid-forties Gillespie began leading his own

---

Since no concerted effort has been made to collect the instruments and memorabilia of one of the founding fathers of modern jazz, most of his possessions are in the hands of private collectors. Fortunately, Gillespie's custom-made King Silver Flair trumpet and case has found a home and is on display at the Smithsonian National Museum of American History in Washington, D.C. (One story goes that during a tour in 1954, a member of the band stepped on Gillespie's horn and bent the bell section. When Gillespie played the damaged horn, he not only thought the horn sounded better, but he could also hear himself play better with the unusual alteration.)

small groups on a permanent basis, with Max Roach on drums and bassist Oscar Pettiford, and recorded "Disorder at the Border." Convinced that this new music should be considered serious jazz, he continued to perform with his own small group and made a series of impressive recordings with Dexter Gordon and Milt Jackson. In 1946 he formed his first large orchestra, in which he enjoyed commercial and critical success. Often considered the peak of Gillespie's career, the titanic sound produced by such a large and enormously talented group was disbanded due to financial considerations. After an ill-fated attempt at owning his own record company, Gillespie came under exclusive contract with Norman Granz and was the featured performer in many of Granz's Jazz at the Philharmonic concerts, both in the U.S. and Europe.

In the End . . .

In 1956 the U.S. State Department financed a sixteen-piece orchestra fronted by Gillespie and Quincy Jones on a tour of Latin America and the Middle East. Through the 1960s Gillespie continued to incorporate Latin elements within his various groups, recording on Granz's Verve label with such gifted artists as Stan Getz and pianist Lalo Schifrin. Touring endlessly with both his large and small group ensembles, Gillespie traveled around the world as the unofficial ambassador of jazz.

Invited to the White House by President Jimmy Carter in 1978, hours before the scheduled dinner, Gillespie drove over to a former schoolteacher's house and knocked on the door.

"HAVE TRUMPET, WILL EXCITE!"

DIZZY GILLESPIE

The retired teacher and one-time mentor to Gillespie was surprised to see his former pupil—and even more surprised when Gillespie invited him to join him with the president. That night Gillespie and Carter jammed together for a chorus of "Salt Peanuts" at the dinner.

Though not as dynamic a performer in his later years, Gillespie nonetheless remained quite active, lecturing and performing at high schools and colleges across the country. He spent his later years as the elder statesman and an original American musical legend, collecting awards and charming the world up until the very end. He died quietly at his home in New Jersey of cancer.

Flushing Cemetery
Queens, New York

One of the great geniuses of twentieth-century music was buried in Section 31, Plot 1252-31 in Flushing Cemetery in New York City with little fanfare. Just across the street lies the great Duke Ellington sideman Johnny Hodges and the legendary Louis Armstrong. But unlike his peers, Dizzy Gillespie's grave remains unmarked.

I can hear my mistakes quicker.

Dizzy Gillespie, on the benefits of having a bent horn.

BENNY GOODMAN

BORN May 30, 1909
Chicago, Illinois

DIED June 13, 1986
New York, New York

CAUSE OF DEATH Heart Failure
Age 76

As undisputed leader of the greatest swing band ever, Benny Goodman was also considered one of the finest virtuoso clarinetists in styles ranging from swing, bebop, and classical. With such luminaries in his group as drummer Gene Krupa, guitarist Charlie Christian, bassist Teddy Wilson, vibrophonist Lionel Hampton, and future band leader Harry James, it comes as no surprise that throughout his career he was referred to as the King of Swing.

In the Beginning . . .

Born to a family of eleven brothers and sisters in abject poverty in Chicago's immigrant district, Benjamin David Goodman began his career with the Hull House house band. Although the musical repertoire was limited to marches and popular Americana tunes of the times, Goodman was more inspired by jazz sounds of the King Oliver Band, Bix Beiderbecke, and Dixieland from New Orleans. By age fifteen, he was a member of the Ben Pollack Band, where he made some of his first recordings for the Victor label. Though considered a dance orchestra, the music allowed for solo improvisation and Goodman took full advantage of this opportunity.

After four years with Ben Pollack (whose band by then was considered one of the top three or four dance bands in the country), Goodman stayed on in New York following the musical migration from Chicago to New York City. For the next five years Goodman played on radio shows, theater bands (including the show *Girl Crazy* with Ethel Merman), and a great deal of studio sessions, including Billie Holiday's debut recordings in 1933. A very popular freelance studio musician, Goodman briefly formed a band to front singer Russ Columbo. However, in 1934 Goodman put together his first big band utilizing the talents of Gene Krupa on drums, Jess Stacey on piano, and Bunny Berigan on trumpet. After adding the sophisticated, hip arrangements of Fletcher Henderson, by 1935 success had

---

Goodman's greatest concert, without a doubt, was his 1938 engagement at Carnegie Hall. Two acetates of this concert were made, and twelve years after his death, Goodman's daughter found one of them in the closet of his former New York apartment. This concert is currently available under the title *The Famous 1938 Carnegie Hall Jazz Concert* on the Columbia label and is considered one of the greatest jazz concerts of its era.

Although video footage is limited, he did appear in several films including *Hollywood Hotel* (1937) and *The Powers Girls* (1942). The 1955 biographical film *The Benny Goodman Story* was, unlike *The Glenn Miller Story* starring Jimmy Stewart, a major box office dud. Despite the miscasting of the wooden Steve Allen in the title role, several of his former sidemen, including Kid Ory, made guest appearances in the film. This, however, hardly makes up for the insipid story line that bears little resemblance to Goodman's life.

Upon his death Goodman left his entire estate to Yale University in Hartford, Connecticut, including rare photographs and hundreds of never-before-heard recordings. And alongside Ella Fitzgerald's famous red dress and Dizzy Gillespie's classic bent trumpet stands one of Goodman's clarinets on display at the Smithsonian National Museum of American History in Washington, D.C.

finally caught up with Goodman and his brand of hot swing jazz. Still struggling for recognition, a two-month concert engagement in Los Angeles developed into a national tour that caused riots, crowd-control problems, and dancing in the aisles, then unheard-of. For the next ten years Benny had the hottest band in the nation, but with Gene Krupa, Teddy Wilson, Lionel Hampton, Ziggy Ellman, Bunny Berigan, Lester Young, and Charlie Christian all rotating through the band, this comes as no surprise. The band's success as a live act also translated to recordings, with instrumental hits like "Stompin' at the Savoy," "One O'Clock Jump," "Sugar Foot Stomp" (featuring future band leader Harry James on trumpet), and the immortal "Sing, Sing, Sing" with the signature pyrotechnic drumbeat of Gene Krupa. Despite the Depression and World War II, Goodman was touring the U.S. and Europe, playing three hundred days a year (sometimes up to six performances a day) and making over a million dollars a year.

In the End . . .

A stern taskmaster considered "distant" and "standoffish" by nature, many of Goodman's sidemen considered the Benny Goodman Band a great band to start out from. But some of the musicians that floated through the group claimed Goodman to be cheap at best, and plain dishonest at his worst when it came to paying musicians. Even worse than his allegedly poor business ethics was the infamous Goodman Ray. God help the poor musician who made a mistake and received the forboding glare that came from the strict bandleader. However, if there was ever one thing that Goodman would not tolerate it was being upstaged by his own musicians. When Gene Krupa began getting recognition in reviews and by fans alike, Goodman dismissed the legendary drummer for another drummer with less flash.

By 1940 when Goodman's contract with Victor expired, he had lost Krupa, Berigan, Wilson, and James as they became their own bandleaders with varying degrees of success. For the most part, however, musicians were kind when they spoke of their former boss, fully realizing despite his many disagreeable practices that Goodman was still the King of Swing.

During the 1940s Goodman and his band continued their string of hit recordings for Columbia Records. Adding arranger Eddie Sauter and vocalist Helen Forrest, they released "Perfidia," "I Hear a Rhapsody," and the number one hit "Taking a Chance on Love." In 1942 Peggy Lee replaced Forrest and her first hit, "Why Don't You Do Right," was a million-seller. The group also continued their run of instrumental hits with "The Man I Love," "Mission to Moscow," and "Clarinet à la King."

Just because a record looks old or has been out of print for half a century does not make a vinyl album valuable. For the most part, 78s sold at garage sales are worth about ten cents each. However, if you find a copy of Benny Goodman's "Popcorn Man" on the Victor label, you might want to hold on to it—it's worth about $1,000 in good condition.

If Goodman ever had a misstep, it was during 1948 and 1949 when he tried to give his orchestra a bebop flavor. During the early forties New York musicians Charlie Parker, Dizzy Gillespie, Thelonious Monk, Kenny Clarke, and others began to turn the dominant style of swing into bebop, utilizing uncommon harmonies, unconventional rhythmic accents, and off-tempo phrasing as the new jazz style. As the new musical revolution took hold, Goodman felt increasingly out of place, and shortly after dissolved his orchestra.

Just remember, baby, he's fired the best!
    Former Benny Goodman drummer Gene Krupa, consoling a fellow drummer upon being dismissed.

While his role as an influential musician was over, Goodman continued to perform regularly throughout his entire life. Recording prolifically for RCA, Capitol, London, and other labels, Goodman stayed busy with reunion dates, local tours, and the occasional trip overseas. In 1962 he became the first American musician in forty years to play inside the Soviet Union. In the late 1960s he began to appear regularly with symphonic orchestras, playing not only his swing classics, but also classical clarinet pieces by Bartók and Copland.

As the grand master entered the eighties, Goodman began to suffer from arthritis, chronic knee problems, and a weakened heart (which required a pacemaker). Goodman nonetheless continued to play selected dates and even scheduled a tour for the West Coast. After recording the soundtrack for the TV special *Let's Dance*, Goodman flew down to St. Martin in the Caribbean to his summer home. After a restful vacation he returned to his apartment on Sixty-sixth Street in New York. Goodman died one afternoon while practicing the clarinet. He simply slumped over in his chair with his clarinet in hand and Brahms's Sonata Opus #120 on the music stand beside him.

Long Ridge Cemetery
Stamford, Connecticut

A private ceremony was held in Stamford, Connecticut, where Benny Goodman was laid to rest next to his wife, Alice Hammond Goodman, at Long Ridge Cemetery. From Highway 95 take the Atlantic (104) off-ramp. Atlantic turns into Brookford, but stay to the left, as the road will split off onto High Ridge Road. Continue after the split and turn left at the light (Erskine Road). Drive two miles farther to the entrance of the cemetery. Turn left into the cemetery and drive straight back to the edge of the grounds. Turn right at the end and park. Goodman's simple granite marker is next to the bench under the tree.

THE BENNY GOODMAN BAND

A FEW LEGENDARY PERFORMERS WHO WORKED WITH THE KING OF SWING

Gene Krupa
January 15, 1909—October 16, 1973

With his arms flailing behind the drum kit, Gene Krupa forever changed the role of the drummer and provided his fans with an everlasting visual and musical image of the swing era. He first met Goodman in the orchestra pit for the play *Strike Up the Band*. In 1936 he joined Goodman and Teddy Wilson for the first incarnation of the Benny Goodman Trio (later expanding to a quartet with Lionel Hampton). After several years with Goodman he was fired for drawing too much attention to himself, as the audience screamed for more drum solos. He continued his career fronting his own band, as well as playing with Tommy Dorsey and reuniting with Goodman on several occasions. Krupa died of leukemia just weeks after his last reunion gig with the original Benny Goodman Quartet and was buried at Holy Cross Cemetery in Calumet City, outside Chicago. He was buried in the Krupa family plot in the Immaculata section, Lot 22, Block A, just behind the Sadowska monument.

Teddy Wilson
November 24, 1912—July 31, 1986

Born to parents with teaching positions at Tuskegee University, Wilson began studying violin and piano at an early age. Continuing his studies at college, he began his professional career in Detroit, later moving to Chicago where he worked with Louis Armstrong, Erskine Tate, and Art Tatum. In 1933 he moved to New York, where he made a succession of outstanding records, including many of Billie Holiday's earliest recordings. Often considered the most influential musician contributing to Holiday's success, he joined the Benny Goodman Trio shortly after and remained with Goodman through 1939. After an unsuccessful shot as his own bandleader, he continued touring, teaching, recording, and playing the role of elder statesman of jazz up to the very end. Wilson is buried at Fairview Cemetery in New Britain, Connecticut.

Bunny Berigan
November 2, 1908—June 2, 1942

A virtual unknown in today's contemporary jazz, Berigan and his soaring trumpet helped catapult Benny Goodman, Tommy Dorsey, Paul Whiteman, and a host of other bandleaders into the swing era. But with a quick rise to the top, this giant among his peers also shouldered the burden of alcoholism, exhaustion, and financial ruin. Berigan is buried on the right in the center section of St. Mary's Cemetery, seven rows from the road behind the Burns monument, in his hometown of Fox Lake, Wisconsin.

Lionel Hampton
April 20, 1908—September 22, 1989

Sporting a fabulous array of sidemen, the Lionel Hampton Orchestra was known around the world for its high-energy performances of such Hampton classics as "Sunny Side of the Street," "Hamp's Boogie-Woogie," and his signature tune "Flying Home." A brilliant vibraphonist and composer of over two hundred original songs, Hampton broke racial barriers when he joined the Benny Goodman Quartet. When he died of heart failure at the age of ninety, Hampton had outlasted all his peers and now rests peacefully across the street from Duke Ellington and Miles Davis at Woodlawn Cemetery in the Bronx, New York. Upon his passing, his entire musical collection was donated to the University of Idaho.

THE GRATEFUL DEAD

RON "PIGPEN" MCKERNAN

BORN September 8, 1945
San Bruno, California

DIED March 8, 1973
San Francisco,
California

CAUSE OF DEATH
Liver Failure
Age 27

KEITH GODCHAUX

BORN July 19, 1948
Concord, California

DIED July 23, 1980
Marin County,
California

CAUSE OF DEATH
Auto Accident
Age 32

BRENT MYDLAND

BORN October 21, 1952
Munich, Germany

DIED July 26, 1990
Concord, California

CAUSE OF DEATH
Drug Overdose
Age 37

JERRY GARCIA

BORN August 1, 1942
San Francisco,
California

DIED August 9, 1995
Knolls, California

CAUSE OF DEATH
Heart Attack
Age 53

Over the course of three decades the Grateful Dead were the longest-living freeform, Summer of Love band to come out of San Francisco. Despite the lack of airplay or a media-savvy public relations firm, the Grateful Dead continued their trek around the world, starting in the clubs of San Francisco and going on to the pyramids of Egypt, to stadiums and festivals throughout the world. Producing twenty-nine albums ranging in style from bluegrass, country, jazz, and even pop, the Grateful Dead changed the musical and cultural landscape in the sixties and continued through the 1990s with the support of thousands of Deadheads, keeping the spirit alive.

In the Beginning . . .

The band had its genesis when Ron "Pigpen" McKernan met with Jerry Garcia, Phil Lesh, and Bob Weir in the music stores and nightclubs of Palo Alto. First formed as Mother McCree's Uptown Jug Champions, they later changed their name to the Warlocks. Like all bands at the time, the Warlocks were profoundly influenced by the arrival of the Beatles and various experimental pharmaceuticals. With the introduction of LSD (then legal), the Warlocks expanded their music toward exploratory rock with Pigpen on keyboards and Garcia moving from banjo to the guitar.

With the band gathering a loyal following, and to avoid comparison with another band of the same name, they changed their name to the Grateful Dead. Garcia first spotted the phrase in a dictionary at Lesh's house. With a macabre, suggestive balance of courtesy and mortality, the Grateful Dead encompassed many of the artistic and philosophical trends that would carry the band well into the nineties. With the name change came the release of their first album. Although it was not at the time considered a successful release (it wasn't even recorded in stereo), the live concerts continued to draw increasing crowds. A few years later the band released the live album *Live/Dead* as a record of their escalating success with their experimental approach to music and concerts. Yet along with their fame, little fortune came to the Dead members in the early years. Pigpen was particularly hard hit financially when Mickey Hart's father stole most of the band's money at the time. But his life took a turn for the worse in the summer of 1971 when two weeks after the death of close friend Janis Joplin, he was diagnosed with cirrhosis of the liver. A heavy drinker since his teen years, he kept his terminal illness from the band. The remaining members recruited Keith and singer Donna Godchaux to assist Pigpen with his keyboard duties, but it was

---

The Grateful Dead Organization is one of the best-run musical corporations in existence today. With a secured vault of all the master tapes, a recording of virtually every concert they played, and all the instruments and band equipment in storage, it is just a matter of time before the official Grateful Dead Museum, currently in the planning stages, is open to the public. Naturally, the house at 710 Ashbury Street in San Francisico, where the Grateful Dead took up residence in 1966, is still a favorite of fans worldwide.

not enough. Exhausted, the founding member and leader of the Grateful Dead played his last show on June 17, 1972, at the Hollywood Bowl in Los Angeles, California.

In 1977 the band's growth continued unabated and took its cues from Garcia's inno- vated inspiration derived from sources as varied as blues legend Jimmy Reed and bluegrass legend Bill Monroe. They released the epic *Terrapin Station*, followed six months later with *What a Long Strange Trip It's Been*. In 1979, following the Oakland Coliseum show in February, the Godchauxs were asked to leave the band due to Keith's continued drug use and musical differences. Two months later keyboardist Brent Mydland from Weir's solo project RatDog was asked to join the band. The group finished their second decade in exis- tence with the release of the *Go to Heaven* LP, a fifteen-night run at the Warfield Theater in San Francisco, another long run at Radio City Music Hall in New York, and an appearance before 500,000 fans at the US Festival in 1982.

In the End . . .

As they entered their third decade of performing and recording, the Grateful Dead's prob- lems with drugs started to unravel the tight-knit organization. Garcia's possession charges in 1985, diabetic coma the following year, and years of drug abuse nearly caused the group to disband. Fortunately, the band was rejuvenated following the release of their album *In the Dark*, which not only sold over a million copies, but also produced their first and only Top 10 hit, "Touch of Grey."

In 1990 Brent Mydland was the third member of the group to die, and was replaced by both Vince Welnick (formerly of the Tubes) and Bruce Hornsby, who alternated on key- boards. In 1994 the band was inducted into the Rock and Roll Hall of Fame, followed by the release of *Skeletons from the Closet*, a compilation package of their best-loved songs, which sold over three million copies. In 1995 the band performed their 2,314th and last concert at Soldier Field in Chicago, closing the show with a medley of "Black Muddy River"/"Box of Rain." One month later, Garcia died at a residential treatment center for his addiction to heroin.

FINAL RESTING PLACES
Alta Mesa Memorial Park Cemetery
Palo Alto, California

Once through the gates of the cemetery, stay to the right on Chapel Road and drive straight as it turns into Oak Grove. Follow Oak Grove to the left and at the intersection drive straight ahead onto Almond Drive. Continue about a hundred feet and stop at the Ramirez monument.  McKernan's final resting place is located in the Hillview section, Subsection 16, Lot 374.

Oakmont Memorial Park
Pleasant Hills, California

Mydland was buried in the hillside section Remembrance, seven rows from the top road near the bench under the oak tree. His official address is Plot 265/7w, Lot C, Site 1.

Garcia was cremated and his ashes scattered in India and the San Francisco Bay.

Somebody has to do something, and it's just incredibly pathetic that it has to be us.

Jerry Garcia

WOODY GUTHRIE

BORN July 14, 1912
Okemah, Oklahoma

DIED October 3, 1967
Queens, New York

CAUSE OF DEATH Huntington's Chorea
Age 55

Armed with a guitar pasted with the banner THIS MACHINE KILLS FAS-CISTS!, singer, songwriter, and composer of America's "other" national anthem "This Land Is Your Land," Woody Guthrie was an artist whose uncompromising songs of social commentary and protest perfectly captured the plight of the everyday working man. Considered the primary influence for generations of folk revival artists such as Bob Dylan, Pete Seeger, Phil Ochs, and dozens of others, Guthrie fought for a myriad of social causes the only way he knew how—through heartfelt songs of protest.

In the Beginning . . .

Born in Okemah, Oklahoma, Guthrie's perspective on life was largely formed by several incidents during his childhood. The death of his older sister, the financial ruin of his father's speculative land dealings, and the institutionalization of his devoted mother all played a role in the development of his outlook on life. When the good times of the oil boom went bust in 1931, Guthrie moved to Texas, where he started his music career by adding new words to traditional tunes and began playing with his first group, the Corncob Trio. Newly married, Guthrie found it difficult to support a family during the Depression with the occasional radio broadcast. Inspired by the great dust storm that swept across the Midwest, which caused untold devastation to thousands of farmers, Guthrie wrote his first classic song, "Dusty Old Dust," and, along with many other thousands of unemployed families, left for the promised land of California.

By the time he reached the West Coast in 1937, he was the object of scorn and hatred, feelings that most locals felt toward this sudden influx of "outsiders." Now a regular on radio station KFVD in Los Angeles, Guthrie played a mix of ballads, blues, gospel, and dance tunes and slowly worked into his repertoire classic dust bowl ballads such as "I Ain't Got No Home" and "Dust Bowl Refugees," which showcased his affinity for the downtrodden outsider. He continued to develop his talent for social commentary and criticism of the status quo for two more years, after which he moved to New York City, where he was welcomed with open arms by leftist organizations of artists, writers, and musicians. In 1940 he recorded hours of music and commentary with Alan Lomax for the Library of Congress and released an album, *Dust Bowl Ballads,* for the Victor label. Guthrie continued to write, record, and perform (most often with the Almanac Singers). While he helped establish folk music as a commercially viable entity within the music industry, a disillusioned Guthrie left New York City and the industry he helped invigorate and traveled back to the West

---

The largest collection of Woody Guthrie memorabilia can be found at the Woody Guthrie Foundation and Archives. Located at 250 West Fifty-seventh Street in New York City, the foundation was opened to the public in 1996. Intially started with a donation by Marjorie Mazia Guthrie (Guthrie's second wife), who donated all of Guthrie's books, songs, papers, and the assorted material stored in their homes, the archives contain more than ten thousand items, including the original handwritten lyrics to "This Land Is Your Land." Guthrie's childhood home in Okemah is no longer standing, dismantled by one too many souvenir-seeking vandals.

Coast to begin a series of songs commissioned by the federal government. After a brief tour with both the U.S. Army and the Merchant Marines, Guthrie returned to New York City where he continued his career, appearing frequently with other folk artists such as Leadbelly, Burl Ives, Sonny Terry and Brownie McGhee, and a very young Pete Seeger.

In the End . . .

After his return to New York from the West Coast where he was commissioned to write a series of songs celebrating hydroelectric dams in the Pacific Northwest and had performed at several fund-raising benefits for leftist organizations, Guthrie found himself blacklisted by national radio due to his Communist affiliations. However, in 1943 Guthrie's autobiography, *Bound for Glory*, was released and despite the lack of airplay, Guthrie's fame and recognition were at an all-time high (the book was made into a feature film starring David Carradine in 1976). The following year he began a series of recordings produced by Moe Asch, including the highly acclaimed children's album *Songs to Grow On*.

By the late 1940s, Guthrie's health began to deteriorate, and as a result he became more irrational and increasingly unpredictable with each passing month. Once again he left the comfort of his home in New York and traveled across the country with his friend Ramblin' Jack Elliott, only to return again to New York. Misdiagnosed as an alcoholic, a schizophrenic, and just plain mentally ill, Guthrie was finally properly diagnosed with Huntington's Chorea in 1952, the very same degenerative disease that caused his mother's institutionalization thirty years earlier and which eventually led to her death.

Two years later Guthrie admitted himself into Greystone Hospital in New Jersey. Thus began a slow, lonely decline in which the disease robbed Guthrie of all his talents, abilities, and personality. After thirteen years living at four institutions, Guthrie died at Creedmoor State Hospital in Queens, New York, in 1967.

After his passing, Guthrie was inducted into the Songwriter's Hall of Fame in 1971, the Nashville Songwriter's Hall of Fame in 1977, the Rock and Roll Hall of Fame in 1988, was awarded the Folk Alliance Lifetime Achievement Award in 1996, and received a Grammy Award for Lifetime Achievement from the National Association of Recording Arts and Sciences in 1999. Today the royalties from his songwriting catalog alone are worth in excess of $100,000 per year.

Guthrie was cremated, his ashes scattered in the Atlantic Ocean. Upon his passing a number of memorial services were held, organized by Pete Seeger and featuring the talents of Bob Dylan, Joan Baez, Richie Havens, Country Joe McDonald, and Tom Paxton. Interestingly enough, his son, Arlo Guthrie, had his biggest hit, "Alice's Restaurant," in the same year as his father's death.

Anything more than three chords is just showing off.

Woody Guthrie

JIMI HENDRIX

BORN November 27, 1942
Seattle, Washington

DIED September 18, 1970
London, England

CAUSE OF DEATH Inhalation of Vomit
Age 27

When the Jimi Hendrix Experience took the stage for their first American audience at the 1967 Monterey Pop Festival, the audience (and millions later through the concert film) recognized that a new musical genius had emerged. Amid a firestorm of howling feedback, Hendrix created the soundtrack for the sixties through his definitive appropriations of Dylan's "All Along the Watchtower," the Troggs' "Wild Thing," and through his stunning originals "Foxy Lady" and "Purple Haze."

In the Beginning. . .

Born Johnny Allen Hendrix, Hendrix was a self-taught musician and acquired his first guitar at age twelve. Since he was left-handed, Hendrix restrung the right-handed guitar and played it upside down. A high school dropout, Hendrix spent two years in the military before moving down south. In the early sixties he played the Chitlin' Circuit as a guitarist for Ike Turner and Little Richard. In 1965 he moved to New York City where he played for a time with the Squires. Frustrated musically, he moved to bohemian Greenwich Village and formed his own band, Jimmy James and the Blue Flames (later called Rain Flower). It was at Cafe Wha! that Hendrix was spotted by former Animal Chas Chandler. Mesmerized by his performance, Chas offered to take Hendrix over to England, set him up with a band, secure a recording contract, and manage his career. The following week Hendrix flew to London.

Through auditions, Noel Redding (bass) and Mitch Mitchell (drums) formed the Experience. Despite the existence of over one hundred clubs in London's thriving music scene, getting proper gigs to showcase the Jimi Hendrix Experience proved problematic. The only work Chandler was able to secure was a supporting act for Johnny Hallyday (the "French Elvis"). They were only allowed fifteen minutes a night, which worked great because they only rehearsed about six songs in total.

After the Hallyday tour, the band went back to London for their first recording session. During these sessions they recorded "Hey Joe," "The Wind Cries Mary," and the original Hendrix composition "Stone Free." In 1966 "Hey Joe" was a British Top 10 hit and the following year Hendrix charted again with the psychedelic classic "Purple Haze," "The Wind Cries Mary," and a haunting version of Bob Dylan's "All Along the Watchtower."

In 1997 billioniare and Hendrix fan Paul Allen opened the $60 million, 130,000-square-foot Experience Music Project museum in Seattle, Washington. Housing the largest collection of Hendrix memorabilia in the world, the collection includes Hendrix's favorite guitar, his white Fender Stratocaster used at Woodstock, reportedly costing over one million dollars at auction. Most recently added to the collection was another Fender that Hendrix used at the Miami Pop Festival. Lit on fire during the encore, the guitar was used extensively by Frank Zappa in the 1970s and was found in a closet by Dweezil Zappa in 2000. One guitar that has eluded generations of collectors and Jimiphiles is the smashed and incinerated guitar Hendrix hurled into the audience at the Monterey Pop Festival in 1967. The guitar, as seen in the classic rock documentary film *Monterey Pop,* has yet to surface in any form. If you are at all interested in starting your own Hendrix museum, at an auction house in London items belonging to the guitar legend brought in nearly $300,000 with a muslin Stars and Stripes shirt fetching a mere $26,000, while a black pen Hendrix used to sign a recording contract brought in $5,800.

Later that same year, Paul McCartney recommended the Jimi Hendrix Experience to John Phillips (of the Mamas and the Papas), who was organizing the first Monterey Pop Festival. Following The Who, the Jimi Hendrix Experience began the set with "Killing Floor" and "Foxy Lady," and finished with "Wild Thing" (complete with a burning guitar). For their first concert in America, they essentially stole the show.

In the End . . .

After an abortive tour with the Monkees (yes! Jimi Hendrix actually opened for the Monkees!), the band continued their recording success with *Are You Experienced* (1967) and *Axis: Bold As Love* (1968). With the release of *Electric Ladyland* the following year, Hendrix was reaching a crisis point musically. Jimi wanted to continue to explore groundbreaking studio effects infused with various forms of jazz and R&B. However, audience expectations emphasized feedback and pyrotechnics over progressive musicianship. In addition, Noel Redding was tired of not sharing in the limelight. Nonetheless, the band continued to make live appearances, including an historic 6:00 A.M. appearance at Woodstock.

In 1970 the Experience split and Hendrix began to record with Buddy Miles and Billy Cox. Calling themselves the Band of Gypsies, they released one live album before Mitch rejoined the band at the Isle of Wight Festival. Seven days later they played at the Isle of Fuhrman Concert. Greeted with sporadic booing during the erratic set, Hendrix ended with "Message to Love" and returned to London. On September 16th, 1970, Hendrix made his last public appearance onstage at Ronnie Scott's jazz club in London, joining Eric Burdon and War for an extended jam.

Two days later, Jimi was stuck in traffic back in Kensington, England. Invited to a party by the car next to him, he accepted the invitation. When girlfriend Monika Danneman found him at their room at the Samarkand Hotel around 11:00 A.M., he was no longer breathing. Rushed to St. Mary's Abbots Hospital, he was pronounced dead at 12:15 P.M. At a London inquest ten days later, the coroner blamed the death on "inhalation of vomit due to barbiturate intoxication."

Greenwood Memorial Park
Renton, Washington

In response to the number of visitors to the cemetery, the Hendrix estate moved his remains to an elaborate monument in early 2003. The new domed tomb for the guitar legend features granite walkways, multicolored marble, and a bronze sculpture of Hendrix. Upon entering the cemetery, the Italian marble tomb is easily visible in this small cemetery.

I knew Jimi and I think that the best thing you could say about Jimi was there was a person who shouldn't use drugs.

Frank Zappa

BILLIE HOLIDAY

BORN April 7, 1915
Baltimore, Maryland

DIED July 17, 1959
New York, New York

CAUSE OF DEATH Heart Failure
Age 44

At her peak, in the big band swing era of the 1930s through bebop in the 1940s, Billie Holiday was unquestionably the greatest jazz singer of all times. She was an avant-garde artist who polished unremarkable popular standards into brilliant works of art. It was not until years after her death that we partially understand the insecurities that led to her excessive drinking, drug use, destructive relationships, and untimely demise.

In the Beginning . . .

Billie Holiday (born Eleanora Fagan) was the daughter of an itinerant guitarist and a mother who worked as a domestic. She was introduced to jazz through records that were played at the brothel where she ran errands as a child. After a brief interlude as a prostitute, she began singing at a small nightclub in Brooklyn, New York, sometime after 1930. Though her parents were never married, Billie adopted her father's last name at the start of her singing career. Sadly, her father refused to acknowledge Holiday as his daughter until after her first success.

Holiday played many small places, including Jerry's, a small nightclub in Harlem well known to jazz enthusiasts, and also worked at Monette's, where she was discovered by record producer John Hammond. Hammond arranged for her to record with Benny Goodman in 1933 and moved her to larger venues in New York City. Some of her best jazz recordings, in which she was joined by many great artists such as pianist Teddy Wilson and Lester Young, were made between 1935 and 1942. Her 1937 recording of "Carelessly" was #1 for three weeks and stayed on the charts for a total of twelve weeks. In 1937 she joined the Count Basie Band and the Artie Shaw Band the following year, though not much of her work survived with either group, as they were all signed to different labels. She earned her nickname "Lady Day" from saxophonist Lester Young, who bestowed the surname on the singer when she objected to the coarse language used by some of the members of the Basie Band. In 1939 she sang what was probably the first jazz protest song ever recorded. "Strange Fruit," a rather grotesque song about the lynchings of black youths in the South, was her personal interpretation of a song that made a strong statement against racism. A slow, melancholy song, it became a permanent fixture as her nightclub finale.

In the mid-forties, she appeared in the film *New Orleans*, in which she proved to be a natural actress. Because of her race, she was stuck playing a housemaid. Although she did not appreciate the typecasting, she was happy to have the opportunity to perform in the film with her idol, Louis Armstrong. Her voice seemed its strongest during the 1944 to 1949 period when she recorded her biggest hit, "Lover Man," for Decca, as well as "Good

Erected by the city of Baltimore, Maryland, to honor her lifetime acheivements and accomplishments, the Billie Holiday Statue stands on Pennsylvania Avenue between Lanvale and Lafayette. In 2002 the handwritten lyrics for the 1956 composition "Lady Sings the Blues" were sold for $10,000. Handwritten by Holiday, it was the only piece of memorabilia friend Bill Dufty saved after her death.

Morning, Heartache," and "Don't Explain." However, her continued misuse of hard drugs and alcohol landed Holiday in jail for drug possession. Due to the publicity of her arrest and jail term, her audience grew after she was released from prison.

Lady Day's life began its steady slide downward in 1950. Her voice failing, one final triumph came in 1957 when she sang "Fine and Mellow" accompanied by Lester Young on the televised program *The Sound of Jazz*. However, at the age of forty-three, she sounded more like a woman of seventy-three.

In the End . . .

By 1958, Holiday was living alone in a small apartment near Central Park in New York. With only a small Chihuahua to keep her company, she released two more albums of work, *Velvet Mood* and *Songs for Distingué Lovers*. And though her voice was ravaged by a lifetime of addiction and mistreatment, her technique and choice of material remained supreme.

On May 31, 1959, Holiday collapsed and fell into a coma. Her friend, Frankie Freedom, had her taken to the hospital in an ambulance, but Holiday was left to languish unconscious on a stretcher in the hall, unattended by an overburdened hospital staff. She was diagnosed with a liver ailment complicated by cardiac failure. Two weeks later, the police invaded her hospital room and allegedly found a small amount of heroin. She was placed under arrest and charged with possession. Some of her friends thought the police planted the drugs; others think that a well-meaning fan had left it as a token of affection to help ease her pain. Whatever the case, the police were overly fervent in their pursuit of justice. Since Holiday was too sick to be moved, a police guard was placed outside her room. A judge later removed the guard, but not before Holiday had undergone severe mistreatment by the police. She had all the personal possessions in her room removed, and was subjected to fingerprinting and mug shots while still in her hospital bed. Before she could begin to recover, she suffered a kidney infection the following month, and on July 11 another heart attack. On July 17 at 3:10 A.M., Holiday passed away quietly after sharing one last joke with constant visitor Bill Dufty. After her death $700 in cash, thought to be payment for her autobiography, *Lady Sings the Blues*, was found strapped to her leg.

St. Raymond's Cemetery
The Bronx, New York

Located at the corner of East 177th Street and Lafayette Avenue in New York City, her monument can be found in the St. Paul section, Range 56, Plot 29, Grave 1 and 2. Holiday is in the center of the St. Paul/St. Luke section near the Lafayette and Whitestone Bridge Service Road border.

I had the white gowns and the white shoes. And every night they'd bring me the white gardenias and the white junk. When I was on, I was on and nobody gave me trouble. No cops, no treasury agents, nobody. I got into trouble when I tried to get off.

Billie Holiday

BUDDY HOLLY

BORN September 7, 1936
Lubbock, Texas

DIED February 3, 1959
Clear Lake, Iowa

CAUSE OF DEATH Plane Crash
Age 22

On a cold February morning in an Iowa cornfield, while most of America was home asleep, the cold, lifeless bodies of Ritchie Valens, J. P. "The Big Bopper" Richardson, Buddy Holly, and their pilot lay still under the falling snow. That day marked the end of innocence—the end of the fifties. It was the day the music died.

In the Beginning . . .

Buddy Holly's (born Charles Hardin Holley) brief but spectacular career started in the sleepy southwestern town of Lubbock, Texas. As a child Holly, with the encouragement of his parents, played the guitar and piano. Upon entering high school he formed Buddy & Bob with local musician Bob Montgomery. They recorded a local hit and even opened for Elvis Presley when the future King of Rock 'n' Roll came to town. In fact, on subsequent visits, Buddy and Elvis could be seen cruising downtown Lubbock for girls after the show.

In 1955, Holly traveled to Nashville to record an early version of "That'll Be the Day" and other songs, but those Decca releases failed commercially. He returned to Lubbock and formed the Crickets with drummer Jerry Allison, guitarist Niki Sullivan, and Larry Welborn on bass (later replaced by Joe B. Maudlin). They traveled to Clovis, New Mexico, to meet and record with Norman Petty at his studio. The result was a #1 hit with a more upbeat, rockabilly version of "That'll Be the Day." Their first tour of the U.S. included Eddie Cochran, Frankie Lymon and the Teenagers, Gene Vincent, Jerry Lee Lewis, Paul Anka, and Chuck Berry. They played sixty to seventy back-to-back performances, tour after tour, and released another twenty singles before the year was over.

By the summer of 1958, Buddy amicably split with the Crickets, dropped his longtime

---

🎸— The largest public collection of Buddy Holly and the Crickets memorabilia can be found in Holly's hometown of Lubbock, Texas, at the Buddy Holly Center. Included in their collection is Holly's own handwritten lyric sheets in a bound songbook binder, Holly's Fender Stratocaster that was used on his last tour, and the glasses worn by Holly on that fateful flight (the same glasses that were kept at the Clear Lake Sheriff's Office for years before being discovered and returned to the family). Although there have been rumors circulated for years that all of Holly's homes have been bulldozed or moved to undisclosed locations, the museum has a full list of Holly homes and sites, including the home at 1305 Thirty-seventh Street where the whole Holly family lived in 1957 when "That'll Be the Day" became a nationwide hit. Unfortunately, the one item you will not find at the museum is Holly's favorite guitar—his circa-1950s Gibson leathertop guitar. That belongs to Holly collector and star of the film *The Buddy Holly Story*, Gary Busey. Naturally, fans still make the drive out to the Surf Ballroom in Clear Lake, Iowa, where they have Hall of Fame of photos and posters from over fifty years of music history and the phone (see left photo) that Holly and Ritchie Valens used to place their last phone calls before boarding the plane.

manager and producer Petty under a cloud of financial misdealings, and married Maria Elena Santiago. Living in Greenwich Village, New York City, Buddy wrote songs at a feverish pace. In two short months he wrote and recorded in his apartment, later to be called the Basement Tapes, "That Makes It Tough," "Crying, Waiting, Hoping," and the classic "Peggy Sue Got Married."

In the End . . .

With his funds frozen in New Mexico (Petty said, "I'd rather see you starve to death first") and no new jobs in the foreseeable future, Holly signed a contract with GAC for a two-month tour of the Midwest, called the Winter Dance Party. Holly was now a solo act, and the Crickets returned to Lubbock, Texas, to work with Petty. As for the tour, Holly wasn't excited about a two-month bus tour in the frozen Midwest with no breaks between shows. However, with his wife now pregnant and the bills due, he felt he had no choice.

The conditions on the road were horrendous. There was no heat, no manager to arrange onsite details, and not a single break in the schedule. After several bus breakdowns and being stranded in the cold, Holly chartered a plane for himself and his two remaining band members, Waylon Jennings and Tommy Allsup (drummer Carl Bunch was in the hospital with frostbite). During the evening of February 2nd, the Big Bopper approached Waylon Jennings complaining of the flu and wanting to get to Moorhead early to see a doctor. Waylon was glad to be off the plane (he enjoyed the camaraderie of the bus) and, in return, the Big Bopper gave Waylon his new sleeping bag. Ritchie Valens had bothered Tommy Allsup all evening about giving up his seat, so they flipped a coin. Ritchie called heads and heads it was, so Tommy traveled on the bus. They finished their second set of the night with rousing versions of "Peggy Sue," "Rave On," "Heartbreak," and "Everyday." The Bopper, Valens, and Holly then shared the stage for a number, and then Valens finished the evening with his hit, "La Bamba."

At the Mason City Municipal Airport, the temperature was eighteen degrees, the wind was gusting to forty miles an hour from the south, and the visibility was near zero. The plane took off from Runway 17 into the blinding storm front. Two minutes later radio contact was lost and with the landing gear still retracted, the plane plowed into a picked cornfield. The fuselage split open on impact and Holly and Valens were thrown twenty feet from the plane. The Bopper was hurled more than forty feet from the wreckage over a fence. They were discovered in snowdrifts later the next morning. Scattered about the wreckage lay Valens's crucifix, the Bopper's dice, and Holly's trademark glasses. The pilot, Roger Peterson, was still strapped to his seat.

Once you're dead, you're made for life.

Jimi Hendrix

Meanwhile back in Lubbock, in the three months since the split with Holly, Jerry Allison and Joe B. Maudlin as the Crickets were not releasing any singles, not getting any gigs, and pretty much sick and tired of working with Petty. They put in a call to Maria Elena in New York and asked her where they could reach Buddy. She looked at the tour schedule and replied, "Clear Lake, Iowa." They made a call to the Surf Ballroom in Clear Lake, but the show was over. They were told that Buddy was already on his way to the next city.

City of Lubbock Cemetery
Lubbock, Texas

As you drive into the cemetery, turn right on Azalea, Block 45, and drive about three hundred feet and park. On the left you will find the Holley (the record company misspelled Buddy's last name as Holly and he decided to leave it as is) family plots, located on the first row closest to the road. Bearing the correct Holley spelling, Buddy is buried beside his mother, father, and a cousin.

Crash Site
Clear Lake, Iowa

From U.S. Highway 18 in Clear Lake, drive north on North Eighth Street for 4.7 miles. When the paved road turns to the west (left), take the gravel road to the east for a short distance, then immediately north again on the gravel road. Continue north for .5 miles (just past the grain bins) to the first fence row on the left. Park the car and walk along the fence west about .3 of a mile. A small memorial is located at the place where the plane came to a rest. Please note: This is private property but you are welcome as long as you remain respectful.

RITCHIE, BUDDY AND BOPPER MEMORIAL MARKER
Surf Ballroom
Clear Lake, Iowa

Located on U.S. Highway 18 near the intersection of Route 107, right on the waters of Clear Lake, this monument to the memories of Holly, Valens, the Big Bopper, and pilot Roger Peterson is located just outside the Surf Ballroom.

THE DAY THE MUSICIANS DIED
PASSENGERS WITH BUDDY HOLLY ON HIS LAST FLIGHT

Ritchie Valens
May 13, 1941—February 3, 1959

Valens's brief career took off with his first single, "Come On, Let's Go," which made it to the number two position on *Billboard*'s pop chart in September of 1958. With it Valens had become the first Latino singer to gain success in the pop music industry. A great deal of touring followed with Valens appearing in the Pacific Northwest and Hawaii during October, bringing down the house with "Donna" and his spirited rendition of "La Bamba." Although he was raised in a predominantly Hispanic area of Los Angeles, Valens never spoke Spanish and his cousin had to teach him the words to "La Bamba." In December of 1958 he played at both schools he'd attended in San Fernando, appeared in Alan Freed's Christmas Jubilee show, and performed a lip-sync rendition of "Ooh! My Head" in the Hal Roach film *Go, Johnny, Go!* before accepting the dates with Holly.

Valens was laid to rest in the San Fernando Mission Cemetery in San Fernando, California. As you drive through the gates, stay to the right and drive straight ahead just past the flower shop on the right. Park on the left where it says "247" on the curb and Valens's black-and-silver stone is three rows off the road on the left.

J. P. "The Big Bopper" Richardson
October 24, 1930—February 3, 1959

Make no mistake, the Big Bopper was pure showmanship. Recording during his free time as a disc jockey in Texas, in 1958 his novelty records "Get a Job" and "Short Shorts" began to sell well to the teen market. Richardson was about to drive to Houston to record "The Purple People Eater Meets the Witch Doctor" when he was playing with the lyrics for the flip side (also known as a "throwaway" in the business) single "Chantilly Lace" with the catchphrase, "Oh baby, You KNOW what I LIKE!", which became a hit. J.P. toured the East Coast from Cleveland to Washington, D.C., and down to Atlanta and New Orleans; by the time he appeared on Dick Clark's show, the Big Bopper was a household name. So when he was offered billing with Dion, the Everly Brothers, Buddy Holly, and Ritchie Valens in the SAG Winter Tour in January 1959, he said yes.

He is buried at Forest Lawn Memorial Park in Beaumont, Texas. Turn left as you enter the cemetery at the first road and park on the left. His simple flat marker is located in the Lily Pool Garden section, second row from the road, directly across the street from the funeral home.

Roger Peterson
May 24, 1937—February 3, 1959

Did Buddy Holly fire a gun onboard that caused the plane to crash? That's just one of a number of conspiracy theories that abound. What really happened was that pilot Roger Peterson was too young, too inexperienced, and probably too enamored with his passengers to just say no to taking flight during the storm.

He is buried at Buena Vista Memorial Cemetery in Storm Lake, Iowa, in the middle of the first section on the right.

JOHN LEE HOOKER

BORN August 22, 1917
Clarksdale, Mississippi

DIED June 21, 2001
Los Altos, California

CAUSE OF DEATH Heart Failure
Age 83

In the long and rich history of the blues, there is no larger figure than the King of the Delta Boogie, John Lee Hooker. A Mississippi native who grew up in the shadows of Blind Blake and Blind Lemon Jefferson, he absorbed gospel, country blues, Detroit electric blues, and rock 'n' roll and transformed them into his own brand of heavily amplified, foot-pounding, single-chord blues. When he died at the age of eighty-three, John Lee "The Hook" Hooker's status as a living legend and true musical icon was secure.

In the Beginning . . .

Born one of eleven children of a Baptist preacher and sharecropper in the heart of the Mississippi Delta, John Lee Hooker began his musical interest at the age of thirteen with spiritual music. When he was young his parents had separated and his mother's new husband, Will Moore, worked his own farm and played country blues at the local juke joints. So it wasn't unusual when Charley Patton, Blind Lemon Jefferson, or Blind Blake would stop by his stepfather's house with Hooker watching in awe.

In the early 1930s, Hooker first moved to Memphis but couldn't make any headway in the clubs. He relocated up north to Cincinnati for seven years, followed by the big move to Detroit. In 1948, he made the colorful travelog single of the Detroit blues clubs, "Boogie Chillen," which made him a star at the top of the R&B charts. The following year he had three smash hits with "Crawling King Snake Blues," "The Boogie Man," and "Hobo Blues." And though he signed with Modern Records, that didn't stop him from making records under the surname of Texas Slim, Birmingham Sam and his Magic Guitar, Delta John, or Johnny Williams for a variety of competing labels. After a dozen labels and a dozen psuedonyms, Hooker finally settled down with Vee Jay in 1955 and recorded with backing musicians Jimmy Reed on harp and guitarist Eddie Taylor on "Time Is Marching," "Mambo Chillun," "Baby Lee," and "Dimples" before returning to the charts with "I Love You, Honey."

In the early 1960s Hooker appeared at the Newport Folk Festival, later producing another R&B hit with "Boom Boom," which also entered the British Top 20. Beginning in 1962, Hooker started a succession of tours to the U.K., culminating in several recording sessions with the Animals and the Yardbirds. In fact, the version of "Boom Boom" that the Animals cut outsold Hooker's version in the U.S. By now Hooker's audiences were nearly all white and at the end of the 1960s Hooker recorded the seminal white blues album, *Hooker and Heat*, with the members of Canned Heat and later with Irish rocker Van Morrison.

By the mid-1970s Hooker was plodding along, simply repeating many of his past glories under the guise of new titles. In 1980 the resurgence of blues and blues roots rock began with Hooker's cameo appearance in the film *The Blues Brothers*. Afterward, though, the music world saw very little of Hooker as he had grown tired of the recording and touring.

In the End . . .

Although Hooker declared himself "semiretired," that didn't mean he stopped working. In 1990 Hooker's duet "I'm in the Mood," with Bonnie Raitt from the album *The Healer* (also featuring Carlos Santana and Robert Cray) won the Grammy Award for Best Traditional Blues Recording, and the following year he was inducted into the Rock and Roll Hall of Fame. In 1992 Hooker released the album *Boom Boom* along with two compilation CDs of his early years.

In 1993 the San Francisco nightclub, the Boom Boom Room, opened with Hooker as one of the partners and again, as in the previous year, Ace, Flair, Specialty, and Modern record labels all released best of compilation CDs. By now Hooker himself estimated that he had recorded or played on over one hundred albums. The success of *The Healer* repeated itself the following year with *Mr. Lucky,* which featured Albert Collins, Keith Richards, and Van Morrison sharing the spotlight with the blues legend.

As the 1990s came to a close, Hooker released two more albums of original material, *Chill Out* and *Don't Look Back,* and won two more Grammys. Retired from the road aside from a few selected dates, Hooker died in his sleep at his home, his legacy intact.

Chapel of the Chimes Cemetery
Oakland, California

As you enter the cemetery, head toward the Garden of Ages mausoleum. Walk through the entrance and take the elevator to the third floor. Turn left and John Lee Hooker's final resting place is in the Dedication niche, Crypt 6.

> *Mississippi produced the best blues singers out of all the states. Take Muddy and Jimmy Reed, and there's Arthur Crudup, and you've heard of Robert Nighthawk—all great. But as for me, there's nobody that plays my style. Some of them try, but there're not even close.*
>
> John Lee Hooker

HOWLIN' WOLF

BORN June 10, 1910
West Point, Mississippi

DIED January 10, 1976
Chicago, Illinois

CAUSE OF DEATH Heart Failure during Surgery
Age 65

When Chester Arthur Burnett packed up his new Cadillac, brushed the Delta dust from his new suit, and drove twenty-five hours straight to Chicago to claim his fame, he didn't need any formal introductions. After all, his fans, the club owners, and his record company all knew he would come eventually. They all knew that the legendary Howlin' Wolf would be comin' to town.

In the Beginning . . .

A direct disciple of Charley Patton and Sonny Boy Williamson II, Howlin' Wolf (born Chester Burnett, earning his nickname from his parents due to his rambunctious nature) did not play guitar much before he was eighteen. Moving to Ruleville, Mississippi, Wolf began playing for house parties and on the streets in nearby towns for spare change.

During the early 1930s Wolf met the now legendary Charley Patton, learning the low, guttural moaning style of country blues from the master after work. Working the farmland around Arkansas, Wolf also met seasoned blues musicians Sonny Boy Williamson II (Aleck "Rice" Miller, from whom he was taught the harmonica) and Robert Johnson. In 1941 he was called for military service and upon discharge returned to the Delta and his plow—but only for a short time. In 1948 he formed his first full-time band consisting of James Cotton, guitarist Willie Johnson, Matt "Guitar" Murphy, and Junior Parker. Three years later he was offered a recording contract with the then-unknown Sam Phillips of Sun Records. Released in the summer of 1951, "How Many More Years" and "Moanin' at Midnight" raced up the charts and established Howlin' Wolf as a bona fide country blues artist.

By the start of 1953, Howlin' Wolf was one of Leonard Chess's artists and recorded exclusively for

It is no secret that Howlin' Wolf and Muddy Waters's relationship was a bit strained. Not surprising, since they were both masters of the blues, both vied for the attention at Chess Records, and both sought premium gigs at the local Chicago nightclubs. It probably didn't help that Wolf sued Chess Records for back royalty payments and that songwriter and producer Willie Dixon preferred Waters over Wolf for a majority of his songs. Therefore, the legacy of Howlin' Wolf doesn't get much respect at the Blues Heaven Foundation in Chicago (which is owned and operated by the Willie Dixon family). And while most of his memorabilia is still controlled by his family, several items of the Wolf and dozens of blues artists are well represented in a rotating exhibit at the Chicago Blues Archives, on the eighth floor of the central library in downtown Chicago.

Chess Records. By no means a young man (he was five years older than Muddy Waters, with whom he feuded all his life), he had to constantly work hard to compete with the new generation of artists. Standing six-foot-six and weighing three hundred pounds, Howlin' Wolf held his own, punctuating his performances with whooping and hollering and dropping to his knees, his suit drenched with sweat.

In the End . . .

A regular in Chicago at Sylvio's Lounge and the 708, Howlin' Wolf was also a regular on the U.S. Blues Tour circuit and traveled to Europe as part of the Chess blues revival series. Opening for the Rolling Stones, Howlin' Wolf adjusted nicely to a new generation of blues-influenced rock 'n' roll fans, recording "Wang Dang Doodle" and "Shake for Me" with a commanding energy of men half his age. Unfortunately, in the early 1970s Howlin' Wolf began to suffer from a series of heart attacks, and later a devastating auto accident, which damaged his liver and kidneys. While his trademark "howling" introduction was missing from his performances (in his younger days, he would enter the stage on all fours howling like a mad dog), he still continued a hectic schedule.

Few who ever witnessed a Howlin' Wolf performance in his heyday could ever forget the wail of his harmonica and his big, booming voice over the wall of sound from his band. However, by 1975 the Wolf was tired and suffering from ill health. Plagued with kidney failure and on dialysis, he was also diagnosed with cancer and continuing heart problems. Finally, on a cold winter's morning in Chicago's Veterans Hospital, Howlin' Wolf's legacy came to an end during surgery for an aneurysm.

Oakridge Cemetery
Hillside, Illinois

From Highway 294, take Highway 38 (Roosevelt Road) east to Oakridge. The cemetery is

located on the southwest corner and the entrance is off Oakridge. As you enter the gate, drive straight ahead toward the back of the cemetery to Section 18. Park between Sections 18 and 19 (18 is on your left). Buried under his birth name, his large upright marker is located in the center of the section about a hundred feet from the road in Lot 325.

This is where the soul of man never dies. God, what would it be worth to see the fervor in that man's face when he sang. His eyes would light up and you'd see the veins on his neck, and buddy, there was nothing on his mind but that song. He sang with his damn soul.

Sam Phillips of Sun Records

MAHALIA JACKSON

BORN October 26, 1911
New Orleans, Louisiana

DIED January 27, 1972
Chicago, Illinois

CAUSE OF DEATH Heart Disease
Age 60

Blessed with a rich, expressive contralto voice, Mahalia Jackson is the undisputed Queen of Gospel. During her forty years of performing, she influenced countless gospel singers and introduced white audiences to the joy and beauty of black gospel music. Exemplifyng the links between the religious and secular roots of jazz, her music provided an uplifting experience that allows her fans to feel the strength of voice and conviction this powerful woman possessed.

In the Beginning . . .

Raised in a strict religious atmosphere as the daughter of a Baptist preacher, Mahalia Jackson was one of six children born in a shack on Water Street in New Orleans, overlooking the Mississippi River. Influenced by her father's inspirational style, he would reinforce his congregation's spirit with joyous and triumphant gospel singing. Jackson quickly learned to appreciate the positive experience of, in her words, "making a joyful noise in praise of the Lord."

By age five she was singing every Sunday in her father's church choir. By the age of ten, her strict religious upbringing forbade her from singing anything other than gospel, as such a transgression would not be appropriate for a "sanctified woman." But her love of music included an appreciation for blues and jazz. Regardless of her decision not to perform blues compositions, her style was heavily influenced by blues singers Bessie Smith, Ma Rainey, and Ida Cox. However, as a teenager, Mahalia worked as a maid and laundress, secretly listening to blues records while she worked, confessing, "scrubbin' the floor, I'd turn on a Bessie Smith record to make the work go faster."

In 1927, at the age of sixteen, Mahalia moved to Chicago. After refusing an invitation by Earl "Fatha" Hines to sing the blues with his group, she worked various odd jobs while singing with the choir of the Greater Salem Baptist Church. Oddly enough, she was banned in several mainstream black churches because of her "flirtatious" stage presence. In 1932 she began singing and touring with the Johnson Gospel Singers, managing to save enough money to open her own beauty and flower shops while also investing in real estate.

By the mid-1930s she was working alone, recording such gospel hits as "He's Got the Whole World in His Hands" and "God Gonna Separate the Wheat from the Tares." Mahalia would sing only songs in which she believed, positive anthems that uplifted the spirit. Her personal statement, "I Will Move on Up a Little Higher," sold in the millions due only to word of mouth among black gospel fans.

Her extraordinarily rich, deep contralto voice captured the attention of audiences all over the world. In 1949, her blues-inspired "Let the Power of the Holy Ghost Fall on Me" won the French Academy's Grand Prix du Disque. The success of her recordings led to the first of four sold-out appearances at New York's Carnegie Hall on October 4, 1950. Radio and television appearances were followed by tours at home and abroad. When she sang "Silent Night" on Denmark's national radio, more than twenty thousand requests for copies poured in. In 1952 she teamed with Duke Ellington at the Newport Jazz Festival for his composition *Black, Brown, and Beige.*

Mahalia was active in the black civil rights movement, joining Rev. Martin Luther King's bus boycott in Alabama. In 1963 she sang at the historic Washington, D.C., rally at which King gave his historical speech "I Have a Dream." During her lifetime, she sang for four presidents—Truman, Eisenhower, Kennedy, and Johnson.

In the End . . .

By the sixties Jackson was still the star attraction for mainly white audiences. An astute businesswoman, she became well-to-do through her chain of Mahalia Jackson Chicken diners. However, the lifelong grind of recording, touring, and business and civic duties began to take their toll on the Queen of Gospel. During her final years, Mahalia suffered from a series of illnesses and setbacks. She died on January 27, 1972, at the age of sixty, worn down by a lifelong battle against high blood pressure and heart disease. She never had any doubt about why she sang gospel: "I sing God's music because it makes me feel free. It gives me hope."

Providence Memorial Park
Metairie, Louisiana

A spectacular funeral was held in New Orleans, where Aretha Franklin led the congregation singing the hymn "Precious Lord, Take My Hand." She was laid to rest in Providence

Memorial Park in Metairie (just outside New Orleans) on Airline Highway. From the New Orleans International Airport, drive down Airline Highway toward New Orleans. Turn right into the cemetery and turn left at the first intersection. Drive to the end of the mausoleum at the curve in the road. Her gated, aboveground monument stands alone, about two hundred feet from the mausoleum.

I know what I can do with it, too, baby, and that's not sing it. Child, I been reborn!
Mahalia Jackson to Louis Armstrong, answering Armstrong's request to sing the blues.

ELMORE JAMES

BORN January 27, 1918
Richland, Mississippi

DIED May 24, 1963
Chicago, Illinois

CAUSE OF DEATH Heart Disease
Age 45

When he first entered the recording studio in 1951, Elmore James was already thirty-three years old with less than twelve years left in his life. However, he posthumously became the most influential bottleneck slide guitarist in the history of postwar electric blues. A direct disciple of Robert Johnson and Sonny Boy Williamson II, James's soaring, frenzied blues style had a profound influence on generations of guitarists years after he was gone.

In the Beginning . . .

Born and raised in the heart of the Mississippi Delta, Elmore James spent a good deal of his youth moving from farm to farm with his family in search of work. With the limited education afforded black sharecroppers during the 1920s, James's life from childhood to early adolescence varied little from others of his generation. What separated James from others was his passion for music. Cousins report that from a very early age, James was picking out tunes on homemade instruments. One such instrument was made of only three strings and an empty tin can.

In the late 1920s and early 1930s, James was making a name for himself at Saturday-night dances and barrelhouse functions around the city of Goodman. Yet to develop the bottleneck slide technique, James accompanied himself on six-string guitar, performing standard blues numbers. Moving to the Belzoni area, James met with two musicians who would change his life. Both Robert Johnson, fresh from recording with the American Record Company, and Aleck "Rice" Miller, who was just beginning his colorful career as Sonny Boy Williamson II, were performing in the area. Bored with the monotony of farm-work, Johnson and Miller embodied everything that James longed to be—the hard-living, hard-drinking intinerant life of a bluesman. More importantly, James began to emulate the bottleneck slide technique that Johnson used so well on such numbers as "I Believe I'll Dust My Broom."

James began to work less in the fields and began traveling farther and farther from home, working in a small group that included his brother. His career as a bluesman was cut short when he was drafted into the U.S. Naval Reserves in 1943. He returned home two years later only to find his family had moved. Diagnosed with a heart condition, James stayed in Mississippi, working occasionally with the now-popular Williamson. In 1951 he was asked by Mrs. Lillian McMurry, owner of Trumpet Records, to record his popular song "Dust My Broom" (contrary to popular myth, James was not tricked into recording the single). Released with "Catfish Blues" on the flip side by Bobo Thomas (but credited to James nonetheless), the record went to the #9 position on the Billboard R&B charts. With his

Not exactly a man of wealth and fame, Elmore James died with a little more than a couple of guitars and the clothes he owned. One of those guitars, a circa-1948 National guitar with a missing pickguard, was given by Fire Record label owner and friend Bobby Robinson to the Rock and Roll Hall of Fame in Ohio.

heart ailment troubling James, he took the royalty payments and "retired" from recording with Mrs. McMurry (interestingly enough, McMurry hired veteran bluesman Arthur "Big Boy" Crudup to record as "Elmer James").

Asked to relocate to Chicago, James moved north in 1952, staying with Howlin' Wolf. By the end of 1952, James began recording with a group of musicians that eventually became his backing band, the Broomdusters. Though his chronic heart condition hampered his output, over the next twelve years James recorded more than one hundred songs for Modern, Chess, Enjoy, Chief, Fire, and Fury Records.

In the End . . .

Despite two heart attacks, James signed with Bobby Robinson's Fire Records in New York City in 1959. Recording "The Sky Is Crying," James scored his first R&B Top 20 song in seven years. With an ever-increasing health problem, it would often take James fifteen to twenty false starts before he could get through a song in the studio. Playing live, he left most of the guitar work to one of the Broomdusters, singing and playing guitar on selected songs. In 1962 James became embroiled in a dispute with the musicians' union—the American Federation of Musicians—and was barred from performing. Disillusioned, he retired once again back to Mississippi. The following year, with his union problems all cleared up by a sympathetic fan, James returned to Chicago and his band on May 19th, 1963. Living and playing with cousin Homesick James Williamson, James suffered a third and final heart attack that same week. He died a short time later at Homesick James's apartment.

Newport Baptist Church
Ebenezer, Mississippi

After well-attended services in Chicago, James made his final journey back to the Delta to the small town of Ebenezer, Mississippi. From Jackson, drive one hour north on Highway 55 to exit 146 (Highway 14). Turn left (west) and drive to Highway 17. Turn right on Highway 17 and drive 2.6 miles to the first paved road (called Newport Road, but it is unmarked). Turn left and drive 3.9 miles to the Newport Baptist Church (on your left). His above-ground monument is about one hundred feet from the back right side of the church. Please note, however, that Mr. James is buried in the back in an unmarked grave. The monument was placed in front of the cemetery to keep tourists just like you from trampling though the sacred grounds of the church members.

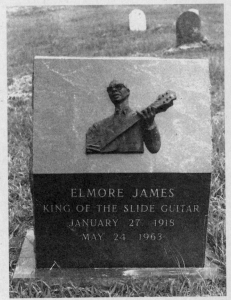

ELMORE JAMES
KING OF THE SLIDE GUITAR
JANUARY 27 1918
MAY 24 1963

Elmore kept playing the same lick over and over, but I get the feeling he meant it.

Frank Zappa

BLIND LEMON JEFFERSON

BORN September 1897
Couchman, Texas

DIED December 1929
Chicago, Illinois

CAUSE OF DEATH Exposure
Age 32

Before 1995 (when his grave was properly marked) to find Blind Lemon Jefferson's grave, one had to navigate the desolate Texas countryside, down a dirt road, to the back of the cemetery to view the small, flat concrete block that marked Jefferson's final resting place. This was an eerie fulfillment of Lemon's plea in his 1928 song, "See That My Grave Is Kept Clean." Neglected and ignored by his home state, Blind Lemon Jefferson is nonetheless revered internationally as a seminal figure in the history of the blues; in just under four years he recorded eighty-nine classic blues songs.

In the Beginning . . .

Little is known about Blind Lemon Jefferson's origins. There are no records regarding his education, his early youth, or how he came to play the guitar. In fact, there is only one known photograph of this celebrated blues musician (see above). That photo was altered with a painted-on tie and autographed by his publicist. It is, however, generally accepted that he was born in Couchman, Texas (about sixty-five miles south of Dallas) in 1897 to Alec and Classie Banks Jefferson. Blind since birth (nobody knows why he wore glasses), Lemon played in the streets of Wortham day and night for nickels and dimes. Blues legend Lightnin' Hopkins remembers hearing him at a church picnic when Hopkins was only eight years old. Finally, toward the end of the day Hopkins sat next to Lemon and tried to play along. Jefferson admonished the youth by saying, "Boy, you've got to play it right!"

By 1910 (dates are sketchy at this point), Jefferson had been traveling between Wortham and Dallas and was quite popular. It was often said that you could find him singing in church in the morning and playing in a whorehouse that night. It was also during this time that he began playing with Leadbelly, who also acted as his guide. Engineers on the Texas & Pacific Railroad would allow them to ride for free just to hear them play guitar. His travels through the South and neighboring states have been well documented by musicians who have reported seeing Jefferson pass through the region in the early 1920s. With a guitar strapped to his large frame and a tin cup dangling from the neck of the guitar, Jefferson would belt out his expressive form of Texas country blues. "Don't play me cheap," he would warn his audience—and he meant it! Although blind, he knew the sound of a penny hitting his cup and would stop to remove it (much to the embarrassment of the donor).

In 1925 Blind Lemon was invited to Dallas to make "race" records for Paramount Records. The following year he recorded his first hit record, "Got the Blues," followed in May with "Long Lonesome Blues." For the next two years Jefferson was considered the most successful country blues singer in the U.S. His subsequent recordings, such as

For the most part, jazz and blues 78s recorded before 1940 are worth more than spare change, but Blind Lemon releases are an exception. While his original release of "Black Snake Moan" on the OKeh label is worth about $300, his first recordings on Paramount released before 1930 are worth over $1,000!

"Matchbox Blues," have been recycled by Carl Perkins, and by Bob Dylan on his debut album in 1962. With his popularity rising, Jefferson's travels took him from Dallas to Chicago, Georgia, Mississippi, and all points in between. At one point he had two cars, a chauffeur, and $1,500 in the bank—unheard of for a black man in postwar America. But it was not to last. By 1929 his trademark phrases and the high-pitched, moving vocal quality of his music became more derivative of his early work. Thus, his enthusiasm deteriorated and his record sales dropped precipitously.

In the End . . .

They say that anyone over the age of sixty-five remembers the day they brought Blind Lemon home to be buried. The circumstances surrounding his death still remain a mystery. Some say he met with foul play during a blizzard one December night in the streets of Chicago. Others say he was drunk when he left the recording studio and passed out in the snow bank (or maybe, they say, it was a heart attack). There are others who claim his chauffeur left him in the street after a fight, only to be found the next day dead from exposure. None of that seemed to matter to the three hundred-plus mourners, black and white, who came to pay tribute to their fallen son.

Wortham Cemetery
Wortham, Texas

Located sixty-five miles south of Dallas, Texas, on Highway 14, take Highway 45 south from Dallas through Ennis and Corsicana to the town of Richland. Look for Highway 14 off to the right and continue on that road for ten miles. Just before you come to "downtown" Wortham, you will find the entrance to the Wortham Cemetery on your right. Pull into the cemetery and immediately turn your car around to exit back out of this cemetery. Turn left back onto the highway and drive fifty feet. Turn left onto the dirt road to the unmarked "colored cemetery." Open the gate and drive ahead about two hundred feet. His large marble marker with the bronze Texas State Historical Society plaque is located in the back along the fence.

I saw Blind Lemon Jefferson one time when I was about nine years old. He came to our house to see my stepfather. Gosh, he was a great guitar player, Blind Lemon Jefferson was. Blind Lemon, Blind Blake, Charley Patton—I remember those three.

John Lee Hooker

WAYLON JENNINGS

BORN June 15, 1937
Littlefield, Texas

DIED February 13, 2002
Chandler, Arizona

CAUSE OF DEATH Diabetes
Age 64

A brash, independent spirit and one of the most influential country singers, songwriters, and performers in the last four decades, Waylon Jennings bristled at the boundries defined by Nashville's Music Row. The creator of the "outlaw" strand of music first defined in the 1970s, Jennings broke rank from the recording executives' stranglehold on creative decisions and pioneered the use of independent songwriters and musicians to produce an impressive catalog of popular music during his forty-four year career.

In the Beginning . . .

Waylon Jennings began his career in his hometown of Littlefield, Texas, making his debut on a local radio station. In 1955 his family moved to Lubbock, where he worked as a disc jockey and first met with local musician and songwriter Buddy Holly. Three years later Holly produced Jennings's first record "Jole Blon" with King Curtis on saxophone. Impressed with the young Texan, Holly hired Jennings as a bass player in 1958 after his split with the Crickets. In early 1959 Holly, Jennings, and guitarist Tommy Allsup began a major national tour with Ritchie Valens, J. P. "the Big Bopper" Richardson, and several other popular groups when tragedy struck. When Jennings gave his seat on the small chartered plane to the Big Bopper (due to Richardson's illness), Holly laughed and said to Jennings, "Well, I hope your old bus breaks down." Jennings replied, "I hope your plane crashes." They were the words that Jennings would regret the rest of his life. Later the next morning the bodies of Holly, Richardson, Valens, and their pilot were found in an Iowa cornfield next to the crumpled plane. They all died on impact.

Shaken by the tragedy, Jennings returned to Texas and continued as a disc jockey and singer, recording for a small, local label. He moved to Phoenix, Arizona, in the early 1960s and was signed by A&M Records shortly after. Recording light pop-rock covers such as "If I Were a Carpenter" and "Four Strong Winds," Jennings was beginning to develop his unique brand of rough-edged, chicken-pickin' rockabilly-and-country style. In 1965, Jennings was signed by Chet Atkins to RCA Records out of Nashville, where he continued to release a variety of country standards preselected for him and recorded by the same cabal of studio session players, their sound designed to be consistent, regardless of the artist they were recording for.

Scoring several hits and keeping his name on the country charts with "Green River" and "Love of the Common People," Jennings was disgusted and disillusioned with the Nashville system. Negotiating a then-unheard of production deal using his own material and own musicians (often his road band, the Waylors), the changes were immediate. With a stripped-down, bass-heavy sound derived partly from honky-tonk, partly from rock 'n'

Granted, a great deal of Waylon "stuff" was sold at Waylon and wife Jessi's moving sale at their home in Arizona prior to his death, including signature boots, guitars, photos, and in the end, even their house. Fortunately, many of those items and several from his son, Buddy Jennings, are on loan to the Buddy Holly Center in Lubbock, Texas, and the CMA Hall of Fame in Nashville, Tennessee.

roll, Jennings began to pull in country fans, college students, blue-collar country fans, and every music lover in between with "Luckenbach, Texas," "I've Always Been Crazy," "Amanda," and "This Time." In 1974, Jennings was named the Country Music Association's Male Vocalist of the Year and four years later won his second Grammy (with Willie Nelson) with "Mammas, Don't Let Your Babies Grow Up to Be Cowboys." Attracting the attention of fans and critics outside of country music circles, Jennings solidified his demographic mix of admirers with the 1976 release of *Wanted: The Outlaws*, the first million-selling album ever recorded in Nashville.

In the end . . .

Acknowledged founder and leader of the "outlaw" brand of music, Jennings often laughed at the record labels' philosophy: "We just couldn't do it the way it was set up. It wasn't until I started producing my own recording and using my own musicians and working with people who understood what I was about that I first started having any real success." By the late 1970s, Jennings was selling albums in record numbers often reserved for rock stars; consequently, Jennings also developed lifestyle habits associated with rock stars. With alcohol and drug abuse rampant in the early 1980s, Jennings eventually cleaned up his act with the help of his fourth (and final) wife, Jessi Colter. In the mid-eighties Jennings formed the supergroup the Highwaymen with Johnny Cash, Willie Nelson, and Kris Kristofferson and released both *Highwayman* and *Turn the Page* in 1985 and successfully toured not only in the U.S., but also in Australia, Singapore, and China.

In 1998, after forty years on the road, in the studio, and on the charts with seventy-two albums and forty million records sold worldwide, Jennings announced his retirement. Fatigued from advancing diabetes and triple-bypass heart surgery in 1988, Jennings noted, "I really went way too long on the road. It wrecked my health for a while." In October of 2001 Jennings was inducted into the Country Music Hall of Fame; however, he was too sick to attend so his son accepted the award for him. Two months later he had to have his foot amputated as the diabetes continued to cause trouble for the ailing legend. In February of the following year, Jennings died in his sleep with his wife by his side.

Mesa City Cemetery
Mesa, Arizona

As you enter the cemetery on Center Street, proceed west on B Street (the main road), turning left on Ninth Street. Go to the sixth tree on your left and park. Walk four rows to the east of the sixth tree and look to the right. Jennings is buried in the family plot.

I'm excited to perform on the same stage as Waylon. Anyone who gives the finger to the lame music business rules and who cuts new trails is all right by me. And hey, the man wears black!

James Hetfield of Metallica

BUNK JOHNSON

BORN December 27, 1889
New Orleans, Louisiana

DIED July 7, 1949
New Iberia, Louisiana

CAUSE OF DEATH Effects of a Stroke
Age 59

The legend of Bunk Johnson, one of the early jazzmen from New Orleans, is clouded by fictional stories and bold exaggerations, usually told by Johnson himself. Although he erroneously claimed to be born in 1879, recorded with legendary Buddy Bolden, and taught Louis Armstrong on cornet, he was nonetheless considered a symbolic figure in the revival of Dixieland and traditional jazz, despite the controversy surrounding the quality of his work.

In the Beginning . . .

Born in New Orleans, Louisiana, as William Geary Johnson, his actual birth has been proven to be unverifiable due to the lack of records kept before the turn of the century. To add to the mystery, much of Johnson's recollections of growing up and playing in New Orleans with Buddy Bolden before the turn of the century have been contradicted by Bunk himself. However, a New Orleans census dated in the year 1900 shows a Geary Johnson born in 1889. In addition, none of Bolden's sidemen ever mention Johnson in interviews and of the surviving photos before 1900, none show Johnson with any of the bands. Therefore, it is highly unlikely that Johnson played with the acknowledged father of jazz, Buddy Bolden, before the age of ten.

What is known is that Johnson was considered a solid ensemble player with a sweet tone and a genuine feeling for the blues. Active in the New Orleans jazz scene from 1905, Johnson started with the Superior Orchestra, later joining the Eagle Band (Bolden's band before he was committed to an insane asylum) as second cornet. In 1914 he moved to Lake Charles and Baton Rouge, teaching and playing in minstrel shows, county fairs, and honky-tonks. A short list of his musical background includes Ma Rainey, W. C. Handy's Orchestra, Tuts Johnson's band, and the American Theater. In the early 1920s he worked with Gus Fortinet's band in New Iberia, then with the Black Eagle Jazz Band in Crowly, Louisiana. In 1932, during a road trip with the Black Eagle Jazz Band, leader Evan Thomas was stabbed to death by an irate customer on the bandstand. Later that month Bunk's trumpet was destroyed during a bar fight, leaving him without an instrument. The final blow came two months later when dental problems forced Johnson into an early retirement. Within a single year Johnson went from nightclub stages to the sugar fields of New

His birthplace on Constance Street in New Orleans may be gone, but the city that Johnson called home today hosts the Bunk Johnson/New Iberia Arts and Heritage Festival every May. The festivities include live bands and the annual second line parade and rededication of Johnson's final resting place. The Iberia Parish Library and Archives house some of Johnson's memorabilia and occasionally display the trumpet Johnson was "buried" with at his funeral. Seems at the time of his death, his widow, Maude, requested that *Life* magazine cover the funeral of her husband. The magazine agreed upon one condition—that Johnson be photographed in his casket with his horn and buried with the valuable instrument. The Widow Johnson agreed, only to pull the horn out just before they closed the lid without anyone looking. The remainder of Johnson's estate went to biographer William Russell who, with 42,500 items in his collection, holds one of the largest private jazz collections.

Iberia, and for the next ten years he worked as a field hand, crane operator, and music teacher—virtually forgotten by the music world.

Six years later Johnson attended a concert by Louis Armstrong in New Iberia. They met after the show, triggering a chain of events that led Johnson back into music. Due to Armstrong's recommendation to writer William Russell in a discussion about the early days of jazz, Johnson was contacted; Johnson was soon back in the spotlight.

In the End . . .

When Johnson was contacted by amateur jazz historians William Russell and Fred Ramsey in 1939, they continued their correspondence over the next year as Johnson became the focus of their New Orleans revival articles. With his ability to perform still hampered by years of dental neglect, it was arranged for Sidney Bechet's dentist brother to provide dentures. In 1942 he was asked to record for two jazz labels, where he appeared and recorded with the Yerba Buena Jazz Band. He moved to New York and worked briefly in 1945 with Sidney Bechet (who found the elder Johnson to be surly and difficult to work with). It was here in New York that Johnson achieved his greatest fame as he played the Stuyvesant Casino in New York City from September 1945 until the following January. Surrounded by other aging New Orleans veterans retrieved from obscurity, he was regarded as a living legend. During the second phase of his career, Johnson recorded over forty times for a variety of radio broadcasts, live performances, and studio sessions dates until 1948.

With his health deteriorating, he went back home to New Iberia after suffering a stroke. A bitter man who drank too much, he had waited years for success and recognition, yet as far as Johnson was concerned, it was far too little too late. In November of 1948 he suffered two more strokes and passed away the following year. But even after a half century since his passing, Johnson's influence and popularity surpass that of Armstrong in Europe, where they have a jazz society and hospital named in his honor.

St. Edward Cemetery
New Iberia, Louisiana

A three-hour drive from New Orleans, the cemetery is located at the corner of French Street and Dale Street near downtown New Iberia. As you enter the cemetery from any of the three entrances, walk to the center of the cemetery, facing the cross at the intersection of the pathways. Turn to the left and his small marker can be found three rows down, six spaces over between the larger tombs.

The fellow they ought to write about is Bunk. Man, what a man! They should talk about that man, that alone.

Louis Armstrong

ROBERT JOHNSON

BORN May 8, 1911 (?)
Hazelhurst, Mississippi

DIED August 16, 1938
Greenwood, Mississippi

CAUSE OF DEATH Murdered
Age 27

The primary influence for Muddy Waters and Robert Jr. Lockwood, and the chief source of inspiration for Eric Clapton and the Rolling Stones, Robert Johnson, undisputed King of the Delta Blues, is probably the most obscure yet fiercely original artist to come out of the Mississippi Delta.

In the beginning . . .

Very little is known (factually that is; there are countless stories) about Robert Johnson's life. What is known is that he was born the illegitimate eleventh child of Julia Major Dobbs and a plantation worker named Noah Johnson. Johnson spent his first years in Memphis, but in his early teens returned to the Mississippi Delta region around Robinsonville, where he was raised by his mother and stepfather, Dusty Willis.

The origins of Johnson's musical development were revealed by Son House to blues folklorist Julius Lester:

"And there was this little boy standin' around. That was Robert Johnson. He blew harmonica and was pretty good with that, but he wanted to play guitar. When we'd get a break and want to rest some, we'd set the guitars up in the corner and go out to cool. Robert would watch and see which way we'd gone, and he would pick one of them up. And such racket you heard. It'd make people mad, you know. They'd come and say, 'Why don't y'all go in and git that guitar away from that boy. He's running people crazy with it.' "

In his late teens (again, dates and places are a bit sketchy), Johnson had learned the rudiments of guitar from House and bluesman Willie Brown. It is believed that he traveled widely, including the East Coast and down to Texas. After two years had passed, when Son House, Johnny Shines, and others caught up with Johnson, they could scarcely believe their ears. In a very short time Johnson had become an incredible, solidly original blues guitarist and songwriter.

This sudden proficiency did not go unnoticed by the locals. Many myths and legends have been retold over the years to account for the supposed "mystery" of Johnson's talent. The most common story was that just before midnight one summer, Johnson traveled to the crossroads and sold his soul to the devil. As legend has it, like Tommy Johnson before and Howlin' Wolf after, Robert played a song for a man dressed in black. He then handed his guitar over to the devil and, after tuning the guitar, proceeded to play the same tune back to Johnson. Upon return of the guitar, in exchange for his eternal soul,

---

Opened in 2002, the Greenwood Blues Heritage Museum boasts the largest collection of Robert Johnson-related memorabilia, including the only two known photographs of the blues master. In Clarksdale, Mississippi, the Delta Blues Museum has the sign from the juke joint in which Johnson was poisoned, at Three Forks. And though sinced moved from the original site, the building that housed the juke joint that Johnson was murdered in has survived all these years and is currently a private residence. From Highway 82 take Highway 7 south through Itta Bena. Continue as the road jogs to the right, then to the left. Approximately 2.3 miles after the left curve, on the left hand side of the road sits the house on the corner just before the bridge.

the devil granted Johnson the absolute ability to play any song in his head. Regardless of how he accrued his amazing talent, this period marked the beginning of his professional career.

In the End . . .

For the next couple years, Johnson traveled and played with Shines, Sonny Boy Williamson II, Robert Nighthawk, and his own stepson, Robert Jr. Lockwood. It was in 1936 that Johnson traveled to San Antonio to cut his first record. In three days he recorded sixteen songs. Six months later in Dallas he recorded another thirteen, for a total of twenty-nine songs (not including outtakes). These would become the only known recordings of Robert Johnson's music. For the two recording sessions he was paid about one hundred dollars.

His last year of life is at best speculative. It is known that Johnson played a while in Dallas, later moving around through Memphis and St. Louis before settling down in Greenwood, Mississippi. Living in a small one-room house, he spent the nights playing juke joints and plantation houses.

The night of his murder still remains shrouded in mystery. Of the three possible scenarios, only one has been substantiated by eyewitnesses. The least credible version has Johnson dying in the arms of Sonny Boy Williamson after being poisoned by a jealous girlfriend. Another version has him being stabbed to death by the father of his girlfriend on Quito Bridge near Greenwood. Both stories, although wildly entertaining in their entirety, remain unconvincing in their lack of evidence.

The most believable story places Johnson at a juke joint Sunday night in Three Forks (fifteen miles from Greenwood). It seems that the owner or operator of the dance had hired Johnson for the weekend, only to discover that Johnson was messing around with his wife. He gave his unknowing wife a bottle of poisoned whiskey to give to Johnson. By around 1:00 A.M., Johnson complained of illness but continued to play. By 2:00 A.M. he was so sick they had to carry him back to his room in Greenwood. For two days he moaned and crawled on the floor in horrifying agony. On Wednesday evening he died, by all accounts of strychnine poisoning.

FINAL RESTING PLACE #1
Payne's Chapel
Itta Bena, Mississippi

Much like his life, his final resting place is in dispute. If you believe statements made by those who claim they were actually at the funeral, then Robert Johnson is buried in the small cemetery adjoining Payne's Chapel. From downtown Itta Bena, drive 4.25 miles to #167 and turn right (just over the bridge). Drive five hundred feet and on the right is Payne's Chapel. Walk to the back of the church and turn left into the cemetery/open field. Walk fifty feet and look for the John White monument. To the right is Robert's monument (directly in front of the three other unrelated Johnson monuments).

They brought him back 'bout three o'clock to Greenwood to his room. And Monday he was so sick he didn't know nothing, hardly nothing. And he was sick Tuesday. He was crawling around, just crawling and crawling on the floor. He died Wednesday evening.

Robert Johnson protégé David "Honeyboy" Edwards

FINAL RESTING PLACE #2
Mt. Zion Church
Morgan City, Mississippi

If you believe the death certificate, then from Payne's Chapel turn right on Highway 7 south and drive two miles. Turn left on #511 just before Morgan City (#511 shares the road with Matthew's Brake and the National Wildlife Preserve). Drive five hundred feet and Mt. Zion Church will be on your left. To the far left on the church grounds you will find an obelisk that reads:

> His music struck a chord that continues to resonate.
> His blues addressed a generation he would never know
> and made poetry of his visions and fears.

However, don't bother looking for his grave as it has always been unmarked. The obelisk is merely a cenotaph.

FINAL RESTING PLACE #3
Little Zion M.B. Church
Greenwood, Mississippi

Often believed by most to be the true location of Johnson's grave, from downtown Greenwood drive north on Fulton Street over two bridges, approximately three miles. Look for the small white church on the left with the address number 63530 on the building and pull up to the front of the church. Like the gravesite, the church name is not marked. However, by the time you read this, there is a good chance that still another tribute/grave marker for the late bluesman will be erected, randomly placed within the cemetery.

THE CROSSROADS
Clarksdale, Mississippi

Once and for all, for all the blues tourists out there who want to see the crossroads where Johnson sold his soul to the devil—THERE IS NO ONE CROSSROADS! The single most-asked question at every information center and blues museum in Mississippi will always yield the same answer. Yet, despite the fact that there are hundreds of crossroads within the Delta region, tourists continue to look for the elusive site. So, in answer to this obviously pent-up demand, the Mississippi Visitors Bureau has marked the "official" crossroads location at the intersection of Highways 61 and 49. Fortunately, the Mississippi Visitors Bureau also has contracted with the devil for him to appear on the third Thursday of each month to buy the souls of aspiring musicians and gullible tourists alike.

I'VE GOT THOSE REALLY OBSCURE MUSICIAN BLUES

If you think Robert Johnson is obscure, here is a few more . . .

Mississippi Joe Callicott
1899—1969

Joe Callicott was born, lived, and died in the town of Nesbit, Mississippi. His first record was "Fare Thee Well Blues" and "Traveling Mama Blues" in 1930. He played the juke joints and house parties of northern Mississippi with Frank Stokes and Garfield Akers for the next thirty-five years before recording again in 1967. One of the songs during that session, "Love My Baby Blues," was covered later by Ry Cooder as "France Chance." Known to only the most diehard of blues fans, Callicott was buried in Mount Olive C.M.E. Church Cemetery in nearby Pleasant Hill. From exit 284 on Interstate 55, drive east on Pleasant Road for approximately three miles to Getwell Road. Turn left and drive a short distance to the church cemetery on your left. Callicott's well-marked grave is easily distiguishable from the handmade gravestones that mark the majority of this cementery's final resting places.

Eugene "Sonny Boy Nelson" Powell
December 23, 1908—November 4, 1998

This longtime bluesman was one of the last surviving musicians from the old-style Delta blues era of the 1930s and '40s. Powell first recorded as Sonny Boy Nelson in 1936 with his future wife, Mississippi Matilda. Playing locally and for Parchman Prison inmates, Powell worked full-time for the John Deere Company before resuming his musical career in the mid-1970s. With good friend Sam Chatmon, they traveled and played on many of the same blues festival gigs for close to twenty years. Buried in an unnamed cemetery, head north from Greenville, Mississippi, on Highway 1 and take the Broadway Road Extension to the first right after the METCALFE 1 1/2 MI. sign. Drive one mile and take the right fork, driving another mile and turning left onto the dirt road. Cross the bridge into the cemetery and Powell's grave is 150 feet to the left.

Frank Frost
April 15, 1936—October 12, 1999

A protégé of the great harp player Sonny Boy Williamson II, Frank Frost began playing in the 1950s with Little Willie Foster. After working with Sonny Boy in the late fifties, Frost, drummer Sam Carr, and guitarist Big Jack Johnson caught the eye of Sun Records founder, Sam Phillips. After recording for his new label, the trio also recorded with Elvis Presley guitarist Scotty Moore, producing the minor hit "My Back Scratcher." Frost continued playing, and

later appearing as a blues muscian in the film *Crossroads*. Frost died of heart failure and was buried at Magnolia Cemetery in Helena, Arkansas, next to fellow bluesman Robert Nighthawk. As you enter the cemetery on College Street (near Perry Street), Frost's and Nighthawk's elaborate headstones are visible from the entrance on top of the hill.

BRIAN JONES

BORN February 28, 1942
Cheltenham, Gloucestershire, England

DIED July 3, 1969
Hartfield, East Sussex, England

CAUSE OF DEATH Accidental Drowning
Age 27

Although most of the Rolling Stones' publicity has been focused on the Glimmer Twins—Mick Jagger and Keith Richards—the fact remains that the Rolling Stones was originally Brian Jones's band. It was Brian who put the group together, named the band, and as the only truly accomplished musician at the time, he established their musical identity. And despite the band's success over the last thirty years since his death, there are some who say the band died with Brian.

In the Beginning . . .

Lewis Brian Hopkins-Jones was born and raised in the working-class town of Cheltenham, Gloucestershire, England. An excellent student, Jones excelled in the sciences and music. His mother was a piano teacher, and his parents fully expected their son to continue his studies toward a career as a classical musician. But like most teens, Jones rebelled against the strict confines of classical music and developed a strong interest in the freeform elements of jazz and blues. At age fourteen, Jones got another classmate pregnant (which, much to the embarrassment of his parents, was announced in the local paper) and was thrown out of school. After the baby's adoption, Jones left his parents' home to fend for himself.

In 1960, Jones, his girlfriend Pat Andrews, and Richard Hattrell shared a small flat in London. To make ends meet, Jones would host rent parties every week where jazz musicians would come by to have a jam session. The parties and impromptu jam sessions became quite popular as news spread about Jones's talents. One night Jones almost passed out when the great Muddy Waters walked through the door. He was even more excited when Muddy asked Jones to join him on a song.

Shortly afterward, Brian ran an ad in *Jazz News*, seeking rhythm-and-blues-style musicians. Mick Jagger, Keith Richards, and Ian Stewart all appeared for the auditions. Later guitarist Geoff Bradford and bassist Dick Taylor were added. Jones named the motley bunch the Rolling Stones, after Muddy Waters's "Rollin' Stone Blues." Officially a band in Jones's eyes, nobody seriously thought they would perform anywhere.

By 1962, the Stones's lineup was complete with Charlie Watts on drums and Bill Wyman on bass. They recorded Chuck Berry's "Come On" and the Lennon/McCartney hit "I Wanna Be Your Man," which became their first Top 20 hit. Over the next six years their albums and concerts drew from an eclectic melange of blues, rock, and country tunes that catapulted the Stones toward unbelievable success.

🎸➤ The former residence of the famed founding member of the Rolling Stones is now a major tourist attraction, with fans traveling the world over to visit the farm and the surrounding woods in Hartfield, England. Unfortunately, most of those tourists are not fans of Mr. Jones per se. For Cotchford Farms was once the summer home of author A. A. Milne and the inspiration for the children's classic *Winnie-the-Pooh and the House at Pooh Corner*. That is not to say you can't still view the very same pool in which Jones took his final swim. Unfortunately for the ex-Stone, most of his personal possessions were stolen as his body lay in the morgue. Even his clothes, according to his former gardener, were dumped outside the estate and turned into a bonfire.

As the songwriting team of Jagger and Richards began to dominate the band, Jones's efforts were marginalized. With the singles "Jumpin' Jack Flash" and "Sympathy for the Devil" receiving heavy airplay, on June 8, 1969, Jagger, Richards, and Watts drove out to Jones's country estate, Cotchford Farm, to advise the founding member that his services were no longer required.

In the End . . .

After the initial rush of media attention, Jones felt alone and defeated. Since being fired from his own group, Jones reduced his considerable consumption of illicit drugs. When offers started pouring in from Alexis Korner, John Lennon, and others to record, Jones finally began to settle down and enjoy the fruits of his labor. He began to work with drummer Micky Walls of the Jeff Beck Group and oversaw the renovation of his English estate.

Those closest to Jones suspected that something was amiss. Hostility was brewing at the estate between Jones, the contractor, and his workers. The former Rolling Stone began to suspect faked bills, stolen furniture, and double billings, which were initiated by the workmen. On the evening of July 2nd, 1969, the laborers quit early, invited their girlfriends down to the estate, and helped themselves to Jones's food and wine. As the guests moved toward the pool, Brian joined the party. The workmen immediately resented his presence as the girls shifted their attention to the rich rock star. Two of the workmen began taunting Brian, holding him underwater as Brian struggled to get out of the pool. What happened next is still a mystery; however, within minutes, his body lay at the bottom of the pool. Brian's death was labeled as "death by misadventure" as a small quantity of barbiturates, two other unknown drugs, and no sign of a struggle were found at the autopsy. And

despite an alleged deathbed confession by one of the workers present (denied by his surviving family), no charges have been filed.

Priory Road Cemetery
Cheltenham, Gloucestershire, England

A two-hour drive from London, take the M40 northwest toward Oxford, then continue on the A40 west all the way to Cheltenham. When you reach the city limits, drive one mile to Priors Road (there will be signs to the cemetery, and if you end up in the town center you went too far) and turn right. The cemetery will be on the right, with Brian's grave on the road near the church in Plot V11393 (not far from his parents' home across from the Parish Church on Hatherley Road).

> He wouldn't come to the studio. He wouldn't do anything. We felt we couldn't go on. We couldn't hold our heads up and play because Brian was a total liability. He wasn't playing well, wasn't playing at all, couldn't hold the guitar. It was pathetic.
>
> Mick Jagger

EDDIE JONES
AKA GUITAR SLIM

BORN December 10, 1926
Greenwood, Mississippi

DIED February 7, 1959
New York, New York

CAUSE OF DEATH Bronchial Pneumonia
Age 32

It has been over forty years since the death of blues pioneer Guitar Slim. So many years, in fact, that most people reply "Guitar Who?" A masterful guitarist who pioneered the use of the distorted guitar solo, Slim would appear onstage resplendent in a blue suit, blue shoes, blue hair, and five hundred feet of microphone cord (to allow his valet to carry him on his shoulders and out into the street during a performance). Thus, the question instead should be, "How could you *forget* Guitar Slim?"

In the Beginning . . .

Despite his flamboyant persona both on and offstage, very little is known about Eddie Jones's early years. Born in the heart of the Mississippi Delta, Jones was five years old when his mother died (he never knew his father), and he moved to Hollandale, Mississippi, to be raised by his grandmother. Living on the L. C. Haves farm, Jones followed in the footsteps of Muddy Waters and Howlin' Wolf—working the rich farmland by day and playing the local clubs on weekends. He started out as a singer and dancer, earning the name Limber Legs for his wild dancing skills. In 1944 he met bandleader Willie Warren, who introduced the guitar to the young singer. After briefly serving in the army, Jones came back to the Delta where he was surrounded by a wealth of blues and slide guitarists. Though his musical styling can be heard in the earlier music of Robert Nighthawk, his primary influences were found in Texas with such artists as T-Bone Walker and Clarence "Gatemouth" Brown (Jones used Brown's "Boogie Rambler" as his theme song for most of his career).

By 1952 Jones was living in New Orleans and was a big draw on the southern R&B circuit. Having first recorded in 1951 and then again a year later, Jones began using the stage name Guitar Slim and stayed on the road a good part of the time. When he was in town, Jones lived upstairs at the Dew Drop on LaSalle Street in New Orleans because not only was it a great place to rehearse, but Jones liked to be close to the action. In fact, everyone knew when Guitar Slim was back in town because after a night of drinking, he liked to turn up the amps and PA system at five in the morning. And more often than not, when neighbors called the police, they would find Guitar Slim dancing amid six or seven women, a couple cases of empty wine bottles, and new song sheets strewn all about the room.

In 1953 Jones signed with the Specialty label and had the biggest hit of his career. "The Things I Used to Do" (featuring Ray Charles), which made pick of the week on both

---

In the few pictures that remain of Guitar Slim during his short burst of fame, he was seen playing with a gold-top Gibson Les Paul guitar. If you were wondering which Hard Rock Cafe or museum that guitar hangs in, look no further. Guitar Slim was buried with his guitar. And those ads in the papers listing a Guitar Slim Jr. performing in New Orleans clubs—yes, that is his son.

Billboard and *Cashbox*. It topped the R&B charts for six weeks and became the biggest-selling R&B record of 1954, with twenty-one weeks on the chart (six on the #1 spot) and selling over a million copies. After a national tour including stops at the famed Apollo in Harlem, and the Howard Theater in Washington, D.C., Jones continued to record for Specialty for two more years. Though he never would top the success he had with "The Things I Used to Do," Jones's writing and performing skills never diminished as he continued to chart with "Sufferin' Mind" and "The Story of My Life." But with an alcohol- and womanizing-rich lifestyle taking its toll on Jones's health, Specialty dropped the flamboyant singer who promptly signed with Atco, releasing several more singles that charted successfully over the next two years.

In the End . . .

Eventually Slim's popularity made it such that he signed with Hosea Hill. Owner of the popular Thibodaux nightspot the Sugar Bowl, Hill booked Slim in Chicago, New York, New Orleans, and everywhere in between. Consequently Slim began to spend more time in Thibodaux.

However, Guitar Slim's days were numbered. Some say he was a pretty good drinker, most would say he was the best. Being on the road and living fast took their toll, and despite doctors' warnings about his lifestyle, by 1958 Jones was in ill health and unable to travel. For his final recording session for Atco he recorded the prophectic "If I Had My Life to Live Over."

After a brief hospital stay in late 1958, Jones and his group began a tour of nightclubs in New York. Before the first show in Rochester, Jones went to one of his men and said, "I'm tired. I don't think I can make it no more. You all got a good band—you can find another singer." The band opened at the dance, but Jones could only make it though the first song. As they drove to Newark for the next concert, Jones played the gig, but collapsed immediately afterward. His valet ran for the doctor, who ordered Jones to check into a hospital. The following day the band carried an incapacitated Guitar Slim to a doctor's office across from the Cecil Hotel in Manhattan, but he died that night.

Moses Baptist Cemetery
Thibodaux, Louisiana

Guitar Slim's body was kept in New York City to see if drugs were involved in his death. When it was determined that he died of bronchial pneumonia, they released his body to Hill, who paid to have Jones flown back to Thibodaux.

Despite all reports otherwise, his grave is neither hidden nor unmarked. He was buried in the Moses Baptist Cemetery located next to the Louisiana National Guard Armory in Thibodaux. From the corner of Twelfth and McCulla (two blocks off Louisiana's Highway 1), park in the gravel parking lot. Walk along Twelfth Avenue away from McCulla, about fifty feet. Jones's stone is located next to Hosea Hill, second row from the sidewalk.

If he had a job in Florida, I'd have to ration him. I'd make sure the valet gave him only a fifth of wine when he left New Orleans, another fifth in Biloxi, and one more by the time he got to Mobile. And don't nobody fool with Slim's wine or he'd be in trouble.

manager Percy Stovall

SPIKE JONES

BORN December 14, 1911
Long Beach, California

DIED May 1, 1965
Los Angeles, California

CAUSE OF DEATH Emphysema
Age 53

Directing his band with a toilet plunger, Spike Jones and the City Slickers would take a sophisticated popular song and subsequently destroy the mood with gunshots, cowbells, horns, doubled tempos, and cornball jazz solos. To the average listener such songs as "Cocktails for Two," "You Always Hurt the One You Love," and "The Nutcracker Suite" sounded like absolute chaos, but it was controlled, hysterical chaos.

In the Beginning . . .

Lindely Armstong Jones was born to a railroad depot agent and schoolteacher just before Christmas in Long Beach, California. By age seven he was taking music lessons for trombone and piano and before his teen years he already had founded a band and switched to drums. By the time he graduated from Long Beach Polytechnic High School, Jones performed for dances and radio with his own Dixieland combo, Spike Jones and his Five Tacks.

After a short stay at college, Jones dropped out for a full-time musical career. During numerous performances in Southern California, he was a drummer for Ray West, Everett Hoagland, and Earl Burtnett. As a regular guest on Bing Crosby's radio show, he established himself as a talented studio musician. Jones later went on to record for Judy Garland, Lena Horne, and Bing Crosby. However, he wanted more solo exposure—Spike Jones wanted to be under the bright lights.

In an often-told story (never told the same way twice—Jones was a master yarn spinner), Jones recalled how he came upon the idea of planned mistakes in musical arrangements: "We went to hear Stravinsky conduct *The Firebird* at the Shrine Auditorium. Stravinsky was wearing new patent leather shoes and I was sitting close enough to notice [that] every time he went up on his toes in preparation for a downbeat, his shoes would squeak. So here go the violins, and here goes his shoes—in perfect harmony!"

Finding other skilled studio musicians to join in the fun, Spike Jones and the City Slickers began rehearsing songs that incorporated parody, cowbells, belches, and a few well-placed raspberries. In 1942, the band had its first national hit, selling 1.5 million copies of "Der Fuehrer's Face."

Crowned the King of Corn by *Downbeat* magazine, Spike and the band continued with a string of hits, including "Cocktails for Two" and "You Always Hurt the One You Love." In 1946 the band engaged in a stage extravaganza entitled *The Musical Depreciation Revue*. The show included skaters, jugglers, midgets, and as always, Spike's maniacal interpretations of the classics.

Aside from studio recordings (which, by the way, were done in one take with no overdubs) and live appearances, Spike Jones and the City Slickers made numerous television appearances, including *The Frank Sinatra Show*, *The Perry Como Show*, and *The Jack Benny Show*. However, despite all the success Jones enjoyed over the course of his career, there is no single museum or exhibit showcasing his considerable talents. All fans are left with is the home at 490 Martin Lane just above Sunset Boulevard in Beverly Hills, where Jones passed away.

The 1950s were a busy decade for the band. They filmed several TV appearances, movies, and began issuing full-length albums. After fathering his fourth child, it became increasingly obvious to friends and associates that Spike Jones was not a well man. Never the picture of health, his undernourished frame and sallow complexion were beginning to raise questions.

In the End . . .

Rapidly aging, Jones was diagnosed with emphysema in the late 1950s. Despite the ever-present oxygen tank and his chronic shortness of breath, Spike was unable to kick his smoking habit. A lifelong smoker, Spike was usually seen with a cigarette in one hand and an oxygen mask in the other.

Public appearances became fewer and far less prestigious with the coming of the 1960s. When just months before he was breaking attendance records, the Riviera, the Flamingo, and the Tropicana stopped calling Spike. The final insult came in 1964 when Spike and the band went on tour with the Show of the Year, a package tour with Homer and Jethro from *The Beverly Hillbillies*. It was a slap in the face when the red carpet was laid out—for Homer and Jethro.

The final appearance of Spike Jones and the City Slickers took place at Harrah's Lake Tahoe on March 23, 1965. Despite the ever-present oxygen, the plane ride and the eight thousand-foot elevation were too much for Jones and he collapsed. Jones was flown back to Los Angeles, where he remained in critical condition for nine days. Returned to his home, Jones remained alert and sharp in his final days. With visits from Danny Thomas and Loretta Young, Jones came to terms with his illness and a couple of months later he died in his sleep at his home in Beverly Hills.

Holy Cross Cemetery
Culver City, California

As you enter through the cemetery entrance off Slauson Avenue, make your way back to the mausoleum. Enter the mausoleum on the first floor and walk past the office on your left, then make the first right. Walk down the hall into the right wing and look to your right, where you will see Fred MacMurray's lengthwise crypt in Room 7. Directly across the hall in Section 70, on the top row, middle column, is Spike Jones's crypt.

> But it was always gags, always a laugh, nothing very serious. He knew he was ill, he knew smoking was at the base of most of what ailed him, and yet he carried on. I never saw anybody before or since that smoked as incessantly as he did.
>
> Harry Geller

JANIS JOPLIN

BORN January 19, 1943
Port Arthur, Texas

DIED October 4, 1970
Hollywood, California

CAUSE OF DEATH Accidental Drug Overdose
Age 27

A central figure in the burgeoning rock music scene in San Francisco in the late sixties, Janis Joplin was and continues to be the premier female white blues singer of the last fifty years. But due to her limited artistic output, to the current generation she remains a historic rather than a legendary figure, not afforded the respect given her contemporaries like Jimi Hendrix and John Lennon. And while her surviving family members continue to recast her life's work within the context of feminism, her music, her life, and her sudden death will forever make Joplin rock 'n' roll's first female superstar.

In the Beginning . . .

Born in the booming oil refinery and seaport town of Port Arthur, Texas, Janis Lyn Joplin was the oldest child in a working-class family. Her father, Seth, worked for the Texas Company as an engineer while her mother Dorothy was a housewife. Though she was considered a bit eccentric by the locals of this once-small Texas town, she nonetheless spent her youth uneventfully.

By the age of fourteen, Joplin began to put on weight, her once flowing hair turned unruly, and acne began to scar her face—in other words, she became a teenager. Unfortunately, at the time Port Arthur was a one-high school town, and you either fit in with the crowd, or you didn't. Rejected and ridiculed by many at school, Joplin sought what few friendships she could find with other "outcasts," mainly the artists and musicians.

For teenagers in east Texas, the promised land of cheap booze and live music lay just across the border in neighbooring Louisiana. With a drinking age of eighteen across the border (Texas was twenty-one), artists such as Tommy McLain, Clifton Chenier, and Slim Harpo lay claim to the roadhouses and nightclubs that dotted the highway between Lafayette and the Texas state line. It was here that Joplin spent many weekends, escaping the boredom of Port Arthur for gritty, hip-grinding, raucous dancing to the blues and R&B.

Running away from home at the age of seventeen, she returned and enrolled at Lamar State College of Technology, later transferring to the University of Texas at Austin. Now more a student of Bessie Smith and Leadbelly than academics, Joplin dropped out in 1963 to pursue a career singing in the honky-tonks of Texas. Singing with a bluegrass group at Threadgill's, Joplin made her way to San Francisco, where she embraced the hippie move-

---

It's ironic that Port Arthur's most famous resident, whom they had no problem rejecting in the late 1950s, is now celebrated at the Coast Gulf Museum. It comes as no surprise that the Joplin family has chosen to leave only a few token items to the museum. All the other items in the Joplin collection are replicas, including Joplin's famed psychedelic Karmann Ghia. All the houses associated with Joplin's youth have been torn down, and all the museum has to offer are bricks from her childhood home at 4048 Procter (on sale in the gift shop of five dollars each). To see the real stuff, you will need to drive 1,500 miles due north to the Rock and Roll Hall of Fame Museum in Cleveland, Ohio. In San Francisco there seems to be some confusion as to which house Joplin called home for the brief time she lived there. Tours that come through the area have identified no less than four different houses on the block as being "the one where Janis slept." However, her driver's license and a paid bill both show her living at 122 Lyon Street in the Haight-Ashbury district.

ment and quickly became a favorite at small clubs in the Bay Area and down around Venice Beach in Southern California. Abusing amphetamines and alcohol, she returned home to Texas in an attempt to fit into small-town life. Unable to cope, Joplin returned to California, when she received a call from friend and concert promoter Chet Helms. Helms called to recommend Joplin to an existing group called Big Brother and the Holding Company. Joplin accepted without hesitation.

In the End . . .

Joining Big Brother and the Holding Company in 1966, Joplin's animated, no-holds-barred stage presence was a perfect match for the then-unknown group. They quickly went into the studio and recorded a poorly produced album that received little notice at the time. It wasn't until the following year, after Big Brother's appearance at the Monterey Pop Festival and Joplin's raw, incendiary performance of Big Mama Thornton's "Ball and Chain" that the group first garnered national attention.

In the audience at the festival were future manager Albert Grossman and Columbia Records executive Clive Davis. Through Grossman the band signed a deal with Columbia and released the renowned *Cheap Thrills* with the classic radio standard "Piece of My Heart." With a #1 gold album and a hit single, Joplin quickly began to overshadow her backing band. Now known as Janis Joplin with Big Brother and the Holding Company, tension in the group began to mount. In addition, several criticisms were leveled at the album, pointing out the ragged character of the instrumental backing. With a desire to go solo, Joplin quit the group, taking only guitarist Sam Andrew with her.

Forming the Kozmic Blues Band in 1970, Joplin recorded the musically uneven but commercially successful album *I Got Dem Ol' Kozmic Blues Again, Mama* with the gutsy, blues-based single "Try (Just a Little Bit Harder)." From the Kozmic Blues sessions she formed her strongest backing band, the Full Tilt Boogie Band, with Brad Campbell on bass, John Till on guitar, Richard Bell on piano, and Clark Pierson on drums. Despite the great band and the progression of her music, Joplin's personal life begin to tailspin with an increasing dependency on alcohol and heroin.

Taping for her next album *Pearl* (that was her nickname) with producer Paul Rothchild (known for his work with the Doors) was nearly finished on the evening of October 3rd when she was pounding down screwdrivers with a band member at Barney's Beanery in Los Angeles. Just after midnight they drove back to the Landmark Hotel (now called the Highland Gardens), a hotel well known then to rock stars who wanted to be close to the

action and their drug dealers. Once in room 105, Joplin shot up a new package of heroin. Some say that was the last time anyone saw her alive; others say she returned to the lobby to get change from the desk clerk. Regardless, Joplin collapsed beside the bed, slamming her face into the nightstand as she dropped face-down in her baby doll pajamas. She died almost instantly from an overdose of an unusually pure grade of heroin. Her body was discovered the next morning when a band member became alarmed when he couldn't reach her.

People, whether they know it or not, like their blues singers miserable. They like their blues singers to die afterwards.

Janis Joplin

Joplin was cremated, her ashes scattered in the Pacific Ocean. After an autopsy found the cause of death to be "acute heroin-morphine intoxication," her body was taken to Westwood Memorial Park for cremation. Her will (yes, she actually had a will!) stipulated that her ashes be scattered over Stinson Beach in Marin County, California, and that $1,500 be provided for a funeral party. After the ashes were scattered, a party was held at the Lion's Share in San Anselmo near San Francisco. The Grateful Dead played for the nearly two hundred invited guests.

The Highland Gardens
7047 Franklin Street
Hollywood, California

Once known as the Landmark Hotel, the name may have changed but the hotel is still the same (although most of the drug dealers have been replaced by tourists). And while management just a short time ago chased anyone out uttering the phrase, "Did Janis really die here?" the new management is much more gracious and accommodating to the fans of Pearl. In fact,

they are more than happy to reserve room 105 for your visiting pleasure. At about ninety dollars a night, the room is complete with everything, including the ghost of Janis (yes, this place is certifiably haunted!). Please note that the room number is the same; however, the furniture is not.

Barney's Beanery
8447 Santa Monica Boulevard
West Hollywood, California

This favorite of rock stars and regulars has been around since 1920 and still retains all the "charm" of a road-house/dive bar. Jim Morrison of the Doors was once a regular and was knocked over the head with a near-full bottle of Jack Daniel's by Janis in the late sixties (and everyone there said he deserved it). The three-room bar now offers over three hundred beers, burgers, and chili to aspiring Morrison and Joplin wannabes seven days a week.

DANCING WITH MR. JITTERS
FORMER HEROIN USERS WHO LIVED TO TELL ABOUT IT

Ray Charles
After signing a sweetheart deal with ABC Records and scoring big with hits like "Hit the Road, Jack" and "Georgia on My Mind," Brother Ray was arrested on drug charges in 1964 and took a year off the road to successfully overcome his addiction.

Eric Clapton
By the time he hit the studio to record "Layla" in 1970 with Duane Allman as Derek and the Dominoes, his addiction was in full force. Not only did he get the monkey off his back, he opened a rehab clinic in the Caribbean to help other musicians.

Anthony Kiedis
Kiedis successfully ended his trip to hell and back, but only after friend and Red Hot Chili Peppers guitarist Hillel Slovak did not.

Courtney Love
Final score for the Seattle grunge marriage made in heaven—Love 1, Cobain 0.

Jimmy Page
And you thought that the former Yardbird and Led Zeppelin guitarist only dabbled in the occult.

Lou Reed
A one-hit wonder with the FM staple "Walk on the Wild Side," Lou Reed has had more of an effect on the art rock scene and punk rock in the seventies than on the charts. His brief dalliance with heroin is a mere footnote in his career.

Keith Richards
I imagine you're as shocked as I am that one of the founding members of the Rolling Stones, with his multiple drug arrests and blood transfusions, would be associated with such misdeeds.

Axl Rose and Slash
After one great album, the entire band had to quit to either escape from the rantings of Rose or just to get clean and sober. Slash chose both.

Johnny Rotten
Former Sex Pistol Johnny Rotten (born John Lydon) was able to come clean. Sid Vicious wasn't as lucky. Neither was Nancy Spungen.

James Taylor
Well, this is a surprise. But I guess it comes with the territory when you hang around John Belushi for too long.

Pete Townshend
Both drummer Keith Moon and bassist John Entwistle died of drugs (or the effects thereof). I guess Townshend didn't want to die before he got old.

Johnny Winter
And I bet you didn't know that Johnny Winter is legally blind, too?

LOUIS JORDAN

BORN July 8, 1908
Brinkley, Arkansas

DIED February 4, 1975
Los Angeles, California

CAUSE OF DEATH Heart Attack
Age 66

The line from big bands through R&B to rock 'n' roll was drawn by the King of the Jukebox, Louis Jordan. Credited as the man who put the jump in the blues, the infectious beat of Jordan's horn-dominated group and the personality of its leader set the stage for rock 'n' roll well before Bill Haley or Buddy Holly. As one of the first bands to incorporate electric guitar, bass, horns, and rap-style rhyming lyrics, Jordan's showmanship and musical talent had huge influences on Ray Charles, James Brown, B. B. King, Chuck Berry, and Dizzy Gillespie.

In the Beginning . . .

Louis Thomas Jordan was taught music by his father, Aaron Jordan, a well-respected director of a local brass band who studied with W. C. Handy. Before his early teen years, Jordan was able to play sax, clarinet, and several horn instruments before turning professional at the age of fifteen. Attending college, he worked weekends with Jimmy Pryor's Imperial Serenaders before moving to Philadelphia in 1930.

Working with the West Coast-based Charlie Gaines Band, Jordan married for the second time to singer and dancer Ida Fields. Traveling to the East Coast often, the band was playing the Apollo Theater in Harlem when the agent convinced Jordan to start his own group. His first aborted attempt as a bandleader lasted almost two years when Jordan joined Chick Webb's Savoy Ballroom Band. Now anchoring the horn section of one of the hottest black bands on the circuit, Jordan enjoyed touring, recording, and performing with the very young Ella Fitzgerald. In 1938 he tried his hand again as bandleader and formed the Tympany Five and signed with Decca Records. Playing five and six shows a night, Jordan took his cues from Cab Calloway and began to enliven the shows with a solid blend of showmanship and musicianship.

 There is no doubt that Louis Jordan wrote the hit song "Caledonia." However, the composer of the song is listed as "F. Moore." Turns out that name belongs to his third wife, Fleecie Moore. As Jordan once explained, "We put it in her name. She didn't know nothin' about no music at all. Her name is on this song and that song, and she's still getting the money!"

By all accounts, Jordan was a strict disciplinarian and perfectionist when it came to performing and rehearsing. But all the hard work paid off in the early 1940s with the string of hits "I'm Gonna Move to the Outskirts of Town," "Five Guys Named Moe," and his smash hit, "Caledonia." Blessed with a great sense of humor and vitality, Jordan was able to reach beyond the racially imposed barriers of contemporary music and routinely charted on the pop, R&B, blues, and country charts over the next fifteen years. Continuing his cross-country tour schedule of one-night stands, Jordan also found time to appear in the

The annual Louis Jordan Tribute takes place each year around the second weekend in July in Little Rock, Arkansas. Along with dozens of Jordan-influenced bands, the tribute also shows vintage film clips of Jordan with proceeds to help fund a memorial to Jordan to be placed in his birthplace of Brinkley, as well as memorabilia for the Visitors Center in the old Brinkley Union Pacific train depot. His saxophone, baton, and music case are on display in the Rock and Roll Hall of Fame.

films *Meet Miss Bobby Socks* and *Swing Parade*, which further exposed Jordan's immense talents to an even wider audience. In all, Jordan charted an amazing fifty-seven *Billboard* R&B hits (twenty-one of them at the #1 spot) and recorded with Fitzgerald, Bing Crosby, and Louis Armstrong.

At age forty-two, Jordan's hits were few and far between as rock 'n' roll began to chip away at his fan base. Bookings of the large venues began to dry up as record sales began to drop. Soon, Hollywood stopped calling altogether.

In the End . . .
In 1954 Jordan moved to Phoenix, Arizona, for his health and dropped Decca, just as they began to record Bill Haley and the Comets, closely modeled on the successful Jordan style. Signing to a Los Angeles-based label, Jordan's output during the late 1950s was beginning to sound dated. Producer Quincy Jones, a great admirer of Jordan, produced remarkably updated versions of "Let the Good Times Roll" and "Salt Pork, West Virginia" that appealed more to the rock 'n' roll crowd. In turn, Ray Charles, another unabashed fan, signed Jordan to his Tangerine label in 1962, but unfortunately the sales were lacking and Jordan was relegated to lounges and small clubs. In the early 1970s he reformed the Tympany Five and in 1974 made one of his final major appearances at the Newport Jazz Festival to enthusiastic crowds. That same year he made his final recordings for Johnny Otis's Blues Spectrum label before passing away suddenly in Los Angeles of a heart attack. Twelve years after his passing he was inducted into the Rock and Roll Hall of Fame.

Mount Olive Cemetery
St. Louis, Missouri
Located in an area called South County, Mount Olive Cemetery is just off Lemay Ferry Road next to Mount Hope Cemetery. Once through the gates (a white fence borders the cemetery with the number 3900 on it), drive to the last section on the right side of the cemetery to the back fence. Jordan's pink granite stone is the twenty-sixth stone from the road and the ninth stone from the back white fence (Section 4, Row 3, Lot 16, Grave 16).

Louis was remarkable, because I think he was so far ahead of his time. What he was doing became the origins of rap. He was rhyming things that nobody else was able to do.

B. B. King

TERRY KATH

BORN January 31, 1946
Chicago, Illinois

DIED January 23, 1978
Los Angeles, California

CAUSE OF DEATH Accidental Gunshot Wound
Age 31

"Don't worry—it's not loaded." These were the chilling last words spoken by prolific songwriter and gifted guitarist Terry Kath, best known as one of the founding members of the rock band Chicago. He spoke them to a horrified friend, who watched as he pointed a gun to his head and pulled the trigger, thus ending his life in an accidental game of Russian roulette.

In the Beginning . . .

Growing up in a musical family in Chicago, Terry Alan Kath had plenty of opportunity for exposure to musical instruments—his brother's drums and his mother's banjo. By the ninth grade, Kath had a guitar and amp of his own and spent much of his free time jamming with friends, trying to duplicate the surf sounds of bands such as the Ventures and Dick Dale. As a teenager he joined Jimmy Rice and the Gentlemen, later playing with Jimmy Ford and the Executives. Upon graduation from high school, Kath was an accomplished and fully self-taught guitarist and bassist.

In 1966, Kath and some friends formed a band called the Missing Links. The lineup featured (in addition to Kath) Peter Cetera, Robert Lamm, Walter Parazaider, Danny Seraphine, Walt Perry, James Pankow, and Lee Loughnane. Before the year was out, they had agreed on a new name, Chicago Transit Authority, and had taken their unique brand of jazz-influenced rock on the road. The band quickly acquired a following, particularly in Los Angeles, where they were a favorite at the Whisky-A-Go-Go on the Sunset Strip. What really set them apart was their horn section—something of an anomaly in rock at that time. Their first album, put out by Columbia in 1969, featured the hit single "Does Anybody Really Know What Time It Is." The following year the band shortened its name simply to Chicago.

The 1970s were the most successful years for the band. The follow-up album, cleverly entitled *Chicago II*, yielded the monster radio hit "Make Me Smile." However, the highlight of the album was their second hit, "25 or 6 to 4." Not only was the song a staple of classic rock radio for thirty years (and counting), but it also introduced Kath as a standout guitarist among his peers. Running his guitar through a tube amp, Kath produced a memorable guitar solo that was often featured as the closing number for Chicago in concert.

Though praise for his talents as a guitarist (he held down both rhythm and lead guitar for the group), songwriter, and vocalist were plentiful from other musicians and fans, pop critics hated the group. With Janis Joplin, Jimi Hendrix, and Jim Morrison all dead, reviewers wanted something more substantial—not horns and melodies. And as Chicago turned more to ballads with "Just You and Me" and "Saturday in the Park," the

Kath was using feedback and distortion before Hendrix, and was double-tapping and slamming the whammy bar before Van Halen, but don't look for Chicago in the Rock and Roll, or Blues, or Jazz, or Country Hall of Fame anytime soon. The home at 5754 Fallbrook Avenue in Woodland Hills, California, where Kath spent his last minutes, is a private residence that reports no sightings of Kath's spirit.

critics went from loathing Chicago to just plain ignoring them. Nonetheless, five consecutive Chicago albums topped the charts from 1972 to 1975. The year 1976 brought their huge #1 hit, "If You Leave Me Now," and in 1977, the album *Chicago X* was awarded the Grammy for Best Album. The band had really hit its stride and with very little turnover in the band, there was nothing left to do but sit back and enjoy their enormous popularity and success.

In the End . . .

Unfortunately, the happiness was not destined to last. On January 23, 1978, Terry Kath and his wife, Camelia, attended a party at the Southern California home of Don Johnson, a roadie for Chicago. Kath, an avid gun collector, brought along two guns—this was not unusual as he was frequently armed when he went out. After the party had broken up, Terry and Don were sitting around talking when Terry began playing with his guns. He spun the .38 revolver on his finger, put it to his head, and snapped the trigger—the chamber was empty. Don nervously asked Terry to stop it. Terry then picked up the nine-millimeter automatic pistol he had brought along, and in an effort to allay his friend's fear, said, "Don't worry—it's not loaded." Then he put the pistol to his head, and pulled the trigger. This time, the weapon was indeed loaded. Terry Kath died instantly, leaving his wife, one-year-old daughter, and legions of friends and fans to mourn his loss. His funeral was attended by then-Governor Jerry Brown, Doc Severinsen, and four hundred other mourners.

Forest Lawn Memorial Park
Glendale, California

As you enter the cemetery, follow the signs up the hill toward the Triumphant Faith Terraces. Stop and park at the Court of the Christus, and walk up the three steps to enter the court. At your immediate left is an entryway to the Garden of Remembrance. Go into the garden and walk all the way through it into the second garden. At the second garden, turn right; then turn left (before you reach the stairway) and follow the path along the ten-foot-high wall. Walk about twenty-five feet, and on your right against the wall you'll find the Kath family plot.

Your guitar player is better than me.

Jimi Hendrix to Chicago's saxophone player Walter Parazaider.

ALBERT KING

BORN April 25, 1923
Indianola, Mississippi

DIED December 21, 1992
Memphis, Tennessee

CAUSE OF DEATH Heart Attack
Age 69

B. B. King may have had a better manager, but Albert King had the tone and the feel. And there was no mistaking the King when you walked into any blues club during his heyday. Standing at six feet, four inches, weighing over two hundred fifty pounds, and playing his trademark Gibson Flying V left-handed, Albert was truly the heavyweight of the blues. His intense, unmistakable fat tones and his deceptively sparse style have been a huge influence on everybody from Eric Clapton and Jimi Hendrix to Stevie Ray Vaughan and Jeff Beck.

In the Beginning . . .

Born Albert Nelson in the Mississippi Delta town of Indianola, Albert's father left after his birth while his mother remarried and moved the family to the farming community of Forrest City, Arkansas. Taking his stepfather's last name, Albert Nelson King's education was limited to the few days of school he actually attended (he learned to read and write as an adult). Like many of the other children of the area, everybody was needed in the farm fields just to survive.

King bought his first guitar at the age of 20 for the grand sum of one dollar and twenty-five cents and used the hollow-body Guild guitar to practice songs by John Lee Williamson (Sonny Boy Williamson I), Blind Lemon Jefferson, and Memphis Minnie. With all guitars at the time built for right-handed players, King was forced to restring the guitar and play it upside down and backward.

King started his career as a professional musician in Osceola, Arkansas, with the In the Groove Boys. As a member of the house band at the infamous T-99 Club (which boasted regular visits by B. B. King, Bobby "Blue" Bland, and Johnny Ace), he was known around town as Big Albert. After two years he traveled north to Chicago, looking for a recording contract, not unlike Elmore James, Muddy Waters, and Willie Dixon. Despite working with Dixon and Odie Payne in the studio, his first record, "Be On Your Merry Way," was a commercial dud. He went back to Osceola for another two years before moving to St. Louis. King finally saw R&B chart success in 1959 with his first hit, "I'm a Lonely Man," and again in 1961 with "Don't Throw Your Love on Me So Strong." It wasn't until he moved to Memphis and signed with the small local label Stax that his long overdue recognition became a reality.

Backed by the infamous Booker T and the MGs, he recorded the classic blues singles "Born Under a Bad Sign" and "Laundromat Blues." A collection of these singles was compiled and released as the album *Born Under a Bad Sign* in 1967. Considered one of the most pivotal recordings in blues history, singles such as "The Hunter" and "As the Years Go Passing By" are the standards with which new blues artists are judged. Eric

---

As you walk down Beale Street in Memphis, Tennessee, take a peek inside any number of bars and live music clubs and you will no doubt see a photo or two of Albert King (if not one of his actual guitars adorning the walls). To date, only St. Louis, Missouri, has chosen to honor the great bluesman with a plaque on the the the St. Louis Walk of Fame. His personal monument is located at 6370 Delmar Street.

Clapton has even admitted that the historic guitar riff from "Layla" was directly lifted from King's "As the Years Go Passing By." With national exposure, King traded the smoky juke joints and nightclubs for the larger venues often reserved for rock stars. Armed with two horn players, a pianist, and backup singers, King shared the bill for the opening night of Bill Graham's Fillmore Auditorium in San Francisco with Jimi Hendrix and John Mayall. In 1968, King returned to the Fillmore West to record the landmark blues album *Live Wire: Blues Power*, which for many people was their introduction to Albert King and the blues.

In the End . . .

In the mid-seventies, with Stax/Volt reeling under the strain of financial difficulties, Albert moved over to RCA. For the next couple of years, his blistering guitar and smooth-as-silk vocals were buried under a mess of strings and studio orchestras. After two miserable albums, King took to the road and recorded his albums in the heart of some of the great music cities—New Orleans, New York, and Detroit. The result was felt both musically and commercially as King regained much of his momentum, commanding soldout audiences in both the U.S. and Europe.

After retiring and returning over a dozen times, King flew to Los Angeles in December of 1992 for what was to be his final concert performance on the 19th. He returned four days before Christmas in preparation for the start of a major 1993 European tour when he suddenly suffered a fatal heart attack at his Memphis home. A few days after Christmas, the Memphis Horns led the procession down Beale Street and a wake was held at the Blues City Cafe Band Box with Joe Walsh singing "Amazing Grace."

Paradise Grove Cemetery
Edmondson, Arkansas

His final resting place is located across the river from Memphis, Tennessee, at the Paradise Grove Cemetery in Edmondson, Arkansas (just outside West Memphis, Arkansas). As you leave Memphis to cross the river to Arkansas on Highway 50, drive five miles to exit 271. Turn left and drive to the intersection of Broadway and Highway 147. Drive three miles south on Highway 147 toward Edmondson. The Paradise Grove Cemetery is on the right, next to the Corner Market. His grave is in the front right section, next to the fountain near the playground.

Albert can take four notes and write a volume. He can say more with fewer notes than anyone I've ever known.

Michael Bloomfield

HUDDIE LEDBETTER AKA LEADBELLY

BORN January 29, 1889
Mooringsport, Louisiana

DIED December 6, 1949
New York, New York

CAUSE OF DEATH Lou Gehrig's disease
Age 60

More than any other folk-blues artist, Leadbelly possessed and recorded a library of ballads, blues, dance songs, and minstrels richer than any other performer in this century. A man of extraordinary talent and a commanding presence, he was also a violent man full of contradiction—a man of great creativity but plagued by self-destruction.

In the Beginning . . .

Huddie William Ledbetter was born on the Jeter plantation, the only child of Wesley and Sally Ledbetter. Born into a sharecropper life, Leadbelly spoke very little of his early years in Louisiana. It is known that he left his birthplace of Mooringsport, Louisiana, at age five for Texas. Inspired by an uncle, Leadbelly (the origins of his nickname seem to be a cross between mispronunciation and his ill-temper) originally began playing the accordion but after a couple of years he switched to the guitar.

At the age of twenty-one, Leadbelly left the abject poverty of farming and took to the road with his guitar in tow. Working as a laborer during the day, he played honky-tonks and work camps at night. For the next ten years he was (according to Leadbelly himself) the world's greatest cotton picker, railroad track liner, lover, drinker, and guitar player. Since everyone did not share Leadbelly's generous assessment of his skills, Leadbelly often found it necessary to forcefully convince his detractors. His violent tendencies would often land him in jail.

In 1915 his path crossed with established bluesman and recording artist Blind Lemon Jefferson and together they traveled extensively through Texas and Louisiana. Acting as Jefferson's guide, Leadbelly's style and mannerisms would echo that of the great Jefferson (especially in his later recordings). During this tour of the South, Leadbelly settled on the twelve-string guitar as his instrument of choice and began to develop a rich, rhythmic guitar style in which he played the walking bass figures commonly used by barrelhouse piano players. This successful pairing of Jefferson and Leadbelly was, however, short-lived. The following year Leadbelly was serving time in Texas on assault charges when he escaped from prison and spent the next two years under the alias of Walter Boyd. Leadbelly was sent back to prison after killing a man in Texas, where his explosive temper landed him a thirty-year jail term at the Huntsville Prison Farm. Though the legend persists to this day, Leadbelly was not released in 1925 after he composed and sang a tune to the governor pleading for his freedom. Rather, it was simply a standard early release for good behavior.

Five years later he was arrested again for attempted murder. Leadbelly was serving time at Louisiana's Angola State Prison when he was first recorded in 1933 by John Lomax for the Library of Congress. With Lomax and Leadbelly pleading for an early parole, he was

To view a small collection of Leadbelly's memorabilia, there is a small museum in downtown Mooringsport, appropriately named the Mooringsport Mini-Museum, which is only open two to four hours a day. One of his surviving twelve-string guitars is on display in Cleveland's Rock and Roll Hall of Fame.

released into Lomax's custody. Leadbelly followed Lomax to New York where he worked as his chauffeur and continued to record for the Library of Congress (over two hundred songs in seven years) and for the American Record Company. After serving a brief sentence for assault in 1939, Leadbelly began working with folk musicians including Woody Guthrie, Pete Seeger, and Brownie McGhee. In 1944 he moved to Hollywood and later toured the U.S. He moved back to New York for good in 1947.

In the End . . .

"Goodnight, Irene," "Midnight Special," "Rock Island Line," "Black Betty," and "Boll Weevil" were just a few of the hundreds of songs Leadbelly produced during his heyday in New York. Though his recordings were powerful examples of black folk music and were held in high esteem by the white, hip New York artists, Leadbelly and his wife lived on the brink of poverty. Since moving to New York, separated from his rural southern roots, Leadbelly failed to build a black audience. What few records he did sell most likely went to white urban listeners. Frustrated, he pulled a knife on Lomax during an argument, effectively ending their personal and professional relationship.

In 1949 he traveled overseas to Paris, hoping to build a European following. Toward the end of the failed tour, he began to suffer muscle spasms and was having difficulty working his guitar strings. Upon his return to the U.S., he was diagnosed with Lou Gehrig's disease and died shortly after at home in New York City, with his wife by his side.

Shiloh Baptist Church Cemetery
Caddo Parish
Mooringsport, Louisiana

From Shrevesport, Louisiana, take the I-20 west toward Texas and take the Highway 169 off-ramp to Mooringsport. Turn right and drive eight miles toward Mooringsport and you will see the general store on your left. Continue on to the next road and turn left and drive about two miles and you will see the small church and adjoining cemetery on your left. Despite the popular myth, he is not buried at Republic Baptist Church, but rather in the center of this small, very rural church cemetery.

Lomax arrives with Leadbelly, Negro Minstrel/Sweet singer of the swampland, here to do a few songs between homicides.

From the *New York Herald Tribune*, January 3, 1935.

LIBERACE

BORN May 16, 1919
West Allis, Wisconsin

DIED February 4, 1987
Palm Springs, California

CAUSE OF DEATH AIDS-Related Heart Failure
Age 67

It didn't matter if he came soaring out from the stage in wings wearing a two hundred-pound cape covered in seashells and pearls, wearing one of his many piano-shaped rings encrusted with hundreds of diamonds, sitting behind his favorite Baldwin concert grand piano with his trademark candelabra—Liberace was foremost a brilliant pianist and entertainer. Critics of his style and panache are loath to admit the astounding array of prestigious awards—two Grammy Awards, Instrumentalist of the Year, six gold albums, two stars on the Hollywood Walk of Fame, and Pop Keyboard Artist of the Year for three straight years. But this Mr. Showmanship never played for his critics—only for his fans.

In the Beginning . . .

Born in Wisconsin to a French horn player for John Philip Sousa, Wladziu Valentino Liberace (Walter to his friends) was popular both in school and in the bars and cabarets where he played nightly all during his teen years. After a visit from renowned pianist Ignacy Paderewski to the Liberace home, the young protégé received a music scholarship to the Wisconsin School of Music. His classical training culminated with his debut as a soloist with the Chicago Symphony at the age of fourteen.

After high school his well-honed nightclub act took him to the Persian Room in New York's Plaza Hotel. After a quick fling at movies, he debuted in the 1952 television show *Liberace* on KLAC in Los Angeles. His approach to editing the classics appalled the critics, but Liberace explained, "I have to know just how many notes my audience will stand for." By "leaving out the dull parts," the show in less than two years was seen on over 175 stations—more than *I Love Lucy*. If his concerts made him popular, television made him a star.

In 1953, Liberace played to a sold-out audience at Carnegie Hall and again at Madison Square Garden. In 1955, he opened in Las Vegas as the highest-paid entertainer in the city's history. Parting company with his brother, George, after moving to Las Vegas, Liberace spent the next thirty years playing every opera house, auditorium, and concert hall in the U.S. and Europe. Whether he made his stage entrance in a $35,000 blue shadow mink coat or the 140-pound black diamond-and-rhinestone-encrusted mink cape, the shows got progressively wilder, and the crowds larger.

The Liberace Museum in Las Vegas, Nevada, is one of the most impressive, single-artist museums open to the public today. Founded in 1979 by the late entertainer, the museum features an incredible array of jewelry, rare antiques, wardrobe, custom cars, and eighteen of his dazzling pianos (including George Gershwin's Chickering baby grand, and this is *after* the three-day auction of his estate after his death!). The recently expanded museum also includes rare Moser crystal from Czechoslovakia, as well as examples of his opulent lifestyle from his home in Palm Springs, California. And though it is one of the most visited celebrity homes in Palm Springs, there is no plan to turn the Cloisters into a museum or home tour in the near future. And believe it or not, the only Liberace piano owned outside of the estate is in the possession of Deborah Gibson (formerly known as Debbie Gibson, former teen mall singer).

In October of 1986, Liberace opened his three-week run at Radio City Music Hall in New York City to sold-out shows. While many critics praised Lee for his showmanship and energy, some reviewers noted he looked gaunt and underweight. With a two-and-a-half-hour show that included flying in the air, six full costume changes, and a dance number with the Rockettes, his friends simply attributed his waning energy to his tough schedule. Retreating to his Palm Springs mansion the Cloisters, Liberace made out his will in late January. Maintaining that he lost thirty to forty pounds on an ill-advised grapefruit diet, Liberace, surrounded by many of his close friends, sought refuge from the hordes of reporters that congregated in the parking lot across the street. For Liberace and the nation, the death watch began.

In the End . . .

On the morning of February 4, 1987, a pale, yellow skeleton of his once-vibrant self, Liberace died quietly in his bedroom with his sister Angie and his beloved shar-pei, Wrinkles, by his side.

That afternoon a station wagon from Forest Lawn Cemetery was dispatched to the home. As the body was driven away from the back of the house, the family held a press conference in front. The cause of death was released by the family as "congestive heart

failure caused by encephalopathy." However, as the funeral home was preparing the body, the Riverside County coroner took possession of it. After an autopsy, amid the glare of photographers and reporters, the coroner's office announced that despite the attempted cover-up by the family and the mortuary, Liberace died from complications caused by AIDS.

Forest Lawn Hollywood Hills
Los Angeles, California

Turn into the entrance and drive through the gates. Drive past the Church of the Hills and turn left on Evergreen Drive. Turn right on Vista Lane and park the car. Walk into the Courts of Remembrance and look straight ahead for the elegant ten-foot-tall crypt and sarcophagus with his signature on the crypt. Liberace is buried with his mother and brother, George.

Go ahead, touch my coat. Really, touch it! You like it? You should—you paid for it!

Liberace, to an admiring fan.

JIMMIE LUNCEFORD

BORN June 6, 1902
Fulton, Missouri

DIED July 12, 1947
Seaside, Oregon

CAUSE OF DEATH Heart Attack
Age 45

Renowned for its showmanship, tight ensemble playing, and imaginative interplay between the soloist and the orchestra, the Lunceford Orchestra was one of the most exciting bands of the thirties. Lunceford's uncompromising demand for perfection earned the group a reputation for ensemble precision that influenced big bands for the next twenty years.

In the Beginning . . .

Born in Fulton, Missouri, and raised in Denver, Colorado, James Melvin Lunceford's musical family enabled him to learn the saxophone, flute, guitar, and trombone at an early age. In his early teens he began to study under the father of bandleader Paul Whiteman and upon graduation from high school he secured a spot in George Morrison's orchestra playing alto sax. A year later he enrolled at Fisk University in Nashville to study music and during holiday and summer breaks from classes, he traveled to New York and Memphis to work in a variety of dance bands. After receiving his degree from Fisk (a rare accomplishment for blacks in the 1920s), he moved to Memphis to begin teaching music classes at Manassa High School.

As a teacher, he began to recruit some of his brightest students for his own band. The first of several student groups, the Chicksaw Syncopators, spent summers and holidays at a resort in Lakeside, Ohio. In late 1929, the group turned professional with the addition of fellow Fisk students Willie Smith (sax), Edwin Wilcox (piano), and Henry Wells (trombone). Under the direction of Lunceford, the band began a series of one-nighters from Memphis to Cleveland to Buffalo and everywhere in between. Although an accomplished pianist and proficient on all reed instruments, Lunceford rarely played with the band, preferring instead to conduct it.

Their big break came when they arrived in New York City and began a residency at the famed Cotton Club in Harlem. Unlike other big bands from the era, Lunceford's group was noted for its ensemble work, rather than for individual soloists. During their run at the Cotton Club, their signature two-beat swing style at medium tempo began to emerge, in large part thanks to the arrangement of new trumpeter and arranger Sy Oliver. Future works such as "For Dancers Only" and "Margie" set high standards for other dance band arrangers, as well as for the Lunceford Orchestra.

Although the band first started recording in 1930, with the addition of Sy Oliver four years later they scored an amazing twenty-two hits between 1934 and 1946, more than any other black swing band (with the exceptions of Duke Ellington and Cab Calloway). This achievement was mostly attributed to Lunceford's strict insistence on precision in per-

---

While Jimmie Lunceford died over a half century ago, the rumor that he died of food poisoning by the hands of an irate cafe owner in Seaside, Oregon, is still presented as fact. With regard to memorabilia, very few personal possessions remain, although he did autograph many photos of himself, which are still available at auction for around $450.

formance, excellence in dress, and a well-planned, sophisticated, yet thoroughly professional stage show.

Never known for paying large salaries, in 1943 Sy Oliver left the Jimmie Lunceford Orchestra for Tommy Dorsey's group. Lunceford continued to record for Columbia, along with maintaining a grueling tour schedule that took the band from New York to Los Angeles and back again. They did occasional work on radio, but opportunities were limited by racial barriers.

In the End . . .

By early 1947, eighteen-plus years on the road had eroded his spirit and his health. As big bands were becoming financial dinosaurs, Lunceford worked harder than ever to keep his band together. Many of the original members had left and were replaced by more polished musicians. However, they could never recapture their early innocence, and future recording sessions were merely remakes of earlier hits.

While touring the West Coast with a series of one-nighters, the band stopped in Seaside, Oregon, for lunch, followed by a public appearance by Lunceford at a local record shop. During the autograph session, Lunceford grabbed his chest and collapsed. He was dead on arrival at the hospital, the victim of a heart attack.

Elmwood Cemetery
Memphis, Tennessee

Returned to Memphis, a procession of family, friends, and band members accompanied Lunceford's casket to the historic Elmwood Cemetery. Located about one mile from famed Beale Street, take the bridge through the cemetery entrance and park at the historic Victorian Gothic Cottage office (ask for the tour map, though Lunceford's grave is not listed). Continue your drive straight down Elm Avenue until it ends on the other side of the cemetery. Turn left and follow Grand Tour around the outside of the cemetery until you come to Gardiner Drive. Turn left at Gardiner Drive and park at the intersection of Grand Tour and Gardiner. Lunceford's monument is four rows from Gardiner and nine rows from Grand Tour, just behind the Pipes monument under the tree.

For combined spirit, enthusiasm, and swinging musicianship, the Lunceford band had no equal. I can't remember any other band swinging as high and with as much fun as this one did.

author George Simon

LYNYRD SKYNYRD

ALLEN COLLINS
BORN August 19, 1952
Jacksonville, Florida

DIED January 23, 1990
Jacksonville, Florida

CAUSE OF DEATH
Pneumonia
Age 37

STEVE GAINES
BORN September 1950
Seneca, Missouri

DIED October 20, 1977
Gillsburg, Mississippi

CAUSE OF DEATH
Plane Crash
Age 27

RONNIE VAN ZANT
BORN January 15,1949
Jacksonville, Florida

DIED October 20, 1977
Gillsburg, Mississippi

CAUSE OF DEATH
Plane Crash
Age 28

LEON WILKESON
BORN April·2, 1952
Jacksonville, Florida

DIED July 24, 2001
Ponte Verde Beach,
Florida

CAUSE OF DEATH
Liver Disease
Age 49

During the sweltering summer stadium tours of the seventies, crowds of rowdy, long-haired rockers armed with the rebel flag surged closer to the stage with every song. With their meticulous, muscular, three-guitar attack, Lynyrd Skynyrd brashly redefined the southern rock genre by downplaying the Allman Brothers' jazz-improv ethos in favor of a raucous hard-rock swagger.

In the Beginning . . .

Lynyrd Skynyrd was formed in the summer of 1964 in Jacksonville, Florida. Throughout high school, Allen Collins, Gary Rossington, and Ronnie Van Zant (along with Bob Burns and Larry Junstrom, later replaced by Ed King, Billy Powell, and Artimus Pyle) found a common bond among the classic radio music of country, British rock, and southern rock and soul. Practicing in Burns's carport, they first called themselves My Backyard. Slowly developing a style of their own (as well as a decent following in the bars in their hometown), they also took the stage as the Noble Five, Conqueror Worm, Sons of Satan, and the One Percent. In addition to music, they also shared a commonality in the length of their hair, eventually running afoul of their high school gym teacher Leonard Skinner. With their collective long hair and bad boy swagger, they eventually dropped out of high school. In a final dig to their former nemesis, one night they introduced themselves onstage as Leonard Skinner. After several spelling changes, the name stuck as Lynyrd Skynyrd.

All good things must come to an end, and nearly twenty-five years after the passing of her husband, Judy Van Zant has closed the doors on the Firebird Foundation. However, the Freebird Cafe on First Street in Jacksonville, Florida, remains open. Owned and operated by Judy and Ronnie's only daughter, Melody, the cafe and live music venue was once home to walls and walls of Skynyrd memorabilia. However, the bright lights and grind of a nightclub do not make a good home for priceless memorabilia, so most of the items have been donated or are on loan to the Rock and Roll Hall of Fame Museum in Cleveland. And yes, the Little Brown Jug, which inspired the song "Gimme Three Steps," is still at the corner of Edison and Acosta in Jacksonville (now called the Pasttime) and is still doing business as a skanky bar. And to answer those last burning questions, yes—Leonard Skinner is still alive, and no—neither Mr. Skinner nor Neil Young are angry with the band. In fact, they all consider themselves good friends to this day.

Several years and numerous personnel changes later, Lynyrd Skynyrd started hitting the road throughout Florida, Georgia, and Alabama on the notorious one-night bar circuit. Despite recording a demo tape at Muscle Shoals Sound Studios and another recording session with producer Jimmy Johnson that produced a seventeen-song demo tape, the elusive big break was still outside their grasp.

Upon being discovered in an Atlanta bar by MCA producer Al Kooper in 1973, they signed with the label and produced their first album, *Pronounced Leh-nard Skin-nerd*. The album started the band on its meteoric rise to fame with rock classics "Gimme Three Steps," "Simple Man," and the incendiary, guitar-driven radio standard "Freebird." Opening on tour for The Who in support of their first album, Lynyrd Skynyrd crossed the U.S. in a frenzy of nonstop interviews, live gigs, and recording sessions. Radio airplay never ceased as the group released their second album, *Second Helping*, two years later. With their first chart hit, "Sweet Home Alabama" (a patriotic retort to Neil Young's "Southern Man"), and another album that same year, the "overnight" success of Lynyrd Skynyrd was finally paying off.

In the End . . .

Boosted by their second release, *Second Helping*, and constant touring, the band's star continued to rise even further. But as the pressure of the road increased, so did the heavy partying. The press began to portray the band as a bunch of drunken, redneck hillbillies hell-bent on self-destruction. Lynyrd Skynyrd found itself at an all-time creative low, with founding guitarist and songwriter Ed King leaving the band in the middle of the '75 Torture Tour.

In 1976 they changed management, added the Honkettes (three female backup singers), and released their fourth album. While the crowds and venues grew in size, some of the trademark cutting-edge sound was missing. They restored their signature three-guitar lineup with the addition of Steve Gaines. Steve, the brother of vocalist Cassie, was playing in a bar band in West Seneca, Missouri, when Skynyrd played nearby. Invited onstage during one of the songs, Gaines played "T for Texas" with the band in front of his hometown. Two weeks later he got the call to join the band permanently. After only two weeks of rehearsal, they recorded the epic live album *One More from the Road*, which perfectly captured the intense power of the band onstage.

When MCA first released *Street Survivors*, the band was ironically depicted surrounded by burning fire. The "flame cover" version of the album was quickly pulled by the record company after the plane crash. However, if you have one of these not-so-rare albums, it is only worth about fifteen dollars. But if you own one of the rarer 8-tracks or cassettes, those are worth two hundred dollars in good condition.

The following year the band returned to the studio to record *Street Survivors*. They hit the road in October for a planned eighty-concert tour of the U.S. They only made it through four shows.

After the concert in Greenville, South Carolina, the band boarded their leased Convair 240 for a show at Louisiana State University in Baton Rouge, Louisiana. Some of the band members were playing poker when keyboardist Billy Powell noticed that the right engine had stopped. He made his way up to the front to ask the pilot what was going on. The pilot told Powell to get back to his seat and strap himself in—the plane was going down.

The plane banked sharply when it clipped the treetops of the Mississippi swamplands below. The aircraft plowed into the swamp, both wings torn from the plane. The fuselage

We wrote "Alabama" as a joke. We didn't even think about it—the words just came out that way. We just laughed and said, "Ain't that funny." We love Neil Young; we love his music.

Ronnie Van Zant

cut a one thousand-foot path through the trees as it came to a stop. As Powell and drummer Artimus Pyle climbed out of the wreckage, six people were dead, including lead singer Ronnie Van Zant, Cassie Gaines, her brother and newest member, Steve Gaines, both pilots, and longtime road manager, Dean Kilpatrick.

FINAL RESTING PLACES
Jacksonville Memorial Gardens
Jacksonville, Florida

The former resting places of Ronnie Van Zant and Steve Gaines can be found two hundred feet to the left of the entrance of the cemetery, to the left of the gardener's shed. In 2002, both graves were opened and desecrated, with Van Zant's coffin removed from the sealed vault and Gaines's cremains scattered just outside his vault. Van Zant was moved to a new monument in the back while the Gaines family has moved his cremains to a private location within the cemetery. Cassie Gaines quietly resides behind the old Van Zant vault.

Riverside Memorial Park
Jacksonville, Florida

In 1986, Allen Collins was driving his new Thunderbird when he rolled the car, killing his girlfriend and causing paralysis to himself. Convicted of DUI and manslaughter, Collins was never the same after the accident. He died in the hospital of pneumonia and liver failure. Leon Wilkeson played with the reformed Skynyrd band up until his passing from chronic liver and lung disease. As you drive into the entrance of Riverside Memorial Park, Collins is buried to the left in the Garden of the Cross, Unit 17 (next to the Collins bench, three rows from the pathway near the large cross). Wilkeson is buried in Unit 2, Lot 172, Space 9.

According to the NTSB report released months after the accident, the crash was simply due to pilot error in calculating the amount of fuel needed for the short flight. And as for the re-formed Lynyrd Skynyrd, only Gary Rossington and Billy Powell remain as original band members.

AND LEAVE THE DRIVING TO US
MUSICIANS WHO SHOULD HAVE FLOWN COMMERCIAL

Buddy Holly (1959)
It all began with Holly, the Big Bopper, and Ritchie Valens and their young pilot. Before this accident, bands toured on the bus.

Patsy Cline (1963)
Country took its first hit four years after rock 'n' roll took theirs. And like Holly, this crash took the lives of two other great performers, Hawkins and Copas, and the pilot.

Jim Reeves (1964)
Country music lost big two years running when, once again, weather was the cause of this crash that also took the life of sideman Docky Dean Manuel.

Otis Redding and the Bar-Kays (1967)
The only two-band crash in history; miraculously enough, one of the Bar-Kays survived the crash in the icy waters of Lake Michigan.

Jim Croce (1973)
Barely made it off the runway, which also claimed the lives of four other band members and the pilot.

Lynyrd Skynyrd (1977)
It's bad enough to have a plane crash due to mechanical failure; it's another thing entirely to just plain run out of gas. Three musicians, one road manager, two pilots, and a lot of people in the hospital spelled the end for this band for ten years (when the band reformed again with rotating musicians).

Randy Rhoads (1982)
Brilliant guitarist and architect of Ozzy Osbourne's return to the stage, Rhoads died from excessive cocaine use (not his own, but the pilot who was flying).

Rick Nelson (1985)
And to think, Jerry Lee Lewis sold the plane to Nelson because he thought it was unsafe. But to clarify a rumor, Rick Nelson's plane did *not* crash because the band was freebasing cocaine in back. Despite the ugly rumors surrounding the cause of the plane crash, it was determined that the accident was not due to drug use by any of the passengers. A year and a half after the accident the NTSB released a report indicating that all evidence pointed to a faulty heater in the rear of the plane.

Dean Martin Jr. (1987)
Not Dean Martin of the Rat Pack, but his son Dean Martin Jr. of Dino, Desi, and Billy. A pilot with the Air Force Reserves, he plowed his plane straight into the ground at Mach I. All that was left was a huge crater and bits of metal. After the accident, the elder Martin was never the same and died a broken man a couple of years later.

Stevie Ray Vaughan (1990)
Never, ever, take off in the fog with a pilot with a spotty flight record. And this had to happen just when SRV was clean, sober, and playing at the peak of his career.

Bill Graham (1991)
Again—never, ever, take off in the fog.

John Denver (1997)
There was a reason the type of plane he was flying is called an "experimental" aircraft.

THE MAMAS AND THE PAPAS

CASS ELLIOT
BORN September 19, 1941
Baltimore, Maryland

DIED November 11, 1972
London, England

CAUSE OF DEATH Heart Attack
Age 31

JOHN PHILLIPS
BORN August 30, 1935
Parris Island, South Carolina

DIED March 18, 2001
Los Angeles, California

CAUSE OF DEATH Heart Failure
Age 65

While they owed an enormous debt to the vocal groups and folk musicians of the forties and fifties, their visual imagery, sixties-inspired lyrics, and carefree California lifestyle made the Mamas and the Papas the vocal leaders of the underground folk music scene of the sixties.

In the Beginning . . .

Possessing a rich and powerful voice, Cass Elliot was in two bands in the early sixties prior to the formation of the Mamas and the Papas. The first was the Big Three, with whom she recorded for Warner Brothers. Later Elliot joined the band the Mugwumps, where she met Denny Doherty. One half of the future Mamas and the Papas group, the other half of the Mugwumps were made up of John Sebastian and Zal Yanovsky (who would later go on to become the Lovin' Spoonful).

The Mamas and the Papas, who wouldn't get that name until halfway through the recording of their first album, were actually born in the Virgin Islands. It was there that John and Michelle Phillips, vacationing with friends Elliot and Doherty, would discover the beautiful harmonies they could create. They stayed on at the island where, much to Phillips's credit, he developed a whole new style of pop music, blending the old style of traditional folk music with the new emerging electric pop music.

The group saw tremendous success upon their return from St. Thomas. Their first two albums sold more than one million copies each with the single "California Dreamin' " hitting the number four position on the pop charts. Their follow-up single, "Monday, Monday," also made the Top 10 and solidified the band as both a top radio and live act. Unfortunately, affairs of the heart, unrequited love, and the dismissal of Michelle from the group made for a tense situation among band members. After a brief replacement, Michelle was invited back and the band continued to record, perform, and organize the legendary Monterey Pop Festival. After the festival, the band took a year off to regroup, including a trip overseas together to reconnect, but whatever magic they once had was now gone. Besides, Cass was a mother now, and she had more important things to worry about besides touring and recording.

In the End . . .

In 1971 the band came together for one last studio effort born out of contractual obligations to their label, ABC. Though the quartet briefly put aside their animosity for the making of *People Like Us*, the halfhearted attempt did not capture the spirit and joy of the early years. After the release of the album in 1971, the original members of the Mamas and the Papas would never perform together again.

No one was more eager to pursue a solo career and shed the "Mama" name than Cass Elliot. She worked to establish herself independently from the Mamas and the Papas, recording six solo albums in the ensuing years. She even had her own television special. But perhaps her proudest accomplishment was playing to sold-out crowds at the London Palladium. "The best thing about Cass," wrote Michelle Phillips in her 1986 book *California Dreamin'*, "was that in a society obsessed with looks, she was fat—cheerfully, superbly, willingly fat." Sadly, it was this excess weight that would ultimately cause her premature death. After completing a two-week run at the Palladium, Elliot, contrary to media coverage that said she had choked to death on a ham sandwich, died of a massive heart attack in her London flat.

John Phillips continued to write and perform, usually under a variety of pseudo-Mamas and the Papas reunion tours. Though given the fact that he was heavily self-medicated throughout much of the 1960s and on through the 1980s, he reached sobriety and continued a successful songwriting career, including the last Beach Boys hit "Kokomo." He underwent a successful liver transplant in 1992 and lived nearly a decade before succumbing to heart failure at a California hospital.

Nearly three decades after their breakup, the Mamas and the Papas were inducted into the Rock and Roll Hall of Fame.

FINAL RESTING PLACES
Mount Sinai Memorial Park
Los Angeles, California
As you enter the park, drive up Mount Sinai Drive on the right and continue on past the Gardens of Heritage on the right. Just past the gardens, park at the Courts of Tanach. Elliot's plot is in Section 7 (the far-right court). As you enter the court, walk to the back left corner and Elliot's plot is in the very back row, the second marker from the left.

Desert Memorial Park
Cathedral City, California
As you come to the entrance of the park, look across the street to the mausoleum annex on the south side of the street. From the parking lot of the annex, take the center walkway all the way to the back of the mausoleum sections, turn left, and Papa John's is the last crypt on the right, third row from the bottom.

The reactions that I heard a lot when he died were, "Oh no," and "I can't believe he lasted this long."
songwriter John Stewart

BOB MARLEY

BORN February 6, 1945
St. Anns, Jamaica

DIED May 11, 1981
Miami, Florida

CAUSE OF DEATH Melanoma Cancer
Age 36

The only reggae artist to achieve legendary superstar status, Bob Marley and the Wailers drew from the well of rock music, African rhythms, and their Rastafarian beliefs to create a type of world music that remains timeless and universal to this day. With a heavy heart, he decried the injustices of the present day Jamaica, yet in the same breath he left the world a positive message dedicated to equal rights and justice.

In the Beginning . . .

In 1945 an eighteen-year-old black girl named Cedella Booker married Captain Norval Marley, a white fifty-year-old quartermaster attached to the British West Indian Regiment. The following year Robert Nesta Marley was born in St. Anns, Jamaica. Although he provided some financial support, the captain seldom saw his son.

In the early fifties, newcomers moved to the small village of Nine Mile, which Bob and his mother called home. The Livingstons, including their young son, Bunny, moved across the street from Bob. Bunny and Bob quickly became best friends and their families moved together to Kingston, where the boys were sent to complete their educations.

Viewed by many islanders as the land of opportunity, Kingston in reality had very few jobs to offer during the fifties and sixties. Bunny, Bob, and their families lived in the notorious shantytown known as Trenchtown (named after the trench that drained raw sewage from Kingston through the village). When Bob finished school at sixteen, he reluctantly took a job as a welder at the insistence of his mother. After almost losing his eye during a welding accident, he quit his job to devote his life to music. Marley first approached Chinese-Jamaican record producer Leslie Kong, who agreed to first record "Judge Not." The initial release went nowhere, as well as the second single, "One Cup of Coffee."

Undeterred, Marley returned to Trenchtown and began singing with Bunny and new acquaintance Peter McIntosh. After two years of rehearsing, working out harmony patterns and singing styles with the help of popular recording artist Joe Higgs, the trio was ready to audition for the biggest name on the island—Clement "Sir Coxson" Dodd of Studio One Records. Along with Beverly Kelso and Junior Braithwaite, they passed the audition and

----

While most tourists are content to park their pasty, fat butts on any number of "exclusive" beach clubs in Montego Bay or Ocho Rios, the more adventurous will grab a short plane ride to the capital of Kingston, Jamaica. Here you will get a real feel for Jamaica and its culture—both positive and negative (Kingston is a very dangerous place for the uninitiated). That should not deter one from visiting Bob Marley's former home and tour at 56 Hope Road. An excellent one-hour guided tour of Marley's life and times and home to one of the two Tuff Gong recording studios (when I visited, Steven Marley was recording and spoke with several visitors).

recorded "Simmer Down." The single went to #1 on the Jamaican charts, selling more than eight thousand copies in the first month.

During the next two years the Wailin' Wailers cut over thirty singles, becoming the hottest group in the dancehalls of the small island nation. Marley moved briefly to Delaware, but returned to Jamaica to continue his musical passion. After a failed business venture on their own record label and failed business dealings with both Kong and Dodd (both stole millions from the group), Aston and Carlton Barrett joined the Wailers in 1970. With Jamaica's hardest rhythm section, Bob Marley and the Wailers were unquestionably the hottest Caribbean band, but outside the islands they were unknown.

In the summer of 1971 Bob accepted an invitation to Sweden to work on a film score. The Wailers joined Marley to begin work on the music, only to find themselves with no money and no ticket home. On a gamble, Marley walked into Chris Blackwell's office at Island Records in England. Though home to Traffic,

Bronze Bob Marley statue across from the National Stadium in Kingston, Jamaica.

Jethro Tull, Cat Stevens, and Free, Blackwell was not unfamiliar with the reggae and ska movement in Jamaica. Initially intimidated by their "gangsta" reputation, he took a chance and gave the band eight thousand dollars and access to the same recording studios afforded their rock group contemporaries. The result was *Catch a Fire*, the Wailers' first album.

A critical success (sales were a bit lacking), the Wailers toured the U.K. for three months in 1973. Between gigs they recorded their follow-up *Burnin'*. In the summer of that same year, they were all given a hundred English pounds each and were told the band owed the record company forty thousand pounds. Enraged, Bunny Wailer (he had since changed his last name from Livingston) quit the group and vowed never to work for the white man again. Peter Tosh felt the strain of touring and Blackwell's preference for Marley over himself was too much. When the second album was released, the Wailers were finished.

In the End . . .

With Bunny and Peter gone, Marley regrouped in 1974 and brought in the I-Threes—a female trio consisting of Marcia Griffiths, Judy Mowatt, and his wife Rita Marley, and renamed the band Bob Marley and the Wailers. Recording *Natty Dread* and the bone-chilling arrangements of "Rebel Music," "Revolution," and the new concert favorite, "No Woman, No Cry," the band released music under Bob Marley and the Wailers.

In 1976 Marley finally cracked the American charts with *Rastaman Vibrations* and survived an attempted assassination. He sought exile in London where he recorded the LP *Exodus* in 1977, yielding the massive hit singles "Jammin'," "Waiting in Vain," and "Exodus." The year 1978 proved to be an extraordinary one for the band. Marley returned to Jamaica to play the One Love Peace concert, received the United Nations Medal of Peace,

Jah, Bob always screwface. I wasn't used to that, so I was scared at times. Terrified actually of everybody. Then I get to find out that it's just like some dogs—the bite is not as heavy as the bark.

keyboardist Tyrone Downie

and performed in Africa, Australia, Japan, and New Zealand. Bob Marley was truly an international musical superstar.

Toward the end of the European tour that year he reinjured his toe while playing soccer during one of the band's off days. After the tour, he flew to Miami to seek treatment for the injury, which had turned cancerous. Given the option to have the toe amputated and the disease stopped, Marley refused, as it was against his Rastafarian beliefs. Given prescriptions and a special diet on an out-treatment basis, there seemed to be no cause for concern.

In 1980, the band opened their American tour with two shows at Madison Square Garden. Feeling weak, Marley went for a jog in Central Park, only to collapse during the first mile. By now the cancer had spread through his entire body as Marley fought the disease for eight months. During his stay at a German clinic for treatment, he was weakening and wanted to return home to Jamaica. It was a journey he would not complete. Too weak to continue, he was rushed to a Miami hospital and died the next day.

Bob Marley Home
Nine Mile, Jamaica

When Marley passed from this world, the entire island of Jamaica came to a stop in what became the largest gathering in Jamaican history. Even Parliament recessed for the week in preparation for his state funeral. Over 250,000 people lined the roads to the small town of Nine Mile to return Marley to the home of his youth. He was buried in a simple cement sarcophagus.

Since then, the simple sarcophagus has become one of the island's biggest tourist attractions. The small village of Nine Mile is nine miles from the nearest town on the north side of the island. It is a one- or two-hour cab ride from most destinations on the island. Admission to the gravesite is four hundred Jamaican dollars (about ten dollars U.S.), plus a tip for your guide. Visitors are allowed into the sanctuary that houses the tomb; however, pictures are not allowed of the actual sarcophagus. The tour also includes the home that he shared with his mother (see below), along with all the original possessions that belonged to Marley. And if you are lucky, Mother Booker (Bob's mom) gives tours a couple times a week when she is in the village.

Bob Marley Museum
Nine Mile, Jamaica

The entrance to the hillside home is flanked by two columns with RESPECT and EXODUS adorning the columns. The colors green, yellow, and red represent the green of the earth, the yellow of the sun, and the red of the blood that is shed.

This is the house that Marley shared with his mother. It still contains his original blankets, furniture, and books.

Located next to the house is the outdoor kitchen. It is common in Jamaica to have outdoor kitchens since most of the cooking is done using open wood flames, both to keep the house cool and to avoid runaway flames which might easily burn down the house.

This is the only addition to the grounds: Naturally, what museum would be complete without a gift shop.

THE MARSHALL TUCKER BAND

Toy Caldwell circa 1983.

TOMMY CALDWELL	TOY CALDWELL
BORN November 9, 1949	BORN November 13, 1947
Spartanburg, South Carolina	Spartanburg, South Carolina
DIED April 28, 1980	DIED February 25, 1993
Spartanburg, South Carolina	Spartanburg, South Carolina
CAUSE OF DEATH	CAUSE OF DEATH
Automobile Accident	Respiratory Failure
Age 30	Age 45

Try as they might, critics (and there are a lot of them) could never pigeonhole the Marshall Tucker Band. A successful blend of country, blues, rock, and a dose of improvisational jazz, the MTB tore through the southern states in the early 1970s with their own style of back-porch pickup-truck rock 'n' roll. And in the fine tradition of the Outlaws, Lynyrd Skynyrd, and the Allman Brothers, the original founding members and brothers Toy and Tommy Caldwell did nothing to disgrace that tradition.

In the Beginning . . .

Both Tommy and Toy Caldwell began their music careers in their hometown of Spartanburg, South Carolina. Toy originally began as a guitarist with several local high school bands that played the usual dance circuit, with a blend of instrumental blues and rock cover tunes. With the British Invasion of the mid-sixties, Toy formed the Rants and recorded three original songs that got the attention of a couple of Nashville producers. Recording follow-up material in Nashville, things just didn't pan out for the struggling group and they returned to Spartanburg and split up shortly after.

With the Rants ancient history, Tommy joined his brother as the bass player for the Toy Factory. After recording more of Toy's original material at Muscle Shoals Sound Studios, Toy and Tommy had a confrontation, splitting the band into two factions for a while. Eventually egos and pride were put aside and the remnants of the two bands grew into a single band. In 1972, with three years of solid club dates under their belt, the band had just finished rehearsal and were discussing a name change. They looked at the name on the door of the person who had rented the building before them. Mr. Tucker was a blind piano tuner who had used the building for his business. The boys in the band looked at one another and agreed—the Marshall Tucker Band was now official.

When their debut album came out in 1973, the MTB struck gold right out of the gate with the classic radio hits "Can't You See" and "Take the Highway." Opening for the Allman Brothers Band allowed the group to move from sold-out clubs to sold-out arenas and coliseums. Playing up to three hundred dates a year, the MTB built a following across the U.S. with a steady output of hit albums, including the Grammy-nominated instrumental "Long Hard Ride" and a double album of live material and new studio tracks. Their greatest achievement was their 1977 release, *Carolina Dreams*, which featured their most requested song "Heard It in a Love Song."

After putting the finishing touches on what was to be their tenth album (and one

From 1973 to 1984, the original band recorded fourteen albums, including seven gold and two platinum. A big part of that sound was made possible by drummer Paul Riddle, who still lives in Spartanburg today. And if you are so inclined, he gives private lessons inside Smith Music and has his own line of drumsticks called the Carolina Stick Company.

month after the death of the Caldwells' younger brother Tim), Tommy was driving his Toyota Land Cruiser north down South Church Street in Spartanburg when his car struck a stalled vehicle and flipped over. Rushed to Spartanburg General Hospital, Tommy suffered massive head injuries despite the fact that he was wearing a seat belt with rollbar protection. He died six days later with his family and band members by his side.

The sudden death of a founding member created a downward spiral for the band. Unable to recapture the spirit or success of the early years, Toy, drummer Paul Riddle, and guitarist George McCorkle left the band in 1984. For brother Toy, it would be another six years before he solidified the Toy Caldwell Band for another go at music.

In the End . . .

In February 1993, on the eve of what should have been a national tour with the new Toy Caldwell Band, Toy developed a severe case of respiratory illness. His hacking cough and inability to breathe worsened. His wife, Abbie, stayed with him until 3:30 in the morning when she dozed off herself. Several hours later she discovered her husband had died in his sleep.

Unlike Tommy's funeral, Toy's farewell was a public affair with over two hundred family, friends, and fellow musicians attending to pay their respects. Founding member McCorkle and Allman Brothers guitarist Dickey Betts were on hand to play "Can't You See." The service concluded with a salute from the Marine Corps (both brothers had served in the armed services) and the playing of "Taps."

Floyd's Greenlawn Cemetery
Spartanburg, South Carolina

As you drive into the cemetery entrance, turn right and park directly behind the large statue and lawn section at the entryway. Toy Caldwell is buried in the middle of Section M-3 on the walkway ten rows down from his father in Plot 239-B, Grave 1.

Now drive over to the cemetery office and turn left at the road leading into the office. Drive past the large mausoleum and park at the corner of Section D-4. Walking toward the two large pillars, Tommy Caldwell is buried twenty feet to the left of the Moore monument.

They would practice in the basement and it would get so loud you could watch a coffee cup dance across the table. They loved it loud.

Toy Caldwell Sr.

MEMPHIS MINNIE

BORN June 3, 1897
Algiers, Louisiana

DIED August 6, 1973
Memphis, Tennessee

CAUSE OF DEATH Stroke
Age 76

Memphis Minnie ranks as one of the blues' most influential and historically significant female artists. Her roots were in country blues, an area dominated by men, where she managed to single-handedly keep a female presence in that genre. She influenced a great number of prominent performers, from Muddy Waters to Bonnie Raitt. An excellent composer, she was also an accomplished guitarist and powerful singer, packing her notes with boisterous and rugged passion. Her talent was such that her career spanned three decades and survived numerous stylistic changes within the blues and her songs "Bumble Bee," "Hoodoo Lady," and "Ain't No Use Tryin' to Tell on Me (I Know) Something on You" are genuine blues classics.

In the Beginning . . .

Born in Algiers, Louisiana, in 1897, Lizzie Douglas (aka Memphis Minnie) was the oldest of thirteen children. Her father was a sharecropper who in 1904 moved the family to Wall, Mississippi, a small town outside Memphis, Tennessee. Lizzie, known in her early years as "Kid" Douglas, received a guitar in 1905, which fueled her already strong desire to leave the grueling farm life. From an early age Kid would often run off to Memphis to play in Church's Park, and listen and learn from important bluesmen of her time, such as Frank Stokes and Furry Lewis. In 1929, while playing amid the Beale Street blues scene, she was discovered and recorded her first song, "Bumble Bee." She could easily play down any competition, and her picking style, even in those early days, showed a great deal of skill and artistry.

Kid Douglas had several musical partners, including Willie Brown, with whom she worked for six years. In 1928 she teamed with and married Kansas Joe McCoy. In 1929 they recorded several numbers for Columbia, at which time "Kid" became Memphis Minnie. During the early thirties, Minnie and Joe moved to Chicago to record for Vocalion, and Minnie regularly began using the steel guitar in her act. Minnie had no problem adjusting to the changing sounds of the industry, maintaining her popularity and ability to support herself throughout the Depression.

Memphis Minnie wasn't exactly known as a prolific recording artist such as Lightnin' Hopkins or Muddy Waters. Therefore, the few singles she did cut are nowadays worth a premium. While 78-rpm recordings of "Broken Heart" on Checker and "Kissing in the Dark" on J.O.B. are worth over a hundred dollars, the same singles on 45s are worth over five hundred dollars.

Unfortunately, her marriage to Kansas Joe ended during this time, possibly due to his jealousy over Minnie's popularity.

Years ago I had the privilege to view the extensive collection of memorabilia at the Memphis Music Hall of Fame. Privately owned and operated by a local Memphis businessman, the museum brought to life the blues from the Mississippi Delta region, the rockabilly movement from the early 1950s, the rise and fall of Elvis, and the rhythm and soul from the Stax era. More importantly for Memphis Minnie fans, he owned virtually every piece of memorabilia to be had from this amazing woman. Included in the Memphis Minnie collection were original releases, photographs, and the dress and guitar in the photo above. Unfortunately, the museum closed in 2000 and there is no plans at this time to reopen.

Between 1934 and 1939 she adopted the Melrose sound (a smoother, less complex urban sound fostered by Lester Melrose) to insure her ability to compete in Chicago and thus began using a piano sideman. She continued her innovative experimentation, as she not only was among the first to use a steel guitar, but Minnie also used mandolin, horn, and clarinet accompaniments. Additionally, she also had a firm grasp of the lyrical quality of the electric guitar. Despite the smoothing and uniform effect of the Melrose sound, Minnie never lost her gritty, down-home quality and the early forties were a prosperous time for Minnie and her new husband and partner, Little Son Joe (Ernest Lawlars), who had joined her in 1939.

In the End . . .

The postwar era gave way to a new generation of blues musicians, and Minnie found it increasingly harder to compete. Washboard Sam and Big Bill Broonzy had given way to Howlin' Wolf and Muddy Waters. Although she supported younger acts by inviting them to perform at her famous Blue Monday house parties, Minnie herself found it necessary to tour more often and farther from home. The late forties were her weakest period, and while she did manage some strong sessions in the early fifties, she never regained her initial popularity.

In 1958, Minnie's waning popularity and Little Son Joe's poor health convinced them to leave Chicago and return to Memphis permanently. She continued to play the guitar until she suffered a stroke. Minnie and Joe then moved in with her younger sister, Daisy Johnson. Joe died in 1961 and Minnie suffered another stoke shortly afterward. Later, Minnie moved into a nursing home after Daisy became too ill to care for her. Confined to a wheelchair the last thirteen years of her life, she died after suffering another stroke. She was inducted into the Blues Foundation's Hall of Fame in 1980.

Morning Star M.B. Church
Walls, Mississippi

Lizzie "Kid" Douglas, aka Memphis Minnie, was properly eulogized in October 1996, over twenty-three years since her passing. Her grave, previously unmarked, was given a proper headstone in 1997 during a service that brought more than fifty members of the Douglas family together. From Memphis, drive ten miles south on Highway 61 and turn west off the highway at the first exit for Walls. Follow the signs to Walls and turn  right on Second Street (before the Amoco station). Drive to the end and turn right, then veer left over the railroad tracks. Drive two miles to Norfolk Road and turn right, driving another half mile to Morning Star M.B. Church. Her upright marker is very visible from the road on the right, the farthest marker from the church.

Wasn't nothing he could teach her. Everything Willie Brown could play, she could play, and then she could play some things he couldn't play.

blues guitarist Willie Moore

FREDDIE MERCURY

BORN September 5, 1946
Zanzibar, East Africa

DIED November 24, 1991
London, England

CAUSE OF DEATH AIDS-Related Pneumonia
Age 45

There was an unmistakable presence surrounding Freddie Mercury, frontman for the hard-rocking quartet Queen. Whether he was the playful pop hipster, operatic diva-in-waiting, or rock demigod delivering unparalleled stadium anthems, Mercury was more than just a singer—he was a performance artist in every sense of the word. A vocalist who could hit the high notes with astonishing ease, his commanding stage presence and lavish stage shows made Freddie Mercury an irreplaceable rock icon.

In the Beginning . . .

Born on the small island of Zanzibar, Farookh Bulsara was the first of two children for Bomi and Jer Bulsara. At the age of eight Farookh was sent to an English boarding school where friends began to call him Freddie. Several years into his education the headmaster wrote to his parents, suggesting an increase in tuition to cover the additional expense of music lessons for their son. With a solid foundation in arts and music, Freddie began taking part in school musicals and formed his first band, the Hectics.

Upon returning to Zanzibar after completion of his education, the family moved to England and Freddie enrolled in college. After aborted attempts with the bands Ibex, Wreckage, and Sour Milk Sea, Freddie became the new lead singer for Smile, a band featuring Brian May on guitar and Roger Taylor on drums. Always a dominant force to be dealt with, Freddie changed the name to Queen (May wanted to call the new band Build Your Own Boat) and changed his stage name to Freddie Mercury.

Adding John Deacon on bass, the quartet signed to Trident Productions in 1972. Their 1973 single of the Beach Boys' hit "I Can Hear Music" stiffed in the record stores while their second album, *Queen II*, yielded the minor hit on the British charts "Seven Seas of Rhye." Their first international hit came the following year with the guitar-driven "Killer Queen" from the album *Sheer Heart Attack*.

In 1976 Queen released their epic album *A Night at the Opera*, which included a six-minute single divided into three equal movements of bombastic opera married to heavy metal—"Bohemian Rhapsody." Staying on the charts for over two months, the band fret-

When Freddie Mercury passed on, he left 25 percent of his estate to his sister, 25 percent to his parents, and the remaining share, including his home, all the associated artwork and furnishings, and his music and publishing rights to his former girlfriend, Mary Austin. Located at 1 Logan Place (see right) in the Kensington district in London, England, the home is not a museum or open to the public; however, it has become a common gathering for Queen fans, who freely leave their signatures and artwork on the sidewalk.

ted over how they would replicate the song live onstage. Nonetheless, the band hit the road to sold-out audiences in stadiums, opera houses, and arenas worldwide. In his trademark white trousers, suspenders, and open-necked shirt, Mercury rushed around the stage like a man possessed. Queen continued their worldwide domination of record charts, videos, and lavish stage shows upon the release of *A Day at the Races* and *News of the World* (1977), featuring the bombastic "We Will Rock You."

In the End . . .

The end of the 1970s brought the band additional success with the musically mediocre album *Jazz* featuring "Fat Bottomed Girls." And while the 1980 release of *The Game*, featuring "Crazy Little Thing Called Love" brought the band their greatest American success, Queen was musically beginning to become stagnant. In 1982 Mercury announced the band would be on hiatus for at least a year.

While his solo efforts never reached the level of grandiose energy of the group, Mercury recorded some outstanding efforts including "Under Pressure" with David Bowie. In 1985, Queen made an acclaimed appearance at Live Aid, in effect leaving no doubt as who the star of the show was. However, all was not well with the band. Everyone had suspected that Mercury was tired and sickly, yet no one knew the extent of his illness. When Queen went on to play their final concert at Knebworth Park in 1986, the 300,000 in attendance never knew that the masterful vocalist and frontman had been diagnosed with AIDS two years before.

Few people outside the band (and they weren't even the first told) knew of Mercury's illness. In his final years he gradually became more ill and was rarely seen in public. At the end of 1990 he began to slowly lose his eyesight and the following summer he was having trouble walking even a few steps. In the fall of 1991, enough was enough and Mercury quit taking the multitude of drugs that were keeping him alive. He died in his sleep at home.

Mercury was cremated, but the disposition of his ashes are unknown. Upon his death, Mercury made his former girlfriend and confidante, Mary Austin, promise to never reveal the location of his final resting place. Although she kept the ashes at the residence in London for a time, she disposed of the cremains in the mid-nineties and in keeping with his wishes, she has remained silent on the matter. The statue to the right, located on the Lake Geneva shoreline in Switzerland, is the only monument or memorial to the great singer, songwriter, and rock icon.

> *He knew how to front a show. It was his way of expressing that side of his personality. Everything he did onstage later in Queen, he was doing with Ibex at his first gig.*
>
> former Ibex bandmate Ken Testi

GLENN MILLER

BORN March 1, 1904
Clarinda, Iowa

DIED December 15, 1944
The English Channel (MIA)

CAUSE OF DEATH Plane Crash
Age 40

Leading the most commercially successful big band of the 1930s, the Glenn Miller Orchestra played swing with a string section, earning the band the distinction of the first gold record (over one million copies sold) ever awarded for their hit "Chattanooga Choo-Choo." With professional skill and dogged determination, Miller almost single-handedly built his band into an international sensation.

In the Beginning . . .

Alton Glenn Miller grew up in a typical midwestern family at the turn of the century. Miller began his musical interest on the cornet and mandolin, while his younger brother (and a future bandleader in his own right) played the trumpet. Miller got his first trombone at the age of thirteen and when the family moved to Fort Morgan, Colorado, the music teacher at the high school allowed Miller to sit in with his own dance band.

Miller continued with music, playing professionally with the Boyd Senter Band to pay for his education at the local university. Miller continued with college for two years, but during his third year he dropped out and moved to California with the Max Fischer Band. While in California he moved over to the Ben Pollack Band where Miller played alongside future legends Benny Goodman and Dick Morgan. After cutting his first record, "Deed I Do," with Pollack, Miller moved to New York, playing and arranging for Red Nichols, Victor Young, the Casa Loma Orchestra, Ozzie Nelson, and the Dorsey brothers. Miller made his first record as the Glenn Miller Orchestra in 1935 for Columbia Records, but it wasn't until two more versions of the orchestra and three years later before Miller's music really caught on. In March of 1939, the band was informed that they were being booked for a lengthy engagement at the Glen Island Casino in New York. With such swing classics as "In the Mood," "Tuxedo Junction," "Chattanooga Choo-Choo," "Pennsylvania 6-5000," and "Moonlight Serenade," the Miller band broke attendance records everywhere they performed. In 1940 they averaged $20,000 in ticket sales every day, where they would play four shows at the Paramount Theater, five sets at the hotel, three radio shows a week,

---

Four generations of the Miller family have lived in the Clarinda, Iowa, vicinity, so it would only be natural that the Nodaway Valley Museum in Clarinda has family memorabilia displayed by the Glenn Miller Birthplace Society. The fully restored birthplace of Miller is located on South Sixteenth Street between the museum and town square. The United States Air Force Museum at the Wright-Patterson AFB in Ohio has an excellent display of Miller memorabilia, including photographs, lead sheets, uniforms, and the cornerstone of their exhibit, Miller's backup trombone with mouthpiece and case. Overseas, the English have a true affinity for Miller evidenced by the Glenn Miller Exhibition at Twinwood Farms in Bedford, England. The control tower from where Major Miller departed on his final flight has been restored and now houses a facinating museum packed with photos, uniforms, a jukebox from 1940, and one of Miller's trombones. Down the road in downtown Bedford you can find a bust and memorial plaque of the legendary bandleader at the Bedford Corn Exchange (why there is a bust at the Corn Exchange, I haven't a clue!). And if you were still wondering, if you dial Pennsylvania 6-5000, the Hotel Pennsylvania will pick up. The New York hotel, which served as Miller's home base in the late 1930s, still has the same phone number.

rehearsals, and the occasional film appearance or recording date. In February of 1942, the Glenn Miller Orchestra was awarded the very first gold record for sales of 1.2 million copies of "Chattanooga Choo-Choo" by RCA Victor. And in a little more than a year later, Miller decided to break up the band and joined the Army Air Corps to serve in his country's war effort.

In the End . . .

Too old to be drafted, Miller first tried the navy (but they couldn't really use the services of a bandleader), but later joined the Army Air Corps. As Captain Miller, he was put in charge of organizing the Army Air Force Band, responsible for reveille, taps, marches, retreat, and the entertainment of over one million service men. And if Miller thought his schedule was busy in the States, his band was often airlifted from one base to the next with shows from 8:00 A.M. in the morning until well past midnight that same day.

Lieutenant Haynes was the last person to see Major Miller (he had been recently promoted from captain) as Miller took his manager's place on the airplane destined for Paris, France. At 1:15 P.M. at Twinwood Farm Airfield in Bedford, England, Major Miller, along with a pilot and another officer, took off in the heavy fog. With no radio contact or wreckage, it was three days before anyone realized the officers were overdue.

Several years after his passing, rumors of the cause of his death began circulating. One unfounded rumor, spread by one of his business associates, was that Miller and another officer were out all night drinking the town dry and demanded the plane take off in the fog. Another rumor hinted at the incompetence of the pilot, or that the ground crew forgot to fuel the plane. However, during the 1990s eyewitness reports and confirmation with military records confirmed that Miller's plane was flying below a returning squadron of fighter aircraft who, before landing back home in England, emptied their load of bombs over the English Channel, hitting what many believe to be Miller's plane. The plane took a direct hit and dove into the sea below without a trace of wreckage.

While it is true that Glenn Miller vanished without a trace, that hasn't stopped anyone from erecting cenotaph memorial markers around the world. With memorials at the Grove Street Cemetery in New Haven, Connecticut, the American Military Cemetery in Hamm, Luxembourg, and on the Wall of Remembrance at the Cambridge American Military Cemetery in England, the family also requested that a stone be placed in Memorial Section H, Number 464-A, on Wilson Drive in Arlington National Cemetery in Washington, D.C.

Grant City, Missouri, in 1917 wasn't a very big place, and when a strong-lunged youngster cut loose on a trombone, you heard him all over town.

neighbor John Mosbarger

BILL MONROE

BORN September 13, 1911
Jerusalem Ridge, Kentucky

DIED September 9, 1996
Springfield, Tennessee

CAUSE OF DEATH Stroke
Age 84

The title Father of Bluegrass Music was bestowed upon Bill Monroe not by a concert promoter or record executive, but rather by the friends, fans, and fellow musicians that grew up in the shadow of this country legend. A member of the Grand Ole Opry for over a half century, a member of the Country Music Hall of Fame, and awarded numerous Grammys and recording achievement awards, Monroe was an American legend who had a profound effect not only on bluegrass, but also folk, country, rock, and jazz.

In the Beginning . . .

Born the youngest of eight children, William Smith Monroe took up the mandolin at the age of ten only because the other children in the family had laid claim to the fiddle and guitar. Born with poor vision and crossed eyes, he was unable to take formal music lessons at school and was taught the rudiments of the instrument from a local farmer.

At the age of eighteen he moved to Indiana, and later to Illinois in seach of work. Exposed to blues and jazz, he joined with his brothers Birch and Charlie playing dances, small package shows, and on local radio stations. In 1934, Charlie and Bill quit their oil refinery jobs and began performing full-time. Known as the Monroe Brothers, they cut sixty sides for Victor Records over the next four years, which included several fast, intense versions of traditional songs such as "On the Banks of the Ohio."

In 1938, Bill parted company with Charlie, who formed his highly successful Charlie Monroe and the Kentucky Pardners. Bill founded the group the Kentuckians, later moving to Atlanta to form Bill Monroe and the Blue Grass Boys. The following year Monroe and his Blue Grass Boys auditioned for the Grand Ole Opry on WSM radio in Nashville. This secured his spot on the show, which he held until the day he died.

The 1940 recordings showed a diverse blend of blues, country fiddling, and western swing. The first elements of bluegrass were forged with his 1945 recording of "Kentucky Waltz." Things really began to move forward the following year when Monroe added Lester Flatt on guitar, Earl Scruggs on banjo, and Chubby Wise on fiddle. Over the next several years the band recorded the core of bluegrass roots with "Blue Moon of Kentucky," "Molly and Tenbrooks," and "Mother's Only Sleeping."

"Bluegrass is the only form of music with origins that can be directly traced to one country, one state, one town, one farm, one house, and one man—Bill Monroe," remarked Campbell Mercer of the Bill Monroe Foundation. And that one house is the fully restored birthplace of Monroe just outside Rosine, Tennessee. In the near future they also have plans for a full restoration of the rest of the farm, brother Charlie Monroe's home, an annual music festival, and a Bill Monroe Museum. Unfortunately, what the museum will not have in its collection is Monroe's prized 1923 Gibson Master Model F-5 mandolin. Bought by Monroe for a hundred and fifty dollars, he played this mandolin almost exclusively throughout his fifty-plus-year career. Similiar instruments would fetch seventy thousand dollars, but since this instrument is so clearly identified with the origin of bluegrass music, it is worth in excess of a million dollars. The new museum could not come up with the cash needed to secure the instrument, so it will go to auction sometime in late 2003.

With Flatt and Scruggs off to form their own group in the late forties, Monroe struggled briefly in the late 1950s as the introduction of electric music diminished the interest in acoustic country. Monroe's career rebounded quickly in the early 1960s as he was embraced during the folk music revival. After several documentaries and festivals, Monroe's legacy throughout the 1960s and 1970s as a living legend was secure.

In the End . . .

During the 1980s his physical strength and stubborn Scottish heritage served him well as he survived colon cancer, a broken hip, and heart bypass surgery. However, his most painful event took place in 1985 when an intruder broke into his home and nearly destroyed his trademark 1923 Gibson mandolin. Smashed with a fire poker, he took the pieces of the instrument and another vandalized mandolin in a paper bag to the Nashville Gibson repair shop. With over five hundred pieces to sort and reassemble, Monroe cried when he first played the fully restored instrument.

Already a member of the Country Music Hall of Fame, Monroe opened the Bluegrass Hall of Fame and Museum in Nashville, was nominated for Grammy Awards in 1987, 1989, and 1995, received the Lifetime Achievement Award by the National Academy of Recording Arts and Sciences, and received the National Medal of the Arts from President Clinton in 1995. With a full tour schedule, Opry performances, and festival engagements, Monroe continued to record and release stellar-quality albums, including

the 1986 *Bill Monroe and Stars of the Bluegrass Hall of Fame* album, which reunited him with fellow contemporaries Ralph Stanley, Jim and Jesse McReynolds, and Carl Story. The only thing that interrupted his schedule was his death from a stroke, four days before his eighty-fifth birthday.

Rosine Cemetery
Rosine, Kentucky

While there is a large Monroe monument near the Roy Acuff grave in Madison, Tennessee's Spring Hill Cemetery, which contains many of Monroe's family, it doesn't have the Father of Bluegrass Music. No, Bill Monroe's final resting place is located in his childhood hometown of Rosine, Kentucky, in a small city cemetery. One does not need directions within the cemetery to find his mammoth thirty-foot monument among the smaller tombstones that make up the bulk of memorial markers.

I never wanted to copy any man. I was determined to carve out a music of my own. Bluegrass is wonderful. I'm glad I originated it.

Bill Monroe

JIM MORRISON

BORN December 8, 1943
Melbourne, Florida

DIED July 3, 1971
Paris, France

CAUSE OF DEATH Heart Failure
Age 27

The Doors were never part of the peace and free love movement exemplified by the Jefferson Airplane or Donovan. They really didn't fit the mold of acid rock, electric folk music, or that of the Grateful Dead. And they certainly wouldn't be confused with the pop sounds of the Beatles. Fronted by Jim Morrison, the Doors were an anomaly in the world of sixties rock. Raw and powerful, dark and explosive, Jim Morrison's Dionysian lyrics and vocal energy were not an act—Jim Morrison was not a rock star. The Lizard King was the real thing.

In the Beginning . . .

James Douglas Morrison was raised, by all accounts, within the normal surroundings of a loving and supportive military family. While studying filmmaking at UCLA, Morrison and future Doors keyboardist, Ray Manzarek, met and became quick friends. Upon graduation, Morrison told Manzarek he was going to New York to try his hand at producing experimental avant-garde films. However, two months later, Morrison and Manzarek met again at Venice Beach. When Morrison told Ray he changed his mind and was writing poetry and song lyrics, Manzarek asked Morrison to read one. Blown away, Ray asked Morrison right off if he wanted to form a band. Borrowing a name suggested by Aldous Huxley's phrase (from a William Blake poem), the Doors of Perception, Manzarek called upon ex-Psychedelic Rangers Robby Krieger and John Densmore, and the Doors were formed.

After rehearsing for over a year, the Doors began playing on the Sunset Strip in Los Angeles, eventually becoming the house band at the Whisky-A-Go-Go. Throughout 1966, The Doors played nightly alongside Love, the Byrds, and Van Morrison's Them. Shortly after they were fired from the Whisky (due to the graphic nature of the *Oedipus*-inspired lyrics of "The End"), they released their first album. From the opening throes of "Break on Through," the hypnotic "Light My Fire," the cover of Howlin' Wolf's "Back Door Man," and the epic eleven-minute "The End," FM radio would never sound the same. By Christmas of 1967, they emerged from the studio with another strong effort, *Strange Days*.

Listening to a Doors record was one thing, but to see the band live was to truly witness a performance. Lyrics, solos, and rhythms were never played the same way twice. With Manzarek's rhythmic pounding of the organ and Krieger's slow, flamenco-tinged guitar stylings, the Lizard King's shrieks and screams came from a subconscious layer—some kind of unique and personal pain. For Morrison communicated with the audience on many levels—not all of them pretty.

Some say that when Morrison died in Paris, France, he died without a will and that his estate was transferred illegally to Pamela Courson. The truth of the matter is that Morrison did have a will, dated 1969 and filed in Los Angeles, California, naming Courson as sole beneficiary of his estate (including his full 25 percent share of the Doors' recording and publishing concern). When Courson died three years later, the Courson family gained control of her estate. Therefore, there is scant evidence of Doors memorabilia to be had. The Morrison family has donated or loaned numerous personal letters and affects to the Rock and Roll Hall of Fame, but little else is available for fans.

The final years of Morrison's life were chaotic. Many attribute the beginning of the end to the Miami concert incident, where Morrison was charged with lewd and lascivious behavior. Others attribute Morrison's downward spiral to his now-legendary consumption of drugs and alcohol. Still others point to the rock star persona that the record company and the press played upon when in fact all Morrison really wanted to be was a serious poet and writer.

In the End . . .

While speculation has run rampant regarding the Doors' and Morrison's seemingly imminent departure, Morrison knew as well as the band—he needed the Doors and the Doors needed Morrison. The respite was to be only a brief one in everyone's mind. To get away from the press and the legal hassles in Florida, Morrison planned a trip to Paris. Two days before he left he gave one last interview to *Rolling Stone* magazine. During the session he said, "For me, it was never really an act, those so-called performances. It was a life-and-death thing. An attempt to communicate, to involve many people in a private world of thought."

According to Pamela Courson, Morrison's girlfriend, Morrison and Courson went to a late-night showing at the cinema of the Robert Mitchum movie *Pursued*, later returning to their Paris apartment. After watching some of Morrison's home movies, they drifted off to sleep. An hour later Courson awoke to Morrison choking and gurgling. Courson slapped Morrison awake, after which he promptly vomited blood in the bathroom. Worried, she offered to call a doctor, but Morrison declined, saying he was feeling better and wanted to take a bath. Courson went back to sleep and Morrison finished his bath. She woke the next morning at approximately 8:00 A.M. to discover Morrison unconscious in the bathtub. A small amount of blood trickled from his nose as Courson tried to wake him. She called her friend Alan Ronay at 8:30, and later the fire department. As the firemen pulled Morrison from the bath and laid him in the bedroom, they began to massage his heart. But it was too late. James Douglas Morrison—the Lizard King, Shaman, Poet—was dead.

By Monday, July 5, rumors reached America that Morrison was dead. Manager Bill Siddons was not concerned for he had heard these rumors before. He finally telephoned Courson and was soon on the next plane for France that very day. As Siddons was flying over the Atlantic, Courson purchased a thirty-year lease on a double plot at Père Lachaise Cemetery just outside downtown Paris. She paid a total of approximately two hundred dollars for both the plot and pine casket—the cheapest the cemetery had available. Siddons arrived at the apartment the next day to view the coffin and death certificate (though he never saw the body). On Wednesday, a hearse with four pallbearers came to collect the casket from the apartment. No clergyman

Morrison's French death certificate.

> I wouldn't mind dying in a plane crash. It'd be a good way to go. I don't want to die in my sleep, or of old age, or OD. I want to feel what it's like. I want to taste it, hear it, smell it. Death is only going to happen once. I don't want to miss it.
>
> Jim Morrison

was in attendance when they lowered his casket into the grave and only five people were present at the funeral. Neither Morrison's family, friends, or the band were contacted.

When Pam arrived back in Los Angeles on Friday, July 9, she released a statement to the press and confirmed what many in the music world had already suspected.

Père Lachaise Cemetery
Paris, France

Entering the cemetery nearest the intersection of Boulevard de Menilmontant and Boulevard de Charonne, Mr. Mojo Risin' can be found in Divison 6, near the intersection of Chemin Maison and Chemin Lebrun (walking toward Chemin de Lessups). And if you have done your math correctly, you have probably figured out that his lease on the gravesite was due in 2001. Fortunately, the Morrison family renegotiated the lease and their son will remain at the cemetery. A good thing, considering that the box Courson purchased for less than a hundred dollars has in all likelihood decomposed, along with the remains of her boyfriend. In other words, there just isn't anything left to move.

Pamela Courson Gravesite
Santa Ana, California

After her boyfriend died, the Doors' answer to Yoko Ono returned to America to live off Morrison's estate, only to die three years later a lonely death due to a heroin overdose. Found dead in her small ground-floor apartment at 108 North Sycamore Avenue in Hollywood, California, on April 25, 1974, her parents had her ashes installed in a small, inexpensive wall unit at Fairhaven Cemetery in neighboring Orange County. The fact that she was buried under the name Pamela Susan Morrison rather than her true name has sparked rumors regarding her relationship to Morrison (they were never married). Her ashes can be found in the Garden Courts mausoleum Rose alcove in Unit 614, four rows from the bottom on the left.

Jim Morrison's Final Residence
18 Rue Beautreillis
Paris, France

Located in the Marais section of the city, the apartment on the third floor (four stories from ground level) was Morrison's last address. They rented the apartment from a French model and her boyfriend, an American producer. The apartment they occupied includes the three windows on the far left, second from the top (just above the balcony window), and the window on the left is the bathroom were Morrison was found dead. According to tenants in the building, the bathroom is much the same, including the bathtub where Morrison took his final soak.

Restaurant Le Beautreillis
18 Rue Beautreillis

A favorite restaurant of Morrison (located just across from his apartment above), this was the hangout for Doors fans worldwide up until 1996, when new owners ripped out all the Doors memorabilia and tried to turn it into a "respectable" restaurant. They failed and it was then turned into a law office.

Vins des Pyrenees
25 Rue Beautreillis

During his months in France, Morrison liked to drink a lot! Witnesses rarely saw him sober from midday through the night, and during his last weeks alive he was coughing up blood and seemed short of breath. Nonetheless, Morrison preferred to buy his wine (usually white Bordeaux) at Vins des Pyrenees just down the street from his apartment. Today the former wine merchant is an above-average restaurant using the same name.

Le Mazet
Rue St. Andres des Arts

This is the last-known public place where Morrison was seen alive. While the restaurant has been extensively renovated into a tourist trap in recent years, the booth on the very left as you enter the building is the same booth Jim occupied, where he had his final meal of white Bordeaux wine and croque monsieur. The setting has a plaque just above stating the historical reference and the booth is exactly the same as the night Morrison sat there.

JELLY ROLL MORTON

BORN October 10, 1890
New Orleans, Louisiana

DIED July 10, 1941
Los Angeles, California

CAUSE OF DEATH Heart Failure
Age 50

Along with Louis Armstrong, Jelly Roll Morton was the most important musical figure to rise from New Orleans. While there are those who dismiss his claim that he alone created jazz, there can be no doubt as to his technical brilliance as a pianist, composer, and arranger. For it was Jelly Roll who transformed the rigid confines of ragtime and ushered in the freeform structures of jazz.

In the Beginning . . .

Born Ferdinand LaMonthe Jr. to a prominent Creole family, Morton's musical education began in his teens under a variety of teachers in prejazz New Orleans. Impressed by the amount of money and female attention a ragtime pianist garnered in the active New Orleans nightlife, Morton joined the fun as a top pianist in the brothels of the notorious Storyville district. His playing style and composing earned him a good living in the sporting houses of the red-light district (much to the surprise of his relatives!) and he adopted a boastful, arrogant attitude that would be one of his trademarks. When his mother remarried, he adopted his stepfather's last name of Morton.

When Storyville was torn down (and most every notable jazz musician from Louis Armstrong to King Oliver left town), Morton moved to Memphis, where he performed in minstrel-type shows. He adopted the name Sweet Papa Jelly Roll, and in 1915 published his first original composition "Jelly Roll Blues." In 1923 Morton recorded for the first time with the New Orleans Rhythm Kings for Gennett studios in Indiana. For the next twenty years Jelly Roll found himself playing virtually every nightclub and honky-tonk from Memphis to Chicago, down to Los Angeles. He further supplemented his income as a pool shark and hustler.

In 1926, while living in Los Angeles, he formed the group that would ensure his footnote in musical history. The Red Hot Peppers, which included Kid Ory on trombone, Barney Bigard on clarinet, and Warren "Baby" Dodds on drums, was formed to fulfill a recording contract that he had signed earlier. Those first sessions included the historic recordings of "King Porter Stomp," "Black Bottom Stomp," and "Dead Man Blues." In a departure from standard convention, Morton encouraged his players to improvise and not just play what was set in front of them. Although Morton and his group's playing was criticized for their less-than-perfect technique, others recognized his sense of swing and musical freedom—a truly original expression of the music.

Morton continued to record through 1930 with the Red Hot Peppers until RCA took over the Victor label and Morton was dropped from the roster. Through much of the

The Historic New Orleans Collection acquired the extensive collection of the late journalist William Russell in 1992, including the entire estate of Jelly Roll Morton. The collection, containing more than thirty-six thousand pieces, including manuscripts, books, sound recordings, and photographs, features material related to Morton, Louis Armstrong, Mahalia Jackson, and Bunk Johnson. The William Russell Jazz Collection goes on exhibit every couple of years at 533 Royal Street in New Orleans.

1930s Jelly Roll was a forgotten man and much of the attention that he had previously received was now focused on Chicago musicians, many of whom he had played with. While his band was considered out of fashion, Morton's compositions were taken up by many of the leading groups of the day. Benny Goodman, Fletcher Henderson, Tommy Dorsey, and Bunny Berigan all scored hits from many of Jelly Roll's compositions. Financial problems also dogged him for much of the 1930s from investments that left him virtually broke.

In the End . . .

In 1938, while listening to the radio at home, Morton heard that W. C. Handy claimed to have originated jazz. Ego still intact, Morton responded in a lengthy, egotistical letter that he, Jelly Roll Morton, alone had invented jazz in the early 1900s. This started a cross-country debate that jump-started Morton's career. The ensuing controversy provoked interest in his music and led to an invitation to record on piano and to recount his life for the Library of Congress. A year later, RCA Victor invited him back to record again, and he began performing onstage, though sporadically, while managing a jazz club in Washington.

With his health declining and money running out, Morton drove to California with the mistaken notion that his recently departed grandmother had left a large quantity of jewels in her home. Broke and too sick to work, Morton was twice hospitalized for heart and respiratory problems that finally claimed his life in 1941.

Calvary Cemetery
Los Angeles, California
Located at 4201 Whittier Boulevard in Los Angeles, California, the entrance to the cemetery can be found at the intersection of Downey and Whittier Boulevard. As you drive through the gates, turn left at the first opportunity past the office. Stay to your left as you pass the Our Lady's Garden mausoleum and once you pass the main mausoleum on your right, look for the number 343 on the curb on your right. Stop at this number and walk nine rows up to the base of the tree to Section N, Lot 347, Grave 4. When his casket was carried to his final resting place by Kid Ory, Papa Mutt Carey, Dink Johnson, Ed Garland, and Fred Washington, Morton's pallbearers were members of an elite group—they were all part of the first black jazz band to make a record.

ORIGINATOR OF JAZZ—STOMP—SWING. WORLD'S GREATEST HOT TUNE WRITER.

Jelly Roll Morton's business card

RICK NELSON

BORN May 8, 1940
Teaneck, New Jersey

DIED December 31, 1985
De Kalb, Texas

CAUSE OF DEATH Airplane Crash
Age 45

The youngest member of America's "perfect family," Rick Nelson parleyed the free publicity that the television show *The Adventures of Ozzie and Harriet* afforded into a musical career. With teen idol good looks and talent to match, Nelson's legacy began with such million-seller pop classics as "Poor Little Fool" and "Hello, Mary Lou" and ended with the more introspective "Garden Party."

In the Beginning . . .

Born to perhaps America's most famous parents, Ozzie and Harriet Nelson, Rick Nelson began to show an interest in rock 'n' roll at an early age. His passion in life was surprisingly not acting, but the rockabilly beat of Memphis' Sun Records—particularly Elvis, Carl Perkins, and Jerry Lee Lewis. In 1967 he was able to display his passion on the national TV show *The Adventures of Ozzie and Harriet* with the Fats Domino song "I'm Walkin'."

The amazing part of Nelson's music was that Ozzie, rather than becoming an obstacle, was his greatest promoter. Ozzie saw the potential and drive in his young son, and having the number one-rated show in the nation didn't hurt the chances for promotion, either. Ricky's first recordings were "I'm Walkin'" with doo-wop ballads "A Teenager's Romance" and "You're My One and Only Love" on Verve. The first two singles reached number four and number two on the *Billboard* Best Sellers In-Store chart. Achieving this without the "Nelson family" byline was an incredible achievement for this teenager—the die was cast.

Filming *The Adventures* series from September to May, Nelson spent his off-time touring and recording with Eddie Cochran, Gene Vincent, the Everly Brothers, and the Burnette Brothers. Ozzie continued his involvement as far as negotiating contracts, scheduling recording dates, and working with his son on song and single selection.

By the late 1960s the musical tide was shifting from the single-oriented pop hit to the Los Angeles-based country-rock sounds evidenced by the sounds of the Byrds, Poco, the Eagles, and Rick Nelson and the Stone Canyon Band. The SCB signature sound was obtained by using the pedal-steel guitar with a rock 'n' roll rhythm. Making their debut at the Troubadour on the Sunset Strip, the band taped four nights for their first album, *Rick Nelson in Concert*. The album sold well, but it was the critical acclaim that Rick coveted. *Rolling Stone* magazine and *Billboard* overwhelmingly praised the effort without once using the "teen idol" label.

The next fifteen years of living life on the road were hard on Nelson, and marriage and the pressures of a family only added to his problems. His personal life began to unravel shortly after Ozzie's death in 1975. Coupled with psychological and drug problems, his wife, Kris, spent almost every dollar Rick earned on houses, cars, and lavish furnishings.

For the ultimate Ricky Nelson fan, the house in which the family grew up and which was featured on their long-running television show can be found one block off Hollywood Boulevard at 1822 Camino Palmero, Hollywood, California. And if you were wondering—yes, it is haunted (but not by Rick). Visitors and former home owners have both admitted to hauntings and apparitions of Rick's dad, Ozzie, who died in the home in 1975.

Once Rick initiated divorce proceedings, Kris spent the next ten years in a vindictive, financially draining divorce whose sole purpose was to make Rick's life a living hell. Consequently, Rick spent two to three hundred nights a year on the road touring just to keep up with alimony and child support payments.

In the End . . .

At Christmas in 1985, Kris's attorney contacted Rick to inform him (erroneously) that he was behind on his court-ordered alimony and support payments, forcing Rick and the band back on the road the day after Christmas. On Monday, December 30, Rick Nelson and the Stone Canyon Band gave their final performance in Guntersville, Alabama. They closed the show with Buddy Holly's "Rave On."

The next day the band left for a New Year's Eve show at the Park Suite in Dallas, Texas. Four hours into the flight, the pilot radioed Fort Worth regarding trouble onboard. Minutes later the pilot radioed again that he could no longer keep the airplane in the air. The DC-3, previously owned by Jerry Lee Lewis, plunged to the ground, severing power lines and slamming into a tree, losing a wing. As the two pilots scrambled from the cockpit windows, flames as high as seventy feet leapt from the wreckage. The inferno, which held seven bodies, burned all night before anyone could get near the plane.

The funeral and private burial in Los Angeles, California, were quite a spectacle—for all the wrong reasons. As the funeral began, Kris stepped from a limousine into a hostile crowd, which included her own children. By the end of the funeral an argument ensued regarding Kris being specifically left out of the will and life insurance money. Before anyone knew it Kris had thrown her daughter Tracy to the ground and started hitting her before others could intervene. Two days later, Rick was laid to rest near his father, Ozzie.

Forest Lawn Hollywood Hills
Los Angeles, California

As you drive through the gates of the cemetery, continue on Memorial Drive until it ends.

Veer right and turn right on Crystal Lane, parking the car at the intersection of Crystal Lane and Evergreen Drive. Rick is buried fifteen rows from Evergreen Drive; walk up the hill toward the large tree directly above where the two roads intersect. With Ozzie and Harriet Nelson buried on the thirteenth row in Plot 3540, their son's grave is two rows above and two markers to the left of his parents' in the Revelation section.

I waited, and I'm sure Elvis did, too, for each Ricky Nelson record like we would a Chuck Berry record or a Fats Domino record, to see what was goin' on.

Roy Orbison

THE NEW YORK DOLLS

Nolan (second from left), and Thunders (right).

JOHNNY THUNDERS
BORN July 15, 1952
New York, New York

DIED April 23, 1991
New Orleans, LA

CAUSE OF DEATH
Drug Overdose
Age 38

JERRY NOLAN
BORN May 7, 1951
New York, New York

DIED February 25, 1991
New York, New York

CAUSE OF DEATH
Stroke
Age 39

One cannot talk about the origins of punk without mentioning the New York Dolls. This underrated American glam band played an important role in influencing bands as diverse as the Sex Pistols to Mötley Crüe. Unfortunately, they were never able to translate the energy of their live shows into their records or airplay.

In the Beginning . . .

The New York Dolls were formed in 1971 when Johnny Thunders (born John Genzale) asked David Johansen to become the vocalist for the remnants of his band, Actress. They rehearsed through the winter of 1971 in the back of a cycle repair shop and by the end of the year were playing live locally in the SoHo district of New York City. Although they only had recorded a handful of demos, the group, comprised of Johnny Thunders, David Johansen, Sylvain Sylvain, Billy Murcia, and Arthur "Killer" Kane, were invited to open for the Faces on a 1972 British tour. While in London their drummer, Murcia, died from a combination of drugs, alcohol, and drowning in the bath Murcia's girlfriend placed him in to wake him after he passed out. Jerry Nolan joined as their new drummer upon their return to America and they soon recorded their only two records, *The New York Dolls* and *Too Much Too Soon.*

Conflicts between Thunders and Johansen, Kane's descent into alcoholism, and their new manager, Malcolm McLaren, prompted Thunders to quit the band midway through a 1975 tour. Together Nolan and Thunders, along with Walter Lure and Richard Hell, formed a new group, the Heartbreakers. Johansen and Sylvain continued with a brief tour of Japan as the Dolls, disbanding the group in 1976.

After a disastrous tour with the Sex Pistols overseas, Thunders went solo in 1978,

---

The story goes that when they discovered Thunders the morning after he OD'd, he was found clutching his guitar in full rigor mortis. The truth of the matter is that he was found dead in his room, partially under the dresser in room 37 of the St. Peter Guest House in New Orleans. When the coroner brought him out on a stretcher, his body formed a grotesque V shape from the rigor mortis. Fortunately, his room and all the furnishings remain the same and is still available for rent (though it still attracts the same seedy element one would expect in this area of the French Quarter). But sad to say, unlike Janis Joplin's or Gram Parsons's, this death room is not haunted.

gathering a network of followers, including Mick Jones of the Clash. The early eighties were no better for Thunders, seeing the creation and quick demise of numerous bands. Thunders's growing dependence on heroin and cocaine made his performances seem more like a dope fiend's bad trip. Fans soon became more curious to know if he would survive the night than in the quality of any new, albeit rare, material. Amazingly, even in his condition, Thunders was able to pull out a critically acclaimed album, *So Alone*, which contains the classic Thunders cuts, "You Can't Put Your Arms Around a Memory" and a searing cover version of "Pipeline."

In the End . . .

Despite his problems, Johnny's managers and friends managed to keep him afloat, and by the end of the eighties, he'd produced some of his best material. After finishing a tour with his last band, the Oddballs, Johnny left for New Orleans with the intention of forming yet another band that would blend jazz with his ferocious style of rock. The next day, Thunders was found in his hotel room dead from a drug overdose. His fans were left to wonder not why the thiry-eight-year-old had died, but how on earth he had managed to live so long! The coroner's report, released several months after his death, cited toxic levels of methadone and cocaine as the primary cause of death. Jerry Nolan performed a tribute concert for Thunders later that year. "Everywhere I look I see Johnny clones—Poison, Mötley Crüe. I could name a hundred bands that had a Johnny clone in them," remarked Nolan about his good friend and bandmate. Sadly, a few months later Nolan died, at the age of forty, from a stroke after undergoing treatment for pneumonia and meningitis brought on by years of drug abuse.

Mount St. Mary's Cemetery
Flushing, New York

As you drive through the entrance, stay to the left and as the road forks, park in front of the Nicholas Patti mausoleum. Thunders is located behind the mausoleum in Section 9, Grave R-78-82 and his upright stone has the name Nicoletti inscribed on it. Nolan can be found close by in the second section on the left from the entrance. Nolan's permanent address is 24-A-89 and his upright monument rests four spaces from the fence.

The only downside of working with the Dolls was dealing with Johnny Thunders. He was a fuckin' dick, a whiny pain in the ass, and he couldn't play guitar. We used to call him "Johnny Blunders."

roadie Nite Bob

JOSEPH OLIVER
AKA KING OLIVER

BORN May 11, 1885
New Orleans, Louisiana

DIED April 10, 1938
Savannah, Georgia

CAUSE OF DEATH Stroke
Age 52

Before Miles Davis, before Satchmo, even before Bix and Bunny, the very first and one of the greatest practitioners of American jazz was Joseph "King" Oliver.

Armstrong and Oliver.

In the Beginning . . .

Although early records of the time are sketchy, young Joseph Oliver first played professionally at age fifteen in the Storyville section of New Orleans. As a young cornetist in a brass band, Oliver was considered a slow learner of music and supplemented his meager earnings as a musician at night by working as a house servant by day. As musical tastes shifted, Oliver started to abandon the strict confines of the brass band marches for a new style that let him improvise around a common theme or melody. As this new style of music caught favor with the public, so did Oliver's reputation. Oftentimes one would find Oliver and his band marchin' down the streets of New Orleans, playing as if he would blow every house down, pulling customers out of the other nightclubs and leading them in a long procession to his club for the night. By this time he was known simply as King Oliver.

Like all the great musicians from New Orleans, King Oliver left for the bright lights and financial stability of Chicago, where he was the featured cornetist in both Eddie Venson's band and the New Orleans Jazz Band. In 1920 he formed his own band called King Oliver and his Creole Jazz Band. With Lil Hardin (later Louis Armstrong's wife) on piano, Johnny Dodds, and Ed Garland on bass, the Creole Jazz Band was the hottest nightclub act in both Chicago and Los Angeles during most of the 1920's. Only one player could challenge the King's title, and that was a young player out of New Orleans by the name of Louis Armstrong. No stranger to Oliver, he was invited to join the Creole Jazz Band. With no music on the stands and a keen sense of timing, the band tore into one stomp after another every night to the crowd's delight. "Jazzin' Babies Blues," "Tomcat," "Tin Roof Blues," and "King Porter Stomp" would never sound right without Louis and Papa Joe together. With Oliver as the leader, he was a strict taskmaster, allowing no alcohol on the bandstands, with musicians only allowed to drink from a bucket of sugar water, sharing a dipper. With the band performing forty-five-minute versions of "Riverside Blues" and "Mabel's Dream" complete with complex "hot breaks" featuring Armstrong on lead cornet, Chicago's Lincoln Garden came alive every night with dancers and other musicians envious of the hottest band in Chicago.

The few items of King Oliver's left after his death eventually found their way to the Old U.S. Mint on Esplanade Avenue in New Orleans, Louisiana. On display is one of the largest jazz collections strictly devoted to Louisiana's musical heritage, including items from Armstrong, Oliver, Buddy Bolden, Jelly Roll Morton, and dozens of exhibits exploring the early development of jazz.

With the Depression on the horizon and the introduction of sound films that didn't need the services of a house band, Louis Armstrong left for a solo career. That left King Oliver with only scattered one-night stands, not the lucrative two- and three-month engagements that he had been so used to receiving. A move to New York proved to be a mistake with even fewer jobs available for musicians and a quick tour through the South was a complete financial disaster when he found out that his name outside Chicago had no influence.

In the End . . .

If times were bad now, they only got worse for the King. His tour bus failed in Kentucky, forcing the cancellation of his remaining shows. One of his sidemen, saxophonist Paul Barnes, wrote in his diary:

1 November—Having bus trouble. Stay on road all night. Weather cold. Orchestra make bonfire with bus tire. Get help next morning.

7 November—Bus seized by clothing store, finally redeemed too late for Orchestra to make date in Cumberland, Kentucky. Woman proprietor of Southern Hotel hold King Oliver's trumpet for rent.

Shortly afterward King developed a severe case of periodontal disease that caused him to lose all his teeth. Unable to play anymore, Oliver stayed in Savannah in a small boardinghouse room. When Louis Armstrong heard of his plight, he drove to Savannah to find his former employer working at a vegetable stand. Armstrong was so moved that he gave Papa Joe all the money he had on him. When Oliver died four months later of a stroke, one of the founding fathers of American jazz only had $1.60 in his pockets.

When his sister in New York heard of his passing, she traveled down to Savannah to claim his body and bring him back to New York. Unable to provide for a "decent burial," she gave her brother her plot at Woodlawn Cemetery. When it was all over, few appeared at his funeral and there was no money left for a headstone.

Woodlawn Cemetery
The Bronx, New York

Take the Bronx River Parkway north and exit at 233rd Street. From the entrance at 233rd Street, enter the cemetery on West Border Road and continue straight as the road changes to Canna Avenue. After passing Alpine Avenue, continue on to the second asphalt walkway. Walk up this walkway and cross the perpendicular asphalt path, continuing up the grass/gravel path. There is a two-trunk tree on the left. Continue up the path to the last row of tombstones and go left past

the tree. The grave is located in the eighteenth space to the left of the tree in Range 16, which is next to the fence at 211th Street.

As long as I got him with me, he won't be able to get ahead of me. I'll still be king!
Joseph "King" Oliver to Lil Hardin, regarding Louis Armstrong.

ROY ORBISON

BORN April 23, 1936
Vernon, Texas

DIED December 6, 1988
Nashville, Tennessee

CAUSE OF DEATH Heart Attack
Age 52

The Beatles called him "one of the great ones." Elvis called him "his favorite singer." But everybody knew him as Roy Orbison— the man with the trademark Ray-Ban glasses and the haunting falsetto voice.

In the Beginning . . .

Born in the Depression-torn west Texas city of Vernon to Orbie Lee and Nadine Orbison, Roy first picked up the guitar at age six and played the songs of Roy Acuff and Lefty Frizzell. Moving from Vernon to Fort Worth, the Orbison family finally settled in Wink, Texas, where Roy grew up and went to high school. An awkward kid with thick glasses, Roy failed in sports and on the social scene. This made him all the more determined as he held on to his music and was involved in high school band, glee club, and the chorus. By age sixteen, Orbison had his first band, the Wink Westerners, and played the hits of Hank Williams, Webb Pierce, and Lefty Frizzell throughout west Texas. In another town about an hour away, Buddy Holly was hosting his own show and Waylon Jennings was also playing around Texas. By 1954 they ocassionally played together on the same bill and often traveled to see one another's shows.

The big break came when Roy cut his first record, "Ooby Dooby," with Norman Petty (Buddy Holly's producer). Eventually Sam Phillips of Sun Records heard the record and signed on Roy and his new band, the Teen Kings. Roy's tenure with Sun Records proved to be a mixed blessing. On the same roster was Carl Perkins, Jerry Lee Lewis, Johnny Cash, and of course Elvis; Roy was never accorded the same attention as the others. When "Ooby Dooby" was recut and released nationally, it broke into *Billboard*'s Top 100, eventually selling over 250,000 copies. A minor hit compared to the number one song "Heartbreak Hotel" and the fact that Elvis had sold over ten million records in 1957 alone.

Roy spent the next couple years on the road with Eddie Cochran, Gene Vincent, Johnny Cash, Jerry Lee Lewis, and Buddy Holly. Tired from the lack of promotion at Sun Records, Roy signed with Acuff-Rose of Nashville and quickly had a hit with "Claudette" as recorded by the Everly Brothers (a song about Roy's soon-to-be-wife). In 1960 he struck gold with "Only the Lonely,'" a song that both Elvis and the Everly Brothers had turned down. The song also was the beginning of a new trend in rock 'n' roll—the melodic ballad. Throughout the sixties the hits kept coming with "Oh Pretty Woman," "Crying," and "Blue Angel." And Orbison was constantly touring with everyone from Patsy Cline to the Rolling Stones, from the Beatles to the Beach Boys in the U.S., Europe, and Australia.

The Roy Orbison Museum in Wink, Texas, gives a whole new meaning to the phrase "lack of adequate funding." With 45s nailed to the wall of this one-room building, the posters, collection of 8-tracks, and newspaper clippings are a bit underwhelming. Be sure to visit in June for the festival dedicated to the memory of Orbison that features a flea market and a "Pretty Woman" beauty pageant.

Orbison's professional and personal life took a turn for the worse when he lost his wife in a motorcycle accident in 1966. Four years later, after a string of album flops, he flew to England for a European tour. While on the road he was called back home after an explosion at his home in Nashville claimed the lives of his two eldest sons. Three years later his brother, Grady Lee, died when his car left the twisting road that led to Roy's new home.

In the End . . .

The 1980s were great for Roy's career, but took a terrible toll on his health. Despite a heart bypass operation, Roy continued to tour heavily and was basking in the light of his peers' recognition, namely his induction into the Rock and Roll Hall of Fame. Newly married, he and his new family moved to the Hollywood enclave of Malibu Beach, California, where he appeared on *Lifestyles of the Rich and Famous*. In 1987 he teamed up with Tom Petty, Bob Dylan, George Harrison, and Jeff Lynne (of ELO) to record *The Traveling Wilburys, Part I*. The album was cited by *Rolling Stone* magazine as one of the Top 100 albums of the decade. It would be the last album released in his lifetime.

After a concert in Ohio and three days before a video shoot in London for the Traveling Wilburys, Roy stopped in Nashville to rest and visit with daughter, Nadine, and his only surviving son with first wife, Claudette, Wesley. On the evening of December 6, 1988, Roy went to use the bathroom. After thirty minutes, Wesley forced the door open only to find his father's lifeless body leaning against the door. Despite resuscitation efforts at the home, Roy Orbison was pronounced dead of a massive heart attack.

Westwood Memorial Park
Los Angeles, California

There were two memorial services after his death. One was held in Hendersonville, Tennessee, with his close family, friends, and fellow musicians. The other service was in California and featured many from Hollywood society, but none of Roy's friends. The Tennessee memorial was open to the public while the Hollywood services were strictly a closed affair. None of the family members were invited by his new wife, Barbara, to the West Coast services.

Nine days after his untimely death at age fifty-two, he was laid to rest, not in the Orbison family plot in Tennessee, but rather in one of the premier cemeteries in Beverly Hills. As you enter the cemetery, drive through the gates and park near the office. Between the office and the gate is a large tree fifty feet from the road in the park area. From the tree, opposite the road, look for the Frank Wright Tuttle marker. Orbison is buried just above Tuttle's bronze marker in an unmarked plot.

At a New Year's dance in 1954 we had to play through the actual time of midnight and when someone requested "Shake, Rattle, and Roll," we struck up on it. By the time we were finished I was fully converted.

Roy Orbison, discussing his conversion to rock 'n' roll.

CHARLIE PARKER

BORN August 29, 1920
Kansas City, Kansas

DIED March 12, 1955
New York City, New York

CAUSE OF DEATH Heart Failure
Age 34

While the audiences were not always able to comprehend what he was playing, Charlie Parker was a living legend to his colleagues. Avoiding standard phrasing, familiar keys, and chord progressions, Bird experimented with passing tones and raised ninths and thirteenths—the more adventurous the better. To the indifference of the masses, pure genius and innovation was always passed over for the familiar. Unlike many artists who have passed on before and since the death of the Bird, deification did not begin with his passing. But despite his legendary status, Charlie Parker invariably demurred: "It's just music. It's trying to play clean and looking for the pretty notes."

In the Beginning . . .

Parker was born and raised in one of the richest musical communities of his time—Kansas City. From 1920 to the present, Kansas City has played host to a variety of swing, folk, and jazz musicians and influences. If Parker was destined to become a legendary musician, there were few early signs. Raised by his mother, Addie Parker, Charlie began skipping school until his freshman year, when he enrolled in the school's marching band.

From the numerous stories involving false starts and career rejection from his peers, it is known that by 1937 Parker was fast becoming known to those in the Kansas City music scene. With his strong presence and a ready smile, in three years' time Parker became an immensely talented jazz musician with a decidedly disheveled look. Considered by his musician peers as an elder statesman, at age twenty-two Parker looked and acted more mature than his age.

Returning to Kansas City after a move to New York, Parker was on the road with the Jay McShann Orchestra in 1940 when the driver hit two farm chickens. Stopping, Parker jumped out and took the two birds to the roadhouse where they were staying. Amused by his unusual request to serve the chickens for dinner, the owner of the roadhouse gave Parker the name Yardbird. Later the name was shortened to just Bird.

Ailing, tired, and moving too fast, Bird was nonetheless a prime force in modern jazz, playing alongside Billy Eckstine, Thelonious Monk, Bud Powell, and Dizzy Gillespie. By 1944 Bird and Dizzy ruled Fifty-second Street in New York with their version of the new jazz music—bebop. Not once since the pairing of King Oliver and Louis Armstrong has the music world seen such a powerfully dynamic matching of talent. However, Parker continually missed more and more gigs, causing Dizzy to carry the show. Within two years heroin completely dominated his life and Parker was arrested and found guilty of

The Kansas City Jazz Museum contains more than eight thousand artifacts and fifteen hundred photographs, with emphasis on the contributions of Louis Armstrong, Ella Fitzgerald, Duke Ellington, and of course Charlie Parker. One of the prize artifacts in their collection is the saxophone once played by Parker, valued at over $150,000. Just outside the museum at the corner of Eighteenth Street and Vine is a sculpture in Parker's honor.

In New York City, Parker's home from 1950 to 1954 is now on the National Register of Historic Places. Located at 151 Avenue B, Parker occupied the ground floor of this Gothic Revival-style rowhouse along with his wife and three children.

"disturbing the peace" and was incarcerated for the next six months at the [...] State Hospital.

Upon his return to New York, the Parker-Gillespie relationship became strained. Parker's more serious endeavors were generally undertaken with Miles Davis and drummer Max Roach. Producing some of his greatest work with the Dial and Savoy labels in 1947, Bird began injecting smack again. He would continue the habit until the day he died.

In the End . . .

The year 1948 saw the further decline of a living legend. The death of his daughter and the parting of Miles and Max, coupled with the breakup of his marriage, all took their toll. Parker was often seen sleeping in taxis as they drove him around town. Considered unreliable by his fellow musicians, he was reduced to paying other people so he could play on their records. Bird's last concert was at Birdland, the very club named after him. Despite being banned, the management invited him back for a chance to redeem himself. Billed as the Charlie Parker All Stars, he arrived thirty minutes late, incapacitated by drink, along with his piano player, Bud Powell (who was also incapacitated). The gig was going badly when Bird started abusing Powell between songs. Powell swung around on the piano stool and shouted, "What key, motherfucker?" "The key of S for shit," shouted back Parker. Powell walked out in the middle of the set, as did most of the patrons.

In the winter of 1955 the Bird paid a visit to the Baroness Pannonica de Koenigswater at the elegant Stanhope Hotel on Fifth Avenue. She took a liking to Parker and offered her suite as a sanctuary from the grinding discomfort of his daily existence. As he walked in the room he collapsed. A doctor was summoned and he asked the legendary jazz figure if he drank. "Well, Doc, just an occasional glass of sherry before dinner," he replied. Parker stayed overnight on doctor's orders and was watching *The Tommy Dorsey Show*. Suddenly his throat filled with blood, caused by his severe bleeding ulcers, and he choked to death as Dorsey played "Maria."

Lincoln Cemetery
Kansas City, Kansas

Upon entering the cemetery, take the first road to the left and the grave is located about 150 feet behind the office, surrounded by a six-inch cement "wall" next to the road. Despite rumors to the contrary, Parker's grave is not going to be moved to the Kansas City Jazz Museum.

GRAM PARSONS

BORN November 5, 1946
Winter Haven, Florida

DIED September 19, 1973
Joshua Tree, California

CAUSE OF DEATH Drug Overdose
Age 26

In marked contrast to other rock musicians who adopted country instrumentation and styles, Parsons, in solo albums and his work with the Flying Burrito Brothers, Emmylou Harris, and the Byrds, melded the power of rock 'n' roll with the passion and sadness of country western music. Commercially unsuccessful, Parsons's various recordings helped shape the vision of such hugely successful artists as the Eagles, Elvis Costello, and the Rolling Stones, whose *Exile on Main Street* was heavily influenced by Parsons's wistful country spirit.

In the Beginning . . .

Born Ingram Connor III, he spent his youth in Waycross, Georgia, in the relative comfort of the Snively orange juice dynasty. Moving to Florida in his early teens, Gram joined his first working band, the Pacers, at fourteen. Within a year, he teamed up with Jim Stafford (of "Spiders and Snakes" fame) in the Legends, covering primarily Elvis, Ray Charles, Duane Eddy, and the Ventures material at nightclubs and dances within a hundred miles of Winter Haven, Florida.

After a brief stop at Harvard (he was enrolled, but despite popular myth, never attended a single class), Parsons moved to New York with the International Submarine Band. Despite plenty of work at hip sixties night spots such as Ondine's, their mix of R&B with country was getting mixed ("redneck shit-kickin' hicks") reviews. Going nowhere fast, the band moved to Los Angeles. Establishing digs near Laurel Canyon (off Sunset Boulevard), Parsons wasted no time immersing the band into the Los Angeles/Everly Brothers/Stone Pony/Rick Nelson-country-rock music scene. With help from pedal steel guitarist, J. D. Maness, then-session guitarist Glen Campbell, and bassist Chris Ethridge, Gram recorded *Safe at Home.* A solid C&W effort with rock 'n' roll attitude, the 1968 release garnered rave reviews. Unfortunately, the album went nowhere.

After a brief three-month stint with the Byrds, Parsons pulled together the Flying Burrito Brothers. It was during this time that Parsons hooked up with Keith Richards and Mick Jagger and became an influential part of the *Let It Bleed* and *Beggar's Banquet* albums. While the Stones' albums took off, the FBB albums failed to sell over fifty thousand copies. The Stones connection did, however, help the FBB connect with their largest audience ever—they played as the opening act in the final concert of the Stones's 1969 tour at Altamont, California, the infamous concert in which the Hell's Angels stabbed to death a young man in the audience, and simultaneously marked the end of the sixties.

━━● The Country Music Hall of Fame in Nashville, Tennessee, has a great display of one of Parsons's custom-tailored Nudie suits (complete with hand-stiched marijuana leaves) and his guitar. And much like Janis Joplin's final hotel room, room 8 of the Joshua Tree Inn (see right) is haunted with the spirit of Parsons. The room, aside from the bed, is exactly as it was the day he was found dead.

After taking a year off in England, Parsons moved back to L.A. and with the help of Elvis sidemen Glen Hardin, James Burton, and Ronnie Tutt, along with newcomer Emmylou Harris, he cut his first solo album, *G.P.* Due to self-destructive alcohol and drug abuse, as well as an underrehearsed band, *G.P.*'s touring efforts were dismal in 1973. After losing several close friends and watching his house burn to the ground, Gram was forced to focus on his music and his life and his follow-up album, *Grievous Angel*, proved to be the highlight of his musical career.

In the End . . .

On September 17, 1973, Parsons headed east of L.A. and booked himself and three friends into the Joshua Tree Inn. After a full day of alcohol and self-medication, the events of Tuesday afternoon have become a mixture of myth and reality. What is known is that Parsons was left alone in his motel room only to be discovered around 11:00 P.M. to have died of, according to the official death certificate, "drug toxicity, days, due to multiple drug use, weeks."

As news of his death spread, Bob Parsons (Gram's stepfather) claimed the body in the mistaken notion that Louisiana law would allow him to claim the estate. Knowing that Parsons's wish was to have his remains "released" at Joshua Tree, road manager Phil Kaufman and friend Michael Mortin borrowed a friend's hearse station wagon and bluffed their way into taking possession of Parsons's coffin. Simultaneously toasting and cursing their "passenger," they drove to Joshua Tree National Park to Cap Rock. Kaufman then placed a can of beer in the coffin, doused the body with gasoline, and lit a match. They said you could see the flames from five miles away.

Cap Rock
Joshua Tree, California

Located within the Joshua Tree National Park, park in the Cap Rock campground. Walk around the left side of Cap Rock for about two hundred feet. The rock tablet marking the site where Parsons's coffin was burned is located in the northwest corner, two hundred feet from the highway.

Garden of Memories Cemetery
New Orleans, Louisiana

Drive through the entrance gates and drive past the Veterans Memorial and follow the road around, staying to the right. When you make a hard left look to your right for a large statue two hundred feet from the road. Park on the right and his small bronze marker is in Section K, R-12-11-3, ten rows from the road to the left of the statue near the oak tree.

Phil kidnapped his coffin from the airport at Los Angeles and burned it in the desert. My first thought was that I wished I could have been there, because I never got a chance to say goodbye to Gram. I respect Phil for doing what he did. It was an act of love and friendship.

Emmylou Harris

JOE PASS

JOE PASS
MEDITATION
Solo Guitar

BORN January 13, 1929
New Brunswick, New Jersey

DIED May 23, 1994
Los Angeles, California

CAUSE OF DEATH Liver Cancer
Age 65

In the last fifty years, few have come to epitomize the image of the jazz guitarist as completely as Joe Pass. As a soloist, Pass redefined the instrument, weaving spontaneous chordal sequences, walking bass lines, and single notes into colorful musical textures. It is safe to say that Joe Pass was the most versatile, well-rounded, mainstream guitar player in the history of jazz.

In the Beginning . . .

Joseph Anthony Jacobi Passalaqua received his first guitar, a seventeen-dollar Harmony steel-string flat top, at age nine. From the very first day, he practiced six hours a day at the insistence of his stern father. At the age of fifteen, Pass dropped out of high school and began working jazz clubs in New York City. Enthralled with the bebop music and lifestyles of Charlie Parker, Dizzy Gillespie, and Bud Powell, Pass began his descent into heroin addiction.

During the early 1950s, Pass was busted for drug use and spent four years at the U.S. Public Health Service Hospital in Fort Worth, Texas. Upon his release he made his way back to Las Vegas and the lounge circuit. Unfortunately, along with his return to music, Pass returned to heavy drug use. He was in such bad shape that he was stealing instruments out of the lounges and pawning them for cash. Pass was again arrested in Sacramento for selling pawn tickets of the stolen merchandise.

At age thirty-one, with no recordings, no guitar, and no money, Pass entered a rehab program in Southern California. Concentrating on staying clean, Pass slowly emerged from his self-imposed "retirement" and began to take selected studio dates with artists as diverse as Julie London and Frank Sinatra. He reemerged as a solo artist, drug free, in 1962 with his first album, *Sounds of Synanon.* By 1963 he left rehab drug free, never to return.

From his new base of operations, he began to work with mostly West Coast artists including Bud Shank, Bobby Troup, Les McCann, and a variety of others. For two years he almost exclusively toured with pianist George Shearing. During a review jazz critic Leonard Feather called Pass "the most exciting new talent on jazz guitar to emerge since Wes Montgomery came to prominence in the 1950s." But it wasn't until the 1970s, when Pass signed with Pablo Records, that the jazz legend came into international prominence. From the mid-1970s on, Pass recorded more extensively than any other guitarist at that

SALARMY MT PLEASANT
THRIFT
261 12TH AVE E
VANCOUVER   BC

CARD   * * * * * * * * * * * *7997
CARD TYPE   INTERAC
ACCOUNT TYPE
               FLASH DEFAULT
DATE   2021/06/10
TIME   8470 11:44:07
INVOICE #   17589
RECEIPT NUMBER
  H84144413-001-001-232-0

PURCHASE
TOTAL

            $3.58

Interac
A0000002771010
CEB2579A9C4E68DA
8080008000-

APPROVED
AUTH# 422480   00-001
THANK YOU

       CARDHOLDER COPY

time. He produced sixteen albums under his own name, as well as accompanying Duke Ellington, Count Basie, Benny Goodman, Sarah Vaughan, Oscar Peterson, and of course, Ella Fitzgerald. It was with Ella that Pass received his greatest recognition. One night, backstage at Carnegie Hall, Pass knocked on Ella's dressing-room door and inquired about the songs they would be performing. With the titles and the keys written on a matchbook, When asked after the concert where it was. Pass replied, "I don't know. I never looked at it."

In the End . . .

As one of the most highly acclaimed modern jazz guitarists, Pass further expanded his fan base with regular trips overseas. He made a yearly pilgrimage to the North Sea Jazz Festival in The Hague in Europe, as well as world-renowned events in Canada, Japan, and the U.S. And while he remained a phenomenal solo guitarist, covering jazz standards as well as new material, Pass never played it safe. His projects became as diverse as a recording date with the Vienna String Quartet or a two-week string of gigs with Danish bassist Niels-Henning Orsted Pedersen.

In the winter of 1992, it was discovered that Joe was suffering from liver cancer. After initially responding to treatment, his health began to decline. He played his last concert at a small jazz club in Los Angeles with longtime friend John Pisano. After their final number, Joe looked at John with a tear in his eye and said, "I can't play anymore."

Three weeks later with his wife, daughter, and son by his side, the reigning jazz guitar virtuoso for the last twenty years died at the USC-Norris Comprehensive Cancer Center.

Resurrection Cemetery
Piscataway, New Jersey

After a memorial service in Los Angeles, Pass's body was flown east for interment in the Passalaqua family plot at Resurrection Cemetery. As you enter the main gate to the cemetery turn left on St. Patrick, then right on St. Paul. With Section 8 on your left, drive five hundred feet to the two private crypts directly behind the large mausoleum complex. Park on the right at the elaborate Rosamilia monument and by the second monument off the road on the left rests the jazz giant.

Drugs didn't help me to play. All it did was to hang me up for about fifteen years.

Joe Pass

JACO PASTORIUS

BORN December 1, 1951
Norristown, Pennsylvannia

DIED September 21, 1987
Fort Lauderdale, Florida

CAUSE OF DEATH Murdered
Age 35

If there was one thing that characterized Jaco Pastorius's music, it was intensity. That intensity, combined with his pioneering techniques on the electric bass, his manic finger speed, and his talent for composing, earned Pastorius the title Greatest Bass Player in the World. For those who question the title, one only need listen to his magic touch on "Stella by Starlight," "Cantaloupe Island," "Fannie Mae," or the entire Weather Report album *Heavy Weather*. Unfortunately, intensity was replaced by drugs, alcohol, and mental illness, resulting in a sudden and tragic end to the music.

In the Beginning . . .

The son of renowned jazz drummer Jack Pastorius, John was born in Norristown, Pennsylvania, in the early 1950s. As the result of a divorce, "Jacko" (as he was then known), along with his two younger brothers, moved to south Florida in the late fifties. An avid sportsman as well as musician, Pastorius was originally a drummer when he broke his wrist in a football game. By age fifteen he had switched to bass and was playing with several bands in the Fort Lauderdale area.

At nineteen he got his first taste of stardom when he joined the C.C. Riders band. After nine months he dropped out of the band and went back to Florida. While most people didn't want to deal with his huge ego, Pastorius befriended Bobby Colomby of Blood, Sweat and Tears. Teaching bass part-time at the University of Miami, Pastorius was introduced through Colomby to several executives from Epic Records. In the back of a small New York City bar, the executives from the record company were absolutely floored at his style and technique. So convinced that they were in the presence of the world's greatest bass player, they offered him a record deal. In the era of disco and leisure suits, it was highly unusual for an unknown Florida bass player to land a recording contract. After the release of his highly acclaimed solo album, *Jaco Pastorius*, Pastorius was working and recording with Joni Mitchell, Pat Metheny, Al Di Meola, Ian Hunter, and Weather Report. Pastorius was sitting on top of the world.

The period from 1976 to 1982 was a whirlwind of activity for Pastorius. He toured with Blood, Sweat and Tears, was nominated for two Grammy Awards for his solo album, and toured with keyboardist Herbie Hancock. He joined jazz fusion group Weather Report, where Pastorius achieved his greatest acclaim, as well as another Grammy nomination for *Heavy Weather*.

During his final year with Weather Report, Pastorius's dark side began to emerge. He had, by all accounts, always been somewhat eccentric and egotistical. However, things were starting to get out of control. During the tour with his new Word of Mouth band, he started painting his face with black markers and appearing in public naked. At the

There are dozens of unreleased gems from Jaco Pastorius's archives; when they will be shown to the public is just a question of determining who owns what. One of the odder albums waiting to see the light of day is a full album of material that he recorded yet signed the rights of over to a fan (in exchange for posting his bail in the late 1980s).

1983 Playboy Jazz Festival he was physically removed from the stage for his odd behavior. In 1984, Pastorius was thrown out of the New York offices of Blue Note Records for violent behavior.

After six weeks of treatment at the psychiatric ward of Bellevue Hospital in New York, Pastorius was released. He headed back to Fort Lauderdale to resume his music career from ground zero after a short stay in San Francisco. But after just two short months Pastorius's mood turned dark again. He stopped his regular routine of exercising and rehearsing, and began drinking heavily. By the summer of 1987 he was out of control—drunk, sleeping in the streets, panhandling, and refusing all offers to help.

In the End . . .

The end came suddenly during the early morning hours of September 12, 1987. After being evicted earlier from a Santana concert for trying to get onstage, Pastorius appeared at the Midnight Bottle Club in Fort Lauderdale. Barred from the seedy, members-only club, Pastorius tried to kick down the door to gain entrance. The manager, Luc Havan, heard the commotion and went outside. Minutes later, the Greatest Bass Player in the World lay facedown in a pool of his own blood, his skull fractured, one eye ruptured, and nearly every bone in his face broken. When the police arrived, Havan stated that Pastorius must have fallen down.

Pastorius was taken to Broward General Medical Center, where he lingered in a coma. Then, quite unexpectedly, seven days after he was admitted, a blood vessel burst in his brain. Two days later, with no brain activity, he died quietly in his father's arms.

Three months after his death, Luc Havan was finally charged with second-degree murder in the death of Jaco Pastorius. A year later he pleaded guilty to the lesser charge of manslaughter. Sentenced to twenty-two months in prison, he spent less than four months behind bars before he was released for "good behavior."

Our Lady Queen of Heaven Cemetery
Fort Lauderdale, Florida
Drive through the gates and turn right at the end of Section A. Continue driving around the side of the cemetery until you can see the rear of the mausoleum. As you walk toward the mausoleum, walk past the hedges and look for the Mother of Mary statue on the Garaventa grave. Pastorius is buried in Section L, Block 219, Grave 8, one row in front of the statue, five rows from the hedges.

It's tough when a guy sets out to join the ranks of the jazz legends that completely fucked up their lives, but Jaco seemed determined to follow [in] the path of guys like Bird. It's so sad. I mean, for a creative instrumental musician to have that much impact.

Peter Erskine

CHARLEY PATTON

BORN April 1891
Edwards, Mississippi

DIED April 28, 1934
Indianola, Mississippi

CAUSE OF DEATH Heart Disease
Age 43

Musically incredible, small in stature, and at times personally rude, Charley Patton was, nevertheless, the most influential artist among singers of the first blues generation. Time has not diminished his celebrity, and his place in history has reached mythical proportions among blues devotees.

In the Beginning . . .

Little is known of Patton's early life. He moved from the hill country of Edwards, Mississippi, to the Dockery plantation near Ruleville, where his family rented land and farmed and where he spent much of his life. It was here that Patton encountered Henry Sloan, one of the earliest (yet unrecorded) Delta bluesmen. By 1915, Patton was regarded as the Delta's most popular bluesman. With fellow guitarist Willie Brown he hoboed around the South playing picnics, juke joints, and levee camps. He gained fame for his loud, brilliant, and inventive guitar style, accentuated by an extraordinary sense of rhythm. He was far from passive when performing for a live audience. It was not uncommon for him to play the guitar behind his back, between his knees, or pounding the back like a drum.

One of the first blues artists to record, Patton first came to the attention of Henry Speir, a Jackson, Mississippi, record store owner. Speir contacted Paramount Records and set up a recording session for Patton in Indiana. The subsequent release of "Pony Blues" followed with "Banty Rooster Blues" introduced his resonant bellow and richly accented percussive guitar style. The records sold well and he made twenty-one singles in all between 1929 and 1930. Patton's third and final recording session for Paramount included Willie Brown and future blues legend Son House.

The great thing about being a Charley Patton record collector is that you have to know absolutely nothing about Charley Patton. So if you see "Pea Vine Blues," "Green River Blues," "Some Happy Day," or any other original seventy-eight single on Paramount or Vocalian, buy it. Because any of those records (and dozens more) are worth in excess of five hundred dollars per single.

Though he was not the first recorded blues artist, he was the first blues celebrity. He drank, smoked, cursed excessively, was easily provoked, and was able to consume huge quantities of food and alcohol in one sitting (often with a woman under each arm). He was married a total of eight times and had several other common-law wives. He was jailed at least once and traveled most of his forty-plus years. Patton was superstitious and experimented with religion, and people in Indianola still remember him today as a violent and quarrelsome individual, cocky and belligerent, and a womanizing illiterate.

No birth certificate has been found, and very little of Charley Patton's possessions remain. Only one known photograph of the bluesman (see above), his original death certificate, six out of his eight marriage records, and one daughter have survived through the years. No guitars, homes, or autographs are known to exist.

Sleepy John Estes once remarked that Patton was the loudest blues singer he had ever heard and, in an often-told story, talked about Patton's ability to sing at an outdoor dance and have patrons hear the words five hundred yards away. And while Patton was only five feet tall and weighed less than 140 pounds, his high-energy singing style made him sound like a man twice his size. It has been said that he was kicked off many plantations during harvest season because he caused too many workmen to stop their work to listen to the bluesman.

In the End . . .

From 1930, Patton led a more settled life in Holly Ridge by staying off the road and playing for local functions. Despite a heart condition, Patton traveled to New York with his eighth wife and blues singer, Bertha Lee, and completed twenty-six songs for Vocalion in 1934. The session did not go well and is considered by blues historians to be his least fruitful.

During his final days, heart disease began to take its toll, as Patton was having trouble walking and could only talk in shallow whispers. Where he died is still in dispute today. The death certificate shows that he died at a relative's house at 350 Heathman Street in Indianola (the house is no longer standing). Other relatives say he died in his home just across the street from the cemetery in Holly Ridge (also torn down). Either place, the end result was still the same.

New Jeruselum Churchyard Cemetery
Holly Ridge, Mississippi

Originally called Longswitch Cemetery, the unmarked cemetery is located to the right of the H.R. Gin Company on Holly Ridge Road. Patton is buried in the back, and his three-foot above-ground marker is the one closest to the company property, roughly two hundred feet from the road on the left. Please note that his marker does not represent his final resting place. His actual gravesite is unknown and like many forgotten Mississippi bluesman, his marker was just placed randomly in the cemetery.

Charley would lie about his love for any female listener, and he was tight with his money.

bluesman Son House

ELVIS PRESLEY

BORN January 8, 1935
Tupelo, Mississippi

DIED August 16, 1977
Memphis, Tennessee

CAUSE OF DEATH Heart Failure
Age 42

From that very first song at Sam Phillips's Sun Records, Elvis Presley was the complete embodiment of rock 'n' roll music. Blessed with incredible good looks, natural rhythm, and a voice that inspired such feelings that (in the words of Carl Perkins) he "could [just] clear his throat and have ten thousand people scream," Presley became the undisputed King of Rock 'n' Roll despite surrounding himself with sycophants, bad management, and the drugs that overtook his life in the end.

In the Beginning . . .

Born in a simple two-room shack in Tupelo, Mississippi, Elvis Aaron Presley was the surviving twin of Vernon and Gladys Presley. Moving from house to house within Tupelo, the Presleys survived day to day with Vernon working odd jobs as they came. At the age of ten, Elvis appeared on his first radio broadcast and sang "Old Shep" at the Mississippi-Alabama State Fair. Broadcast live over WELO radio, Elvis took second prize, which was five dollars and all the rides for free.

The following year Gladys took her only son to Tupelo Hardware, where she purchased the future King of Rock 'n' Roll his first guitar for $12.95. Shortly after the Presley family moved to Memphis in search of work and a better life. Upon graduation from high school Elvis worked odd jobs, taking classes at night to become an electrician. In the summer of 1954, Sam Phillips called the young singer into his studio to record the song "Without You." Disappointed, Phillips tried a number of different songs and styles, but nothing really clicked until a sped-up version of Arthur Crudup's "That's Alright, Mama" backed by Bill Monroe's "Blue Moon of

Thought lost forever, the original acetate that Elvis cut at the Memphis Recording Service for four dollars was purchased in 1993 by collector Sean O'Neal after answering a newspaper ad. "I'll Never Stand In Your Way" and "It Wouldn't Be the Same Without You" are the very first songs Elvis recorded and the Elvis Presley estate is doing everything in their power to prevent its release to the public.

Kentucky" became the first of five smash hit singles for the Sun label. Within two short years Elvis Presley would become the biggest international recording star the world has ever seen.

After a brief interruption with army duty in Germany, Elvis returned to the States in 1960. Managed by the inept Colonel Tom Parker, Elvis walked through thirty-three generally forgettable movies as the British Invasion led by the Beatles swept the nation. Despite

He may have died with only one million dollars in his bank account, but today Elvis Presley Enterprises is a one hundred million-dollar industry that centers around Graceland in Memphis, Tennessee. With over 700,000 visitors a year, the Presley "estate" is one of the most visited homes in the nation (and at twenty dollar a head just for the home tour, one of the most expensive). For an extra five dollars you can tour the two private jets in the Presley fleet, the *Lisa Marie* and the *Hound Dog II.* And for a mere six dollars you can continue the tour at the Automobile Museum, which includes Presley's collection of fine cars, including the 1956 Lincoln Continental that Priscilla drove to high school, the famous 1956 pink Cadillac Fleetwood, and the custom-made screaming purple Cadillac Eldorado. Naturally, your tour is greatly enhanced if you time your visit during death week in August, when every tour is packed with Elvis imitators from around the world.

the infamous 1968 Comeback Special, the Beatles, the Beach Boys, Jimi Hendrix, the Doors, and others succeeded in making Presley an anachronism before the King turned thirty. Still, Elvis's fans remained loyal, helping push record sales to over 200 million albums, with fourteen Grammy Award nominations (three actual wins), and hundreds of sold-out concerts in the U.S. (Elvis never toured overseas due to Parker's potential immigration problems). By 1970, Elvis was the forgotten icon, suffocated by the demands of stardom and drug dependency.

In the End . . .

Beginning in late 1976, Elvis literally cut himself off from the rest of the world. Staying in his upstairs bedroom at Graceland with the black curtains closed tight behind the aluminum foil-covered windows, Elvis continued to gain weight as his drug abuse continued unabated. Rehospitalized the following April for "exhaustion," his return to the stage in May was ill advised as fans began to boo the once-thin heartthrob. Forgetting lyrics, shaking uncontrollably, stumbling around the stage, and panting between songs, his fans, the band, and friends continued to watch his decline from the sidelines.

At 5:00 in the morning of August 16, Elvis was swatting at balls in the racquetball court behind Graceland before retiring upstairs to sleep for the rest of the day. After three hours and multiple drug injections to help him sleep, Elvis grabbed some reading material and closed the door to the bathroom. At 2:30 that afternoon girlfriend Ginger Alden went to check on the King. As she opened the door she saw the King's contorted body lying face-down, buttocks pointed skyward with his feet tucked behind him, bloated, blue, cold, and very much dead.

Graceland
Memphis, Tennessee

Originally buried at Forest Hills Cemetery in Memphis (the estate still owns the original tomb in the mausoleum in the back of the cemetery), Presley was moved to Graceland in the middle of the night after an attempt to steal the coffin and other security issues became a problem. He is buried next to the swimming pool, which you'll see at the end of the tour, with his mother, father, and grandmother, Minnie Mae Presley.

Mr. Presley has no discernible singing ability. His specialty is rhythm songs, which he renders in an undistinguished whine; his phrasing consists of the stereotyped variations that go with a beginner's aria in a bathtub. For the ear he is an unutterable bore.

From a 1956 *New York Times* review

Bill Black
September 17, 1926—October 21, 1965

When Elvis cut his first ground-breaking single "That's All Right, Mama" he was backed by Sun Studio musicians Scotty Moore on guitar and Bill Black on bass. With D. J. Fontana later added as drummer, the four hit the road and played at every dancehall, fairground, and club that manager Tom Parker could book. But what could have been the first great rock 'n' roll band fell apart when Parker paid and treated the backing musicians as just hired help. They left Elvis in 1959 with Black releasing his first single that same year. As the Bill Black Combo he released twenty-two singles, fourteen albums, and sold over five million records before succumbing to a brain tumor. Black was buried in Section 15 at Forest Hills Cemetery in Memphis. As you enter the cemetery, stay to the left, drive over the bridge, turn left at the circle and left again at the intersection of Sections 8, 9, and 19. Park behind the single-story mausoleum (the very same one that Elvis would be placed in twelve years later), and walk to the center of Section 15. Look for the Morrison marker and Black is buried ten feet away.

Jesse Garon Presley
January 8, 1935—January 8, 1935

Elvis's twin brother died at birth and was buried in an unmarked grave at Priceville Baptist Cemetery in Tupelo. Don't ask cemetery workers where he is buried—they won't tell you as his grave remains unmarked.

When the Presley estate sold a large chunk of Elvis memorabilia at auction, a number of privately held museums began to open around the country. Naturally, both the Rock and Roll Hall of Fame and the Country Hall of Fame and Museum both pay tribute to the King through their collections and temporary loans through the Presley estate. Here are three more collections that I have personally visited out of the dozens in operation:

Elvis Presley Birthplace and Museum
Tupelo, Mississippi

Built by Vernon Presley for only $180, his birthplace has been nicely restored. Though it is worth the one dollar to walk through the small home, none of the furniture is authentic. Next to the home is the Elvis Presley Museum, which is really just the personal collection of Janelle McComb, who knew Elvis for a number of years. The highlight seems to be a pair of Holiday Inn towels that Elvis used when he was on tour in the sixties. The remaining collection is just records, photos, and some items of clothing that have no descriptions.

Elvis Presley Museum
Kissimmee, Florida

Located in Old Town just outside Disney World, this museum's collection highlight seems to be a pair of bell-bottom pajamas, a gold lamé jumpsuit, and a replica of the dining room at Graceland amid lots of cars and really bad velvet murals.

Elvis-a-Rama Museum
Las Vegas, Nevada

If you're going to have an Elvis museum, then spend three million dollars on memorabilia and do it right. Lots of cars, jumpsuits, and over two hundred personal items of the King. Definitely worth the $7.50 price of admission.

THE FAT ELVIS PRIMER
ELEVEN THINGS YOU REALLY DIDN'T WANT TO KNOW ABOUT THE KING

1. On the day Elvis died, his estate was only worth about seven million dollars (with one million dollars of that in his checking account). Conversely, John Lennon, who recorded less often, toured less than Elvis, and split his earnings four ways, was worth about two hundred million.

2. Manager Colonel Tom Parker received 50 percent of the gross proceeds of all income derived from Elvis. In addition, the William Morris Agency received another 10 percent (the industry standard is 10 percent to 20 percent total for representation). Add to that the contract that Parker negotiated with RCA Records on behalf of Elvis, which only paid the singer five cents per album. Adding insult to injury, father and financial manager Vernon Presley allowed the IRS to calculate Elvis's tax returns each year. All in all, Elvis only saw a small fraction of the estimated four billion dollars in sales he generated during his lifetime.

3. On the day he died, Elvis was an exhausted, puffy 350-pound caricature of his former self who suffered from an enlarged heart, glaucoma, hypertension, chronic water retention, severe constipation, and a twenty-year dependency on prescription drugs.

4. All of the jumpsuits worn by Elvis during his bloated Las Vegas days on display at Graceland have had five to fifteen inches taken in along the waistband (ostensibly to make room in the display cases for other items).

5. By 1970, Elvis was spending over five hundred thousand dollars a year on prescription drugs supplied by over a hundred physicians and pharmacists. His "ailments" were treated with a wealth of drugs, including Placydil, valmid, Valium, Dilaudid, Dexedrine, morphine, codeine, Quaaludes, pentobarbital, and a whole host of amphetamines, steroids, and twenty-five different types of barbiturates.

6. After Priscilla left him, Linda Thompson fell under the Presley charm to become his next girlfriend/baby-sitter. During the tour in 1973, Thompson's main duty was to feed Presley, engaging him in baby talk to get him to eat caramel popcorn balls as he leaned back, burbling and drooling because he was so doped up with Valium. He also had to wear a diaper to control his weakened bladder.

7. Bobby Mann, Elvis's cousin, was the one who took the picture of Elvis lying in his casket at Graceland and sold the photo for $78,000 to the *National Enquirer.* The reason he looked so healthy and thin in the casket was that the doctor who performed the autopsy removed 150 pounds of organs and water before releasing the body to the funeral home.

8. Elvis was not originally buried at Graceland, but rather with his mother at the Presley family crypt at Forest Hills Cemetery in Memphis. He was moved to Graceland a month later when three men were caught trying to open the burial vault. To thwart future attempts, his 1,800 pound copper casket was encased in a 3,000-pound vault covered by a 2,000-pound granite slab and topped off with an 1,800-pound bronze plaque.

9. Despite PR claims to the contrary, Priscilla Presley did not rescue the Presley estate from almost certain bankruptcy. After the death of financial guru Vernon, Priscilla was about to renew the relationship with Parker until Probate Judge Joseph Evans and Memphis attorney Blanchard Tual (acting as guardian for Lisa Marie) stepped in to evaluate, and eventually terminate, the contract with Mr. Parker.

10. EPE has registered "Elvis," "Elvis Presley," "Elvis in Concert," and "Graceland" as trademarks. "The King" was applied for, but rejected. The inscription on Grandma Minnie Mae Presley's tombstone is also protected.

11. The King's name for his penis was "Little Elvis."

PROFESSOR LONGHAIR

BORN December 19, 1918
Bogalusa, Louisiana

DIED January 30, 1980
New Orleans, Louisiana

CAUSE OF DEATH Heart Failure
Age 71

With all of the music that originated from the streets of New Orleans—Louis Armstrong, King Oliver, Jelly Roll Morton, Buddy Bolden—few of them stayed home. One of those who did was Henry Byrd, better known as Professor Longhair.

In the Beginning . . .

Born Henry Roeland Byrd and raised in New Orleans, Professor Longhair began his musical training early. From being among the "second line" musicians that followed the band during a parade to impromptu street performances, Professor Longhair played a variety of instruments. Exposed to everything from Dixieland, ragtime, and blues, the Professor explained how he discovered his calling: "It [a piano he found in an alley] was broken, but I bought some strings and hammers and just kept fumblin' and foolin' with it. I finally patched it up till one or the other key would play, even if four or five wouldn't. It didn't matter to me. I just wanted to play so bad I'd just match 'em up and sound 'em off. That's when I started cross-chording the piano—putting alias keys in there to give it a better blend. Where you would use three keys, I would use the whole five. You've got so much space when you're playin' music."

The Professor continued his musical odyssey through the whorehouses, lumber camps, and honky-tonks found in Memphis, Houston, New Orleans, and Helena. With a strong left hand and steel-tipped shoes (to literally pound the beat into the piano), the Professor kept everyone dancing and drinking until dawn.

By 1949, everyone was talking about Professor Longhair and his powerful blend of barrelhouse, rollicking piano with syncopated blues-rhythm undertones. After recording and touring for some ten years, the Professor vowed never to leave New Orleans again.

For the next fifteen years he recorded and played sporadically, but only in New Orleans. It was not, however, the time to be a part-time, party-time barrelhouse pianist. Rock 'n' roll was coming into fashion and blues and traditional jazz were fast becoming unhip. Professor Longhair had to take odd jobs, including sweeping out a record store, to make ends meet.

In 1971 his career started to slowly recover when he first appeared at the New Orleans Jazz and Heritage Festival. By 1973, he was a coveted headliner at many emerging music festivals around the world, including the Newport Jazz Festival and the Montreux Jazz Festival. In

New Orleans may be known for the French Quarter, but Tipitina's is still considered the premier nightclub in the city. It is also a veritable museum of Professor Longhair photographs and memorabilia. His final place of residence is located at 1740 Terpsichore Street. The house is brown, wooden, and typically New Orleans.

1974, he released his first album of new material in a decade, titled *Rock 'n' Roll Gumbo* and was invited to perform for a party given by ex-Beatle Paul McCartney, which was later released as *Live on the Queen Mary*.

In the End . . .

Once again, even occasional traveling was hard on the Professor. Fortunately, a group of local blues enthusiasts and promoters pooled their resources together and, along with Professor Longhair, bought a rundown warehouse in 1977 and opened the doors as Tipitina's. Now the Professor always had a place just around the corner from his home to "bang the rocks" until all hours of the night. Word eventually spread and Tipitina's was a resounding success. However, forty-five years of club dates and travel had taken their toll. When Professor Longhair opened Tipitina's in 1977, he was in a totally depreciated state physically. When he sat down, he couldn't stand up. When he did stand up, his knees rattled until he could feel the rhythm enough to walk a short distance. The Professor's teeth were almost nonexistent, he suffered from vitamin deficiency, and he was unable to digest solid foods. Onstage was another matter, for whatever his physical state indicated, his fingers and his heart had lost none of their soul.

In the final week of January 1980 his newest release, *Crawfish Fiesta*, was sold-out just one week in the record stores. The Professor was set to begin filming a documentary on his life when he died quietly in his sleep.

Mount Olivet Cemetery
Gentilly Parish,
New Orleans, Louisiana

Professor Longhair was originally laid to rest beneath a beautiful piano-shaped tombstone; unfortunately, when his wife died, he was moved into the new (and somewhat boring) mausoleum in the front of the cemetery. Enter the cemetery near the corner of Foy and Norman Mayer (the New Orleans Public Library is on the corner), park your car at the office, and walk toward the new outdoor vaults. He is interred next to his wife in the Corridor of Grace, Lot C-17 on the first story of the two story structure.

He and his friends went out in the alley and got an old piano that only had a certain number of keys because someone had left it for the trashman. Now how many piano players in their childhood only had eight or ten keys to work with?

Allen Toussaint

THE RAMONES

JOEY RAMONE
BORN May 19, 1951
New York, New York

DIED April 15, 2001
New York, New York

CAUSE OF DEATH
Lymphatic Cancer
Age 49

DEE DEE RAMONE
BORN September 18, 1952
Fort Lee, Virginia

DIED June 5, 2002
Hollywood, California

CAUSE OF DEATH
Drug Overdose
Age 49

With a frenzied "one-two-three-four" that introduced every song, the Ramones delivered two-minute, three-chord punk anthems with all the subtlety of a jackhammer in church. With "brothers" Joey, Johnny, Dee Dee, and Tommy, the Ramones stripped away all the pretensions of rock music, and in the process influenced every punk, new wave, and indie band that ever took to the stage. But the fact of the matter was there were nary four more dysfunctional misfits who were less equipped to lead a rock 'n' roll revolution. But as Joey once said, "Hey man, it was just chemistry—a chemical imbalance."

In the Beginning . . .

Formed in Queens, New York's Forest Hills neighborhood, Joey (lead singer Jeffrey Hyman), Johnny (guitarist John Cummings), Dee Dee (bassist Doug Colvin), and Tommy (drummer-turned-producer Tommy Erdelyi) began the group in the basement of Johnny's house when Johnny and Dee Dee both became unemployed. Unable to play standard cover tunes (mainly because they could barely play their instruments), they decided it would be easier to write their own songs than play someone else's. Without understanding the basics of chord progressions or song structure, Dee Dee wrote "Loudmouth," "I Don't Wanna Walk Around with You," and together they wrote "Havana Affair." After rehearsing for seven months starting in February 1974, they adopted a common surname and played their first show at CBGB down in the Bowery district of Manhattan. Despite sharing the stage with Blondie, Talking Heads, and Television, the Ramones were soon the headlining band, packing the small club with the hipper-than-thou crowd. As Johnny once said, "They think this is good, what we're doing? Maybe we can fool everyone. Fool the whole country."

Signed by Sire Records in 1975, they recorded their first self-titled, newly branded "punk rock" album the following year with such punk classics as "Blitzkrieg Bop" and "Judy Is a Punk." The Ramones' second and third albums were quite easy to finish because the band had most of the material already written, with many of the songs established as concert standards at this point. But unlike most bands, the Ramones recorded and released their songs in chronological order as they were written. Because they withheld some of their material from the record company, the Ramones were able to control the release of songs so there would be a natural progression from one album to the next. And when *Rocket to Russia* and *Road to Ruin* were released in 1977 and '78 respectively, the gamble paid off. With punk anthems "Sheena Is a Punk Rocker," "Rockaway Beach," and "I Wanna Be Sedated" part of their live concerts, the Ramones were an international success.

Dee Dee Ramone's last residence in Los Angeles, and where he was found dead by his wife, Barbara, is 6740 Franklin Place, Apartment 204 in Los Angeles. Joey Ramone's home in New York was at 115 E. 9th St. The Rock and Roll Hall of Fame in Cleveland has the last word in memorabilia with the New York Hard Rock Cafe displaying a couple of minor items.

After fifteen years, fifteen albums, and one great rock 'n' roll movie (Roger Corman's *Rock 'n' Roll High School)*, Dee Dee Ramone called it quits. Tired from his recent battles with drugs, alcohol, a failed marriage, and the constant travel, Dee Dee continued to write songs (he was the chief songwriter for most of the Ramone hits) for the group as he took a break from the band. Replaced by C. J. Ramone, the band continued on, selling more records each year, yet they were "always kind of the underdogs. I guess I liked that, but it got to be a pain in the ass," as Joey recalled. Though they were the legends of punk, the Ramones never had a Top 10 hit (they topped out with "Rockaway Beach" at #66) and only had two albums make it into the Top 100.

In the End . . .

After twenty-two years, twenty-four or so albums, and 2,262 shows, the Ramones called it a day in 1996. Already diagnosed with lymphoma, Joey kept a low profile while working on his solo album for the last three years of his life. But after a brief phone call with Bono from U2, Jeffrey Hyman, the rail-thin, pallid-skinned lead singer of the greatest punk rock band, lost his seven-year battle with cancer on Easter Sunday.

Just months after the remaining Ramones were inducted into the Rock and Roll Hall of Fame, Doug Colvin was found slumped over on a couch at 8:25 P.M. by his wife in their Hollywood Hills home in California. Though he candidly discussed his drug problems and professed to kicking the habit in the early 1990s, drug paraphernalia was found next to the body. Toxicology reports issued the following month indicated that Colvin died of a heroin overdose.

Mt. Zion Cemetery
Lyndhurst, New Jersey

From the main entrance at the intersection of Rutherford Avenue and Orient Way, turn onto Orient Way and enter at the third gate on your left just before the caretaker's shed. Drive down until you see the gates for the New York Social Club on your right. Walk through the gates and look for the Hyman monument three rows from the road, ten headstones to the right.

Hollywood Forever
Hollywood, California

As you enter the gates of the cemetery, turn left and drive along the border until you reach Section 8 (Garden of Legends). Colvin is buried thirty feet from the corner nearest the office, under the large tree, next to the Klarquist bench, behind the large Grass mausoleum in Section 8, Plot L-2003, Space 4.

We started in '74 and the only thing that you heard on the radio was disco, whereas you used to hear great, great music like the Kinks and the Who and the Beatles and all that stuff.

Joey Ramone

OTIS REDDING

BORN September 9, 1941
Dawson, Georgia

DIED December 10, 1967
Lake Monona, Wisconsin

CAUSE OF DEATH Plane Crash
Age 26

As one of the most original vocal stylists of the sixties, Otis Redding's emotional and soulful qualities brought him fame on both the pop and R&B charts. As a singer, producer, songwriter, and arranger, Otis, along with famed Memphis musicians Al Jackson, Duck Dunn, and Steve Cropper, were the architects of the Stax sound—a blend of rough-edged rhythm and sixties R&B soul.

In the Beginning . . .

A native of Dawson, Georgia, Otis Redding was born the son of a Baptist minister. At the age of five the Redding family moved to Macon, Georgia, and he began singing with the Vineville Baptist Church choir at an early age. While Redding went to high school and played in the school band, he was forced to drop out before graduating to help his family financially. After a short stint with the Upsetters (Little Richard's former band), Redding went to work as a member of Johnny Jenkins and the Pinetoppers in 1960. While the band, with Redding, was recorded on the Bethlehem, Finer Arts, and Alshire labels, they failed to attract attention outside of Macon and the singles subsequently failed to chart. It wasn't until 1962, during a Johnny Jenkins recording session in Memphis, that Redding was given a chance to prove his talents outside the band. During the recording session there was some extra time already booked, so Stax co-owner Jim Stewart allowed Redding to record a couple of songs. The result was a R&B Top 20 hit with the Redding original composition "These Arms of Mine." His follow-up single "Pain in My Heart" proved that his first hit was no fluke. By 1964, Phil Walden (founder of Capricorn Records and future manager of the Allman Brothers) nurtured Redding's talent and helped establish Redding as one of the top R&B artists on the southern tour circuit.

During the years 1964-'65 all the classic elements of the Stax sound—tight call-and-

---

The largest collection of Otis memorabilia resides in the den of Zelma Redding on the Big O Ranch. If you decide to make the trip to Macon, Georgia, to Karla's Shoe Boutique at the corner of Second and Cherry Street (Karla is Otis and Zelma's daughter, and Zelma can be found working there in the afternoons), you had better be looking for shoes and not an invitation to view her collection. Better yet, drive over to the Georgia Music Hall of Fame in Macon. In addition to several items on loan from the Redding estate, they also feature items from the Allman Brothers Band, the B-52s, Little Richard, and over three hundred Georgia musicians.

One piece of Redding-related memorabilia that has yet to be recovered is Steve Cropper's guitar, which was on the plane that fateful night. It remains on the bottom of Lake Monoca to this day. As an author of over four hundred songs and dozens of hits during the Stax/Volt days, Cropper never had another hit record after that night.

response interplay of voice and horns—were well represented by "Mr. Pitiful," "Chained and Bound," and one of his most covered songs, "I've Been Loving You Too Long." His choice to record the Rolling Stones' "I Can't Get No Satisfaction" (considered by Mick Jagger to be his favorite cover version of any Stones song) as a single in 1966 only served to increase his popularity in Europe. A tour of England and other European countries proved to be a resounding success.

In the End . . .

By 1965 Redding had established himself through constant touring and slowly climbing record sales. With strong record sales in Europe, major crossover appeal to both black and white audiences in America still eluded him. While "I've Been Loving You Too Long" became his first Top 30 hit on the pop charts, Redding finally gained popularity with the white American audience following his 1967 appearance at the Monterey Pop Festival. Backed by Booker T. and the MGs, Otis brought the audience to their feet with such hits as "My Lover's Prayer," "Respect," and "Try a Little Tenderness." That same year he had his biggest hit with the Sam Cooke composition "Shake."

In the summer of 1967, Redding spent a week on a houseboat overlooking the San Francisco Bay during his appearance at the Fillmore West. Mesmerized by the just-released Beatles album *Sgt. Pepper's Lonely Hearts Club Band*, Redding set out to write the ultimate crossover hit that would appeal to audiences worldwide. Returning home, he finished the lyrics and music with Stax/Volt guitarist and songwriter, the extraordinary (and future Blues Brother band member) Steve Cropper. Together they put the finishing touches on a solemn, acoustic ballad called "(Sittin' on) the Dock of the Bay."

Three days after recording what would be his last single, Redding was back on the road with his backing band, the Bar-Kays. As they finished their concert in Cleveland, the group boarded their twin-engine Beechcraft and left Cleveland, heading for Madison, Wisconsin. Just as the plane was about to land, it pulled up and circled the airport to make another approach. During the final approach, the plane suddenly plunged into the icy waters of Lake Monona. Splitting the fuselage open, several members of the Bar-Kays were able to swim free of the wreckage. Unfortunately, only trumpeter Ben Cauley survived the crash and the icy-cold waters of Lake Monona.

> *I'm still married. I just don't see him here with me. When it seems like a long time, I just put me on Otis Redding, and I just listen to him and it seems like yesterday. It's like he's talking to me.*
>
> Zelma Redding

The Big O Ranch
Round Oak, Georgia

Music was so much of Otis Redding's life, and it was an impressive part of his funeral service back home in Macon, Georgia. Booker T. Jones of Booker T and the MG's played organ. Blues singer Johnny Taylor broke down as he sang "I'll Stand By." Those who attended included Aretha Franklin, Joe Tex, James Brown, and virtually all the session players from Otis's Stax/Volt days. After the public memorial, private graveside services were held at the three hundred-acre Big O Ranch in nearby Round Oak, Georgia. Buried in an above-ground, white-marble mausoleum with a perpetual flame, the remains of Otis Redding are on very private property and are absolutely not open to the public. As Zelma once remarked to trespassers who drove onto the property, "This ain't no Graceland! I live here." However, you are more than welcome to take your picture at the entry gate to the property. From downtown Macon, take the Gray Highway to the city of Gray and turn left onto Highway 11 (just before the railroad tracks). Drive seven miles into Round Oak and con-

tinue another mile just past Dove's grocery store. At the railroad crossing sign, take a right and drive another mile to the Big O Ranch sign on your right. And if you look close enough down the driveway, three hundred feet away you can just barely see the grave of the late singer.

The Otis Redding Statue
Macon, Georgia

Dedicated in the fall of 2002, the Otis Redding statue is another contribution to the continuing efforts to honor the great musicians that came out of Macon, Georgia. The life-size bronze statue of the singer and songwriter can be found at the trailhead of Gateway Park along the Ocmulgee River, just a few blocks from the historic downtown.

As expected, all of the Redding singles he cut as a member of the Pinetoppers from 1961 through 1964 are worth anywhere from forty to four hundred dollars a side. However, Redding's stunning performance at 1967's Monterey Pop Festival is only valuable from the aspect that it has long been out of print and due to legal considerations from the Hendrix estate, probably will never see the light of day in rerelease form.

THE BAR-KAYS

RONNIE CALDWELL 1948—1967,
CARL CUNNINGHAM 1948—1967,
PHALON JONES 1949—1967,
JIMMIE KING 1949—1967

Formed in 1965 in Memphis, Tennessee, when they were only in their teens, the original line-up of the Bar-Kays included James Alexander on bass, Ronnie Caldwell on organ, Ben Cauley on trumpet, Carl Cunningham on drums, Phalon Jones on sax, and Jimmie King on guitar. In early 1967, they were signed by the Stax sub-

sidiary Volt Records as the in-studio house band. Under the tutelage of drummer Al Jackson of Booker T. and the MGs, the quintet was groomed into a great, funky R&B instrumental combo and played on the records of Otis Redding, Sam and Dave, and most of the premier artists that came through the Stax studio doors. Shortly after they were signed, the Bar-Kays had a minor hit of their own on the R&B charts called "Soul Finger" and an album of the same name was issued that same year. That summer, Redding asked the young band if they wanted to back him on selected dates through the U.S. Given that most of the band had never set foot out of Memphis, much less traveled around the U.S., they quickly packed their bags and hit the road. After the show in Cleveland, Ohio, the small Beechcraft they were traveling in with Redding on the way to Madison, Wisconsin, plunged into the fog-shrouded icy waters of Lake Monona. Only Ben Cauley sur-

vived the crash, with Caldwell surviving the initial impact, only to die of hypothermia waiting for the rescue boat. James Alexander had taken a different plane, and was not onboard the fateful flight.

Cunningham, King, and Matthew Kelly (not a member of the Bar-Kays, he was the band's valet during the tour) were buried together in New Park Cemetery in Lake Horn Mississippi (just outside Memphis, Tennessee). From the entrance, go straight down the

road and stop six rows before the ditch. Look for the large King and Cunningham monuments on your left. Jones, whose body was found several days after the crash, was not buried with the group, but also resides at New Park Cemetery, while the only white member of the Bar-Kays, Ronnie Caldwell, was buried in another cemetery in Memphis.

JIM REEVES

BORN August 20, 1923
Galloway, Texas

DIED July 31, 1964
Brentwood, Tennessee

CAUSE OF DEATH Plane Crash
Age 40

Thirty-plus years since his untimely death, Gentleman Jim Reeves is still one of country and western's most important crossover artists. With singles still charting in the U.S. and U.K., sales of his records continue unabated worldwide. Initially labeled "hillbilly," Jim's velvety-smooth vocals continue to draw hundreds of fans daily to his impressive roadside monument in east Texas.

In the Beginning . . .

Raised by his mother (his father died shortly after Jim's birth), James Travis Reeves was one of nine children born into this working-class family. At age five he retrieved a broken guitar from the trash and had it repaired by a family friend. However, Jim's sights were set on an athletic career, not music. Unfortunately, in 1944, after a couple of years playing semipro baseball, Jim injured his ankle sliding into second base, effectively ending his baseball aspirations.

Newly married, Reeves worked as a shipping clerk, insurance salesman, truck driver, and boxer. In possession of a fine speaking voice, Reeves found success as a broadcaster. Working with a small band in the evenings, Reeves was asked to appear on the Louisiana Hayride when Hank Williams failed to show. In the audience that night was the owner of Abbott and Faber Records. Fabor Robinson was so impressed that he signed Reeves to a recording contract. Four weeks later, "Mexican Joe" became a number one hit for nine weeks and Jim became an official member of the Louisiana Hayride.

In 1955, Jim became a member of the Grand Ole Opry and after two years of solid hits on the Abbott label, Reeves moved to the more prestigious RCA/Victor label. In 1957 Gentleman Jim scored six Top 10 hits (including one on the pop charts), toured Europe again, and had his own ABC radio series. In 1955, Reeves began to widen his exposure through television appearances, beginning with *The Ed Sullivan Show* in New York City. In 1958, he filled in for Red Foley as the host of *Jubilee U.S.A.* on the ABC television network. His good looks, clean image, and slow melodic delivery made him a success nationwide. And most every Sunday night he was back in Nashville, often holding court at Tootsie's Orchid Lounge after his appearance on the Grand Ole Opry.

"Four Walls" may have made Reeves a crossover artist on both the country and pop

Until 1995, Mary Reeves was the owner and operator of the Jim Reeves Museum at Evergreens Place (the home they once shared) at 1023 Joyce Lane, Nashville, Tennessee. Due to health reasons, Mary sold the entire estate to Ed Gregory Jr., a Brentwood carnival operator with several convictions stemming from financial misdealings. Shortly after taking over the operation of the museum, Gregory and his company declared bankruptcy, all the while selling off Reeves's memorabilia on eBay, through newspaper ads, and to private collectors, essentially selling off the assets and bleeding the museum dry. Upon Mary's death in 1999, Mary's second husband didn't even have the decency to bury her with Reeves in Texas. So if it's memorabilia you want, your only option is either the Heritage Hall in downtown Carthage, Texas (home to both the Jim Reeves and Tex Ritter collections), or the Country Music Hall of Fame Museum in Nashville.

charts, but it was with "He'll Have to Go" that Reeves scored his only million-selling hit during his lifetime. "He'll Have to Go" reached number one on the country charts, number one on the R&B charts, and number two on the pop charts with a staying power of nearly half a year. In 1961, Reeves was one of the first country artists to record an album entirely composed of pop songs, *A Touch of Velvet*. Recording country, folk, honky-tonk, western swing, pop, and popular ballads, Reeves continually varied his songs, backing musicians, and styles to avoid the strict confines of being just a "country" singer.

In the End . . .

From 1956 until 1964, a year didn't go by without Reeves's name being at the top of the charts. Cultivating the image as the master of soothing love songs and not restricting himself to the "country and western" label, Gentleman Jim was a demanding perfectionist in the studio. Reeves was never one to allow others to dictate his choice of material, and agressively marketed his music to station owners and fans alike.

In 1962, Reeves, along with Chet Atkins, Docky Dean Manuel, Floyd Cramer, and a whole host of country artists flew down to South Africa, where they were treated like royalty. The following year Reeves's first starring role in a feature-length film, *Kimberley Jim*, opened to enthusiastic audiences worldwide. And at the end of 1963 he embarked on a tour of England, Ireland, and several European nations as Reeves topped the pop charts, dethroning the Beatles' "I Want to Hold Your Hand."

At the end of July 1964, Reeves and Manuel were returning from a business trip from Arkansas. Despite warnings of bad weather, they continued on in their rented single-engine Beechcraft airplane with Reeves at the controls. Long overdue, the plane and two musicians were found three days later just a couple miles from the Nashville airport.

Private Cemetery
Carthage, Texas

Jim was taken back to his boyhood home of Carthage, Texas, for burial. His wife, Mary Reeves, purchased a two-acre plot of land three miles outside Carthage on Highway 79, just past the airport. Reeves's fifteen-foot statue is visible from the highway and the turnoff is well marked by signs. Please note that the only other resident of this private cemetery is his faithful dog.

Dean Manuel was buried at Spring Hill Cemetery in Nashville, Tennessee, in the Crestview section toward the back of the cemetery. His upright monument is three rows off the road that borders the Crestview and Sunnymeade sections.

I frequently hire a commercial plane to get from one place to another, and generally it is piloted by someone whom I have never met before or know anything about. I just want to be prepared to land the plane in case something should happen to the pilot.

Jim Reeves, responding to why he took flying lessons.

RANDY RHOADS

BORN December 6, 1956
Santa Monica, California

DIED March 19, 1982
Leesburg, Florida

CAUSE OF DEATH Plane Crash
Age 25

Everybody laughed when Ozzy Osbourne quit heavy metal masters Black Sabbath and announced his solo career. After all, what could this burned-out, vocally limited rock 'n' roll warrior offer in the way of new music? When *Blizzard of Ozz* was released in 1980, nobody was laughing anymore. With Randy Rhoads on guitar, his two-handed tapping hammer-ons and double-tracking, signature shredding guitar attracted thousands of guitar-worshiping fans. Ozzy was back and rock 'n' roll had a new guitar hero, and his name was Randy Rhoads.

In the Beginning . . .

Born the youngest of three children in Southern California, Rhoads began playing guitar at a very early age. As he once explained, money was tight and the family had no television or radio for entertainment. Since his mother ran a music store, Rhoads picked up various instruments to entertain himself. After one year of formal lessons by the guitar instructor at the store, the instructor told Delores Rhoads that he couldn't teach her son anything new. Already a talented musician as a teenager, he started giving lessons himself at the store.

By the early 1970s he began playing with a variety of garage bands. As he began looking at bands along the Sunset Strip in Los Angeles, one of the first musicians he met was Kevin DuBrow, lead singer of Quiet Riot. As DuBrow remembers, "He plugged his guitar into a little portable amp he had brought along and suddenly my living room was filled with the most amazing guitar sounds in the world. He played for about ten minutes, then turned to me and said, 'Okay, let's hear you sing.' I just looked at him and smiled and said, 'After what I just heard, I'm not opening my mouth.' " Quiet Riot with DuBrow and Rhoads lasted three years, beginning in 1977. After two musically uneven albums that were released in Japan only, Rhoads left Quiet Riot in 1980 after the band failed to secure an American recording contract.

During this time Black Sabbath frontman Ozzy Osbourne was tired of the grind and was in Los Angeles in search of musicians for his new band. After auditioning dozens of guitarists with lots of hair but little talent, Ozzy was about to leave for England when a member of his crew suggested a local guitar instructor. Amid towers of Marshall amps and miles of PA cables, Rhoads walked in at 2:00 A.M. with his little practice amp and played some soft fretboard harmonics. After weeks of listening to high-volume heavy metal clones, Ozzy offered him the gig on the spot.

Randy left for England and holed up with Ozzy to write and record *Blizzard of Ozz*. From the opening track, "I Don't Know," Randy established his signature sound with dark,

🎸—Delores Rhoads continues to own and operate the Musonia School of Music in Burbank, California. For several years she could be seen at various Ozzy concerts, always happy to talk to fans about her son. Through her son's estate, she has helped fund the International Guitar Reseach Institute at the California State University at Northridge.

minor-tonality riffs and lightning-fast chops. Rockers like "Crazy Train" and "Mr. Crowley" thrust Ozzy and Rhoads equally into the limelight.

After a short tour, the band went back into the studio to record their second album. Randy was now a rising star in the guitar world and won several awards for best new guitarist. Proving it wasn't just beginners luck, *Diary of a Madman* featured more of Rhoads's signiture harmonics, tremolo effects, and modal runs on more Ozzy classics.

In the End . . .

The band left England for the much-anticipated U.S. tour in the winter of 1982. They had just finished a show and on the tour bus with Osbourne were his fiancée and manager Sharon Arden, bassist Rudy Sarzo (asleep on the bus), and keyboardist Don Airey (awake and a witness to the accident). On the morning of March 19th, Rhoads and band cook and seamstress Rachel Youngblood boarded a plane that driver and part-time pilot Andrew Aycock stole from an adjacent airport hangar. During the flight Aycock was flying as low as ten feet off the ground as he buzzed the band bus three times. On the fourth pass the left wing of the plane clipped the back of the bus as the aircraft then crossed over the top of the bus, hit a pinetree, and crashed into the garage of an adjacent mansion. The plane exploded on impact and caused a fire that burned the house and all of its contents down to the ground. All the victims in the plane were burned beyond recognition and Rhoads had to be identified by his jewelry. Wreckage from the plane was scattered across one acre with no piece of the aircraft, aside from the detached left wing, larger than a football. Toxicology reports later confirmed that cocaine was found in Aycock's urine, while no traces of drugs or alcohol were found in Rhoads's system.

Mountain View Cemetery
San Bernardino, California

From the main entrance at Highland Avenue and Waterman, drive straight ahead one hundred feet. The large private mausoleum on your left at the intersection holds the young guitarist. Rhoads was moved to the private mausoleum two years after the crash. Paid for in part by Ozzy, the elaborate tomb took just under a year to plan and complete.

He had hair down to his waist and a thumbnail about four inches long. I looked at him and thought, no way can this guy play. He plugged in, and I thought that my head was being plastered against the wall. Every lead that I could imagine, he played them better.

Kevin DuBrow of Quiet Riot

BUDDY RICH

BORN September 30, 1917
Johnstown, Pennsylvania

DIED April 2, 1987
Los Angeles, California

CAUSE OF DEATH Brain Cancer
Age 69

Beyond his flamboyant, sometimes volatile character, beyond his tasteful wardrobe and his status as a preferred guest on the *Tonight* show with Johnny Carson, Buddy Rich was a magnificent drummer. His recording and performance résumé— Bunny Berigan, Harry James, Artie Shaw, Tommy Dorsey, Charlie Parker, Bud Powell, Dizzy Gillespie, Art Tatum, Lionel Hampton (to name just a few)—is unparalleled by any other artist.

In the Beginning . . .

Born into a vaudevillian family, Rich (by his own accounts) was performing onstage with his family act, Wilson and Rich, at age two. He started playing the drums and tap dancing for the Broadway show *Pinwheel*. With little time for a formal education, Buddy toured Australia at age six as "Baby Traps—the Drum Wonder" under the guidance of his parents, who also doubled as his managers.

By the age of eleven, Rich was playing his first jazz gigs with Art Shapiro and Hot Lips Page, and two years later moved into the big leagues of swing. By age twenty-one, he had successfully recorded with Harry James, Artie Shaw, and Tommy Dorsey. With the Tommy Dorsey Orchestra, Buddy stayed on from 1939 through 1946 (with two years off for military duty). At his best he pushed the band with flair and fire, playing on several of Tommy's two hundred-plus hit numbers. At his worst, he was brutally outspoken and made no effort to hide his intense dislike of Tommy and his choice of music.

In 1946, Frank Sinatra bankrolled the first of many Buddy Rich Big Bands, but it was a critical and financial failure (one of many things that dissolved their friendship). During the late forties, Rich modernized his drum style in response to bebop. Touring with Norm Granz's Jazz at the Philharmonic show, he also cut sides with Dizzy Gillespie and Charlie Parker and before the end of the decade, managed to appear in three films, *Symphony of Swing*, *Ship Ahoy*, and *How's About It*.

Throughout the fifties and most of the sixties, Rich teamed up with Harry James on many of his recordings and live performances. Rich's showmanship, flashy drumming, and talent for self-promotion made him the group's centerpiece. Aside from a two-year hiatus due to a heart attack, Rich was now the highest-paid orchestral musician at fifteen hundred dollars per week. Not bad for a musician who never took a formal lesson and refused to practice outside of performances.

Buddy left James for good in 1966 to re-form his own group. Fronting a sixteen-piece big band, Rich emphasized raw power over tone, color, or mood. He toured the world, play-

There is a select group of recordings that are very valuable to collectors; however, you won't find them in stores. These are secret rehearsal tapings created by his musicians during the eighties. Rich's maniacal, abusive, obscenity-filled diatribes are prized among bootleg recording collectors. Mel Tormé's comprehensive biography contains a whole chapter listing Buddy Rich's infamous enemies list, starting with the Chairman of the Board, Frank Sinatra (who deliveried the eulogy at Rich's funeral).

ing for Queen Elizabeth of England, President John F. Kennedy, King Hussein of Jordan, and the King of Thailand. Much to the howl of critics, he even began adding Beatles and Paul Simon tunes to his records. Rich dismissed the critics with a wave of his hand (and some choice adjectives). After all, they came to see first-rate arrangements with flashy, technically brilliant drum solos. It didn't matter in the least to him that swing bands were out of favor.

In the End . . .

Touring nine months out of the year, Rich starred in his own TV variety show in 1968. In the early seventies, Rich trimmed his band down to a combo, only to re-form the full orchestra again for the remainder of the decade. During the 1970s, Rich also opened two nightclubs, Buddy's Place and Buddy's Place II, in Los Angeles. And despite bypass surgery in 1985, Rich was back on the road and in the studio two weeks later. Rich's many appearances on TV talk shows and his flamboyant condemnation of certain types of music made him a controversial figure whose public personality often obscured his talent. But that didn't seem to bother Rich; after all, he had been selling out show after show, year after year, for the last fifty years.

The jazz legend was also acknowledged by his peers through numerous awards and honors, including the *Modern Drummer* Magazine Hall of Fame and the *Downbeat* Magazine Hall of Fame Award. Unfortunately, his active schedule came to a halt in the summer of 1987 when Rich was diagnosed with brain cancer. He passed away of heart failure following surgery for the malignant brain tumor. On the day before Rich died, a new nurse came to his room and asked if the legendary drummer was allergic to anything. "Only two things," Rich replied, "country and western."

Westwood Memorial Park
Los Angeles, California

As you enter the cemetery (on Glendon, one block off Wilshire Boulevard), take an immediate left and walk to the Sanctuary of Tranquillity. As you enter the alcove, he is the second tomb on the bottom row. Rich shares this permanent residence with neighbors such as Dean Martin, Frank Zappa, Roy Orbison, Minnie Riperton, Peggy Lee, Les Brown, Carl Wilson, and Mel Tormé.

The greatest drummer ever to have drawn a breath.

drummer Gene Krupa

TEX RITTER

BORN January 12, 1905
Murvaul, Texas

DIED January 2, 1974
Nashville, Tennessee

CAUSE OF DEATH Heart Attack
Age 68

The only entertainer to be elected to both the County Music Hall of Fame and the Cowboy Hall of Fame, Tex Ritter helped give the country and western sound a degree of dignity that often was lacking. Once called the Voice of the Western, Ritter was the most influential and successful singing cowboy to emerge from the shadows of Gene Autry.

In the Beginning . . .

Born in eastern Texas and raised in Beaumont, Ritter attended the University of Texas to study law. Through contact with Alan Lomax, he moved to New York to land a role in a Broadway play. His role as a singing cowboy in *Green Grow the Lilacs*, his radio program *Tex Ritter's Campfire*, and as a member of Bobby Benson and the B-Bar-B Riders' radio program, Tex drew plenty of attention and fans. In 1933, he began recording sessions for the newly formed Decca label—twenty-nine singles in all for the next four years.

In 1936, Hollywood was looking for another singing cowboy to emulate the success of Gene Autry and William "Hopalong Cassidy" Boyd. Producer Ed Finney arranged for a screen test and signed Ritter to a five-year personal contract. His first movie, *Song of the Gringo*, starred Ritter with William Desmond and the following year he was in *Trouble in Texas* with Rita Cansino (later known as Rita Hayworth). During his first five years in Hollywood, Ritter made thirty-two B westerns. In the mid-forties he starred in his movie industry swan song, *The Texas Rangers*, which marked his 85th film.

After 1945, his acting career began to fade while his recording career continued without interruption. His distinctive voice provided the soundtrack to such western film classics as *High Noon* (1952) and *Wichita* (1955). Since signing with the new Capitol label in the early forties, he recorded at least one session every year for the remainder of his life. He

There seems to be no shortage of Tex Ritter memorabilia to be had by fans of this country legend. He shares honors with Jim Reeves and a whole host of great Texas musicians at the Texas Country Music Hall of Fame in Carthage, Texas (just a mile or so down the road from Jim Reeves's cemetery and monument). There is also a small museum in downtown Nederland (known as the Windmill on Boston Street, three miles from the cemetery), where there are a few photos and items belonging to the Ritter family. Both museums are open every day except Sunday. Naturally, Ritter is also respresented along with the other singing cowboys at Nashville's Country Music Hall of Fame. And if you were wondering, the answer is yes, John Ritter from *Three's Company* fame is related. He is one of Tex Ritter's two sons.

scored a series of Top 10 hits throughout the 1940s, including "Rye Whiskey," "Boll Weevil," "Wayward Wind," "You Are My Sunshine," and "High Noon" as Tex Ritter and His Texans.

In the End . . .

In 1960, Ritter turned his attention back to the cowboy songs he had collected during his youth. With the success of Marty Robbins's gunfighter ballads, Ritter released "Blood on the Saddle" and had a number one hit on the country charts with "I Dreamed of a Hillbilly Heaven." After a two-year stint as president of the Country Music Association, Ritter moved to Nashville, where he became a member of the Grand Ole Opry. Although he was more known as a singing cowboy than a country star, after Ritter joined the Opry he consistently made the charts every year. In 1959, he had began a successful three-year run as the star of the TV series *Ranch Party*. In 1964, Ritter became only the fifth person to be honored as an inductee to the Country Music Hall of Fame in Nashville, Tennessee.

In 1970, Ritter launched an unsuccessful campaign for the U.S. Senate from Tennessee. Four years later and after a half century of classic C&W recordings, Tex Ritter died of a heart attack in a Nashville police station while bailing out a band member on the eve of another concert tour.

Oak Bluff Memorial Park
Port Neches, Texas

From downtown Port Neches, turn right on Block Street and drive to the end of the road. Turn left into the cemetery at the last entrance. Drive straight ahead past the office (on your right) and follow the road as it curves to the left (past the gazebo). Stop at the three pine trees that surround the Tex Ritter Texas Historical Commission plaque. With your back to the plaque, walk straight ahead, fifteen plots from the road, and you will find his marker.

We moved every two years. All I remember about Phoenix is cactus—and meeting Tex Ritter.

Stevie Nicks

MARTY ROBBINS

BORN Sept 26, 1925
Glendale, Arizona

DIED December 8, 1982
Nashville, Tennessee

CAUSE OF DEATH Lung and kidney failure
Age 57

Marty Robbins was country music's most versatile singer and consistent hitmaker. His early recordings saw him veer from tear-stained ballads and honky-tonks to rockabilly and pop. Best known for his series of gunfighter ballads, Robbins's musical and personal integrity made him one of the most beloved entertainers by his fans and within the music industry alike.

In the Beginning . . .

Born Martin David Robinson in extreme poverty in Arizona, Robbins spent his youthful days watching Gene Autry movies and listening to tales of the Old West as told by his grandfather. After his discharge from the navy, he changed his name and began playing nightclubs around Phoenix, eventually securing his own local radio and television show. When country singer Little Jimmie Dickens made an appearance on Robbins's show in 1951, he was so impressed by Robbins that he recommended him to Columbia Records. Signed to the label the following year, Robbins's first two outings failed to chart. The following year Robbins recorded "I'll Go on Alone," which soared to number one on the country charts. On the strength of that one single, Robbins was invited to join the Grand Ole Opry in Nashville, Tennessee.

In 1959, he released "The Hanging Tree," which was featured in a movie of the same name starring Gary Cooper. The song revealed Robbins's original ambition of becoming a singing cowboy. In 1959, he released his landmark concept album, *Gunfighter Ballads and Trail Songs*, which featured the classic Mexican-flavored ballad "El Paso." The single went straight to number one and was awarded a Grammy for Best Country Song.

Several years (and hits) later, the Nashville community was stunned at the sudden deaths of Patsy Cline, Cowboy Copas, and Hawkshaw Hawkins. Robbins wrote "Two Little Boys" for Hawkshaw's widow, Jean Shepard. He then transferred the copyright to Hawkshaw's sons so they would receive royalties from the sales. It turns out that the singing cowboy was also a gentleman with class.

In 1968, Robbins began the tradition of closing the Grand Ole Opry show every Saturday night. He had always requested the 11:30 slot so he could be at the racetrack on Saturday afternoons. Robbins's unrehearsed, freewheeling sets often stretched far past the show's midnight ending. That same year he suffered his first of many serious heart attacks. The following year, while on a bus to a show in Cleveland, he suffered chest pains and was

Outside the family, the Roy Acuff Museum at the Grand Ole Opry entertainment complex in Nashville contains the most memorabilia, including furniture, cars, guitars, and mementos from his forty-plus years in music. They even have his entire office (orange shag carpet and all!), reassembled within the museum. The admission is free and it is open most every day.

taken to the hospital. Despite tests showing he had suffered another heart attack, he performed his scheduled concert before checking into the hospital.

In the End . . .

In 1969, Robbins suffered another heart attack. Hospitalized in serious condition, Robbins underwent the then-new procedure of heart bypass surgery. Advised to take it easy, Robbins was soon back on the road performing, as well as back at the racetrack. The following year he was awarded his second Grammy with the song "My Woman, My Woman, My Wife," which he had recorded just weeks before his surgery. In 1975, Robbins charted for the final time with the number one singles "El Paso City" and "Among My Souvenirs."

In 1975, Marty was inducted into the Nashville Songwriters Hall of Fame and in the fall of 1982 he was inducted into the Country Music Association Hall of Fame. Robbins accepted the award saying, "There are other people that deserve it before I should get it.

[But] I think, possibly, it might not happen again, so I'm gonna take it home tonight!" It was a tragic prophecy. Two months later, he was hospitalized with those now-familiar chest pains. With four blocked arteries, he survived the initial nine-hour heart surgery only to succumb six days later to lung and kidney failure.

**Woodlawn Cemetery
Nashville, Tennessee**

Marty is buried in the Garden of Gethsemane at Woodlawn Cemetery in Nashville. As you enter the cemetery, drive past the large office building to the road behind the office. Turn left and drive while staying to the right. Drive past the historic wood house and pond (on your left) and park one hundred feet past the pond. Walk three hundred feet to the top of the hill on your left. Laid to rest near his good friend Webb Pierce, his flat, six-foot tablet and ever-present flowers are easy to find.

The great songs just come out. If it comes quick, just leave it that way.

Marty Robbins

JIMMIE RODGERS

BORN September 8, 1897
Meridian, Mississippi

DIED May 26, 1933
New York, New York

CAUSE OF DEATH Tuberculosis
Age 35

Known to millions as the Singing Brakeman, Jimmie Rodger's entire recording career lasted only six short years. Before he died at the young age of thirty-five, he had recorded 111 songs and sold over twenty million records. Second only to the great opera singer Enrico Caruso, Jimmie's work lived on to inspire Gene Autry, Hank Williams, Lefty Frizzell, Merle Haggard, and Ernest Tubb.

In the Beginning . . .

James Charles Rodgers was born in Meridian, Mississippi, to Aaron and Eliza Rodgers. He was only four when his mother died, and his father moved from state to state in search of work in the railroad yards. Living in a series of boardinghouses and freight yard shanty-towns, Rodgers's playgrounds were the cabs and engines of the great trains on which his dad worked.

Rodgers was deeply influenced by the black workers in the construction gangs, who would allow the young boy to join them during breaks while they sang spirituals and traditional songs. Around the age of ten, Rodgers learned to play the banjo and guitar and four years later dropped out of school to become a full-time apprentice railroad employee. About the same time he won an amateur talent contest in his hometown of Meridian. While he dreamed of becoming a wandering musician, his future as a railroad worker seemed more secure.

Rodgers worked as a flagman, a baggage master, and brakeman for ten years on the New Orleans and Northeastern Railroad. As Rodgers traveled the endless miles of track, it wasn't unusual to see him performing for the white crew in the afternoon between stops, then play the blues that evening for the black construction workers. Unfortunately, Rodgers's health began to deteriorate in 1915 and he lost his job three years later. Six years later he began to cough up blood during one of his coughing spells. The diagnosis was grim—tuberculosis. The doctor's advice was simple for such a fatal disease: "Stop working for the railroads." That left only one occupational choice.

Now that he had no job, no money, and a wife and children to support, Rodgers had no

The Jimmie Rodgers Museum, located in an old railroad station in downtown Meridian, is open every day and provides the largest collection of Rodgers memorabilia (including his prized Gibson acoustic guitar, which is kept in a fire-proof vault on the right). The annual Jimmie Rodgers Festival (held the last week of May) convinced RCA to re-release all of Jimmie's songs on seven albums. In 1961, the Country Music Association Hall of Fame honored Jimmie Rodgers, the Father of Country Music, as the first inductee into the Hall of Fame. If at all possible, make your visit to Meridian during the day, then keep driving to the next town. Sad to say, the once thriving downtown is merely a shell of its glorious past.

alternative. Playing banjo in a local string band, he heard that Ralph Peer planned to produce records in Bristol, Tennessee. In August 1927, just three days after the recording debut of the Carter Family, Rodgers cut his first solo record. It wasn't meant to be a solo audition. However, when Jimmie Rodgers and the Entertainers arrived in Bristol, the Entertainers left Jimmie, forcing him to record solo. Unfazed, he recorded two songs, accompanied only by his Gibson guitar. Peer signed Jimmie to a recording contract on the spot. The Entertainers went home with nothing.

In the End . . .

Barely one step ahead of poverty, his first royalty check of $27.43 was only the beginning. Rodgers traveled to Washington to record "Blue Yodel No. 1 (T for Texas)." Within three months the Victor label had the biggest-selling records in the nation. Rodgers immediately summoned his sister-in-law, Elsie McWilliams (who performed with Rodgers during the early years), to cowrite more songs. By now he was earning two thousand dollars a month in royalties, plus fees for concert appearances as the variety of musical themes expressed in "Train Whistle Blues," "Yodeling Ranger," "Frankie and Johnny," and "TB Blues" caught the imagination of the American public.

From 1928 until 1932, Rodgers recorded twenty singles a year and made an average of two hundred appearances a year. However, the busy schedule was beginning to wear him down as his coughing spells would sometimes last for days. Finally, in 1932, he was hospitalized, then confined to bed at home for nearly two months. He knew his time was coming.

In May of 1933, Rodgers took one last trip to New York for another recording session. He was scheduled to record twenty-four new songs, yet he had to be carried into the studio, with a private nurse by his side. The session went slowly, as Rodgers laid down on a cot next to the microphone after each take. Sometimes it would be hours before he had the energy to sing again. On May 24th, he sang his last note and had to be carried back to the hotel. Two days later, in the early morning hours, Jimmie Rodgers died in his hotel room.

Oak Grove Cemetery
Meridian, Mississippi
As you drive through Meridian, take the 154A (Butler-South) exit off Interstate 20. Turn left at the first light, then turn right at the first road. Drive up Azalea Drive, turning left on Oak Grove Road. The cemetery will be on your right, just past the Oak Grove Baptist Church. Rodgers's monument is two rows from the road in the center of the cemetery.

There are only four musical stylists—Jimmie Rodgers, Al Jolson, Hank Williams, and myself.

Jerry Lee Lewis

BON SCOTT

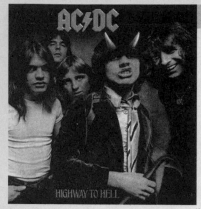

Scott (far right) looks over Angus Young's shoulder on his final album with the band.

BORN July 9, 1946
Kirriemuir, Scotland

DIED February 21, 1980
London, England

CAUSE OF DEATH Death by Misadventure
Age 33

With an abundance of ear-bleeding guitar riffs supplied by the Young brothers and the whiskey-soaked lyrics and vocals of Bon Scott, AC/DC became the most successful and often imitated heavy metal band from the late seventies until present. Possessing one of the most unique voices in rock, Bon Scott's throaty drawl coupled with the thunderous guitars of Angus and Malcolm made AC/DC heavy metal's preeminent rock 'n' roll troubadours.

In the Beginning . . .

Bon Scott spent the first six years of his youth in the small town of Kirriemuir, Scotland. The family moved to Melbourne, Australia, then to Sunshine, and finally to Fremantle just outside the coastal town of Perth. The frequent moves made it difficult for the young Scott to adjust to new schools and he dropped out of school for good at the age of fifteen. He worked a series of odd jobs, including driving a tractor, as a mechanic, and laborer on a fishing boat. At the age of twenty, Scott began to look toward music as an escape

Scott's first musical duty came as the drummer and vocalist for the Spectors in Perth. He then joined the Valentines, releasing a single "Every Day I Have to Cry" that made it to number five on the local Australian charts. The band moved to Melbourne, where they recorded three more singles by the Easybeats. Unfortunately, shortly after, the band was arrested for possession of narcotics, and their clean-cut image was destroyed. In 1970 the band dissolved and Scott joined Fraternity as their new lead singer. The band gained in popularity and toured Australia, Germany, and the U.K. with limited success. When the band returned to Australia, Scott was in a severe motorcycle accident and was kicked out of the band.

Just as Scott was getting out of the hospital, another Australian band, AC/DC, founded by Angus Young and brother Malcolm, had recorded the lifeless single "Can I Sit Next to Your Girl." Discouraged, the brothers relocated to Melbourne, Australia, where they languished in the bar circuit. One day their new driver, Bon Scott, suggested that he should become their lead singer and the whole band exploded in laughter. But the joke was on the Young brothers when they discovered that Bon's gravelly, no-nonsense vocals were a perfect match for Angus's intense bad-boy guitar solos.

With the addition of Phil Rudd (drums) and Mark Evans (bass), AC/DC recorded two excellent albums, *TNT* (1975) and *High Voltage* (1976). They relocated to England during the high point of the punk movement, but unlike other standard rock 'n' roll bands, AC/DC

AC/DC was finally inducted into the Rock and Roll Hall of Fame in Cleveland, Ohio, in 2003, and with the honors goes a small display of memorabilia, including one of Scott's leather jackets. In his hometown of Kirriemuir, Scotland, a museum was opened to celebrate the town's rich Celtic history and culture and there is a display honoring the town's most famous (or infamous) resident. When in London, fans from around the world make the pilgramage to No. 67 Overhill Road in East Dulwich, where Scott lost his life in the driveway to the garage.

began to draw a strong following for their over-the-top live shows and for their highly evolved musical skills (at least compared to punk's relative lack of musical ability).

In 1977, AC/DC hit the airwaves big with "Whole Lotta Rosie," "Problem Child," and "Dirty Deeds Done Dirty Cheap." The following year the live release *If You Want Blood, You Got It* became their biggest hit album to date. AC/DC's follow-up studio album, *Highway to Hell*, despite being dismissed by the critics, sold over one million units upon release, and secured AC/DC's spot as the top metal band on both sides of the Atlantic.

In the End . . .

Despite his various indulgences, Scott was in good spirits at the beginning of 1980 as the band made an appearance (and to collect a boatload of gold albums) at the annual Midem music industry convention in France. The band continued on to the U.K. for a short tour before settling back in England for the all-important follow-up to *Highway to Hell*.

On the night of February 20th, Scott had been drinking with friend Alistar Kinnear until about 3:00 A.M. By the time they left the Music Machine in London's Camden Town, Scott had consumed seven double whiskeys (certainly a considerable amount, but not remarkable considering Scott's prodigious standards for consumption). After driving to Kinnear's home, Kinnear was unable to wake Scott and left him in the car to sleep it off. After sleeping fifteen hours, Kinnear awoke the next day only to find that Scott had shifted during the night and had choked to death on his own vomit. Pronounced dead on arrival at Kings College Hospital, the coroner later reported that Scott's stomach contained "the equivalent of half a bottle of whiskey" and labeled the cause as "death by misadventure."

Fremantle Cemetery
Fremantle, Australia

Scott was cremated and returned to Australia, where a private service was held at the Fremantle Cemetery in Fremantle, Australia (about fifteen miles south of Perth). His bronze marker can be found in the Memorial Garden section, GN3 Garden of Remembrance, about thirty feet from the Bon Scott memorial bench.

We'd play anywhere, anytime, and not always to adoring fans. But we never stopped playing, mostly in fear of what would happen if we did.

Angus Young

TUPAC SHAKUR

BORN June 16, 1971
New York, New York

DIED September 13, 1996
Las Vegas, Nevada

CAUSE OF DEATH Murdered
Age 25

During the 1980s, as violence replaced drug abuse as the leading cause of death for urban American black men, angry and provocative gangsta rap emerged on the forefront of American pop culture. The most popular and controversial artist was Tupac (aka 2Pac) Shakur whose lifestyle and lyrics of ghetto culture were admired and emulated by countless middle-class suburban gang-banger wanna-bees. So it came as no surprise that the young artist who rapped his way out of the poverty and despair of the ghetto was gunned-down in a hail of bullets—a victim of the street violence he could not leave behind.

In the Beginning . . .

After dropping out of high school, running with gang members in North Carolina, and joining the Black Panther Party, Alice Williams (who used the name Afeni Shakur) gave birth to Tupac Shakur just one month after leaving prison. Shuttled between shelters and halfway homes, Shakur was raised absent a father or close friends. Turning to music and poetry, his mother enrolled him in the 127th Street Ensemble in Harlem at the age of twelve. A struggling theater group in the wrong neighborhood, Shakur thrived on stage and began to develop a talent of music and songwriting.

In 1986 the family moved to Baltimore where the young Shakur fell into the rap movement. With a cocky swagger and New York attitude, Shakur began to call himself MC New York and cultivated a reputation as the tough rapper from New York City. Enrolled in the Baltimore School for the Arts, he was now surrounded by middle-class white kids, yet by all accounts, loved the school and the opportunities it provided. Still the pull of the street was too strong and by the age of twenty, Shakur had been arrested eight times and served nearly a year in prison after his conviction for sexual abuse.

In the late 1980s Shakur joined forces with several other Oakland, California based rappers to form Digital Underground. Based on the bass-heavy beats of Parliament/Funkadelic, Digital Underground released their Grammy-nominated debut album *Sex Packets* to excellent reviews that bore two hit singles, "Humpty Dance" and "Doowutchyalike." Digital Underground continued for another year with two more successful releases, *Sons of the P* and *The Body-Hat Syndrome*, on Tommy Boy Records.

In 1992 Shakur began his rapid rise to stardom with his first solo release *2Pacalypse Now* quickly follwed by *Strictly 4 My N.I.G.G.A.Z.* Nominated for Best New Rap/Hip Hop Artist for the American Music Awards in 1993, he also starred opposite Janet Jackson in

Financial arrangements are still pending as plans are in the works to construct the Tupac Amaru Shakur Center for the Arts just outside Atlanta, Georgia. The site considered is a ten-acre wooded lot in the suburb of Stone Mountain near the home Shakur purchased just before his death. The Center will be constructed in three phases including a Tupac Museum, art gallery, screening room, a 400-seat theater, and an artists' village. In addition to a lifetime of memorabilia. It is rumored that Tupac's final remains will be interred at the Center upon completion. Until then, Death Row Records is said to have in its possession over 100 completed unreleased tracks recorded prior to Shakur's death—enough for a new release every year for the next decade.

the film *Poetic Justice*. Unfortunately fame and fortune did not keep Shakur off the police blotters. In 1993 Shakur's extreme lifestyle resulted in charges of assaulting two off-duty policeman in Atlanta, assaulting a movie director, and various weapons charges. Yet in interviews Shakur maintained that he was misunderstood and that the "thug" image he cultivated was just an act. However just two years later a judge in Manhattan found Shakur guilty of sexual assault and sentenced the rapper to four and a half years in prison.

In the End . . .

In November of 1994, just one day before his verdict for sexual assault was handed down, Shakur was shot five times in the lobby of a New York recording studio in an apparent robbery. At 12:20 A.M. Shakur and his entourage (including manager Freddie Moore) entered the recording studio where the Notorious B.I.G. (aka Biggie Smalls) and Sean "Puffy" Combs were working upstairs. Once in the lobby, three men stopped the group before they got on the elevator and demanded Shakur's jewelry and money. Shakur lunged at one of the gunman and gunfire erupted, wounding Moore and Shakur. As Moore gave chase, the remaining group pulled Shakur into the elevator. Bleeding with three bullet wounds to the body and two to the head, Shakur was dragged into the upstairs studio. According to witnesses, Combs and Biggie did nothing for the wounded rapper who had to make his own call to the police. He then laid against the wall and smoked a joint as he waited for the ambulance.

After a three-hour surgery, Shakur left the hospital fearing for his life. He made his appearance in a Manhattan courtroom the following day and was found guilty and later sentenced to fifty-four months in jail. After serving less than a year, Marion "Suge" Knight of Death Row Records posted bail for Shakur's appeal in exchange for a three-record deal. Suspecting that the shooting was a setup by Biggie and Combs, Shakur felt safe signing with Death Row for the protection Suge Knight could offer his clients.

Despite the prison sentence and attempts on his life, Shakur released *Me Against the World* in 1995 quickly followed by the double-CD *All Eyez On Me*, both of which sold in excess of two million copies. But in September of the following year Shakur's luck had run out. After leaving the Mike Tyson–Bruce Seldon boxing match in Las Vegas, Knight and Shakur were driving down East Flamingo Road near the Strip when a late-model white Cadillac with four passengers pulled alongside. A gunman in the back seat emptied a semi-automatic pistol into the passenger side of Knight's black BMW. Shakur took four shots to the chest and abdomen.

FINAL RESTING PLACE
Cremated
Ashes returned to the family

In critical condition with four bullet wounds, Shakur was rushed to the nearby University Hospital where he was operated on immediately. After his right lung was removed, Shakur began to show signs of improvement four days later. However he fell into a coma and died of respiratory and cardiac arrest six days after the shooting. After the autopsy, his mother had his body cremated with no further details offered to the press.

What I learned in jail was that I can't change. I can't live a different lifestyle—this is it. This is the life that they gave me and this is the life that I made.

Tupac Shakur

THE NOTORIOUS D.E.A.D.

NEW MEMBERS OF THE DEAD RAP STAR CLUB

Christopher "The Notorious B.I.G." Wallace
May 21, 1972—March 9, 1997

Raised in the rough Bedford-Stuyvesant section of Brooklyn, New York, by his unmarried mother, Christopher Wallace (street name Biggie Smalls, stage name the Notorious B.I.G.) lived the life of the gangsta rapper he portrayed on his albums. An ex-convict and one-time crack dealer, B.I.G. dropped out of high school and before the age of twenty had been either charged or convicted of drug possession, assault and battery, robbery, and multiple weapons charges. Fortunately for B.I.G. these proved to be excellent creditials for entree into the world of music—specifically the violent and provocative world of gangsta rap. Drawing from his world of violence, drugs, and death, B.I.G. released his debut album, *Ready to Die*, under the Bad Boy Entertainment label (run by Sean "Puffy" Combs) in 1994. The album chronicled life in the hood and closes with the haunting death of its rapping narrator. With the hit single "One More Chance" B.I.G. was catapulted to stardom and was named Rap Artist of the Year by *Billboard* magazine and was awarded Rap Singer of the Year in 1995. And though rap artist Tupac Shakur and B.I.G. were once friends and contemporaries, Shakur was angry with B.I.G. accusing rap's latest star of ripping off Shakur's musical style and being involved with the near fatal shooting and robbery of Shakur in 1994. When B.I.G. made references to Tupac in his music, Shakur countered with a rap and video alleging that Shakur had slept with B.I.G.'s wife, singer Faith Evans. The rivalry escalated to such a point that Combs, Death Row founder and CEO Marion "Suge" Knight, the East Los Angeles street gangs the Bloods and the Crips, and rap groups the Dogg Pound, Junior M.A.F.I.A., and Mobb Deep all became involved in the feud. In the fall of 1996 Shakur was fatally gunned down in Las Vegas and though the East Coast/West Coast feud was viewed as a possible motive for murder, no arrests were made. Then just six short months later, after attending the Soul Train Music Awards and an industry party, a dark car pulled alongside B.I.G.'s GMC Suburban at a stoplight and fired several shots into the passenger-side door. The Notorious B.I.G. was pronounced dead on arrival at nearby Cedars-Sinai Medical Center. At the time of his shooting, B.I.G. was listening to a tape of his newest album, *Life After Death*. The CD was released three weeks after his murder and sold over a million copies before the month was over.

So the question remains: Who killed Tupac and Biggie? Investigations by both private and public organizations point to numerous potential suspects. One theory holds Crips gang member Orlando Anderson as the triggerman in Tupac's murder. Interestingly enough, the car used in the B.I.G. killing was registered to Anderson's cousin (Anderson himself was murdered in 1998). Another theory points to B.I.G. offering one million dollars to the triggerman in the Shakur slaying, only to have the assassin turn the gun on B.I.G. after being short-changed. Still another theory leads straight to Death Row CEO Marion "Suge" Knight and Bad Boy Records executive Puffy Combs over money and ego (Shakur was about to leave Death Row for another label). It probably didn't help investigators any when various witnesses to the slayings such as Yafeu Fula (a member of Shakur's entourage) were found murdered shortly after the rapper's homicide. Regardless of the various stories and alibis offered in the press, the fact remains that two rappers are dead, both slayings remain unsolved, neither murders are being actively investigated by the Los Angeles Police Department, and both rappers were cremated with their ashes returned to their families.

Lisa "Left Eye" Lopes
May 27, 1971—April 25, 2002

As a member of one of the most popular hip-hop R&B groups during the 1990s, TLC burst onto charts in 1992 with their platinum selling debut album *Ooooooohhh On the TLC Tip.* With a condom in place of the left-eye lens on her glasses, Lisa "Left Eye" Lopes, along with childhood friends Rozonda "Chinin" Thomas and Tionne "T-Boz" Watkins, formed the trio which quickly garnered international fame with the hits "Ain't 2 Proud 2 Beg" and "Baby-Baby-Baby" off their first album. Two years later they had even a bigger success with their second album *CrazySexyCool* selling over four million albums—one of the biggest selling albums by an all-female group. That same year Lopes pleaded guilty to arson and was sentenced to a half-way house and probation after torching her boyfriend's home, baseball player Andre Rison. In 1994 the group collected two more of their four Grammy Awards,

but tension between the group members was obvious. After the release of another multiplatinum album in 1999, Lopes challenged the other members of TLC to release solo efforts so fans could choose their favorite member. Lopes's solo effort, *SuperNova,* received little airplay and suffered from poor sales. Lopes was on vacation in Honduras when the minivan she was driving was struck head-on in a dangerous two-lane road just outside the town of La Ceiba. Although Lopes died instantly at the scene, the other seven passengers in the van were not injured. Funeral services were held in Atlanta, Georgia, with burial at Hillandale Memorial Gardens in Lithonia, Georgia. As you enter the cemetery, park near the entrance by the mausoleum. Walk toward the lake and Lopes's grave can be found fifty feet above the lake shore in Garden J, Space 38,

Eric "Easy-E" Wright
September 7, 1963—March 26, 1995

Cofounder of the influential Compton, California, gangsta rap group N.W.A., Easy-E (along with Dr. Dre and Ice Cube) won acclaim for portraying life on the streets of east L.A. in the 1980s as one of the premier West Coast rappers. Upon his death from AIDS, then-mayor of Compton Omar Bradley (who once chastised Wright for portraying the city as a gang ridden cesspool) proclaimed the day of his funeral as "Easy-E Day" for making Compton famous around the world. Driving up the hill of Rose Hills Memorial Park in Whittier, California, turn left at the bottom of the Lupine Lawn Section and drive about 200 feet to the next intersection. Walk about 25 rows up the hill to Lot 3113, Grave 1, to his simple flat marker.

Jason "Jam Master Jay" Mizell
January 21, 1965—October 30, 2002

The first rap group ever to appear on the cover of *Rolling Stone* magazine, Jam Master Jay was the DJ for the group Run-DMC. With fellow rappers Russell Simmons (Run) and Darryl McDaniels (DMC), Run-DMC catapulted to stardom in the 1980s as the first rap/hip-hop group to garner mainstream fame. The trio's minimalist style (often just a drum machine and the turntable scratching by Jay) served them well as the group became the first rap group to make it into the Top Ten charts, have the first rap video aired on MTV, and star in the first rap-oriented movie *(Krush Groove).* Teaming with members of the hard-rock group Aerosmith, Run-DMC achieved worldwide success with a remake of "Walk This Way" in 1986. Out of the limelight for several years, Jay was shot in the head in his New York City studio by two unknown gunman. He was laid to rest at Ferncliff Cemetery in Hartsdale, New York, in the Hillcrest Garden C, Plot 1120.

FRANK SINATRA

BORN December 12, 1915
Hoboken, New Jersey

DIED May 14, 1998
Los Angeles, California

CAUSE OF DEATH Heart Attack
Age 82

He wasn't called the Voice for nothing, for Francis Albert Sinatra possessed probably the finest voice of any singer in the twentieth century. The epitome of cocktail cool, Sinatra was the first modern pop star, provoking mass adolescent pandemonium that would later dog Elvis Presley and the Beatles. A master of phrasing and style, a series of brilliant conceptual albums with an incredible array of songwriters, lyricists, and arrangers at his disposal assured his legacy as the Chairman of the Board.

In the Beginning . . .

Frank Sinatra, the only child of boxer-turned-fireman Anthony and former barmaid Dolly, was born in the shadow of Manhattan in Hoboken, New Jersey. An amateur singer in high school, Sinatra worked at the local newspaper and sang in the evening in various talent contests, either solo or with the Hoboken Four. In his early twenties he began working his first professional job as the singer, emcee, and waiter at the Rustic Cabin roadhouse in Englewood Cliffs, New Jersey. During one of his shows in 1939, famed bandleader Harry James heard Sinatra perform over the radio and hired him to front his band. At the end of the year, Sinatra met another one of his idols and went to work for Tommy Dorsey. For the next three years Sinatra learned all the elements of phrasing, song selection, and awesome breath control (he could go sixteen bars without taking a breath) that catapulted the young singer into a star.

In 1942, Sinatra thought he was out of his contract with Dorsey and started his solo career. Dubbed the Voice That Is Thrilling Millions by a manager, Sinatra recorded the signature tunes that defined his earlier career, such as "When Your Lover Is Gone," "Fools Rush In," and "I've Got a Crush on You." Struggling to be taken seriously as opposed to being just another teen idol, in 1946 Sinatra had all teenagers banned from his radio shows and began adjusting his repertoire to include slower but still swinging arrangements of the classics.

As all artists will encounter, Sinatra hit a dry spell in the late forties as he was labeled a bully by gossip columnist, was seen in the company of notorious underworld figures, and left his wife and three children for actress Ava Gardner. But in 1953 he won the part of Private Maggio in the film *From Here to Eternity*, which won him an Academy Award and the respect of his peers.

🎻➡ While there are no less than one hundred informal and unauthorized collections of Sinatra memorabilia on the drawing boards of those wishing to cash in, only two under consideration are authorized by the family. Both the Smithsonian on the East Coast and a proposed Frank Sinatra Museum in Palm Springs, California, on the West Coast have plans for a permanent Sinatra exhibit. In Sinatra's hometown of Hoboken, the options are a little bit underwhelming. The Hoboken Historical Society has made available for one dollar a walking tour map of relevant Sinatra sites throughout the town. The highlights of the tour include Lepore's Chocolates and the owner's vast collection of Sinatra stuff on the walls, the building shell at 415 Monroe Street (it burned down in 1967) where Sinatra spent his youth, and the Frank Sinatra Museum next door (that, other than photographs, seems to be lacking in actual memorabilia). Naturally, after a two-hour walking tour you can have lunch at Piccolo's or Leo's Grandevous in Hoboken, which are virtual shrines to the memory of Old Blue Eyes.

For the remaining 1950s through the 1960s, Sinatra threw himself into both films and music. Making a return to the recording studios he recast himself as the sophisticated, worldly hipster and surrounded himself with some of the top arrangers and songwriters of the time—Sammy Cahn, Nelson Riddle, Gordon Jenkins, and Jimmy Van Heusen to name a few. All in all, Sinatra recorded fifty-one albums of timeless music from 1954 to 1975 including *Songs for Young Lovers* and *Only the Lonely.*

In the End . . .

The 1980s were rather sedate for Sinatra as he was honored with numerous awards, including the Presidential Medal of Freedom (the highest honor awarded a civilian of the U.S.). And while his musical output slowed (he recorded only five albums during his last fifteen years), his legend only grew as several unauthorized biographies were released and cartoonist Garry Trudeau featured several strips with Sinatra cavorting with his mobster friends.

In 1985, Sinatra insisted on hitting the road with his son, Frank Jr., as his long-suffering band leader. Despite his advanced age and need for TelePromTer assistance with the lyrics, Sinatra sold out night after night with fans fearing this would be the last time to see the Voice in person. Sinatra still had a little bit of fire in him as he closed out the decade with a pair of albums, *Duets I* and *Duets II*, that paired Sinatra with recording stars as diverse as U2's Bono and Tony Bennett, with both albums winning Grammy Awards.

With his memory fading, his eyesite eroded, and his heart weakening each day, Sinatra refused to age gracefully. Continually fighting to stay out of the hospital and refusing to keep doctor's appointments, Sinatra tried to control his failing health as he had tried to control everything else in his life. Out of the public eye since 1997, Sinatra died at Cedars Sinai Hospital with his family by his bedside.

Desert Memorial Park
Cathedral City, California

The Chairman of the Board was laid to rest in the Sinatra family plot just outside the resort community of Palm Springs. As you drive into the side entrance, turn left toward the cemetery office. From the front gate of the cemetery, count twenty-two rows from the entrance and four rows from the road and Francis Albert Sinatra is buried with his mother, father, and good friend Jilly Rizzo.

Rock 'n' roll is the most brutal, ugly, degenerate, vicious form of expression. Lewd, sly, in plain fact, dirty. A rancid-smelling aphrodisiac and the martial music of every side-burned delinquent on the face of the earth.

Frank Sinatra

THE RAT PACK PRIMER

THE CHAIRMAN OF THE BOARD AND HIS PACK OF COOL

When cool came to town in Las Vegas during the 1960s, the defining element of "cool" was the Rat Pack—Sinatra, Dean Martin, Sammy Davis Jr., Joey Bishop, Peter Lawford, and various other pallies, *paisans*, and hanger-ons. With a scotch in one hand (except for Bishop, who was the group's token teetotaler), a cigarette in the other, and tuxedoed to kill, the crew ruled the strip at night. Interesting enough, Sinatra was not the original Chairman of the Board, nor did the group even begin with Old Blue Eyes; rather, the genesis of the Rat Pack began with close Sinatra friend Humphrey Bogart.

In the 1950s an informal social club called the Holmby Hills Rat Pack (named by Lauren Bacall when the boys came in from drinking one night and she commented that they all looked like "a pack of drowned rats") formed around Bogart and his friends. With original members Bogart, Bacall, Sinatra, Judy Garland, agent Swifty Lazar, and songwriter Sammy Cahn, Sinatra took control of the group as Bogart's health began to decline in his later years. Pulling in his friends Sinatra was dubbed the Chairman of the Board by the press whenever the social club was spotted at a popular Hollywood hotspot. The group really took off after Vincente Minnelli directed Sinatra and Martin in their first movie together, *Some Came Running.* Shortly after Sinatra produced and directed Martin's album, *Sleep Warm,* the duo shared the stage at the Sands on the Vegas strip, trading ad libs that became the beginning of early sixties Rat Pack hipness. With the addition of Sammy Davis Jr., Joey Bishop (who scripted most of the group's jokes and ad-libs) and Peter Lawford (a bit actor with close ties to the Kennedys), the group's hard-swinging, hot-chicks, hazy booze-filled reputation was sealed with the film *Ocean's Eleven.* With Sinatra's death in 1998, Bishop became the only surviving member of either Rat Pack social club.

DAVIS

SAMMY DAVIS JR.
December 8, 1925—May 16, 1990

A flamboyant entertainer firmly trained in the vaudevillian tradition, Sammy Davis Jr. first appeared on the stage at the age of two. Four years later, he made his film debut in the Ethel Waters film *Rufus Jones for President.* At the age of seven he joined his father and his uncle in the family song-and-dance act, the Will Maston Trio but within a couple of short years the young Davis was the star of the act. In 1946 the group finally broke out of the one-night stand chitlin circuit and became headliners. Losing an eye in an automobile accident forced Davis to concentrate on his singing, and his strength remained in his nightclub act, with only one hit to his credit, "Candy Man." He died of cancer in 1990 and was buried at Forest Lawn Memorial Park in Glendale, California, at the top of the cemetery in the locked Garden of Honor section.

DEAN MARTIN
June 7, 1917—December 25, 1995

Throughout his career, he slyly and hilariously exploited the myth that his supreme relaxation was the result of knocking back a few too many martinis. In fact, Dean Martin was the master of the insinuating ad-lib and a natural at self-parody. When he died at the age of seventy-eight, Dean Martin was the quintessential lounge lizard.

The son of an Italian immigrant barber, Dino Paul Crocetti was born in 1917 in the working-class town of Steubenville, Ohio. He began his singing career at a local spaghetti restaurant, copying the style of Bing Crosby "one hundred percent." As Dino Martini, he slowly worked his way up the lounge and nightclub circuit until he was headlining at most of his shows. His relaxed, easygoing charm won him only moderate success until in 1946, billing himself as Dean Martin, he teamed up with rising comic Jerry Lewis.

With Dean and Jerry booked on the same bill at the Club 500 in Atlantic City, they began to improvise, with Martin as the straight man trying to sing to the audience, and Lewis always interrupting and talking to the patrons and staff. After a couple shows they became a team, and within two months they moved the act to the Copacabana in New York City for a twelve-week run. At a salary of five thousand dollars a week, they were one of the highest-paid nightclub acts in postwar America.

Word of mouth spread quickly and they soon found themselves on the West Coast filming television specials. In 1948, they signed a long-term movie deal with director Hal Wallis at Paramount. The following year the wildly successful *My Friend Irma* was released and for the next seven years they released a total of sixteen films, all of which were commercially successful. Outside of films, Martin continued to record and released a number of minor hits, including "I'll Always Love You" and "That's Amore."

As is often the case with any successful team, the Martin/Lewis relationship began to show signs of fatigue after time. While completing their final picture, *Hollywood or Bust* (where Martin was practically written out of the first forty minutes in favor of Jerry's clowning antics), they announced their breakup. Some years later Martin said "the two biggest turning points in my career were meeting Jerry Lewis and leaving Jerry Lewis."

Dean continued to play the slightly amused, fraternally indulgent, and faintly patronizing straight man, successfully mixing cabaret and film work for several years, but without any recording success. That all changed in 1964 when he reached number one with "Everybody Loves Somebody," which became the theme song of his long-running television series *The Dean Martin Show*. However, it was his antics offstage as a member of the notorious Rat Pack that drew the attention of the press. The consulship of cool had its origins in 1959 during the filming of *Some Came Running* with Martin and Sinatra. During the recording of Martin's *Sleep Warm* album, Sinatra conducted the orchestra by day, and by night the two were joined by Peter Lawford, Joey Bishop, Sammy Davis Jr., and Shirley MacLaine (in her present life) onstage at the Sands in Las Vegas. During the early 1960s, the Rat Pack filmed by day, took the stage of the Sands by night, and in between drank, smoked, and sat around telling stories. John F. Kennedy, an honorary member, was often seen at ringside.

After forty years in the public eye, Dean semiretired from the business to his home in Beverly Hills, making the occasional appearance with Frank in Vegas or with Jerry on his famous telethon. He took a turn for the worse, however, when his son, Dean Paul, died in a fiery plane crash in 1987. He never made a public appearance after his son's death—the sardonic wit gone along with his will to live.

Martin was buried at Westwood Village Memorial Park in Los Angeles in the Sanctuary of Love mausoleum.

BESSIE SMITH

BORN April 15, 1894
Chattanooga, Tennessee

DIED September 26, 1937
Clarksdale, Mississippi

CAUSE OF DEATH Automobile Accident
Age 43

If Robert Johnson, Son House, Charley Patton, and Muddy Waters were all considered the King of the Blues at one time or another, then Bessie Smith was most certainly their queen, or as she was later referred to, Empress of the Blues. The highest-paid black entertainer of her time, she recorded over 160 sides and left a rich legacy that influenced generations of artists, including Billie Holiday, Dinah Washington, Aretha Franklin, and Janis Joplin.

In the Beginning . . .

Raised in a one-room cabin on Cameron Hill in Chattanooga, Tennessee, with her parents and six brothers and sisters, Bessie emerged from abject poverty by singing and dancing in the streets for change. By age twelve she was already on the road with a theater group, which also starred blues legend Ma Rainey. Although she was only paid ten dollars a week by the show manager, audience members would sometimes throw that same amount up on the stage during one of her numbers. Despite popular legend, Ma Rainey took no credit for the young teenager's talent—she was a natural.

Bessie was rejected for a recording contract by a number of companies up north. One notable rejection came from Thomas Edison, who rejected Smith by entering "NG" (no good) next to her name when she auditioned for his label. Smith ultimately cut her first songs—"Gulf Coast Blues" and "Downhearted Blues"—for Columbia Records on February 15, 1923, and within six months sold more that 800,000 copies.

For the next four years Bessie Smith's review was the hit of the theater circuit and she even had her own private rail car with an entourage of forty-five people. Her record contract called for twelve new songs per year (Smith did much more than that), and she spent the rest of her time on the road. Her shows were constantly sold out as Smith commanded two thousand dollars per night.

As time passed, Smith's talents grew enormously, but what should have been her glory days seemed to produce failure after failure. She was involved with a doomed Broadway musical, *Pansy*, which closed after only four shows as the grip of the Great Depression was too much for many theater owners. Columbia Records even dropped Smith from their roster when they almost sank into bankruptcy. The Empress of the Blues was even forced to suffer the indignity of having Hack Back, the Ukelele Wonder, accompany her onstage.

Blues folklore has held that when Bessie Smith was brought to the G. T. Thomas Hospital in Clarksdale, she was turned away because she was black. The only problem with this legend is that the Thomas Hospital was a black hospital. Today it is better known as the Riverside Hotel, once home to Sonny Boy Williamson II and Ike Turner. Smith's memorabilia can be found at the Rock and Roll Hall of Fame, where she was one of the original inductees.

Smith's career began to turn around when she met Richard Morgan, a dapper and charming bootlegger for Al Capone. By 1933, Smith began to record again for OKeh Records and was recording and performing with Benny Goodman and other stars of the swing era. She was about to sign a contract to perform with Lionel Hampton, Johnny Hodges, and Nat "King" Cole, but it was not to be.

In the End . . .

At one o'clock in the morning, Bessie's companion Richard Morgan pulled Smith's old Packard onto Route 61 with Smith as its other passenger, leaving Memphis for Clarksdale, Mississippi. Smith fell asleep as Morgan drove down the dark, narrow highway. Suddenly the rear end of a large truck appeared in front of the Packard and the car slammed into the back of the truck, throwing Bessie onto the highway. As the truck quickly drove away, Richard frantically waved at an approaching car. The car shined its headlights, highlighting the unconscious figure lying near the wreckage. As one of the occupants ran to a nearby house to call for an ambulance, the other driver, Dr. Hugh Smith, examined Bessie and determined her condition was critical. Smith was taken to the Clarksdale hospital, but died at 11:30 that morning of intra-abdominal injuries.

Mount Lawn Cemetery
Sharon Hill, Pennsylvania

Drive though the gates and turn left. Go to the last road in the cemetery and then turn right. The grave is located on the left just before the first row of trees, and the large upright stone is visible from the road. If the stone looks "new," you are correct. Her grave remained unmarked until 1970, when Janis Joplin and a local nursing home owner, Juanita Green, split the cost of the stone.

Bessie showed me the air, and taught me how to fill it.

Janis Joplin

ART TATUM

BORN October 13, 1909
Toledo, Ohio

DIED November 5, 1956
Los Angeles, California

CAUSE OF DEATH Kidney Failure
Age 47

Art Tatum transported the art of jazz piano improvisation beyond the real and imagined confines of his day. Technically the most advanced and respected pianist in the 1920s and 1930s, his influence on later jazz pianists—Bud Powell, Oscar Peterson, and Erroll Garner—was unparalleled.

In the Beginning . . .

Art Tatum was born a visually impaired child prodigy in Toledo, Ohio. Completely blind in one eye with limited vision in the other, he was encouraged by his musically talented mother (piano) and father (guitar) at an early age. By the age of three, he was able to play music by ear and as a teenager Tatum developed his talent at the Toledo School of Music, where he was encouraged to pursue a career as a classical pianist. However, Tatum found the pull of Fats Waller stronger than the limited prospects for a black concert pianist.

At age eighteen he was already well known in the clubs around Toledo and Cleveland. Strongly influenced by Waller, Tatum made a name for himself among musicians with his ability to take complex passages and transform a standard jazz melody into a blindingly rapid run up and down the keyboard, varying tempos, styles, and passing harmonies. Whether he was playing as a soloist or in a small trio, Tatum enjoyed impressing and intimidating would-be competitors in cutting contests and after-hours jam sessions. In 1932, Tatum moved to New York where he was the featured after-hours pianist at the Onyx Club in Harlem. He cut his first records in 1933, recording songs that would become staples in his live act, including "Tiger Rag," "Indiana," and "Body and Soul." Despite his notoriety among musicians, Tatum was unable to support himself in New York and slowly made his way through the Midwest for much of the thirties. From 1938 to 1942 he found himself in Los Angeles, where he was in high demand to play at celebrity parties. Through his connections in Hollywood, he was featured on one of Bing Crosby's television specials in the early 1940s.

Although working primarily as a soloist, he was equally comfortable working with his trio with Tiny Grimes on guitar and Slam Stewart on bass. Patterned after Nat "King" Cole's successful trio, the group matured in jam sessions at Tatum's after-hours jobs. Growing more successful with each passing year, Tatum began splitting his time between New York and Los Angeles, playing in New York at the Three Deuces, the Downbeat, and the Famous Door, or in Los Angeles at a variety of hot jazz clubs on Central Avenue or in Hollywood.

Tatum signed with Capitol in 1949, which led to four productive years of recording. His endless flow of melodies were surrounded by detailed counter melodies, all the while

Every year in the month of June the Toledo Jazz Society pays tribute to the legendary pianist with the Art Tatum Jazz Heritage Festival in the pianist's hometown of Toledo, Ohio. The festival honors the memory of Tatum with an all-day outdoor program with individual performances and special events lasting until 2:00 A.M.

hinting at the underlying theme. In 1953, Tatum began an association with record producer Norman Granz that led to a marathon series of 120 tracks over the next year. Granz also organized small group combos pairing Tatum with Lionel Hampton, Ben Webster, Barney Kessel, Benny Carter, and drummer Buddy Rich. Tatum went into the studio one final time in early 1956 to record his last album, *Art Tatum in Person.*

In the End . . .

Because of this series of sessions and the friendship that evolved, Granz was determined to advance Art's career. A series of U.S. and European concert hall-style dates were planned. The plans had progressed so far that Tatum had already purchased the traditional white tuxedo and tails. Unfortunately, Tatum's health had already begun to deteriorate in 1953 when he was diagnosed with kidney disease. Tatum continued a limited number of live engagements in Los Angeles and New York, but was forced to return home in the summer of 1956. In November, he was hospitalized and died of uremia shortly thereafter.

FINAL RESTING PLACES
Rosedale Cemetery
Los Angeles, California

Ella Fitzgerald sang "God Will Take Care of You" as pallbearers Benny Carter and Eddie Beal, along with honorary pallbearers Oscar Peterson, Erroll Garner, Dizzy Gillespie, and Cozy Cole escorted his casket to Section 5, Plot 173-2NW. However, in 1991 Tatum was disinterred and the monument serves as a cenotaph to the legendary pianist.

Forest Lawn Memorial Park
Glendale, California

Art Tatum was laid to rest in the Great Mausoleum in 1991. As you enter the cemetery gates, drive up the hill, turning left into the parking area of the great mausoleum. Tatum's

final resting place is locked and not open to the general public. However, if you park at the entrance on the right farthest from the main entrance and walk in behind a keyholder, Tatum can be found on the ground floor near the entrance in the Jasmine Terrace, Sanctuary of Restful Peace on the bottom row in Crypt 16107.

Not just anyone could get to hear Tatum at his best. It is generally accepted. . . . that his most formidable playing was displayed only in circumstances and before audiences largely of his own choosing. After hours, the man played strictly as he pleased.

jazz critic Orrin Keepnews

THE TEMPTATIONS

MELVIN FRANKLIN
BORN
October 12, 1942
Montgomery,
Alabama

DIED
February 23, 1995
Los Angeles,
California

CAUSE OF DEATH
Heart Failure
Age 52

EDDIE KENDRICKS
BORN
December 17, 1939
Union Springs,
Alabama

DIED
October 5, 1992
Birmingham,
Alabama

CAUSE OF DEATH
Lung Cancer
Age 52

PAUL WILLIAMS
BORN
July 2, 1939
Birmingham,
Alabama

DIED
August 17, 1973
Detriot,
Michigan

CAUSE OF DEATH
Suicide
Age 34

DAVID RUFFIN
BORN
January 18, 1941
Meridian,
Mississippi

DIED
June 1, 1991
Philadelphia,
Pennsylvania

CAUSE OF DEATH
Drug Overdose
Age 50

With a history stretching over four decades, the Temptations were destined to become one of the most successful, long-lived, and beloved vocal groups in pop music history. With a catalog of popular songs, finely tuned harmonies, smooth, precision choreography, shimmering, suave costumes, and perfectly blended vocals, the Temptations were able to appeal far beyond their core black audience.

In the Beginning . . .

The history of the Temptations begins with two competing vocal groups—a trio called the Primes (with Eddie Kendricks, Paul Williams, and Kell Osborne) and the Distants (a quintet featuring Melvin Franklin, Otis Williams, Eldridge Bryant, and two other singers). Shortly after the Distants recorded their one single, "Come On," they broke up, thus allowing Franklin, Williams, and Bryant to join forces with Kendricks and Williams to form the Elgins in 1960.

The newly formed quintet was asked to audition for Berry Gordy Jr., but were notified that they would need to change their name if they wanted a contract. They came up with

---

A former Ford assembly-line worker, Berry Gordy Jr. borrowed seven hundred dollars to open his own independent recording studio and record label. Today Motown Records, also called "Hitsville U.S.A.," is one of the best examples of what a music-oriented museum and tour should be. Tours begin with Gordy's humble residence and continue with the business office, the studio (aka the Snakepit), the control room, finishing with the Motown Historical Museum (complete with costumes of the Supremes and the Temptations). What makes this museum a cut above the rest is it looks and feels like the Motown Records of the 1970s. The studio has all the original mics, instruments, and music stands complete with sheet music still on them. The control room still boasts the original 3-track and 8-track tape machines used to record the Temptations' "My Girl" and "Papa Was a Rolling Stone." The historical display includes memorabilia from the Temptations, Marvin Gaye, Mary Wells, the Four Tops, Stevie Wonder, the Pips, and everyone else who walked through the doors of 2648 West Grand Boulevard in Detroit, Michigan. The future looks bright for the museum as talks are underway to add a new Motown museum in the downtown historic district. Currently the museum displays less than 5 percent of the costumes, instruments, gold records, sheet music, and videotapes that are in Motown's vast archives.

the Temptations on the front lawn of the offices, and later that same night passed the audition and signed with Motown Records.

The group released their first two singles, "Oh, Mother of Mine" and "Check Yourself" for Miracle Records in 1961 without much success. They were switched to Motown's newly formed Gordy Records and released "Dream Come True," which topped out at number twenty-two on the R&B charts. Their next four singles all failed to chart, causing concerns with Gordy and Motown Records. In 1963, famed Motown choeographer Cholly Atkins worked with the group to add polish to the show, adding slick new routines to the struggling singers. Fortunately, things then began to change for the group, with the addition of Smokey Robinson as their principal songwriter and the addition of David Ruffin to replace Bryant after Bryant attacked Paul Williams after a Christmas show. With Ruffin's gruff baritone vocals providing a perfect balance to Kendricks's silky falsetto, Robinson scored a chart hit for

the group with "The Way You Do the Things You Do." In 1965, the Temptations scored their first number one hit with "My Girl" with Ruffin on lead vocals. For the next four years Motown Records and the Temptations altered the public's perception of black music. Combining the elements of gospel, blues, pop, and swing with the backing of an incredible studio band known as the Funk Brothers, and the amazing stable of in-house songwriting talent, the Temptations were unstoppable on the charts. The group remained at the forefront of radio and record sales with such Top 10 hits as "Ain't Too Proud to Beg" (featuring the famous Temptation "walk"), "I Know I'm Losing You," "All I

The Temptations from left to right: David Ruffin, Melvin Franklin, Paul Williams, Otis Williams, and Eddie Kendricks.

Need," and "You're My Everything." In 1968, a dispute arose with Ruffin, though it is unclear who initiated the action. Some say Ruffin wanted more say in the group (such as Diana Ross had within the Supremes) and independent songwriting credits, and he quit of his own volition. Others say that Ruffin was fired for asking too many question regarding the business dealings, wondering why the group pulled in ten thousand dollars a night, yet each member was only paid five hundred a week. Either way, Ruffin departed in early 1968 after recording the Top 10 R&B hit "Please Return Your Love to Me."

The group rebounded by summer and replaced Ruffin with ex-Contour singer Dennis Edwards. In 1969, the recording of "Cloud Nine" brought both Motown and the Temptations their first Grammy Award. But two short years and several more hits later, Kendricks departed the group after recording "Just My Imagination" and Paul Williams was released due to his struggle with drugs and alcohol. The changing of the guard was complete, with only Franklin and Otis Williams left from the original Temptations. Still, they were able to maintain their position on the charts when Damon Harris replaced Kendricks and sang lead on the number one pop hit "Papa Was a Rolling Stone," adding two more Grammy Awards to their collection.

I've been praying hard for him to come back to life. Tell him to call me if you see him. I just want to talk to him face to face. I want to tell him to look up instead of down. If he would just go right, he would be a famous man someday.

Earline Ruffin, David's stepmother, one year before he died

In the End . . .

For the departing former Temptations, being an "ex" Temptation was both a blessing and a curse. Paul Williams was unable to control his demons and was found dead in his car in an abandoned parking lot just around the corner from Motown Records. He died from a self-inflicted bullet wound to the head.

For Ruffin, his recording career in 1975 began with the number one R&B album *A Song for You*. After several Top 10 hits on both the pop and R&B charts, including "Walk Away from Love" and "Everything's Coming Up Love," Ruffin's career began to suffer as he started using cocaine more and more frequently. And like Ruffin, Kendricks's solo efforts began with the R&B hit single "Keep on Truckin' " and began to flounder by the late 1970s. And as for the remaining Temptations, no longer working with their principle songwriters Smokey Robinson and Norman Whitfield, the group left Motown in 1975 for Atlantic Records. After two years with limited success, the Temptations returned to Motown, but they were no longer regarded as a leading force in R&B or pop music.

The 1980s saw a resurgence of the Motown sound and the Temptations reunited with Kendricks and Ruffin for a reunion tour in 1982. After producing another hit single, "Standing on the Top," and selling out shows across the U.S., tensions within the band and Ruffin's continued drug use caused the band to split apart again after an engagement in New York City. The group continued on with Williams and Franklin as they appeared at the Motown twenty-fifth Anniversary Show and then headed back out on the road, selling out show after show for the next three years.

By 1988, Ruffin was a virtual recluse, living in a mobile home owned by a friend in rural Green Oak Township near South Lyon, Michigan, with his old Cadillac rusting in the front yard. Despite selling millions of albums, Ruffin had been convicted for tax evasion, receiving and concealing stolen property, charged at various times with assault and battery, and most recently convicted of using crack cocaine. He didn't own a home, a car that ran, or have a bank account. In 1991 after completing a short tour with Kendricks and former Temptation Dennis Edwards in England, Ruffin went to a well-known crack house in Philadelphia with a briefcase full of cash and British traveler's checks (some say as much as forty thousand dollars' worth) and a need for a quick high. At 2:45 A.M. a limousine dropped an unconscious Ruffin at the front of the emergency entrance of the University of Pennsylvania Hospital. An hour later Ruffin was pronounced dead, and due to lack of identification, was tagged in the morgue as a "John Doe." He was positively identified three days after his death. Police later retrieved the briefcase, but the money and traveler's checks were gone.

After his arrest for failure to pay child support at Ruffin's funeral, Kendricks began experiencing health problems and that following November had his right lung removed to stop the spread of lung cancer. The remaining Temptations continued on and released their fiftieth album, *Milestone.* The following month the group was honored by the NAACP Hall of Fame, to add to their induction to the Rock and Roll Hall of Fame in early 1990. But nearly one year after his surgery and a pending lawsuit over missing royalty payments from Motown Records, Kendricks lost his battle with lung cancer. Without health insurance, Kendricks died leaving his family penniless.

In 1995, original member Melvin Franklin was stricken with a brain seizure in Los Angeles, California. Rushed to Cedars Sinai Hospital, Franklin died of heart failure a week later. With only Otis Williams remaining as an original member, the Temptations entered their fourth decade of performing stronger than ever. In 1998, the group made an appearance at the Super Bowl football championship halftime show and later that month released the album *Phoenix Rising*, featuring the hit single "Stay." In November of that same year the premier of the made-for-TV movie *The Temptations*, based on Williams's book, brought a renewed interest in the vocal group. After their inductions into the Vocal Group Hall of Fame, the group released still another album, *Earresistable*, in 2000, and received another Grammy Award that same year.

FINAL RESTING PLACES
Woodlawn Cemetery
Detroit, Michigan

As you enter the cemetery, turn left before the office and drive around the back of the office building. David Ruffin's large, flat marble stone memorial is just off the road on the right-hand side, behind the office, directly in front of the black Teamer/Smith monument.

Lincoln Park Cemetery
Clinton Township, Michigan

Paul Williams was quietly buried in Section G, Lot 275, Grave 4 under a simple, flat bronze marker.

Forest Lawn Hollywood Hills
Los Angeles, California

As you enter the cemetery, turn left and drive toward the large outdoor mausoleum. On the outside wall toward the right, Melvin Franklin (born David English) can be found in the Courts of Rememberance, Crypt C-3571.

Elmwood Cemetery
Birmingham, Alabama

Eddie Kendricks was laid to rest in Block 47, Lot 257, approximately forty feet from the road with his monument facing away from the road of this very large cemetery.

Eddie Kendricks Memorial Statue
Birmingham, Alabama

Located in a corner park in downtown Birmingham at Fourth Street and Eighteenth Street North, you will find this excellent tribute to one of the founding members of the Temptations.

PETER TOSH

BORN October 9, 1944
Church Lincoln,
Westmoreland, Jamaica

DIED September 11, 1987
Kingston, Jamaica

CAUSE OF DEATH Murdered
Age 42

As Jamaica's most iconoclastic reggae singer, Peter Tosh was an unapologetic ganja-smoking rude boy turned revolutionary whose music was squarely aimed at the political and social elite. His life-long advocacy of the legalization of marijuana and radical political views inevitably led him to confrontations with the police. And many believe to this day that Tosh's inflexible sense of right and wrong cost him his life.

In the Beginning . . .

Born Winston Hubert McIntosh on the southwest coast of the island of Jamaica, Peter Tosh (he changed his name in his teens) never lived with his father and his mother, who sent him to live with his aunt. Moving to Kingston during his teens, Tosh met Bob Marley and Bunny Wailer in the ghettos of Trenchtown. In 1964, they formed the Wailin' Wailers and the following year cut their first release, "Simmer Down."

As the only musician in the group, Tosh taught both Marley and Wailer how to play guitar. After a couple of singles, the group began to gain momentum and their music started to chart well on the Jamaican music charts. Though unbeknowst to Tosh, many of his rehearsals were being taped and sold in England under the name of "Peter Touch." Also they were only getting paid three pounds a week, while their singles were consistantly in the Top 20 and receiving heavy airplay on the radio. Bouncing from one producer to another didn't seem to help either as the group failed to see any royalty payments from albums selling in the U.K.

In 1972, they met with producer and owner of Island Records Chris Blackwell, who was determined to give reggae music an international audience. Their first release, *Catch a Fire*, propelled the Wailers to popularity beyond their small island nation. Their second release, *Burnin'*, saw the hit "Get Up, Stand Up" become the anthem for the group's sense of social awareness. Yet Blackwell saw success solely in the voice of Marley rather than the outspoken, candid approach of Tosh. Soon the focus shifted all to Marley and Bunny, and then Tosh left the group.

After Tosh left the Wailers, his music and views became more politicalized. In 1975, he was arrested for possession of marijuana and brutally beaten by Jamaican police.

In addition to the private mausoleum filled with photographs and memorabilia, ask your guide to take you up back to see the house where Tosh lived for many years. The house closest to the mausoleum is the home of his mother and uncle, who can be found sitting on the porch, happy to allow a few pictures for a modest donation. The half-built Tosh Museum next to the mausoleum remains just that—due to lack of funding.

Nonetheless, he recorded his first solo project in 1976, *Legalize It*, which was promptly banned in Jamaica by the government. Now Tosh was seen by friends and foe alike as an outlaw and revolutionary who was not afraid to expose the inequities of the establishment. His next effort, 1977's *Equal Rights*, delivered such stinging broadsides as "Apartheid" and "Equal Rights" aimed at the racial inequalities within South Africa long before it was considered fashionable or politically correct.

In the End . . .

When Bob Marley died of cancer in 1981, Tosh expected that his records would garner more international attention as the natural successor to Marley's fame and glory. But his hard-edged, militant stance against inequities inherent in the Jamaican "shit stem" (as Tosh would call it) and the rise of dancehall music kept Tosh on the sidelines. In 1978, he was signed by Rolling Stone Records, but those releases were arguably the weakest recordings of his career. The only hit to come of the two records was the Tosh and Mick Jagger composition "(You've Got to Walk and) Don't Look Back." His relationship with Jagger and Keith Richards quickly soured when the records failed to chart and Tosh blamed the Glimmer Twins for failing to use their vaunted influence to market or distribute his music.

After four years of contract disputes and personal problems, by 1987 Tosh realized that his brand of music and the Rasta reggae movement had lost its soul. In August of that year he released *No Nuclear War* a clean mix of reggae beats and pop hooks clearly aimed at the international market. Yet Tosh was struggling to find financing for a worldwide tour. The following month three intruders broke into Tosh's Kingston home in an alleged botched robbery attempt. Led by Dennis "Leppo" Lobban, the three demanded money when they simply shot Tosh, musician Wilton "Doctor" Brown, Tosh's girlfriend, Marlene Brown, and four others. Tosh and Doc Brown were killed instantly while the others sustained severe injuries. Lobban was quickly convicted and sent to prison while the other two were never caught (some say they were later killed by the government). Many to this day still suspect that it was a planned execution by the government who for years wanted to silence the singer.

Peter Tosh Monument and Mausoleum Bluefields, Jamaica

Located twelve miles southeast of Savanna-la-Mar, the Peter Tosh monument and mausoleum is located about one mile past the jerk stalls at Bluefields Beach Park on the left. A small donation is requested for viewing the tomb and Tosh memorabilia lining the walls surrounding his final resting place.

> *All in a Buckingham Palace, the queen dance. You think is a joke business because you know say—God Save the Queen. The queen dance to reggae music, because reggae music is the only music that has that spiritual ingredient that can heal a sick nation.*
>
> Peter Tosh

SARAH VAUGHAN

BORN March 27, 1924
Newark, New Jersey

DIED April 3, 1990
Hidden Hills, California

CAUSE OF DEATH Lung Cancer
Age 66

Second only to Ella Fitzgerald, Sarah "Sassy" Vaughan was one of the greatest lyrical interpreters and jazz singers to emerge after the Second World War. A talented jazz vocalist and pianist famous for her rich voice, wide range, and inventive, spirited spontaneity, she could change a song's mood simply by altering her enunciation or delivery.

In the Beginning . . .

Sarah Lois Vaughan was born in New Jersey into a family that cherished music. With her mother a member of the church choir and her father a skilled after-hours guitarist, it wasn't long before Vaughan was singing in the choir herself. In addition to singing gospel music, Vaughan studied piano and at the age of twelve she became the church organist. Soon after, she began playing piano in the high school orchestra and at school functions, as well as entertaining her friends and family with popular standards at parties. In 1942, she won a talent contest singing "Body and Soul" at Harlem's Apollo Theatre in New York. And though her mother was disappointed at her decision (she preferred her daughter to continue on to college to become a choir director), Vaughan entered the world of entertainment as a vocalist.

One of those in the audience at the Apollo Theatre was bandleader Billy Eckstine, who recommended Vaughan to Earl "Fatha" Hines. That summer she joined the Earl Hines big band as a pianist and vocalist. At the age of twenty, Vaughan joined Billy Eckstine's new big band and made her recording debut with him that year. Most of those first recordings were small group combo, including a well-crafted reading of "Lover Man" in which she was partnered with Charlie Parker and Dizzy Gillespie. "I thought Bird and Diz were the end," Vaughan reminisced, "At the time I was singing more off-key than on. I think their playing influenced my singing. Horns always influenced me more than voices."

After a short stint with John Kirby, Vaughan went solo at the young age of twenty-two. She continued to record cool, hip jazz albums in small combos with Parker, Gillespie, and Eckstine, along with Clifford Brown and other great artists. Among her most memorable recordings include 1948's "Nature Boy" and her million-seller "Broken Hearted Melody."

Vaughan continued to gain popularity by performing pop ballads and show tunes, while still recording numerous jazz anthems. During the 1950s she recorded songs for the Mercury label, which were decidedly more pop oriented. She was also not above recording show tunes, including "C'est la Vie," "Whatever Lola Wants," and the popular Harry Belafonte Calypso song, "Banana Boat Song."

In addition to the numerous artists she recorded with, Vaughan was also heavily influenced by the men in her personal life. Married for ten years to trumpeter George Treadwell (who later became her manager), Treadwell encouraged Vaughan to take voice lessons after she had become a professional singer. He also arranged for Vaughan to undergo plastic surgery, dental reconstruction, and he upgraded her wardrobe. The effect was so dramatic she was later nicknamed "Sassy." Her second marriage to taxicab company owner and businessman C. B. Atkins in 1958 added a layer of business acumen that was missing from her professional life. After the marriage, Atkins put Vaughan's business affairs in order, ridding her of parasites and hangers-on that so often permeate the music industry. Vaughan continued to record for a variety of different labels between 1960 and 1967 before taking a five-year break. In 1971, she returned to music under the Pablo label with Norman Granz.

In the End . . .

During the 1980s, Vaughan became a bit reclusive, rarely allowing access for interviews or stories about her personal life. Self-concious more than reclusive, she once bristled, "They always ask me the same questions. Where was I born? When did I start singing? Who have I worked with?" So naturally, many believed she was retired or just plain stand-offish. Nothing could be further from the truth as the readers of *Down Beat* magazine voted her into the Down Beat Hall of Fame in 1985, joining famed female vocalists Billie Holiday and Ella Fitzgerald. During her final recording period in the late 1980s, she recorded two well-received albums of Duke Ellington material to add to the nearly two dozen albums that were still in print at the time. However, the one record she always longed to make was an all-piano album in the vein of the work of the Nat "King" Cole Trio or Art Tatum. An accomplished pianist, Vaughan rarely played outside her close circle of friends, always modest about her abilities outside of singing. Unfortunately, she never got to make that record as she was diagnosed with lung cancer in the late 1980s and died shortly after at the age of sixty-six.

Glendale Cemetery
Bloomfield, New Jersey

Located at 28 Hoover Avenue near J.F. Kennedy Drive South, Sarah Vaughan's magnificent stone is located in the Crestwood section at the corner of Cypress Road and Pine Road.

Sarah Vaughan makes all other singers sound like they were in rehearsal.

Charles Bourgeois

STEVIE RAY VAUGHAN

BORN October 3, 1954
Dallas, Texas

DIED August 27, 1990
Alpine Valley, Wisconsin

CAUSE OF DEATH Helicopter Crash
Age 35

With bristling chops and fiery phrasing, guitarist and bona fide Texas blues legend Stevie Ray Vaughan did not so much reinvent the blues as add a renewed passion. A master of fills, intros, and imaginative solos, he created piercing rhythms and riffs that were equal parts blues, rock, and pure showmanship.

In the Beginning . . .

Born to Big Jim and Martha Vaughan in 1954, Stevie Ray and big brother Jimmie Lee spent their early years in the Dallas suburb of Oak Cliff. They started their musical studies in early childhood. Like many musicians before them and since, Vaughan had little interest in school. Rather, he spent most of his time practicing to Albert King records and playing with several local bands. Big Jim and Martha were losing faith in their boys and Vaughan was coming home in the wee hours of the morning with alcohol on his breath. Try as they could to instill some sense of normalcy to the boys' lives, it was too late. Jimmie left home at fifteen to live with other band members and SRV continued to play two to four shows every night until he was eighteen.

Slowly but surely, this scrawny kid from the wrong side of Dallas was beginning to make his mark. In 1975, he was invited to play onstage with his idol Albert King at Austin's renowned blues club, Antone's. The skinny kid with the hip-hugger bell-bottoms, beret, and downcast eyes blew old Albert away. With brother Jimmie and Buddy Guy in the audience, the seeds of a legend were planted.

The first version of Double Trouble was formed in 1978. With Chris Layton, Lou Ann Barton, Jackie Newhouse, and Johnny Reno, SRV and Double Trouble were touring the major cities. By 1980, Vaughan re-formed Double Trouble, keeping Layton on drums and replacing Newhouse with Tommy Shannon on bass (Barton and Reno left the band). With the re-formed group, SRV also brought with him a well-formed cocaine and alcohol habit.

Vaughan then spent another six weeks with David Bowie cutting the intricate guitar parts for the landmark *Let's Dance* album. Scheduled as the lead guitarist for the Let's Dance tour, he pulled out two days before the first show over a contract dispute.

With four albums under his belt and twenty years of one-night stands, Stevie Ray Vaughan was a walking sheet of death by the time his *Live/Alive* album was released. The

After a visit to his gravesite, get back on I-35 north (going back toward Dallas) and exit on Illinois Avenue to visit the simple ranch-style home at 2557 Glenfield, where Vaughan lived during his youth. Head back to downtown Dallas to the Hard Rock Cafe, where on the wall next to ZZ Top's fur-lined guitars you will find SRV's lime green Stratocaster. The other thirty-five guitars are in the possession of brother Jimmie Lee or his former guitar tech, Rene Martinez.

long road of drug and alcohol abuse was not an easy route. The photographs used for the inner sleeve of the live album told the whole story. Ghost white and emaciated, the blues great had to make a decision. After a lifetime of substance abuse and with the support of family and friends, he enrolled himself into a drug treatment center. Vaughan had taken his last drink and his last line of cocaine.

In the End . . .

By 1989, after several years of talk, SRV and Jimmie finally began work on an album together. The animosity that dogged their lives for years was gone. In its place, *Family Style* was finally recorded and set for release in the fall of 1990.

It was a hot, sticky night in Wisconsin when SRV and Double Trouble took the stage on August 26, 1990. Vaughan looked resplendent in his flowing purple outfit—his whole body was caught in the throes of the performance. That night was truly special, as Vaughan claimed his place beside Eric Clapton, Buddy Guy, Robert Cray, and Jimmie at the Alpine Valley Music Festival. For their final number, Robert Johnson's "Sweet Home Chicago" was extended for over twenty minutes when Vaughan launched into another solo—passionate, beautiful, and LOUD! Eric Clapton looked shyly over to Vaughan, knew he couldn't top that solo, and brought the tune to a close. All holding hands, SRV took his final bow.

After the show, one of the stage managers asked Stevie, Jimmie, and Jimmie's wife, Connie, if any of them wanted to go by helicopter back to Chicago. As they stood on the tarmac, only one seat was left. Stevie grabbed the seat and with his big toothy grin, hugged Jimmie and said, "See you back in Chicago." SRV's chopper, with booking agent Bobby Brooks and assistant tour manager Nigel Browne, banked sharply to the right as the other chopper flew to the left in the heavy fog. Within fifteen minutes, at exactly 1:00 A.M., the helicopter slammed directly into a mountainside, killing everyone instantly.

Laurel Land Cemetery
Dallas, Texas

As you enter the cemetery parking lot, drive through the left-most entrance (closest to the office) and drive straight ahead about a third of a mile. Stop at the rock-lined intersection now known as the Vaughan Estates. Please note that Vaughan is no longer buried at Section 25, Lot 194, Space 4.

Telling Bowie to fuck off was the greatest factor for establishing Stevie Ray Vaughan as the working-class guitar hero.

former manager Chesley Millikin

GENE VINCENT

BORN February 11, 1935
Norfolk, Virginia

DIED October 12, 1971
Newhall, California

CAUSE OF DEATH Chronic Bleeding Ulcers
Age 36

More threatening than Elvis, wilder than Jerry Lee Lewis, and sexier than Buddy Holly, Gene Vincent was the real thing. A swaggering, unrepentant rock 'n' roll singer, he represented a dangerous embodiment of the defiant tension that gave birth to rock in the 1950s. While Presley made the transition from a defiant, rebellious rock icon to a Vegas lounge lizard, Vincent was, remained, and died a rocker.

In the Beginning . . .

Vincent Eugene Craddock acquired his first guitar at the age of twelve, learning the fundamentals of blues and country amidst the working poor in Munden Point, Virginia. In 1952, with limited opportunities, Vincent joined the U.S. Navy (though he never saw active duty). Three years into his hitch, Vincent was knocked off his Triumph motorcycle and transported to the local naval hospital. While surgeons agreed that the crushed leg needed to be amputated, Vincent and his mother pleaded with the doctors not to remove the damaged limb. Discharged from the service, Vincent spent the next year in and out of hospitals with his leg in a cast with a steel brace attached.

In 1956, Vincent, a regular performer on the WCMS *Country Showtime* program, would often perform his new composition "Be-Bop-a-Lula" with his band, the Virginians. With Capitol Records' desire to sign their very own Elvis Presley, Vincent and the band flew out to Nashville to audition. On May 4th, Vincent and his renamed band the Blue Caps recorded their first single, and The 1956 seven-inch single of Gene Vincent's "Be-Bop-a-Lula" issued by Capitol Records with the white label with promotional insert is worth over one thousand dollars to collectors on both sides of the Atlantic.

by the first week of June the record was selling over fifty thousand copies a week. The follow-up, "Race with the Devil," was a hit in England, but failed to chart in the U.S. The following year Vincent released the double-sided hit, "Lotta Lovin'"/"Wear My Ring," that returned Gene Vincent and the Blue Caps to the charts on both sides of the Atlantic.

The image was intriguing—a youthful, greasy, working-class lad clad in black leather confirmed his role as the keeper of the rock 'n' roll flame. But the image ultimately became dark and tragic. During a concert tour of England with Eddie Cochran, Vincent, Cochran, and Cochran's girlfriend, Sharon Sheeley, were in a tragic auto accident, killing Cochran and severely injuring Vincent.

In constant pain and limping badly from the accident, Vincent continued to record and

---

Very little memorabilia exists from a man who practically invented rock 'n' roll with an attitude. Former Blue Cap musician Dickie Harrell has Vincent's old road-tested suitcase (with Vincent's autograph on the case) and Jerry Merritt has Vincent's custom-made Fender amplifier. In Hollywood, California, Vincent's star on the Hollywood Boulevard Walk of Fame can be found at 1751 Vine Street (just a stone's throw from Chuck Berry's). In Nashville, at the high-tech, glass-and-chrome steel structure of Columbia/Sony headquarters, they have enclosed the studio space where "Be-Bop-a-Lula" was recorded.

tour but as a raging alcoholic who was rarely seen sober, those who knew Vincent the best moved far away as soon as possible. Prone to violence and unexplained rage, Gene would go on a bender and pull out his pistols, shooting at people in the hotel. As one of the Blue Caps remembered, "Man, the cat was wild!" In 1965, Vincent's career and health had bottomed out. Watching from the sidelines as the Beatles and the subsequent British Invasion captivated teen audiences on both sides of the Atlantic, Vincent went into a self-imposed retirement.

In the End . . .

By 1967, Vincent was back on the road, shuttling between England and Los Angeles, falling further and further into the same predictable, self-destructive lifestyle. While in Los Angeles, Vincent would find company with a young singer named Jim Morrison, and together they could be seen drinking heavily at the Shamrock on Santa Monica Boulevard. It was also Morrison, lifting the singer's leather-clad outfit and rock star swagger, who insisted that Vincent open for the Doors at the 1969 Toronto Rock and Roll Festival. Vincent was backed that night by the Alice Cooper band.

Upon returning from England for the last time, Vincent was barely holding on when he went on a three-day drinking binge in October of 1971. Worried about their son, Vincent's parents drove out to his home to find him heartbroken and disoriented. They took him to their house only to have Vincent trip and rupture his chronic ulcers. An ambulance was summoned to their house and Vincent, vomiting blood, was taken to the Inter-Valley Hospital where he died an hour later in his mother's arms. She later reminisced, "After he died, he had the sweetest smile on his face."

Eternal Valley Cemetery
Newhall, California

As you enter the cemetery, turn left at the first intersection. Continue up the hill past the historic horse-drawn hearse and park at the Repose section. Vincent's permanent address is Lot 91, Grave A, and is located six rows from the curb on the left, just below the intersection.

When I first started I never meant to make money. My only thought was to make a living singing, but all of a sudden I was getting fifteen hundred dollars a night. And if you take a nineteen-year-old boy and put him in those circumstances, it was a bad scene. I didn't know how to handle a hit.

Gene Vincent

T-BONE WALKER

BORN May 28, 1910
Cass County, Texas

DIED March 16, 1975
Los Angeles, California

CAUSE OF DEATH Stroke
Age 64

Infusing the blues with an electrifying, yet sophisticated uptown flavor, T-Bone Walker was the driving force that redirected the course of the blues, moving it from juke joints and roadhouses to swank nightclubs and theaters. Favoring hot swing rhythms with a big band accompaniment, Walker seamlessly blended jazz and Texas blues to become a seminal figure in the development of rock 'n' roll.

In the Beginning . . .

Movelia Jimerson Walker gave birth to her only son in rural Cass County, Texas. Aaron Thibeaux Walker ("T-Bone" was his mother's way of saying his middle name) and his mother left their sharecropper lives behind for big-city opportunities in Dallas. Everybody in the extended family played guitar, so it was not unusual for musicians like Huddie Ledbetter, Blind Lemon Jefferson (for whom he worked as a guide in exchange for learning some blues fundamentals), and Cab Calloway to spend the evening playing and storytelling until the early-morning hours.

When Movelia remarried, she naturally chose a musician, Marco Washington. When Walker turned ten, he began his life as an entertainer and was a member of the Washington Brothers. A natural performer, Walker played the guitar, banjo, mandolin, and danced with his extended family.

When Cab Calloway came through town in 1930, Walker won first prize during the talent portion of the concert and toured with the band for a week. Columbia Records recorded two sides, but since they didn't know how to market "race" records, the singles failed and Walker wasn't called back. Undaunted, he made his way to Los Angeles where Jim Wynn had a band with Zutty Singleton on drums. From the Little Harlem Club, Walker moved on to the upscale Trocadero Club on Sunset Strip, and then later to Billy Berg's club on Vine Street. His reputation as a jazz guitarist sealed, he joined the Les Hite Orchestra, plugged his guitar into an amplifier, and the rest, as they say, is history. Along with Charlie Christian, Walker used this new instrument to revolutionize both blues and jazz—introducing a single-note style of guitar solo which has since become the dominant lead-guitar technique in blues, jazz, rock, and most every other type of popular music.

Walker moved to Chicago in the early forties after the rhythm section in the Les Hite Orchestra objected to the electric guitar. He opened as a headliner at Rhum Boogie, where he enjoyed a three-month stint. In the fall of '42 he got his chance to record his electric guitar when he cut "I Got a Break, Baby" and "Mean Old World" on Capitol. His biggest hit, "Call It Stormy Monday But Tuesday's Just as Bad," was issued in late '47 and made him a household name from coast to coast.

Walker was at the peak of his career when he hit the road with a series of all-star revues and tours. Sharing star billing with such greats as Ray Charles, Big Joe Turner, and Lowell Fulson, he inevitably was asked to close the show because of his high-energy performances. A natural on guitar, he also stole the show with his duck walking, behind-the-back guitar playing, and hip-swinging dance routines that predated Chuck Berry by a full decade. The only thing harder to follow onstage was Walker off-stage. His gambling and drinking were legendary, as was his generosity. Unfazed by the competition, he willingly shared his songs, billings, money, and time with fellow musicians just for the asking.

In the End . . .

In 1960, with blues dropping in popularity, T-Bone traveled to Europe as part of the Rhythm and Blues USA package tour, which also featured Willie Dixon, John Lee Hooker, and Memphis Slim. Fans were ecstatic at having such luminaries sharing their stage.

Suffering from arthritis, ulcers, and other such maladies that occur from fifty years on the road, T-Bone never lost his passion for playing. He hit the road again in 1974, but his drinking took a heavy toll on his health. In June, he played his last concert with John Lee Hooker in Pittsburgh.

On New Year's Eve he suffered a debilitating stroke. Good friend and protégé Pee Wee Crayton, along with his wife, mother, and daughter, all visited him daily at the West Vernon Convalescent Home. Three months later he was gone.

Inglewood Park Cemetery
Inglewood, California
Angelus Funeral Home was not prepared for what was to be a simple ceremony. In a matter of minutes after the viewing had begun, there was a line of friends and fans that stretched around the block and the viewing had to be extended an additional day to accommodate the thousands of fans who had come to pay their respects. From the entrance

of the cemetery, drive through the gates to the Mausoleum of the Golden West. Park and walk to the Capistrano Garden, which is to the left of the mausoleum. The courtyard is square with wall crypts on the three outer walls. Walk through the center of the courtyard to one of the last panels on the right, marked Memorial 25 Panel. T-Bone Walker's memorial is just above eye level.

You my pimp, and I'm yo' ho'. Yo' job is to find me the best money and the best corners to work!
T-Bone Walker to his manager, Robin Hemingway

DINAH WASHINGTON

BORN August 29, 1924
Tuscaloosa, Alabama

DIED December 14, 1963
Detroit, Michigan

CAUSE OF DEATH Drug Overdose
Age 39

One of the most versatile vocalists in the history of American pop music, Dinah Washington would be considered a cross-over superstar in today's market. Variety could have been her middle name, as her style was generously spread across classic and jump blues, standard ballads, and traditional pop. Her clear enunciation and incredible sense of timing, coupled with her penetrating multi-octave voice, enhanced her ability to sing anything with distinction. She possessed a strong command of the passion and sensitivity required to bring depth to songs ranging from bawdy and sad, to rousing, high-spirited, and celebratory.

In the Beginning . . .

Born Ruth Lee Jones in Tuscaloosa, Alabama, she and the family moved to Chicago in 1927. Raised on the South Side of Chicago in a strictly religious atmosphere, Jones began her musical training in the world of gospel, learning to play the piano in church, where she was a member of the choir, as well. As a teenager she joined the Sallie Martin Singers, a gospel group led by a former associate of Thomas A. Dorsey. At the age of fifteen, she won a talent contest at Chicago's Regal Theater. But what really impressed the budding singer was hearing Billie Holiday during an engagement in Chicago. Afterward she returned to the stage and to secular music, singing in local blues clubs. Though Jones was equally happy singing R&B, jazz, or classic standards of the day, she was crowned the Queen of the Blues by local musicians—a title she did nothing to discourage.

In 1942, she began a regular run at Chicago's Garrick's Stage Bar, where Lionel Hampton saw one of her shows. Whether it was the manager at the club or Hampton who changed her name, Dinah Washington became a member of Lionel Hampton's band until 1946. During downtime with the orchestra, Washington would book time at the studio with several Hampton sidemen, and in 1943 released her first of many singles "Evil Gal Blues." When it came time for her to leave Hampton for a solo career, Washington was already a headliner on the R&B circuit.

After leaving Hampton's orchestra, she began recording what some have come to call reverse cover versions. Releasing a diverse catalog of hits for the mainstream black population, Washington recorded Hank Williams's "Cold, Cold Heart," the Orioles' "It's Too Soon to Know," and her biggest R&B hit of the forties, "Baby, Get Lost." Washington continued her chart success, maintaining a spot on the Top 10 R&B chart between 1949 and 1955 with "I've Got You Under My Skin" and "What a Diff'rence a Day Makes."

Washington refused to be pigeonholed into any one category of music, demanding to play what she liked without regards to whether it was considered "suitable" in that day's market. Although her blues recordings demonstrate her gospel origins, she didn't

In 1991, the state of Alabama awarded Washington its Lifework Award for Performing Achievement. In 1993, she was inducted into the Rock and Roll Hall of Fame, and in the following year the United States Postal Service issued a twenty-nine-cent stamp in her honor.

believe in mixing the spiritual with the secular and refused all offers to include gospel in her repertoire.

By the mid-fifties, Washington began to concentrate more on straight jazz sessions with both big bands and small combos. After an appearance in the film *Jazz on a Summer's Day*, she recorded many memorable releases with Clifford Brown (on *Dinah Jams*), Ben Webster, Wynton Kelly, Clark Terry, and future Miles Davis collaborator Joe Zawinul.

In the End . . .

As her career progressed, Washington crossed over into the popular music market and enjoyed tremendous commercial success while still maintaining her earlier fans. She teamed with many great musicians of the late 1950s, including Wynton Kelly, Clifford Brown, Maynard Ferguson, Andrew Hill, Clark Terry and Joe Zawinul. She sang two duets with Brook Benton in 1960, "You've Got What It Takes" and "A Rockin' Good Way," which both enjoyed spots on the Top 10 charts for both pop and R&B.

Although she enjoyed immense popularity, the Queen of the Blues suffered a turbulent private life involving seven failed marriages and alcoholism. And beginning in 1957, critics started slagging Washington hard, accusing her of selling out, turning her back on her roots by recording several mundane, commercially oriented albums. In addition, even those close to Washington weren't aware of her lifelong struggle with her weight and use of diet pills. In the winter of 1963 just two weeks after a well-received engagement in Los Angeles, Dinah Washington died in Detroit, Michigan, from an accidental overdose of diet pills and alcohol.

Burr Oak Cemetery
Alsip, Illinois

As you enter the cemetery off 127th Street, park at the office. Walk straight ahead out of the front of the office down the road that divides the two sections. Count eight rows on the right section (Elm Grove), turn right, and walk twenty graves into the Elm Grove section. Her final address is Lot 155, Grave 4. About one hundred feet away in the other section lies the great Willie Dixon.

There's a quality in her voice. I mean, she's, of all the great jazz singers, she was more than a jazz singer. You hear about Sarah Vaughan, you hear about Billie Holiday, you hear about Ella Fitzgerald. But you just don't hear enough about Dinah Washington.

jazz producer Joel Dorn

MUDDY WATERS

BORN April 4, 1915
Rolling Fork, Mississippi

DIED April 30, 1983
Westmont, Illinois

CAUSE OF DEATH Lung Cancer
Age 68

If blues is an original American art form, then Muddy Waters should be considered an original American icon. An extraordinarily potent singer, songwriter, and guitarist, Waters was the architect of Chicago blues. Backed by Little Walter Jacobs, Otis Spann, and Jimmy Rogers, his music was the greatest single influence on the British blues artists of the sixties. Active up until his death at age sixty-eight, he was and always will be the original Hoochie Coochie Man.

In the Beginning . . .

Raised from a young age on the Stovall plantation in Clarksdale, Mississippi, McKinley Morganfield (nicknamed Muddy Waters by his grandmother) supplemented his income by sharecropping, running moonshine, gambling, and playing guitar with a local country string band. Taught slide guitar by Son House and influenced by Robert Johnson, Muddy developed as one of the original innovators of the Delta blues. His deep bass style was recorded by Alan Lomax for the Library of Congress in 1941 in the same cottonfield shack he shared with his grandmother, uncle, and new bride.

Tired of southern culture and lack of opportunity, Muddy packed his bags and Silverton Sears electric guitar, and headed for Chicago. Within a year he began to play in the clubs, aided by Big Bill Broonzy and Sonny Boy Williamson I. In 1946, he recorded his first sides for Columbia records, but they did not release them that year. The following year Leonard Chess's Aristocrat label released the first of many singles to come. From 1948 until 1960, he fronted the finest blues band with assistance from blues legends Little Walter, Jimmy Rogers, Otis Spann, Ernest "Big" Crawford, and Baby Face Leroy. With gigs every night and widespread airplay, Muddy Waters reigned supreme over the Chicago, Cleveland, Detroit, and Memphis blues scenes. His amplified Delta music had come to define the Chicago Sound.

As television grew in popularity, Muddy's sales began to slide. However, as interest in the "old music" dropped in the U.S., it grew in amazing popularity across the Atlantic. Muddy toured Europe several times to appreciative audiences in England. Much to his

---

The first home Muddy bought and lived in until his first wife died can be found at 4339 South Lake Park Avenue. Currently owned by Muddy's son Charles Morganfield, this was the house where B. B. King, John Lee Williamson (Sonny Boy Williamson I) Chuck Berry, and a whole host of blues greats spent a night or two. Unfortunately, the old screen door that at one time was inscribed with Muddy's name is long gone. The old cabin (see right) that once stood at Stovall's plantation has since been restored and moved indoors to the Delta Blues Museum in nearby Clarksdale, which also boasts one full room dedicated to Waters. In downtown Chicago at Buddy Guy's Legends blues club the walls are filled with blues memorabilia of Waters, as well as that of several of his sidemen.

surprise, his English tours brought Muddy to the attention of folk and blues purists back in the States. In April 1959, he played a blistering set with Otis Spann and James Cotton at New York's Carnegie Hall. The following year the Newport Jazz Festival booked the full Waters band to headline the blues program. Chess issued the classic performance as *Muddy Waters at Newport*.

In the End

In the late 1960s, Waters released two horrific albums, *Electric Mud* and *After the Rain*, which one reviewer went so far as to call "dog shit." Fortunately, after a short tour together with Johnny Winter, who played the role of producer, bandmate, friend, and protector of the classic Muddy Waters sound, there resulted four albums of his most moving records in the last twenty years.

Diagnosed with lung cancer in 1982, Waters underwent surgery to remove a lung and began radiation therapy. On June 30th, Waters graced the stage for the final time when he surprised Eric Clapton in Miami, joining him for the final number, "Blow Wind Blow."

Upon his return, the cancer began to spread and Waters rarely left home. When former bandmate Bob Margolin paid a visit to his former boss, he inquired if Waters was practicing guitar at home. Waters quietly replied, "Naw, I've been playing for years." Several days after that last visit, Waters was rushed to nearby Good Samaritan Hospital in Downers Grove, Illinois, where he was pronounced dead from cardiac arrest.

Restvale Cemetery
Chicago, Illinois

Located on the corner of 117th Avenue and Laramie Avenue, drive through the entrance on Laramie to the office and park. Walk just to the left of the office; in Section H his black marker is three graves away from the front door of the office.

When Muddy Waters passed away at the age of sixty-eight, he had recorded with hundreds of musicians and appeared on just as many albums. Jimmy Rogers, Ernest "Big" Crawford, Leroy Foster, Sunnyland Slim, St. Louis Jimmy Oden, Junior Wells,

Willie Dixon, Fred Below, James Cotton, Odie Payne, Matt "Guitar" Murphy, Earl Hooker, Luther Tucker, Sonny Boy Williamson II, Eric Clapton, Memphis Slim, Willie Smith, Hubert Sumlin, Pinetop Perkins, Bo Diddley, Buddy Guy, and Howlin' Wolf were just a few that joined Waters live or in the studio. But perhaps the most famous of his sidemen were:

I do well on the South Side here because my audience are older people; they drink whiskey. Now, you get the bands who play the Key Show Lounge, their audiences drink beer. There's no money in that. I get good money for playing because my public drinks whiskey.

Muddy Waters

LITTLE WALTER JACOBS
May 1, 1930—February 15, 1968

At the young age of twelve, Little Walter ran away from home to make his living on the streets and by age fifteen, he found himself in the center of the blues universe—Chicago. With little money but an abundance of talent, Little Walter joined the ever-changing group of musicians who played for free on Maxwell Street. In 1947, Little Walter was asked to join the Muddy Waters band. With Waters on guitar, Little Walter on harp, Baby Face Leroy on drums, and Jimmy Rogers on guitar, Little Walter was now a member of one of the greatest blues ensembles.

After three years with Waters, Little Walter recorded the concert opening instrumental used to introduce Muddy. While on the road with the Waters band, Little Walter's "Juke" became the biggest-selling record of the year. From 1954, Little Walter charted a hit every year for the next nine out of ten years. "Mean Old World," "Last Night," and the Willie Dixon hit "My Babe" kept Little Walter on the charts and in the best nightclubs. Yet as the 1960s ushered in the British Invasion, Walter's career began to fade. Never a pleasant man to begin with, he became even more disagreeable as his drinking increased. In February of 1968, Little Walter was involved in a street fight where he was seriously hurt. Injured, he went

home to bed, only to die in his sleep at the age of thirty-seven. Little Walter was laid to rest at St. Mary Catholic Cemetery in Evergreen, Illinois, on the South Side of Chicago. His grave is in the narrow border strip in Grave 5, Lot 5, Block 28, Section SW (across from Section Q). His flat bronze monument is four rows from the water spigot and fifteen plots from the road.

OTIS SPANN
March 21, 1930—April 24, 1970

Otis Spann's first paying gig was at the age of eight when he won first prize of twenty-five dollars at a blues competition in Jackson, Mississippi. After high school, Spann moved to Chicago where he fell under the supervision of Big Maceo who, after suffering a stroke, Spann would fill in for at gigs, sometimes even playing one hand for him in the studio. As one of Waters's favorite musicians, Spann also played on the side with Little Walter, Buddy

Guy, Sonny Boy Williamson II, and Chuck Berry. Though he was the house pianist for Chess Records, he recorded his first solo album in 1960 and continued to appear solo and with the Waters's group up until his passing from liver cancer at the age of forty. He was buried at Burr Oak Cemetery in Alsip, Illinois (outside of Chicago), in Section 6, Lot 13, Row 8, Grave 31 in the back of the cemetery. His grave remained unmarked until June 1999.

BUT MY HEAD'S IN MISSISSIPPI

Muddy Waters, Otis Spann, and Little Walter may have left Mississippi, but the blues still remain behind.

Blues and Legends Hall of Fame Museum
Robinsville, Mississippi

Okay, so some of the display facts are erroneous and the museum is located inside a casino (the Horseshoe), this still doesn't take away from the high-class presentation with a good selection of memorabilia. And you can't beat the price of admission—it's free!

Delta Cultural Center
Helena, Arkansas

This small but nicely done museum on Cherry Street features a continuous video presentation on the blues, traveling exhibits, a section of the museum dedicated to the blues, and Sonny Payne's legendary KFFA *King Biscuit Time* radio show is still broadcast here most weekdays starting at noon.

Delta Blues Museum
Clarksdale, Mississippi

This museum features Muddy Waters's restored cabin inside the very same train depot from which he left in 1943 to seek his fortune in Chicago. Other highlights include sculptures by Son Thomas and signed guitars by John Lee Hooker and other blues luminaries. Live music is featured in the adjacent blues alley every Friday night during the summer months.

Ground Zero Blues Club
Clarksdale, Mississippi

Co-owned by actor Morgan Freeman, this club is Clarksdale's most reliable source for out-of-town national blues and roots artists. Live music is available most Friday and Saturday nights. Freeman also owns the fine restaurant Madidi just down the street.

Sarah's Kitchen
Clarksdale, Mississippi

Easily the funkiest, coolest juke joint running in Clarksdale today. Most Thursdays feature the Deep Cuts, a local band featuring the best musicians in town. Sarah also books the best of the traveling acts for the weekend and will book an act if you've got a large enough group visiting from out of town.

Cat Head Delta Blues and Folk Art
Clarksdale, Mississippi

This is the very first place to stop before you begin your quest of blues sites. Run by the very knowledgeable Roger and Jennifer Stolle, this is a one-stop blues heaven of CDs, albums, original Delta folk art, maps, books, and a clearing house for weekly blues events throughout the region. But most importantly, they can answer every really dumb question ("Where is the crossroads so I can sell my soul to the devil?") with a great story.

Greenwood Blues Heritage Museum and Gallery
Greenwood, Mississippi

A small but noteworthy museum started and funded by Robert Johnson expert Steve LaVere (he knew Johnson's mother), this museum has assembled a great collection of photos and artifacts.

New Jerusalem Churchyard Cemetery
Holly Ridge, Mississipppi

If you only visit one cemetery during your visit, this is the one—a blues trio featuring Charley Patton, Asie Payton, and Willie Foster. Unlike Patton, Payton and Foster are actually buried underneath their monuments.

LAWRENCE WELK

BORN March 11, 1903
Strasburg, North Dakota

DIED May 17, 1992
Los Angeles, California

CAUSE OF DEATH Pneumonia
Age 89

With a cheery "ah-one an' ah-two," Lawrence Welk traded his plow for a squeezebox to become the second-highest-paid entertainer (behind Bob Hope), and his band and production company became the second-biggest tourist attraction, just behind Disneyland, in California. With his television program the most watched in PBS history, his name became inextricably linked with "champagne music."

In the Beginning . . .

Born in a sod farmhouse in the prairie village of Strasburg, North Dakota, Lawrence Welk dropped out of the fourth grade to work his family's farm with his seven other siblings. At night his father, Ludwig, taught him to play an inexpensive accordion. From the age of thirteen he played local social gatherings. Within five years he was performing professionally with several bands in the area.

On his twenty-first birthday, he left the family farm and lived on buses and in backs of cars as an itinerant accordion musician. After a brief business venture selling "squeezeburgers" on an accordion-shaped grill, he slowly drew a loyal following, playing progressively larger ballrooms and hotels. By the 1930s, Welk's band grew to ten musicians, performing all the standards using simple arrangements. "Keep it simple so the audience thinks they can do it too," he once remarked.

Oddly enough, Welk rarely addressed the audience during a performance, and never acted as a musical host until the mid-1940s. Self-conscious about his thick German accent, Lawrence preferred to let the music do the talking. When the manager of a Milwaukee theater asked Welk to announce the other acts on the bill, he replied that he couldn't do it—he didn't speak well. The manager offered him an extra hundred bucks. "For a hundred dollars, I'll say anything you want," was his reply. His folksy charm and bubbly brand of music were a perfect combination.

Welk's band was headquartered in Chicago with road shows all over the U.S. After a routine show in Los Angeles that was broadcast on television, the reaction from the viewers was so strong that Lawrence moved the whole group to Los Angeles to begin his highly successful, long-running series. In 1956, ABC-TV broadcast Welk coast to coast, and

Perhaps the only mobile home retirement park, country club, and museum combination in existence, the Lawrence Welk Museum will appeal to, well, only Lawrence Welk fans. You will be greeted by a bronze statue of the man himself as you enter the museum, which is full of history in the land of happy thoughts, polkas, waltzes, and champagne music. His birthplace is also a shrine of sorts, for Welk fans only, in Strasburg, North Dakota.

over a sixteen-year period the Welk show only missed one performance—the week President Kennedy was assassinated.

Looking for a more youthful and affluent market, ABC dropped the show in 1971. Not surprisingly, his two largest sponsors were Geritol and Sominex. Undeterred, Welk responded by syndicating the show himself to over 250 stations nationwide—more than previously aired on ABC. The program was a hit and the Lawrence Welk organization became a recording, publishing, and real estate empire.

In the End . . .

Building an empire came at a cost. Welk was a stern taskmaster, demanding from his performers hard work, dedication, thrift, and self-discipline. He kept his musical family (the Champagne Lady, Norma Zimmer, and the Lennon Sisters) intact, even if at times that meant arbitrating marital disputes backstage. Still others grew frustrated by his methods, which included total control over music, costume, and hairstyle selection (which proved to be a problem when working with younger performers in the 1970s). There were some left-over money disputes with Welk, who paid the cast minimum union scale (then a mere $110 a week). To his credit, Welk did set up a generous profit-sharing plan for his performers while giving them the freedom to appear on other shows and to make personal appearances.

After Welk took over the syndication, the program did not miss a week of airtime until weekly production of the show ended in 1982. Still, it proved to be the show that would not go away. When a PBS documentary on Lawrence Welk was aired in 1987, there was a huge request to air the old shows. The show was re-released and appeared on more than two hundred stations coast to coast.

At the grand age of eighty-nine, Lawrence Welk slipped away quietly at his Santa Monica home in the Champagne Towers, with his wife of sixty-one years, his son, and two daughters by his side.

Holy Cross Cemetery
Culver City, California

As you drive through the gates off Slauson, drive straight through the cemetery, making your way toward the mausoleum. As you approach the mausoleum, you will find the flower shop on the right side, across the road. Park behind the flower shop on the main road and walk toward the center of the large grassy section. Welk's flat marker is virtually in the center of this large section, known as Section Y (St. Francis). His official grave location is 110-T9-Y.

Keep it under three minutes, just in case they don't like it.

Lawrence Welk, revealing his secret to success.

THE WHO

Entwistle, Daltry, and Moon.

KEITH MOON
BORN August 23, 1946
Willesden, England

DIED September 7, 1978
London, England

CAUSE OF DEATH Drug Overdose
Age 32

JOHN ENTWISTLE
BORN October 9, 1944
London, England

DIED June 27, 2002
Las Vegas, Nevada

CAUSE OF DEATH Heart Attack
Age 57

During the early seventies, Led Zeppelin, the Rolling Stones, and The Who were all touted at one time or another to be the greatest rock 'n' roll band in the world. Yet while Zeppelin and the Stones were firmly rooted in the past in a melange of blues, The Who were forever looking forward. Led by the ambitious designs of guitarist Pete Townshend, drummer Keith Moon's cataclysmic drumming and John Entwistle's intricate bass lines provided the rhythmic thunder for one of rock 'n' roll's most aggressive and fabulously successful bands.

In the Beginning

The origins of The Who began in the early 1960s in London's West End with banjo player Pete Townshend and trumpetist John Entwistle as part of the traditional jazz group the Confederates. Switching to guitar and bass respectively, the two teenagers were asked to join the Detours by lead singer, Roger Daltrey. After a bit of shuffling of personnel, the Detours consisted of Daltrey, Townshend, Entwistle, and drummer Doug Sandom. After two years on the club circuit, it was obvious that Sandom would not be able to perform in the style that the group wanted. After a revolving door of drummers, the band spotted the unorthodox style of Keith Moon, who was with the popular surf group the Beachcombers. In 1963, they added Moon and changed their name to The Who.

After a brief foray as the High Numbers, during which they released two singles aimed at the mod crowd, they changed their name back to The Who and signed a production deal with Shel Talmy. During a gig at the Railway Hotel in London, Townshend was having technical problems with his guitar and, in a fit of frustration, smashed the instrument to pieces at the end of the set. The audience went wild, so naturally the wholesale destruction of instruments became the norm at every Who concert.

With a worldwide distribution deal with Decca Records, The Who released their first album, *My Generation*, in 1965. Even with "I Can't Explain" already climbing the charts in England and appearances on *Ready, Steady, Go*, it still took a full two years for their initial success to reach the U.S. After several months of legal wrangling, The Who bought out the contracts of Decca and Talmy and brought in Kit Lambert as their producer and Townshend's musical mentor.

By the end of the sixties The Who had gained notoriety, with solid records and a great live show. Following the release of the ambitious rock opera *Tommy*, the group performed at the Woodstock Festival, followed by the release of *Live at Leeds*, featuring a blistering ver-

When the Hard Rock Cafe hung one of Eric Clapton's guitars in their London restaurant in 1971, they received another guitar with the note, "Mine's as good as his. Love, Pete." Thus a dynasty was born. Now Who memorabilia can be found in virtually every one of their restaurants. And the number at the end of each of his guitars was used by Pete to identify his guitars onstage.

sion of Eddie Cochran's "Summertime Blues." The following year the group released the album *Who's Next* with the song of teenage disillusionment "Won't Get Fooled Again" (often mistakenly called "Baba O'Rily"). After three more albums in two years, the group released another ambitious rock opera *Quadrophenia*, which followed the life of mods in the early sixties and their experiences. Unlike *Tommy*, which stayed on the charts for two years, *Quadrophenia* died quietly in the stores.

As everyone went their separate ways doing solo projects in music and film, the band released *The Who by Numbers*, featuring "Squeeze Box" and again three years later the album *Who Are You*, with the single by the same name. While both efforts charted, fans and critics alike were wondering if the creative output of The Who had peaked.

In the End

Upon returning from a party given by Paul McCartney in celebration of the British premiere of *The Buddy Holly Story*, instead of indulging in his habitual partying into the wee morning hours, Moon left the party around midnight and went straight home. The following morning Keith awoke hungry and ate breakfast, only to go to sleep again. At 3:40 in the afternoon his companion Annette was unable to wake Moon up and soon discovered he had been dead for some time. Two weeks later the coroner's report indicated that Moon had swallowed a total of thirty-two Heminevrin tablets (used to control his alcoholism), of which twenty-six had remained undissolved in his stomach. This amount "constituted a vast overdose," according to the report. At the same time, only a trace amount of alcohol and no cocaine or other hard drugs were found in his system.

After a near fatal overdose and two really bad solo albums, Pete Townshend was nearly bankrupt. With The Who in a tailspin of mediocrity since the death of their drummer, they criss-crossed the U.S. numerous times under the guise of a "farewell" tour (a technique later perfected by KISS) to replenish everyone's bank account. Suffering from severe hearing loss and a weak heart, Entwistle was staying at the Hard Rock Hotel in Las Vegas prior to the following night's opening of the newest Who reunion/farewell tour in 2002. Although he was under a doctor's care and taking prescription medication for his ailing heart, he saw no harm in indulging in heavy drinking and several lines of cocaine on the night of June 26th. The next day he was found face-down in his hotel room, dead of an apparent heart attack. A postmortem revealed that the cocaine had constricted the arteries leading to his heart, causing the fatal attack. Three days later The Who (or what was left of them) continued with the tour.

FINAL RESTING PLACES
Golders Green Crematorium
London, England

Daltry, Entwistle, and Townshend were joined by rock's royalty, including Eric Clapton, Charlie Watts, and Bill Wyman, at a very private service in the Garden of Remembrance at Golders Green. Afterward Moon was cremated, his ashes were scattered in Section 3P (yes, that's exactly what those small mounds of gray "dirt" scattered over the lawn are!).

St. Edward's Church
Gloucester, England

Entwistle was given a similar sendoff before his casket was lowered at this small church cemetery in Stow-on-the-Wold. His plot, located in the center of the cemetery, is quite easy to find.

It was a shame, because Keith was having such a great time. At one time it looked like we were all set to become film moguls, and then he went and dropped dead. Most inconvenient; his timing was a bit off at the end.

Pete Townshend

HANK WILLIAMS

BORN September 17, 1923
Georgiana, Alabama

DIED January 1, 1953
Oak Hill, West Virginia

CAUSE OF DEATH Heart Failure
Age 29

Often described as being fiercely driven, drug-addicted, and stubbornly drunk, Hank Williams was none-the-less the finest songwriter and song stylist of the twentieth century.

In the Beginning . . .

Born to Lonnie and Jessie Lillybelle "Lilly" Skipper Williams in the fall of 1923, Hiram Williams was raised in Alabama in absolute poverty. Sitting beside his mother at the Mount Olive West Baptist Church, Williams's musical training began with singing in church. By age eleven, Hank was sneaking hard liquor on the days he skipped school to perform on the streets of Georgiana and nearby Greenville for loose change. Never one to waste his time with formal education, Hank (as he preferred to be called) dropped out of school and began playing guitar, shining shoes, and selling newspapers in Greenville, Alabama. It was during his teen years that Hank began hanging out with a local black musician named Rufus Payne (who went by the name Tee-Tot), paying the itinerant musician and laborer fifteen cents for guitar lessons.

At the age of thirteen, Williams and family had moved to Montgomery, Alabama, where Williams earned the name the Singing Cowboy for his two fifteen-minute programs on radio station WSFA. For the next seven years, Williams cut his teeth in some of the worst Alabama honky-tonks and dive bars, often with his mother acting as his agent.

In 1943, Williams met the woman who would become a driving force in his life—for both good and bad. Caught between two strong-willed women, girlfriend Audrey Sheppard Guy and mother Lilly Williams, Williams was no match and continued his spiral into unremitting alcoholism. In 1944, Hank and Audrey were married by a justice of the peace at a Texaco station.

Williams achieved his first small measure of success when he sold his first song, "I Am Praying for the Day Peace Will Come," to country singer Pee Wee King. Three years later he delivered a batch of songs to Fred Rose, co-owner of the Acuff-Rose publishers along with Roy Acuff. Looking for new material for their growing company, Rose signed Williams and eventually placed him with MGM Records in 1947. With MGM he charted his first release "Move It on Over," followed by "Honky-Tonkin' " and "I Saw the Light." The following year Rose got Williams a spot on the Louisiana Hayride, broadcast live on

One would think that the first place to go for Hank Williams memorabilia (and there is a lot of it out there) would be the Country Music Hall of Fame in Nashville, Tennessee. Unfortunately, you would be very disappointed to find that the museum's sole artifacts currently consist of a pair of boots and a stage outfit. Based on current exhibition space, LeAnn Rimes and Billy Ray Cyrus have made more of a contribution to country music than Williams. Interestingly enough, the few artifacts that are available are on loan from country artist Marty Stuart, who has the largest collection of Hank Williams memorabilia in the world. Even more ironic is that the Rock and Roll Hall of Fame in Cleveland, Ohio, has an entire room devoted to the Lonesome Cowboy (with artifacts on loan from daughter Jett Williams and son Hank Williams Jr.). As for the Martin guitar with the mother-of-pearl inlay created by an inmate of the Alabama prison system in the late 1940s, that is in the possession of Jett Williams and proudly hangs in her home today.

KWKH out of Shreveport. Even with his well-known reputation for his hard-drinking lifestyle, the Hayride was willing to gamble on the new talent, even though the Grand Ole Opry and the National Barn Dance already passed on the troubled country singer. Williams proved them wrong when he gave his all for the Hayride, with the country hit "Lovesick Blues," which remained on the charts for six months. Suddenly, the Opry came calling.

"Lovesick Blues," which was not an original Hank Williams song, provided the opportunity for Williams to make his Opry debut in June 1949. Following performances by Ernest Tubb and Bill Monroe and his Blue Grass Boys, Williams took to the stage with a mere smattering of applause. After the first refrain of "Lovesick Blues" the audience was on their feet, forcing the young new star back for six more encores. Host Uncle Dave Macon had to beg the audience to quiet down and let them continue with the show.

With the Opry as his launching pad, Williams's position among the leading artists of country music was unassailable. His records such as "Mind Your Own Business," "Long Gone Lonesome Blues," and "Why Don't You Love Me" unfailingly reached the charts more often than not at the number one position. But Rose felt that Williams's classic tales of heartbreak and hard living could also have an impact in mainstream pop. Rose's lobbying efforts paid off as Tony Bennett, Frankie Laine, and Jo Stafford were just a few of the pop artists who had hits with Williams's songs.

In the End . . .

Williams continued his assualt on the country charts with good-natured classics like "Hey, Good Lookin' " and "Jambalaya" well into the 1950s. However, acceptance by his peers and the Nashville establishment did nothing to curb Williams's insatiable appetite for drinking and prescription painkillers for a back injury. As his addictions began to affect his performances, Williams was suspended by the Opry in 1952. In that same year Audrey filed for divorce, taking their children with her. Williams took his pain out in his songs as he recorded "You're Gonna Change (Or I'm Gonna Leave)," "Why Don't You Love Me," and "Your Cheatin' Heart."

Statue of Hank Williams across from the Municipal Auditorium in Montgomery, Alabama, where Williams was eulogized at his funeral.

Williams spun out of control as the consequences of his self-destructive lifestyle began to play out. He headed back to Shreveport and rejoined the Louisiana Hayride the summer of 1952, broke and broken-down. By now Williams was dividing his time between the road, Lilly's boardinghouse, and a variety of sanitariums for the treatment of acute alcohol and drug intoxications. Performing to less-than-enthusiastic audiences (he was often literally run out of town), Williams married the young Billie Jean Jones Eshlemar (much to the disgust of Lilly and Audrey) in three well-publicized ceremonies within twenty-four hours. Two of the weddings were part of a gala Hank Williams Homecoming concert event. Finally it all seemed to be going Hank's way.

If Hank could raise up in that coffin, he'd say, "See, I told you I could draw more folks dead than you SOBs could alive."

Grand Ole Opry manager Jim Denny

On the morning of January 1, 1953, Williams was carried unconscious by his driver from the hotel room to his Cadillac. Williams was sleeping off the effects of two morphine injections, a pint of vodka, and chloral hydrate tablets. Stopped in Tennessee for speeding, driver Charles Carr was told that his passenger looked dead. Accepting his ticket, Carr reassured the officer that Williams was just tired. Pulling his car over on Main Street in Oak Hill, West Virginia, Carr tried to rouse his passenger, but to no avail. Hank Williams was dead of heart failure at the age of twenty-nine.

With cars lining all highways leading to Montgomery and over twenty thousand descending on Montgomery's Municipal Auditorium on Perry Street, Williams was given the funeral of the decade. All of Opryland was in attendance, along with his fans, when his concrete-and-copper-lined, steel-reinforced silver casket was removed from the boardinghouse at 318 North McDonough Street. He lay in state for two days and was carried to the auditorium, where Williams had performed many a time. The casket was carried to the foot of the flower-covered stage and the top half was opened for the mourners.

Ernest Tubb, Roy Acuff, Bill Monroe, and Red Foley all performed at the service, which was carried live over two radio stations. As the service ended, the crowd made its way up Jefferson Street to the Oakwood Cemetery Annex, where Hank Williams was lowered into the ground as his hit record "I'll Never Get Out of This World Alive" still hung on the charts.

Oakwood Cemetery
Montgomery, Alabama

At the corner of Ripley and Jefferson, go past the entrance of the cemetery, over the bridge, to the last entry road into the cemetery. Turn left at the Oakwood Cemetery Annex sign. Go up to the fork in the road and veer right. Drive two hundred feet and the giant sixteen-foot monolith of Hank and Audrey Williams (surrounded by artifical turf) is clearly visible on your left. The cemetery is open from 7:00 A.M. until dusk.

The Hank Williams Museum
Montgomery, Alabama

Once the Hank Williams Jr. Family Tradition Museum closed in the late 1990s, treasures from the museum in the back of the store were transferred down to the Hank Williams Museum in Montgomery. Opened in early 1999, the museum contains Williams's 1944 D-28 C.F. Martin guitar (the eleventh of only twelve made), an assortment of hand-painted ties, great photos, his personal shaving kit, the stage outfit he wore when he took that final sleep, and his famous White Music Note Nudie of California suit he wore in concert. The star attraction of the museum is the completely restored 1952 Cadillac in which he died. This is the very same car that Hank Williams Jr. once drove to high school every day.

The Hank Williams Boyhood Home and Museum
Georgiana, Alabama

This is the home where Williams spent his early years before moving to Montgomery. The home now serves as a museum, housing pictures and artifacts from various parts of Williams's life. Funded entirely by donations, the staff has done a wonderful job of preserving and documenting Williams's life and impact on country music. Just behind the museum is the Hank Williams Memorial Park, which is home to the annual fund-raising drive known as the Hank Williams Festival held in June. Jett Williams and the remaining Williams backing band, the Drifting Cowboys, usually make an appearance.

Rufus Payne Memorial

Born in Alabama in 1884, but raised in New Orleans, Rufus "Tee-Tot" Payne grew up during the formative years of jazz amid the street musicians in the historic Storyville district. Upon the death of his parents, Payne moved back to Greenville, where he achieved a following of fans from both races, playing a variety of instruments at parties and picnics. In nearby Georgiana, he met an eager young student named Hank Williams, whom he taught guitar and songwriting. When Williams moved to Montgomery Tee-Tot followed and lived there until his death in 1939. A good friend of the family, Williams has stated publicly that Payne was his only teacher. He died a pauper and was buried in an unmarked grave at Lincoln Cemetery in Kirkland, Alabama. The monument was placed at the entry of the cemetery in the early 1990s.

Lake Martin Cabins
Lake Martin, Alabama

The cabins just off Highway 63 outside Alexander City along the lake are enjoyed by visiting travelers during the hot summer months. One cabin was discovered in the 1990s to be the actual cabin that Hank Williams would escape to in order to get a little privacy. The cabin was then moved back to its original spot along the lake and restoration was begun. Photos of the cabin and the actual furniture that Williams once used to write "Kawliga" and "Your Cheatin' Heart" have been found and incorporated into the restored cabin. Restoration was completed in 2002 and it is now used as part of the Children's Harbor nonprofit organization. While you cannot actually stay in the cabin, visitors are welcome.

SONNY BOY WILLIAMSON II

BORN March 11, 1905
Glendora, Mississippi

DIED May 25, 1965
Helena, Arkansas

CAUSE OF DEATH Tuberculosis
Age 60

Sonny Boy Williamson II was one of the most influential harmonica players in blues history. Often compared with Little Walter and John Lee Williamson (Sonny Boy Williamson I), Sonny Boy II was a legendary blues character whose colorful personality, superb musicianship, unpredictable actions, and frequent stretching of the truth only served to enliven his blues with a warm eccentricity.

In the Beginning . . .

Born Aleck "Rice" Miller to a sharecropper family in the Mississippi Delta region, Miller began his career as a self-taught itinerate musician in the early 1900s. As the Reverend Blue, Miller played gospel and blues on street corners and picnics for tips as a child. For the next twenty years he traveled through most every dance hall, carnival, lumber camp, plantation, and juke joint in Arkansas, Mississippi, Missouri, and Tennessee.

As legend has it (and there are a lot of stories and legends surrounding him), Miller was arrested for stealing a mule and sent to Parchman Farm State Penitentiary. Sentenced to hard labor on the prison farm, Miller charmed the prison guard, who allowed him to escape (not surprising, given that Miller hated farmwork and his lack of productivity in the fields probably didn't even cover the cost of feeding and housing him in prison). After his escape, he was constantly changing his name and performing under a variety of aliases, including Slim, Little Boy Blue, and finally Willie "Sonny Boy" Williamson.

As he learned very early, church music may get you noticed, but the blues got you paid; through a combination of raw talent and self-promotion, Miller became known as the blues' first radio star. His daily performances on the Helena, Arkansas, radio station KFFA not only made him a celebrity but influenced a generation of musicians living in the Delta. Armed with a superb sense of timing, intricate phrasing, and bold sonic vibratos, his radio shows were second to his live performances. Often seen performing with Robert Johnson, Robert Jr. Lockwood, Elmore James, and Howlin' Wolf (whom Sonny Boy personally tutored), his playing would always be the center of attraction. Yet Sonny Boy was more than a blues harp genius and potent performer. He went on to display his songwriting skills with such classics as "One Way Out," "Don't Start Me Talkin'," and "Nine Below Zero"—all acknowledged blues classics. Despite his popularity, he recorded for the first time after 1951, teaming with Elmore James to record the infamous "Dust My Broom."

The quality of his first recordings were heightened when he signed on with Chess Records in Chicago. Here he recorded with the best blues musicians the city had to offer— Muddy Waters, Otis Spann, Jimmy Rogers, and Robert Jr. Lockwood. While he relocated to Chicago (and later to Cleveland), he always considered the Delta home and returned often, continuing to broadcast on the *King Biscuit Time* radio show out of Helena.

In 1963, Sonny Boy returned to Europe for the second time for the American Folk Blues Festival tour. Captivating his fans with his stage presence and musical excellence, he stayed on for several months to perform and record with the Yardbirds (with a very young Eric Clapton) and the Animals.

In the End . . .

In the summer of 1964, Sonny Boy returned to Chicago for his final recording session at Chess Records where he cut "Understand My Life" and "Find Another Woman" with Buddy Guy on guitar. He then flew back to Europe for the 1964 American Folk Blues Festival tour featuring Howlin' Wolf, Lightnin' Hopkins, Sleepy John Estes, and Willie Dixon.

In April of 1965, Sonny Boy returned from Europe, his tuberculosis and alcoholism now out of control. Spitting up blood between sentences, Sonny Boy was met by the band Levon and the Hawks at the Rainbow Inn Motel in West Helena, where they jammed with the blues master into the late night. They parted company that night, agreeing to record together in the coming months. Within months the Hawks would be renamed The Band and would become the backing band for a young Bob Dylan.

A couple of weeks later, Sonny Boy failed to show up for his regular spot for the *King Biscuit Time* show. The producer sent James Peck over to Sonny Boy's apartment at 421 ½ Elm Street in Helena to wake the bluesman. He was too late. Sonny Boy Williamson II died sometime in the early morning in his sleep.

The mural depicting a map to the gravesite of Sonny Boy Williamson II outside Tutwiler, Mississippi. The mural is on the backside of the old train station in downtown Tutwiler.

First of all, I got shocked at how much he drank. But after a while, I understood that he needed his bottle of whiskey, and then he performed perfectly. I only had a problem one time. He was drinking two or three bottles and he didn't want to leave the stage.

Frank Lippman

Whitfield Church Cemetery
Tutwiler, Mississippi

From Greenwood, take Highway 49 south about eight miles. Once you see the Tutwiler city sign, look for Hancock Street. Turn right and go to the end of Hancock Street and turn left, driving over the railroad tracks. Turn left after the tracks and then right onto Second Street and drive 0.4 miles to a fork in the road (there is an above-ground natural gas meter on the right). Turn right and drive one mile to the intersection of Gibbons and Prairie. Stay to your right, going another 0.5 miles and the church cemetery will be on your right (the actual church burned down several years ago). Facing the former church site, walk on the left side, and about thirty feet from the back of the building you will find a row of graves. Turn left, walking about fifty feet over toward the tree and you will find Sonny Boy Williamson II's magnificent tombstone.

If these directions fail to help you locate his grave, then go back to downtown Tutwiler and look at the giant mural and map at the former train station. It takes up an entire city block!

John Lee Williamson (Sonny Boy Williamson I)
March 30, 1914—June 1, 1948

Considered by blues enthusiast as the first true blues harmonica virtuoso, Sonny Boy Williamson I (as he is now known) began working professionally in the late 1920s, traveling with James "Yank" Rachell and Sleepy John Estes. In the early 1930s, he moved to Memphis, where he worked with Sunnyland Slim down on Beale Street. At the age of twenty, Sonny Boy I moved up to Chicago, where he worked on famed Maxwell Street and at the local clubs with a variety of blues artists. He made his first, and most successful, recording of the blues classic "Good Morning Little Schoolgirl" at the Leland Hotel for the Bluebird label in 1937 and continued recording for Bluebird until 1948. After that first recording he began working with the biggest acts on the South Side, including Muddy Waters, Big Bill Broonzy, and Big Joe Williams. In 1948, just after his thirty-fourth birthday, Sonny Boy was leaving the Plantation Club after a gig when he was mugged and clubbed on the side of the head with a block of cement (not an ice-pick, which has been

previously reported). Staggering home beaten and bloody, Sonny Boy was taken to the Michael Reese Hospital, where he died of a skull fracture. Buried in the old Blair's Chapel C.M.E. Church cemetery, from Jackson, Tennessee, go west on Bemis Lane, turn right on Missouri, then left on D Street. When D Street becomes Steam Mill Ferry Road, drive six miles to Blair's Chapel Road. Turn left and drive another half mile to the cemetery on your left. Williamson's marker is toward the back of the cemetery.

OBSCURE BLUES MUSICIANS PART II
FOR THOSE WHO CAN'T TELL THE DIFFERENCE BETWEEN SONNY BOY I AND II.

FURRY LEWIS
March 30, 1914—June 1, 1948

A notable guitarist in both bottleneck and finger-picking styles, Furry Lewis, one of the first generation of Memphis-based blues artists, contributed his style of blues, ballads, and minstrels to the collection of recorded black music. An associate of W. C. Handy, Furry played the medicine-show circuit in the early 1910s and in the 1920s he began to record for Vocalion and Victor, preserving for generations his classic renditions of "Kassie Jones" and "John Henry." After a hard life of some fame and even less fortune, Furry was rediscovered by blues enthusiasts in  1963. Since he lived in a high-crime area of Memphis, Furry's red Martin guitar would hang on the wall of Capital Loans and Pawn, where it wouldn't get stolen. After each gig he would pawn his guitar, and whenever someone wanted him to play, he'd ask them for money to get his guitar back. Of course, he would always ask for a little extra to make a few bucks on the side. At Memphis's Hollywood Cemetery, drive through the entrance gates past the first section on your left. As the road begins to veer left, park at the intersection. His stone is on the road in the second section on your left, about ten graves from the intersection.

BIG JOE WILLIAMS
October 16, 1903—December 17, 1982

As a first-generation Mississippi bluesman, Big Joe Williams recorded more often, performed longer, and lived longer than almost all of his contemporaries. But what is even more remarkable is that in six decades of performing, little changed in his music. He didn't electrify, and he didn't need a drummer. He just played deeply expressive country blues on his hand-made nine-string acoustic guitar. Best known for the blues classic "Baby, Please Don't Go" (1935) and "Crawlin' King Snake" (1941), Williams achieved his unique sound from his very own custom-made nine-string guitar. From Crawford City Hall in downtown Crawford, Mississippi (the tin shed on the left), drive 4.3 miles to Bethesda Road (unpaved). Turn left on Bethesda and drive .5 miles to the fork at the church on your right. Stay to the right and drive one mile to the end of the road. Turn left and drive to the first curve in the road, just past the house on your right. Look to your right and you will see his upright monument from the road in an overgrown cemetery.

GUS CANNON
September 12, 1883—October 15, 1979

As the leader of one of the finest jug bands from Memphis, Gus Cannon began recording in 1928 and played with blues greats guitarist Jim Jackson and Blind Blake. With his style of music passed over for the guitar-driven boogie of the Delta blues, Cannon continued to perform sporadically for various roots-oriented projects, festivals, and documentaries up until his death at age ninety-six. Cannon was buried ten miles south of Memphis at the Oak Grove M.B. Church cemetery in Nesbit, Mississippi.

JACKIE WILSON

BORN June 9, 1934
Highland Park, Michigan

DIED January 21, 1984
Mount Holly, New Jersey

CAUSE OF DEATH Pneumonia
Age 49

Known thoughout his career as Mr. Excitement, Jackie Wilson was one of the all-time great performers of R&B and early rock 'n' roll. Projecting a sweat-drenched sexuality onstage, he performed spins and splits with a style and panache that matched his full-range, flamboyant singing. With his hair fashioned into a shiny pompadour and wearing a black, sharkskin suit, Wilson would curl his lips and shake his hips, punctuating every song with his vocal gymnastics until he brought the audience to the brink of hysteria.

In the Beginning . . .

Jack Leroy Wilson was born and raised in a suburb of Detroit, Michigan, where he developed a love of sports. While attending high school he began to train as a boxer, later lying about his age to enter local matches. While it is true he did fight professionally, rumors that he was a Golden Gloves champion have been proven false. After winning only two out of ten matches, he turned his attention toward his other passion—music.

As is true of many black singers at the time, Wilson developed his vocal and phrasing technique singing gospel music in church choirs and quartets. Wilson released his first recordings in 1951 under the name of Sonny Wilson and two years later was asked to replace the great Clyde McPhatter as lead singer of the Dominoes. Wilson stayed with the Dominoes for three years and made several notable recordings that scored on both the R&B and pop charts.

In 1957, manager Al Green (no relation to the singer) secured Jackie a solo contract with Brunswick Records. Wilson's first hit was the Berry Gordy composition "Reet Petite" quickly followed by the hit "To Be Loved." With enough songs for an album, they released *He's So Fine*, which peaked at number seven on the R&B charts. The lavish arrangements and astounding vocal presense made Wilson's first album quite an impressive first outing.

When Green died the following year, his assistant, Nat Tarnopol, directed Wilson toward the more lucrative, upscale cabaret market. The period from 1957 to 1959 proved to be Wilson's greatest recording success. "Lonely Teardrops," "That Is Why," "You Better Know It," and others all held top positions in both the pop and R&B markets.

In the early sixties, Jackie's career move in a variety of new directions. From ballads to soul and operatic pop standards, Jackie remained in top form. However, he didn't earn the title Mr. Excitement from his recordings. To fully appreciate Wilson was to see him live onstage. Sweating through his silk shirt by the end of the first song, he would jump up, landing in a split while still hitting a high note. He would then pull himself up by the collar, and twist through a double spin while kicking the mic stand into his right hand.

The impassioned, full-tilt hysteria he generated worked against him in 1961, when he was shot and seriously wounded by a girlfriend outside his New York apartment. But losing a kidney in the incident wasn't his only problem. Tarnopol always believed that rock 'n' roll was just a passing fad, and that Wilson's future lay with the supper club crowd. Odd interpretations of "Danny Boy" and "Swing Low, Sweet Chariot" began to turn up regularly on his albums and in his live act. At the same time, acts from across the Atlantic such as the Beatles, the Yardbirds, and later the Rolling Stones began to erode his popularity. By 1975, Wilson was relegated to the rock 'n' roll revival circuit, a little paunchy and looking a bit tired, yet his voice was still as strong as ever.

In the End . . .

In 1975, Wilson was working on the road again to enthusiastic audiences when he agreed to headline Dick Clark's Good Old Rock 'n' Roll Show. He was well on his way to a comeback when, while performing at the now-defunct Latin Casino in Cherry Hill, New Jersey, he collapsed onstage of a heart attack while singing "Lonely Teardrops." Cornell Gunter of the Coasters was the first one to reach Wilson and administered resuscitative efforts before the ambulance arrived. After another thirty minutes spent stabilizing the singer, oxygen starvation to the brain caused irreversible brain damage.

Wilson remained in a coma for over three months before he gradually improved to a semiconscious state. Limited in movement and unable to talk, lawyers, insurance providers, and his record company argued over who was responsible for his rehabilitation. Consequently, little was done early in his illness, and Wilson suffered further deterioration due to lack of adequate treatment. In 1976 Joyce McRae, a fan visiting from Chicago, was appalled at the lack of therapy and became a one-woman crusade on behalf of the semi-comatose performer. But just as one treatment option was started and began showing results, it was invariably terminated by the estate or insurance providers. Eventually McRae's funds were exhausted and she returned to Chicago. While Wilson was in the hospital, Tarnopol was convicted on several federal charges stemming from an investigation into Wilson's missing back royalties. Wilson died receiving rudimentary care at Burlington County Memorial Hospital, eight years after singing his last note. His estate has yet to recover the missing royalty payments.

Westlawn Cemetery
Wayne, Michigan
A very private ceremony was held for Wilson upon his death. His grave remained unmarked until 1987, the same year Wilson was inducted into the Rock and Roll Hall of Fame. The rose marble crypt with matching bench lies fifty feet from the office, toward the fence.

My heart is cryin', cryin'.
Jackie Wilson's final words before collapsing onstage, from his hit song "Lonely Teardrops."

LESTER YOUNG

BORN August 27, 1909
New Orleans, Louisiana

DIED March 15, 1959
New York, New York

CAUSE OF DEATH Heart Failure
Age 49

Leading the way from big band to bebop and cool jazz, tenor saxophonist Lester "Prez" Young was one of the true giants of jazz. Young introduced a light, darting, soulful lyricism to a medium dominated by a brash, heavily ornamented sound. A warm and witty man, Young struggled with prejudice and alcoholism to produce consistently brilliant music up until his death.

In the Beginning . . .

Lester Willis Young was raised for the first ten years of his life near New Orleans. Having only completed his education through grade four, Young earned his living by shining shoes and passing out handbills for King Oliver, Louis Armstrong, Sidney Bechet, and other great New Orleans musicians. When his father remarried, the Young family moved to Memphis, then later to Minneapolis, where his father and stepmother decided to form a family band. The three children were taught a variety of instruments and went on the road as soon as they were old enough.

Lester switched from drums to alto sax while playing in the family group, the Billy Young Band. In an argument with his father over bookings, Young left the band while in Salina, Kansas. He played with Art Bronson's Bostonians, covering the western states through much of 1928. For the next ten years he played in countless nightclubs and bands, including King Oliver, Bennie Moten, Hot Lips Page, Count Basie, and Fletcher Henderson. He also recorded some of his finest work with Billie Holiday (with whom he remained close his entire life). It was during his stay with Henderson's band that Lester began to receive rave reviews. These reviews suggested he would dethrone the reigning master, Coleman Hawkins, whom he had replaced in the band. Forced out of the band by the other musicians (who held Hawkins in very high regard), Young told his side of the story: ". . . And this bitch would take me down, Fletcher Henderson's wife, [would] take me down in the basement and play one of them old windups and shit, and actually said, 'Lester, can't you play like this?' Coleman Hawkins's playing. But I mean, don't you hear this? Can't you get with this? You dig! I split! Every morning that bitch would wake me up at nine o'clock to try to teach ME to play like Coleman Hawkins. And she played trumpet— circus trumpet! [Laughing] Fuck those motherfuckers! I'm gone!"

He rejoined Basie in 1936 and continued his association for four more years, recording some of his best work to date. Young left Basie in 1940 to front his own group with his brother, Lee, and freelanced on other recording dates. He returned to Basie in 1943 for the chance at steady work again. The following year the army tried to draft Young into service. The FBI served induction papers after a gig in Los Angeles, and despite showing up for the physical drunk, he was inducted into the army.

Stationed at Fort McLellan in Alabama, Young was ironically named the number one tenor saxophone player by *Down Beat*. Unfortunately, the military was trouble for Young as his hair was cut, his sax was confiscated, and his warrant officer refused to allow Young to play in the base's jazz band. After only two months, he was arrested for possession of marijuana and barbiturates. Young was given the maximum sentence—a dishonorable discharge and a year in prison at Fort Gordon, Georgia. Fortunately, it was during his ten months at the disciplinary barracks that he was able to play every Sunday in the dance band.

In the End . . .

Upon his release from prison, Young's income and popularity soared. He was making about fifty thousand dollars a year in the late forties, commanding five hundred or more for a solo engagement. But the bitterness and increased consumption of alcohol made Young moody and unapproachable to all but his close friends. His speech, always peppered with slang, was now almost incoherent. After a show, he would leave the bandstand and go directly to the dressing room, not coming out until one minute before the next show. When he went on the road, he wouldn't leave the room, rarely eating. Rather, he got most of his energy from a bottle of gin. While the personal damage was great, no musical damage had been done, and his playing, if anything, became even more emotional.

Young remained with Basie until the end of 1949, after which he made a series of incredible recordings with Billie Holiday. However, in the winter of 1955, and again in 1957, Lester was hospitalized at Bellevue for depression and alcoholism. He entered King's County Hospital in 1958 for a combination of ailments, including cirrhosis of the liver, malnutrition, and severe depression. Healthy enough to leave and record again, he moved into the Alvin Hotel (across from Birdland) in Manhattan. When not performing at the legendary nightclub, he spent his days watching westerns on TV and drinking gin. In July of 1958, he was strong enough to make an appearance at the Newport Jazz Festival. Pleased with his playing, he made plans to rejuvenate his career and accepted a series of concert dates in Paris. After an engagement at the Blue Note Club in Paris, Prez became very ill and was unable to perform. He flew back to the states in dire condition, returning back to the Alvin where, drinking heavily, his condition went from bad to worse. At 3:00 A.M. on March 15th, Young died of heart failure.

Evergreen Cemetery
Brooklyn, New York

Young was interred in Grave 11418 in the Redemption section. Located on the east side of the cemetery, the section borders the Interborough Parkway at the edge of the cemetery between Orient Hill and Ascension. His upright monument is located in the middle of the section near the back row.

In those days before hearing Charlie Parker and Dizzy, and before learning of the so-called bebop era, my first jazz hero ever, jazz improviser hero, was Lester Young. I was a big Lester Young-oholic and all my friends were Lester Young-oholics. He was our god.

jazz trombonist J. J. Johnson

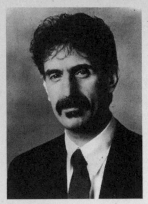

FRANK ZAPPA

BORN December 21, 1940
Baltimore, Maryland

DIED December 3, 1993
Los Angeles, California

CAUSE OF DEATH Prostate Cancer
Age 52

When Frank Zappa died, the obit writers discovered, to their chagrin, that all attempts to neatly classify the late, great iconoclast would fail miserably. Our language is simply inadequate to effectively describe the fierce independence, the musical genius, and the innovative thought that made Zappa, well . . . Zappa. Rock star? Producer? Politician? Satirist? Monster guitar player? Zappa would've been bemused by the writers' quandary. As he himself might've put it, it's hard to find "the crux of the biscuit."

In the Beginning . . .

Frank Vincent Zappa Jr. was born in Baltimore, Maryland, the oldest of four children. At eleven, Frank and the family moved to Monterey, California, where Zappa's interest in music began to develop. By the time he was twelve he had a powerful fascination with sound in general, and with drums in particular. In high school Zappa was in the marching band (although he was eventually kicked out for smoking under the bleachers while in uniform). It was during his high school years that Zappa became interested in the guitar, and formed his own group called the Black-Outs. He also spent time writing classical pieces while pursuing his interests in orchestral music, and rhythm and blues. He was already exhibiting the multifaceted talent and individualism that would become his trademark.

By the time Zappa was in his early twenties, he was firmly ensconced in the music world. He played cocktail lounges, scored some B movies, and collaborated with friend Don Van Vliet (Captain Beefheart). In 1964, he bought a recording studio and formed a band called the Mothers (to be renamed the Mothers of Invention by nervous record executives at MGM Records). The Mothers had become a popular fixture on the L.A. club scene when they released their first studio album of the modern rock era, *Freak Out*, in 1966. *Freak Out* along with its follow-ups *Absolutely Free* and *We're Only in It for the Money* were truly inspired theatrical works providing commentary on the upheaval of the sixties. (At the time, in true Zappa style, the Mothers managed to offend both middle America and the love bead set.)

By the early seventies the original Mothers lineup had disbanded, and Zappa was pursuing other projects, such as signing acts (including Alice Cooper) to his record label. He produced and scored the satirical rock 'n' roll film *200 Motels*, all the while reinventing the Mothers of Invention over again and again in varying incarnations. Although many critics tried to dismiss Zappa as finished after the dissolution of the original Mothers, the fans would have none of it; in the mid-seventies the solo album *Apostrophe* earned Zappa his first gold record and his 1979 release, *Sheik Yerbouti*, placed in the Top 30.

In the 1980s, Zappa continued to break musical ground, including the release of *Shut Up 'n Play Yer Guitar* and *You Can't Do That Onstage Anymore*, Vols. 1-6. *Shut Up* firmly established Zappa—in case there was any question—as one of rock's most ingenious guitarists. The conservative eighties also saw Zappa's highest visibility as a political activist when he testified at a Senate subcommittee hearing investigating the content of pop music lyrics. Frank was a rabid opponent of the Parents Music Resource Center

(PMRC), headed by Tipper Gore, which called for the institution of a ratings system for records. Sound bites from the Senate hearings turned up on the delightfully titled album *Frank Zappa Meets the Mothers of Prevention*. On June 29, 1991, Zappa made an appearance as a guest guitarist at a concert in Budapest. It would be his final appearence as a performer and in November the Zappa family announced that Frank had been diagnosed with prostate cancer.

In the End . . .

During the final years of his career and life, Zappa was as busy and prolific as ever. He oversaw the reissue of his albums on CD, undertook a world tour in 1988, and completed work on his much-anticipated sequel to *Lumpy Gravy, Civilization, Phaze III* (a two-CD work performed entirely by Zappa on the Synclavier digital synthesizer). Even after he was diagnosed with prostate cancer in January 1990, Zappa continued to work, perhaps even more feverishly than before, in an effort to complete the many unfinished projects he had going. When he died at his Laurel Canyon home on December 4, 1993, he left behind an incredible catalog of music for which he will be remembered for many decades—if not longer. Zappa also has been honored with an asteroid named for him: Zappafrank. In perhaps the greatest irony of all, Frank Zappa was posthumously inducted into the Rock and Roll Hall of Fame in 1995. You can almost hear him laughing.

Westwood Memorial Park
Los Angeles, California

It was not unexpected when Frank Zappa died at his Laurel Canyon home and he was quickly buried in the predawn hours. As you enter the cemetery (on Glendon, one block off Wilshire Boulevard), keep going straight toward the office, stopping halfway at the large tree just to the left. Walk onto the grass area toward the tree and look for the flat bronze marker of Charles Bassler. Zappa is located in the unmarked and unadorned plot just above Bassler's. Roy Orbison spends his days about twenty-five feet away, also in an unmarked grave. There are no plans in the future to place a marker at either gravesite.

I write the music I like. If other people like it, fine, they can go buy the albums. And if they don't like it, there's always Michael Jackson for them to listen to.

Frank Zappa

HAS BEENS,
SHOULD-HAVE BEENS,
ONE-HIT WONDERS,
AND A FEW
REALLY GREAT ARTISTS

AALIYAH
January 16, 1979—August 25, 2001
CAUSE OF DEATH Plane Crash

A native of New York and niece of Gladys Knight, Aaliyah Haughton's talent surfaced early when she opened for her aunt in Las Vegas at the age of eleven. Three years later she released her first album, *Age Ain't Nothin' but a Number,* which sold more than a million copies. Secretly married to troubled rapper R. Kelly at age fifteen (Kelly was twenty-seven at the time—they divorced shortly after), that same year she released her second album, *One in a Million,* that went on to sell two million copies. Now modeling for fashion designer Tommy Hilfiger, she appeared in the film *Romeo Must Die,* released her third album, and was scheduled to appear in the sequel to the film *The Matrix* when she died in a crash aboard a small private aircraft. She had just finished a video shoot in the Bahamas to the third single, "Rock the Boat," off her new album when the ten-seater Cessna 402B went down less than a minute after takeoff. Overloaded with luggage, all eight passengers and

the pilot either died at the scene or shortly after at the hospital. Aaliyah was laid to rest at Ferncliff Cemetery in Hartsdale, New York in the mausoleum in Unit 11, Alcove BBB. As you enter the building, walk upstairs to the second floor and walk to the end of the hallway toward the window. Her crypt is located on the left, three spaces from the floor.

JOHNNY ACE
June 9, 1929—December 25, 1954
CAUSE OF DEATH Accidental Shooting

When Johnny Ace (born John Alexander Jr.) put a bullet into his head while playing Russian roulette backstage in Houston in 1954 (in front of blues singer Big Mama Thornton no less), he assured himself a minor place in pop culture's mythology of the damned. An R&B ballad singer in the style of Charles Brown and Nat "King" Cole, Ace started out by playing the piano in Memphis with the Beale Streeters in the late 1940s. In 1952, Ace recorded two songs for the well-known Memphis-based Sun label (both songs were never issued and are today considered "lost"). His first released single, "My Song," went to number one on the R&B charts in 1952 and he quickly followed with six more Top 10 R&B hits. On Christmas Eve in 1954 while on a promotional tour, Ace was playing Russian roulette backstage at the City Auditorium in Houston when he accidentally shot himself. He died the next day (Christmas Day), yet his new single, "Pledging My Love," went on to become one of the biggest hits of 1955. Ace was buried at New Park Cemetery,

Lake Horn, Mississippi, in old Section C. From the entrance of the cemetery, go straight down the road and cross the ditch at the bottom. Going back up the hill, park at the large tree on the left. The stone is second from the road just below the tree.

JULIAN "CANNONBALL" ADDERLEY
September 15, 1928—August 8, 1975
CAUSE OF DEATH Stroke

NAT ADDERLEY
November 25, 1931—January 2, 2000
CAUSE OF DEATH Diabetes

Originally a music teacher in Fort Lauderdale, Florida, Cannonball Adderley was a talented jazz soprano and alto sax player who moved to New York City to seek his fame shortly after the passing of Charlie Parker in 1955. First recording with his trumpeter brother, Nat, in 1955, the quintet featuring the Adderley brothers and Kenny Clarke was a commercial dud. In 1957, Cannonball then had the good fortune to join the Miles Davis group, first recording *Somethin' Else*, then expanding the group to include John Coltrane. Their second album together was one of jazz music's most classic recordings, *Milestones*, with Cannonball taking the lead solo during "Straight No Chaser." Leaving the Davis group, during the 1960s, Cannonball was best known for his style of "soul jazz" and had several hits with Bobby Timmons ("Dat Dere") and the Staple Singers ("Why Am I Treated So Bad"). After Cannonball's passing in 1975, Nat continued on both as a session player and fronting his own groups. Although Nat had played with Woody Herman, J. J. Johnson, and Lionel Hampton, he was still best known for the time spent with his elder brother's groups. Nat was also the composer of "Work Song" and "Jive Samba," which are frequently attributed to Cannonball. Buried at Southside Cemetery in Tallahassee, Florida, Julian can be found in Block E, Section 1, Lot 15, while brother Nat is found in Block E, Section 1, Lot 45.

LAURINDO ALMEIDA
September 2, 1917—July 26, 1995
CAUSE OF DEATH Heart Failure

Born in Brazil, Laurindo Almeida began his career as a guitarist in Rio de Janeiro with Radio Ipanema. Considered one of South America's greatest musicians, he left Brazil for California in 1947 and shortly after joined the Stan Kenton Orchestra as a soloist, composer, and arranger. By 1950, Almeida had released four of his own records. In 1960, the bossa nova craze really took off and Almeida was one of the first to bring a more gentle Brazilian influence into the jazz context. Over the next forty years he could be heard performing on over eight hundred film soundtracks and completed scores to ten major motion pictures (including the award winning *Old Man and the Sea*). His own featured groups included the Laurindo Almeida Quartet and the L.A. 4 (with Bud Shank, Ray Brown, and Shelly Manne). All told, his group recordings received over twenty major musical award nominations and he was awarded five Grammy Awards during his long career. Continually working, his international touring schedule continued on into the nineties to Japan, Europe, and Brazil. Even in the last weeks of his life, he completed his last CD with Danny Welton and performed at the Santa Cruz Jazz Festival with Charlie Byrd. He was laid to rest at

the San Fernando Mission Chapel and Cemetery in Mission Hills, California. His simple grave is located in Section J, Tier 15, Grave 275. He shares this cemetery with Ritchie Valens and actors Chuck Connors and William Frawley (of *I Love Lucy*).

LUTHER ALLISON
August 17, 1939—August 12, 1997
CAUSE OF DEATH Lung Cancer and Brain Tumors

When blues legend Luther Allison passed away at the age of fifty-seven, he was finally achieving the mainstream popularity often reserved for rock stars. Named Entertainer of the Year two years in a row and Best Male Contemporary Blues Artists with five W. C. Handy Blues Awards and fifteen Living Blues Awards in the last two years, Allison was set to assume his rightful place next to Muddy Waters, Buddy Guy, and Robert Nighthawk as a living Chicago blues legend. Born the fourteenth of fifteen children in Widner, Arkansas, Allison began his education in the blues when the family migrated to Chicago in 1951. A classmate of Muddy Waters's son, Allison began playing guitar in earnest at the age of eighteen and was soon jamming with the best the West Side of Chicago had to offer— Otis Rush, Magic Sam, and future bandmate Freddie King. By 1969, Allison was headlining major festivals in the U.S., but moved to Europe shortly thereafter due to the declining interest in the blues domestically. He lived outside of Paris and performed to sold-out venues all throughout Europe, releasing twelve albums in as many years as a bona fide superstar. Allison revived his long-dormant career back home by signing with Alligator Records in 1994, and in the year preceding his death, Allison's North American tour alone included appearances at the Montreal Jazz Festival, the Beale Street Music Festival in Memphis, and the Monterey Bay Blues Festival. Just four weeks after his diagnosis of lung cancer, Allison was buried at Washington Memory Gardens Cemetery in Homewood, Illinois, directly across the road from the main office in the Sanctuary of Prayer, Lot 48-A.

THE ANDREWS SISTERS
LAVERNE ANDREWS
July 6, 1911—May 8, 1967
CAUSE OF DEATH Cancer

MAXINE ANDREWS
January 3, 1916—October 21, 1995
CAUSE OF DEATH Heart Attack

One of the most popular vocal acts of the forties, the Andrews Sisters recorded an amazing eighteen hundred songs and sold over ninety million records. The sisters' big break came in 1938 with "Bei Mir Bist du Schoen," which became the first million-selling record for an all-female group. They went on to appear in seventeen movies (usually as themselves), but in 1954, Patty left the group to try a solo career, with Maxine following in her sister's steps a year later. However, the separation did not last long and the sisters reunited in 1956. They are both buried at Forest Lawn Memorial Park in Glendale, California.

Located in the Grand Mausoleum, walk through the entry to the end of the hallway. Turn right and walk to the end of the hallway to the Columbarium of Memory on the right. They are at the end of the hallway directly under the stained glass window.

CHET ATKINS
June 20, 1924—June 30, 2001
CAUSE OF DEATH Cancer

Known as Mr. Guitar, Chet Atkins was a Country Music Hall of Fame player, producer, and record executive whose name was synonymous with the Nashville Sound. His career began in 1943 touring as a sideman with Kitty Wells and Johnny Wright, and ended almost six decades later with over forty million albums sold, fourteen Grammy Awards, and nine Country Music Association Awards. With over a hundred solo albums to his credit, Chet was also one of the most-recorded musicians in Nashville history, recording with Hank Williams ("Jambalaya"), Faron Young, Webb Pierce, Porter Wagoner, Kitty Wells, Elvis Presley ("Heartbreak Hotel"), and Hank Snow, to name but a few. In 1957, as manager of operations for RCA Records, Chet convinced executives of the need for their own recording studio and the infamous RCA Studio B in Nashville was born. Chet then proceeded to record and produce some of the greatest records for RCA, including Eddy Arnold, Hank Snow, Jim Reeves, Dottie West, Roger Miller, Elvis, Jerry Reed, and Waylon Jennings. Up until his death after a long battle with cancer, he continued to record, tour, and design guitars for Gibson. He is buried at Harpeth Hills Cemetery just south of downtown Nashville, Tennessee. From the cemetery entrance off Highway 100, drive into the main entrance and follow the signs to the cemetery office. Continue past the Cross section and take the next right, parking at the sidewalk just past the Fountain section. Walk down the sidewalk toward the fountain and his grave is to the left of the Atkins bench on the sidewalk. His memorabilia, including guitars and sheet music, can be found in town at the Country Music Hall of Fame.

HOYT AXTON
March 25, 1938—October 26, 1999
CAUSE OF DEATH Heart Disease

It probably came as no surprise that Hoyt Axton enjoyed a successful forty-plus-year run as a singer, songwriter, actor, and performer. After all, his mother, Mae Boren Axton, did cowrite Elvis Presley's smash hit "Heartbreak Hotel." Unlike his peers, Hoyt spent his youth mostly involved in athletics and later spent time in the navy. Upon his discharge in 1961, he joined the emerging folk music scene. After a brief stint in Nashville, he headed for California and played the coffeehouse circuit for ten years. In 1963, Axton had his first hit with "Greenback Dollar" for the Kingston Trio. However, financial success didn't come until Axton wrote "The Pusher" and "Snowblind Friend" for the prototype metal band Steppenwolf. Two years later he wrote a string of hits, including "Joy to the World," "Never Been to Spain" (both for Three Dog Night), "The No No Song" for Ringo Starr, and a duet with Linda Ronstadt that went to number one on the Canadian charts. In the late 1970s he found a home among the Nashville songwriter elite and had a hit record with "Della and the Dealer" and "Rusty Old Halo." In addition, Axton also recorded for A&M, MCA, and his own Jeremiah label. In the 1980s he cut back on his touring and recording schedule and spent more time in Hollywood in films and TV. Upon his passing, Hoyt was buried at Riverview

Cemetery in Hamilton, Montana. As you drive through the cemetery entrance, continue straight toward the office. After you drive through the intersection in the center of the cemetery, look to your left on the road for the large Axton memorial. His mother was buried at Woodlawn East Memorial Park in Hendersonville, Tennessee, in the main mausoleum.

BADFINGER
PETE HAM
April 27, 1947—April 23, 1975
CAUSE OF DEATH Suicide by Hanging

TOM EVANS
June 5, 1947—November 23, 1983
CAUSE OF DEATH   Suicide by Hanging

The story of Badfinger is the story of every musician's nightmare—lots of talent, great songs, millions of fans, hit records, and really, really bad management that guarantees your failure. Originally called the Iveys, Badfinger was brought to the attention of the Beatles and were signed to Apple Records. They released "Without You" in 1969 and "Come and Get It" in 1970. Dogged by accusations that they merely replicated the Beatles' sound, they quickly followed up with "No Matter What," as well as appearing on all of the solo Beatles records, including John Lennon's *Imagine*. After leaving Apple amid rumors of fraud, the band suffered both artistically and financially. Distraught over personal and professional problems, Peter Ham was found dead in his home studio. Joey Molland and Tom Evans re-formed the group, changing the subsidiary members frequently over the next few years. Commercial success proved elusive and in November 1983, history repeated itself when Evans hung himself from a tree at his Surrey home. Oddly enough, the remaining members continued their lawsuits over missing royalties through the 1990s. Both Ham and Evans were cremated.

PEARL BAILEY
March 29, 1918—August 17, 1990
CAUSE OF DEATH Heart Failure

Established primarily as a cabaret singer in her later years, Pearl Bailey's catalog of recordings shows her to be an incredible vocal stylist who was at home in the company of some of the greatest jazz musicians, including Hot Lips Page, Jackie "Moms" Mabley, Charlie Shavers, and her husband, jazz drummer Louis Bellson. Her rise through the ranks of the jazz elite at age fifteen started with her brother, Willie, who became famous as the tap dancer Bill Bailey. She would hang around the Pearl Theatre in North Philadelphia where Bill was rehearsing. As happens with younger sisters, Pearl would tag along and pester Bill, who in turn would often hit her. In retaliation, Pearl entered the theater's talent contest and won first prize—five dollars and an offer for a week's work. This initial success led to more gigs in several Philly clubs. Her big break came in 1941 with gigs at two of New York's biggest jazz clubs, the Blue Angel and the Village Vanguard. Her first film appearance came in 1947 with *Variety Girl*, which also produced her first hit, "Tired." Soon other films followed, including *Carmen Jones* and *Porgy and Bess*. Her most memorable performance came in 1966 when she starred on Broadway in an all-black production of *Hello Dolly*, for which she won a Tony Award. Bailey won numerous awards during her extensive career, including a special appointment by President Richard M. Nixon as Ambassador of Love. She was named Woman of the Year in 1956 by the United Services Organization, for whom she had entertained troops since 1941. In 1975, she was appointed as a goodwill ambassador to the United Nations. In 1978, she was given an honorary degree in the arts from Georgetown University in Washington, D.C. All the while she continued to work internationally with her husband, Louis Bellson, as a cabaret artist and in television. On August 17, 1990, she and her husband of thirty-eight years were staying at a hotel in Philadelphia. Pearl was undergoing rehab after having knee surgery. She had just finished a phone conversation with her sister and gone back to her needlepoint when Bellson noticed that she dropped something. "There's something wrong with my hands," she told him as he rubbed them for her. Then, as Bellson remembered, "The kind of look you never want to see crossed her face" as she slumped in her chair, dead from heart failure. Bailey rests at the Rolling Green Memorial Cemetery in West Chester, Pennsylvania. As you enter the cemetery stay to the left and park about sixty feet in from the gate at the MEDITATION GARDENS sign. Walk approximately twenty feet and Bailey's modest ground marker is right along the road.

CHET BAKER
December 23, 1929—May 13, 1988
CAUSE OF DEATH Fall from a Hotel Room Window

Crowned the Great White Hope of Jazz at the young age of twenty-three, it was a burden to which the musician would never get accustomed. With his Hollywood good looks, bad-boy reputation, and a lifelong addiction to drugs, Baker became the poster boy for West Coast cool jazz. With a style that combined a certain nervous agitation and a strong dose of sentimentality, Baker captured the imagination not only of jazz lovers, but of a general public fascinated as much by his lifestyle as his music. His career began in San Francisco in 1950 while he was stationed at the Presidio with the U.S. Army Band. A regular at the city nightclubs, he received an audition with Charlie Parker, but became famous from his groundbreaking recordings with Gerry Mulligan. He went on to form his own groups and became a legend in Europe. However, his heroin addiction insured that he spent more time avoiding arrest (he spent time in prison in both the U.S. and Italy) than recording and performing. After losing his front teeth in a fall in 1966, living on welfare in the 1970s, and a halfhearted attempt at drug rehab in the 1980s, he returned to Europe to become one of the most recorded jazz musicians ever, with over two hundred albums to his credit. He died

under mysterious circumstances, falling out of a second-story window in Amsterdam. (Murder, suicide, or accident? Nobody seems to know.) Baker played himself in a revealing documentary by Bruce Weber, *Let's Get Lost*. His body was returned to the U.S. and was buried in the Elm Section, Plot 152, at Inglewood Park Cemetery in Inglewood, California.

JOSEPHINE BAKER
June 3, 1906—April 25, 1975
CAUSE OF DEATH Cerebral Hemorrhage

Born in the slums of St. Louis, Missouri, Josephine Baker rode the wave of French enthusiasm for American jazz to become deified in France as a music hall legend and enthusiastic patriot. Baker's career began in 1923 as a member of a Philadelphia dance troupe, followed by a position as a chorus girl in Eubie Blake's show *Shuffle Along*. She appeared briefly (and scantily clad) at Harlem's Cotton Club before traveling overseas to Paris to appear in La Revue Nègre with Sidney Bechet. The show was an enormous hit and made Baker a star. She moved to Paris and began recording for Odeon and became the star of the Folies Bergère within the year. Soon Baker became known as much for introducing the Charleston (dressed only in a girdle of bananas) to Parisians as she was for walking her pet leopard down the Champs-Élysées. In 1937, Baker became a naturalized citizen of France and joined the French Resistance during the Second World War. She returned briefly to America after the war, only to return to France permanently. Upon her death just four days after a well-received return to the stage, Baker became the first American woman buried in France with military honors. Her well-marked gravesite is in the Cimetière de Monaco in Monaco. Not far out of Les Eyzies in France, as you go through the town of St. Cyprien (a picture-book village clinging to the north bank of the Dordogne), you will pass Les Milandes, former home of Josephine Baker and her "world village" of adopted children of all races.

FLORENCE BALLARD
June 30, 1943—February 22, 1976
CAUSE OF DEATH Heart Failure

The most successful female group of the 1960s, the Supremes came into the hits when Berry Gordy teamed the trio with the songwriting team of Holland, Dozier, and Holland. The first of the Motown groups to be processed through its charm school, they hit international fame with "Where Did Our Love Go?" and "Baby Love." All told, they had twelve number one hits and sold over 20 million records during the 1960s. The problem arose in 1968 when Gordy and Ross orchestrated the removal of Florence, renamed the group Diana Ross and the Supremes, and forced Florence to relinquish her rights for $140,000. Three years later, she sued Motown but the judge dismissed the lawsuit in favor of Motown. She eventually lost her home, separated from her husband, and went on welfare with her three children. In 1975, she began a solo career, only to die suddenly the following year. At Florence's funeral, Ross was booed as she made a grand entrance into the chapel (she even had the nerve to take a seat in the front row with the family). Florence was laid to rest at Detroit Memorial Park in Warren, Michigan, in Section D, Lot 291A, Grave 1, under her married name of Florence Chapman.

Florence, Mary Wilson, and Diana Ross in the early 1960s.

THE BAND
RICHARD MANUEL
April 3, 1943—March 4, 1986
CAUSE OF DEATH Suicide by Hanging

RICK DANKO
December 9, 1942—December 10, 1999
CAUSE OF DEATH Heart Attack

The Band made two undeniable contributions to rock. First, they were one of the most famous backing bands that propelled Bob Dylan to the forefront of popular music when Dylan made the transition from acoustic to electric. Second, they ushered in an era of AOR rock not previously heard with *Music from Big Pink* (1968) and *The Band* (1969). Pieced together in Canada by Ronnie Hawkins and Levon Helm, Hawkins recruited future members of the Band as his backing group, only to have the group leave to form Levon Helm and the Hawks. In 1965, Dylan invited the group to back him during his world tour; then, following Dylan's 1966 motorcycle crash, they joined him in Woodstock, where they recorded *The Basement Tapes*. Those recordings showcased the writing talents of members Rick Danko, Robbie Robertson, and Richard Manuel as they began to write their own material. The 1970s proved to be their most productive period with a schedule of nonstop touring and recording. By 1976, the group decided to disband, documenting their final concert with Martin Scorsese's *The Last Waltz*. Reformed in 1983 (sans Robertson), The Band had just finished a gig at the Cheek to Cheek Lounge in Winter Park, Florida, when Richard Manuel returned to his hotel room and hung himself. Whether it was the lack of respect he felt The Band was getting or a relapse of his addiction to drugs and alcohol that caused his demise, no one can say for sure. No note was left and no warning signs were offered. Several days later, he was buried in Avondale Cemetery in Stratford, Ontario, Canada in Section 23A, Lot 193. In January of 1994, The Band was inducted into the Rock and Roll Hall of Fame with longtime friend and fan Eric Clapton doing the honors. Five years later, Rick Danko died in his sleep the night after his fifty-seventh birthday. A public memorial service was held at the Bearsville Theater in Woodstock, New York, and he was buried that week in the back row of Woodstock Cemetery in an unmarked grave.

SIDNEY BECHET
May 14, 1897—May 14, 1959
CAUSE OF DEATH Cancer

This nearly forgotten jazz legend was considered a child prodigy, playing both clarinet and soprano saxophone in his youth. Having played with King Oliver, Bunk Johnson, Louis Armstrong, and Buddy Petit in his hometown of New Orleans, Louisiana, Bechet left New Orleans for Texas, then on to Chicago in 1917. Within two years, he had completed his first tour of Europe with Louis Mitchell's Jazz Kings and four years later he made his recording debut with the Clarence Williams Blue Five, featuring a still-young Louis Armstrong on cornet. Bechet played briefly with Duke Ellington's Washingtonians in 1925 (and again briefly in 1932; however, he never recorded with the Duke) before moving overseas. While living in Paris, his notorious temper got the best of him and he was involved in a gun battle with banjoist Little Mike McKendrick (injuring three other bystanders). He spent eleven months in prison and upon release briefly toured Germany before returning to the U.S. Spending most of his time in New York City, he played with a variety of musicians, including Eddie Condon and Bunk Johnson. Bechet returned to France in 1952 a bona fide jazz legend and was a celebrated artist with the Left Bank intelligentsia of Paris. Although he never reached the level of fame of Louis Armstrong (mainly due to his distrust of agents and managers), he lived a rich life in a small estate just outside Paris until his final days. Bechet is buried in an elegant, black tomb at the Cimetière de Garches in Hauts de Seine, France. Bechet's Armstrong clarinet is on display in the jazz museum in the old U.S. Mint Building in New Orleans, while his home from 1945 to 1952 at 160 Quincy Street in Brooklyn, New York, is visited regularly by jazz purists.

CHRIS BELL
January 12, 1951—December 27, 1978
CAUSE OF DEATH Auto Accident

The story of Chris Bell begins with Alex Chilton of the Box Tops in Memphis, Tennessee (yes, the very same Memphis that gave the world the Bar-Kays, the Rock 'n' Roll Trio, Furry Lewis, the Bill Black Combo, Rufus Thomas, Stax, Bukka White, and some guy named

Elvis). Alex and the Box Tops scored a Top 10 smash hit with "The Letter" in the summer of 1967. They went on the road and performed with the Beach Boys and others until three years later when Alex left everything for the bright lights of New York City. It was Chris Bell who urged the one-hit wonder back to Memphis to form Big Star and produce a critically acclaimed album that subsequently died due to lack of distribution. Bell took the songs he collaborated with Chilton on and began recording a solo album—*I Am the Cosmos*—that he would never see released in his lifetime. In the early morning hours of December 27, 1978, Bell was driving his 1977 Triumph sports car east on Poplar when he struck the curb, careened out of control across a private driveway, and struck a utility pole on the corner of Poplar and Grove Park. The utility pole snapped at the base and landed on the car, killing him instantly. Bell was laid to rest at Memory Hill Gardens in Germantown, east of downtown Memphis, in the mausoleum garden behind the second oak tree on your left in Lot 54C-4. Alex Chilton continued with Big Star through three albums and continues to live in Memphis, performing a couple times a year locally.

JOHN BELUSHI
January 24, 1949—March 5, 1982
CAUSE OF DEATH Drug Overdose

Known primarily as a comic actor, John Belushi, along with friend and partner Dan Aykroyd, made music history with their creation of the Blues Brothers. Their use of classic blues numbers helped revitalize the careers of many blues legends, who were experiencing difficult times in the mid-seventies. Always a fan of music, Belushi's odyssey into music began in 1977 during the filming of the movie *Animal House*. While on location, he met singer Curtis Salgado of the Robert Cray Band when Belushi mentioned Ray Charles would be appearing in the film. Salgado gave Belushi a lesson in the history of the blues. Belushi asked him for advice on his idea for a blues act, ultimately adopting Salgado's performance style and manner of dress, wearing similar dark shades, with his hair and mustache just like the blues singer's, and even doing his between-song dialogs. "He basically lifted my whole act," said Salgado, who also taught Belushi to sing like Belushi. "The first time he sang, he tried to sing like Joe Cocker. I told him to sing like himself." Belushi went back to New York and, along with fellow performer Dan Aykroyd, got some of the best names in the music business to work with him in the Blues Brothers Band—Matt "Guitar" Murphy, Lou Marini, Alan "Mr. Fabulous" Rubin, Donald "Duck" Dunn, and Steve "the Colonel" Cropper (the latter two from Booker T. and the MGs). Unfortunately, Belushi seemed to live by the adage "everything in excess, moderation is for monks." His use of alcohol and drugs grew with his fame, to the point that even fellow cocaine users were alarmed by the amount he regularly self-administered. On March 5, 1982, Belushi was staying in bungalow three at the historic Chateau Marmont Hotel in West Hollywood, working on a new movie script with comedian Robin Williams, actor Robert DeNiro, and writer Nelson Ryan. Shortly after they left, Cathy Smith (a would-be singer, groupie, and former girlfriend of musician Gordon Lightfoot) injected Belushi with a speedball (a mixture of cocaine and heroin). The

actor/musician had wanted to go a little further than he ever had before but the mixture of heroin and cocaine had a cumulative effect on the brain. The dose slowed down John's breathing, resulting in complete respiratory failure. At the age of thirty-three, John Belushi died alone of a drug overdose. John Belushi was buried on March 9, 1982, in Abel's Hill Cemetery on Martha's Vineyard off the coast of Massachusetts. His best friend, Dan Aykroyd, performed as pallbearer and also led the funeral procession on his motorcycle. Located three miles from the Martha's Vineyard airport, the cemetery is on your right. Upon entering the cemetery look to the left and you will see his cenotaph. Originally buried more toward the center of the cemetery, he was moved over three spaces in 1985, while his tombstone was moved to the front to keep the tourists from trampling through the cemetery. Unfortunately, during the move, John's wooden casket had rotted through and he fell out (so to speak). In the spring of 2000, a marker was erected indicating his current resting place, although this also is in dispute. It has also been rumored that brother Jim had John moved to Elmwood Cemetery in Chicago, Illinois, to be with his parents in the Belushi family plot.

JESSE BELVIN
December 15, 1932—February 6, 1960
CAUSE OF DEATH Auto Accident

As author of the best-known doo-wop hit "Earth Angel" and "Good Night, My Love," Jesse Belvin was one of the premier voices of West Coast black vocal music. Born in Texas and raised in Los Angeles, California, he was a featured vocalist as a teenager on the single "All the Wine Is Gone" by Big Jay McNeely in 1950. After a quick tour with the U.S. Army, he recorded his first major hit, "Earth Angel," by the Penguins, which sold over two million copies. He recorded a follow-up hit with "Goodnight, My Love," which was adopted by disc jockey Allan Freed as the closing theme to his highly rated radio show. Jesse achieved more chart success with the Top 10 R&B hit "Dream Girl" (1953) and the Top 20 hit "You Cheated" (1958). That same year he signed with RCA Records, the owners of which had hoped to develop the talented singer and writer into another Nat "King" Cole. So it came as a great shock when the singer met his untimely end outside Hope, Arkansas. Jesse performed at the first integrated-audience concert in Little Rock, Arkansas, and it did not go smoothly—white supremacists managed to halt the show several times and Belvin and his wife had received numerous death threats. Four hours after the concert, Belvin's driver lost control of their Cadillac due to tire failure and the car exploded on impact (some say the scorch marks were still visible on the highway twenty-five years after the accident). Both Jesse and his driver died at the scene, while Belvin's wife died shortly after at the hospital. They were brought back to Los Angeles and buried side-by-side at Evergreen Cemetery in Section G, Lot 41. Despite a cloud of suspicion, there has never been an investigation into the cause of the accident.

FRANCIS "SCRAPPER" BLACKWELL
February 21, 1903—October 27, 1962
CAUSE OF DEATH Murdered

Had he not been found shot to death in an alley in his hometown of Indianapolis, Scrapper Blackwell would have taken his rightful place next to Lightnin' Hopkins, Mississippi John Hurt, and Sleepy John Estes during the late 1960s country blues revival. As it stands, Blackwell is best remembered for his work with pianist Leroy Carr. A successful moonshiner in the early 1920s, Blackwell played his distinctive style built around single-note picking at dances and house parties. In 1928, he was persuaded by Carr to record for

Vocalion and for the next seven years he recorded both with Carr and solo sides that sold very well. A little-known fact is that Blackwell's "Kokomo Blues" was "lifted" by Kokomo Arnold, which in turn was "borrowed" by the legendary Robert Johnson and recorded as the seminal blues classic "Sweet Home Chicago"). After the death of Carr in 1935 from alcoholism, Blackwell stopped playing music and became a day laborer. It wasn't until 1959 that he was rediscovered by blues fan Duncan Scheidt. Unfortunately, one of the blues' first guitar virtuosos was murdered before he had a chance to realize his influence on a generation of up-and-coming artists, such as Muddy Waters and the Rolling Stones. He was buried at New Crown Cemetery in Indianapolis, Indiana. From the main entrance drive straight ahead toward section marker 21, turn right and drive to Montgomery Road to Section 21. Go to the far end of the section and look for the large tree on the left. His simple black marker can be found behind the tree, fifteen rows from the road in Plot 27-426.

EUBIE BLAKE
February 7, 1883—February 12, 1983
CAUSE OF DEATH Natural Causes

A legendary figure for not only his contribution to ragtime jazz but for his longevity, James Herbert "Eubie" Blake's career as a pianist spanned an incredible eighty-five years. The son of former slaves, Blake began playing Atlantic City, New Jersey, nightclubs at the age of fifteen and by the following year he began composing original ragtime music, including "Charleston Rag" and "The Chevy Chase." In 1914 while performing with Joe Porter's Serenaders, Blake began a partnership with the band's vocalist, Noble Sissle. For the next ten years the duo joined James Europe's Society Orchestra, produced the first musical by blacks on Broadway (the successful *Shuffle Along)* and worked on a number of musicals featuring such future legends as Paul Robeson and Josephine Baker. When Sissle left for Europe, Blake continued writing, producing, and performing until 1948, when he retired to study composition. Ten years later Blake released a new album and reestablished his partnership with Sissle. In 1978, a reworked *Shuffle Along* was successfully transformed into the hit Broadway show *Eubie.* Blake continued to perform live and appear at special events honoring his contribution to jazz up until just two months before his passing. He died just five days past his one hundredth birthday and was buried at Cypress Hills Cemetery in Brooklyn, New York in Section 11, Lot 98, Grave 1. Following his death, the Eubie Blake National Jazz Institute and Cultural Center was opened to honor the legacy of a number of jazz greats born or raised in Baltimore, Maryland. Memorabilia and exhibits featuring the music of Blake, Billie Holiday, Cab Calloway, and others is open to the public at 847 North Howard Street in Baltimore, Maryland.

MICHAEL BLOOMFIELD
July 28, 1944—February 15, 1981
CAUSE OF DEATH Suicide

Bloomfield was the highly talented, Chicago blues guitarist who provided the controversial electric accompaniment (along with Paul Butterfield's rhythm section) for Bob Dylan at the 1965 Newport Folk Festival. Later that year, he played lead guitar in sessions for Dylan's

Highway 61 Revisited (that's Bloomfield on "Like a Rolling Stone"). As the lead guitarist in the Butterfield Blues Band, Bloomfield reached the pinnacle of his performing career, mixing rapid-fire blues-inspired solos with blues/jazz-based instrumentals that fit well within the late 1960s psychedelic surroundings. Those performances with Dylan and Butterfield established Bloomfield as an American guitar hero on the same level as Eric Clapton and Jeff Beck. At the height of

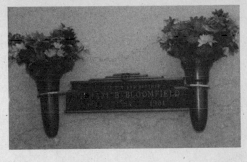

his fame, he walked out of the BBB to form the Electric Flag. He left after two uninspired albums and more or less slowly withdrew from music, only to surface occasionally for an odd jam session or live appearance. Although heroin was Bloomfield's drug of choice, he was found dead of an apparent self-induced cocaine overdose in his San Francisco garage. He was buried at Hillside Memorial Park in Los Angeles, California. As you enter the gates, turn right just past the office (that's the Al Jolson memorial and waterfalls to your left), and drive to the top of the hill. Walk to the front of the Courts of the Book mausoleum (Al Jolson will be directly behind you) and veer left into the north wing from the rotunda. Turn right into the Corridor of Love, then turn left into the Sanctuary of Meditation. Bloomfield is in Crypt 314, third row from the bottom on the left.

MARC BOLAN
September 30, 1947—September 16, 1977
CAUSE OF DEATH Auto Accident

When Marc Bolan died at the age of twenty-nine, he had sold millions of records, toured both Europe and America, and drew hordes of screaming fans usually reserved for the Beatles and The Who. Unfortunately, Marc Bolan, founder and driving force behind T. Rex, never gathered as huge a following in the U.S. Add to the mix an orgy of booze, drugs, and a fatal car crash and you end up with the tragic and early demise of one of glam rock's founding fathers.

Born Marc Feld, Marc Bolan's elusive search for fame began at age fifteen, when he dropped out of school and worked briefly as a model. He recorded a few singles with Decca Records as Marc Bowland, then briefly joined the group John's Children. The following year he joined with drummer Steve Peregrine Took to form Tyrannosaurus Rex. Dressed in love beads, hippie threads, and singing of fairies and gnomes, the acoustic duo recorded two albums and toured the U.K. for a year. In 1969, T. Rex (the name had now been shortened) added a bass player and a second guitarist to the group and embarked on a disastrous U.S.

tour. By the time the band reached New Orleans, tension between Bolan and Took was at a breaking point (mostly due to Took's increasing dependency on drugs) and Took was asked to leave the band. Upon returning home to England, the period from 1970 through 1975 is often regarded as the band's most productive, producing twenty-five chart-topping singles and one major U.S. hit "Get It On" (later retitled "Bang a Gong"). However, a consistent rotation of musicians, increasing drug and alcohol abuse, and a sud-

den massive weight gain proved fatal to Bolan's popularity. The end came suddenly early in the morning of September 16, 1977, when Marc and his girlfriend/backup singer Gloria Jones left London's Mortons Club and began their drive home. With Gloria at the wheel, the Mini left the road near Barnes Common on Queens Ride in a blanket of fog. As the car crossed over the guard rail, it struck a small sycamore tree just off the road, killing Bolan instantly as he was thrown into the backseat of the small sports car.

Upon his passing, Bolan was cremated and his ashes scattered over the grave of his parents at Golders Green Crematorium on Hoop Lane in London, England. As you enter the grounds, follow the signs to the Tea Rooms. To the left of the Tea Rooms, take the door to the West Memorial Court. Look to your left on the top row and you will see Marc Bolan's memorial plaque (to the left and down you will see jazz artist Ronnie Scott's plaque). Walk through the courtyard and leave opposite the door you entered, turn left, and walk along the Cloister Walk in front of the crematorium buildings. At the end you will see a brick mausoleum (the Martin Smith mausoleum), then turn right onto the Eastern Path and stay on this path until you reach the Keats rosebed on your left. The Feld bush is about halfway along the grass side on Plot 46087 (a bit hard to find due to the fact that the plaque gets stolen by fans all the time).

The Bolan Memorial plaque placed by his son, Rolan, can be found at the crashsite on Queens Ride just off Upper Richmond Road near Gipsy Lane (just a five-minute walk from the Waterloo Underground station, at the Barnes station).

In one of rock's saddest ironies, Steve Peregrin Took died in 1980 by choking on a cocktail cherry. Cruelly referred to as the Pete Best of Glam Rock, Took spent his life attempting to retrieve what he perceived as his lost fame. As Marc Bolan became more successful, Took began to receive royalty checks from sales of the early T. Rex recordings. It was with a newly cashed royalty check that Took purchased the drink (along with heroin and hallucinogenics) that proved fatal. He was laid to rest at Kensal Green Cemetery on Harrow Road in London, England. From Harrow Road just past a pub called the Masons Arm, look for the sign for St. Mary's Cemetery. Follow the sign and look for the entrance to Kensal Green on the left. Just inside the cemetery, get a map of the cemetery grounds and look for section 103, just past the chapel in the center of the cemetery. About fifty yards from the chapel on the main path you will come to a roundabout—turn left here along the grassy path for about thirty yards and to your left you will come upon a smaller path. Took's grave is about another thirty feet along this path on your right in Plot 61065, Section 103-2.

BUDDY BOLDEN
February 7, 1883—November 4, 1931
CAUSE OF DEATH Cerebral Arterial Sclerosis

The beginnings of jazz and the story of Buddy Bolden are inextricably intertwined. Because he never recorded, Bolden remains a shadowy figure in the prehistory of jazz. With no formal training, Bolden fused his cornet playing with ragtime, dance rhythms, and early blues, making him the first King of Jazz, and to many, the official First Man of Jazz. In 1907, he began a slow decline into insanity and was committed to the Louisiana Insane Asylum in Jackson, where he died twenty-five years later. His last trip through the streets of New Orleans was to Holt Cemetery on City Park Avenue. From City Park Avenue, turn into the administrative office parking lot of Delgado Community College. Look closely and you will see the cemetery corner toward the back of the parking lot. From the cemetery office/shed, walk over one hundred feet to the large, white monument commemorating the final resting place of Buddy Bolden. While his pine-box coffin was originally buried in Section C-623, it is impossible to know exactly where he is buried as cemetery records were not accurately kept until 1940. The only memorabilia remaining of this elusive figure is the Bolden family home, which is still standing at 2309 First Street in New Orleans. The last direct link to the King of Jazz, Bolden's old neighbor and New Orleans musician Papa John Joseph remained musically active to the end. In 1965, at the age of eighty-five, Papa John had just finished a bass solo on "When the Saints Go Marching In" at the historic Preservation Hall when he turned to the piano player and said, "That number just about did me in," and then died.

TOMMY BOLIN
August 1, 1951—December 4, 1976
CAUSE OF DEATH Multiple Drug Overdose

Best known as Ritchie Blackmore's replacement in Deep Purple and Joe Walsh's replacement in the James Gang, Tommy Bolin was a brilliant guitar player whose life was tragically cut short due to his intense consumption of alcohol, barbiturates, and heroin. Born and raised in Sioux City, Iowa, Bolin began his career with local bands Energy and the more popular Zephyr. His reputation among guitar purists soared when Bolin was invited by drummer Billy Powell to play on the now-classic *Spectrum* album. He recorded in 1975 with Deep Purple on *Come Taste the Band* and released his first solo album, *Teaser,* that same year. The following year he released his second solo album, *Private Eyes,* and set off on a three-month tour with Blue Öyster Cult. The tour was a disaster with missed dates due to overconsumption or bad weather, eventually ending with what would be Tommy's final performance in his hometown at the Sioux City Auditorium. The following day his family drove him to the airport for a flight to Miami. After a week of vacation, Bolin was to begin a tour opening for Jeff Beck, followed by a tour with Fleetwood Mac. After the opening night of the tour with Jeff Beck, Bolin was found dead of a drug overdose in his hotel room. Returned home, Bolin was buried in the Bolin family plot at Calvary Cemetery in Sioux City. From the entrance of the cemetery, drive to the back of the cemetery and turn left. Drive to the top of the hill and turn left again to the Golatha section. The grave is four rows from the road, in the Golatha Section, Plot 51, Grave 3. Until funds can be secured to build the Iowa Museum of Rock 'n' Roll History in Lake Okoboji, Iowa, brother John Bolin retains ownership of the vast majority of Tommy's guitars and memorabilia.

SONNY BONO
February 16, 1935—January 5, 1998
CAUSE OF DEATH Skiing Accident

Fortunately (or unfortunately, depending on your point of view), Sonny Bono's legacy is secure in the knowledge that every night, in karaoke bars throughout the world, someone is singing "I Got You, Babe." Formerly a sausage truck driver, Bono got his first job in the music business working as a gofer and backup singer for record producer Phil Spector. Married to Cher in 1964, they first performed as Caesar and Cleo before settling on Sonny and Cher. They signed with Atco the following year and had a string of minor hits over the next four years. After a four-year hiatus they recorded several more singles before launching *The Sonny and Cher Comedy Hour* on TV. Built around Sonny's straight man routine to Cher's designer outfits and semiwitty banter, the show lasted three years before being canceled. The couple divorced that same year, with Sonny drifting on the fringes of the entertainment business with guest shots on *Fantasy Island* and *The Love Boat.* Legend has it Sonny quit show business when he called *Fantasy Island*'s Tattoo "Pontoon." When the diminutive actor started screaming at Bono, he walked off the set and never looked back. Outside of Hollywood, Sonny moved to Palm Springs, California, and opened a restaurant, remarried, got elected mayor, and later elected to the U.S. Congress. His life ended suddenly on a clear, sunny day on the ski slopes in Lake Tahoe. Sonny decided to take one last run for the day; when he didn't return his family alerted the ski patrol to organize a search team. They found him that evening slumped near a lodgepole pine tree—dead from injuries sustained when he hit the tree. Interment was at Desert Memorial Park in Cathedral City outside Palm Springs, California. As you drive into the cemetery, proceed to the back to the Americas Plaza. He is buried just outside the plaza to the right of the flagpole, in Section B-35, Space 294.

JAMES BOOKER
December 17, 1939—November 8, 1983
CAUSE OF DEATH Drug Abuse

Known in the Crescent City as the Bayou Maharajah, Little Booker, and the Piano Prince of New Orleans, James Booker was the finest blues pianist to come out of the Big Easy since Jelly Roll Morton. A musician of far-reaching depth and talent, Booker formed his own band while still in his teens and was a member of the house band at Cosmo Studios on the early Ace Records releases. In the late fifties, he toured and recorded with Joe Tex, Wilson Pickett, B. B. King, and Aretha Franklin. It was during this period that his legendary consumption of drugs and alcohol began to take their toll (he served time at both

Parish Prison and Angola State Prison in Louisiana and later lost his left eye to drug abuse). But regardless of his personal shortcomings, he was without a doubt the finest, wildest, and most unpredictable pianist of his time. Upon his early and not surprising death, he was interred at Providence Memorial Park on Airline Highway outside New Orleans. As you drive through the entryway, drive straight back to the small mausoleum in the rear. His crypt is located on the left outside wall, third from the bottom, third space from the left.

D. BOON
April 1, 1958—December 22, 1985
CAUSE OF DEATH Auto Accident

As guitarist and founding member for L.A.'s seminal punk band the Minutemen (they got their name because in the beginning most of their songs were only about a minute long), D. Boon mixed funk, punk, metal, country, and a healthy dose of rage that influenced the likes of Nirvana for generations. Like peers Black Flag, Hüsker Dü, and the Meat Puppets, the Minutemen built a solid cult following throughout the U.S. the old-fashioned way—by living in a van on the road for six years. The end came tragically one night after a concert when D. Boon was driving home with his girlfriend. His van caught on fire and he was killed. The well-

attended services at his gravesite were held at Green Hills Memorial Park in San Pedro, California. As you drive through the entrance of the cemetery, turn right and then turn left, and drive past the Garden of Reflection on your left. Turn left at the next intersection, turn right onto Lake View Road, and drive approximately halfway the length of the road and park. D. Boon's gravesite is on your right in the Lake View Lawn section in Plot 365, five rows from the road.

WILLIAM "BIG BILL" BROONZY
June 26, 1893—August 15, 1958
CAUSE OF DEATH Throat Cancer

Big Bill Broonzy is one of the select few bluesmen whose recorded body of work is still considered an essential building block of the blues we hear today. Based in Chicago, he recorded 78s as early as 1926 and worked with Memphis Minnie and Sonny Boy Williamson I. In 1938, he became the first African American to play Carnegie Hall when he replaced the recently deceased Robert Johnson. Among the hundreds of titles Broonzy cut for Paramount, Bluebird, Columbia, and OKeh Records are the standards "All by Myself" and "Key to the Highway." After a thirty-year career, he retired from music to become a janitor at Iowa State University.

Rediscovered by author and radio personality Studs Terkel, he billed himself as the Last Blues Singer Alive to European audiences. They didn't know any better, so the ruse worked (at least in Europe). Luckily, Broonzy had the skills to pull off such a stunt, and in the thirty-plus years since his death, his reputation remains intact. Despite seven different grave locations that various biographies have printed, he truly can be found at Lincoln Cemetery on the corner of Kedzie and 123rd Street in Chicago, Illinois. As you enter the cemetery, park at the office and walk over to the section directly across from the office and behind the mausoleum. He resides in Section TLA, Lot 289, which is seven rows behind the mausoleum (in the same row as the Larrey monument).

CHARLES BROWN
September 13, 1922—January 21, 1999
CAUSE OF DEATH Heart Failure

A tall, gentle soul who was an essential force in postwar West Coast R&B, Charles Brown was a pianist and vocalist whose style of cool blues was a study of low-key expression and sophistication. Born in Texas City, Texas, Brown graduated from UC Berkeley with a degree in chemistry, working as a teacher and chemist before he found work in the piano lounges of Los Angeles. He joined the Three Blazers with Johnny Moore (brother of guitarist Oscar Moore of the Nat "King" Cole Trio). They soon released Brown's "Driftin' Blues," which knocked Louis Jordan off the top of the R&B charts. The always dapper Brown soon became an R&B star nationwide with the hits "Merry Christmas, Baby" and "Sunny Road." At the height of his popularity he was fronting an eight-piece orchestra that became a training ground for such future stars as Ray Charles, Ruth Brown, and the Dominoes. But with success came frustration with the "blues singer" label. "I consider myself to be an artist," Brown once remarked. "People think a blues singer is someone in overalls and a straw hat, but man, we were sharp! Wore silk suits and changed clothes three times a night." As the rock 'n' roll explosion took hold in the sixties, Brown was relegated to small clubs, playing the same set night after night. It wasn't until the late 1980s that musicians—both rock and blues—sat up and took notice of his talent and contributions. Brown was all ready for his induction into the Rock and Roll Hall of Fame when he passed away from congestive heart failure in an Oakland hospital. He was interred at Inglewood Park Cemetery in Inglewood, California, in the Sunset Mission mausoleum upstairs in the Sanctuary of Bells, in Plot 926, just below Lowell Fulson.

DENNIS BROWN
February 1, 1957—July 1, 1999
CAUSE OF DEATH Respiratory Failure Due to Substance Abuse

If Bob Marley was the King of Reggae, then Dennis Brown certainly earned his title of Crown Prince of Reggae. Brown's musical career began at age nine and he is credited with over sixty albums and touring relentlessly throughout the world up until his early demise. Blessed with a melodic vocal quality with a roots-conscious message to his lyrics, Brown scored his first hit in 1969 with "No Man Is an Island." He spent much of the 1970s moving between studios and recording a series of now-classic albums before he had an international hit with "Money in My Pocket." After the death of Bob Marley, Brown was signed by A&M Records in an attempt to corner the international crossover market. He also recorded with K.C. and the Sunshine Band in an effort to expand his American audience—both efforts failed. He continued with his pop hits set to a reggae beat for much of the 1980s, during which he also became

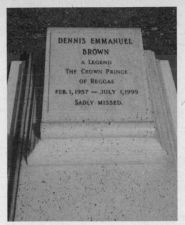

a fixture at the Reggae Sunsplash Festival in Jamaica. After an extensive tour of Brazil with close friend and peer Gregory Isaacs, Brown fell ill and checked into the University Hospital in Kingston, Jamaica, where he died shortly thereafter. Brown was the first entertainer to be buried at Kingston's National Heroes Park, an exclusive cemetery reserved for such notables as independence leaders Alexander Bustamente, Norman Manley, and black nationalist leader Marcus Garvey. As you enter the cemetery in the center of Kingston, you will need a guide to take you past the guards toward the back of the cemetery (be sure to tip the guide one hundred Jamaican dollars, about three bucks) to his simple monument (there are only about ten people buried in this large cemetery).

ROY BROWN
September 10, 1925—May 25, 1981
CAUSE OF DEATH: Heart Attack

Had Roy Brown written only "Good Rocking Tonight," that would have been enough to label him great; however, he was also a gifted singer and performer—a flamboyant, emotional blues shouter whose style was later copied by Jackie Wilson and Bobby "Blue" Bland. After "Good Rocking," Brown continued with a string of hits in the early 1950s, including "Hard Luck Blues," "Love Don't Love Nobody," and "Cadillac Baby."

However, by the late 1950s prevailing tastes shifted and the tide of rock 'n' roll left Brown without a recording contract, little money, and a hefty IRS bill. Times got so bad he sold the rights to "Good Rocking Tonight" and later spent time in jail for tax evasion. After a ten-year hiatus, he was featured at the 1970 Monterey Jazz Festival with Johnny Otis, which marked the beginning of his return. He toured England in 1978 and was about to embark on a major U.S. tour when he was suddenly stricken by a heart attack near his home in Los Angeles. Roy Brown was buried at Eternal Valley Memorial Park in Newhall, California. Upon entering the cemetery, take the middle left road toward the top of the hill. Turn left at the second intersection and drive to the top of the right section. Walk nine rows from the top and fifteen rows over from the road to Plot 202-E in the Garden of Meditation. He shares this cemetery with Gene Vincent.

JIMMY BRYANT
March 25, 1925—September 22, 1980
CAUSE OF DEATH Lung Cancer

When Jimmy Bryant passed away of lung cancer at his sister's home in Moultrie, Georgia, the loss of this talented guitarist barely made a ripple in the newspapers outside his hometown. If Jimmy Bryant wasn't the first country-jazz guitarist, then he was without a question the best—period! Known for his fluent lines, dizzying technique, mind-bending, innovative chops, and speed—my God, was this man fast on the fretboard! Hence his title of Fastest Guitar in the Country was well deserved.

Bryant got his start on guitar when upon discharge from the army in 1945 he used his military discharge pay to buy a guitar and amp. After playing small jazz clubs around the Washington, D.C., area as Buddy Bryant, he loaded up his car and along with a new wife moved to California. The first couple of years were tough, barely making a living as an extra in B-type western films and playing the low-rent country bars of Southern California. It wasn't until around 1950 when Bryant teamed up with pedal-steel guitarist Speedy West that things really began to click. They released five albums by the mid-fifties and had over fifty singles with Capitol Records. Along with heavy airplay, they played on sessions with Bing Crosby, Gene Autry, Nelson Riddle, Jim Reeves, and Dinah Shore. If that wasn't enough, they were in demand for radio and television at a pace of two to three shows per week, including most of Roy Rogers's movies at the time. All in all, it is estimated that during the 1950s the duo played with over two hundred different artists. Always the innovator, Speedy was credited with being the first pedal steel on a record, while Jimmy's claim to fame was being the first to play a Fender Telecaster on record—in fact, he owned the very first Telecaster ever made!

Speedy and Jimmy went their separate ways in 1955, with Bryant alternating between Nashville and Los Angeles as a much-requested session player. In the mid-seventies, Bryant moved to Nashville but soon found that he was considered a musical outsider. In a town that wanted only commercial players, Jimmy was considered a hot player—and a great one at that! But it really didn't matter too much, as time was running out for the guitar master. A heavy smoker, he died two years after being diagnosed with lung cancer.

Jimmy Bryant was buried in the Pleasant Hill Cemetery in Berlin, Georgia. From downtown Berlin (and I use that term loosely), drive north on Highway 133 just outside of Berlin and turn left on Wesley Chapel Road. Drive 2.5 miles to Pleasant Hill Baptist Church Road and turn right on Pleasant Hill. Drive a half mile to the cemetery, pull into the entrance to the cemetery on the left directly across from the church. Walk to your left a short distance to the cemetery's only guitar-shaped headstone.

ROY BUCHANAN
September 23, 1939—August 14, 1988
CAUSE OF DEATH Suicide

Roy Buchanan was destined for fame at an early age. He acquired his first guitar at the age of nine and in his early teens had dropped out and traveled across the country, answering to no one. By sixteen he was leading his own band and in 1961 while on tour in Canada met Ronnie Hawkins, briefly playing with the Hawks (later renamed the Band). By this time, Buchanan began a three-year run of steady studio and session work with a variety of artists. Tired of the grind, he moved to Virginia and recorded and played locally to the critical acclaim of such luminaries as John Lennon, Eric Clapton, and eventually the

Rolling Stones. In the often-told story, after the death of Brian Jones, the Stones offered the guitar spot to Buchanan, who turned it down, stating, "I don't want to be another rock 'n' roll casualty." Unfortunately, that's what he became. Several years later, with multiple critically and commercially successful albums behind him, he was arrested just outside his home on a charge of public drunkenness. What happened afterward is a mystery to this day. What we do know is that approximately thirty minutes after being locked in his cell, he was "found" hanging  from his shirt around his neck. What many people, including his widow, Judy, question is why? While Roy had a dark side to his personality, many dispute the conclusions of the official police report. Even odder still was the fact that years after his death, Fairfax County Police still refused to answer basic questions regarding the events of that night. Eventually, after being kept in storage for two years pending an independent autopsy, Roy Buchanan's body was buried at Columbia Cemetery in Arlington, Virginia, just outside of Washington, D.C. As you enter the cemetery, veer left at the fork in the road and turn left onto Azalea at Oak Hill Road. Drive three hundred feet to a black marble bench on the left and park in front of the Hilleary monument. Walk to the top of the hill and look to the right for the black marble monument in Section 2.

DORSEY BURNETTE
December 28, 1932—August 19, 1979
CAUSE OF DEATH Heart Attack

JOHNNY BURNETTE
March 28, 1934—August 1, 1964
CAUSE OF DEATH Drowning

Johnny was best known for the hit singles "You're Sixteen" and "Dreamin' " while Dorsey had a minor hit with "Tall Oak Tree." However, they should be remembered for their collective recordings as the Rock 'n' Roll Trio. One of the first (and arguably the best) rockabilly groups, the Trio was rejected by Sam Phillips as sounding too similar to Elvis (as if that's a problem!). They signed with Coral Records and had hits with "Tear It Up," "Blues Stay Away from Me," and "Train Kept a-Rollin' " (complete with a distorted guitar solo, later made popular by the Yardbirds and Aerosmith) and appeared in the movie *Rock, Rock, Rock!* in 1956. Shortly after, the Trio disbanded and the brothers moved to Hollywood to establish themselves as songwriters. Upon their deaths they were laid to rest in Forest Lawn Memorial Park in Glendale, California. Following the directions for Sam Cooke or Sammy Davis Jr., turn back around from the Garden of Honor, staying to the right as the road splits and park at the Chotimer monument on Freedom Way. Walk to the left of the Chotimer monument and follow the sidewalk away from the monument to the statue of the woman holding a child. Turn right into the lawn area at the statue and walk down the hill fourteen rows to the Dorsey marker. They are buried near each other with Dorsey in Lot 8319 and Johnny in Lot 8276 in the Garden of Ascension. The largest collection of Burnette memorabilia can be found at the Memphis Music Hall of Fame, across from the Peabody Hotel in downtown Memphis.

CLIFF BURTON
February 10, 1962—September 27, 1986
CAUSE OF DEATH Auto Accident

Cliff Burton was one of those rare individuals—an extremely talented bassist in a field of mediocrity during the formative years of heavy metal in the early 1980s. Picking up the bass in his early teens, Burton played in the Bay Area bands Easy Street, Agents of Misfortune, and Trauma before being invited to play with Metallica in 1983. Cliff agreed on one condition—that Metallica relocate to San Francisco. Since the band had no problem leaving Los Angeles, Burton joined the band. They recorded three now-classic metal albums and quickly distanced themselves from the glam-rock poseurs and the punk rock scene. In 1986 they were asked to join Ozzy Osbourne's Ultimate Sin tour in support of their new album *Master of Puppets.* After a successful show in Stockholm, the tour was traveling to the next gig on a narrow, two-lane road when the bus carrying the members of Metallica and some of their road crew hit a patch of black ice. The bus began to skid out of control when the driver overcorrected, throwing the bus on its side into a ditch. During the rollover, Burton was thrown from his bunk, out the back window, with the bus landing on top of him—killing him instantly. Metallica returned home minus one of their own and shortly after attended the memorial services for the young bassist. His cremated remains were scattered in and around some of his favorite San Francisco haunts.

GLEN BUXTON
February 11, 1947—October 19, 1997
CAUSE OF DEATH Pneumonia

"I grew up with Glen, started the band with him, and he was one of my best friends. He was an underrated, influential guitar player and a genuine rock 'n' roll rebel," said Alice Cooper upon hearing of the passing of the original guitar player for the Alice Cooper Band. Though kind of Buxton's musical talent, the Alice Cooper Band didn't exactly start with a bang when the band first got together. Born out of the Phoenix, Arizona, club scene, Buxton and guitarist Michael Bruce provided the three-chord crunch behind Cooper's swagger and attitude. The first two albums, *Pretties for You* and *Easy Action,* were universally panned by critics and what few fans the band had. But the 1971 release of *Love It to Death* with the single "I'm Eighteen" landed the band on the radio, on the charts, and out on the concert trail. The next two releases, *Killer* and *School's Out* showed the best of Buxton and Bruce—a solid two-guitar fuzztone attack minus the clichés of seventies rock. But like most bands then and now, cracks began to show as the band's popularity soared. Cooper began to assume the position of lead spokesman for the band, relegating

the others as sidemen while Buxton's substance abuse problem made it difficult for him to show up to recording sessions and concerts. It got so bad that during the recording of *Billion Dollar Babies,* guitarists Dick Wagner and Steve Hunter were brought in to cover for the ailing Buxton, while still another guitarist, Mick Mashbir, was used on the road playing for Buxton offstage while Buxton's guitar was turned off. It finally got too much for the band and Cooper when, during the recording of *Muscle of Love,* there were more studio musicians than band members. Shortly thereafter, Cooper dismissed the band to continue on as a soloist. Buxton and Bruce went their separate ways with Buxton

briefly forming the band Virgin in 1980. He died in his hometown of Clarion, Iowa, and was buried at Evergreen Cemetery. As you drive into the cemetery, go past the caretaker's shed on the right and park. Walk to the edge of the cemetery and look for the upright black monument (note—his name faces away from the road).

THE BYRDS
MICHAEL CLARKE
June 3, 1946—December 19, 1993
CAUSE OF DEATH Liver Disease

GENE CLARK
November 17, 1944—May 24, 1991
CAUSE OF DEATH Heart Attack

CLARENCE WHITE
June 7, 1944—July 14, 1973
CAUSE OF DEATH Hit by a Drunk Driver

With the opening riff of Jim (later changed to Roger) McGuinn's electric twelve-string Rickenbacker guitar, there are few more immediately recognizable songs than the Byrds' "Mr. Tambourine Man" or "Turn! Turn! Turn!" With their perfect blend of folk, rock, and country, the Byrds not only went on to influence the Beatles and Bob Dylan, but subsequent generations of bands from Tom Petty and the Heartbreakers to innumerable alternative bands of the postpunk era, including REM and the Gin Blossoms. Initially founded by the vocal trinity of McGuinn, Gene Clark, and David Crosby, the trio made a primitive demo for the record companies as the Jet Set, later recording a single as the Beefeaters. Renamed the Byrds, they added Michael Clarke on drums and fan Chris Hillman on bass. Of their debut single as the Byrds, the only instrument from the original group to make it on the 1965 chart-topping hit single "Mr. Tambourine Man" was McGuinn's guitar (session players for this hit included future solo artist Leon Russell and drummer Hal Blaine). What they lacked in musical ability (what they also lacked was instruments—most members still didn't have their own), they more than made up for with their determination to master an alt-folk country-rock sound that would change the pop scene before the end of the year. Within ten months the quintet had recorded material for two full album releases, their second number one pop hit, "Turn! Turn! Turn!," and one of the bands most-covered songs (most recently by Tom Petty), Gene Clark's "I'll Feel a Whole Lot Better." As principal songwriter and lead vocalist for the formative years, Clark left the band amid a growing tension among the founding members and a fear of flying on tour. But in his absence, Crosby and McGuinn established themselves as formidable songwriters, penning the latter-day Byrds hits "Eight Miles High" (with Clark on one of the first rock songs to be banned for its alleged drug reference) and "So You Want to Be a Rock 'n' Roll Star" (by McGuinn and Hillman, on the group's last Top 20 hit). The 1968 album *The Notorious Byrd Brothers* saw the departure of Crosby (who left to form a band that only lasted three decades, Crosby, Stills, and Nash), and the addition of guitarist Clarence White and later short-lived member Gram Parsons. With McGuinn as primary songwriter, the members of the original Byrds then embarked on what was to be their most influential album, *Sweetheart of the Rodeo*. With songs by Bob Dylan ("Nothing Was Delivered"), Merle Haggard ("Life in Prison") and Gram Parsons's "Hickory Wind," the album began a musical style that would be the precursor to the Eagles. But after years of a succession of various members and studio musicians,

McGuinn disbanded the group in 1972 to re-form with the original lineup. The failed lineup only served to showcase Clark's past contributions, and thus the Byrds were formally disbanded, with members going on to continue their sporadic solo careers. In 1973, while loading his equipment into his car after a gig in Palmdale, California, White was run over by a drunk driver (and even more tragically, his wife and two children were killed in a traffic accident shortly after his death). White was buried at Joshua Memorial Park in Lancaster, California, in the section 300 feet from the entrance to the right of the praying hands statue. Both Clark and Clarke suffered from the long-term effects of alcohol abuse. Clark was buried in his hometown of Tipton, Missouri, at the St. Andrew's Cemetery in the Calvary section (twelve rows from the back fence). Clarke, who passed away in Florida, was reported to have been cremated, with the ashes returned to his family.

SAMMY CAHN
June 18, 1913—January 15, 1993
CAUSE OF DEATH Heart Failure

One of the most prolific, if not commercially successful, songwriters of the twentieth century, Sammy Cahn amassed twenty-six Oscar nominations with four Academy Awards spread over four decades. Born Samuel Cohen (later changed to Kahn) in New York City, he began as an itinerant violinist playing with a variety of dance bands before turning to songwriting with his first partner, Saul Chaplin. One of their first efforts, "Rhythm Is Our Business," became a hit and was soon adopted by the Jimmie Lunceford Orchestra as their signature tune. In 1937 the duo had a multimillion seller with "Bei Mir Bist du Schoen" for the Andrews Sisters. The pair traveled to Hollywood where they went their separate ways, and thus began a fruitful partnership with Jules Styne that yielded such hits as "I'll Walk Alone," "Saturday Night Is the Loneliest Night of the Week," and "Come Out, Come Out." In the 1940s Cahn met a young singer with the Tommy Dorsey Orchestra by the name of Frank Sinatra. At the time Sinatra was signed by MGM to appear in the movie *Anchors Aweigh*. Sinatra refused unless Cahn wrote the material. The Sinatra-Cahn magic worked, and in 1954 when Cahn and Styne wrote "Three Coins in a Fountain" used in the movie of the same title, Cahn was awarded his first Academy Award for the effort. In the late 1950s, Cahn teamed with composer Jimmy Van Heusen and over the next six

years the team garnered three more Academy Awards and numerous nominations and were considered the de facto personal songwriting team for Sinatra. In 1974, Cahn starred in his own Broadway show *Words and Music* which ran nine months on Broadway and for nearly two decades on tour before declining health ended his illustrious career. Upon his passing he was buried at Westwood Memorial Park in Los Angeles, California. His simple flat marker can be found in the center of the central lawn area, Section D, near actress Donna Reed and the unmarked grave of Roy Orbison. The Academy of Motion Picture Arts and Sciences now houses the entire Sammy Cahn collection, which encompasses his personal collection of production, television, and movie notes, along with manuscript files, sheet music, handwritten lyric sheets, and rare commercial and noncommercial disc recordings.

RANDY CALIFORNIA
February 20, 1951—January 7, 1997
CAUSE OF DEATH Accidental Drowning

Hard to argue the talents of a guitarist who, at the young age of fifteen, played in Jimi Hendrix's band for a summer in New York. But that was indeed the start of Spirit guitarist Randy Wolfe (nicknamed "California" by Hendrix), stepson of celebrated jazz drummer Ed Cassidy. Shortly after the stint with Hendrix, Cassidy and California moved back to the West Coast and with Jay Ferguson on bass and pianist John Locke formed the quartet Spirits Rebellious in 1967. Their first album yielded the hit "I Got a Line on You" and the band quickly became one of the most admired West Coast rock bands of the late sixties. With a unique mix of jazz, rock, and fusion backed by solid songwriting, the band released three more albums during the next four years featuring the classic tracks, "Nature's Way," "Animal Zoo," and "Mr. Skin." In 1969, they made the mistake of refusing an offer to open for Hendrix at Woodstock and shortly thereafter the original band broke up, with members regrouping occasionally through the nineties. In 1995, reissues from their classic 1960s recordings were selling well to a new generation of fans and plans were made to release a rarities compilation when during a family vacation, Randy was pulled out to sea off the coast of Molokai by the strong current while pushing his twelve-year-old son, Quinn, to safety. A search was called off the following day and he was officially declared lost at sea.

CANNED HEAT

BOB "THE BEAR" HITE
February 26, 1943—April 6, 1981
CAUSE OF DEATH Cocaine and Heroin Intoxication

HENRY "THE SUNFLOWER" VESTINE
December 25, 1944—October 20, 1997
CAUSE OF DEATH Heart and Respiratory Failure

ALAN "BLIND OWL" WILSON
August 4, 1943—September 3, 1970
CAUSE OF DEATH Barbiturate Overdose

Founded in 1966 by record store manager Bob "the Bear" Hite (named for his massive three hundred-plus-pound frame) and blues collector Alan Wilson, Canned Heat was the only white American blues group to chart a Top 10 hit during the 1960s. Their debut album in 1967 featured classic Chicago blues tracks such as Elmore James's "Dust My Broom" and Howlin' Wolf's "Goin' Down Slow." But it wasn't until their performance of "Rollin' and Tumblin' " at the Monterey Pop Festival and a subsequent drug bust in Denver that the band's reputation as rock's bad boys of blues boogie was solidified. For their second album the following year, Wilson wrote their first hits, "On the Road Again" (featuring Wilson's high-pitched vocals) and "Going Up the Country." This was the band's high point, with Canned Heat performing at the Isle of Wight Festival, the Newport Pop Festival, and of course their electrifying set at the original Woodstock. The band struggled after the untimely death of harmonica and vocalist Alan "Blind Owl" Wilson—found

dead in his backyard of a drug overdose in Los Angeles. Wilson's death was followed ten years later by the discovery of Hite's body in a parked van outside a home in Los Angeles. Both founding members were subsequently cremated and their ashes scattered. Former guitarist for Frank Zappa's Mothers of Invention and founding member Vestine was found dead in a hotel room outside of Paris, France. He was cremated and returned to the U.S. to Oak Hill Cemetery on South Danebo Street in Eugene, Oregon. As you enter the gates of the cemetery, drive past the office on your left and veer to the right through the first turn. Park thirty feet past the curve in the road and Vestine's grave is on the second row in the Oak Cress Garden (Crypt 4, Space 44b).

HOAGY CARMICHAEL
November 22, 1899—December 27, 1981
CAUSE OF DEATH Heart Attack

Composer, performer, lyricist, and occasional actor, Howard Hoagland "Hoagy" Carmichael will probably always be remembered as the author of one of the most recorded standards ever written—"Stardust." A self-taught pianist (with a little help from his mother), Carmichael came into prominence after the family moved to Indianapolis. Here he followed his mother to movie houses and university dances as she supplemented the family's income performing ragtime. In 1920, he attended Indiana University where he formed his own jazz combo named Carmichael's Collegians. During this time, he met and befriended his idol, Bix Beiderbecke, who encouraged Carmichael to consider composing in addition to performing. So upon graduation, he briefly practiced law before concentrating on music full-time and in 1929 wrote the now classic "Stardust." Over the next ten years the song was recorded by the likes of Louis Armstrong, Bing Crosby, Benny Goodman, Tommy Dorsey, Artie Shaw, and a whole host of prominent artists. Unlike most composers, Carmichael never worked steadily with just one collaborator—rather, he preferred to work with such luminaries as Johnny Mercer and Frank Loesser. Upon his death in California, he was returned to his hometown of Bloomington, Indiana, and buried at Rose Hill/White Oak Cemetery. His upright granite monument is located in Section G between the Hinkle building and the maintenance building along the wall. Shortly after his passing, his entire estate, of over 3,500 items spanning five decades, was willed to the Indiana University at Bloomington and is now open to the public.

ERIC CARR
July 7, 1950—November 24, 1991
CAUSE OF DEATH Cancer

Eric Carr (born Paul Caravello) worked in a deli, as a gas appliance repairman, a clerk, and as a drummer in a disco cover band before riding his bicycle to an audition to fill the drum stool for the hottest band in the world—KISS. As he left the audition he asked Paul Stanley, Gene Simmons, and Ace Frehley for their autographs. Little did he know that three days later he would be named the new drummer for the supergroup in 1980. During his decade with the band he recorded on eight albums and played live on countless tours. In the spring of 1991, Carr was diagnosed with a heart tumor. After successful cancer treatment he attended the MTV Music Video Awards ceremony, only to suffer

a devastating cerebral hemorrhage two days after the event. He suffered a second hemorrhage later in the week and fell into a coma. By now the cancer had returned and he died peacefully at New York's Bellevue Hospital. He was buried with his drumsticks at the Cedar Hill Mausoleum on Route 9 in Middlehope, New York. As you drive into the cemetery grounds, stop at the first mausoleum on the right and walk into the center entryway. His final resting place is the fan-adorned crypt on the right.

LEROY CARR
March 27, 1905—April 29, 1935
CAUSE OF DEATH Nephritis Due to Acute Alcoholism

Leroy Carr and Scrapper Blackwell are arguably the two most underrated blues musicians of the late 1920s through the 1930s. What is undeniable is that the two musicians together created some of the most recorded classic blues standards, including "How Long, How Long Blues," "Mean Mistreater Mama," and "When the Sun Goes Down." Carr, a former meat packer and bootlegger, began earning a living as a musician full-time in the early 1920s. Playing piano at house parties and dances up and around Indiana Avenue (where one could hear great jazz, buy bootleg whiskey, and get robbed—usually all in the same night!) in Indianapolis, Indiana, Carr met Blackwell at one of these parties in 1928. For the next seven years the duo sealed their reputation primarily in the Midwest through local touring and their seminal recordings for the Vocalion label. Two months before he died, Carr entered the recording studio for the last time without his partner and recorded the eerily prophetic "Six Feet Into the Ground." He was buried two months later

in an unmarked grave (a stone was added more than five decades later) at Floral Park Cemetery in Indianapolis. As you drive into the cemetery, proceed straight ahead toward the Sunset Lawn section. Park at the gravel road opposite Sunset Lawn that leads into the Home Lawn section across the street. The grave address is Home Lawn H3-3-26, with the monument twenty-six rows from the paved road, three rows from the gravel path opposite a small white wooden gate.

PETER "MEMPHIS SLIM" CHATMAN
September 3, 1915—February 24, 1988
CAUSE OF DEATH Kidney Failure

A self-taught blues pianist well versed in South Side Chicago blues and boogie-woogie, Memphis Slim was also an amusing storyteller and a charismatic figure during blues' formative years. Born in Memphis, a young Chatman started his career in Beale Street honky-tonks and dancehalls, calling the Midway Cafe on Beale and Fourth Street home for many years. After Prohibition, Chatman settled in Chicago in 1937 and shortly after teamed with Big Bill Broonzy in clubs, later recording his first sides for Bluebird in 1940. A member of the well-respected artist group that included Roosevelt Sykes, Arthur "Big Boy" Crudup, Broonzy, Lonnie Johnson, and Memphis Minnie, the newly dubbed Memphis Slim formed Memphis Slim and the Houserockers and introduced a new sound to the evolving South Side blues—a seven-piece ensemble that added horns in place of the harmonica parts of traditional blues. Before the end of the decade, Memphis Slim had recorded on no less than eight labels, performed at Carnegie Hall and the Newport Folk Festival, and sold hundreds of thousands of albums throughout the world. When rock 'n' roll

pushed the blues off the charts in the early 1960s, Memphis Slim visited Europe with Willie Dixon and moved permanently to Paris shortly after. In Europe, Slim was treated as a true artist and genius and often spoke bitterly in interviews of his treatment in postwar America. And while he returned for the occasional concert or recording date, Memphis Slim became quite wealthy and content to record and tour in Europe for the remainder of his life. Upon his death in Paris, he was returned to Memphis, Tennessee, and buried at Galilee Memorial Gardens. As you park at the office in the small cemetery, walk to the center of the grounds to the circular sections. Walk over to the lectern holding a bronze Bible and Memphis Slim's bronze monument is positioned directly in front of the seating area.

CHARLIE CHRISTIAN
July 29, 1916—March 2, 1942
CAUSE OF DEATH Tuberculosis

Despite a sudden death at the age of twenty-five, Charlie Christian did more to advance the development of modern jazz guitar than any single artist before or since his passing. His use of amplified single-note runs coupled with rhythmic and harmonic complexities bridged the gap from big band to bebop. Born in Dallas, Texas, and raised in Oklahoma City, Christian was inspired to concentrate his efforts on the amplified guitar after seeing Jimmie Lunceford's guitarist play locally. Influenced by the fluid lead lines of saxophone legend Lester Young, Christian developed a style that brought the guitar from behind the bandstand and to the front as a lead instrument. In 1939, he was discovered by John Hammond, who persuaded bandleader Benny Goodman to audition the young artist. Goodman hired Christian, who quickly became a fixture in the Benny Goodman sextet, recording such jazz classics as "Flying Home," "Seven Come Eleven," and what is considered his finest recording, "Solo Flight." To stretch his incredible improvisational skills, after a performance with Goodman, Christian would seek out jam sessions in the nightclubs of New York City. He would often jam with legends Charlie Parker, Thelonious Monk, and Dizzy Gillespie, improvising altered chordings and unrestricted offbeats that became the birth of bebop jazz. In the spring of 1941, while on tour with Goodman, Christian was diagnosed with tuberculosis and by the following year he had died in New York City. Fifty-two years after his passing, his grave was finally located and marked with a headstone at Gates Hill Cemetery in Bonham, Texas.

JOHN CIPOLLINA
August 24, 1943—May 29, 1989
CAUSE OF DEATH Emphysema

Though never as successful as the Jefferson Airplane or the Grateful Dead, guitarist and founding member of Quicksilver Messenger Service John Cipollina represented the archetypal late-sixties San Francisco musician. Formed in 1965, the band was featured in the film *Revolution*, featuring several up-and-coming San Francisco artists such as Steve Miller. Their debut release in 1968 showcased the band's unique blend of jazz, rock, and a healthy dose of psychedelic instrumental jams. However, studio recording was never the band's strong suit as evidenced by their more successful live release *Happy Trails*. A heavy smoker, Cipollina was confined to a wheelchair and crutches in his final years due to treatments related to his advancing emphysema. Upon his death he was cremated and his ashes scattered on Mt. Tamalpais in San Francisco, California. In 1995, the massive amp stack he used for much of his career was donated to Cleveland's Rock and Roll Hall of Fame, where it was prominently displayed at the entrance to the museum.

John Cipollina (second from left) in the early days of Quicksilver Messenger Service.

STEVE CLARK
April 23, 1960—January 8, 1991
CAUSE OF DEATH **Accidental Nondependent Abuse of Drugs and Alcohol**

The prototypical guitar slinger for the most successful hard rock group of the eighties, Def Leppard, Steamin' Steve Clark cut an impressive figure onstage—lean with long, blond hair and his trademark Gibson Les Paul hung low to his knees. But more importantly it was Clark's soaring, dynamic six-string chorales, evident on the hits "Photograph" and "Rock of Ages," that separated Def Leppard from the plethora of conventional heavy metal groups from the same era. Born in Sheffield, England, Clark picked up his first guitar at age eleven with the provision that he study classical guitar. With a few lessons under his belt, he began to stretch his knowledge of Bach and Vivaldi and apply them to the more popular riffs of Led Zeppelin and Thin Lizzy. He auditioned for Def Leppard, a group of lads still in their teens desperately seeking a way out of Sheffield, and was immediately added to the lineup after his note-for-note rendition of Lynyrd Skynyrd's "Free Bird." But even after the successes of the albums *On Through the Night*, *Pyromania*, and *Hysteria*, Clark was by all accounts the most miserable millionaire rock star of the decade. With Robert "Mutt" Lange as producer, cosongwriter, and well-known studio perfectionist, Clark began to drink during downtime in the studio. As he began to drink more, Lange preferred to use guitarist Phil Collen for the precise, repetitive demands of recording. By the end of 1988 and several detox clinics and rehab centers later, the writing was on the wall—Clark was in trouble. So it came as no surprise to family members and bandmates when Clark was found dead by his girlfriend at his Chelsea apartment after a particularly adventurous night of heavy drinking. It was later determined that in addition to a blood alcohol level in excess of .30 (triple the British legal limit for driving), Clark had consumed various amounts of Valium and morphine, along with a lethal dose of codeine. Upon his passing, he was laid to rest in Wisewood Cemetery in the Hillsborough section of Sheffield, England, in Plot 1697D. As you enter the main gate of the cemetery, take the main road to the left at the fork and look to your left, three rows off the path, for his spectacular memorial.

THE COASTERS

CORNELL GUNTER
May 18, 1912—May 12, 1990
CAUSE OF DEATH Murdered

WILL "DUB" JONES
May 14, 1928—February 2, 2000
CAUSE OF DEATH Diabetes

BOBBY NUNN
September 20, 1925—November 5, 1986
CAUSE OF DEATH Heart Attack

Hailed as the preeminent vocal group from the first origins of rock 'n' roll, the Coasters not only sang of teenage angst but also deeply influenced vocal groups for the next thirty years. A virtual creation of the songwriting team of Jerry Leiber and Mike Stoller, the Coasters were created from remnants of the Robins (with Johnny Otis, Carl Gardner, and Bobby Nunn) when the songwriters persuaded Gardner and Nunn to leave the group to form the Coasters. With the addition of Billy Guy and Leon Hughes (soon replaced by Young Jessie), the Coasters (so named by their manager to identify them with the West Coast) made their debut recording in 1957 with the massive hit "Searchin'." The song remained on the charts for six months with the flip side of the single, "Young Blood," achieving Top 10 status. After several other minor recordings, the Coasters moved to New York with Will "Dub" Jones of the Cadets and Cornell Gunter of the Flairs replacing Guy and Jessie. They were joined in the studio by saxophone master King Curtis, whose solo interjections became a mainstay of the Coasters's hits. Their record, "Yakety Yak," raced up the charts with vocal characterizations that captured the frustrations of teenage life through parental instructions and threats ("If you don't scrub that kitchen floor, you ain't gonna rock 'n' roll no more!"). The groups next hit, "Charlie Brown," was enlivened by the dead-panned reading of the line "Why's everybody always picking on me?" by the floor-rumbling bass of Jones. Known as the Classic Coasters, the quartet from 1958 through 1961 were responsible for the majority of the Coasters' hits both on the pop and R&B charts. Except for "Wake Me, Shake Me," all their chart success was due to Leiber and Stoller, with the hits "Poison Ivy," "Along Came Jones," and their final Top 40 hit, "Little Egypt." Parting ways with Leiber and Stoller in 1963, the Coasters' hits and sales began to slump. And aside from Gardner, numerous versions of the group continued to record but with little success. Gunter left the group in 1961 (replaced by Earl Carroll of the Cadillacs) who joined Dinah Washington on tour as a backup singer before starting his own competing Coasters group. Both Jones and Guy left shortly after for sporadic success as solo artists. Gardner, Jones, Guy, and Gunter reunited occasionally, including an appearance at the fortieth anniversary celebration for Atlantic Records. A popular main-stay on the revival circuit, Gardner continued to performer with the "original" Coasters while Gunter formed his "Fabulous" Coasters group. To add to the confusion, Guy also performed with his own "Coasters" group. In 1987, the original group (Gardner, Guy, Jones, and Gunter) were the first vocal group to be inducted into the Rock and Roll Hall of Fame. Three years later, Gunter was found shot to death in his car in Las Vegas

(his murder was never solved) and was buried at Inglewood Park Cemetery in Inglewood, California, in the El Sereno section, Plot 151, Space E (eight rows from the bottom road). Nunn was buried in an unmarked grave at Evergreen Cemetery in Los Angeles, California, while Jones was cremated and his ashes returned to his family.

PERRY COMO
May 18, 1912—May 12, 2001
CAUSE OF DEATH Natural Causes

Bing Crosby may have started it all, Mel Tormé was the Velvet Fog, and Frank Sinatra was the Chairman of the Board, but Perry Como had the last laugh as he outlasted them all. Dubbed the Man who Invented Casual by Bing himself, Perry Como's relaxed manner and trademark cardigan sweaters lasted through sixty-five years of changing styles and musical taste. Born the seventh of thirteen children, Pierino Como worked his way through school as a barber in the gritty steel town of Canonsburg, Pennsylvania, before auditioning for the Freddie Carlone band in 1933. He toured the Midwest for three years as Carlone's featured singer before moving to Ted Weems's band in 1936. He continued with the Weems band until the early 1940s when he signed with NBC as costar of the *Chesterfield Supper Club* radio show with Jo Stafford. In 1943, he signed with RCA Records as a solo artist and released his first million seller, "Till the End of Time," in 1945. For the next two decades Como recorded twenty-seven gold records, received five Emmy Awards for his work in television, and sold over 100 million albums during his lifetime (in 1945, he sold over one million albums in one week!). Although critics would poke fun at his casual, somnambulant style, Como had a good sense of humor about it and often remarked that he found the Como impersonation on the Second City TV comedy show (featuring a lounge singer lying on the floor, nearly comatose, singing into a microphone while dancers leapt all around him) quite amusing. He semiretired in the 1970s, recording less often and appearing in Las Vegas and on selected television specials through the 1990s. Como was honored in 1999 by his hometown of Canonsburg with a life-size statue in the town square. He died peacefully in his sleep two years later at his home in the exclusive Jupiter Beach Inlet Colony in Palm Beach, Florida. He was buried at Riverside Memorial Park in Tequesta, Florida, next to his wife of sixty-five years, Roselle Como.

JOHNNY COPELAND
March 27, 1937—July 8, 1997
CAUSE OF DEATH Complications from Heart Surgery

Johnny Copeland was at home, whether it be Texas blues, jazz, jump blues, or eclectic African instrumentation, in front of an audience. Born in Louisiana and raised in Texas, Copeland got his first break in 1958 when he recorded his first regional hit, "Rock 'n' Roll Lilly." He toured through the 1960s with his group the Dukes of Rhythm and backed some of the great blues artists of the early 1960s, including Big Mama Thornton, Freddie King, T-Bone Walker, and Sonny Boy Williamson II. By 1970, blues had taken a backseat to the British Invasion and Copeland moved to New York City, appearing regularly in Greenwich Village coffeehouses and Harlem nightclubs. Copeland fell "back in style" to those who recognized his talent and he began recording again on a number of Rounder Records releases. In 1985, Copeland recorded *Showdown!* with Albert Collins and Robert Cray, which won a Grammy Award for Best Traditional Blues Album, thus introducing Copeland to a whole new generation. Over the next ten years he recorded five more albums, was rewarded with five W. C. Handy Awards and was a regular on the U.S. and European blues festival circuit. In 1994, Copeland was diagnosed with a heart condition and over the next two years he underwent seven operations, culminating with a heart transplant in 1997. He died seven months later after an eighth operation to repair a defective heart valve. He was buried outside of Houston, Texas, at Paradise Memorial Cemetery (South) in Block 3, Section 149N, Number 4 in a plot behind the McDanial monument.

NOËL COWARD
December 16, 1899—March 26, 1973
CAUSE OF DEATH Heart Failure

A prolific English playwright, performer, and raconteur, Noël Coward was also a talented songwriter whose acerbic wit (both on and offstage) and sophisticated British persona were recognizable worldwide. Coward first appeared onstage at the young age of twelve, had his first success as a lyricist at the age of twenty-six, and by the end of the 1930s had nine hit musical productions. In the 1940s, he spent much of his time traveling the world, entertaining war troops, and he starred in the movie *In Which We Serve*, which won him his only Oscar. After 1945, his clipped, lisping speech and languid Englishness were wearing thin on the public and his career never regained the momentum of the prewar era. And

though his stage productions and movie appearances in the 1950s never garnered the critical praise of his earlier works, he nevertheless had one of the highest-paid nightclub acts on the road. Upon his passing, Noël Coward was buried at his beloved Firefly estate overlooking Blue Harbour on the island of Jamaica. The home, open to the public with all the original artwork and furniture, appears exactly as when Coward lived there.

DARBY CRASH
August 24, 1958—December 6, 1980
CAUSE OF DEATH Suicide

Darby Crash was to vocals what Sid Vicious was to the bass—that is to say, not much. But that didn't stop Darby Crash (born Jan Paul Beahm) from fronting the seminal Los Angeles punk band the Germs. A typical show featuring Crash would consist of a wretched version of the Archies' "Sugar, Sugar" (complete with Crash pouring sugar over the audience), food fights, a revolving door of untalented musicians, and a lead singer so loaded on smack he would smear the audience with blood from self-mutilation. All this and more was perfectly captured in Penelope Spheeris's landmark 1981 film *The Decline of Western Civilization*. Even more appalling than his limited vocal range was his lack of timing—days after his drug-induced suicide a deranged "fan" shot John Lennon. Thus his death, if even reported, was pushed below the obvious headlines. He was buried at Holy Cross Cemetery in Culver City, California, in Section R, Tier 8, Grave 114 overlooking the freeway.

PEE WEE CRAYTON
July 15, 1914—May 18, 1985
CAUSE OF DEATH Heart Attack

Incorporating the styles of Charlie Christian and T-Bone Walker, this Texas-born blues guitarist moved to the West Coast and became an integral part of the 1950s Central Avenue jazz scene in Los Angeles. Recording and performing with Walker, Big Joe Williams, and Roy Brown, Crayton was a talented musician gifted with warm vocals and simple but elegant guitar lines. Despite having the distinction of being the first guitarist to use a Fender Stratocaster, his career was spotty at best, and he never was able to profit from the blues revival of the sixties, spending most of the decade driving a truck. Fortunately, during his last ten years of life he was recognized for his talent and appeared in concerts all over the world. Crayton is interred at Inglewood Park Cemetery in Inglewood, California, in the Cascade Garden mausoleum in Crypt 180, facing the road.

IAN CURTIS
July 15, 1956—May 18, 1980
CAUSE OF DEATH Suicide

Ian Curtis was the talented, if not troubled, vocalist for England's Joy Division. Formed in 1978, success in the U.K. came quickly with the release of the record *A Factory Sample EP* and the first album four months later. This garnered solid reviews by fans and critics alike, with Warner Bros. offering the group one million dollars for distribution rights. The group rebuffed the offer—twice!—and continued to tour England through much of 1979. Diagnosed with epilepsy, Curtis was suffering from exhaustion and depression when he hung himself at his home in Macclesfield, England, just two days before the start of their first American tour. His cremated remains were buried at Macclesfield Cemetery, where a map to his final resting place can be found at the entrance.

BOBBY DARIN
May 14, 1936—December 20, 1973
CAUSE OF DEATH Faulty Heart Valve and Septicemia

A finger-snapping hipster of the 1950s, Bobby Darin (born Walden Robert Cassotto) made the successful leap from the calculated, cutesy recordings such as "Splish Splash" to swinging lounge standards such as "Mack the Knife." Raised by his mother (his father died before he was born—actually Bobby discovered his "mother" was really his grandmother and his "sister" was in reality his mother, but that's a whole other story) in New York, Darin found his start in the coffeehouses and small clubs in New York City as a teenager in the mid-1950s. In 1956, with good friend Don Kirshner, they wrote Darin's first song, "My First Love," and he was signed to his first recording contract. After several unsuccessful singles and a new label, Darin wrote and recorded his first hit, "Splish Splash," which was quickly followed by "Queen of the Hop," "Plain Jane," and his smash hit, "Dream Lover." In 1960, Darin made the successful transition from pop singer to swinging hipster with a series of recordings that started with the million-seller "Mack the Knife" and continued with "Beyond the Sea," "Lazy River," "You Must Have Been a Beautiful Baby," and "Nature Boy." Playing to standing room-only audiences, Darin was a popular draw in Las Vegas at the Flamingo, the Sands, the Hilton, and at the

Copacabana in New York City. But unlike many performers during his time, Darin was not only a talented singer, but also a gifted songwriter (writing many of his own hits), played several instruments, and was a composer of film scores (including four of the thirteen films he appeared in), and was a half-decent actor with an Academy Award nomination in 1963. After the assassination of Senator Robert Kennedy, Darin's career made another successful transition to political activist in both his personal and professional life. Thus the combination of pop, rock, and lounge standards kept Darin in the public eye as a top performer. Generous to a fault, he helped a young Wayne Newton by giving him his trademark song, "Danke Schoen," and was good friends with Elvis Presley, Sammy Davis Jr., Johnny Mercer (with whom he cowrote "Two of a Kind"), and future Byrds member Roger McGuinn (who played guitar in Darin's backing band). Despite his quick rise to fame, time was not on Darin's side. Suffering from rheumatic fever as a child, his heart was damaged, which caused Darin problems all of his life. During a second heart operation to correct a defective heart valve, Darin died on the operating table. As per his instructions upon his death, Darin's body was donated to UCLA's Medical Center for study and research. Aside from some furniture and a piano that was donated to a nonprofit in Las Vegas, Dodd Darin (his son from his marriage to Sandra Dee) manages the bulk of his memorabilia. Darin was inducted into the Rock and Roll Hall of Fame in 1990.

REVEREND GARY DAVIS
April 30, 1896—May 5, 1972
CAUSE OF DEATH Heart Failure

Gary Davis was a gifted guitarist who influenced generations of listeners of blues, jazz, folk, and other forms of traditional American music not normally associated with rural black artists. Born partially blind, Davis began his odyssey as a street musician in North Carolina in the 1930s. Now completely blind, Davis continued to play from his vast repertoire of nonsecular songs, but was primarily known for the sacred songs he recorded after becoming an ordained minister and a traveling gospel preacher in the mid-1930s. After World War II he moved to New York City and began recording again, where he had a profound influence on the burgeoning folk music scene in the 1950s. After the release of "Harlem Street Singer" in 1960, he was a common sight on the blues and gospel festival circuit in both the U.S. and Britain. He was interred at New York's Rockville Cemetery in Lynbrook, Long Island, in Section 68, Plot 1078, Grave 3. From the entrance on Merrick Road, drive past the office to the end and follow the road around. Look for the Garden of Prayer sign on the left and Section 68 will be directly on the right. The simple bronze marker is approximately fifty feet off the road.

SANDY DENNY
January 6, 1947—April 21, 1978
CAUSE OF DEATH Cerebral Hemorrhage

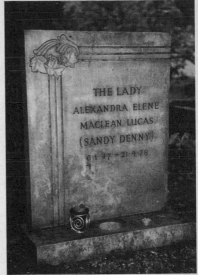

Pete Townshend of The Who labeled Sandy Denny the Perfect British Folk Voice. Perhaps best known as the female lead on Led Zeppelin's "The Battle of Evermore" (where she remains the only vocalist outside of Robert Plant to appear on a Led Zeppelin album), Denny's talent was never fully recognized either critically or commercially until after her untimely death at age thirty-one. A one-time nursing student, she left school to sing cover tunes in British pubs before joining the Strawbs in the mid-sixties during the burgeoning folk scene. After one album, Denny was asked to replace Judy Dyble in Fairport Convention, where she transformed the north London cover band into a successful leader of the English electric folk rock genre. In 1969 alone, they recorded three albums, including the classic *Liege and Lief*, which became a Top 20 hit. Unfortunately, the following year two key members, Denny and Ashley Hutchings (who went on to found Steeleye Span), left the group. It was after Denny was awarded *Melody Maker*'s Best Female Vocalist two years running that a chance encounter with Led Zeppelin's Robert Plant resulted in a guest appearance on Zep's classic fourth album. After a brief venture with future husband Trevor Lucas to form the group Fotheringay, Denny spent the next several years as a solo artist before rejoining Fairport for several albums. After leaving again, she planned to move to America with her husband and child to start a new solo career when, while visiting a friend's home, it has been reported that she accidentally fell down a flight of stairs and suffered a brain hemorrhage. She lapsed into a coma and died three days later without recovering. She was buried in Putney Vale Cemetery in London, England. From the entrance of the cemetery, go up Central Drive and turn right on Richards Way. Take the fourth path on the left and Denny is on the right side in front of the maple tree.

JOHN DENVER
December 31, 1943—October 12, 1997
CAUSE OF DEATH Plane Crash

Proving that nice guys do finish first, John Denver's breezy tenor voice and middle-of-the-road songs served him well during his three decades and thirty albums in the limelight. Born John Henry Deutschendorf (he adopted his stage name after his home state's capital), Denver first entered the public eye when he replaced Chad Mitchell himself in the Chad Mitchell Trio as singer and songwriter in 1965. He toured with the group for four years when, based on the strength of his hit single "Leaving on a Jet Plane" for Peter, Paul and Mary, he signed on as a solo act with RCA Records. In 1971, after two lackluster albums, he scored a number two hit on the pop charts with "Take Me Home Country Roads" and by 1975 he had charted five more additional Top 10 hits, including "Sunshine on My Shoulders," "Annie's Song," and his best-known song, "Rocky Mountain High." Now in demand internationally as a pop/country crossover artist, Denver earned international acclaim as a singer, songwriter, performer, TV and movie actor, and as an outspoken advocate for social and environmental causes. So it came as a great shock to fans, friends, and family when Denver, piloting a Long-EZ experimental airplane (which he had just taken delivery of the day before), plunged 150 yards off the shore of Lover's Point in Pacific Grove, California. Witnesses to the accident reported seeing a puff of smoke and hearing quick *pop* before watching the plane drop suddenly into the bay. Per his wishes, his remains were cremated and his ashes were scattered in his beloved Colorado Rocky Mountains. Two months after his passing, the City Council of Pacific Grove rejected plans to build a public memorial to the artist.

ERIC DOLPHY
June 20, 1928—June 29, 1964
CAUSE OF DEATH **Heart Attack**

Despite a mere six years on the music scene, Eric Dolphy continues to influence countless musicians to this day. Prior to Dolphy, virtually all jazz musicians were identified with one main instrument. Dolphy's mastery of three instruments—alto sax, flute, and bass clarinet—was a rarity during his time. Born and raised in Los Angeles, California, Dolphy began his musical training in school playing oboe and clarinet. Influenced by Charlie Parker, he switched to alto sax and played in a big band led by Parker's former drummer, Ray Porter. After two years, with the band, Dolphy served in the U.S. Army for two years, where he then transferred to the U.S. Naval School of Music. In the mid-1950s, Dolphy returned to Los Angeles, where he first met John Coltrane and Ornette Coleman. After forming his own group, Men of Modern Jazz, and a short residency with Chico Hamilton, Dolphy moved to New York to record with Charles Mingus. Shortly after, Dolphy made his own debut album, but subsequently found his greatest success working as a sideman for others such as Mingus, Coleman, Coltrane, and Max Roach. After spending a year with John Coltrane, he left for Europe as a sideman for Charlie Mingus in 1964. Upon completion of the tour, Dolphy undertook his own engagements in small cafés and nightclubs throughout Germany. Just one week after his thirty-sixth birthday, Eric Dolphy suffered a fatal heart attack as a result of undiagnosed diabetes. Dolphy's body was returned to the U.S. and interred at Rosedale Cemetery in Los Angeles, California. Located at the corner of Washington Boulevard and Normandie Avenue, enter the cemetery off Washington and turn right at the first road (just past the office). Drive straight ahead until the road makes a sharp left. Park here and walk on the walkway toward Washington Boulevard. He is buried in Grave 10-14-1 NE, in the second row from the fence, second monument over from the walkway.

THOMAS A. DORSEY
July 1, 1899—January 23, 1993
CAUSE OF DEATH **Natural Causes**

Known as the Father of Gospel Music, Thomas A. Dorsey was one of America's greatest and most prolific songwriters, as well as a respected pianist and singer. Originally recording under the name of Georgia Tom, Dorsey and his band, the Wildcats, toured from 1924 to 1928 with Ma Rainey, Dorsey acting as musical director. In 1928, with band member and slide guitarist Tampa Red, Dorsey recorded and released the blues hit "It's Tight Like That,"

selling over a million copies and later covered by over a dozen artists. Four years later, Dorsey gave up the Georgia Tom moniker and worked exclusively within a religious setting, where he created a new type of music, which he called gospel music. Shortly afterward he formed his own publishing company and sold copies of his music on the streets for ten cents apiece. He became known for the greatest gospel song ever written, "Precious Lord," written after the death of his wife and baby. Applying blues melodies and rhythms to spiritual compositions, Dorsey is credited with over 1,800 gospel songs during his lifetime. Though he stopped recording

in 1934, he continued to perform live well into the 1940s. Before his death in 1993, Dorsey founded and served as president for forty years of the National Convention of Gospel Choirs and Choruses, was elected to the Nashville Hall of Fame for Composers, was awarded a Grammy, and discovered and trained gospel legend Mahalia Jackson. He was buried at Oak Woods Cemetery on the South Side of Chicago, Illinois, on Marquette Street. Dorsey's final resting place is in the Tower of Memories in the Sanctuary of Rest on the bottom tier on the right. His robe and an excellent taped interview can be found at the Georgia Music Hall of Fame in Macon, Georgia.

NICK DRAKE
June 19, 1948—November 25, 1974
CAUSE OF DEATH Suicide (Disputed)

Deemed to wallow in rock 'n' roll obscurity under the category Tragic Romantic Artist, Nick Drake was lifted to the level of cultural icon with a simple commercial for the zippy Volkswagen Cabrio that featured his haunting single "Pink Moon." Dead for over a quar-

ter of a century, Drake is now the subject of more media attention than during his short four-year career. Discovered in Cambridge by Fairport Convention producer Joe Boyd, Drake recorded his first album at the age of twenty in 1968. Produced with a minimum of musicians in addition to Drake and his guitar, the album was a perfect reflection of his songs—simple, quiet, and reflective without the usual self-pity or bitterness. After the commercial failure of his second album in 1970, he began a slow descent into clinical depression that was, after the intervention of several psychiatrists, starting to subside with medication. In his final months, he moved to Paris to begin a new phase of his life but died in his sleep from an overdose of Tryptizol (an antidepressant he was taking as a sleeping aid). Though the coroner ruled the death a suicide, friends and family strongly dispute this conclusion. He was buried in a simple church cemetery located in the center of Tanworth in Arden, England. His headstone can be found behind the church, in front of the oak tree.

PETE DRAKE
October 8, 1932—July 29, 1988
CAUSE OF DEATH Heart Attack

One of the truly talented and innovative artists of the Nashville sound, Pete Drake was one of the greatest pedal-steel players, equally at home with country (Ernest Tubb and George

Hamilton IV) and rock (Bob Dylan, Ringo Starr, and George Harrison). His session work alone on Dylan's *John Wesley Harding* and *Nashville Skyline* made him the choice session player for any and all artists who passed through Music City. A self-taught guitarist, Drake switched to the pedal steel early in his career and played on sessions and the radio in his hometown of Atlanta before moving to Nashville in the late 1950s. Equally in demand on the Grand Ole Opry and for recording sessions, Drake was always an innovator. He has been credited with popularizing the "talking" guitar long before Peter Frampton and Jeff Beck made it to the airwaves, releasing several instrumental albums utilizing the technique throughout the sixties. As Drake's career and reputation grew, he diversified into production, publishing, and became owner of a highly successful recording studio. His work with Ernest Tubb alone (he produced over twenty of Tubb's greatest hits) would qualify him as a leader of the Nashville sound. Upon his passing, he was buried at Nashville's Spring Hill Cemetery. From the front office, take the second left at the Valley Vista section and follow the road so that the Laurel Hill section is on your left and Section 17 is on your right. Parking in the middle of the two sections, Drake's impressive monument stands approximately thirty feet from the road. His memorabilia can be found at both Nashville's Music Hall of Fame and Georgia's Music Hall of Fame in Macon, Georgia.

IAN DURY
May 12, 1942—March 27, 2000
CAUSE OF DEATH Colon and Liver Cancer

Afflicted with polio at the age of seven, Ian Dury of Ian Dury and the Blockheads authored the seventies' U.K. anthem "Sex and Drugs and Rock and Roll" and the British number one single "Hit Me with Your Rhythm Stick." An emblem of the seventies English punk music movement and a seminal influence on pop music groups such as Madness and Blur, Ian Dury studied, and later taught painting at the Royal College of Art in London before recruiting several students to form Kilburn and the High Roads. A regular on the pub circuit, Kilburn even went as far as to open for The Who, but never achieved any acclaim above cult status. It wasn't until 1977 with the release of *New Boots and Panties* as Ian Dury and the Blockheads that Dury enjoyed a yearlong ride on the charts of the new wave/British punk movement. The new band was featured with newcomers Elvis Costello and the Attractions, Nick Lowe, Wreckless Eric, and Larry Wallis, but it was the Blockheads who were the surprise hit of the summer tour. Over the next three years the band enjoyed five hit singles and two Top 10 albums. After twenty years working as a screenwriter, playwright, actor, and television host, Dury returned to the music scene when he reunited with the Blockheads to produce *Mr. Love Pants* and a tour of the U.K. Already diagnosed with cancer, the gravel-voiced singer once remarked to the BBC, "I don't care if I'm immediately forgotten. I'm not here to be remembered, I'm here to be alive." Upon his death at his home in Hampstead, London, England, he was cremated.

NELSON EDDY
June 29, 1901—March 6, 1967
CAUSE OF DEATH Stroke

JEANETTE MACDONALD
June 18, 1903—January 14, 1965
CAUSE OF DEATH Heart Failure

Known as America's Singing Sweethearts, Nelson Eddy and Jeanette MacDonald starred in eight films together and recorded dozens, together and separately, of hit singles from their many musical performances. While fans have often felt that the two were "made for each other," they came from very different backgrounds. MacDonald was a successful Broadway musical comedy star before making her film debut in 1929. Eddy was a gifted opera singer with a solid classical background. They starred together in their first film *Naughty Marietta* in 1935 and the following year they sold a million copies of "Indian Love Call" from their movie *Rose-Marie*—the first million-seller for a show tune! They worked together for the next six years, after which Eddy continued with movies until 1947, when he retired from Hollywood to concentrate on his nightclub and cabaret appearances. MacDonald also faded away from Hollywood and worked in a number of regional revivals of Broadway musicals. She passed away in 1965 in a Houston, Texas, hospital while awaiting heart surgery. She is interred at Forest Lawn Memorial Park in Glendale, California, in the top floor of the Freedom mausoleum alongside Nat "King" Cole, George and Gracie Burns, Alan Ladd, and actress Clara Bow. Eddy was onstage at the Sans Souci Hotel in Palm Beach when he collapsed midsong and died two hours later at a local hospital. He was returned to California, where he was buried at Hollywood Forever in Los Angeles in the Garden of Legends. As you enter the park, make your way to the back left of the grounds and park in front of the Cathedral mausoleum entrance. Walk across the road and in the fourth row from the road near the palm tree lies the grave of Eddy and his wife. Eddy's memorabilia was divided between Occidental College Music Library (California) and the American Music Research Center at the University of Colorado.

SLEEPY JOHN ESTES
January 25, 1899—June 5, 1977
CAUSE OF DEATH Natural Causes

The story goes that Sleepy John Estes was so poor that, when he died, they had to borrow dirt to fill the hole. Born in 1899 (some say 1904), Estes was one of the more significant prewar bluesmen from the South. A solid guitar player, his legacy has been in his songwriting. His catalog of songs has been recorded by Ry Cooder, Eric Clapton, Led Zeppelin, and dozens of other blues and rock artists worldwide. After his peak period during the 1920s and '30s, many thought he had died and subsequently was not heard from much until his rediscovery during the 1960s. He toured through much of the decade, including stops in Europe for the American Folk Blues Festival on three occasions. Estes is currently buried next to his sister Daisy in an unmarked grave behind the Elam Baptist Church in Durhamville, Tennessee. Estes's home in neighboring Brownsville is now a tourist attraction with some of his memorabilia on display at the Elma Ross Public Library on East Main Street.

GIL EVANS
May 13, 1912—March 20, 1988
CAUSE OF DEATH Pneumonia

Gil Evans was easily one of the most original and influential jazz arrangers in the postwar modern period. A central figure in the era's cool jazz, Evans perfected a style that was both ethereal and deeply expressive, culminating in a trio of landmark albums with Miles Davis that marked the "birth of cool." Born in Toronto, Canada, Evans settled in California, where his musical training began. Enrolled in school in Berkeley, he was introduced to jazz through the concerts and recordings of Duke Ellington, Louis Armstrong, and Earl "Fatha" Hines. In 1933, he formed his first group in Stockton, where three years later they opened for Benny Goodman. By 1938, Evans was in full command of writing and conducting while several prominent musicians filtered through the group, including Stan Kenton on the piano. After a quick tour with the army, Evans moved to New York to a small room on now mythical Fifty-fifth Street, where he renewed his association with Claude Thornhill and re-formed his orchestra. In time Evans's room became a central meeting place for some of the most talented and creative artists of jazz—Gerry Mulligan, John Carisi, Charlie Parker, Dave Lambert, and of course Miles Davis. Though short-lived, a band formed with Miles Davis as the leader that incorporated the experimentation of bebop with the textures of the Thornhill orchestra recorded twelve sides that were later released under the title *The Birth of the Cool*, a monumental recording that marked a turning point in jazz history. The 1950s marked Evans's high point of creativity and productivity, working with Pearl Bailey, Charlie Parker, then several Miles Davis albums including *Miles Ahead, Sketches of Spain,* and *Quiet Nights*. Evans also continued releasing albums through the 1960s under his own name and began a collaboration with Jimi Hendrix that was cut short by the guitarist's untimely death. In the 1980s, Evans remained busy with the sound track to *The Color of Money* and an extended European tour that included a concert with Sting. Evans was in Cuernavaca, Mexico, when he passed away and was cremated shortly after.

PERCY FAITH
April 7, 1908—February 9, 1976
CAUSE OF DEATH Cancer

A piano prodigy at the age of fifteen, Percy Faith was on the road to becoming an accomplished concert pianist when an accidental fire injured his hands in 1926. The following year he began a new career in music as an arranger, later becoming a conductor and composer. Appointed the staff conductor of the Canadian Broadcasting Company at the age of twenty-five, Faith went on to star in his own radio show, *Music by Faith*, as well as arranging and conducting radio shows for both CBS and NBC. In 1950, he accepted an appointment with the

Columbia Records A&R staff where he worked with, among others, Tony Bennett. The team of Faith and Bennett scored gold record status on a number of the crooner's hits, including "Rags to Riches," "Because of You," and "Cold, Cold Heart." In the mid-1950s, Faith began working in several classic B films, including the Doris Day release *Love Me or Leave Me*, which earned Faith an Academy Award nomination. Now considered the master of full orchestral arrangements of popular songs, his "Theme from A Summer Place" was the biggest-selling record in America in 1960. By the mid-1960s the hits he once enjoyed were now history; however, he did continue to produce an amazing fifty-plus albums of his particular style of "mood music" for Columbia up until the end of his life. Faith's final resting place is located in Culver City, California, at Hillside Memorial Park. As you enter the cemetery, drive to the first section on your left and Faith's grave is located along the sidewalk in the Garden of Memories, Court of Honor, Lawn Space 407.

LEO FENDER
August 10, 1909—March 21, 1991
CAUSE OF DEATH Parkinson's Disease

Keith Richards once said, "Thank God for Leo Fender." For it was Leo Fender who created the standard dress code for guitarists of all musical genres—the Fender Telecaster, Stratocaster, and guitar amplifiers. With six hundred dollars in hand, Fender started the Fender Radio Service during World War II, which eventually led to a lifetime obsession of building the best guitars and amplifiers. Played by Dylan, Springsteen, the Beatles, and nearly every garage band wannabe, Fender continued designing and building his creations up until the day he passed away at the age of eighty-one. He was buried at Fairhaven Memorial Park in Santa Ana, California, in Lawn Section J, eleven rows up and eighteen spaces south from the northeast corner. A display of fifty years of design and innovation (including a number of rare guitars and prototypes) can be found nearby at the Fullerton Museum Center.

LESTER FLATT
June 19, 1914—May 11, 1979
CAUSE OF DEATH Stroke and Heart Disease

Lester Flatt was one half of one of the most celebrated duos in bluegrass history, the legendary team of Flatt and Scruggs. With Flatt on lead vocals/guitar and Earl Scruggs on banjo, the duo dominated the bluegrass scene from 1948 to well into the 1960s. Leaving school at an early age, Lester Flatt worked at a variety of jobs before getting his start with Charlie Scott's Harmonizers, then later with Charlie Monroe's Kentucky Pardners. He moved to Nashville in 1944 to work with Charlie Monroe's brother, the legendary Bill Monroe. When Earl Scruggs joined the band shortly after, the effect on the band was immediate. Billed as the Blue Grass Boys, incessant touring, radio broadcasts, live appearances, and Columbia Records releases guaranteed that the Monroe band would become the most influential roots-based group in country music. By 1946, Monroe bought a stretched automobile and at the end of the *Grand Ole Opry* radio show Saturday nights, the band would all head for the car and hit the road for the next seven days, often driving all night to make the Sunday matinee performance. After two years, Flatt and Scruggs decided to leave Monroe and signed with Mercury Records as Flatt, Scruggs, and the Foggy Mountain Boys. Through vigorous promotion by Scruggs's wife, Louise, the duo soon became more successful than their ex-employer (almost twenty years passed before Bill Monroe would

speak to either of his former bandmates), and for a time usurped Monroe's position as country music's top act. Throughout the 1950s and early 1960s, the Foggy Mountain Boys released vocal, banjo and guitar instrumentals, bluegrass standards including "Flint Hill Special," "Crying My Heart Out Over You," and the 1962 million-seller "The Ballad of Jed Clampett" (the theme from the TV show *The Beverly Hillbillies*). Unfortunately, as folk rock and blues began to emerge in the early 1960s, Scruggs wanted to move the band toward a more contemporary sound while Flatt wanted to remain true to their traditional country roots. Their musical differences came to a head, and by 1969 the duo split, with Flatt continuing to tour and record the original acoustic bluegrass sound up until his death. Today Lester Flatt's grave is in Oakwood Memorial Park in Sparta, Tennessee. His simple, flat bronze marker can be found in the first section on the left in the fourth row. Six years after his passing, Flatt and Scruggs was the second bluegrass act elected to the Country Music Hall of Fame. In 1991, Lester Flatt and Earl Scruggs were individually inducted into the Bluegrass Hall of Honor.

RED FOLEY
June 17, 1910—September 19, 1968
CAUSE OF DEATH Heart Attack

One of country music's most versatile artists, Red Foley found fame as the first country singer to have his own national radio show with comedian Red Skelton *(Avalon Time)* in 1939. His success as a radio star led to a lifetime recording contract with Decca Records, which released his first hit, "Old Shed," in 1941 followed by "Smoke on the Water" in 1944. In fact, Foley was one of the first country acts to record in Nashville and was responsible (along with Ernest Tubb) for persuading the music companies to change the label from "hillbilly" to the less derisory "country." But Foley was more than just a simple country singer and guitarist. He learned to play bottle-neck guitar from blues artists in Chicago and also added elements of comedy, bluegrass, rockabilly, and gospel into his repertoire of hits. After selling millions of records through the 1940s, Foley teamed up with Ernest Tubb in 1950 for a number of hits and found major success with his gospel recordings through the remainder of the decade. In addition to his hit records, Foley was a successful radio show host, starting with the *Renfro Valley Barn Dance,* moving to WLS in 1940, then joining the Grand Ole Opry in 1947, ending with the *Ozark Jubilee* in Missouri in 1954. Shortly after his admission to the Country Music Hall of Fame, Foley suffered a fatal heart attack hours after finishing with "Peace in the Valley" at a Grand Ole Opry roadshow in Fort Wayne, Indiana. He was returned to Nashville, where he was laid to rest in Woodlawn Cemetery. As you drive up to the cemetery entrance, turn into the small section across the street from the main cemetery grounds. Drive past the small Companion Terrace section and park about one hundred feet past the section. He is buried in the Graceland section, Lot 290, Space 5, three rows from the road across from the Hillcrest section.

TENNESSEE ERNIE FORD
February 13, 1919—October 17, 1991
CAUSE OF DEATH Liver Disease

Ernest Jenning Ford began an impressive fifty-year run in the entertainment business in California as both a serious disc jockey and as his drawling, hillbilly alter-ego, Tennessee Ernie. Singing along with records to elicit a few laughs, Ford was signed to sing on Cliffie Stone's various live radio and TV shows in the Los Angeles area. Signed to Capitol Records in 1949, Ford scored a hit single the first time out with "Tennessee Border." That was quickly followed by "Mule Train," "The Shotgun Boogie," and the million-seller "Sixteen Tons." By 1976, he had recorded over eighty albums and sold more than sixty million records worldwide. But just as Ford's popularity was beginning to decline, he began recording and marketing gospel music exclusively, which kept him in the forefront of popular music. Already in possession of a Grammy, in 1984 he was awarded the Presidential Medal of Freedom, and in 1990 was inducted into the Country Music Hall of Fame. The following year, after having dinner with President Bush, Ford fell ill en route to the airport and was rushed to the hospital. Upon his passing several days later, he was laid to rest at Alta Mesa Memorial Park Cemetery in Palo Alto, California, in the Urn Garden in Lot 242, Subsection 1.

BLIND BOY FULLER
July 1905—February 13, 1941
CAUSE OF DEATH Kidney Disease

Born Fulton Allen, Blind Boy Fuller was one of the best-selling bluesman of the 1930s and was a seminal figure in the development of the Piedmont style of blues that emerged from the southeastern U.S. Little is known about Fuller's early life, and he only began to play guitar seriously when he went blind in the early 1920s. Tutored by the Reverend Gary Davis, Fuller made a living as a street musician, playing his loud steel-body National guitar outside the factories and workplaces in Durham, North Carolina. Discovered by James Baxter Long, a local store manager who heard Allen playing outside his store, Long drove Allen to New York, where he recorded for the American Record Company. Named Blind Boy Fuller by Long, Fuller recorded over 125 sides over a five-year period, occasionally using harmonica player Sonny Terry as his only accompanist. Songs such as "I'm a Rattlesnakin' Daddy," "Truckin' My Blues Away," and "Step It Up and Go" not only sold well, but were also recorded by black and white musicians alike. In 1940, Fuller was diagnosed with kidney disease, a failing bladder, and arrested syphilis. In 1941, he recorded for the last time before he was hospitalized, dying a short time later. He was buried in Grove Hill Cemetery in Durham; however, only a single cemetery marker remains on the property and his exact grave location is unknown. On July 16, 2001, the city of Durham recognized the legacy of Blind Boy Fuller and unveiled a monument to his artistic achievement on the American Tobacco Trail, located behind the Fayetteville Street Elementary School. The monument is located on the trail at the foot bridge.

LOWELL FULSON
March 31, 1921—March 6, 1999
CAUSE OF DEATH Kidney Disease

A major blues figure in California, Lowell Fulson developed a solid West Coast jump style of blues by way of Louisiana and Texas. Originally playing country and gospel, Fulson switched to the blues full-time when he replaced Chester Burnett (later to be known as Howlin' Wolf) in a band led by Texas Alexander while still in his teens. He moved to the West Coast in the forties and released his first hit on the R&B charts with "Three O'Clock in the Morning." While he continued to score hits on the R&B charts throughout his career, his widest exposure came from cover versions of his songs by such artists as Elvis, B. B. King, Otis Redding, and Eric Clapton. Fulson also was known for the company he kept—Ray Charles, Stanley Turrentine, David "Fathead" Newman, Ike Turner, and King Curtis all played in his touring bands at one time or another. In 1993, he received the Rhythm and Blues Foundation's Pioneer Award and in that same year won five W. C. Handy Blues Awards. A member of the Blues Hall of Fame, Fulson received a Grammy nomination for his second-to-last album, *Them Updated Blues*, released in 1995. Upon his passing at the age of seventy-seven, he was buried above fellow blues artist Charles Brown at Inglewood Park Cemetery in Inglewood, California, in the Sunset Mission Mausoleum upstairs in the Sanctuary of Bells in Space 926.

SERGE GAINSBOURG
April 2, 1928—March 2, 1991
CAUSE OF DEATH Heart Attack

Aside from "Je T'aime Moi Non Plus," very few people outside of Europe are familiar, much less understand, the impact that Serge Gainsbourg made on French music. With over two hundred songs covered by a variety of artists worldwide, one cannot dismiss Gainsbourg as a mere scandalous figure once gracing the covers of the popular press. Born Lucien Ginzburg in Paris, France (his father changed Lucien's name to Serge

Gainsbourg shortly after his birth), Serge got his first break at the age of thirty when one of his nightclub dates was covered in the French press by a notable jazz critic. Faced with the notion that he might have the talent and potential for the big time, Serge plunged into a period of songwriting and performing that included influences from jazz, rock 'n' roll, soul, and even reggae. His choice of material often found him at odds with the French establishment; however, he was the darling of the Left Bank crowd with his songs about lost love, alcohol, politics, and sex. Thus Serge emerged as a scandalous, self-promoting womanizer who became a cultural icon within French society. But toward the end, he wistfully remarked that he "succeeded at everything except my life." When he died of a heart attack brought about by a lifetime of excess, all of Paris came to a standstill. He is buried at Cimetière du Montparnasse in Paris, France. Located on the main road, the map at the entrance of the cemetery will guide you to his final resting place.

RORY GALLAGHER
March 2, 1948—June 14, 1995
CAUSE OF DEATH Complications After a Liver Transplant

One of Europe's great guitar players, Rory Gallagher's single-minded dedication to the blues and his refusal to change his style for radio success forever relegated him to small clubs and college circuit tours. Born in Ballyshannon, Ireland, Gallagher formed his first professional band, Taste, in 1968. A blend of heavy metal power chords and American blues, Taste recorded several well-received albums for the ATCO label. With so few Irish rock bands apart from Van Morrison and Them, Taste began to garner critical and popular acclaim, touring with Peter Green's Fleetwood Mac, Yes, Cream, and Blind Faith before disbanding under a cloud of financial mismanagement. Gallagher continued as a solo act, touring the U.S. no less than twenty-five times. Voted Musician of the Year by *Melody Maker* in 1972, Gallagher's popularity in the States dropped considerably during the 1980s. In 1994, during a tour in Europe, Gallagher fell seriously ill and received a liver transplant the following year. Unfortunately, complications arose and he passed away at King's College Hospital in London, England. He was taken back to his hometown in Cork, Ireland, where friends, fans, and family members lined the streets as his funeral cortege made its way to the Church of the Descent of the Holy Spirit. Gallagher was laid to rest in nearby St. Oliver's Cemetery under a golden, five-fingered fan monument in the center of the cemetery.

ERROLL GARNER
June 15, 1921—January 2, 1977
CAUSE OF DEATH Cancer

A gifted jazz pianist who could play stunningly complex runs without once looking at the keyboard, Erroll Garner exemplified the sophisticated, accessible jazz style that followed him throughout his three decade career. First appearing on the radio at age ten, Garner moved to New York City in the early forties, working briefly with Slam Stewart before forming his own trio in 1945. After working with Charlie Parker on his now famous "cool blues" sessions in 1947, Garner's reputation with fans and fellow musicians soared. By 1950, he had graduated from bars and jam sessions to top-level international tours and concert appearances. In 1954, he recorded his classic "Misty," and with lyrics by Johnny Burke (Jimmy Van Heusen's partner), the song would later become a million-seller for Johnny Mathis. Garner continued his successful routine of recordings (he once recorded three albums of material in one day!) and concert appearances up until 1975 when, for health reasons, he was forced to retire. Upon his passing two years later, he was buried at the Homewood Cemetery in Pittsburgh, Pennsylvania, in Section 12-2, Lot 19-E, Grave 3.

DANNY GATTON
September 4, 1945—October 4, 1994
CAUSE OF DEATH Suicide

His flawless technique, versatility, blinding speed, and his effortless ability to mix rock, jazz, blues, and country made the troubled but colorful Danny Gatton a true master on the Telecaster. Dubbed by musicians and the press alike as the Greatest Unknown Guitarist, he was a master at a variety of styles, regardless of whether the song called for slide, flat-pickin', pedal-steel, or funky chicken-pickin' style. Born and raised in a musical Washington, D.C., family, Gatton was already considered a virtuoso when he began to make home recordings and perform at high school dances at the age of twelve. By the age of fourteen he was playing in clubs with the Offbeats to patrons twice his age. One gig led to another and soon he was in Nashville trying to break into the tightly controlled world of studio session work. Frustrated, he moved back to Washington, D.C., and went through a variety of bands and styles. In 1980, he was invited to audition for Roger Miller and began touring with the legend. Shortly after, he got a call from rockabilly artist Robert Gordon and toured for another year playing strictly three-chord, fifties retreads. Discouraged, Gatton was dismissive of the music and the travel. To continue playing, he would only go back on his terms—his music and absolutely no travel outside his Maryland farm. Finally, at the age of forty-six, Gatton signed with a major label and recorded the instrumental *88 Elmira Street* in 1991. Despite a Grammy nomination and being named Hot Guitarist by *Rolling Stone* magazine, album sales for a nontouring musician were limited. After a follow-up recording, he was dropped by Elektra Records. One month after his forty-ninth birthday, Gatton stormed out of his house and toward the barn after a brief argument with his wife. He was found dead hours later of a self-inflicted gunshot wound. Whether Gatton's suicide was the result of a stalled career, financial difficulties, or the devastation over the death of his close friend and bandmate Billy Windsor, we will never know. No note was left when his body was discovered. Upon his passing, he was cremated and six years later Gatton's home at 11085 Lloyd Point Road on Route 257 in Newburg, Maryland, and much of his memorabilia, were sold at auction.

STAN GETZ
February 2, 1927—June 6, 1991
CAUSE OF DEATH Cancer

Known as The Sound for his golden tone on the saxophone, Stan Getz's résumé reads like a Who's Who of American jazz, recording with Jack Teagarden, Stan Kenton, Jimmy Dorsey, Dizzy Gillespie, Benny Goodman, and Woody Herman during his career. Getz was a mere teenager when he began his career in New York City with Teagarden in 1943, moving from one major swing band to another before working with Woody Herman's Thundering Herd in 1947. Getz left Herman two years later and led his own group for the remainder of his career. A major figure of cool jazz in the fifties, Getz ushered in the bossa nova craze of the sixties with *Jazz Samba* (with Charlie Byrd) and later with the worldwide pop hit "The Girl from Ipanema" with composer/guitarist João Gilberto. Although he could have coasted on his reputation, he chose to keep bossa nova a small part of his repertoire and continued to advance his brilliant improvisational skills, recording with younger musicians such as Chick Corea and Gary Burton through much of the eighties. In 1986, he became an artist-in-residence at Stanford University and made the occasional concert appearance while under the shadow of terminal cancer. When Getz died at the age of sixty-four, he was considered by many to be one of the most lyrical voices in jazz, whose five decades in the limelight made him the premier mainstream saxophone player. Upon his passing, he was cremated and his ashes were scattered in the Pacific Ocean.

ANDY GIBB
March 5, 1958—March 10, 1988
CAUSE OF DEATH Viral-related Heart Inflammation

The 1970s and early 1980s are often remembered as the decade that wrought disco, greed, cocaine, and unending excessive wealth and consumption. With this seemingly limitless party there were bound to be casualties. Andy Gibb was one of them. Born on the Isle of Man in the U.K., Andy was the youngest of the four handsome and talented brothers Gibb. While his brothers were enjoying international success in the early seventies as the Bee Gees, Andy was garnering attention as a teen heartthrob in

Australia, where he was raised. By the late 1970s, the Bee Gees were considering whether to add their younger sibling to the group. But before a decision could be made, Andy hit the U.S. pop scene with his album, *Flowing Rivers*, produced by brother Barry. The first single from that album, "I Just Want to Be Your Everything," hit number one on the charts in 1977 and Gibb was nominated for two Grammy Awards. His next two singles, "(Love Is) Thicker than Water" and "Shadow Dancing" also topped the charts, making Andy Gibb the first solo performer to have three consecutive singles hit number one. By the age of twenty-one, the youngest Gibb had sold over fifteen million albums. It was during this time that Gibb developed a ferocious cocaine habit and his addiction was causing him serious problems by the early 1980s. Although his pop star/teen idol status had begun to diminish, he was working as a host of the television dance program *Solid Gold*, and had been signed to star in the Broadway production of *Joseph and the Amazing Technicolor Dreamcoat*. Fired from *Solid Gold*, he struggled with unemployment and was plagued by personal and financial problems, including bankruptcy. Though he sought help from a treatment center for his cocaine addiction, the damage had been done. Just five days after his thirtieth birthday, Gibb died while recording a new album for Island Records. The death certificate listed the official cause of death as a viral-related heart inflammation. However, at the time of his passing, rumors had been circulating that his lifestyle had caused permanent damage to his heart. His body was flown back to the United States to his final resting place in Crypt 2534 in the Courts of Remembrance at Forest Lawn Hollywood Hills in Los Angeles, California.

STEVE GOODMAN
July 25, 1948—September 20, 1984
CAUSE OF DEATH Leukemia

One of America's finest songwriters of the 1970s, Steve Goodman's traditional brand of folk music was augmented by his clever lyrics and appealing melodies. Best known for penning the hit "City of New Orleans" (a major hit for Arlo Guthrie), Goodman was first discovered by Paul Anka during a bar gig and shortly after he was signed to Buddah Records. Supplementing his meager earnings by writing commercial jingles for advertising, he released his first album in 1971. While his first record was a critical success, sales were not. However, he did gain a cult following on the college circuit and always made more money in concert appearances than in sales of records. And while Guthrie was riding the hit wave off Goodman's song, Goodman was the hit of the Cambridge Folk Festival during his first visit to England. While he never attained star status for himself, his songs became hits for dozens of other artists, including Johnny Cash, Joan Baez, and Jimmy Buffett. The end did not come as a surprise to family and close friends who knew of Goodman's lifelong battle with leukemia. A longtime Chicago Cubs baseball fan, per his wishes upon his untimely death, he was cremated and his ashes were interred under home plate at Wrigley Field in Chicago, Illinois.

BILL GRAHAM
January 31, 1931—October 25, 1991
CAUSE OF DEATH Helicopter Crash

Technically not a musician (though he may have picked up a tambourine at one of his live events), promoter, manager, and concert impresario Bill Graham was responsible for developing the organizational structure to showcase rock 'n' roll events that is still in use today. His first job found him managing the San Francisco Mime Troupe, but as the years passed by, he graduated to owning several concert venues (the Fillmore East and West, as well as working with the Jefferson Airplane, the Grateful Dead, Janis Joplin, Quicksilver Messenger Service, Santana, Bob Dylan, and the Rolling Stones. After attending a concert by Huey Lewis and the News, the helicopter ferrying him back to San Francisco struck a high-voltage power line in the fog near Vallejo, California. He was buried at Eternal Home Cemetery in Colma, California. Use the northern-most entrance into the cemetery and take a left at the first road. Walk through the Court of the Twelve Tribes of Israel monument and count six rows from the road, where Graham's monument address is 700-G-8.

W. C. HANDY
November 16, 1873—March 28, 1958
CAUSE OF DEATH Bronchial Pneumonia

Creator of "St. Louis Blues," "Beale Street Blues," and "The Memphis Blues," William Christopher "W. C." Handy was often referred to as the Father of the Blues. In reality, he really should be referred to as the First Person to Copyright the Blues. Though he claimed at one time to having invented both blues and jazz, this part-time cornet player was most influential as a music writer and publisher. His final recordings as a performer occurred in 1939 with New Orleans artist Edmond Hall and two years later he published his autobiography, *Father of the Blues.* After an eye disease and a fall off a subway platform left him totally blind in 1943, his role as guardian, promoter, and publisher of the blues was secure and his contribution to an emerging black culture was immeasurable. When he died at the age of eighty-four, he was put to rest at Woodlawn

Cemetery in the Bronx, New York. Following the same directions as Joseph "King" Oliver, take Alpine Avenue down to Canna Avenue. Turn right and park twenty feet from the intersection. Look for a weathered asphalt path leading into the Cosmo section on your left. Walk up the path toward the fence. Handy's weathered, upright monument is in the third row from the fence, third row to the right.

Back in Memphis, Tennessee, the Memphis Music Hall of Fame Museum (located across from the Peabody in downtown Memphis) has the largest collection of W. C. Handy items in the world. In addition, a lifesize statue of Handy is located just off Beale Street. In his hometown of Florence, Alabama, the log cabin where he was born has been restored and turned into a museum, which houses a nice collection of memorabilia from his life. In addition, a Handy memorial statue can be found in Florence's Wilson Park.

TIM HARDIN
December 23, 1941—December 29, 1980
CAUSE OF DEATH Heroin and Morphine Overdose

As Neil Young wrote, "It's better to burn out than fade away." Unfortunately for Tim Hardin, he managed to do both. Although he was the author of the folk classic "If I Were a Carpenter" made famous by Bobby Darin, Hardin had little success as a recording or live concert artist. Born in Eugene, Oregon, and the son of classically trained parents (but not a distant relative of the outlaw John Wesley Hardin as has been rumored), Hardin became an influential member of the East Coast folk revival in the early 1960s. After a well-received appearance at the Newport Folk Festival in 1966, Hardin recorded *Tim Hardin* and the more popular *Tim Hardin II* (which included the evocative "Reason to Believe" later recorded successfully by Rod Stewart) for Verve Records. However, after the second album, Hardin failed to capitalize on the success by touring due to an ever-increasing heroin and alcohol addiction. He moved briefly to Europe to take advantage of their liberal methadone treatment programs, but it was to no avail. When he returned to the States, it is rumored Jim Morrison once took Doors staff members to see Hardin to show them the dangers of drug addiction. Not surprisingly, Hardin died of an accidental overdose at his apartment at 625 North Orange Street in Hollywood, California (see photo above). He was cremated after his death, and his ashes returned to his family.

COLEMAN HAWKINS
November 21, 1904—May 19, 1969
Cause of Death Effects of Alcoholism

Considered by many to be the first great saxophonist of jazz, Coleman Hawkins became the dominant voice on the tenor sax by creating a sound and improvisational vocabulary that few could equal. Already playing professionally at the age of twelve, Hawkins was spotted playing in the pit band at a local Kansas City theater by blues singer Mamie Smith. He joined Smith's backing band, the Jazz Hounds, where he played with the group until 1923. He moved to New York City and freelanced a bit before he made his first recordings with Fletcher Henderson. Duly impressed, Henderson invited Hawkins (and later, a young Louis Armstrong) along when Henderson formed a permanent band. A fixture at New York's Roseland Ballroom, Hawkins was not only the star tenor sax player—he was the star of the band! Known for always having the most expensive suits and fastest car, Hawkins proved

his worth on such classics as "The Stampede," "St. Louis Shuffle," and "Wherever There's a Will, Baby." But after ten years with the Henderson band they parted amicably, with Henderson moving to England for the next five years. Returning to New York in 1939 after several successful recording sessions and tours, Hawkins re-established his importance by his historic recording of "Body and Soul." With this landmark recording, he continued his dominance within the emerging bebop scene and became a fixture at New York's Fifty-second Street nightclubs. Always the innovator and leader, he recorded with Dizzy Gillespie and Thelonious Monk and used Oscar Pettiford, drummer Max Roach, and Miles Davis as sidemen during their early years. However, by the early fifties, Hawkins was relegated to mostly club and hotel dates along with a steady stream of recording dates, as Lester Young began to emerge with a whole new style of playing. By the mid-1960s, Hawkins rarely made a public appearance and was suffering from emotional problems, refusing to eat, and from alcoholism. Upon his passing, he was buried in Woodlawn Cemetery in the Bronx, New York, in the Yew section. Park at the intersection of Canna and Park Avenue and walk up five rows from the road and five markers to the right to his granite marker.

MICHAEL HEDGES
December 31, 1953—December 2, 1997
CAUSE OF DEATH Automobile Crash

"Watching Michael play guitar was like watching the guitar being reinvented," remarked Windham Hill Records cofounder Will Ackerman. One of the most innovative, talented, and acclaimed acoustic guitarists of his era, composer and performer Michael Hedges was known for his unique picking style that gave the impression of multiple guitarists playing simultaneously. Although his first record was released on the New Age music label Windham Hill, he was embarrassed by the tag and often referred to his music as "acoustic thrash," "heavy mental," and "new edge." In addition to helping establish the Windham Hill record label in the early eighties, he also collaborated with such diverse musicians as guitarist Dweezil Zappa (son of Frank Zappa); Crosby, Stills, and Nash; as well as with San Francisco–Bay Area bassist Michael Manring. A Grammy Award nominee, Hedges was returning from a Thanksgiving visit with his girlfriend when, upon driving from the San Francisco Airport up to his home in Mendocino County, his 1986 BMW skidded off a curve and down a steep embankment off of State Route 128. The car and Hedges were discovered by a road crew that happened upon the site two days after the accident. He was cremated and a memorial service was held several days later.

FLETCHER HENDERSON
December 18, 1897—December 28, 1952
CAUSE OF DEATH Effects of a Stroke

A gifted musician, arranger, and a true bandleader, Fletcher Henderson was instrumental in the development and growth of the big band era that began in the 1920s. With an ear for talent, Henderson's band members included Louis Armstrong, Coleman Hawkins, Rex Stewart, Don Redman, and Benny Carter—a veritable list of Who's Who of American jazz. Moving to New York City in 1920 to continue his studies in chemistry at college, Henderson took a part-time job as a song demonstrator for W. C. Handy's publishing firm. He continued as a recording manager for the Black Swan label, always with an eye on leading his own band. That opportunity came when the Roseland dance club needed a resident band and Henderson auditioned for the opening. With Hawkins on tenor sax, the Fletcher Henderson Orchestra

remained at Roseland for the next ten years, augmented by the occasional tour to the Midwest and down south. One of the first black big bands, the orchestra was known for its chop-busting arrangements and powerhouse rhythm section that was second to none. After a near-fatal car accident in 1928, Henderson seemed to slow down and by the mid-thirties, he was rarely performing with a band, preferring to work as the staff arranger for Benny Goodman's orchestra, providing the master plan for the swinging Goodman sound on such classics as "King Porter Stomp" and "Honeysuckle Rose." By the 1940s, he was back leading a variety of bands in both New York and Chicago, as well as arranging for a number of new bands. He rejoined Goodman in 1947, but in 1950 suffered a debilitating stroke that ended his career. When he passed away two years later, he was returned home to Cuthbert, Georgia, and buried at the old Eastview Cemetery. From the left-most entry

onto the grounds, drive up the dirt path approximately one hundred feet. Walk to the left to the three graves surrounded by a simple granite border. Listed as an historical site, his home at 1016 Andrews Street is sorely lacking in adequate funding and will not be opening soon to the public. In addition, no memorabilia exists in the house or within the town itself.

Z. Z. HILL
September 30, 1935—April 27, 1984
CAUSE OF DEATH Automobile Crash

Z.Z. Hill's contribution to the blues stems largely from the fact that he was one of the few performers who could draw a reluctant southern black audience back to the blues in the early eighties. But one could not call Hill an overnight success. He spent twenty years in the music business, on a variety of labels and playing to mostly empty clubs, until his first release in 1982 on Malaco Records, *Down Home*, landed Hill on the R&B charts for nearly two years. He followed his hit album with two more well-received releases in as many years and sparked a revival of southern blues and soul that helped the careers of Bobby "Blue" Bland, Robert Cray, and Stevie Ray Vaughan. But sadly, just as his career was at a high point, rivaling that of longtime blues legends B. B. King and Buddy Guy, he died from injuries sustained in an automobile accident. He was buried just outside his hometown of Naples, Texas, at Gethsemane Cemetery. As you drive into the center of the cemetery, look to the center for his dark red granite monument with the musical notes and his birth name Arzell Hill etched in the granite.

AL HIRT
November 7, 1922—April 27, 1999
CAUSE OF DEATH Liver Failure

Known around the French Quarter as Jumbo and the Round Mound of Sound due to his massive three hundred-pound, six-foot, two-inch frame, Al Hirt was one of New Orleans's favorite sons. But unlike Louis Armstrong, Al Hirt never really left New Orleans during his five-decade, fifty-five-album run as one of the true gentlemen of jazz. Born and raised on the Dixieland of his native New Orleans, Al Hirt was given his first trumpet at the age of six and ten years later he landed his first professional gig, earning the princely sum of forty dollars a week. As the story goes, his first mouthpiece on the trumpet was flawed, so to compensate Hirt developed a powerful playing technique—one that in later years left fellow musicians in awe. After studying the trumpet at the Cincinnati Conservatory of Music, he joined the army for two years before going on the road with such big band legends as Tommy Dorsey, Jimmy Dorsey, Horace Heidt, and Benny Goodman. Tired of the road and longing for the improvisation that Dixieland music allowed, he moved back to New Orleans for much of the 1950s. In the 1960s, Al Hirt and the Dixieland Six were playing Las Vegas when they were seen by Dinah Shore, who promptly booked them on her popular TV show. Shortly afterward Hirt signed with RCA Records and recorded several gold records, won a Grammy in 1963 for his million-seller "Java," and was named *Billboard* magazine's Top Instrumentalist in 1965. During this time Hirt opened a popular nightclub on Bourbon Street in the French Quarter—right across the street from Fountain's place. Good friends, they often played at each other's clubs. However, as time went by, the good life (and a few extra pounds) began to take their toll and in his later years he performed from a wheelchair. True to his nature, he waited until the annual New Orleans Jazz and Heritage Festival to pass away after several months of ill health. Wearing a powder blue suit and sporting his trademark cigar, he was cremated and his ashes interred in the mausoleum at Metairie Cemetery outside New Orleans, Louisiana. As you enter the All Saints mausoleum, walk upstairs and go toward the left side and make your way to the St. Thomas Apostle Quarter, Tier E, Crypt 68.

JAMES HONEYMAN-SCOTT
November 4, 1956—June 16, 1982
CAUSE OF DEATH Drug Overdose

Taking their name from the Platters' hit "The Great Pretender," Chrissie Hynde and boyfriend Pete Farndon joined forces with drummer Martin Chambers and guitarist James Honeyman-Scott to form one of the classic eighties rock bands—the Pretenders. In 1978, just one year after their formation, the band released their eponymous first album, which included the staples of FM airplay "Brass in Pocket," "Mystery Achievement," and "Stop Your Sobbing." While the band members' inspiration lies with British punk, ska, and new wave, the Pretenders were more clearly defined by Hynde's sensual, husky growl and Scott's syncopated rhythms and sustained melodic chordings. When their second album came out in 1981, it yielded another hit in "I Go to Sleep," along with unbearable tension and feuding within the band. Just two days after Farndon was kicked out for drug abuse, Scott was found dead in his London apartment of an overdose. Scott was taken back to his hometown of Hereford, England, where he was buried at the historic St. Peter's Church in Pipe-Cum-Lyde. Located on the A49, enter through the heavy iron gates and walk back to the new section on the right side of the cemetery and his grave is three rows from the back on the right.

EARL HOOKER
January 15, 1930—April 21, 1970
CAUSE OF DEATH Pulmonary Tuberculosis

Boasting a fretboard touch so smooth and clean, one would be hard-pressed to find a more brilliant and more underrated slide guitarist residing in Chicago during the fifties and sixties than Earl Hooker. A cousin to John Lee Hooker, he learned the essentials of the blues from Robert Nighthawk and performed or recorded with Ike Turner, Sonny Boy Williamson II, Pinetop Perkins, Otis Rush's band, along with his own band, the Roadmasters. If not for his modest vocal abilities and constant health problems, he would have emerged as a major Chicago blues legend like Muddy Waters or Howlin' Wolf. However, Hooker spent much of his time on the road as he made his living playing full-time, he had very little time to cut a full album and much of his recorded work was released locally as singles. In 1969, he finally got his chance to record beyond the three-minute limit of the singles market and Hooker cut some of his best work for Arhoolie Records. He then took his band to Europe, where they played in the American Folk Blues Festival along with Magic Sam and Clifton Chenier. Upon his return to the States he was admitted into Chicago's Municipal Tuberculosis Sanitarium where he died of pulmonary tuberculosis. He was buried in an unmarked grave at Restvale Cemetery in Worth, Illinois, in Section K, Lot 33, Grave 4.

SHANNON HOON
September 26, 1967—October 21, 1995
CAUSE OF DEATH Cocaine Overdose

So this is how it ends—an unsold final album, a few band members that drift quietly away, a bee girl, and dead at age twenty-eight in the back of a tour bus in New Orleans. As it turns out, death was not a good career move for the lead singer of Blind Melon, Shannon Hoon. The product of heavy MTV rotation, Blind Melon came into national recognition with the 1993 video for "No Rain," featuring a young girl dancing in an oversize bee costume. Selling over two million copies of their debut album, Blind Melon became a national sensation with a cover on *Rolling Stone* magazine, nominations for both Grammy and American Music Awards, and a frenzy of live shows with Neil Young, the Rolling Stones, Soundgarden, as well as a prime spot at Woodstock II. As for Blind Melon today, they have been relegated to the discount bin and Shannon Hoon is merely a badly painted mural on the exterior wall of JL Compact Discs in Hoon's hometown of Lafayette, Indiana. As you enter Dayton Cemetery in Dayton, Indiana, continue through the cemetery to the very back section. His elongated, flat marble monument is located ten rows from the back fence in the center section.

LIGHTNIN' HOPKINS
March 15, 1912—January 30, 1982
CAUSE OF DEATH Cancer

As a youth, Sam "Lightnin'" Hopkins was introduced to the blues as he accompanied Blind Lemon Jefferson as his guide through Texas. Through much of the 1920s, thirties, and forties, Hopkins worked as a farmer and played blues on the weekends, recording with his

cousin Alger "Texas" Alexander for twenty-five years before performing on his own. A man who loved to drink, smoke, gamble, fight, and chase women, Hopkins had the scars from prison leg irons to show that he had lived the life of which he sang. With over eighty albums to his credit, Hopkins opened for such acts as the Jefferson Airplane and the Grateful Dead. Whether he performed on an acoustic or electric guitar, or whether he played solo or with a combo, Hopkins was an astonishingly skillful artist who influenced musicians from all genres. Hopkins died in 1982 and with over four thousand in attendance at his funeral he was interred at Forest Park Cemetery in Lawndale, Texas. As you enter the cemetery, drive around toward the left to Section 23. Look on your left for the Vaughan monument and one row behind, you will find Hopkins in Section 23, Lot 266, Number 11.

JOHNNY HORTON
APRIL 3, 1925—NOVEMBER 5, 1960
CAUSE OF DEATH Automobile Accident

You've just got to love a guy who, after having fame and fortune heaped upon him, goes out and buys a bait factory in Natchitoches, Louisiana, just so he could go fishing more often. Dubbed the Singing Fisherman, Horton is best known for "The Battle of New Orleans" and "Johnny Reb." He is also remembered as the man who married Billie Jean Williams, Hank Williams's widow. In what has to be one of the true ironies in country music, Johnny was killed by a drunk driver after performing at the Skyway Club in Austin, Texas—the very same club where Hank Williams played his last performance. The story goes that at about 2:00 A.M. after the gig, the group was traveling near Milano, Texas, in Horton's Cadillac. As they were crossing a bridge a truck came at them, hitting both sides of the bridge before slamming into Horton's car. Horton had no opportunity to avoid the oncoming truck and took the full force of the collision. Still breathing when he was pulled out of the car, Horton died on the way to hospital. It came to light that the nineteen-year-old truck driver, James Davis, was intoxicated at the time of the accident. He was buried at Hillcrest Memorial Park in Haughton, Louisiana, on Highway 80 (ten miles east of Shreveport). As you approach the cemetery from the west, take the second driveway (just past the office and parking lot) and turn left into the cemetery. Drive to the first section and park. His flat monument is easy to find, thanks to the loving guitar-encased monument maintained by his daughter, Melody, and her husband, Larry (by the way, they would like you to know that the guitar is NOT a real guitar, so stop trying to steal it!). With regards to Horton memorabilia, Billie Jean Williams Horton is alive and well and still maintains all of the items at her home in Shreveport.

WALTER "SHAKEY JAKE" HORTON
April 6, 1918—December 8, 1981
CAUSE OF DEATH Cancer

Sometimes known as Shakey Jake or Mumbles (a pseudonym he disliked), Big Walter Horton's harmonica saved a great number of albums from mediocrity. Not as well known as Sonny Boy Williamson II or Little Walter, he was still considered one of the greatest harp players in the history of the blues. While he recorded very little under his own name, his talent graced the records of Memphis Minnie, Muddy Waters, Big Joe Williams, Willie Dixon, and Eddie Taylor. The end of Big Walter's life was marked by disenchantment at lost opportunities and lack of work. Though he was considered one of Chicago's finest, he was without a band, a recording contract, or regular income at the time of his death. He was buried at Restvale Cemetery on Chicago's South Side. As you drive through the gates off Laramie Road, turn left and drive to the end, past the war memorial on your left. Look for Section J-1 (just past Section J). His marker is located nine rows from the fence bordering Laramie, and fourteen plots from the hedges in Section J-1, Lot 39, Grave 5.

SON HOUSE
March 21, 1902—October 19, 1988
CAUSE OF DEATH Natural Causes

Though mostly uncredited in the annals of blues history, Eddie James "Son" House was the role model for two of the blues' greatest legends—Robert Johnson and Muddy Waters. Born in Riverton, Mississippi, at the turn of the century, blues music came late in House's life. An avid choir singer and later a Baptist preacher, House spent his early years on the road traveling between Clarksdale, Memphis, Helena, and Baton Rouge in search of farm work and other rudimentary jobs. His life began to take a turn toward the blues when he met Blind Lemon Jefferson and later, Frank Stokes and Jim Jackson. Impressed by the small medicine bottle Stokes used as a slide on the guitar, House bought an old used guitar for $1.50 from a friend and began to learn slide guitar in the tradition of Mississippi country blues. After House adapted two songs as his own, he was promptly hired to play a country dance—playing the same two songs over and over all night. In 1929, he moved to Lula and met with the King of the Delta Blues, Charley Patton, and they performed together at dances and house parties in the area. Hired to record for Paramount, Patton recommended that House and fellow artist Willie Brown and pianist Louise Johnson be added to the session. Recording eight to ten sides, including a recently discovered "Walking Blues," House was paid forty dollars for his efforts and was now considered a recording star on par with Blind Lemon Jefferson and Patton. Now working with Brown, it was during the midthirties that a young Robert Johnson pestered the two musicians, wanting to learn slide guitar. House was annoyed that Johnson would break a string or scare away paying customers with his rudimentary knowledge of the blues. Nonetheless, they let Johnson sit in on occasion and were astonished when he returned two years later, having acquired impressive skills earned during his short career playing jukes in Mississippi. His connection with Johnson, and later with Muddy Waters, led to his being recorded for the Library of Congress by Alan Lomax in the early forties. After Brown's death, for the next twenty years, House remained musically inactive until 1964, when he was found to be living in retirement in a small apartment with a bottle of whiskey and a wife of thirty years. Though he hadn't played for a long time, he had one last hurrah that lasted eleven years and included a new album and concert appearances in Europe and America. He retired due to health reasons and died in a nursing home in 1988 at the age of eighty-six. He was buried in the lower section of Mt. Hazel Cemetery in northwest Detroit, Michigan.

MISSISSIPPI JOHN HURT
March 8, 1892—November 2, 1966
CAUSE OF DEATH Natural Causes

Of all the Delta bluesman still alive in the sixties, none enjoyed the fruits of rediscovery as much as Mississippi John Hurt. Possessing a quiet charm and a superb guitar style, Hurt was a collector of songs that he arranged into his own unique style. Originally recorded in 1928, Hurt was amazed thirty-five years later when folklorist Tom Hoskins came to his home in Avalon, Mississippi, and remembered his six 78s that he recorded and coaxed him out of retirement. Hurt's new career lasted only three years, but during that time he played the Newport Folk Festival, on numerous college campuses, and was in big demand in Europe

before he died in 1966. He is buried in his hometown of Avalon, Mississippi, in the St. James Cemetery. From Highway 7 in Avalon, turn east after the post office, heading toward the bluffs. Drive 3.7 miles (the road will turn to gravel) and then turn left into the woods toward the gravel quarry (there will be a trailer on your right and please note, you are now on private property). The ten or so graves that make up the graveyard lie two miles down the rut-filled dirt road on the left with Hurt's grave in the back row.

MICHAEL HUTCHENCE
January 22, 1960—November 22, 1997
CAUSE OF DEATH Suicide

Possessing good looks and stage presence, INXS lead singer Michael Hutchence was able to back up the style with musical substance. Supplementing dance rhythms with guitar-based rock separated INXS from the rather more mundane Australian eighties exports, such as Air Supply and Men at Work. Formed as the Farriss Brothers in Perth, Australia, in the mid-seventies, they were originally signed to RCA Records in 1981 and changed their name to INXS. With an eye on American radio, they changed record companies and in 1982 released their second album *Shabooh Shoobah*. Opening for the Kinks and Adam Ant in the U.S., the relentless roadwork and PR produced their first major hit, "The One Thing," making the Top 30 in America. Their next album was produced by legendary eighties producer Nile Rodgers, who guided the band to their first hit album, *Original Sin*. But it wasn't until 1988, eleven years since the group first formed, that they became an international sensation with the album *Kick*, which produced several hit singles, including "Need You Tonight," "Devil Inside," and "Never Tear Us Apart." By now, INXS was an international success and Hutchence, with the usual string of beautiful models, excessive drug and alcohol intake, and a lame solo album, was front-page fodder for gossip columns around the world. With the band set to embark on a worldwide tour in support of a new album and twenty-year anniversary, Hutchence left a note with tour manager John Martin, stating that he would not be attending the final rehearsal. The next morning he made several disturbing phone calls, including one to his personal manager in New York, stating that "I fucking had enough!" Another call was to Bob Geldof, where Hutchence heaped abusive and threatening remarks at Geldof regarding a custody/visitation battle over Paula Yates's (Hutchence's arm decor and Geldof's ex-wife) children. Hutchence was found dead several hours later in room 524 of the Ritz-Carlton Hotel at Double Bay in Sydney, Australia. He had apparently hung himself with his own belt off the door to his room and was discovered by a maid with the body kneeling on the floor, facing the door. A service was held five days later and his body was cremated, with the ashes scattered in Sydney Harbor at dusk. In early 1998, a large cenotaph was erected at the Northern Suburbs Memorial Gardens in Sydney. Four months after his passing, the coroner ruled the death a suicide after finding the presence of alcohol, cocaine, Prozac, and other prescription drugs present. There was no evidence, despite the tabloid headlines, that Hutchence died while performing auto-eroticism.

BURL IVES
June 14, 1909—April 14, 1995
CAUSE OF DEATH Cancer of the Mouth

Famous for such folk songs as "Blue Tail Fly," "Jimmy Crack Corn," and "Big Rock Candy Mountain," Carl Sandburg called Burl Ives "the mightiest ballad singer of this or any other century." Although best known as the narrator and singer for the classic Christmas holiday program *Frosty the Snowman*, he is remembered by friends and fans alike as one of the great folksingers from the 1940s and fifties in the vein of Woody Guthrie and Pete Seeger. In addition to recording over a hundred albums during his lifetime, he was an accomplished actor, starring in several films, including *East of Eden, Cat on a Hot Tin Roof,* and *Big Country* (for which he won an Academy Award). Upon his passing at the age of eighty-five, Ives was buried at Mound Cemetery in Jasper County, Illinois, near Hunt City. His large, black marble monument is in the center of this small country cemetery. In 1997, the impressive Burl Ives Collection, displaying his vast collection of memorabilia from his career, was opened in the Scottish Rite Temple located at 1733 Sixteenth Street in Washington, D.C.

AL JACKSON
November 27, 1935—October 1, 1975
CAUSE OF DEATH Murdered

With Al Jackson on drums, Booker T. and the MGs were the heart and very soul of Stax Records and founding members of what is known as the Memphis sound. Formed in 1962 with Steve Cropper on guitar, Donald "Duck" Dunn on bass, and Booker T. Jones on the keyboards, Booker T. and the MGs continued throughout the sixties to write, produce, and play on over six hundred Stax recordings, including ten albums under their own name. One of the more prolific groups in popular music, the songs "Soul Man" by Sam and Dave, "In the Midnight Hour" by Wilson Pickett, and every single hit with Otis Redding, including ("Sittin' on the) Dock of the Bay," were made with the famous foursome. With Al Jackson as the acknowledged musical and spiritual leader, the band also played on hits with Albert King, Carla Thomas, Eddie Floyd, Johnnie Taylor, and anyone else who walked through the Stax studio doors. When Stax was sold in 1968, the band drifted apart to work on their own projects. Jackson was kept busy as a session drummer and continued working with and produc-

ing albums with Albert King. In 1975, Jones called upon the other three members to reunite and the group worked with Rod Stewart, as well as on some solo material for a new album. Unfortunately, work came to a halt in the fall of 1975. Earlier that year Jackson's wife shot him during a domestic dispute; however, Jackson wasn't hurt and charges were dropped over a claim of self-defense. That following October, Jackson's wife opened the door to an alleged intruder, who threw Jackson down on the floor and shot him five times in the back. Police described the scene as a botched robbery attempt and the crime remains unsolved. Jackson was buried in New Park Cemetery in Lake Horn, Mississippi. Upon entering the cemetery grounds, turn left and then turn right at the second road. Drive 150 feet and Jackson's monument is just off the road on the left.

HARRY JAMES
March 15, 1916—July 5, 1983
CAUSE OF DEATH Cancer

Born to a circus trumpeter father and a mother who was a trapeze artist, Harry began his lifelong musical odyssey as a drummer at the age of four. At the age of eight he began playing trumpet and four years later he was leading the Mighty Haag Circus band. The family eventually settled in Beaumont, Texas, where a teenage James began playing in local dance bands, eventually joining Ben Pollack's band. By the age of twenty, James was playing trumpet with the renowned Benny Goodman Orchestra, alongside Ziggy Ellman and drummer Gene Krupa, and was featured on BG classics "Sing, Sing, Sing" and "One O'Clock Jump." With Goodman's blessing, James started his own band at the age of twenty-three and over the next forty years, James had some of the jazz world's greatest talent join his band, including Frank Sinatra, Connie Haines, Buddy Rich, Corky Corcoran, Vido Musso, and Willie Smith. Considered the number one dance band in the country in 1942, James

sold over a million copies each of "Velvet Moon," "You Made Me Love You," "All or Nothing at All," and his biggest hit, "I've Heard That Song Before." Upon his passing just nine days after his final show, James was interred at Eden Vale Memorial Park in Las Vegas, Nevada. As you drive into the cemetery, park in front of the Chapel of Eternal Peace. Through the front doors of the mausoleum, locate the Remembrance corridor and James resides in a crypt on the second row.

BEAU JOCQUE
November 1, 1953—September 10, 1999
CAUSE OF DEATH Heart Attack

In the ten years preceding the new millennium, the classic sound of zydeco music, pioneered by the great Clifton Chenier, was revitalized by the hulking zydeco bandleader Beau Jocque and his band the Zydeco Hi-Rollers. Often compared to Howlin' Wolf and James Brown, Beau Jocque incorporated the rhythms of hip-hop, the funk of War, and the blues rock of ZZ Top to create one of the hottest, funkiest zydeco bands that ever hit the dance

floor. Born Andrus Espre, Jocque didn't start playing music until 1987 after an accident at work and
a ten-month recuperation period (when he learned
to play his father's button accordion) allowed the
budding musician to change careers. After watching the mainstays of the southwest Louisiana zydeco circuit, including Boozoo Chavis, C. J. Chenier,
and the legendary Buckwheat Zydeco, Jocque
formed a band around a mix of historic Cajun
rhythms, heavy bass lines and guitar solos, along
with contemporary rhythm and blues. Already a
legend from New Orleans to Baton Rouge down to
Lafayette, when Jocque released his first album featuring zydeco's first "modern" hit "Give Him
Cornbread," fans would pelt the band with chunks

of cornbread in appreciation. Now the top zydeco act in Louisiana, the owner of the nightclub Rock 'n' Bowl in New Orleans, John Blancher, had to reinforce the dance floor after a
set by the Zydeco Hi-Rollers due to the crowd's response to the propulsive, hypnotic brand
of music. As word spread outside the South of this "new" type of music, Jocque began to
make forays outside of his home in Kinder, Louisiana, with performances in England,
Turkey, as well as appearances on the David Letterman and Conan O'Brien shows. When
the Rolling Stones came to town during the Jazz and Heritage Festival in New Orleans,
vocalist Mick Jagger and drummer Charlie Watts made it a point to catch the double bill
featuring Beau Jocque and Boozoo Chavis. So it came as quite a shock when Jocque, after
a double show at Rock 'n' Bowl, drove home and kissed his wife good night, then was discovered by his wife the next morning, slumped over in the shower after a heart attack.
Efforts by a crew of workmen, and later paramedics, to revive the musician were futile. His
funeral was attended by the zydeco world, including Boozoo Chavis, the Dopsie family,
Buckwheat Zydeco, Willis Prudhomme, and the Delafose brothers. Jocque was buried near
his father, who had died just two weeks earlier at the St. Matildas Cemetery in Eunice,
Louisiana, four rows from the back of the cemetery.

TOMMY JOHNSON
?, 1896—November 1, 1956
CAUSE OF DEATH Heart Attack

With the fourteen sides he recorded between 1928 and 1930, Tommy Johnson exhibited
all the qualities of a great Delta bluesman—dramatic, intense vocals coupled with superb
compositions and guitar accompaniment. A contemporary of Charley Patton (from whom
he drew inspiration), he was discovered by H. C. Speirs (a talent scout for RCA Victor), who,
in Jackson, Mississippi, rented a bus bound for the studios in Memphis to record what have
now become fourteen of the greatest blues standards ever recorded. Unfortunately, Tommy
was drawn more to the bottle than to his music; hence he became increasingly unstable
and gambled most of his money away (including the rights to his hit single "Big Road
Blues"). He lived the last twenty-five years of his life as an alcoholic, eventually succumbing to the effects of overindulgence. His unmarked grave is located at Warm Springs
Cemetery in Crystal Springs, Mississippi. From I-55 south, exit at Crystal Springs and turn
east onto Highway 27. Cross over the railroad tracks and turn left on Cherry Grove Road,
then right on Henry Road. The cemetery is located about one mile back into the woods on
private property, with his final resting place just to the right of B. W. Johnson.

AL JOLSON
May 26, 1886—October 23, 1953
CAUSE OF DEATH Heart Attack

Al Jolson's forty-year career moved from stage, screen, radio, and vaudeville to early phonograph recordings when he became the most popular recording artist in America. Billing himself as the World's Greatest Entertainer, he would often sing for three hours only to call out, "You ain't heard nothin' yet!" Acclaimed as the most complete entertainer of the twentieth century, he sold over one million records as early as 1912 ("Raggin' the Baby to Sleep") and as late as 1950. Born Asa Yoelson, he was considered a pioneer in the world of entertainment. He was the first to take a Broadway show on the road, the first to make a talking picture (the historic film *The Jazz Singer*), the first to record a long-playing album, and he gave both Irving Berlin and George Gershwin their first big breaks in the music business. But there was a dark side to his success. By the mid-1940s he had been divorced three times and was considered a wealthy show business has-been. Known as one of the most ruthless men in Hollywood, Jolson was one of the most disliked men in show business and was even barred for a time from the set of his own film biography. But with the release of the film *The Al Jolson Story* in 1946, his career was resurrected and he became immensely popular again with the release of *Al Jolson Sings Again*. He had just returned from Korea, where he was entertaining the troops, when he fell ill while with some friends at a San Francisco hotel. "It looks like the end," Jolson remarked as his companions called for a doctor. When a doctor did arrive, he motioned for the physician to "pull up a chair and hear a story or two." Moments later he was dead. Jolson was buried at Hillside Memorial Park in Los Angeles, California. Wanting to be buried near water, Jolson's sarcophagus is located above the waterfall, just to the left of the cemetery office.

SCOTT JOPLIN
November 24, 1868—April 1, 1917
CAUSE OF DEATH Syphilis-related Pneumonia

It may have taken over a half century since his passing, but Scott Joplin, known as the King of Ragtime, was finally recognized as the greatest ragtime composer of all time. Credited with over sixty compositions, including his most famous "Maple Leaf Rag" (which sold over a million copies of sheet music alone), Scott enjoyed a revival when the 1972 movie *The Sting* used his song "The Entertainer" in the score. Shortly after, his opera *Treemonisha* (the first full-scale opera composed by an African-American) was awarded the coveted Pulitzer Prize. And while he was paid a modest royalty rate for his efforts, he was never recognized for his talent as a composer like his white contemporaries of Tin Pan Alley during his lifetime. By 1916, Joplin had begun to suffer the deteriorating mental and physical effects of syphilis that he contracted in the late 1890s. In January 1917, he was hospitalized and subsequently transferred to a mental institution, where he died four months later. Joplin was buried in a simple grave at St. Michael's Cemetery in Astoria, New York. As you enter the cemetery his grave is well marked with a historical plaque on the right-hand side, fifty feet from the road.

STAN KENTON
December 15, 1911—August 25, 1979
CAUSE OF DEATH Stroke

It seems that Stan Kenton's reputation as a jazz innovator has outlived the criticism that his music was experimental at best, and pretentious at its worst. A student of piano and composition who studied under Earl "Fatha" Hines, Kenton began playing piano in the big bands of Southern California during the early 1930s. Realizing the only way to feed his creative vision was to front his own band, he auditioned his practice band (they had only been together a few months) at the Rendezvous Ballroom on Balboa Island off Newport Beach, California. Initially called Artistry in Rhythm, the band played from 1941 until 1947 as the Progressive Jazz Band, adding and adjusting instrumentation as the band's reputation grew. By 1950 he fielded one of the largest bands on the road—forty musicians including strings, congas, horns, and guitar. In addition to the large group, Kenton's band made an effort to avoid the dance halls during the tour stops to allow for the exploring of new musical (and nondanceable) territory. Not all of Kenton's experiments worked. Critics will be more than happy to point you toward the country album with Tex Ritter and the horrid concept album featuring jazz themes centered around Richard Wagner operas. Despite those (and other) failures, Kenton never stopped taking his music further into the future rather than safely repeating the past. After a year of ill health, Kenton died just days after a massive stroke and was cremated, with his ashes scattered in the rose garden at Westwood Memorial Park in Los Angeles, California. As you drive into the cemetery, park in front of the rose garden at the small church. A small nameplate adorns the memorial marker in front of the roses.

JUNIOR KIMBROUGH
July 28, 1930—January 17, 1998
CAUSE OF DEATH Heart Failure

This northern Mississippi bluesman may be remembered for his hypnotic guitar rhythms and his vocal stylings reminiscent of Bukka White and Mississippi Fred McDowell. But most

of his close friends and family around Holly Springs, Mississippi, will remember David "Junior" Kimbrough for his rollicking house parties. Born in 1930 in nearby Hudsonville, Kimbrough first recorded in 1966 and cut his first single, "Tramp," in 1968 for a local label. For the next two decades Kimbrough didn't have much opportunity to tour, so he began having house parties in his modest home in the

Mississippi hill country and playing the local juke joint circuit on weekends. In the late 1980s, Kimbrough was featured in the Delta blues documentary, *Deep Blues*, which led to a national recording contract with the Fat Possum label. In 1992, he released his first full-length album, *All Night Long*, to critical acclaim in both blues and mainstream publications. Now at age sixty, Kimbrough was in demand outside of Mississippi, playing in England, and his popular house parties had moved down the road to an old abandoned church-turned-juke joint called Junior's. Legend has it that the Rolling Stones once paid a visit to Junior's but were booed off the stage by the patrons because they just couldn't grasp the feel for the Delta blues. Whether this oft-told story is true or not, Junior's was now an institution in the hill country of northern Mississippi, with Kimbrough and his band, the Soul Blues Boys, taking the stage every Sunday afternoon he was in town. Upon his passing at the height of his popularity, he was buried in an unnamed cemetery just outside Holly Springs. Traveling north on Highway 7, turn left onto Clear Creek Road. Drive 1.1 miles to Kimbrough Church Road and then after a short distance you will see the cemetery on the left. His marker is halfway back to the side of the cemetery. Burned to the ground in 1998, Junior's has since been rebuilt at the same location on Highway 4 ten miles west of Holly Springs.

FREDDIE KING
December 15, 1911—December 28, 1976
CAUSE OF DEATH Heart Attack

Unrelated yet equally talented as Albert and B.B., Freddie King was the stylistic heir to T-Bone Walker and B. B. King. He would have been remembered as a great Texas blues guitarist had it not been for the fact that his family moved to Chicago, where he was duly influenced by Big Bill Broonzy, Elmore James, and Hound Dog Taylor. Between 1960 and 1964 he recorded over one hundred songs that, for the most part, are now considered the definitive interpretations of classic blues standards. There's hardly a bar band in Chicago that can't leave the stage without playing "Hideaway," "Goin' Down" "Palace of the King," or "I'm Tore Down." An impressive figure on stage (he was six-foot, seven-inches tall and weighed over three hundred pounds!), he could tear to pieces anyone—

including Ted Nugent and Eric Clapton—who dared challenge him with his intense, yet soulful artistry on the guitar. After a slack period in the late sixties, King came back with a vengeance with three great albums for Shelter Records and toured with the popular blues/rock singer Leon Russell. King was in the prime of his life when he suffered a heart attack during a Christmas Day Dallas concert and died shortly thereafter. He was buried just after the New Year at Hillcrest Memorial Park on Northwest Highway in Dallas, Texas. As you enter the gates, veer left at the intersection just past the office. Stay to the left past the Mother of Mary statue and drive past the large mausoleum on your right. Continue straight ahead, past the fireman statue, and head for the white boundary fence. Park thirty feet past the large aboveground Adams monument on your left (across from the Garden of Devotion). Walk through the section on your left (just to the left of the Lipscomb bench) and continue into the Garden of Prayer section, another fifty feet to Block 6, Column 35, Plot C.

PAUL KOSSOFF
September 14, 1950—August 25, 1979
CAUSE OF DEATH Cerebral and Pulmonary Edema

The late 1960s produced a number of great bands and guitarists born out of the post-British blues invasion. The era began with Eric Clapton and Cream and continued with Mick Taylor (Rolling Stones), Jeff Beck, Jimmy Page (Led Zeppelin), and Peter Green (Fleetwood Mac). Arguably one of the most talented, yet most underrated musicians to join this fraternity was Paul Kossoff and his band Free. Originating out of the same clubs that gave us Jethro Tull and Procol Harum, Free was comprised of Kossoff on guitar, Simon Kirke on drums, Paul Rodgers on vocals (Kirke and Rodgers went on to found Bad Company), and Andy Fraser on bass. After recording a couple of mediocre albums, they were able to secure the opening spot for the Blind Faith tour (featuring Eric Clapton) in 1969. The following year they released the classic album *Fire and Water*, which contained the monster FM radio hit "All Right Now." Now bona fide rock stars, Free played alongside Jimi Hendrix, the Doors, and The Who at the infamous Isle of Wight concert. Barely out of their teens and selling millions of records worldwide, the pressure to succeed was tremendous and their follow-up efforts failed to grasp airplay or sales. The band broke apart as a result in part to Kossoff's increasing drug use and inability to make concert dates and recording sessions. As rehearsal dates were being made for Kossoff's new band, Back Street Crawler, the young guitarist died on a plane en route to New York City from Los Angeles. His remains were cremated and his ashes were interred in his brother's home garden just outside London, England.

MARIO LANZA
January 31, 1921—October 7, 1959
CAUSE OF DEATH Heart Attack

Celebrated voice coach Enrico Rosati said that Lanza had one of the finest voices he had ever heard. Conductor Arturo Toscanini remarked that he possessed "the greatest voice of the twentieth century." Unfortunately the life of Mario Lanza, although exciting, was much like the operas he sang in his youth—tragic. Born into a loving family that recognized his talents at an early age, Lanza began serious musical training in his teens, only to be discovered by conductor Serge Koussevitzky, who recommended the young Lanza for a scholarship at the Berkshire Music School. He made his singing debut at the Berkshire Music Festival in 1942 and was on his way to an illustrious career when the army called. Upon discharge, he continued studying under master voice coaches and began performing solo and with the Bel Canto Trio. After a performance at the Hollywood Bowl in 1947, he was signed by Louis B. Mayer to a seven-year contract with MGM studios. His first film, released in 1949, *That Midnight Kiss*, cast Lanza as a singing truck driver—a typecast that he would never escape. The following year he starred as a singer (again!) in *Toast of New Orleans*, which yielded his first gold record, "Be My Love." It wasn't until his fourth film, *The Student Prince*, that Lanza began to run into troubles that would follow him through his career. Whether it be directors, contracts, musical control, or drugs and alcohol, Lanza never really rebounded from his career high as the star of the 1951 release *The Great Caruso*. In 1957, he moved his family to Rome, where he was treated like royalty and made numerous appearances including two films, a Royal Command Performance in England, as well as concerts in Holland, France, and Germany. Unfortunately, Lanza was missing or cancelling almost as many concert dates as he was attending. Suffering from depression, hypertension, exhaustion, and phlebitis, Lanza checked into the Valle Giulia Clinic in Rome in the fall of 1959. After a two-week stay he called his wife on October 6th, telling her that he would be coming home the next evening. He died the following morning of a massive heart attack. Ironically, he had more recording dates and concerts booked for the next year than at any time in his life. Lanza was laid to rest in Culver City, California, at the mausoleum at Holy Cross Cemetery. As you enter the grounds, drive to the back mausoleum and park near the front entry. Walk through the doors and Lanza can be found in the center of the mausoleum in Section D-2, Space B-46, with the crypt facing the entry, two rows from the left column, three rows from the floor, next to actress Joan Davis. His distraught wife died a short six months later.

NICOLETTE LARSON
July 17, 1952—December 16, 1997
CAUSE OF DEATH Complications Due to Cerebral Edema

What do you say about a vocalist who has worked with no less than Hoyt Axton, the Beach Boys, Jimmy Buffett, Commander Cody and his Lost Planet Airmen, the Dirt Band, the Doobie Brothers, Michael McDonald, and Neil Young? Well, it turns out that Nicolette Larson was more than just a celebrated backup singer. Voted *Performance* magazine's Best

Female Vocalist (1979), Best New Vocalist by both the Academy of Country Music (1984), and *Cashbox* magazine (1985), Larson found herself on the top of the charts with the definitive recording of Neil Young's "Lotta Love" and continued with a number of hits on both the country and pop charts before her death at age forty-five. Her burial was at Forest Lawn Hollywood Hill in Los Angeles, California, in the Murmuring Trees section, Plot L-7036, Space G-1.

FRANKIE LYMON
September 20, 1942—February 27, 1968
CAUSE OF DEATH Heroin Overdose

While Frankie Lymon and the Teenagers were the inspiration for other black teen groups such as the Students, the Chanters, and many of the early Motown groups, Frankie Lymon, as lead singer, teenage idol, and drug addict, became a trendsetter of a different type for musicians through the years. Formed in 1955, Frankie Lymon and the Teenagers released their first (and biggest) hit of their careers, "Why Do Fools Fall in Love," in early 1956. The record sold over 100,000 copies by the end of January and the group played their first live concert the following month, opening for Bo Diddley, Fats Domino, and the Cadillacs. In March the record went international with the song reaching number one on the charts in England—not bad for a thirteen-year-old and four high school students. Before the year ended, the group released several more singles, appeared in Alan Freed's classic teen movie *Rock, Rock, Rock!* and toured Europe, including a Royal Command Performance for England's Princess Margaret. And just as quickly as it started, it all came to a slow, painful end. After the tour overseas, Lymon was persuaded to go solo and released a couple of singles that stiffed. Likewise, the Teenagers tried a host of replacements for the diminutive soprano, but never had much luck. Lymon and the Teenagers reunited briefly for a tour in 1965, but no record deal was forthcoming and Lymon had already been arrested twice for narcotics possession with a failed stay at a drug rehab center. He died in the bathroom of his grandmother's apartment in New York in the winter of 1968—an empty syringe by his side. He was buried at St. Raymond's Cemetery in the Bronx, New York. As you drive through the gates of the cemetery, park at the St. Anthony section on the left and look toward the center of the section. Lymon's grave is visible at Range 13, Grave 70. In the early 1980s, a fight for the rights to Lymon's estate (and songwriting royalties valued at over one million dollars) began among the newly discovered Lymon widows—all three of them! The movie, *Why Do Fools Fall in Love*, was released in 1989, chronicling the personal and subsequent legal problems of the last years of Lymon's life. In 1993, Frankie Lymon and the Teenagers were inducted into the Rock and Roll Hall of Fame. Today Lewis Lymon, Frankie's brother, continues to perform and record with his own doo-wop groups in the New York area.

PHIL LYNOTT
August 20, 1949—January 4, 1986
CAUSE OF DEATH Kidney, Liver, and Heart Failure Due to Septicemia

One of the great, hard-working, twin guitar bands of the seventies, Thin Lizzy was formed and led by bassist and principal songwriter Phil Lynott. While during the band's twelve-year run, they managed to chart a few FM radio standards like "Jailbreak" and "The Boys Are Back in Town," the combination of Hendrix riffs, Celtic folk songs, and a boatload of drugs was not conducive to creating hard rock hits in the States. After Thin Lizzy broke up and Lynott's solo career floundered, his lifetime of partying caught up with him on Christmas Day, 1985, when he collapsed at his Kew, England, estate. He died after the New Year due to blood poisoning from heroin addiction. He was buried at St. Fintan's Cemetery in Sutton County, Dublin, about eight miles from the northeastern border of the town. As you enter the cemetery by the first gate, walk straight across the field to the very last section. Phillip Parris Lynott's flat memorial stone is in Row 1, Plot 13 of the St. Polans section.

KIRSTY MACCOLL
October 10, 1959—December 18, 2000
CAUSE OF DEATH Boating Accident

Ex-Pogues frontman Shane McGowan posed the question in the liner notes to the album

Galore: The Best of Kirsty MacColl, "Why is she not massively famous?" While fans in the U.K. need not respond to the query, those left in the U.S. are still pondering the question in light of the fact that she is really only known in the States as the girl who wrote Tracey Ullman's hit "They Don't Know." To add insult to injury, very little of her work can be found in print in the States even today. Fortunately, many in the music industry did not overlook her talent and she can be found on albums by groups as diverse as the Smiths, the Pogues, the Rolling Stones, Van Morrison, Talking Heads, and Simple Minds, as well as on her solo works. MacColl had just released a critically acclaimed album of acoustic Cuban-inspired music, *Tropical Brainstorm*, and was on vacation in Cozumel, Mexico, when she met her tragic end. She was swimming in the ocean with her two teenage sons when a speedboat strayed into an area reserved for swimmers. Witnesses to the tragic event attest to the fact that MacColl pushed one of her sons to safety before she was fatally struck by the boat. One year after her cremation, a bench in central London's Soho Square was dedicated in her honor.

MISSISSIPPI FRED MCDOWELL
January 12, 1904—July 3, 1972
CAUSE OF DEATH Abdominal Cancer

Unlike Muddy Waters and Elmore James, Mississippi Fred McDowell secured his reputation as a blues legend without a back catalog of historic blues recordings. Discovered by Alan Lomax in 1959, his remaining twelve years left an indelible legacy for many white blues musicians in Europe and the U.S. Born in Tennessee, tired of farm life, McDowell moved to Mississippi at a young age where he saw the great Charley Patton at a juke joint. Inspired, this self-taught guitar player wasn't discovered until 1959 at the age of fifty-five. During one of his famous trips through the South, Alan Lomax was looking for authentic American music to record for the Library of Congress. When he arrived in Como, everyone told Lomax he had to visit Fred. Lomax went over to his house that night and McDowell played nearly twelve hours—straight through the night. As he departed the next morning, Alan promised that fortune and fame would be knocking on Fred's door based on the recordings. Rightfully so, McDowell was soon heralded as the great new discovery in the blues world. Word of mouth spread quickly and a whole new world of opportunities became available. In quick succession, McDowell recorded several solo albums, toured the U.S. via bus (he absolutely hated to fly), received a standing ovation at the 1964 Newport Folk Festival, and toured Europe with the American Folk Blues Festival the following year. It was during his second solo tour of England in 1969 that Keith Richards of the Rolling Stones heard McDowell sing "You Gotta Move." Richards promptly went back to the studio to record the Rolling Stones' version for their landmark album *Sticky Fingers*. Unfortunately, due to severe stomach pains, McDowell canceled his latest tour and returned home to Mississippi in the winter of 1971. Despite an operation, Fred would never leave home again and two years later passed away from cancer. Buried in Como, Mississippi, McDowell was laid to rest in the Hammond Hill Church Cemetery. Located on an unmarked dirt road just outside of "downtown" Como off Highway 51, turn west on the dirt road when you see the sign for the church. Drive down the road about one mile and the church will be on your right. The cemetery is also on the right (just past the church), with McDowell's monument up the short hill in the back of the cemetery.

CLYDE MCPHATTER
November 15, 1932—June 13, 1972
CAUSE OF DEATH Heart Attack

One of the supremely talented New York–style R&B vocalists of the 1950s, Clyde McPhatter's gospel-rich high tenor graced many of the classic doo-wop, R&B, and pop recordings of the times. The son of a Baptist minister and a regular in the church choir, McPhatter crossed over to R&B when he joined the Dominoes in 1950. With McPhatter on lead vocals, the Dominoes exploded onto the R&B charts with "Do Something for Me" and "Have Mercy Baby." After three years and one fight too many with leader Billy Ward, McPhatter

signed with Atlantic Records and began his association with the Drifters. He charted six singles before being drafted into the army. Upon his release, he remained at Atlantic as a solo artist (the Drifters continued on with a variety of lead singers) and scored the biggest hit of his career, "A Lover's Question." Had he stayed with Atlantic, McPhatter would have been remembered as a great soul singer throughout the sixties. Rather, he chose to switch labels, where he recorded more mundane pop numbers, and wallowed in the oldies circuit until his early death from a heart attack brought on by a lifetime struggle with alcohol. McPhatter was buried at George Washington Cemetery in Paramus, New Jersey, in Block O, Lot 121, Section D, Grave 4. From the cemetery gate, drive straight ahead, turning left at the main mausoleum. Drive to the end and turn right on the border road to Block O. Count four maple trees on the left and park. Walk eleven rows into Block O to his simple bronze marker.

BLIND WILLIE MCTELL
May 5, 1901—August 19, 1959
CAUSE OF DEATH Cerebral Hemorrhage

Born at the turn of the twentieth century, Blind Willie McTell was one of the most prolific traditional blues performers of the early twentieth century. During the late 1920s and early 1930s, McTell recorded under a variety of names, including Blind Willie, Blind Sammie, Georgia Bill, and Red Hot Willie Glaze, searching for the right moniker and song combination that would make him commercially viable. Though his repertoire included blues, gospel, ragtime, pop, and country, McTell was never considered a hitmaker for the variety of labels for whom he recorded. When the Depression hit, McTell made money by traveling from Maine to Miami, performing such classics as "Statesboro Blues" (famously covered by the Allman Brothers Band) in every nightclub, fish fry, and house party that would have him. By the 1950s, McTell was relegated to the status of a blues curiosity, only recording sporadically for small private labels. He hung up his guitar for good in 1957 and became a preacher, singing only the occasional gospel number. Unfortunately, McTell didn't live long enough to witness the blues revival of the sixties and died in his hometown of Thomson, Georgia. He was buried at the Jones Grove Baptist Church just outside Thomson. From the center of his hometown, take I-17 south seven miles and turn right on Happy Valley Road (at the Happy Valley store). Drive just under two miles and the church and adjoining small cemetery will be on the right. McTell's grave is five rows from the entrance to the church.

SAMUEL "MAGIC SAM" MAGHETT
February 14, 1936—December 1, 1969
CAUSE OF DEATH Heart Attack

A Chicago blues musician in the style of Otis Rush and Buddy Guy, Magic Sam was a gifted singer, songwriter, and guitarist who was a major influence on Chicago musicians during the fifties. His two original albums on Delmark, *West Side Soul* and *Black Magic*, are considered classic Chicago West Side sound blues without peer. After moving from his hometown in Mississippi to Chicago, he initially worked and recorded with singer and harmonica player Walter "Shakey Jake" Horton. After a year in the army, he returned to Chicago and established himself as a West Side club regular until his two albums for Delmark revitalized his career. His final year of life looked promising—a new recording contract, a new album, and a tour in Europe—but a heart attack took him away. He is buried (along with 90 percent of all Chicago bluesmen) at Restvale Cemetery in Chicago, Illinois. From the entrance on Laramie, drive up to the office and park. Walk around to the right side of the office and count two rows past the end of the office from the section across the road. Walk down that row to the middle of Section D. He is buried in Section D Lot 106, Grave 3 next to the Grahmn monument and a stone's throw from the newly marked Hound Dog Taylor grave.

HENRY MANCINI
April 16, 1924—June 14, 1994
CAUSE OF DEATH Cancer

One of Hollywood's most prolific composers, Henry Mancini enjoyed a five-decade career in an industry not known for longevity. A gifted piano player schooled at Juilliard, Mancini began his life as an arranger after he sent a couple of sample charts to Benny Goodman. He worked with Goodman for a short while before serving in the military during World War II. Working with the rearranged Glenn Miller Orchestra after the war, Mancini was given a two-week work assignment in Hollywood scoring for an Abbott and Costello movie. He continued with Universal Studios as a staff arranger/composer and received his first Academy Award nomination for *The Glenn Miller Story*. Injecting elements of jazz into the staid, traditional orchestral music used in sound tracks, Mancini quickly developed a name and reputation that often not only put movies on the map to success, but also helped establish the growing sound track album sales category by the charting of several of his movie theme instrumentals. Nominations, awards, and record sales began to flow unabated with the songs "Theme to Peter Gunn," "Charade," "Dear Heart," "Moon River" (with Johnny Mercer), and his most popular theme, "The Pink Panther." When all was said and done, Mancini was nominated for eighteen Oscars (winning four), won twenty Grammy Awards, received two Emmys, and released over fifty albums during his lifetime. Before his passing in 1994, he published his autobiography, *Did They Mention the Music?* Upon passing, he was cremated, with the ashes returned to the family.

STEVE MARRIOTT
January 30, 1947—April 20, 1991
CAUSE OF DEATH House Fire

As a singer, songwriter, and consummate blues-rock guitarist, Steve Marriott was often reported to be the first
choice to replace departing members of many super-
groups of the seventies, like the Rolling Stones and Led
Zeppelin. Marriott first shot to fame in the mid-sixties
with the group the Small Faces (featuring Ronnie Lane)
with the hits "Lazy Sunday" and "Itchykoo Park." But
Marriott left the group, disillusioned over the screaming
girls and pinup status of the band (Rod Stewart came in
and the band went on to become Rod Stewart and the
Faces). Marriott's next project included Spooky Tooth
bass player Greg Ridley and a young guitarist named
Peter Frampton. Humble Pie was quickly formed and though album sales were slow, the
band became the "must-see" live act on the road. In May 1971, the band released
Performance: Rockin' the Fillmore, which went on to sell two million albums within the
year. Capturing the raw energy of their live shows, combined with the hard rock
approach to their earlier releases, the band were now considered bona fide rock stars in
the U.S. Frampton left shortly thereafter, with Humble Pie soldiering on on the road and
in the studio. After twenty tours and eight studio albums in less than six years, the band
broke apart under a haze of exhaustion and rampant drug use. Marriott continued to
record and re-form bands throughout the remainder of his career, although he would
never regain the past glory of his Small Faces and Humble Pie years. In late 1990,
Marriott received a visit from Frampton, during which they began to write and record a
set of new material with an eye on re-forming Humble Pie. After a six-week visit in L.A.
with Frampton the following year, Marriott flew back home to England. Jet-lagged and
exhausted, he made it home only to be discovered in the early-morning hours by the fire
department, dead of smoke inhalation from a house fire started from a smoldering cigarette. Along with Marriott, twenty-five years of rock 'n' roll memorabilia was lost in the
fire. Shortly after a memorial service and disposition of his cremated remains, an autopsy report suggested that Marriott probably would not have survived the night given the
levels of alcohol, cocaine, and sedatives in his bloodstream.

CURTIS MAYFIELD
June 3, 1945—December 26, 1999
CAUSE OF DEATH Long-term Effects of Paralysis

As a member of the Impressions and as a solo artist, composer, songwriter, and singer,
Curtis Mayfield was one of the most influential individuals in soul music during the sixties
and seventies. Initially a self-taught guitarist from Chicago, Mayfield first began his musical journey as a founding member of the Alphatones. Joining forces with three members
of the Roosters to become the Impressions in 1956, they charted their first hit, "For Your
Precious Love," two years later. Infused with a mixture of gospel harmonies, Jamaican
rhythms, and Chicago soul, Mayfield continued through much of the sixties, charting
eighteen hits for the group, including "It's All Right," "Woman's Got Soul," and "Gypsy
Woman." In 1970, Mayfield left the Impressions and he created his own record label and
began writing, arranging, and producing a host of other artists. He released two successful solo albums when he was approached by film producer Sig Shore to create the score for
his latest movie. In time *Superfly*, proved to be one of the most successful sound tracks and

black action movies in the history of film. Receiving four Grammy nominations and a gold record for his efforts, Mayfield was now a star in his own right and continued recording solo albums and working with such artists as Aretha Franklin, Gladys Knight and the Pips, and the Staple Singers. The 1980s proved to be an equally productive decade with more hits, a heavy touring schedule in the U.S., Europe, and Japan, and the occasional reunion tour with the Impressions. Mayfield's world changed in one tragic moment when before an outdoor concert in Brooklyn, New York, a lighting rig came crashing down on the singer, damaging his spine and leaving him a quadriplegic. He lived quietly in Atlanta, Georgia, during the nineties with his wife and ten children. In 1994, he received a Grammy Legend Award and one year later received a Grammy Lifetime Achievement Award. In March 1999, Mayfield was inducted into the Rock and Roll Hall of Fame, but was too ill to attend the ceremony. He died quietly in his sleep nine months later and his cremated remains were returned to his family.

THE MC5
ROB TYNER
December 12, 1944—September 18, 1991
CAUSE OF DEATH Heart Attack

FRED "SONIC" SMITH
September 13, 1949—November 4, 1994
CAUSE OF DEATH Heart Failure

Originally formed in Detroit as the Motor City Five, the MC5 held the spotlight briefly on the late sixties national music scene as a counterculture, high-energy rock 'n' roll band that would later be elevated to cult status by the punk movement. In the beginning, with Tyner on vocals and Smith on rhythm guitar, the MC5 started as a house band at Detroit's Grande Ballroom for John Sinclair's White Panther Party. Appearing onstage wearing American flags and shouting profanities and anti-everything slogans between songs, the group was signed to Elektra after a performance at the 1968 Democratic Convention. They released their controversial first album, *Kick Out the Jams*, in which profanities could be clearly heard and understood. Elektra quickly dropped the group and the album from their catalog (they re-released the album fifteen years later) and the group signed with Atlantic after Sinclair was jailed on drug charges. Disillusioned with the revolutionary/political aspect of the music, they returned with a new album in 1970 called *Back in the USA* and toured the U.S. and Europe extensively. But after three albums and no sales, the band broke up and continued with minor projects, never able to translate their cult status into rock 'n' roll success. Upon his passing, Tyner was buried at Roseland Cemetery in Berkeley, Michigan. As you drive into the cemetery entrance, turn left at the third section and Tyner's monument is on the left. Upon his passing, Fred "Sonic" Smith was cremated.

JOHNNY MERCER
November 18, 1909—June 25, 1976
CAUSE OF DEATH Brain Tumor

As singer, actor, lyricist, and composer, Johnny Mercer is credited with over one thousand songs covered by no less than Frank Sinatra, Billie Holiday, Bing Crosby, and Judy Garland during a career that spanned nearly fifty years. Beginning his career as a vocalist for the Paul Whiteman Orchestra, he later sang with the Rhythm Boys (with Bing Crosby) and

then later moved over to the Benny Goodman radio show, *The Camel Caravan*, as the featured vocalist. He cowrote the lyrics for his first musical in 1940, which began a long career of penning both lyrics and music for a number of Broadway shows, movies, and popular recordings, including "Jeepers Creepers," "That Old Black Magic," "On the Atchison, Topeka, and the Santa Fe," and his best-known number, "Moon River" (with Henry Mancini). All told, he collaborated with Jerome Kern, Jimmy Van Heusen, Hoagy Carmichael, Harold Warren, and Michel Legrand and won four Academy Awards for Best Song. In his spare time he also founded Capitol Records in 1942 with two partners, and with Mercer serving as president, the company sold over forty million records a year by 1946. He continued his work as a composer and lyricist up until his death. Having never recovered from an operation on a brain tumor, Mercer's remains were returned to his hometown of Savannah, Georgia, and buried in the family plot at Bonaventure Cemetery. As you enter the cemetery, drive on Bay Street to the end and turn left. Turn right onto Mass Street, then left on Bonaventure, driving until it ends. The Mercer family plot is in Section H, shaded by a large oak tree with two smaller date palms lying within the low, granite curbstone. His boyhood home in Savannah still stands at 226 East Gwinnett Street and a modest collection of his memorabilia can be found at the Georgia Music Hall of Fame in Macon, Georgia.

ETHEL MERMAN
January 16, 1909—February 15, 1984
CAUSE OF DEATH Natural Causes

A symbol of Broadway during her time, Ethel Merman was known as one of the hardest-working, most flamboyant, demanding, and professional voices that graced the musical stage. Possessing a rich and powerful voice, there was no need for hidden microphones for Merman, with her dead-on delivery of every note making her the darling of composers Cole Porter, Irving Berlin, and George Gershwin. Her booming voice was first heard in 1930 when Merman sang her trademark number, "I've Got Rhythm," by Gershwin. She continued in

thirteen Broadway shows during her twenty-nine-year run with Broadway standards like "I Get a Kick Out of You," "You're the Top," "Take a Chance," and "You're Just in Love." In 1959, her run on Broadway had stopped, but she continued on, appearing in fourteen films, including a humorous parody of herself in *Airplane*, as well as hosting her own radio show. A year before she died, she remarked, "Broadway has been very good to me—but then, I've been very good to Broadway." Upon her passing, she was cremated and her remains were allegedly scattered along Broadway in New York City.

ROGER MILLER

January 2, 1936—October 25, 1992

CAUSE OF DEATH Lung Cancer

Singer, songwriter, guitarist, and Broadway musical composer, Roger Miller was one of the most durable and successful country artists during the sixties. A dropout before he even made it to high school, Miller served in the military, ultimately transferring to Atlanta, Georgia, where he played in a service country band. Moving to Nashville, Miller became a bellhop at the Andrew Jackson Hotel, where he hustled gigs playing with Minnie Pearl and Faron Young. His first taste of success came in 1957 when he had two of his songs recorded by George Jones and Jimmy Dean. Finding work in Nashville was difficult, so Miller moved down to Texas, where he continued to write during the slow times at the fire department where he worked. Eventually he was recognized as the hottest songwriter in country music, with songs covered by Ernest Tubb, Jim Reeves, and Porter Wagoner. When he moved from RCA to Smash Records, the hits really came out. Miller released his three biggest hits, "Dang Me," "Chug-a-lug," and "King of the Road," all within a two-year period in the mid-sixties. For the next four years, Roger Miller was truly the King of the Road as he traveled around the country, making concert appearances and collecting music awards, magazine covers, and his own short-lived television show. However, by the 1970s, his star began to fade as his folksy musings and novelty songs began to grow tired. It wasn't until twelve years later that Miller had another hit when he teamed together with Ray Price and Willie Nelson on the album *Old Friends*. In 1984 he was contacted by the Broadway producer of *Big River* (the award-winning adaptation of Mark Twain's *The Adventures of Huckleberry Finn*) and was given the task of producing the musical score for the show. Miller pored over the project for two years, and when the play hit the stage, the show won seven Tony Awards, including one for Miller for Best Score. Sadly in 1990, Miller learned he had lung cancer and began treatments in Los Angeles, California. Although his disease fell into remission, it came back with a vengeance and he died in the hospital. Miller was cremated, with his ashes returned to his wife and children. In Erick, Oklahoma, they have begun a fund-raiser to start a Roger Miller Museum. Unfortunately, due to lack of funding and interest, the museum has yet to open.

THE MILLS BROTHERS

JOHN MILLS SR.
February 11, 1882—December 8, 1967
CAUSE OF DEATH Natural Causes

JOHN MILLS JR.
October 11, 1910—January 24, 1936
CAUSE OF DEATH Pneumonia

HERBERT MILLS
April 2, 1912—April 12, 1989
CAUSE OF DEATH Pneumonia

HARRY MILLS
August 19, 1913—June 28, 1982
CAUSE OF DEATH Diabetes

DONALD MILLS
April 29, 1915—November 13, 1999
CAUSE OF DEATH Pneumonia

They began their singing career in the small town of Piqua, Ohio, with the brothers ranging from seven to ten years of age. In the nearly sixty years in the spotlight, the Mills

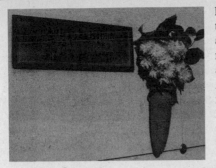

Brothers (and their father) produced over two thousand recordings, sold nearly fifty million albums, appeared in more than ten feature movies, were rewarded with thirty-six gold albums, and ended their career with a Grammy Award for Lifetime Achievement. Originally formed as a quartet when the youngest, Donald Mills, was only seven, in just three short years the group was performing on radio in nearby Cincinnati, and by the late 1920s they were heard nationwide from New York City on CBS.

Performing alongside Bing Crosby and Kate Smith, the Mills Brothers cut their first hit, "Nobody's Sweetheart," in 1931 that went on to sell over a million copies. Two years later they were featured in their first film, *The Big Broadcast*, in 1932, with George Burns and Gracie Allen. After several other films, they expanded their audience to the U.K., and throughout the 1930s through the 1950s the Mills Brothers were synonymous with smooth, sweet harmonies coupled with popular songs of the times. More than just singers, they were also known for the "bass" and "trumpet" accompaniment on their records (even though the only actual instrument was a guitar). They were also among the first black groups to cross racial lines, playing for both blacks and whites in the same audience, as well as for kings and queens around the world. Although the eldest brother died suddenly at a young age, the remaining brothers and their father lived long and healthy lives. John Mills Sr. retired in the 1950s and the brothers carried on as a trio. Upon his passing, John Mills Sr. was buried with his first son at Bellefontaine Cemetery in Bellefontaine, Ohio, in Section 4, Lot 586 between two pine trees. Harry was the first of the trio to succumb and was buried at Forest Lawn Hollywood Hills in Los Angeles, California. As you drive through the gates of the cemetery, take the first left and weave around to the large outdoor mausoleum area. Harry is located in the interior wall in Crypt 3446 in the Court of Remembrance (three rows from the bottom). Herbert was cremated and his ashes scattered at a private memorial, while Donald joined his younger brother Harry at Forest Lawn Hollywood Hills in the mausoleum. Donald can also be found in the Court of Remembrance, but you will need to walk around to the Columbarium of Radiant Dawn. His small niche marker is located directly across from the opening, five spaces from the right wall, seven spaces from the floor (next to popular actor Forrest Tucker, best known as Sgt. Morgan O'Rourke in the TV series *F Troop*).

CHARLES MINGUS
April 22, 1922—January 5, 1979
CAUSE OF DEATH Amyotrophic Lateral Sclerosis

A talented pianist, bandleader, jazz composer, and a virtuoso on the bass, Charles Mingus was one of the most important figures of American music in the mid-twentieth century. Although he formally studied the double bass and composition from the masters of his time, Mingus grew both personally and professionally from playing and touring with the grand masters Kid Ory, Barney Bigard, the Louis Armstrong Orchestra, Lionel Hampton, and the Red Norvo Trio. But unlike most bassists, Mingus became a leader of the jazz movement during and after the 1940s bebop era. Settling in New York, he quickly made a name for himself working as a sideman, recording and performing with Charlie Parker, Miles Davis, Art Tatum, and Duke Ellington. But fans and fellow musicians agree—Mingus was at his best as a soloist. In the 1950s, he formed his own publishing company and recording label to protect his interests as his repertoire of original music and scores grew. With the 1950s recognized as the high point of his career, he played and recorded on over 150 albums and wrote well over double the amount of original music. Albums such as *Pithecanthropus Erectus, East Coasting, Tijuana Moods,* and *Duke's Choice* all featured complex creativity and arresting solos. Mingus was considered no less a genius overseas as he traveled and played in Japan, Europe, Canada, South America, as well as in the U.S. In the 1960s, Mingus began his collaboration with Eric Dolphy and continued his prodigious output. It was during the 1970s when his travel schedule intensified that Mingus began to suffer financial, physical, and psychological problems. Mingus gladly accepted a Guggenheim Fellowship in composition in 1971 that coincided with the release of his autobiography, *Beneath the Underdog.* Mingus also received grants from the National Endowment for the Arts and the Smithsonian Institute that complemented his honorary degrees from Brandeis and Yale universities. By the mid-seventies Lou Gehrig's disease began to take its toll on his body and he was confined to a wheelchair. Unable to write, he began to record his thoughts and music exclusively on tape. Upon his death in Cuernavaca, Mexico, he was cremated, with his ashes spread in the Ganges River.

THELONIOUS MONK
October 10, 1917—February 17, 1982
CAUSE OF DEATH Stroke

Neglected by jazz audiences throughout the forties, Thelonious nevertheless became a central figure in the development of bebop. More advanced harmonically and rhythmically than his contemporaries, he has influenced hundreds of jazz musicians—pianists and others alike. Influenced by Fats Waller and Earl "Fatha" Hines, Monk made his recording debut in 1941 accompanying Charlie Christian. During the next thirty-five years he played with Sonny Rollins, Max Roach, Art Blakey, John Coltrane, and dozens of other groundbreaking jazz legends. He made a world tour with Gillespie's Giants of Jazz in 1971, but his musical activities were curtailed by a stroke. He gave his last performance in 1976 and died six years later in his New York apartment. His last known address is now Ferncliff Cemetery in Hartsdale, New York. From the Secor Road entrance, take the first entrance to the cemetery. Take the driveway past the front of the mausoleum and turn right on the first road that goes alongside the mausoleum. Go to the Hillcrest Section I. The grave is located in the third row and fifth marker up toward the circle turnaround. His grave is directly opposite Grave 305. In a fitting tribute to his genius, shortly after his death the Thelonious Monk Institute of Jazz in New York City was created to promote jazz education and to train and encourage new generations of musicians.

WES MONTGOMERY
March 6, 1925—June 15, 1968
CAUSE OF DEATH Heart Attack

Guitar historians can easily trace a line through all the major influential artists from Lonnie Johnson to Eddie Lang, Charlie Christian and Django Reinhardt. Often that line of brilliance ends at Wes Montgomery. Noted for his incredible single-note runs using his thumb (versus finger picking or strumming), his style of jazz guitar was relaxed, unencumbered, yet full of beauty and genius. A self-taught guitarist (he never did learn to read music), Montgomery spent most of the late forties and early fifties in relative obscurity playing first with his brothers, Monk and Buddy, and later for Lionel Hampton. It wasn't until one night in 1959, while performing in a small jazz club in his hometown of Indianapolis, that Montgomery's life would change

forever. Jazz artist Cannonball Adderley sat at the table in front of the future jazz legend and was in such awe of Montgomery's style, phrasing, and technique that Adderley called his friends at Riverside Records to sign the guitarist. Within the next year, Riverside recorded a series of groundbreaking albums, including *Guitar on the Go!* and *Incredible Jazz Guitar of Wes Montgomery*, that catapulted Montgomery to international recognition. After considerable touring and an offer to play with John Coltrane on a permanent basis (Montgomery declined), he returned to play in small clubs in Indianapolis to be closer to his family. But despite the low profile, Montgomery released several more albums and guested on others and was awarded the *Downbeat* Critic's Poll Award for Best Jazz Guitarist in 1960, '61, '62, and '63. Though he moved toward more commercial adaptations of pop songs, he continued to receive praise from fans and critics alike, including two more *Downbeat* Poll Awards and a Grammy award. But the strain of touring and a weak heart had taken their toll on his health. One afternoon in June 1968, after coming off the road with his quintet, Montgomery suffered a fatal heart attack and died in his wife's arms. He was buried at New Crown Cemetery in Indianapolis, Indiana. Upon entering the cemetery drive straight ahead to Section 21 and turn right to Montgomery Road. Turn left to Section 20 and the grave is the ninth space from the corner in the third row. After his death, his custom-made Gibson L5 guitars were sold to private collectors; however, they occasionally can be seen during special exhibitions at the Country Music Hall of Fame in Nashville, Tennessee, and the traveling Gibson guitar exhibits.

ROBERT NIGHTHAWK
November 30, 1909—November 5, 1967
CAUSE OF DEATH Congestive Heart Failure

Taught guitar by his cousin Houston Stackhouse, Robert Nighthawk (born Robert Lee McCullum) was considered the premier blues slide guitarist during the Chicago blues boom of the fifties and early sixties. Unfortunately, during his lifetime Nighthawk never received the recognition that his predecessors Elmore James, Muddy Waters, and B. B. King enjoyed. Born in Helena, Arkansas, Nighthawk first learned blues harp in his teens before asking Stackhouse to teach him guitar. Nighthawk learned three Tommy Johnson tunes (Johnson had taught Stackhouse guitar) and soon after he began traveling throughout the South, playing house rent parties and fish fries. He began meeting the likes of Robert Johnson, Will Shade, and Charley Patton as he made his rounds in juke joints scattered around the farms of Mississippi. A good friend of Muddy Waters before Waters could even pluck a note, Nighthawk played at the reception for Muddy's first wedding. Recording sporadically and his dislike of Chicago relegated the talented slide guitarist to a footnote in blues lore. When he died in a local Helena hospital, he was buried in an unmarked grave at Magnolia Cemetery in Helena. And while a stone at the front entrance pays tribute to the mysterious blues master, his exact grave location is unknown due to lost cemetery records.

HARRY NILSSON
June 15, 1941—January 15, 1994
CAUSE OF DEATH Heart Attack

A leading pop songwriter first, and a performer a distant second, Harry Nilsson never was able to fully develop his talent and instead was more widely regarded for his erratic rock 'n' roll lifestyle. Nilsson began writing songs in the early sixties while working in the computer department of a large California bank. After struggling for five years, he sold the songs "Paradise" and "Here I Sit" to Phil Spector and the Ronettes. He signed a recording contract with RCA after he sold another song to the Monkees and yet another song to the fledgling Yardbirds. In 1967, he released the critically acclaimed album *The Pandemonium Shadow Show*, showcasing his three-octave range while still working at the bank. The album did not go unnoticed by the Beatles and soon Nilsson became good friends with the Fab Four. Nilsson scored his first Top 10 hit with "Everybody's Talkin'," the theme from the movie *Midnight Cowboy*, ironically enough written by someone else. In 1971, he scored big with his most commercially successful album *Nilsson Schmilsson*, which included the emotive ballad "Without You" (later covered by Badfinger) and the harder-edged "Jump into the Fire." But much of Nilsson's problems began with the infamous yearlong "lost weekend" with John Lennon during Lennon's split with Yoko Ono. The yearlong session of drinking and debauchery stayed with Nilsson the rest of his life. Another blow came when, after Lennon offered to produce Nilsson's next album, Nilsson lost the upper register of his voice for much of the recording sessions. Failing in health during the nineties, Nilsson passed away of a massive heart attack just two days after putting the final vocal tracks down on his last album. He was buried at Valley Oaks Memorial Park in Westlake Village, California, in the Garden of Gethsemane, Plot 830, Grave A.

BRAD NOWELL
February 22, 1968—May 25, 1996
CAUSE OF DEATH Heroin Overdose

In the world of punk, it is sometimes hard to find multitalented artists. Brad Nowell was one of them. Nowell was the talented guitarist and frontman for Sublime who successfully mixed reggae, punk, rock, hip-hop, dub, and blues into a genre of ska not heard then or since his passing. Formed in 1988 with some friends from Long Beach, California, Sublime soon became the band everyone loved to hate, but always wanted to play at their party. They made a name for themselves by playing every backyard party in Southern California in exchange for beer and pot. With no record deal, they recorded their first CD, *40 oz. to*

Freedom, which they sold from the trunk of their car at parties. Selling over fifty thousand copies within the first six months, Sublime by then had graduated to the club circuit. It was also during this time that Nowell began experimenting with heroin to boost his creativity. In 1995, they signed their long-sought-after record deal with MCA and began recording their first "official" release, *Sublime*. On May 18th of the following year, Nowell married his longtime girlfriend and two days later Sublime began their first major national tour. After the fourth show of the tour, Nowell was found dead of an overdose in his hotel room. He was buried at Westminster Memorial Park in Westminster, California, in the Ivy Block 31, Section 112, Space 1, two rows from Shakespeare Drive between the third and fourth tree on the road. Within the first year of his death, Sublime went on to sell over three million albums. Nowell was now officially a rock star.

PHIL OCHS
December 19, 1940—April 9, 1976
CAUSE OF DEATH Suicide

Much like Woody Guthrie, folksinger Phil Ochs was as much a critic as he was a fan of America. Oddly enough, Ochs's musical career did not start in the nightclubs and coffee-houses one associates with folksingers, but rather with the Columbus, Ohio, Capital University Conservatory of Music as the lead chair on the clarinet. In 1958, he enrolled in Columbus University but dropped out four months later to pursue his dream of becoming a singer in Florida. After a couple of odd jobs, an arrest for vagrancy, and a healthy dose of reality, Ochs returned to Ohio with his family and re-enrolled in college. In college Ochs became more politically involved and began writing and performing with a small duo. In 1961, Ochs got the break he was looking for when the Smothers Brothers saw him play in a small coffeehouse in Cleveland and he was asked to open for the popular duo. He spent the next ten years as one of the finest folk-singers of his generation. The best of his early protest songs include "Draft Dodger Rag" and the Joan Baez hit "There but for Fortune." But as the liberal climate changed, coupled with a near-fatal attack in Africa that left him unable to sing, Ochs's popularity began to slide. He tried desperately to attract a new audi-ence with covers of Buddy Holly and Elvis songs, but the obvious ploy did not register with the public. In 1976, after a sustained bout of depression coupled with writer's block, Ochs hung himself at his sister's home in Far Rockaway, New York. Per his wishes his final remains were cremated, with his ashes scattered in Scotland.

KID ORY
December 25, 1886—January 23, 1973
CAUSE OF DEATH Natural Causes

If Edward "Kid" Ory wasn't the most famous trad jazz New Orleans–style trombone player ever to blow the horn, then he certainly played with some of the most famous musicians ever. Forming his first band in 1913, he recruited Johnny Dodds, Sidney Bechet, Joseph "King" Oliver, Jimmie Noone, and a very young Louis Armstrong. After six years in New Orleans he moved to Southern California for health reasons and formed his own Sunshine Orchestra. It was with the Sunshine Orchestra in 1922 that Kid Ory became the first

black musician to cut a jazz record. He went on to work with King Oliver, Dave Peyton, Clarence Black, and Mutt Carey, and was featured in Louis Armstrong's infamous Hot Five band that cut Ory's composition "Muskrat Ramble" and "Heebie Jeebies." For almost ten years in the 1930s he dropped out of music to run a chicken ranch with his brother, but in 1942 he was back with the Barney Bigard Combo and played briefly with Bunk Johnson. Poor health in the 1950s forced Ory to limit his performances and he can be seen in many music-related movies from that era (playing himself in the band sequences). Opening his own club in San Francisco, Ory could be seen playing live during the early sixties and he made his final performance at the New Orleans Jazz Festival in 1971. He died two years later at the age of eighty-six in Hawaii and was buried in Culver City, California, at Holy Cross Cemetery. As you enter the cemetery, turn left and drive past the former office up the hill and you will see the grotto cave on your left. Park about thirty rows downhill from the caves. Ory's simple monument is in the second row from the curb.

CHRISTA PAFFGEN AKA NICO
October 16, 1938—July 18, 1988
CAUSE OF DEATH Cerebral Hemorrhage Following a Bicycle Accident

Better known as Nico, the German-born model and chanteuse began her musical career with the Velvet Underground in 1965. Already considered a successful model and budding film actress in Europe, Nico was looking more to the U.S. to start fresh as an unknown singer. She cut a single, "The Last Mile"/"I'm Not Saying," with producer Jimmy Page, after arriving in New York City. She caught the attention of Bob Dylan, who wrote a song for her, as well as modern artist Andy Warhol. Nico gravitated toward Warhol and the Factory (a loose collection of artists, singers, and hangers-on), who persuaded the Velvet Underground to allow Nico to sing with the band. The result was the 1967 release *The Velvet Underground and Nico*, as well as a whole lot of frustration toward the demanding singer. Nico departed the Velvet Underground shortly after and worked with arranger and producer John Cale in conjunction with her solo works. As the sixties came to a close, and with the deaths of friends Jim Morrison and Brian Jones, Nico moved back to Europe to begin a two-decade descent into heroin addiction. Always searching for that one big hit, Nico experimented with a wide range within the dance and rock genres, but her fading vocal qualities and unpredictable, unprofessional behavior relegated her to occasional club dates and forgettable albums. In 1988, while staying at her home in Ibiza, she was discovered unconscious alongside a road. Whether she fell off her bicycle or suffered a heart attack is still up for debate. Nonetheless, Nico died several days later in the hospital. She was buried in Grunewald Forest Cemetery, a small cemetery within the Grunewald Forest in Berlin, Germany. Nico's black, marble monument that she shares with her mother can be found just a couple of rows to the left as you enter the cemetery.

JOHN PANOZZO
September 20, 1948—July 16, 1996
CAUSE OF DEATH Gastrointestinal Hemorrhage
Due to Chronic Alcoholism

Drummer and founding member of America's leading exponent of pompous theater rock, Styx, John Panozzo provided the churning rhythms that made Styx one of the top stadium acts in the late 1970s. Born just twenty minutes after his twin brother bassist Chuck, the brothers first formed Tradewinds with songwriter and neighbor Dennis DeYoung in 1968. They changed their name and released their first album in 1968, but struck Top 10 gold when the single "Lady" from their fifth album

Equinox was released in 1975. By now the young guitarist Tommy Shaw had joined the band and their 1977 release, *Grand Illusion*, put the band solidly into the stadium-level tour schedule, much like Foreigner and Peter Frampton. With hits like "Come Sail Away," "Babe," and "Too Much Time on My Hands" and a mix of theatrical elements infused with state-of-the-art light shows, Styx was a hard act to follow from 1979 to 1981. After the lukewarm response to *Kilroy Was Here* (featuring the annoying "Mr. Roboto"), the band took what was to be a short hiatus that extended seven years before they reunited in the early 1990s. Though Panozzo continued to be the only drummer Styx has ever known, he was too weak to join the band during their tour in 1995. He passed away quietly and was buried in a private ceremony at Holy Sepulchre Catholic Cemetery in Worth, Illinois. As you enter the cemetery, take the first road just to the left of the center road leading into the cemetery. Drive approximately 200 feet and park just past the large Kuhn mausoleum on your left. Walk six rows into Section 19 and Panozzo's unmarked grave is just to the left of the Rogers memorial in Block 15, Lot 24, Grave 1.

FELIX PAPPALARDI
1939—April 17, 1983
CAUSE OF DEATH Murdered

Formed in the void left by the disbanding of the supergroup Cream, Mountain was the bombastic rock quartet featuring Corky Laing on drums, Leslie West on guitar, Steve Knight on organ, and Felix Pappalardi on bass. Born in New York, Pappalardi first made a name for himself in the Greenwich Village folk scene of the early 1960s. As a backing guitarist and producer for such artists as Joan Baez, Tom Rush, the Lovin' Spoonful, and Tim Hardin, Pappalardi graduated

to the big leagues when he was asked to produce Cream (featuring Eric Clapton, Ginger Baker, and Jack Bruce) on their next album. The result was the gold record *Disraeli Gears* and international recognition. In 1969, after producing West's solo album, Mountain was formed and quickly rose to the top with a triumphant performance at the original Woodstock Festival followed by the hit song "Mississippi Queen." The band continued for two more years and two more albums before Pappalardi, plagued by hearing problems due to the excessive volume onstage, left the band to continue studio work. He returned briefly in 1974 for a Mountain reunion, but the following year all the members left to pursue mediocre solo careers. In 1983, after a heated argument with his wife, Gail Collins, Pappalardi was found dead at their fifth floor apartment at 30 Waterside Plaza on 28th Street in New York City. When police arrived at the apartment, they said they found the musician lying on the bed in his underwear, a single bullet in the neck, and a .38-caliber derringer lying next to the body. Refusing all questions at the scene, Collins was charged with second-degree murder and criminal possession of a weapon. And while she was later only found guilty of the lesser charge of criminally negligent homicide, the trial judge was so disgusted with the verdict that he lectured the courtroom before sentencing Collins to the maximum of four years allowed by law. Pappalardi was buried in a private ceremony in the neighboring Bronx at Woodlawn Cemetery in the Cliff Plot, two rows from the road, and thirty-three spaces from the corner at the top of the hill.

ART PEPPER
September 1, 1925—June 15, 1982
CAUSE OF DEATH Cerebral Hemorrhage

If he had not spent almost ten years in prison between 1953 through 1966, jazz saxophonist Art Pepper would probably stand alongside Coltrane and Lester Young as one of the great jazz artists of his time. As it stands, after drug rehabilitation in the early 1970s, Pepper redeemed himself nicely through the remainder of his career. Born in Los Angeles, California, Pepper began playing professionally while still in his teens on Central Avenue in Los Angeles, jamming with primarily all-black groups, such as the Lee Young Sextet. He briefly played with Shorty Rogers and His Giants, Benny Carter, and the Stan Kenton Orchestra before serving in the army in the mid-forties. After freelancing in both Europe and back in the States, Pepper rejoined Kenton for five years, playing some of his most passionate, emotive solos with the group. He went solo in 1952, but his demons (primarily heroin, pills, and alcohol) got the better of him and his musical career took a backseat to his prison career at San Quentin. He only recorded twice between 1961 and 1975, briefly playing with Buddy Rich before taking the cure and beginning his slow comeback in 1975. He appeared at the Newport Jazz Festival in 1977, later doing full tours of the East Coast, Europe, and Japan to great acclaim. Upon his passing he was interred at Hollywood Forever in Hollywood, California, in the Abbey of the Psalms mausoleum on the bottom row, eighteen spaces from the side entrance on the right.

CARL PERKINS
April 9, 1932—January 19, 1998
CAUSE OF DEATH Complications from Stroke

While there are those who consider Carl Perkins a one-hit wonder, the less ignorant of the masses has come to remember Perkins as the quintessential rockabilly singer, songwriter, guitarist, and musician. As the author of the classic "Blue Suede Shoes," Perkins wrote songs for Johnny Cash, Patsy Cline, and the Judds, in addition to influencing artists ranging from the Beatles to the Stray Cats. Born to sharecroppers in a one-room shack shared by his mom, dad, and two brothers, Perkins began playing a secondhand guitar before the age of ten. While in his teens, he recruited his two brothers, Jay and Clayton, to form the Perkins Brothers Band. After an audition with Sam Phillips at Sun Records in Memphis, they changed the structure of the band from Ernest Tubb–style country and instead

brought the focus to Carl's singing, guitar playing, and songs. Four short months later they released their first single "Turn Around," but it was the next single, "Blue Suede Shoes," that produced not only a huge hit on the pop and country charts, but also Sun's first million-selling record (earning the band twenty thousand dollars a week in royalties for several months!). Ready to parlay the hit into international fame, the band was traveling to New York City for an appearance on *The Perry Como Show* when their car slammed into the back of a poultry truck, putting Carl and Jay into the hospital, where Carl watched as Elvis Presley stole the fame by showcasing the song on national TV and radio. And while Perkins never achieved the fame that "Shoes" provided, he continued to write, perform, and record over the next thirty-five years, accumulating a number of hits and election into the Rock and Roll Hall of Fame in the mid-eighties. Today he is interred in the mausoleum at Ridgeview Cemetery in Jackson, Tennessee, third row from the bottom in the center of the left-most outdoor mausoleum. His first guitar can be seen at the Memphis Rock 'n' Soul Museum on the second floor of the new Gibson guitar factory, just one block south of Beale Street.

LONESOME DAVE PEVERETT
April 16, 1943—February 7, 2000
CAUSE OF DEATH Kidney Cancer

There was nary a male teenager in America in 1975 who didn't play air guitar to "Slow Ride." And it was all due to one of the hardest-working musicians in the business—Lonesome Dave Peverett, founding member, lead singer, and guitarist for the seminal seventies stadium band Foghat. Formed in 1971 from the remnants of Savoy Brown, Foghat released their first record in 1972 to yawns from critics and what few fans they had at the time. The album stalled at number 127 on the charts with the single "I Just Want to Make Love to You" receiving scant airplay. Over the next three years the band released a total of four uneven albums with a variety of producers. All the while, Foghat continued to tour America, garnering a name for themselves as a great live act. It wasn't until the release of *Fool for the City* in 1975, with the monster FM radio staple "Slow Ride," that the band become an "overnight" sensation. Filling stadiums all across

America, Foghat continued with their commercially successful, blues-based music with two more albums featuring hits such as "Drivin' Wheel," "I'll Be Standing By," as well as the double-platinum live album *Foghat Live.* But by 1980, Peverett was getting tired of the formula perpetuated since *Fool for the City* and by 1985, Peverett left Foghat after sixteen years of constant touring and recording. Foghat continued (if in name only) as band members drifted in and out, with two competing versions of the band touring simultaneously from 1990 to 1993. In 1993, Peverett and original drummer Roger Earl patched things up and the original Foghat began touring and recording again, playing up until Peverett's death. He was buried at Woodlawn Memorium/Funeral Home in Gotha, Florida, in Section 35, eighteen rows to the right of the statue.

ESTHER PHILLIPS
December 23, 1935—August 7, 1984
CAUSE OF DEATH Liver and Kidney Failure

A versatile singer who was equally at home singing blues, jazz standards, and pop, Little Esther Phillips was the reigning blueswoman after the death of her mentor, Dinah Washington. If it weren't for her intermittent battles with drug addiction, she would have made a name for herself alongside Washington and Aretha Franklin. Born in Galveston, Texas, Phillips came into prominence after winning a talent contest in Los Angeles in 1948. At the age of fourteen, she recorded "Double-Crossing Blues" with Johnny Otis, which went on to sell almost half a million copies. She continued with blues and R&B singles with the Savoy and Federal labels through the early 1950s. She toured around the U.S. with the Johnny Otis show and continued with Top 10 hits on the R&B charts with "Cupid's Boogie" and "Mistrusting Blues." She stopped touring altogether in 1954 and rarely left her Houston, Texas, home, recording only six songs during the remainder of the decade. She scored a minor hit with the country song "Release Me" in 1962 and in 1965 she appeared on the British TV show *Ready, Steady, Go!* with the Beatles (who commended Phillips on her cover version of their song "And I Love Him"). She appeared at the Newport Jazz Festival the following year before admitting herself into a drug rehab program. Phillips marked her return to music with an appearance with Johnny Otis at the 1970 Monterey Jazz Festival and re-signed with Atlantic Records. She promptly released two live recordings and signed the following year with the Kudu/CTI label, which released the critically acclaimed *From a Whisper to a Scream.* Nominated in 1973 for a Grammy for Best Female R&B Vocalist, Aretha Franklin was so enamored by Phillips that when the Queen of Soul was awarded the Grammy for her *Young, Gifted, and Black* album, she handed her awarded to Phillips, stating that she deserved it more. In the mid-seventies she scored the biggest hit single of her career with the disco remake of "What a Diff'rence a Day Makes." She continued to perform and record up until her untimely death at the age of forty-eight, at which time she was buried at Forest Lawn Hollywood Hills in Los Angeles, California.

EDITH PIAF
December 19, 1915—October 11, 1963
CAUSE OF DEATH Complications from Drug and Alcohol Dependency

The most popular singer in France during the 1950s, Edith Piaf gained international recognition through her emotional songs of doomed and tragic love. Unlike her contemporaries Charles Aznavour and Maurice Chevalier, Piaf achieved stardom through her French recordings, not English translations of her hits. Abandoned by her mother and raised in a brothel in her early years, Edith Gassion began her career singing in the streets and in workcamps as a teenager. At the age of twenty, just one year after she lost her only child to meningitis, Piaf came to the attention of Paris nightclub owner Louis Leplee, who handed the young singer ten francs and the number to his club, Gerny's. There was little Leplee wanted to change about the singer, yet he considered her name unsuitable for the stage and changed it to the Parisian translation for "sparrow"—Piaf. Her opening night made Piaf an overnight success and with her new-found popularity, she began associating with singers Chevalier, Mistinguett, and Left Bank poet Jacques Borgeat. Unfortunately, Piaf also was known to continue her associations with seedier characters from her street days and when Leplee was found murdered in his apartment, she became the prime suspect. While the murder was never solved, the sordid affair soiled Piaf's image for several years. During the war years, Piaf remained in Paris during the German occupation, during which making a living in the nightclubs proved difficult. She scored two of her biggest hits of her career, "La Vie en Rose" and "Les Trois Cloches," immediately after the war and continued to record over two hundred more songs for Pathé-Marconi. Piaf visited the U.S. in 1947, but her greatest success was limited to France and the surrounding countries. In the spring of 1949, Piaf was to begin an engagement in New York City when her lover, boxer Marcel Cerdan, died tragically in a plane crash. He had been on his way to meet with Piaf. After losing another lover and surviving three car crashes that aggravated her rheumatism, the singer began a lifelong descent into morphine and alcohol dependency. In 1952, she married singer and composer Jacques Pill and together they recorded a number of sides destined for posterity, including "L'Accordioniste" and "La Foule." In 1959, she continued with a string of hits in America, Italy, Germany, Holland, and her home country while sordid affairs of the heart and drug dependency began to take their

toll. Despite her personal problems and declining health, she still managed to sell over a million copies of one of her last engagements, *Live at the Olympia*. She was hospitalized in the spring of 1963 and was on the French Riviera to convalesce when she relapsed and died in the arms of her new husband, Theo Sarapo. Sarapo drove through the night to return to Paris with Piaf's corpse, where she was buried at Père Lachaise Cemetery. During the funeral procession, forty thousand Parisians broke down the barricade before the diminutive singer could be laid to rest in Division 97, four rows off Avenue Transversale Number 3. Shortly after her death, the city of Paris named a street in her honor and her apartment at 67 Boulevard Lannes now has a plaque in her honor. Piaf fans can also be seen at 72 rue de Belleville, where Piaf was allegedly born under the streetlamp on a policeman's cloak.

WEBB PIERCE
August 8, 1921—February 24, 1991
CAUSE OF DEATH Pancreatic Cancer

If Webb Pierce had not become one of the best-selling, most successful honky-tonk country singers ever to emerge since Hank Williams, then he might have continued his job as a Sears shoe salesman. But as it stands, Webb achieved a number of firsts in the annals of country and western music—he was the first to record using a pedal-steel guitar, he was the first to wear Nudie-designed rhinestone suits, and he was the first to have a guitar-shaped pool in Nashville. Pierce first started playing guitar at the age of twelve, and four short years later he had his own radio show on KMLB out of Monroe, Louisiana. After serving three years in the army, he moved to nearby Shreveport and quickly became a featured performer on KWKH, home of the Louisiana Hayride. He signed a record deal with Decca in 1951 and had his first hit with a remake of the Cajun song "Wondering." The song became the inspiration for his backing

band, the Wondering Boys, featuring future legends Floyd Cramer on piano, Tillman Franks on bass, and a young upstart named Faron Young. With the death of Hank Williams in 1953, Pierce became the reigning honky-tonk artist, along with a weekly spot on the Grand Ole Opry. He continued to dominate the chart throughout the 1950s with "Slowly," "That Heart Belongs to Me," "Back Street Affair," and "Love, Love, Love." In the ten years following Williams's death, Pierce chalked up ninety-seven chart-topping hits, including thirteen number one hit records and fifty-four Top 10 singles. On the road, Pierce commanded the unheard of fee of $1,300 a performance, allowing the King of Fifties Honky-Tonk Music to indulge his tastes for his much-publicized silver-dollar Cadillac, many Nudie suits, and a guitar-shaped swimming pool (which became a prized Nashville tourist site). Such a flamboyant lifestyle put him at odds with the conservative leanings of the Grand Ole Opry and the Nashville music elite. In addition, Pierce was also purchasing radio stations and had a highly successful publishing and booking agency. While the wealth to be had on the business side of music was frowned upon by his contemporaries, Pierce finally left the Opry in 1956 for the lucrative Saturday night concerts, rather than the union scale the Opry offered. This also allowed Pierce to appear on TV and films, increasing the singer's exposure and concert billings. Through the 1960s, Pierce continued to chart, but not as frequently, as rock 'n' roll continued to build its audience. A successful artist, musician, and businessman, Pierce's career came to a close shortly after he was diagnosed with pancreatic cancer. Pierce was laid to rest next to fellow artist Marty Robbins in the Garden of Gethsemane, Space 1D-1 at Woodlawn Cemetery in Nashville, Tennessee. As you enter the cemetery, drive past the large office building to the road behind the office. Turn left and drive while staying to the right. Go past the historic wood house and pond (on your left) and park one hundred feet past the pond. Walk three hundred feet to the top of the hill on your left and look for the ever-present flowers marking his flat, six-foot bronze tablet. A decade after his passing, he was finally elected to the Country Music Hall of Fame.

LONNIE PITCHFORD
October 8, 1955—November 8, 1998
CAUSE OF DEATH AIDS-related Pneumonia

Dedicated to reviving early Delta blues, Lonnie Pitchford was able to get more out of his self-constructed one-string Diddley bow than most musicians get from a complete guitar. Born just outside of Clarksdale, Mississippi, Pitchford began playing in his youth but became an overnight sensation in 1972 when he began performing for the Smithsonian Institution's Festival of American Folklife. Although he only released one full-length album during his lifetime, by the 1990s he had toured in Europe, Australia, and much of the U.S. Married to the daughter of Elmore James's girlfriend, Pitchford was buried in the same small cemetery, Newport Community Cemetery, located just outside the town of Ebenezer, Mississippi.

JEFF PORCARO
April 1, 1954—August 5, 1992
CAUSE OF DEATH Coronary Artery Disease Caused by Cocaine Abuse

It's certainly tragic when a well-liked and much-respected musician dies too young, leaving a young family—as well as many fans—with nothing but memories. It's even sadder when that loss is overshadowed by controversy concerning the cause of death. Such is the case of Toto drummer, Jeff Porcaro. Porcaro's musical career began in Southern California at Grant High School in Van Nuys. Unbeknownst to anyone at that time, Jeff's casual jam sessions with friends and with his brother, Steve, would form the basis for one of the hottest bands of the 1980s—Toto. After touring with Sonny and Cher and Boz Scaggs, Jeff, along with David Paich, Steve Lukather, Steve Porcaro, Bobby Kimball, and David Hungate, formed Toto in 1978. As talented session players and gifted songwriters (Paich wrote most of Boz Scagg's *Silk Degrees* album), Toto found success right away with their debut album, which sold more than four million copies. By the early 1980s, they had hit their stride with FM radio rock standards such as "Africa," "Hold the Line," and "Rosanna." The music industry loved the band, too, awarding them six Grammys for their *Toto IV* album. One hot summer day in 1992, after spraying his yard with a pesticide, Jeff fell seriously ill. Paramedics were called to his home in an exclusive, gated community in the San Fernando Valley. By that time, according to a fire department representative, "He was in critical condition. . . . There was no breathing, no pulse. He was in full cardiac arrest." Since heart attacks are uncommon among thirty-eight-year-old people and cocaine is known to cause heart problems, there was immediate speculation that Porcaro's fatal heart attack was caused by drug use. But initial doctor's reports indicated that the heart attack was triggered by an allergic reaction to insecticide. Jeff's family vehemently denied, and continues to deny, that he had a drug problem. The L.A. County Coroner's Office had the final say, ruling that Jeff's death was caused by "occlusive coronary artery disease caused by hardening of the arteries," brought on by cocaine use. Results of blood tests and an autopsy showed that cocaine was found in his blood; insecticide was not. Although Jeff's widow, Susan, hired several experts to look into the cause of her husband's death, no other cause was ever publicized. All controversies aside, Porcaro was laid to rest at Forest Lawn Hollywood Hills in Los Angeles in the Lincoln Terrace section. As you drive through the gates and up Memorial Drive, stay to the right as Memorial Drive splits into two roads. Go past the church on your left, staying to your right to the Lincoln statue (on your right, near the very top of the cemetery). Walk all the way up to the statue of Lincoln, turn right, and walk to the hedges and the bench.

COLE PORTER
June 9, 1891—October 15, 1964
CAUSE OF DEATH Heart Failure

Known for his popular Broadway show *Kiss Me Kate*, Cole Porter's strength lies not with his twenty Broadway productions, but rather his individual songs of simple elegance and witty, urbane lyrics that continue to be found in modern day movies, plays, and on CDs long after his death. Born into one of the richest families in Indiana at the time, Porter was spoiled during his formative years, beginning piano and violin lessons at the age of six. By age eleven he had "published" his first composition (actually his mother paid to have a hundred copies made to distribute within her social circle) and was afforded guaranteed solos during his time with the student orchestra because financing for the school music program came from his parents. Attending Yale University, he was known as much for his playboy lifestyle as he was for his musical programs and Yale fight songs (many of which survive to this day). Since his grandfather subsidized his college years, he was forced to attend Harvard Law School after his graduation; however, he switched to the arts after a year. In 1916, he produced his first Broadway show, *See America First*, which also became his first bomb. Cole moved to Europe shortly after, returning with stories of his alleged involvement with the French Resistance movement and the Foreign Legion. He completed his social climbing, marrying socialite Linda Thomas in 1919. The marriage was considered a financial arrangement as Cole pursued an alternative, closeted lifestyle so as not to ruin his reputation or music career. Cole continued writing, with little success during the 1920s until he published "Let's Do It (Let's Fall in Love)" in 1928. He followed that with hit after hit, including "The Gay Divorcee," "Night and Day," and "I Get a Kick Out of You." In the mid-thirties he began writing for Hollywood movies and was equally at home with the liberal lifestyle of the Beverly Hills elite. In 1937, Cole suffered a severe injury while horseback riding, fracturing both legs. For a person who prided himself on his personal appearance and athleticism, the injury was devastating for Cole, both personally and professionally. Losing the use of both legs, Cole continued to write; however, many of his songs during this period simply parodied his earlier work or evoked cheap sentimentality. He did manage to write for the production of *Kiss Me Kate* (based on William Shakespeare's *Taming of the Shrew)*, which included several classic Porter songs, like "Always True to You in My Fashion" and "Another Op'nin', Another Show." His major success in the fifties was the upbeat score to the film *High Society*, starring Bing Crosby, Frank Sinatra, and Louis Armstrong. By now Porter had begun to retreat from social outings becoming more reclusive as his alcohol intake and smoking had increased. In 1958, he had to have one of his legs amputated, causing severe depression and his retirement from show business. Suffering from a broken hip, a bladder infection, delirium tremens, and malnutrition, Cole's heart simply stopped beating as he was resting at home after surgery. His body was returned to his hometown of Peru, Indiana, for burial in the family plot at Mount Hope Cemetery. The simple obelisk surrounded by smaller matching obelisks for each family member is on the road in Section C, Lot 22, Space 1. His home in Peru at 102 East Third Street still survives today and looks much the same as when Porter lived there as a youth.

DAVE PRATER
May 9, 1937—April 9, 1988
CAUSE OF DEATH Automobile Accident

As one half of the gospel-influenced soul duo Sam and Dave, Dave Prater provided rougher, blues growl to Sam's higher-pitched lead vocals. Best know for the signature tune, "Soul Man," Sam and Dave hit the big time when they signed with Atlantic Records in 1965 and were leased to the Memphis-based Stax Records. The Stax house band provided the perfect punch for their hits "Hold On, I'm Comin'," "You Got Me Hummin'," "Soul Man," and "You Don't Know Like I Know." After breaking up and reuniting several times during the 1970s, Sam and Dave's popularity surged again when the film *The Blues Brothers*, featuring John Belushi, Dan Aykroyd, and several members of the Stax house band, featured "Soul Man" in the film. They reunited again briefly after the film was released, only to call it quits for good after a New Year's Eve concert in San Francisco in 1981. Prater died in a car accident when his vehicle left the road near Syracuse, Georgia. Prater was laid to rest at Holy Sepulchre Cemetery in Totowa, New Jersey, and eleven years later Sam and Dave were inducted into the Rock and Roll Hall of Fame.

LOUIS PRIMA

December 7, 1910—August 24, 1978

CAUSE OF DEATH Complications from Brain Stem Tumor Surgery

Son of Italian immigrants and a talented band leader, trumpeter, composer, and singer, Louis Prima developed his talent into the title, the undisputed King of the Vegas Lounges and would also become known as the Wildest Act in Las Vegas. With poker-faced Keely Smith's cool image and melodic vocals coupled with Prima's inspired clowning and fractured Italian-dialect scat singing, augmented by the backing band of Sam Butera and the Witnesses, Prima would wail wildly into the wee hours of the morning. Picking up the trumpet during his teens in New Orleans, Prima formed his first group, New Orleans Gang, in the 1930s. Recording over seventy titles (including their signature hit, "Way Down Yonder in New Orleans") with future jazz greats Frankie Frederico on drums and Pee Wee Russell on clarinet, Prima composed "Sing, Sing, Sing," during this time, the signature closing number of Benny Goodman, now considered a jazz standard. After a brief stint in Hollywood working in several feature films, Prima met his future singing partner and fourth wife, Dorothy Keely Smith in 1948. After having a hit with their song "Oh, Babe," Prima finally hit his stride with swinging arrangements filtered through his unique humor, Neapolitan slang, and hep-talk jivespeak. With songs like "Pleese No Squeeza da Banana," "Hitsum Kitsum Bumpity Itsum," and his biggest hit, a hot version of Johnny Mercer and Harold Arlen's "That Old Black Magic," there was no mistaking that Prima was a natural showman. When he sang "Angelina" (a song about a waitress at a pizzeria), fans would run down the aisles to deliver pans of fresh pizza and lasagne to the stage. Prima wouldn't miss a beat when he turned to the band and exclaimed, "Hey boys, we eat tonight!" In 1961, Prima signed a lucrative deal with Dot Records, lost Smith in a divorce (but thankfully kept Sam Butera and the Witnesses), and took a fifth wife as a new singing partner. In 1967, Prima gave an inspired performance as the voice of King Louie in the animated feature *The Jungle Book*. But with musical tastes changing in the late sixties, Prima and company decided to bring it all back home where it started—New Orleans. A fixture in the clubs in the French Quarter, Prima delivered a lifetime of hits for his hometown before he was stricken with a brain tumor. In October of 1975, he underwent surgery to remove the tumor, lapsed into a coma, and never regained consciousness. Prima died almost three years later in a New Orleans nursing home of pneumonia and was buried in the Prima family tomb in the Metairie Cemetery outside New Orleans, Louisiana. As you enter the cemetery, drive toward the left into the old section, toward the large, aboveground mausoleums. Located in Section 88, Lots 1 and 2, look for the angel playing the trumpet atop the family mausoleum.

TITO PUENTE

April 20, 1923—June 1, 2000

CAUSE OF DEATH Complications from Heart Surgery

When Mambo King Tito Puente took his final bow at the age of seventy-seven, he had recorded over 110 albums, received five Grammy Awards, and played his way through six decades of music, including the rumba-crazed forties, the mambo phase of the fifties, the Latin jazz of the sixties, and through the hot salsa dance craze of the nineties. Traveling with his twelve-piece orchestra, the energetic timbalero never failed to fill a dance floor with

his brass-heavy band and furious, infectious Latin beat. Born Ernesto Puente in Harlem, New York, the young artist began as a dancer before a torn ligament turned him toward music. Playing drums professionally for the Noro Morales Orchestra at the age of thirteen, Puente moved to a band led by Frank Grillo, who suggested the young percussionist play the timbales. He was quickly moved to the front of the stage, where he enthralled audiences with his natural showmanship and humor. In 1948, Puente formed his own band, the Piccadilly Boys, before renaming it Tito Puente and His Orchestra. The following year the band rose to the top of the mambo craze with the national hit "Abaniquito" and a star was born. Of his many hits over the years, Puente's "Oye Como Va" found an even larger audience when Carlos Santana covered the song in 1970. Puente often joked about the large royalty check he received every time Santana's version was played. During his long career, Puente recorded and performed with some of the biggest names in music, including Woody Herman, Lionel Hampton, George Shearing, Ruben Blades, and a whole host of salsa luminaries. Continually touring his entire life, his family urged him to slow down, but he continued playing five nights a week, stating, "If I die, I want to die onstage." Hospitalized during his final months with heart problems in his parents' native Puerto Rico, Puente underwent open-heart surgery but fell into a coma and died shortly after. Following a wake at Riverside Memorial Chapel in New York, Puente was buried at St. Anthony's Church Cemetery in Nanuet, New York. Facing St. Anthony's Church, drive through the parking lot on the right and in the back corner of the lot you will see the Iveli mausoleum. Drive down that road to the end and at the corner on the right is a green pole with 2A on it. At the next pole down, walk into the section, approximately forty feet to Puente's aboveground marker. For music fans, Puente's restaurant and night spot, Tito Puente's on City Island in the Bronx, is a virtual Tito Puente theme park. Pictures and gold records adorn the walls, while pictures from his six-decade career are laminated into the tables and conga drums serve as bar stools.

SUN RA
May 22, 1914—May 30, 1993
CAUSE OF DEATH Effects of Multiple Strokes

With over two hundred albums in six decades, Sun Ra was revered in Europe as a genius, and staged hundreds of concerts, at times with one hundred-piece orchestras. Taking the stage with his Arkestra members wearing wild costumes and flowing cloaks, shows would include long percussion jams, poetry, light shows, dancers, marches through the audience, squealing sax solos, and if he was in the mood, Ra would take a synthesizer solo that inevitably erupted into a volcanic crescendo. This self-proclaimed immortal avant-garde musician can be found by driving through the gates of Elmwood Cemetery in Birmingham, Alabama. Driving toward the middle of this expansive cemetery to Block 25, circle the section until you see the Christu headstone, about forty feet from the road. Sun Ra's simple, flat marker is two rows in front of Christu.

EDDIE RABBITT
November 27, 1941—May 7, 1998
CAUSE OF DEATH Lung Cancer

With a thousand dollars in his pocket and a bus ticket to Nashville, Eddie Rabbitt made the move to the capital of country music in 1968 and two years later got his first break as a songwriter when Elvis Presley recorded his song "Kentucky Rain." Best known for the number one hit "I Love a Rainy Night," Rabbitt signed his first record deal in 1974 and had his first hit as a singer and performer two years later with "Drinkin' My Baby (Off My Mind)." With a gift for writing clever lyrics, pretty melodies, and delivering a clean, family-oriented show, Rabbitt managed to chart twenty-six number one country hits, including "Drivin' My Life Away," "Every Which Way But Loose," and "Two Dollars in the Jukebox." Rabbitt's duet with Crystal Gayle in 1982 also reached number one and his song "American Boy" was popular across the U.S. and with the armed forces during the Gulf War. Voted Top New Male Artist by the Academy of Country Music and awarded a plaque on the Country Music Walk of Fame in Los Angeles, Rabbitt nonetheless scaled back his tour schedule in the early eighties to spend more time with his family and his youngest son Timmy (who died of liver cancer just one month shy of his two-year birthday). And though he spent more time with his family and continued to record, he never felt secure in his success, remarking, "A writer has to keep one foot in the street and one pocket empty and be hungry for it." Diagnosed with lung cancer in 1997, he had part of a lung removed and was in remission when the disease came back with a vengeance. Shortly after the release of his last album, *Beating the Odds*, he passed away and was buried in a private ceremony at Calvary Cemetery in Nashville, Tennessee. After you enter the cemetery, follow the road to the right and stay right through the next two forks in the road. At the yellow building, turn left and drive two hundred feet and park at the intersection. The Rabbitt family cross is on the hill to the left.

JAMES "YANK" RACHELL
March 16, 1910—April 9, 1997
CAUSE OF DEATH Natural Causes

One of the few prewar blues recording artists to continue performing into the 1990s, James "Yank" Rachell was the primary exponent of the blues mandolin. Self-taught at the age of eight, Rachell began to work dances around the Tennessee and Mississippi area with Sleepy John Estes and Jab Jones in the early 1920s. Recording fourteen singles for the Victor label, the Three J's Jug Band split during the Depression. Seeking their fortune in Chicago, Rachell, Estes, and harmonica player Hammie Nixon teamed up for the nightclub circuit on the South Side. This was short-lived as Rachell began to work outside of music, which he did for most of his life. Discovering a young harmonica player by the name of John Lee Williamson (aka. Sonny Boy Williamson I), Rachell recorded several sides with Sonny Boy, from 1938 through 1941. Holding on to his day job, Rachell left the business when Sonny Boy was murdered in 1948. Settling permanently in Indianapolis, he continued to work a regular job until his wife's passing in 1961. Afterward Rachell reunited with Nixon and Estes, taking full advantage of the blues resurgence of the 1960s. After Estes died in 1977, Rachell continued his solo career, and he was most often found playing the Slippery Noodle in Indianapolis, where he was a regular. He died at the age of eighty-seven while working on a new album in the late 1990s. Buried at the New Crown Cemetery in Indianapolis, Indiana, Rachell's well-appointed monument is in Section 42, in the eighth row, twenty-three spaces from the corner.

MA RAINEY
April 26, 1886—December 22, 1939
CAUSE OF DEATH Heart Attack

Although she wasn't the first, Gertrude "Ma Rainey" Pridgett and Bessie Smith were the first to popularize rural southern blues through tent shows, vaudeville troupes, and minstrel shows during the early 1900s. Known as the Mother of the Blues, Ma Rainey joined a traveling black vaudeville troupe at the age of fourteen. At the age of eighteen she married Will "Pa" Rainey and they began billing themselves as "Ma and Pa Rainey and the Assassinators of the Blues." She left her husband and began a solo career but never signed a recording contract until 1923—after nearly twenty-five years of performing. She released approximately one hundred singles during the 1920s, including "Bo Weevil Blues," "See See Rider Blues" (with Louis Armstrong and Fletcher Henderson), and "Oh My Baby Blues" (with Coleman Hawkins). Often accompanied by Georgia Tom (gospel music pioneer Thomas A. Dorsey), the Depression ended both her recording and traveling show career. Afterward Rainey moved back to Columbus, Georgia, where she successfully operated two movie houses and owned her own home. When this future Blues Foundation Hall of Fame and Rock and Roll Hall of Fame inductee died, the local paper listed her profession as "housekeeper." Rainey is buried in Columbus at the Porterdale Cemetery one hundred feet past the gardner's shack on the left, fifty feet from the road.

JOHNNIE RAY
January 10, 1927—February 24, 1990
CAUSE OF DEATH Liver Failure

Labeled at times throughout his career as the Nabob of Sob and the Prince of Wails for his onstage histrionic performances—where he would literally break down sobbing midsong—Johnnie Ray was a controversial artist whose musical exuberance predated rock 'n' roll. Partially deaf from the age of fourteen, Ray had a minor hit with the self-penned song

"Whiskey and Gin." It wasn't until 1951 when he recorded two songs (backed by the Four Lads), "Cry" and "The Little White Cloud That Cried," that Ray became an overnight international sensation. "Cry" was a smash, reaching number one on the pop charts, staying there for eleven weeks and selling over a million copies. But more unsettling to many was his presentation in concert. Ray was the first white singer to stand on the piano and kick the bench into the audience while carrying about onstage, gesturing in a wild, convulsive manner. And partially due to his hearing loss, his singing style was equally as radical, with Ray phrasing on each syllable, a technique popularized in rock 'n' roll twenty years later. While fans in England and Australia worshiped Ray, the press in the U.S. were unmerciful when it became known that Ray was an unrepentant boozer and closeted bisexual. But as his popularity grew, Ray moved easily toward Hollywood, with his first film an Irving Berlin musical, *There's No Business Like Show Business,* in 1954. All in all, Ray put twenty-five hits into the Top 30 from 1951 to 1957 and toured Australia more than twenty times. During the 1980s, after hundreds of low-rent cabaret shows and Vegas lounges, the Halcyon and alcohol had taken their toll, with Ray's performances merely parodies of his old self, as he struggled to remember the words to his songs. He was buried near his hometown of Dallas, Oregon, at the Hopewell Cemetery in the city of Hopewell in the center of the lower section in this small, rural cemetery.

RAZZLE
1960—December 9, 1984
CAUSE OF DEATH Automobile Accident

Nicholas "Razzle" Dingley was the hard-partying, heavy-hitting drummer for the underrated glam-rock group Hanoi Rocks. When Razzle joined the fledgling group in 1982, he injected a level of energy into the band that was sorely needed. Following a brief stint with The Dark, he saw a photo of Hanoi Rocks in *Sounds* magazine and hounded the band until they gave him an audition. After passing the audition, Razzle joined the group and followed them around the world through Thailand, Israel, India, Canada, Japan, England, and the United States. After befriending fellow headbangers Mötley Crüe at the Donnington Festival, the band was in Los Angeles taking a break at Mötley Crüe singer Vince Neil's home in Redondo Beach. When the booze ran low, Neil, with Razzle as passenger, jumped into his brand-new cherry red Pantera sports car for a quick drive to the liquor store. On the way back Neil lost control of the car, skidded across the lane, and smashed head-on into oncoming traffic. Neil was uninjured; however, two occupants of the other car were seriously injured. Unfortunately, the passenger side of the Pantera took the brunt of the impact, throwing one of Razzle's shoes out into traffic as the Hanoi Rocks drummer lay dying in the car. CPR was performed as he was raced to the area hospital, only to be pronounced dead shortly after. Razzle's body was returned to his hometown on the Isle of Wight, U.K., where a service was held and his cremated remains were interred at the Holy Trinity Church in Binstead. From the church courtyard, go to the smaller of the two gates at the end of the wall. Follow the path down between the cremation markers, where Razzle's small marker can be found at the end of the path. Neil was fined $2.6 million and spent thirty days in the hole. Hanoi Rocks disbanded two months later.

JIMMY REED
September 6, 1925—August 29, 1976
CAUSE OF DEATH Respiratory Failure Due to Epileptic Seizure

The Bossman of the Blues, with twenty-two chart-topping hits, Reed was more popular than Muddy Waters and Howlin' Wolf between 1953 and 1966. Unfortunately, he was unable to handle the fame and money that came his way, suffering terribly from alcoholism. Regardless of his shortcomings, his long association with Eddie Taylor produced some of the finest blues to come out of Chicago. "Honest I Do," "Bright Lights, Big City," and "Shame, Shame, Shame" came alive with Reed's readily identifiable hypnotic guitar and slack-jawed singing, becoming instant classics. While he was the favorite of European

groups such as the Beatles, the Animals, and the Rolling Stones, he was too far gone to benefit from the blues revival during the 1960s due to illness. After taking the cure from alcohol and a couple of years of inactivity, Reed slowly returned to the concert dates, where he was a big draw on the black tour circuit. Visiting England for the first time in 1963–1964, Reed returned in 1968 with the American Folk Blues Festival and toured the U.S. with zydeco star Clifton Chenier in 1970. With new recordings issued every two years, Reed's health began to suffer and his later recordings found his guitar skills sluggish and his diction almost indecipherable. Reed died suddenly in 1976 after an epileptic seizure while on tour in Oakland, California. Despite reports that his grave is unmarked, he has found peace at the Lincoln Cemetery South Annex on Kedzie (across from the cemetery office) in Chicago, Illinois. As you drive through the gates, stay to your left for about 150 feet. His simple marker is in Section N, Lot 335, three rows from the road directly across from the mausoleum.

KEITH RELF
March 22, 1943—May 14, 1976
CAUSE OF DEATH Electrocution

One of the most underrated bands in the history of rock 'n' roll, the Yardbirds not only invented the idea of a guitar hero by employing Eric Clapton, Jeff Beck, and Jimmy Page at various times, but also developed from a standard British rhythm and blues pub band into a psychedelic, and later early heavy metal band. With lead singer Keith Relf, the band went through several personality changes, but always with Relf lending his vocal talents to the guitar heavyweights. The band, formed in 1963, didn't really take off until Relf's friend and guitarist Eric Clapton joined the band in 1964. They had already cut a live album with Sonny Boy Williamson II and opened for the Beatles, yet all they needed was a hit to put them on the charts. They got their wish with "For Your Love" in 1965. Now moving away from strict rhythm and blues, Clapton choose to leave the band (he hated "For Your Love" and anything else not blues), and was replaced by Jeff Beck. The match was excellent as Beck loved to experiment with new sounds and music. Using distortion and other new technology, this was the high point of the Yardbirds, with "Heart Full of Soul," "Train Kept a Rollin'," and "Still I'm Sad." In June of 1966, Jimmy Page joined the band (first as bass player, then switching to guitar) but this lineup only lasted six months, as the two guitar

masters became one too many, and Beck left the group. The band began a creative downward spiral and Relf (along with Jim McCarty) left two years later. Page, in order to fullfill scheduled tour dates, recruited future Led Zeppelin band mates and the rest, as they say, is history. Relf continued with a number of projects, but in 1976 he was found dead in his living room (not in the bathtub as previously rumored) from an electric shock from his guitar. Relf was buried at

Richmond Cemetery in Richmond, Surrey, U.K. As you enter the cemetery at Grove Road, drive straight back to the Star and Garter military monument. Relf's unmarked grave, adorned by a simple rose bush, is in Section 21 (located in front of the memorial), next to the perimeter path, to the right of the grave of Anatol Niemyski.

CHARLIE RICH
December 14, 1932—July 24, 1995
CAUSE OF DEATH Blood Clot in the Lung

One of the more critically acclaimed yet commercially erratic country singers, songwriters, and performers of the 1960s and 1970s, Charlie Rich blended country, gospel, rockabilly, and soul through a four-decade run in the business. Initially rejected by Sun Records for sounding too jazzy, after absorbing a few Jerry Lee Lewis records, Rich returned to become a piano session player at Sun. After playing for dozens of popular artists (including Lewis), he turned his talents to songwriting, creating the hits "Thanks a Lot" for Johnny Cash, "I'm Comin' Home" for Elvis Presley, and "The Ballad of Billy Joe" for himself. After a string of mediocre songs, he hit number one on the country charts with "Behind Closed Doors," followed by another number one hit with "The Most Beautiful Girl in the World." Voted Entertainer of the Year by the Country Music Association in 1974, Rich lost a lot of support (as well as record sales) when he refused to read the name of the winner at the awards ceremony the following year. Rather than read the winner, John Denver, he burned the envelope and walked offstage. He continued recording on autopilot for the remainder of his career, occasionally placing a song on the charts. Upon his passing, Rich was buried in Section R-3, Space FR 31-36 in Row 13 near the bench at Memorial Park in Memphis, Tennessee.

NELSON RIDDLE
June 1, 1921—October 6, 1985
CAUSE OF DEATH Cardiac and Kidney Failure

Beginning his career as a trombonist with the Charlie Spivak and Tommy Dorsey big bands in the 1940s, Nelson Riddle went on to become one of the most versatile arrangers and composers for films, television, radio, and studio recordings. Known as one of the top arrangers for singers such as Peggy Lee, Ella Fitzgerald, and Dean Martin, Riddle is probably best remembered for his classic "mood" music arrangements for Nat "King" Cole and Frank Sinatra in the 1950s for Capitol Records. Riddle's career as an arranger didn't really begin until after his discharge from the army after World War II. Hired as a staff arranger for NBC Radio in Los Angeles, he secured work for Nat "King" Cole as a "ghost" (uncredited) arranger. After the successes of "Mona Lisa" and "Too Young" for Cole, he was not only Cole's primary arranger and collaborator, but also the conductor of the orchestra. In 1953, Frank Sinatra was looking to record in New York City among familiar surroundings and friends. Fortunately, he took a chance on the young arranger, which resulted in the classic Sinatra recordings "I've Got the World on a String," "Nice n' Easy," and his most commercially successful album, *Songs For Swingin' Lovers*. Riddle's association with Sinatra during Sinatra's seven-year run at Capitol resulted in film and television work, including the first TV theme to top the charts, "Route 66." With the advent of electronic music, disco, and heavy metal during the 1970s and 1980s, Riddle's recording and arranging career tapered off. It wasn't until a phone call from Linda Ronstadt requesting an arrangement of "I Guess I'll Hang My Tears Out to Dry" that Riddle's dry spell came to an end. They collaborated on three highly successful albums of standards, introducing a whole new generation to Riddle's style and elegance. Although listed as buried at Westwood Memorial Park by several guidebooks and by the cemetery itself, Riddle is really interred at Hollywood Forever in Los Angeles. As you drive through the gates onto the hallowed grounds behind the Paramount Studios in Hollywood, turn right and drive over to the New Beth Olam Mausoleum on the far left of the Abbey of the Psalms on West Avenue. Walk into the Hall of David, turn right, and go to the second narrow niche on the left. Riddle's small plaque is on the right at eye level.

MINNIE RIPERTON
November 8, 1947—July 12, 1979
CAUSE OF DEATH Breast Cancer

Blessed with a five-octave range and the voice of an angel, Minnie Riperton studied to become an opera singer, only to become one of soul music's most gifted artists. Born and raised in Chicago, Riperton began voice lessons at the age of nine and studied opera under the direction of the legendary Marion Jeffries. However, Minnie was more attracted to R&B and rock 'n' roll and signed her first recording contract with Chess Records while still in her teens. Recording first with the Gems, then later with the Rotary Connection, Riperton became well known in music circles as she sang backup for Quincy Jones, Etta James, Freddie Hubbard, and Stevie Wonder. In 1974, she released her first solo album, *Perfect Angel*, and scored the international hit "Lovin' You." She released three more moderately successful albums during her short lifetime. One of the most fan-adorned graves at Westwood Memorial Park (other than Marilyn Monroe's) in Los Angeles, California, she is resting quietly in Section D, Space 41 in the far corner of the grass section, opposite the entry gate, next to Carl Wilson of the Beach Boys.

ROY ROGERS
November 5, 1911—July 6, 1998
CAUSE OF DEATH Congestive Heart Failure

He was the quintessential singing cowboy—white Stetson hat, hand-tooled boots, a guitar at his side, and his six-shooters holstered on his hips. He never used his spurs on his golden palomino Trigger, and he never shot a man, preferring to shoot the pistol out of an adversary's hand. In an era when men tipped their hats to ladies and sang sentimental ballads around the campfire, Roy Rogers was an American hero aptly named King of the Cowboys. Born a poor shoe factory worker's son in Cincinnati, Ohio, Rogers (born Leonard Slye) began playing the guitar and mandolin at barn dances on the weekends during the Depression. After the family moved to California in search of work, Rogers was picking peaches and living in a labor camp when his sister suggested he try out for the *Midnight Frolic* radio show. Two days after the audition, Rogers got a call from a band called the Rocky Mountaineers and became a member. After a year, Rogers left and formed several

other bands, eventually continuing as a solo act on a local Los Angeles radio station. In search of the perfect western-style harmonizing group, Rogers formed the Sons of the Pioneers in 1934 and after radio stations began broadcasting across the country, the Pioneers's national exposure led to their first feature film appearance, in *Radio Scout*. They continued recording for Decca and OKeh along with personal appearances when the enormous success of Gene Autry caused studios throughout Hollywood to jump on the "singing cowboy" bandwagon. When Autry let it be known that he might not show up for his next feature film, a general call went out from Republic Pictures and by the end of the week, the newly named Roy Rogers had just signed a seven-year contract. After his first film (in which Rogers was billed as Dick Weston), he starred in *Under Western Stars* and became an overnight sensation. By 1944, he had starred in close to forty pictures and received over 75,000 pieces of fan mail a month when he was teamed opposite Dale Evans. After the death of his first wife two years later, Evans and Rogers were married and over the course of his career, Rogers starred in over ninety feature films and 102 half-hour television shows. Always ending their shows with "Happy Trails," Rogers kept busy with his growing family, personal appearances, and a very popular rodeo show that once sold out Madison Square Garden in New York City. In the mid-sixties Roy and Dale moved out to the desert in California and purchased the Apple Valley Inn. Although not cut out for the hotel business, Rogers partnered with Marriott to open a chain of Roy Rogers Family Restaurants across the country. At the height of their popularity, there were close to eight hundred restaurants across the nation. He also opened the Roy Rogers Museum, later moving to and

expanding the museum in Victorville, California. And despite all his success, by all accounts Rogers remained true to his fans and himself and was the same humble, decent man offscreen as he was on film. After his passing at age eighty-six, he was buried at the Sunset Hills Memorial Garden in Apple Valley, California, in the Rogers family plot (to the left as you enter the cemetery). His lifetime of memorabilia can still be found at the Roy Rogers Museum, where you will often be greeted or given a tour by one of his many children. And yes, his faithful steed of thirty-one years, Trigger, will greet you at the museum entrance (though please note, he is not "stuffed," but rather "mounted").

MICK RONSON
May 26, 1946—April 29, 1993
CAUSE OF DEATH Liver Cancer

The primary influence for generations of glam-rock guitarists, Mick Ronson was a talented songwriter, excellent producer, and a monster guitar player. Born and raised in the

small town of Hull in northern England, Ronson switched from violin to electric guitar after hearing early recordings of Duane Eddy, and later his idol Jeff Beck with the Yardbirds. Ronson played in a number of local bands and recorded with the Rats in the late 1960s. After a disastrous tour of France, the disgruntled guitarist returned to Hull to become a gardener. In 1970, he got a call from David Bowie to fill the lead guitar position for a new project he was working on. Soon they began work on Bowie's album *The Man Who Sold the World*. After the session finished, Ronson returned to Hull to concentrate on a solo career, only to have Bowie call again. The result was Bowie's *Hunky Dory* album, featuring a heavy fuzz-tone guitar and lots of production work with strings and horn. Building on previous success, Bowie went into the studio, with Mick handling much of the production work, as well as keyboard and guitar duties. The result was the groundbreaking *The Rise and Fall of Ziggy Stardust and the Spiders from Mars*. The production work, featuring keyboards, horns, strings, and acoustic guitars, was matched with excellent songwriting to create one of the great classic albums of all time. Ronson, as leader of the Spiders, became a superstar in his own right. The Bowie-Ronson team continued with *Aladdin Sane* and *Pin-Ups* before Bowie announced his retirement, when in reality he was only retiring the band. Ronson wasted no time turning to a solo career, as well as handling production duties for Mott the Hoople, Lou Reed, John Cougar Mellencamp, Pure Prairie League, as well as handling guitar duties for Bob Dylan's Rolling Thunder Revue tour in 1975. Ronson was working on his third solo album in the early nineties when he was diagnosed with cancer. He was buried in his hometown of Hull, in the Eastern Cemetery on Preston Road. As you enter the cemetery, walk to the chapel and his black marble grave that he shares with his father is to the left of the chapel, third monument from the end of the row.

PEE WEE RUSSELL
March 27, 1906—February 15, 1969
CAUSE OF DEATH Liver Failure

Louis Prima called him "the most fabulous musical mind I know." Neither a virtuoso nor a star, clarinetist Charles "Pee Wee" Russell was nonetheless a central figure in Chicago jazz history, with a musical sincerity rarely seen during the 1930s and forties. In fact, if it wasn't for his hunger for liquor, Russell would be remembered in the same company as contemporaries Benny Goodman and Artie Shaw. Russell, who cut his chops for twenty years with the best in St. Louis, Chicago, and New York, took up permanent residency in New York City with Eddie Condon in 1935, and for the next twenty-five years they ruled the clubs on Fifty-second Street, and later at Condon's own club on West Third Street. In 1962, he moved to form his own groups and recorded more progressive-type jazz before returning as a featured soloist with old friends George Wein and Condon. Upon his passing, his remains were cremated and his ashes were returned to his family.

DOUG SAHM
November 6, 1941—November 18, 1999
CAUSE OF DEATH Heart Disease

They say when they buried Doug Sahm, they buried Texas music. A colorful blend of country, blues, R&B, western swing, and rock, Sahm went from playing on Hank Williams's knee, to working with an English rock star, to becoming a member of the highly regarded Texas Tornadoes. Performing on the radio at the young age of five, Sahm was known on the Louisiana Hayride show as "Little Doug," the pint-size steel-guitar prodigy. He was called up on stage by Hank Williams at Williams's next-to-last show at the Austin Skyline Club, at the age of eleven. During his teen years, Sahm began gravitating toward the early rock 'n' roll explosions of both Texas (Buddy Holly and Roy Orbison) and England (the Yardbirds and the Kinks). His first big hit came in the mid-sixties with "She's About a Mover" by the Sir Douglas Quintet, a group formed by Sahm in answer to the British Invasion. Drawing from a repertoire of Bob Wills, T-Bone Walker, and Junior Parker, during the seventies Sahm collaborated with Bob Dylan while cutting critically acclaimed records under his own name. But the same versatility that made Sahm a favorite of fellow musicians made it very difficult to promote his music commercially. One of the last great American hippies, Sahm's garb of tie-dye and Texas cowboy boots embodied the higher ideals of the counterculture. Taking his son, Shawn, to a Metallica concert, the elder Sahm remarked to the group's manager that he was the oldest one attending. Metallica manager Cliff Burnstein shot back, "Yeah, but you're also the hippest." Living comfortably off his songwriting royalties, Sahm returned to the limelight with the Texas Tornadoes, which also featured Freddy Fender and Flaco Jimenez. The group went on to record several albums, winning a Grammy for Best Mexican-American Album in 1990. Complaining of tingling in his fingers and stomach problems, Sahm was discovered dead in his hotel room at the Kachina Lodge in Taos, New Mexico. He was returned home to San Antonio, Texas, where his viewing at the funeral home had to be extended several hours due to the hour-long wait in a line that stretch around the block. He was buried in the family plot in Section 20, Lot 201 at the Sunset Memorial Parks in Alamo Heights, Texas.

RONNIE SCOTT
January 28, 1927—December 23, 1996
CAUSE OF DEATH Fatal Mixture of Brandy and Barbiturates

A talented jazz tenor and soprano sax player, Ronnie Scott became one of the most important figures within the British jazz community during the 1950s until the end of his career. His London-based club, Ronnie Scott's Jazz Club, featured a veritable Who's Who of American jazz, including Wes Montgomery, Zoot Sims, Dizzy Gillespie, and Stan Getz. Best known for his work with the Jazz Couriers (formed with his good friend and gifted jazz saxophonist Tubby Hayes), Scott opened his club in 1959, which rapidly became world-renowned, receiving the OBE (Order of the British Empire) for his "services to jazz" in 1981. A heavy smoker all his life, he began to suffer severe health problems in 1994. He suffered a thrombosis and had two operations on his legs before dental problems (a disaster for sax players) set in. After only partially successful implant surgery, he began to drink heavily, and the combination with sleeping pills proved fatal. He was cremated. His memorial plaque at Golders Green Crematorium in London, England, in the West Memorial Court, is near the memorials for Marc Bolin and Tubby Hayes.

SELENA
April 16, 1971—March 31, 1995
CAUSE OF DEATH Murdered

With bright red lips and spandex outfits, Selena Quintanilla Perez became the first female Tejano recording artist to score a gold record. Considered the ruling diva of Tejano music,

she was viciously gunned down in a cut-rate hotel in Corpus Christi, Texas, by the then-president of her fan club, at the age of twenty-three. Born and raised in humble surroundings, Selena's short career began with her father, Abraham Quintanilla, a blue-collar worker with a Tex-Mex band that played weddings and small parties on the weekends. Teaching his children simple songs, he was impressed by Selena's emerging talent. Quitting his day job, he and the family opened a restaurant with Selena singing classic Latino songs to patrons. When the oil economy went bust in Texas, the restaurant closed down and the family was forced to go on the road, performing at any opportunity to put food on the table. Soon, Selena y Los Dinos were a favorite on the west Texas music circuit, with the band mixing Tex-Mex and classic American rock 'n' roll. With word of mouth growing, Jose Behar, then president of EMI Records' Latin division, saw the group perform at a festival rodeo. In 1990, she made her first album, but it wasn't until the following year when "Ven Conmigo" catapulted the singer into gold record status. In 1992, she married guitarist and Los Dinos member Chris Perez, and the best-seller *Selena Live* soon followed, which was awarded a Grammy for Best Mexican-American Album. Selena's world came to an end in the winter of 1995 when her father discovered a discrepancy in the financial records from the Selena Etc. Boutique and Salon, Selena's merchandising and nail salon outlet. While many surrounding Selena suspected for some time that Yolanda Saldivar was embezzling money from her friend and employer, it took a discussion with her father before Selena would act. On the day before her death, husband Chris and Selena went to the Days Inn Motel in Corpus Christi, Texas, to recover missing records for the business. When they got back to the car, they noticed several more records were missing. Since it was late, Selena decided to go

back the following day to retrieve them. When Selena arrived early the next morning at room 158, an argument quickly ensued and a shot rang out. Clutching her chest and bleeding profusely, Selena was chased by Saldivar out of the room before Saldivar lowered the gun and returned to the room. Selena burst through the doors of the motel office screaming, "Lock the doors!" before collapsing. When she was wheeled

into the emergency room at the hospital, she was clinically dead from blood loss with no blood flow to the brain, no heartbeat, and unable to breath on her own. The day before Selena's funeral, the Quintanilla family tastefully opened a 900 phone line so fans could leave their condolences for $3.99 a minute. At the funeral, the family was forced to open the casket when a rumor spread that Selena, much like Elvis and Jim Morrison, was not really dead, before graveside services at Seaside Memorial Park in Corpus Christi, Texas. From the entrance off Ocean Drive, take the first left and park at the war memorial flagpole, where Selena's grave is twenty feet off the road on the right. Since her death, the gun used in the murder has been destroyed, room 158 is constantly renumbered to deter fans (hint: it is exactly 392 feet from the office entrance), and the new Selena Museum at 5410 Leopard Street is not worth the suggested one dollar donation. To avoid the drive, just go to the Hard Rock Cafe in San Antonio to see the white suit she wore for the video *No Me Queda Más*, where, unlike at the museum, you can at least drink a beer.

DEL SHANNON
December 30, 1934—February 8, 1990
CAUSE OF DEATH Suicide

Destined to become a one-hit wonder, Del Shannon (born Charles Westover) sold carpet during the day while hitting the lounge circuit at night. In 1961, he penned the song "Runaway," which sold over a million copies in twenty-one countries and inspired close to two hundred cover versions. In an interview in *Rolling Stone*, cowriter and pianist Max Crook said, "I had this tape recorder going. I hit a series of chords and Del said, 'Let's build something.' He was humming a melody and I put that bridge in just the way it is on the record. The next day, Del wrote the words while working in the carpet store." When his manager at work overheard the song, he had Del record it and by March of 1961 it was a hit, selling eighty thousand copies a day in the United States and reaching number one on the pop charts. It would prove to be his only gold record. After a smash tour of England (where the Beatles opened for him), it seemed to all go downhill.

With alcoholism consuming much of his time, he had the occasional chart topper, and his last hit, "Sea of Love," charted in 1982. By the mid-eighties, he was poised for a resurgence with Tom Petty, set to produce his next album, and rumored as a possible replacement for the recently deceased Roy Orbison in the Traveling Wilburys. Unfortunately, Shannon descended into the depths of depression and whether it was the effects of the Prozac he was taking or other personal problems in his life, his fans will never know. In the den of his newly purchased Canyon County, California, home at 15519 Saddleback Road, Shannon put a .22 to his head and pulled the trigger. He was cremated and his ashes were scattered. A memorial to his achievements can be found in his hometown in Coopersville, Michigan, on Main Street just outside the museum which contains several items of Del Shannon memorabilia. He was elected to the Rock and Roll Hall of Fame in 1999.

ALLAN SHERMAN
November 30, 1924—November 20, 1973
CAUSE OF DEATH Heart Attack

A comic best known for satiric songs in the sixties, including the Grammy-winning "Hello Mudduh, Hello Fadduh," Allan Sherman was considered America's greatest musical parodist. Starting out as a gag writer for Joe E. Lewis and Jackie Gleason, Sherman was a television producer when friends persuaded him to record some of his musical parodies. The result was *My Son the Folksinger*, recorded live at a Hollywood studio with a bar and one hundred of Allan's closest friends, including Harpo Marx and Johnny Mercer in attendance. The entire album was recorded in one take in less than an hour, and it went on to become the number one album in America, selling over 900,000 copies! He went on to record several more best-selling albums, write two books, and was a regular on the *Tonight* show with Johnny Carson. At Hillside Memorial Park in Los Angeles, California, drive to the top of the waterfall on the right. Upon entering the mausoleum rotunda, turn right into the Sanctuary of Benevolence, then left into the Corridor of Contentment. Walk down three sections to the Columbarium of Hope on your left. Look five rows from the bottom, thirteen rows from the left, and you will see (barely) Sherman's niche.

DINAH SHORE
February 29, 1916—February 24, 1994
CAUSE OF DEATH Ovarian Cancer

Okay, so Dinah Shore was not exactly Janis Joplin. She was, however, one of the most popular recording stars of the forties and in her fifty-five years in show business she amassed more than seventy hit recordings, a Peabody Award, eight Emmy Awards, and a place in history as the first female entertainer to host a television variety show. Just another hopeful recently arrived in New York City, Shore got her start with Xavier Cugat in 1939 as a vocalist and was a regular on Eddie Cantor's radio show. In 1943, she was signed to host her own radio show, *Call to Music*, and that same year her first movie, *Thank Your Lucky Stars*, starring Eddie Cantor, was released. In a country in the depths of World War II, Shore became a favorite with the troops and her records "Blues in the Night" and "I'll Walk Alone" both went to number one. With the introduction of rock 'n' roll in the fifties, she made the move over to television, hosting a number of chatfests. Upon her death in 1996, she was buried at Hillside Memorial Park in Los Angeles. Following the same directions for Allan Sherman, walk past his section toward the Jack Benny vault, turn left, and exit out the side door. Turn right and walk back to the outside wall units, where you will find Ms. Shore interred in Isaiah-V-247 (please note that only 25 percent of the singer's cremated remains are located here; 25 percent went to her daughter Shirley Shore, and the remaining 50 percent went to her friend Murray Niedorf). She shares this wall with Max Factor (Hollywood makeup artist), Hank Greenberg (baseball great, who was only two homeruns shy of Babe Ruth's

record), and directly behind her crypt on the lawn is Lorne Greene (of *Bonanza* fame). A trip out to the Mission Hill Country Club in Rancho Mirage, California, will allow fans a view of the lifesize statue of Shore that marks the entrance to the memorial course named in her honor. Her home in Beverly Hills, California, where she lived and subsequently passed away, is located at the corner of Glen and Oxford Road just off Sunset Boulevard.

HILLEL SLOVAK
April 13, 1962—June 25, 1988
CAUSE OF DEATH Heroin Overdose

With a lethal combination of metal and funk, as a founding member of the Red Hot Chili Peppers, Hillel Slovak was one of the most innovative guitarists during the 1980s. Formed among a close group of friends (including lead singer Anthony Kiedis and bassist Flea) from Fairfax High School in Los Angeles, California, the RHCP lineup didn't really come together until the second album. With Slovak rejoining the group (it's a long story) and funk master George Clinton handling the production duties, *Freaky Styley* featuring the explosive "Catholic Schoolgirls Rule" propelled the quartet to the top. Unfortunately, it was during the prolonged tour and subsequent media frenzy for *Freaky Styley* that Slovak (along with Kiedis) began experimenting with hard drugs. The band maintained their insane tour and recording schedule, producing two more albums before Slovak's drug habit became unmanageable. But before the band and friends could address the problem, Slovak was found dead in his apartment of a heroin overdose in Los Angeles. He was buried at Mount Sinai Memorial Park in Los Angeles in the Maimonides section, Plot 26, L-4613, eight rows from the road to the left of the tree.

CLARENCE "PINETOP" SMITH
January 11, 1904—March 15, 1929
CAUSE OF DEATH Accidental Shooting

Pinetop Smith is generally regarded as the inventor of boogie-woogie, a style of music best characterized by the continuous pounding of the left hand while the right hand plays the melody on the piano. Part of the first generation of great boogie-woogie pianists including Jimmy Blythe, Cow Cow Davenport, Little Brother Montgomery, "Cripple" Clarence Lofton, and Jimmy Yancey, Smith wrote one of the great blues and jazz classics, "Pinetop's Boogie Woogie" in 1928, the distinctive theme of which continues to influence R&B and rock 'n' roll compositions to this day. The following year, at the age of twenty-five, Smith was killed by a stray bullet during a fight at a Chicago dancehall. Since his premature death his songs have been recorded by such legends as Big Maybelle, Count Basie, Tommy Dorsey, and Woody Herman. Smith's permanent residence is the familiar blues resting place, Restvale Cemetery in Worth, Illinois. All mail can be forwarded to his unmarked grave at Lot 122, Row 2, Grave 16.

KATE SMITH
May 1, 1907—June 17, 1986
CAUSE OF DEATH Diabetes-related Illness

Known by most as the voice behind the classic "God Bless America," Kate Smith recorded nearly three thousand songs (of which over five hundred made the Hit Parade), did over fifteen thousand radio and television broadcasts, and received more than twenty-five mil-

lion fan letters during her lifetime. Although Smith was born into a musical family and spent her youth singing in her church choir and at community events, her parents were dead set against Smith becoming a professional singer. And while she had hoped to move to New York City to work in Broadway musicals, she honored her parents' wishes and went to nursing school instead. Nonetheless, after a year at nursing college, Smith secured a part in the Broadway musical *Honeymoon Lane*. During her fours years on Broadway she starred in five major productions and made a name for herself as a stage comedienne. Unfortunately, being laughed at at the expense of her girth rather than appreciated for her genuine talents as a singer was exactly what she didn't want. Lucky for Smith that during one of the last nights for the musical *Flying High*, a young Columbia Records manager saw Smith and persuaded her to make a record. Early successes begat more records and SRO dates at the Apollo Theatre and the Palace. In 1931, *The Kate Smith Show* debuted and both Smith and her manager Ted Collins were making six-figure salaries. The next thirty years was a non-stop whirlwind of radio, television, recording dates, and concert appearances. Only after partner and manager Collins died in 1964 did Kate slow down, doing only the occasional nightclub appearance. With additional homes in New York City and Arlington, Virginia, she chose to be buried near her summer home of forty years at St. Agnes Cemetery in Lake Placid, New York. Her large, private mausoleum, which backs up to the forest, is easy to find in this small cemetery.

SCOTT SMITH
January 11, 1904—November 30, 2000
CAUSE OF DEATH **Missing, Presumed Drowned**

We've all seen it before—you watch your favorite fifties doo-wop group or eighties classic rockers take the stage, only to be disappointed to find out that the only original member was the second, nonsinging drummer who purchased the name and hit the road with a bunch of second-rate studio hacks. Such is not the case with Loverboy. Still together after two decades, lead singer Mike Reno (think red spandex pants and a white headband) was still performing with the same guys in 2000 as he did twenty years ago. Remembered for such FM radio staples as "Working for the Weekend," "Turn Me Loose," "The Kid Is Hot Tonite," and "Hot Girls in Love," Scott Smith was the bass player and founding member for one of the most successful eighties rock 'n' roll bands. Although Loverboy was inactive from 1989 to 1992, they continued to play fifty to sixty dates a year with their original lineup until the end of 2000. That is when Smith was sailing off the coast of California, six kilometers off San Francisco's Ocean Beach in an area where the sea floor shallows and wave heights can be unpredictable. With fiancée Yvonne Mayotte and friend William Ellis below deck of the eleven-meter boat the *Sea Major*, a sneaker wave swept both Smith and the steering wheel out to sea. Wearing only track sweats and two sweaters (but no life jacket), Smith was gone the minute the wave swept across the deck. And while the Coast Guard searched for two days afterward, cold water survival is generally limited to less than three hours. No body was recovered and no memorial service was held as Smith was presumed drowned and was swept out to sea.

HANK SNOW
May 9, 1914—December 12, 1999
CAUSE OF DEATH Heart Failure

He bought his first guitar for $5.95, but when he was finished, Hank Snow was a member of the Grand Ole Opry with over one hundred records, selling over seventy million units, eighty-five charted singles, and was elected to eight music halls of fame. The last of the hard-drinking, hard-living, rhinestone-encrusted country and western stars was born in Nova Scotia, Canada, but left home at the age of twelve due to an abusive stepfather. By age nineteen, the young Snow had his own radio show, billed as "Hank Snow—the Yodeling Ranger." Three years later he made his first recordings for the RCA/Victor–owned Bluebird label and signed a contract that would last for almost half a century with RCA. But it wasn't until 1950 when Snow penned his first hit, "I'm Movin' On," which still holds the country music record for number of weeks at the number one position on the charts for nearly a full year. Never one to mince words, he made his feelings known about the new breed of country stars, remarking, "I don't believe real country music will ever come back. This young generation is not familiar with Roy Acuff or Hank Williams." He made his opinions about music videos quite clear with a simple, "I'm glad my time is done with recording. I got out at the right time." Buried under a

black granite monument at the Spring Hill Cemetery in Madison, Tennessee, Snow is resting in the Hill Crest section, just a few feet off the main road in the center of the cemetery. His extensive collection of guitars, photos, rhinestone suits, and music is scattered among the Country Music Hall of Fame in Nashville, the Nova Scotia Music Hall of Fame, the Canadian Country Music Hall of Fame, and the Hank Snow Country Music Centre in Liverpool, Nova Scotia, Canada.

JOHN PHILIP SOUSA
November 6, 1854—March 6, 1932
CAUSE OF DEATH Heart Attack

Remembered as the March King of America, John Philip Sousa was not only the composer of "Stars and Stripes Forever," he was the first bandleader to record with any commercial success. Born the son of a trombone player in the U.S. Marine Band, Sousa began his musical study at the age of six. Threatening to join a circus band, his father enlisted the young Sousa into the Marine Band at the age of thirteen. By age eighteen, he had already published his first composition and upon discharge from the Marines, he began performing in, and eventually conducting, many theater productions, including Gilbert and

Sullivan's *H.M.S. Pinafore* on Broadway. In 1880, he began his long association with the U.S. Marine Band, successfully conducting the band under four presidents from 1880 to 1892, when it was the most popular marching band in America. In 1890, his recording of "Semper Fidelis" was number one on the music charts in America, followed by the equally successful "The Washington Post" and "The Thunderer." Sousa formed his own band in 1892 and toured the U.S. and Europe to great acclaim. Though he disdained the recording process, he left the conducting to his concert master Arthur Pryor, who continued releasing hit singles under Sousa's name. He died at the age of seventy-seven after conducting the Ringgold Band in a rousing version of "Stars and Stripes Forever." Sousa was buried in Washington, D.C., at the Congressional Cemetery in Range 77, Site 163-S, just off the main path.

RED SOVINE
July 17, 1918—April 4, 1980
CAUSE OF DEATH Heart Attack

Perfecting the genre of the country and western truck-and-trailer tragedy ballad, Woodrow Wilson "Red" Sovine was a minor star with a solid following both in the U.S. and the U.K. Taught guitar by his mother as a youth, Sovine worked professionally on WCHS in Charleston with Johnny Bailes at the age of seventeen. After kicking around as a member of other bands and a short stint at a factory job, Sovine formed his own band in 1948 and acquired the nickname the Old Syrup Sopper, partly because of his association with sponsor Johnny Fair syrup, but mostly because of his syrupy rendition of such narrative ballads as "Daddy's Girl." Discouraged over his prospects, he was ready to give up his music career when Hank Williams stepped in and got him a good time slot on a radio show in Montgomery, Alabama. Sovine received a warm reception from the audience and later joined the Louisiana Hayride as the star. He scored his first hit on the country charts with a duet with Goldie Hill entitled "Are You Mine" and later with "Why, Baby, Why," a duet with Webb Pierce. By 1954, Sovine was a regular on the Grand Ole Opry, ending his performances with a tear-jerking rendition of "Little Rosa." During the 1960s, Sovine became a legend in truckers' eyes with the release of "Phantom 309" (a truck driver ghost story) "Giddyup Go" (a story about a truck driver reuniting with his son), and his only gold record "Teddy Bear" (a story about a crippled boy and his CB radio). A solid performer with a track record of honky-tonk material, Sovine suffered from the fact that he refused to bow to contemporary trends, nor did he bother with fostering an image to satisfy the Nashville elite. After thirty-one country chart entries, Sovine died of a heart attack at the wheel of his van as he was driving through Nashville. He was buried in the country and western–friendly Woodlawn Cemetery in Nashville, Tennessee, alongside his wife, directly across the street from the main office in the Good Shepherd section, Lot 111, Space C1, approximately thirty feet from the statue in the center of the section.

VICTORIA SPIVEY
October 15, 1906—October 3, 1976
CAUSE OF DEATH Heart Failure

Unlike many of her contemporaries, Victoria Spivey (aka Jane Lucas) was able to emerge from the classic blues era of the late 1920s and 1930s not only as a fine blues singer and recording artist, but also as a superb songwriter and record company owner. While she never attained the status of her mentors Bessie Smith or Ida Cox, what Spivey lacked in range and refinement she more than compensated for with phrasing and emotion. Recording for Decca, OKeh, Victor, and Vocalion beginning in the late twenties, Spivey wrote and recorded some of the most deeply personal and penetrating blues songs, including "TB Blues," "Dope Head Blues," and the highly suggestive "Organ Grinder Blues." In the late 1950s, she left the road and the music business and dedicated her life to the religious world. She returned to the blues in the early 1960s, just in time for the blues revival in the U.S. and Europe. Spivey started her own recording company and was able to persuade blues legends Lonnie Johnson and Roosevelt Sykes to record on her label. For her own debut album, she secured the talents of a young Bob Dylan as one of the backing musicians. Spivey continued to record and tour up until her death in 1976. She was buried without fanfare at Greenfield Cemetery in Hempstead, New York, in Space 396-6.

No, the above photo is not mislabeled. Much like Big Mama Thornton and Joseph King Oliver before her, Victoria Spivey shares a grave with Elton Harris. Her name does not appear on the marker.

DUSTY SPRINGFIELD
April 16, 1939—March 2, 1999
CAUSE OF DEATH Breast Cancer

Hailed as Britain's best pop singer, Dusty Springfield made full use of her husky, breathy voice to exude white soul from her early classic hits "I Only Want to Be with You" and "You Don't Have to Say You Love Me." She began her career singing briefly with the Lana Sisters before joining her brothers Tim and Tom Field to form the Springfields. After a string of hits in Britain, the trio hit pop chart gold with the million-selling "Silver Threads and Golden Needles." Shortly thereafter, Dusty decided to go solo and scored several more R&B and ballad-style hits throughout the sixties, including "The Look of Love" for the James Bond film *Casino Royale*. After dabbling in cabaret, Springfield signed to Atlantic Records, moved to the U.S., and recorded what is considered to be her classic album, *Dusty in Memphis*. She left Atlantic in the mid-seventies and floundered in a sea of mediocrity, including a disco album entitled *White Heat*. Fortunately, Springfield came back to her senses and returned to the pop charts with "What Have I Done to Deserve This," a collaborative effort with the Pet Shop Boys. She also went on to record a duet with Richard Carpenter of the Carpenters (his first project after the death of his sister, Karen). In 1994, she was discovered to have cancer, but remission followed intensive treatment of the disease. Unfortunately, the cancer returned again, and this time the condition was terminal. Springfield was awarded the OBE just days before her passing. After her funeral, she was cremated, with her ashes scattered in Ireland. The week following her funeral, Dusty Springfield was inducted into the Rock and Roll Hall of Fame.

JOHN DANIEL "J. D." SUMNER
November 19, 1924—November 16, 1998
CAUSE OF DEATH Heart Attack

J. D. Sumner was performing at an all night gospel show at the Ellis Auditorium when an impressionable sixteen-year-old named Elvis Presley was captivated by the powerfully rich bass singer. Soon the men would form a friendship that lasted until Elvis's final days. Born in Lakeland, Florida, Sumner escaped the boredom of fruit picking for the uncertainty that gospel singing had to offer. After developing his talent with the Sunshine Boys starting at the age of eighteen, he joined the Blackwood Brothers and stayed with the successful group until 1965. After purchasing the Stamps Music Company, he began performing with his longtime friend Elvis in 1970 and was featured with his group, the Stamps, in concert and on all but one album during the 1970s. Upon the King's passing, Sumner and his group continued through the 1990s with Sumner earning a Grammy Award and a spot in the *Guinness Book of World Records* as the World's Lowest Bass Singer, with his voice plunging to a double low C. Sumner was performing in Myrtle Beach, Florida, when he suffered a fatal heart attack after the concert. He was returned home to Nashville, Tennessee, where he was buried at Woodlawn Cemetery in the mausoleum on the third floor in Space 383 on Level B.

THE SWEET

BRIAN CONNOLLY
October 5, 1945—February 9, 1997
CAUSE OF DEATH Kidney Failure

MICK TUCKER
July 17, 1947—February 14, 2002
CAUSE OF DEATH Leukemia

One of the leading exponents of glam rock from the U.K. during the early seventies, the Sweet enjoyed modest success with hits like "Ballroom Blitz" and "Love Is Like Oxygen." Originally formed as Sweet Shop with the remnants of an earlier band, they shortened their name to the Sweet and released several singles to the sound of one hand clapping. The band, with Connolly on vocals and Tucker on drums, enlisted the help of the songwriting team of Nicky Chinn and Mike Chapman. The band signed with RCA Records and released a series of bubblegum hits. However, by 1971, the band ordered the team to come up with a harder sound while the band extended their use of makeup and costumes. By 1974, the band was writing most of their own songs and released *Desolation Boulevard* with the hit "Ballroom Blitz." The following year the band had two more hits with "Fox on the Run" and "Action," yet despite the success, Connolly left the band while in the middle of recording the follow-up album. The Sweet continued through 1981, releasing three more albums, but never capturing the audience they once had with Connolly. Through the late eighties and early nineties, one could either catch new lead singer Andy Scott's Sweet (billed as A.C. Sweet with Mick Tucker) or the Brian Connolly version (billed as B.C. Sweet). After leaving the band, Connolly's solo career never quite took off, as his heavy drinking continued to wreak havoc on his health (it has been said that Connolly suffered more heart attacks than anyone alive) and wealth (he died virtually penniless). Tucker retired in 1995 due to ill health. Upon Connolly's death due to poor lifestyle choices (officially kidney failure), he was cremated, with a memorial plaque placed at Breakspear Crematorium in Ruislip, Middlesex, U.K. on the wall near the West Chapel. After a five-year fight with cancer and a bone marrow transplant, Tucker was buried at Chorleywood Cemetery just outside of London, in an unmarked grave.

BUDDY TATE
February 22, 1913—February 10, 2001
CAUSE OF DEATH Cancer

One of the few remaining alumni of the Count Basie Orchestra alive at the turn of the century, saxophonist Buddy Tate came into national prominence during the swing era of the 1930s and 1940s with his Texas-style, upper-register phrasing and thick, broad vibrato. Born and raised in Texas, Tate honed his craft in the clubs of the Southwest when swing ruled popular music. Tate played awhile with McCloud's Night Owls and the St. Louis Merrymakers, learning from the examples of Lester Young, Coleman Hawkins, and Herschel Evans before him. He played briefly with Basie in 1934 when Young took flight, but left, only to be called back five years later when Evans died suddenly. Tate continued with Basie for nine years, cementing his legacy among the giants of the tenor saxophone. When the economics of keeping a big band on the road forced changes in the lineup, Tate decided to look for work that would keep him closer to New York. After a stint for bandleaders Lucky Millinder and Hot Lips Page, he spent time with former Basie singer Jimmy Rushing's Savoy band. Eventually Tate secured a residency at the Celebrity Club on 125th Street in Harlem, and stayed for twenty-one years until, according to Tate, "the clientele changed—they wanted rock and didn't appreciate what we were doing, so we quit." The last link to the stellar Count Basie Orchestra also toured Europe, played a command performance for the Queen of England, and shared the stage with Lester Young, Sweets Edison, and Buck Clayton; he was buried at Pinelawn Memorial Park in Farmingdale, New York (on Long Island) in Section 70, Lot 4, Range 15, Plot Z, Grave 123.

MEL TAYLOR
September 24, 1933—August 11, 1996
CAUSE OF DEATH Lung Cancer

His name might not be familiar, but music fans young and old would recognize his signature drumbeat on one of the most popular instrumental songs ever recorded—"Hawaii Five-O" by the Ventures. Since their formation in the early sixties, Mel Taylor sat behind the drum kit through an extraordinary thirty-seven charting albums that made the Ventures one of the biggest recording acts in history. Born in Brooklyn, New York, Taylor moved to Tennessee in his early teens and began as a rhythm guitarist with his younger brother Larry (bass player for Canned Heat) in a rockabilly group before switching to drums. In the late fifties, the Taylors moved again, this time to Southern California, where Taylor worked as a meat cutter by day and a session drummer by night. As the house drummer for the renowned North Hollywood nightclub the Palamino, he had worked with Buck Owens, Herb Alpert and the Tijuana Brass, Bobby "Boris" Pickett ("The Monster Mash") when the Ventures (sans drummer) walked into the club after appearing on a TV show. Taylor filled in for the set and stuck around,

recording and touring on their surf-instrumental hits "Walk Don't Run," "Perfidia," and "Tequila" for over thirty years. In July 1996, during a tour of Japan (where the Ventures tour was considered a major cultural event), Taylor was suffering from pneumonia, later diagnosed as a malignant tumor in his lungs. He returned home on August 2nd, but the cancer aggressively advanced and Taylor died ten days later. At Mount Sinai Memorial Park in Los Angeles, California, turn left onto King David Drive and proceed about one hundred feet and park on the right. Walk up the twenty-seven rows into the Maimonides section, where Taylor is buried in Lot 3708, Space 2DD.

HOUND DOG TAYLOR
April 12, 1915—December 17, 1975
CAUSE OF DEATH Lung Cancer

Although not the most accomplished blues–slide guitarist in Chicago, Theodore Roosevelt "Hound Dog" Taylor was the definitive Chicago houserocker during the fifties and sixties. Born with six fingers on each hand, legend has it he was chased out of Mississippi by the Klan after having an affair with a white woman (hence his nickname "Hound Dog"), and arrived in Chicago two days later, never to return to his hometown of Natchez, Mississippi. He appeared on Sonny Boy Williamson II's KFFA *King Biscuit Time* radio broadcast and worked frequently with Elmore James, Robert Jr. Lockwood, and Sonny Boy II in the late 1930s before moving to Chicago in 1942. Working fabled Maxwell Street for tips with an occasional gig at Stormy's Club or the AT&T Club in Chicago, it took Taylor another fifteen years before he would play music full-time. A favorite of both the South and West Sides of Chicago, Taylor attained national and international acclaim through extensive touring (where future rocker George Thorogood served as his driver on the East Coast), and three excellent albums on Alligator Record in the 1970s. Upon his passing, he was buried at Restvale Cemetery in Worth, Illinois, in Section D, Lot 257, Grave 12. Located about eight rows above Magic Sam, it took nearly a quarter of a century to mark his grave with a proper monument. He was inducted into the Blues Foundation's Hall of Fame in 1984.

JACK TEAGARDEN
August 20, 1905—January 15, 1964
CAUSE OF DEATH Heart Failure

Until Jack Teagarden, jazz trombone sounded (in trombonist Vic Dickenson's words) "like a dying cow in a thunderstorm." Like musical innovators Louis Armstrong and Charlie Parker before him, Teagarden developed new ideas and a close-to-the-chest slide technique that revolutionized jazz trombone. A leading exponent of traditional and early big band jazz and also an accomplished vocalist, he collaborated with Glenn Miller on the jazz standard "Basin Street Blues." In addition, Teagarden played with Paul Whiteman, Louis Armstrong, Benny Goodman, Hoagy Carmichael, as well as fronting his own "all star" orchestra. In 1957, Teagarden toured Europe with Earl "Fatha" Hines and continued to tour solidly for the next five years. A hard life on the road, five marriages, and a full fifty years of excessive alcohol consumption all took their toll. Teagarden played his last engagement at the Dream Room (now the Sea Port) on Bourbon Street in New Orleans's French Quarter. He was found dead around the corner at the Prince Conti Motor Hotel (the exact room number has been long forgotten) the following day, from heart failure. Teagarden was returned to California, where he was buried at Forest Lawn Hollywood Hills, in Los Angeles. Following the same directions for Rick Nelson, Teagarden is buried seven rows from the intersection in Plot 3821 in the Revelation section. Following his death, his family donated a number of personal effects to the Red River Valley Museum in Vernon, Texas. Included are his desk, trombone, and

personal correspondence. The rest of the museum is dedicated to cattle drives and other cow-related stuff. A plaque outside of the Sea Port marks his final gig and his home at 504 Twenty-sixth Street, Pompano Beach, Florida, is still standing.

TAMMI TERRELL
April 29, 1945—March 16, 1970
CAUSE OF DEATH Brain Cancer

Tammi Terrell with Marvin Gaye, just moments before she collapsed onstage.

Blessed with an incredibly romantic, soulful voice, Thomasina "Tammi Terrell" Montgomery was Philadelphia's hometown sweetheart who died much too young and well before she reached her fullest potential. Beginning with talent contests at the age of eleven, Terrell began her recording career at the age of fifteen when the Godfather of Soul James Brown spotted her one night and asked her to join the James Brown Revue (rumor has it Terrell was romantically linked with Brown, and later with David Ruffin of the Temptations). She left after a year and recorded several singles for Checker Records, languishing in obscurity until Berry Gordy heard her in a Detroit nightclub in 1965 and signed her to Motown Records. Two years later, Terrell was teamed with Marvin Gaye and the collaboration was a resounding success for both singers. Together with the songwriting team of Ashford and Simpson, they produced the hit duets "Ain't No Mountain High Enough," "Your Precious Love," "Ain't Nothing Like the Real Thing," and "Good Lovin' Ain't Easy to Come By." Unfortunately, Terrell never had a chance at a solo career, collapsing into Gaye's arms while singing "Ain't No Mountain High Enough" during a performance at Virginia's Hampden-Sydney College. Days later, the awful truth was known—Terrell was suffering from a brain tumor. After two years and nine operations, Terrell was blind and confined to a wheelchair when she passed away. From the main office at Mount Lawn Cemetery in Philadelphia, Pennsylvania, walk toward the hedges bordering the road for Terrell's final resting place. Her grave is one row from the hedge.

JAMES "SON" THOMAS
October 14, 1926—June 26, 1993
CAUSE OF DEATH Stroke and Heart Attack

A leading figure of traditional Delta blues, James "Son" Thomas, unlike Muddy Waters and Howlin' Wolf, never moved from his home in the heart of the Mississippi Delta for the

bright lights and better opportunities in Chicago, for his music and his life were insepara-
ble from the Delta farmlands he knew and loved. Influenced at an early age by his uncle
Joe Propper and seminal blues figures Skip James, Arthur "Big Boy" Crudup, and Tommy
McClennan, Thomas frequented the juke joints of Yazoo City, where he was taught the
fundamentals by the legendary Elmore James. Playing house parties alongside his uncle
for a dollar a night, Thomas built a repertoire of traditional Delta blues, including "Cairo
Blues" and "Catfish Blues." Unfortunately, Thomas's refusal to hire an agent or manager

made him a relative unknown until late in his life. A
gravedigger by trade, he was also a talented sculptor
whose traditional African-inspired folk art has been
sold in art galleries in New York and Los Angeles. In
1967, a struggling documentary producer William
Ferris featured Thomas in one of his books and five
documentary films. By the following year, Thomas
was a featured performer at festivals around the
world. He also released a handful of albums of new
material, as well as reissues of his earlier works.
Suffering from ill health much of his life, including
back pain, emphysema, a brain tumor, a gun-shot
wound, and a stroke, Thomas succumbed to a heart
attack in a nursing home at the age of sixty-six.
Buried at Bogue Memorial Cemetery in Leland,
Mississippi, the cemetery is just before the river crossing on the left, where his upright monument is easy
to see.

WILLIE MAE "BIG MAMA" THORNTON
December 11, 1926—July 25, 1984
CAUSE OF DEATH Heart Attack

Janis Joplin called her one of her inspirations and *Living Blues* magazine described her as
"two hundred pounds of boogaloo." Of course, fans and musicians alike simply called
her Big Mama Thornton. A native of Alabama, Thornton began her career in earnest in
1941 as a singer and comedienne. Watching such blues greats as Junior Parker, Bessie
Smith, and Ma Rainey from the side of the stage, she began to develop an earthy, feisty
style with her huge, deep voice and even larger body frame. After her debut at the Apollo
Theatre, she cut her first record in 1951 for E&W Records, with Mel Walker and Little
Esther Phillips. She recorded her first hit, "Hound Dog," the following year. Although
she only received five hundred dollars for the session, a young Elvis Presley recorded the
song four years later and made well over a million dollars on that single alone. By 1957,
after a solid fifteen years of touring and selling records, Big Mama's career began to
wind down. Leaving her record company over a dispute over royalty payments (or lack
thereof), she played up and down the California coastline in small clubs, her talents generally unnoticed by most of the patrons. With the growing popularity of blues-
influenced rock 'n' roll, her career once again took flight in the late 1960s. Recording
with such greats as Muddy Waters, Lightnin' Hopkins, Mississippi Fred McDowell, and
B. B. King, she began touring and recording heavily, despite continuing health problems
due to excessive weight and alcohol consumption. On the afternoon of July 25, 1984,
while playing cards with her sister and two other friends at her small apartment in
Inglewood, California, Thornton slumped over the table—dead of a heart attack. Today
she shares a grave with two other deceased members of her family at Inglewood Park
Cemetery in Inglewood, California. Parking at the intersection of Regent and Avenue of

Champions, walk across the expansive lawn to the chain-link fence and turn right, walking an additional fourteen spaces along the cemetery border. Thornton is buried in Section M, Lot 2486.

MEL TORMÉ
September 13, 1925—June 5, 1999
CAUSE OF DEATH Stroke

A multitalented composer, arranger, musician, and respected jazz and pop singer for more than six decades, Mel Tormé's fluid, silky voice and interpretations of the classics earned him the moniker the Velvet Fog (a title he neither liked nor encouraged). Born in Chicago, Illinois, Tormé made his professional debut at the age of three and by the age of ten, he was already fully immersed in the demanding world of vaudeville. At the age of sixteen, he was playing drums in the Chico Marx Band, who introduced the young talent to RKO Pictures in Hollywood. Working as an actor and singer on television, Tormé was lounging poolside in Hollywood when he penned what would become his biggest seller—"The Christmas Song,"—a huge hit for Nat "King" Cole and later recorded by over one hundred different artists. Tormé was now in demand as a singer (often with George Shearing as his pianist), with a repertoire that reached five thousand songs (with 250 songs his own). He recorded over fifty albums during his lifetime and though much of his talent was lost among the lush, cheesy string arrangements of the 1960s, Tormé regained solid footing within the jazz community during his final two decades of performing. His ear for melody, his ability to swing, and a talent for scat enabled Tormé to appeal to a whole new generation in the eighties and nineties. This was never more apparent than at the 1995 Bumbershoot Music Festival in Seattle, Washington, where Tormé was a featured performer alongside the Ramones and Mudhoney—and was called back for eight encores! Today Tormé resides at the star-packed Westwood Memorial Park in Westwood, California, near the entrance on the left, in front of Truman Capote's wall crypt.

MERLE TRAVIS
November 29, 1917—October 20, 1983
CAUSE OF DEATH Heart Attack

A talented guitarist and musician, Merle Travis not only revolutionized guitar picking but also played a major role in the development of the first solid-body guitar. The Travis picking style was developed early as a young boy imitating his father on banjo. After learning a few chords, Travis carried over the five-string banjo style of picking and applied it to the guitar. While still in his teens Travis took a job with the Tennessee Tomcats, playing on the radio and touring locally for thirty-five cents (on a good day). In the late 1930s, Travis moved to California and soon his luck began to change. He signed with Capitol Records and immediately scored hits with

"No Vacancy," "Divorce Me C.O.D.," and his million-seller "So Round, So Firm, So Fully Packed." With songwriting partner Cliff Stone, he also scored big with the Tex Williams hit "Smoke, Smoke, Smoke (That Cigarette)" in 1947, adding to his *Billboard* Award for Top Record Sales. After his most-covered song, "Sixteen Tons," was successfully revived by Tennessee Ernie Ford in 1955, Travis spent much of the 1960s at festivals and in films. After a memorable performance of "Re-enlistment Blues" in the film *From Here to Eternity*, Travis joined the cast of the Grand Ole Opry. And while the hits were few and far between, Travis was nominated for two CMA Awards in the Instrumental category and was inducted into the Country Music Hall of Fame in 1977. When he died while on tour in Oklahoma, he had earned seven gold records, twelve BMI Awards for hit songs, and induction into the Gibson Hall of Fame for his contributions to the design of the guitar. Travis was returned to his hometown of Ebenezer, Kentucky, where his ashes were scattered at the monument dedicated in his honor in 1956. Located at Ebenezer Missionary Baptist Church on Merle Travis Highway, the monument is just to the left in front of the church.

BOBBY TROUP
October 18, 1918—February 7, 1999
CAUSE OF DEATH   Heart Attack

JULIE LONDON
September 26, 1926—October 18, 2000
CAUSE OF DEATH   Effects of a Stroke

While they were perhaps best known to American audiences as Dr. Joseph Early and Nurse Dixie McCall on the TV show *Emergency*, accomplished jazz pianist Bobby Troup authored one of the coolest songs ever, "Route 66," while wife Julie London was a successful actress and torch song vocalist with thirty albums to her credit. Troup was introduced to music at an early age through his family's music stores. Upon graduation from college, Troup moved to New York as a songwriter for Tommy Dorsey. After serving in the Marines during World War II, Troup was driving on the venerable highway when he penned the words to the definitive West Coast travel song "Route 66." Upon arrival in Los Angeles, he showed the lyrics to Nat "King" Cole, who loved the song. After a hit with Cole, Troup led a charmed life, penning the hits "Daddy," "Baby, Baby All the Time" (another hit for Cole), and "Meaning of the Blues." After twenty years as an active participant in the West Coast cool jazz scene, he hosted the KABC-TV series *Stars of Jazz* for two and a half years, which featured some of the finest jazz with performances by Stan Getz, Errol Garner, and soon-to-be wife Julie London. Married in 1960, London toured extensively with the Matty Malneck Orchestra early in her career. Retired briefly, she began recording again in the 1950s and was voted *Billboard* magazine's Top Vocalist in 1955 three years running. After their respective TV and film appearances in the 1970s, they both lived quietly at their home in California and raised their family. Upon their passing, one year apart, their ashes were interred at Forest Lawn (Hollywood Hills, in Los Angeles, California). As you enter the cemetery gates, turn left toward the large outdoor mausoleum. They can be found side-by-side in the top row over the doorway of the Columbarium of Providence.

ERNEST TUBB
February 9, 1914—September 6, 1984
CAUSE OF DEATH   Emphysema

Considered unique but not necessarily great, it never came as a surprise to his loyal audience when he missed a note when switching from a Jimmie Rodgers–inspired tenor yodel to his granite baritone. But as Ernest Tubb once said, "I don't care whether I hit the right

note or not. I'm not looking for perfection—I'm looking for individuality!" In fact, Tubb got his start in 1937 after contacting Carrie Rodgers (Jimmie's widow), who agreed to listen to his modest radio show out of San Antonio, Texas. A close friendship ensued in which Rodgers not only helped Tubb in his career, but also gave the young singer Jimmie's prized C.F. Martin guitar (now on display at the Country Music Hall of Fame in Nashville, Tennessee). After recording six songs for RCA, only two were released due to poor sales. After playing countless honky-tonks and dive bars, Tubb didn't record again until 1940, this time for Decca. The difference between the two dates was a completely new sound. Since having his tonsils removed, Tubb could no longer yodel and was forced to develop his own style (as opposed to being just another Rodgers clone). The following year, Tubb cut more sides for Decca, including his biggest hit, "Walking the Floor Over You," which went on to become his first million-seller. After moving to Nashville, in 1943 he joined the Grand Ole Opry and was the first who dared to use an electric guitar on its proud and sacred stage. And whether onstage or just walking down the street, Tubb always wore a hand-tailored western suit and a ten-gallon hat—bound and determined to rid the association of "hillbilly" with country and western music. By 1947, Tubb was a bona fide honky-tonk country star who had his own record store directly across from the Ryman Auditorium, where he broadcast his *Midnight Jamboree* at midnight (after the Opry broadcast had ended). Always willing to help fellow performers such as Hank Snow and Hank Williams (he sang "Beyond the Sunset" at Williams's funeral), Tubb spent most of the 1950s on the road with his band the Texas Troubadours, always returning to Nashville for his Saturday-night performance with the Opry. By now his son Justin, an accomplished songwriter and performer in his own right (he wrote "Lonesome 7-7203," a hit for Hawkshaw Hawkins) began to work on the business side of the family business. Elected to the Country Music Hall of Fame in 1965 and the Nashville Songwriter's International Hall of Fame in 1970, Tubb was forced to slow down due to the ill effects of emphysema, first diagnosed in 1965. Resting between shows in his custom touring bus with oxygen, Tubb retired from the road in 1982. His grave was properly marked after the passing of his son Justin at the Hermitage Memorial Gardens in Nashville. Tubb is buried in Section A of the Garden of Peace in Lot 28C, five spaces in from the road on the path through the middle of the section.

BIG JOE TURNER
May 18, 1911—November 24, 1985
CAUSE OF DEATH Heart Attack

He had little more than a five-note range, but that didn't stop Big Joe Turner from becoming one of the premier blues shouters. A seminal figure in the history of the blues, Turner's sixty-plus-year career spanned a musical variety to include ballads, jump blues, boogie-woogie, and rock 'n' roll. The only thing larger than his massive physique was his powerful voice, which could cut through the din of any bar, house party, or juke joint—with or without a microphone. The soon-to-be Boss of the Blues began as a fourteen-year-old bartender in Kansas City, Kansas, fronting big bands like Bennie Moten and Count Basie before he joined forces with pianist Pete Johnson in the 1930s. After a stunning performance at Carnegie Hall, Turner and Johnson became regulars at Cafe Society in New York City, alongside boogie-woogie piano legends Meade "Lux" Lewis and Albert Ammons. At the same time Turner began recording for a number of record labels, including Vocalion ("Cherry Red"), Decca ("Corrine, Corrina" with Art Tatum), and with Freedom ("Still in the Dark"). But it wasn't until the 1950s, when he was well into his forties, that Turner recorded "Chains of Love," "Sweet Sixteen," "Honey Hush," and his biggest hit, "Shake, Rattle and Roll" (which made it to number one and was covered by Bill Haley and the Comets). After making the successful transition from big bands to boogie-woogie to R&B, Big Joe Turner was now the undisputed Boss of the Blues and a father figure of rock 'n' roll. Now popular with white audiences, Turner toured with Alan Freed's rock 'n' roll package shows and appeared in the movie *Shake, Rattle and Rock*. However, Turner recognized that he was too big, too old, and too black for early rock 'n' roll audiences and wisely signed with Atlantic Records to concentrate on his R&B roots. Based in New Orleans in the 1960s, Turner toured Europe once again with Humphrey Lyttelton in 1965 and then again the following year with the American Folk Blues Festival. In the 1970s, Turner remained on the road, returning to Europe with stops at the Newport Jazz Festival (as part of the Johnny Otis show) in 1970 and the Monterey Jazz Festival. Featured in the brilliant *Last of the Blue Devils*, a film about Kansas City jazz from 1974 to '79, Turner began to suffer the effects of his on-the-road lifestyle and was troubled by illness late in life. Using crutches to get around, Turner continued to work in the studio with Count Basie and Jimmy Witherspoon, unwilling to retire. Upon his death in 1985 at age seventy-four, he was interred at Roosevelt Memorial Park in Los Angeles, California. From the Vermont Street entrance, drive into the cemetery and stay to the right. Drive three hundred feet and park at Marker 3355 on the

"BOSS OF THE BLUES"
BIG JOE TURNER
1911 ♪ 1985
PATRICIA TURNER
PARTNER IN LIFE
1923 ♪ 1990
KATIE BRYANT
JOE'S SISTER
1908 — 1983
DONATED BY FRIENDS OF THE BIG JOE TURNER MUSICIAN'S FUND

right-hand curb. Walk four rows into the section on your right (Section 3358, Space 4). In a fitting tribute, Big Joe Turner was elected to both the Blues Hall of Fame and the Rock and Roll Hall of Fame.

CONWAY TWITTY
September 1, 1933—June 5, 1993
CAUSE OF DEATH Aneurysm

Born Harold Jenkins, Conway Twitty was better known by a number of monikers—Mr. T, the Heartland Heartthrob, Lonely Boy Blue, the High Priest of Country Music, and his favorite, the Best Friend a Song Ever Had. Born in Friars Point, Mississippi, Jenkins formed his first band at the age of ten and made his radio debut two years later. Drafted into the army, he continued with his own band, playing to servicemen while stationed in Japan. Influenced by the surge of popularity of rock 'n' roll and the Elvis mania, Jenkins changed his name (a combination of Conway, Arkansas, and Twitty, Texas) and signed with MGM. Twitty released several pop/rock-oriented songs, including "Lonely Boy Blue" (a song written for Presley's *King Creole* movie) and his breakout hit, "It's Only Make Believe." After several quickie teen rock 'n' roll movies *(Platinum High School* and *Sex Kittens Go to College)* Twitty floundered in the cabaret market before close friend and top Nashville songwriter Harlan Howard convinced Twitty to cut a demo of country songs. That demo tape landed on MCA-Decca Records producer Owen Bradley's desk, who immediately signed the singer to the label. That deal began a string of fifty-five hit records, starting with "Guess My Eyes Were Bigger Than My Heart" and ending with his posthumous release, "Final Touches" twenty-seven years later. An astute businessman, Twitty opened his home/theme park to fans as Twitty City (which closed shortly after his death). Returning home after a string of shows in Branson, Missouri, Twitty collapsed in his tour bus and died a short time later at a Springfield hospital. He is interred in the back of the main outdoor wall mausoleum on the bottom row on the left-most corner crypt at Sumner Memorial Park in Gallatin, Tennessee.

RUDY VALLEE
July 28, 1901—July 3, 1986
CAUSE OF DEATH Heart Attack

Originally singing through a megaphone, Rudy Vallee is generally considered to be the first teen idol. With female fans swooning in the aisles, Vallee was the model which Russ Columbo, Bing Crosby, Frank Sinatra, and Johnny Ray all emulated. Born in Vermont but raised in Maine, Vallee was initially a serious student of the saxophone. It wasn't until he enrolled in Yale that he became a bandleader of a dance band popular with the country club set. A firm believer that sweet, melodic dance music was preferable over the blaring and honking jazz and swing music of the era, Vallee moved to New York City were he formed Rudy Vallee and His Connecticut Yankees. The band soon found themselves playing live nationwide on New York's WABC radio. And Vallee's formula was simple: a strict tempo for dancing, a drummer brushing lightly, plenty of soft strings, and Vallee's relaxed, clearly enunciated lyrics. In 1930, he recorded "The Vagabond Lover"—and the moniker stuck. Throughout the 1930s and 1940s, Vallee recorded and performed dozens of hits, most derived from films and Broadway shows. After World War II, Vallee returned to radio, nightclubs, and making more forgettable movies. Gone were the straitlaced, pompous characters of his early efforts and Vallee reinvented himself as more of a comic actor. During his last twenty years, Vallee mostly played the talk show circuit with the occasional nightclub appearance. Returned to Maine for burial, Rudy was buried in the Vallee family plot at Saint Hyacinthe Cemetery in the town of Westbrook. While his personal stone was stolen years ago, the family monument remains intact, just off Stroudwater Street.

JIMMY VAN HEUSEN
January 26, 1913—February 6, 1990
CAUSE OF DEATH Heart Attack

One of the most successful and prolific songwriters of his era, Jimmy Van Heusen once said that his interests were "chicks, booze, music, and Sinatra, in that order." Born Edward Babcock in Syracuse, New York, Van Heusen got his start playing piano in a brothel while attending Syracuse University in the early 1930s. After writing songs for the famed Cotton Club in Harlem, Van Heusen was hired as a songwriter for a Tin Pan Alley publisher, where he sold his first song, "It's the Dreamer in Me," which was recorded by both Bing Crosby and Jimmy Dorsey in 1938. After a rocky run writing for Broadway, Van Heusen began a long and successful collaboration with Johnny Burke. Together they wrote "Imagination" and "Polka Dots and Moonbeams" (both hits for Frank Sinatra with Tommy Dorsey's band) before moving to Hollywood and working with Crosby (who gave them the nickname the Golddust Twins). In 1940 alone, Van Heusen had written over sixty songs and by 1944, the two had worked on twenty Crosby productions, including the Academy Award–winning picture *Going My Way*. In the 1950s when Burke became ill, Van Heusen teamed with close Sinatra friend Sammy Cahn. Together they wrote some of the most memorable Sinatra tunes, including "High Hopes," "Come Fly with Me," "The Tender Trap," "September of My Years," and that Sinatra classic ode to Chicago, "My Kind of Town." After a few unsuccessful attempts at Broadway shows, the nature of the business had changed, and, as Cahn put it, "the phones just stopped ringing." During the 1970s and

1980s, Van Heusen was busy administering several of his publishing companies, as well as being an active member of the Songwriters Hall of Fame. He passed away quietly at his Palm Springs, California, home and was buried at nearby Desert Memorial Park in Cathedral City outside Palm Springs, California, in Section B-8, Space 63, close to his friend Sinatra.

R. J. VEALEY
September 29, 1962—November 13, 1999
CAUSE OF DEATH Heart Attack

Born from Roy Orbison's backing band, the cream of Atlanta, Georgia's studio musicians came together in the mid-seventies to form the Atlanta Rhythm Section. Best remembered for their MOR classic songs "So Into You" and "Imaginary Lover," the group faded away in the late eighties amid falling sales. Devoted fans continued to support the re-formed group during the 1990s with Vealey on drums. The group had just finished a concert at Orlando's

University of Central Florida when Vealey sat down on one of the equipment trucks and slumped over, suffering a massive heart attack. Paramedics on the scene were unable to revive him. Burial followed at Crest Lawn Memorial Park in Atlanta, Georgia, where Vealey's monument can be found in /the Jewish Summit on top of the hill in the Ahavath Achim lawn section, twenty feet from the road. Two months after his death, the Orange-Osceola Medical Examiner's Office issued their report indicating that the heart attack that killed the Atlanta Rhythm

Section drummer was caused by chronic cocaine abuse. The autopsy report revealed that the talented drummer and family man had the heart of a "very sick, old man," and that his arteries were 90 percent blocked.

SID VICIOUS
May 10, 1957—February 2, 1979
CAUSE OF DEATH Heroin Overdose

Only rivaling G. G. Allin as one of the most overrated, untalented musicians since recorded times, Sid Vicious was the "bass" player for the punk group the Sex Pistols. Born John Simon Ritchie, Vicious was given his nickname by friend and future bandmate John Lydon (named Johnny Rotten while in the Sex Pistols) for his unpredictable, violent outbursts. In 1975, Vicious was asked to join the band after a falling out with original bassist Glen Matlock in 1977. Among the most notable exponents of punk rock, the Sex Pistols enjoyed brief fame in the late seventies with their two singles, "God Save the Queen" and "Anarchy in the U.K." Fronted by singer Johnny Rotten, Sid Vicious "played" bass and vomited on the audience. Even after Vicious met former New York Dolls groupie and heroin addict Nancy Spungen, Vicious's own habit didn't seem to improve his musicianship. As drummer Paul Cook remembers, "We were trying to think of ways to get him out of the studio. Then he got hepatitis—it was a godsend." In concert, Vicious was so god-awful that a real musician played bass behind the speakers while roadies turned off Sid's instrument. After the Sex Pistols' final gig (due in part to Vicious's drug habit) in 1978, Spungen became Vicious's manager and savant as he attempted to go solo. But Chrissie Hynde of the Pretenders summed it up best when she said, "To tell the truth, at the time it wouldn't have surprised me if he or anyone killed her. She was that obnoxious." And kill her he did. After selecting a lock knife as a present for Vicious, Sid and Nancy went back to room 100 of the Chelsea Hotel in New York City. On the night of October 12, 1978 at 1:30 A.M., a small amount of morphine was delivered to the couple. When Spungen was discovered the next morning, her body was slumped over next to the toilet with a single knife wound to her abdomen. Three months later, after being released from Riker's Island on various charges, Vicious was met by his mother, who purchased heroin for her son upon his release. After watching her son inject himself, Anne Beverley went to sleep, as did Sid—permanently—and it was later determined that Beverley had purchased pure heroin. After an autopsy was completed, Vicious was cremated, with the ashes returned to his mother. While it has been widely rumored that Beverley climbed the wall to the King David Cemetery in Bensalem, Pennslyvania, and scattered her son's ashes in the snow over Nancy's grave (against the wishes of the Spungen family), those close to Vicious report that his remains were accidentally dropped in the middle of busy Heathrow Airport and the ashes were distributed among the busy travelers. And though the home at 63 Bank Street in Greenwich Village, New York, where Vicious died is still standing, room 100 at the Chelsea Hotel has been remodeled and sectioned off to adjoining rooms due to one too many curious tourists.

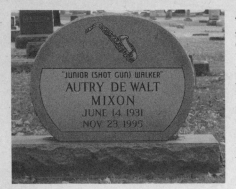

JUNIOR WALKER
June 14, 1931—November 23, 1995
CAUSE OF DEATH Cancer

As one of Motown's premier saxophone players, Junior Walker, along with his band the All Stars, was one of the blues' most dynamic tenor saxophonists. Born Autry DeWalt Mixon, Walker was inspired to pick up the saxophone in high school after listening to the jump, jive, and wail of Louis Jordan. Upon graduating, Walker went professional, forming the All Stars and hitting the road. During his heyday between 1965 and 1970, Walker recorded several Top 20 hits, such as "Shotgun," "Do the Boomerang," "How Sweet It Is (To Be Loved by You)," and "These Eyes." After leaving Motown in 1970, he continued to record and perform (Walker provided the saxophone solo on the Foreigner hit "Urgent"), yet he never regained the popularity he had in the late 1960s. In 1988, Walker made his film debut with Sam Moore in *Tapeheads*, where they play (convincingly) fictional R&B legends, the Swanky Modes. Walker was buried in his hometown of Battle Creek, Michigan, at Oak Hill Cemetery in Lot 998, just off Oak Avenue between Sixth and Seventh Street.

FATS WALLER
May 21, 1904—December 14, 1943
CAUSE OF DEATH Bronchial Pneumonia

When asked, "What is swing?" Thomas "Fats" Waller replied, "If you have to ask, you ain't got it." An unforgettable character, Fats Waller was one of the most gifted and exceptionally creative jazz pianists and composers of the 1930s and 1940s. Raised in abject poverty in a tenement in Harlem, the Reverend Waller initially did not approve of his son playing "the devil's music." And while the father encouraged his son musically by paying for violin lessons, Waller also continued with his studies on the organ and piano. At the time he

was earning seventy-five cents a week running errands for a local grocer, but in 1918, at the age of fourteen, he dropped out of high school and began earning twenty-three dollars a week as a silent movie organist. The following year Waller joined a vaudeville act and learned to do three things that would follow him the rest of his life— how to drink, eat, and write music. By age nineteen he was commanding one hundred dollars per recorded piano roll and two hundred fifty dollars per recording engagement with some of the major artists of the day, including Bessie Smith. Waller even performed a solo engagement at Carnegie Hall, which unfortunately went badly due to his excessive drinking. Waller moved beyond rent parties and nightclubs and along with mentor James P. Johnson, composed the music for several Negro musical comedies, including *Keep Shufflin'* and *Connie's Hot Chocolates* (which included one of his most recognizable hits, "Ain't Misbehavin' "). In 1933, he made a trip to Europe where he played across the Continent with performances at the infamous Moulin Rouge in Paris and the Kit Kat Club in London. Upon his return to the States, though he was still considered a minor musical figure, he was still the highest-paid jazz artist in America. With over four hundred songs under his wing, Waller was making fifty to seventy-five thousand dollars per year. In the prime of his life, Waller contracted the flu during a six-week engagement at the Florentine Gardens in Hollywood, California. After an all-night party following the final show, then an all-night party after the premiere of the film *Stormy Weather* (in which Waller had a cameo appearance), Waller boarded a train for New York. After another all-nighter in the club car, Waller went to sleep in the early morning. That evening as the train pulled into Kansas City, Waller's breathing was labored and a doctor was summoned. Unfortunately, his lifestyle had caught up with the jazz giant and he died in his bunk. Upon his return to New York, Waller was cremated and his ashes were flown over his home and scattered across his beloved Harlem neighborhood.

ETHEL WATERS
October 13, 1896—September 1, 1977
CAUSE OF DEATH Kidney Failure and Cancer

Reportedly the first professional black singer broadcast nationwide on radio in 1922 and the first to star on Broadway in a dramatic role, Ethel Waters's seventy years in show business included radio, TV, films, and recording and performing with the likes of Benny Goodman, Fletcher Henderson, Duke Ellington, and the Dorsey Brothers. Originally billed as "Sweet Mama Stringbean," Waters went from the blues of the twenties to swinging jazz in the thirties and forties, working every nightclub and stage from Los Angeles to London. Noted for such songs as "Dinah" and "Stormy Weather," Waters also had a successful run in both TV and films, nominated for an Academy Award in 1953. Upon her passing, she was buried at Forest Lawn Memorial Park in Glendale, California. Waters's final resting place is located along the walkway in the Garden of Ascension, near Space 7152.

JOHNNY "GUITAR" WATSON
February 3, 1935—May 17, 1996
CAUSE OF DEATH Heart Attack

"I thought his fall was part of the show," said blues fan Gemi Taylor. "Johnny was such a smooth entertainer, he turned death into another funky move." And die he did. Johnny "Guitar" Watson was onstage at the Blues Cafe in Yokohama, Japan, when he fell to the

stage during "Superman Lover," thus magnifying the mythology that had surrounded Watson. Born in Texas, he spent his youth awash in the influences of T-Bone Walker, Clarence "Gatemouth" Brown, and Lightnin' Hopkins. A student of both piano and guitar, he moved with his father to Los Angeles and at the young age of thirteen joined the Mellotones on piano. After a year, Watson switched to guitar and formed his own band, where he developed his spectacular stage presence. Sharing the stage with Guitar Slim on occasion, he would hang from the club ceiling, play guitar with his teeth, jump from the stage onto patrons' tables, and together they would jump on each other's shoulders and walk out into the audience—trading solos. Watson finally scored a hit in 1955 when he label-hopped to Modern and released "Those Lonely Nights" and "Three Hours Past Midnight," showing vocally and musically he was a superb blues artist. Proving himself a versatile player, Watson moved from R&B of the fifties to blues and soul of the sixties, reinventing himself once again with funk and disco into the eighties. While Watson was lost in a sea of drugs and financial problems in the late eighties, he returned in the nineties to the hard funk and R&B that made him famous, collecting a Pioneer Award from the Rhythm and Blues Foundation along the way. So while some artists choose to end it with a bullet to the head, or die on the toilet singing "Unchained Melody," Watson died doing what he did best—laying the funk down. Watson is currently resting in a well-appointed mausoleum crypt at Forest Lawn Memorial Park in Glendale, California, in the Great Mausoleum upstairs in the Sanctuary of Enduring Honor, fourth crypt from the floor (#14247) on the left.

JUNIOR WELLS
December 9, 1934—January 15, 1998
CAUSE OF DEATH Lymphatic Cancer

When Junior Wells blew into one of his trademark Lee Oskar harmonicas, one heard a blues harp style that was based on first-hand knowledge of the legends Little Walter, Big Walter Horton, and Sonny Boy Williamson I and II. Born in Memphis where he learned to play harmonica from Junior Parker, Wells was raised in Arkansas before moving to Chicago in 1945. As the story goes, Walker had his eye on a harmonica costing two dollars in a pawn shop in Chicago. Short fifty cents, Wells put down all his money and grabbed the harp and ran out of the shop. Caught by the police, Wells went before a judge, pleading, "I just had to have it!" When asked to play, the judge was so impressed he paid the fifty cents to the pawn shop owner and dismissed the case. At the age of eighteen, Wells joined the Muddy Waters band and recorded his first solo efforts "Hoodoo Man Blues," "Cut That Out," and the instrumental "Junior's Wail." After a stint with Waters, Wells became a storied partner with Buddy Guy and together the two friends recorded a number of albums over their thirty-year on-again, off-again partnership. Even into the 1990s, Wells's schedule never let up. He recorded an acoustic album of blues that was nominated for a Grammy and won the Handy Award for Best Traditional Blues. In 1997, Wells performed live on the Grammy telecast and was a performer in the 1998 film *Blues Brothers 2000*. Wells had just completed tracks for the album *Paint It Blue: Songs of the Rolling Stones* when he was diagnosed with cancer (oddly enough, both Luther Allison and Johnny Copeland also died after recording for the same album). When Wells died four months later, a cortege of six hundred friends and family made their way to Oak Woods Cemetery in Chicago, Illinois, where he is buried just off Magnolia Drive.

MARY WELLS
May 13, 1943—July 26, 1992
CAUSE OF DEATH Cancer of the Larynx

Auditioning as a songwriter for Berry Gordy, Mary Wells was instead signed as a performer, becoming the first female star of Gordy's Motown label and a vital ingredient of the famous Motown sound. Scoring her first hit in 1961 with the self-penned "Bye Bye Baby," Wells charted her first number one hit song "My Guy" three years later. A

favorite singer of the Beatles, Wells went on to tour with the Fab Four in England and came back with a number of songs that she recorded as *Love Songs to the Beatles.* Along the way she scored ten Top 40 singles and two hit records as duets with Marvin Gaye. Diagnosed with cancer of the larynx in 1990, she was unable to sing and retired from the business. Wells's ashes are interred at Forest Lawn Memorial Park in Glendale, California, in the Freedom Mausoleum. As you enter the Columbarium of Patriots, look right four spaces from the floor for her small niche.

KEITH WHITLEY
July 1, 1955—May 9, 1989
CAUSE OF DEATH Alcohol Poisoning

Keith Whitley's immense musical talent manifested itself early in life when at the age of nine he made his radio debut singing a Hank Williams song. Developing quickly, by his early teens he was singing bluegrass/gospel harmonies with longtime friend Ricky Skaggs in Ralph Stanley's legendary Clinch Mountain Boys. By the age of twenty he was a headliner on the bluegrass tour circuit. As driven as Keith was for a successful music career, he was also equally fearful of failure. "Every time I'd get close to something happening, I'd get drunk," Keith told *Music City News.* Consequently he was well known for seeking solace and comfort in a bottle. After a three-year run as the lead singer of J. D. Crowe's band the New South, Whitley's first full-length solo album, *A Hard Act to Follow,* was only marginally successful. His follow-up album in 1986 yielded a minor hit but was considered by most as a lightweight, sultry ballad-style of country. With the two releases failing to capture the quintessential Whitley at his best, he finally seized the reins of musical control (scrapping an album he had already completed) and teamed up with producer Garth Fundis. The subsequent album, *Don't Close Your Eyes,* yielded the elusive number one hit. He also seized control of his personal life by renouncing alcohol (or so it seemed) and marrying the famed singer Lorrie Morgan. The following year Whitley produced two more hits, a sold-out concert tour, and a son, Jesse. In March of 1989, Keith was working on his next album, the session at which he recorded "I've Done Everything Hank Did but Die." Her career just taking off, Lorrie boarded a plane for a concert in Alaska. The next day she got the news—Keith was found dead in their home. He died at age thirty-two with a blood

alcohol level of 0.477 (a lethal level is 0.30) and a trace amount of Valium and cocaine in what appeared to be an isolated bender. As you drive into Spring Hill Cemetery in Nashville, Tennessee, park at the intersection of Meadow Ridge, Laurel Hill, and Crestview. Walk into the Crestview section (it's the section with a pool in the center) and between the road and the pool, look for the Whitley/Morgan upright, dual monument.

BOB WILLS
March 6, 1905—March 13, 1975
CAUSE OF DEATH Pneumonia

Influenced by a diverse combination of folk, country fiddle, blues, and ragtime, Bob Wills was the acknowledged father of western swing music. Dressed onstage in a white suit, Stetson hat, and custom-made cowboy boots, the King of Western Swing (although Wills preferred to call it "Texas fiddle music") would lead his band the Texas Playboys through a blazing set that might include one of his several hundred titles, such as "San Antonio Rose," "Worried Mind," or "Lone Star Rag." Born the first of ten children, Wills's father was a skilled fiddle player who taught his son mandolin at age five. By age ten, Wills switched to fiddle and accompanied his father at local dances. While still in his teens, Wills was one of the more popular musicians on the barn dance and church social circuit. Moving to Amarillo, Wills began his first radio broadcast, and with the money from odd jobs and music he saved enough to purchase his own fiddle, along with a Model T Ford to travel to music dates. Recording for the first time in 1929 with guitarist Herman Arnspiger (but never released), the duo became a quartet, eventually becoming the Light Crust Doughboys, named for their sponsor, Light Crust dough. After a feud over the band's name, Wills went on to form the Playboys (later becoming the Texas Playboys). Named for their sponsor, Play Boy dough, Bob Wills and the Texas Playboys were just one of many bands categorized under the "western" label touring the Southwest. But somewhere along the way Wills became the acknowledged leader. Not through any musical revolution, mind you, but rather because of Wills's showmanship, musicianship (he employed as many as twenty-four musicians on his bandstand), and the need to put on a good dance show for the fans. Though World War II proved to be a bit of an inconvenience to Wills and the band, they nonetheless managed to appear in eight B-movie westerns, make the U.S. pop and country charts with "New San Antonio Rose" and "You're from Texas," get married for the sixth (and final) time, and lose his shirt financially after several bad investments. And through it all, Wills still managed to write, arrange, and record new material and manage several other bands with his brothers (who were at one time Texas Playboys themselves). Selling off his dancehall in the late fifties, Wills sold the rights to the band after a second heart attack in 1964. And while he would occasionally sit in with the band, he soon realized his name was a big

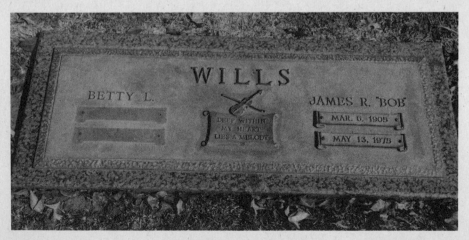

enough draw on its own. So it wasn't unusual to find Wills with just a singer at a local dance-hall or tavern on a Saturday night in the mid sixties. Unfortunately, Wills's lifestyle of heavy drinking and generally declining health caught up with him in the early 1970s. After several heart attacks and strokes, he was confined to a wheelchair and in the fall of 1973, just hours after a recording session with several members of the Light Crust Doughboys and the Texas Playboys in attendance, Wills suffered a debilitating stroke that left him in a coma the remaining eighteen months of his life. Today, Wills lies beneath a simple marker at Memorial Park Cemetery in Tulsa, Oklahoma. As you enter the cemetery, follow the yellow line, drive across the bridge, and follow the road to the right of the chapel. Continue right around Section 15 and take the first road on the left. Park at the sidewalk at the sign SECTION 15—GARDEN OF THE CHRISTUS. Take the sidewalk into the section and walk to the left to the grave marker of Marie M. Hill, and Bob Wills's marker is just over Hill's marker looking toward the center of the section. Established by the Wills family in the early 1980s, The Bob Wills Museum in Turkey, Texas, pays tribute to the legend of western swing with a museum packed full with photos, fiddles, stage outfits, and awards from his days with the Light Crust Doughboys through his nights on the road and all the records and films in between.

RICKY WILSON
March 19, 1953—October 12, 1985
CAUSE OF DEATH AIDS-related Cancer

With their bouffant coifs, thrift store fashions, and dance-infected, retrofitted sound, the B-52's rocked the house in the early eighties by capturing the attention of the "so what?" generation. Founded by Ricky Wilson and his fellow killer B's, they appropriated everything that was tragically unhip and whipped up (via hook-laden pop songs) an ultra-cool, totally fab pop confection. Born and raised in the small university town of Athens, Georgia, upon graduating from high school in 1971, Wilson attended the University of Georgia in Athens. Under the influence of potent tropical drinks at one of the many student bars that surround the university, the B-52's were formed. Named for the tall, beehive hair style of Kate Pierson and Cindy Wilson, the B-52's debut was on Valentine's Day In 1977. Originally performing with pretaped guitar and drum parts (Fred Schneider, Keith Strickland, and Kate had virtually no performing experience), the band became a bigger hit locally when the plug was pulled on the tape player and the band was

actually forced to play their own instruments. The gleeful party music of the B-52's—stripped-down, eclectic pop/funk topped with chirpy lyrics and sixties trivia—garnered a huge following in Georgia. Their initial release, *The B-52's*, sold two thousand copies around Athens. When Chris Blackwell (of Island Records) heard the self-produced record, he signed them to his label, thus securing radio airplay and sales of 500,000. The first two singles from the album, "Rock Lobster" and "Private Idaho," combined

Ricky's Dick Dale–esque guitar lines with Fred's frontman goofing to make music that was mindless fun. In short, if you couldn't dance to the B-52's, then you couldn't dance. After their first national gig at Max's Kansas City, the often cynical New York City crowd found it hip to be square. Armed with go-go boots, miniskirts, and lots of neon colors, the B-52's introduced a whole new way to party—including demonstrations of such dance steps as the Shy Tuna and the Camel. Unfortunately, the party had to end when, during the recording of *Whammy*, Ricky was diagnosed with AIDS. Two short years later, he died of AIDS-

related cancer in New York City at Memorial Sloane-Kettering Hospital at the age of thirty-two. The memorial service was held five days later at the First Assembly Church of God in Athens, with burial at the historic Oconee Hills Cemetery. As you take I-78 east from Atlanta into Athens, the interstate turns into Broad Street. Enter the cemetery across from University Stadium, and drive toward the well house to take the first right, then the first left, and stay right through the curve on the road over the bridge. Drive to the gate in the back and turn right at the road nearest the gate (Section G). Follow the road around and look to the left for the aboveground Westervelt stone marker. Turn left at the road preceding the marker and look for the only pyramid-shaped stone with a bench nearby. Four years after Ricky's death, the B-52's returned to the studio to record their most successful album, *Cosmic Thing*. In 1996, the Georgia Music Hall of Fame in Macon, Georgia, opened its doors, featuring a full display case of B-52's memorabilia.

TAMMY WYNETTE
May 5, 1942—April 6, 1998
CAUSE OF DEATH Heart Failure

With a robust voice seemingly on the verge of tears, Tammy Wynette sang about the classic themes of lost love, loneliness, and divorce so convincingly that she earned the title the Heroine of Heartbreak. Also known as the First Lady of Country Music, Wynette's personal life and mysterious death have often overshadowed her contributions to country music. Born Virginia Wynette Pugh (she lifted the stage name "Tammy" from old Debbie Reynolds and Sandra Dee movies), Wynette was born into a farming family with no plumbing or electricity in rural Mississippi. Married at age seventeen (still with no plumbing or electricity) with two children shortly thereafter, Wynette enrolled in beauty school, singing gospel on the weekends in church. With dreams of becoming a singer, she divorced husband number one (she was married five times) and moved to Birmingham, working as a waitress and singer in various nameless bar bands. Moving to Nashville in 1966, she was signed to Epic by Billy Sherrill, who proved to be the perfect musical partner and mentor for Wynette. She recorded her first hit single, "Apartment No. 9," in 1966 and within four years recorded some of her most classic recordings: "Your Good Girl's Gonna Go Bad," "I Don't Wanna Play House," "D-I-V-O-R-C-E," and "Stand by Your Man." During her twenty-four-year association with Sherrill, Wynette ultimately walked away with twenty number one hit records, the Country Music Association's Female Vocalist of the Year Awards (1968 to 1970), two Grammy Awards, released more than forty albums, and sold more than twenty-five million albums. Though considered one of country music's great success stories, Wynette's personal life threatened to undermine her credibility. Following a stormy, tabloid-ridden marriage to singer George Jones, she was abducted in 1978 by a masked man from the parking lot of a Nashville shopping center. Driven away, beaten, and released by her abductor, the crime was never solved. Wynette also battled a series of health issues during her last fifteen years, a bankruptcy at the height of her popularity, and several break-ins at her home. With a fifth (and final) marriage to her manager George Richey in 1988, her life seemed to settle down during the 1990s. Voted a TNN/*Music City News* Living Legend Award in 1991, she continued to perform and record, releasing the critically acclaimed *Honky-Tonk Angels* (with Dolly Parton and Loretta Lynn) in 1993. At the age of fifty-five, Wynette was found dead by her husband on the couch of their Nashville home. Buried at Woodlawn Cemetery in Nashville, Tennessee, in the Cross mausoleum (on the third floor, Crypt 274-275 B), Wynette was unable to rest in peace for very long. Exhumed shorty after her death, she was the subject of a lawsuit brought on by her daugh-

ters naming Richey, her doctors, and her pharmacy. The suit, which was settled out of court, alleged that those named in the lawsuit "improperly and inappropriately maintained her narcotic addiction" and "failed to see that she would receive necessary medical treatment." Returned to her final resting place, Wynette was inducted into the Country Music Hall of Fame later that year.

JIMMY YANCEY
February 20, 1898—September 17, 1951
CAUSE OF DEATH Diabetic Stroke

Gifted with a light, simple touch, Jimmy Yancey was one of the most dynamic of the early blues/jazz pianists and a leading figure in the development of boogie-woogie. Self-taught at an early age, Yancey began as a song and dance man in vaudeville before concentrating on the piano. By age seventeen he was in high demand at rent parties and after-hours nightclubs. Despite a successful tour of Europe and his obvious talent as a pioneer of the boogie-woogie piano style, Yancey was overshadowed by his contemporaries Meade "Lux"

Lewis and Albert Ammons. Thus Yancey left the music scene in 1925 to become a full-time groundskeeper for the Chicago White Sox baseball team. It wasn't until the late 1930s that Yancey began playing part-time in small clubs, which led to his first recording dates in 1939. Occasionally backed by his wife, Estella "Mama" Yancey, he recorded for the Atlantic and Victor labels and made an appearence at Carnegie Hall in 1948. With diabetes slowly affecting his health, he died of a diabetic stroke in 1951 and was

buried on the South Side of Chicago at Lincoln Cemetery. As you drive through the gates of the cemetery, stay to the left and take the road to the first intersection past the office and park. Yancey's marker is on the right at the intersection. In 1986, Jimmy Yancey was inducted into the Rock and Roll Hall of Fame as an early influence.

FARON YOUNG
February 25, 1932—December 10, 1996
CAUSE OF DEATH Suicide

Originally highly imitative of Hank Williams, Faron Young developed into a talented country artist who never felt he received the proper recognition from fans or the Nashville music industry elite. Born in Shreveport, Louisiana, Young formed his first band in high school and quickly dropped out of college to eventually become a member of the Louisiana Hayride show. Thus began the long road to Nashville via a string of one-night stands in nightclubs and honky-tonks all across the southern states. Complete with nasal whine vocals and similar mannerisms, Young lifted a good portion of Williams's act as a featured vocalist for Webb Pierce before signing with Capitol Records as a solo artist. In 1953, Young and his band moved to Nashville, where at the age of twenty Young became a member of the Grand Ole Opry. After a brief military service interruption, Young returned to Nashville and immediately scored his first country hit, "Live Fast, Love Hard, Die Young." A gifted songwriter, Young also had a talent for picking the very best songs by young, hungry songwriters, thus jump-starting the careers of Don Gibson, Kris Kristofferson, and Willie Nelson (with whom he had the number one hit "Hello Walls"). As Young's popularity rose, he began filming a series of B-movie westerns, which earned him the nickname the Young Sheriff. After quitting the Opry in 1965, Young's popularity soared with tours and chart hits in the U.K., France, and Germany. And though he continued to chart successfully into the 1970s, Young's abusive behavior and penchant for lifting material from other acts did not endear him to his fellow performers. Once stating "I'm not an alcoholic, I'm a drunk," it was not uncommon to hear about Young discharging his gun in a crowded Nashville bar. With few bookings during the 1980s, Young's career was slowing down when he got the news in 1990 that he was suffering from emphysema. Six years later, semiretired and recuperating from prostate surgery, Young shot himself in the head in a fit of depression over his health. Discovered by band member Ray Emmett, Young died the following day. Per his wishes, Young was cremated and his ashes scattered in the rose garden at Johnny Cash's Nashville home. Regardless of the slight he felt from the country music industry, Young was elected to the Country Music Hall of Fame in 2000.

Index by Name

Aaliyah, 276
AC/DC, 222–23
Ace, Johnny, 146, 276
Ackerman, David "Stringbean," 83
Ackerman, Will, 324
Acland, Chris, 49
Actress, 182
Acuff, Roy, 4–5, 42, 43, 173, 186, 260, 262, 377
Adam Ant, 330
Adderley, Cannonball, 68, 277, 349
Adderley, Nat, 277
Aerosmith, 227
Agents of Misfortune, 296
Airey, Don, 213
Air Supply, 330
Akers, Garfield, 131
Alexander, Alger "Texas," 318, 328
Alexander, James, 209
Ali, Rashied, 57
Allen, Paul, 106
Allin, G. G., 391
Allison, Jerry, 110, 112
Allison, Luther, 278, 394
Allman, Duane, 6–9, 141
Allman, Gregg, 6–9
Allman Brothers Band, 6–9, 164, 206, 341
Allman Joys, 6
All Stars, 12, 392
Allsup, Tommy, 111, 124
Almanac Singers, 104
Almeida, Laurindo, 277–78
Alpert, Herb, 34, 36, 381
Alphatones, 343
Ammons, Albert, 388, 399
Anderson, Cat, 76
Anderson, Orlando, 226
Andrew, Sam, 139
Andrews Sisters, 278–79, 298
Anglin, Jack, 53
Animals, 106, 114, 265, 366
Anka, Paul, 110, 321
Archies, 306
Arden, Sharon, 213
Ardoin, Amade, 40
Arkestra, 362
Arlen, Harold, 94, 361
Armstrong, Louis, 10–13, 26, 37, 40, 54, 75, 76, 77, 78, 95, 97, 101, 108, 119, 126, 127, 143, 178, 184–85, 188, 202, 270,

283, 300, 314, 323, 324, 326, 347, 351, 360, 364, 382
Army Air Force Band, 171
Arnold, Eddy, 45, 279
Arnold, Kokomo, 286
Arnspiger, Herman, 396
Artistry in Rhythm, 335
Asch, Moe, 105
Asher, Tony, 19
Ashford and Simpson, 90
Astaire, Fred, 93, 94
Atkins, C. B., 242–43
Atkins, Chet, 49, 124, 211, 279
Atkins, Cholly, 237
Atlanta Rhythm Section, 390
Austin, Mary, 168, 169
Autry, Gene, 14–15, 216, 218, 220, 294, 369
Avcock, Andrew, 213
A Way of Life, 32
Axl Rose and Slash, 141
Axton, Hoyt, 279–80, 338
Aykroyd, Dan, 284, 360
Aznavour, Charles, 356

B-52, 6, 397–98
Bacall, Lauren, 230
Back Street Crawler, 337
Bad Company, 337
Badfinger, 280, 350
Baez, Joan, 105, 322, 351, 353
Bailes, Johnny, 378
Bailey, Bill, 280
Bailey, Mildred, 64
Bailey, Pearl, 12, 280–81, 314
Baker, Chet, 281
Baker, Ginger, 353
Baker, Josephine, 281–82, 286
Baker, Shorty, 76
Ballard, Florence, 282
Band, The, 265, 282–83, 294
Band of Gypsies, 107
Band of Joy, 32
Bar-Kays, 157, 207, 209
Barnes, Paul, 185
Barrett, Carlton, 61, 161
Bartók, Bela, 100
Barton, Ann, 244
Basie, Count, 16–17, 54, 76, 78, 108, 192, 193, 270, 271, 375, 381, 388
B-Bar-B Riders, 216
Beach Boys, 18–21, 159, 186, 199, 284, 338

Predoehl, Eric, 30
Presley, Elvis, 5, 23, 59, 66, 67, 110, 180,
    186, 190, 198–201, 228, 246, 279, 308,
    318, 351, 355, 363, 367, 373, 380, 384,
    389
Pretenders, 326–27, 391
Price, Ray, 346
Prima, Louis, 361, 370
Primes, 236
Prince, 69
Prince, Wesley, 54
Progressive Jazz Band, 335
Prudhomme, Willis, 333
Pryor, Arthur, 378
Pryor, Jimmy, 142
Puente, Tito, 361–62
Pure Prairie League, 370
Pyle, Artimus, 9, 154, 156

Quarrymen, 22
Queen, 168–69
Quicksilver Messenger Service, 302, 322
Quiet Riot, 212
Quintanilla, Abraham, 372

Rabbitt, Eddie, 363
Rachell, James "Yank," 363–64
Rainey, Ma, 118, 126, 232, 364, 384
Rain Flower, 106
Raitt, Bonnie, 115, 166
Ramone, Phil, 35
Ramones, 204–5, 385
Ramsey, Fred, 127
Rants, 164
Rapp, Danny, 49
RatDog, 103
Rathbone, Basil, 84
Rat Pack, 230–31
Ray, Johnnie, 364–65, 389
Razzle, 53, 365
Redding, Noel, 106, 107
Redding, Otis, 6, 9, 58, 60, 157, 206–8, 209,
    318, 331
Red Hot Chili Peppers, 141, 375
Red Hot Louisiana Band, 41
Red Hot Peppers, 178
Redman, Don, 324
Red Norvo Trio, 347
Reed, Jerry, 279
Reed, Jimmy, 103, 114, 115, 365–66
Reed, Lou, 141, 370
Reeves, Jim, 157, 210–11, 279, 294, 346
Reiner, Fritz, 28
Reinhardt, Django, 348
Relf, Keith, 366–67
REM, 297
Reno, Johnny, 244

Reno, Mike, 376
Rhoads, Randy, 157, 212–13
Rhythm Boys, 64, 344
Rich, Buddy, 73, 214–15, 235, 332, 354
Rich, Charlie, 367
Richard Carpenter Trio, 34
Richards, Keith, 115, 132–33, 141, 190, 241,
    315, 340
Richardson, J. P. "Big Bopper," 110, 111, 112,
    124, 157
Richey, George, 399
Riddle, Nelson, 229, 294, 367–68
Riddle, Paul, 164, 165
Riders, C. C., 194
Ridley, Greg, 343
Rigby, Eleanor, 25
Rinker, Al, 64
Riperton, Minnie, 20, 215, 368
Ritter, Tex, 216–17, 335
Rizzo, Jilly, 229
Roach, Max, 76, 97, 189, 310, 324, 348
Roadmasters, 327
Robbins, Marty, 5, 217, 218–19, 358
Robert Cray Band, 284
Robertson, Robbie, 283
Robeson, Paul, 286
Robins, 30, 304
Robinson, Bobby, 120, 121
Robinson, Fabor, 210
Robinson, Smokey, 90, 237, 238
Rocky Mountaineers, 368
Rodgers, Carrie, 387
Rodgers, Jimmie, 82, 220–21, 252, 253, 254,
    264, 386
Rodgers, Nile, 330
Rodgers, Paul, 337
Rodgers, Richard, 92, 95
Rodzinski, Arthur, 28
Rogers, Ginger, 93, 94
Rogers, Roy, 294, 368–69
Rogers, Will, 14
Rolling Stones, 50, 70, 71, 117, 128, 132–33,
    141, 186, 207, 258, 269, 286, 295, 322,
    327, 333, 337, 340, 343, 366
Rollins, Sonny, 57, 68, 348
Ronettes, 350
Ronson, Mick, 369–70
Ronstadt, Linda, 279, 368
Roosters, 343
Rose, Axl, 141
Rose, David, 87
Rose, Fred, 260–61
Rose, Tim, 32
Rosolino, Frank, 49
Ross, Diana, 237, 282
Rossington, Gary, 154, 156
Rotary Connection, 368

Index by Cemetery

Alabama Eddie Kendricks, Elmwood Cemetery, Birmingham; Sun Ra, Elmwood Cemetery, Birmingham; Hank Williams, Oakwood Cemetery Annex, Montgomery.

Arizona Waylon Jennings, Mesa City Cemetery, Mesa; Frankie Carle, Mountain View Cemetery, Mesa.

Arkansas Albert King, Paradise Grove Cemetery, Edmondson; Frank Frost, Magnolia Cemetery, Helena; Robert Nighthawk, Magnolia Cemetery Helena.

Australia Bon Scott, Fremantle Cemetery, Fremantle.

California Roy Rogers, Sunset Hills Memorial Gardens, Apple Valley; Sonny Bono, Desert Memorial Park, Cathedral City; John Phillips, Desert Memorial Park, Cathedral City; Frank Sinatra, Desert Memorial Park, Cathedral City; Jimmy Van Heusen, Desert Memorial Park, Cathedral City; Louis Charles "L.C." Robinson, Cypress Lawn Memorial Park, Colma; Bill Graham, Eternal Home Cemetery, Colma; Jack Benny, Hillside Memorial Park, Culver City; Michael Bloomfield, Hillside Memorial Park, Culver City; Percy Faith, Hillside Memorial Park, Culver City; Al Jolson, Hillside Memorial Park, Culver City; Sam Lerner, Hillside Memorial Park, Culver City; Allan Sherman, Hillside Memorial Park, Culver City; Dinah Shore, Hillside Memorial Park, Culver City; Darby Cras,h Holy Cross Cemetery, Culver City; Bing Crosby, Holy Cross Cemetery, Culver City; Spike Jones, Holy Cross Cemetery, Culver City; Mario Lanza, Holy Cross Cemetery, Culver City; Kid Ory, Holy Cross Cemetery, Culver City; Lawrence Welk, Holy Cross Cemetery, Culver City; Karen Carpenter, Forest Lawn Memorial Park, Cypress; Eddie Cochran, Forest Lawn Memorial Park, Cypress; Laverne Andrews, Forest Lawn Memorial Park, Glendale; Maxine Andrews, Forest Lawn Memorial Park, Glendale; Dorsey Burnette, Forest Lawn Memorial Park, Glendale; Tommy Burnette , Forest Lawn Memorial Park, Glendale; Nat King Cole, Forest Lawn Memorial Park, Glendale; Russ Columbo, Forest Lawn Memorial Park, Glendale; Sam Cooke, Forest Lawn Memorial Park, Glendale; Sammy Davis Jr., Forest Lawn Memorial Park, Glendale; Terry Kath, Forest Lawn Memorial Park, Glendale; Jeanette MacDonald, Forest Lawn Memorial Park, Glendale; Art Tatum, Forest Lawn Memorial Park, Glendale; Ethel Waters, Forest Lawn Memorial Park, Glendale; Johnny "Guitar" Watson, Forest Lawn Memorial Park, Glendale; Mary Wells, Forest Lawn Memorial Park, Glendale; Nelson Eddy, Hollywood Forever, Hollywood; Woody Herman, Hollywood Forever, Hollywood; Art Pepper, Hollywood Forever, Hollywood; Dee Dee Ramone, Hollywood Forever, Hollywood; Nelson Riddle, Hollywood Forever, Hollywood; Chet Baker, Inglewood Park Cemetery, Inglewood; Richard Berry, Inglewood Park Cemetery, Inglewood; Charles Brown, Inglewood Park Cemetery, Inglewood; Pee Wee Crayton, Inglewood Park Cemetery, Inglewood; Ella Fitzgerald, Inglewood Park Cemetery, Inglewood; Lowell Fulson, Inglewood Park Cemetery, Inglewood; Cornell Gunter, Inglewood Park Cemetery, Inglewood, Donald Myrick, Inglewood Park Cemetery, Inglewood; Big Mama Thornton, Inglewood Park Cemetery, Inglewood; Aaron "T-Bone" Walker, Inglewood Park Cemetery, Inglewood; Gram Parsons, Cap Rock, Joshua Tree; Clarence White, Joshua Memorial Park, Lancaster; Jelly Roll Morton, Calvary Cemetery, Los Angeles; Jesse Belvin, Evergreen Cemetery, Los Angeles; Bobby Nunn, Evergreen Cemetery, Los Angeles; Johnny St. Cyr, Evergreen Cemetery, Los Angeles; Gene Autry, Forest Lawn Hollywood Hills, Los Angeles; Bobby Fulle,r Forest Lawn Hollywood Hills, Los Angeles; Melvin Franklin, Forest Lawn Hollywood Hills, Los Angeles; Andy Gibb, Forest Lawn Hollywood Hills, Los Angeles; Horace Heidt, Forest Lawn Hollywood Hills, Los Angeles; Nicolette Larson, Forest Lawn Hollywood Hills, Los Angeles; Liberace, Forest Lawn Hollywood Hills, Los Angeles; Julie London, Forest Lawn Hollywood Hills, Los Angeles; Shelly Manne, Forest Lawn Hollywood Hills, Los Angeles; Donald Mills, Forest Lawn Hollywood Hills, Los Angeles; Harry Mills, Forest Lawn Hollywood Hills, Los Angeles; Rick Nelson, Forest Lawn Hollywood Hills, Los Angeles; Esther Phillips, Forest Lawn Hollywood Hills, Los Angeles; Jeff Porcaro, Forest Lawn Hollywood Hills, Los Angeles; Jack Teagarden, Forest Lawn Hollywood Hills, Los Angeles; Bobby Troup, Forest Lawn Hollywood Hills, Los Angeles; Mama Cass Elliot, Mount Sinai Memorial Park, Los Angeles; Ziggy Elman,

Mount Sinai Memorial Park, Los Angeles; Hillel Slovak, Mount Sinai Memorial Park, Los Angeles; Mel Taylor, Mount Sinai Memorial Park, Los Angeles; Big Joe Turner, Roosevelt Memorial Park, Los Angeles; Eric Dolphy, Rosedale Cemetery, Los Angeles; Art Tatum (former), Rosedale Cemetery, Los Angeles; Les Brown, Westwood Memorial Park, Los Angeles; Stan Kenton, Westwood Memorial Park, Los Angeles; Peggy Lee, Westwood Memorial Park, Los Angeles; Dean Martin, Westwood Memorial Park, Los Angeles; Roy Orbison, Westwood Memorial Park, Los Angeles; Buddy Rich, Westwood Memorial Park, Los Angeles; Minnie Riperton, Westwood Memorial Park, Los Angeles; Mel Torme, Westwood Memorial Park, Los Angeles; Carl Wilson, Westwood Memorial Park, Los Angeles; Frank Zappa, Westwood Memorial Park, Los Angeles; Laurindo Almeida, San Fernando Mission Cemetery, Mission Hills; Ritchie Valens, San Fernando Mission Cemetery, Mission Hills; Roy Brown, Eternal Valley Cemetery, Newhall; Gene Vincent, Eternal Valley Cemetery, Newhall; John Lee Hooke,r Chapel of the Chimes Cemetery, Oakland; Jesse "Lone Cat" Fuller, Evergreen Cemetery, Oakland; Tennessee Ernie Ford, Alta Mesa Memorial Park, Palo Alto; Ron "Pigpen" McKernan, Alta Mesa Memorial Park, Palo Alto; Brent Mydland, Oakmont Memorial Park, Pleasant Hills; Patsy Montana, Riverside National Cemetery, Riverside; Randy Rhoads, Mountain View Cemetery, San Bernardino; Pamala Courson, Fairhaven Memorial Park, Santa Ana; Leo Fender, Fairhaven Memorial Park, Santa Ana; D. Boon, Green Hills Memorial Park, San Pedro; Harry Nilsson, Valley Oaks Memorial Park, Westlake Village; Marty Paich, Valley Oaks Memorial Park, Westlake Village Brad Nowell, Westminster Memorial Park, Westminster; Eric "Easy-E" Wright, Rose Hills Memorial Park, Whittier;

Canada Richard Manual, Avondale Cemetery, Stratford, Ontario; Glenn Gould Mount Plesant Cemetery Toronto

Colorado Ronnie Lane, Masonic Cemetery, Trinidad.

Connecticut Teddy Wilson, Fairview Cemetery, New Britain; Benny Goodman, Long Ridge Cemetery, Stamford.

Denmark Ben Webster, Assistens Cemetery, Copenhagen.

England Nick Drake, Church Cemetery, Arden; Razzle Holy, Trinity Church, Binstead; Brian Jones, Priory Road Cemetery, Cheltenham; Mick Tucker, Chorleywood Cemetery, Chorleywood; John Entwistle, St. Edward's Church, Gloucester; Mick Ronson, Eastern Cemetery Hull; Stu Sutcliffe, Huyton Parish Church Cemetery, Huyton; Brian Epstein, Liverpool Jewish Cemetery, Liverpool; Marc Bolin, Golders Green Crematorium, London; Tubby Hayes, Golders Green Crematorium, London; Ronnie Scott, Golders Green Crematorium, London; Steve Took, Kensal Green Cemetery, London; Sandy Denny, Putney Vale Cemetery, London; Joe Strummer, St. Martin's Church, London; Ian Curtis, Macclesfield Cemetery, Macclesfield; James Scott-Honeyman, St. Peter's Church, Pipe-Cum-Lyde; Keith Relf, Richmond Cemetery, Richmond, Surrey; John Bonham, St. Michael's Church, Rushock; Steve Clark, Wisewood Cemetery, Sheffield; Eleanor Rigby, St. Peter's Parish Church, Woolton.

Florida Jaco Pastorius, Our Lady Queen of Heaven, Fort Lauderdale; Lonesome Dave Peverett, Woodlawn Memorium/Funeral Home, Gotha; Cassie Gaines, Jacksonville Memorial Gardens, Jacksonville; Steve Gaines, Jacksonville Memorial Gardens, Jacksonville; Ronnie VanZant, Jacksonville Memorial Gardens, Jacksonville; Allen Collins, Riverside Memorial Park, Jacksonville; Leon Wilkeson, Riverside Memorial Park, Jacksonville; Cannonball Adderley, Southside Cemetery, Tallahassee; Nat Adderley, Southside Cemetery, Tallahassee; Billy Jones, Garden of Memories Cemetery, Tampa; Perry Como, Riverside Memorial Park, Tequesta.

France Django Reinhardt, Cimetiere de Samois-sur-Seine, Fontainebleau; Sidney Bechet, Cimetiere de Garches, Hauts de Seine; Josephine Baker, Cimetiere de Monaco, Monaco; Serge Gainsbourg, Cimetiere du Montparnasse, Paris; Frederic Chopin, Pere Lachaise, Paris; Stephane Grappelli, Pere Lachaise, Paris; Jim Morrison, Pere Lachaise, Paris; Edith Piaf, Pere Lachaise, Paris;

Georgia Ricky Wilson, Oconee Hills Cemetery, Athens; R.J. Vealey, Crest Lawn Memorial Park Atlanta; Hank Ballard, Greenwood Cemetery, Atlanta; Jimmy Bryant, Pleasant Hill Cemetery, Berlin; Ma Rainey, Porterdale Cemetery, Columbus; Fletcher Henderson, Eastview Cemetery, Cuthbert; Lisa "Left Eye" Lopes, Hillandale Memorial Gardens,

Lithonia; Duane Allman, Rose Hill Cemetery, Macon; Barry Oakley, Rose Hill Cemetery, Macon; Otis Redding, Big O Ranch, Round Oak; Johnny Mercer, Bonaventure Cemetery, Savannah; Blind Willie McTell, Jones Grove Baptist Church, Thomson.

Germany Nico Grunewald, Forest Cemetery, Berlin.

Ireland Rory Gallagher, St. Oliver's Cemetery, Cork; Phil Lynott, St. Fintan's Cemetery, Dublin.

Illinois Gene Krupa, Holy Cross Cemetery, Calumet City; Willie Dixon, Burr Oak Cemetery, Alsip; Otis Spann, Burr Oak Cemetery, Alsip; Dinah Washington, Burr Oak Cemetery, Alsip; Lovee Lee Watson, Burr Oak Cemetery, Alsip; Lillian "Lil" Hardin, Armstrong Lincoln Cemetery, Chicago; Big Bill Broonzy, Lincoln Cemetery, Chicago; Jimmy Reed, Lincoln Cemetery, Chicago; Jimmy Yancey, Lincoln Cemetery, Chicago; Thomas A. Dorsey, Oak Woods Cemetery, Chicago; Little Brother Montgomery, Oak Woods Cemetery, Chicago; Junior Wells, Oak Woods Cemetery, Chicago; Steve Goodman, Home plate at Wrigley Field, Chicago; Little Walter, St. Mary Catholic Cemetery, Evergreen; Howlin' Wolf, Oakridge Cemetery, Hillside; Burl Ives, Mound Cemetery, Hunt City; John Panozzo, Holy Sepulchre Catholic Cemetery, Worth; Doc Clayton, Restvale Cemetery, Worth; Jazz Gillium, Restvale Cemetery, Worth; Earl Zebedee Hooker, Restvale Cemetery, Worth; Walter Horton, Restvale Cemetery, Worth; Kansas Joe McCoy, Restvale Cemetery, Worth; Magic Sam, Restvale Cemetery, Worth; Pine Top Smith, Restvale Cemetery, Worth; Hound Dog Taylor, Restvale Cemetery, Worth; Muddy Waters, Restvale Cemetery, Worth; Valirie Wellington, Restvale Cemetery, Worth;

Indiana Hoagy Carmichael, Rose Hill/White Oak Cemetery, Bloomington; Shannon Hoon, Dayton Cemetery, Dayton; Leroy Carr, Floral Park Cemetery, Indianapolis; J.J. Johnson, Crown Hill Cemetery, Indianapolis; Scrapper Blackwell, New Crown Cemetery, Indianapolis; Wes Montgomery, New Crown Cemetery, Indianapolis; James "Yank" Rachell, New Crown Cemetery, Indianapolis; Cole Porter, Mount Hope Cemetery, Peru.

Iowa Glen Buxton, Evergreen Cemetery, Clarion; Bix Beiderbecke, Oakdale Cemetery, Davenport; Tommy Bolin, Calvary Cemetery, Sioux City; Roger Peterson, Buena Vista Memorial Cemetery, Storm Lake.

Jamaica Peter Tosh, Private Residence, Bluefields; Noel Coward, Firefly Estate, Blue Harbour; Dennis Brown, Kingston's National Heroes Park, Kingston; Bob Marley, Private Residence, Nine Mile.

Kansas Charlie Parker, Lincoln Cemetery, Kansas City.

Kentucky Merle Travis, Ebenezer Mission-ary Baptist Church, Ebenezer; Bill Monroe, Rosine Cemetery, Rosine.

Louisiana John Delafose, St. Matildas Cemetery, Eunice; Beau Jocque, St. Matildas Cemetery, Eunice; Johnny Horton, Hillcrest Memorial Park, Haughton; Rockin' Dopsie, St. Genevieve Catholic Church, Lafeyette; Clifton Chenier, All Saints Cemetery, Loreauville; James Carroll Booker, Providence Memorial Park, Metairie; Mahalia Jackson, Providence Memorial Park, Metairie; Huddie Ledbetter, Shiloh Baptist Church, Mooringsport; Gram Parsons, Garden of Memories Cemetery, New Orleans; Buddy Boldon, Holt Cemetery, New Orleans; Jessie Hill, Holt Cemetery, New Orleans; Al Hirt, Metairie Cemetery, New Orleans; Louis Prima, Metairie Cemetery, New Orleans; Professor Longhair, Mount Olivet Cemetery, New Orleans; Ernie K-Doe, St. Louis Cemetery #2, New Orleans; Bunk Johnson, St. Edward Cemetery, New Iberia; Eddie "Guitar Slim" Jones, Moses Baptist Cemetery, Thibodaux.

Maine Rudy Vallee, St. Hyacinthe Cemetery, Westbrook.

Massachusetts John Belushi, Abel's Hill Cemetery, Martha's Vineyard.

Michigan Junior Walker, Oak Hill Cemetery, Battle Creek; Rob Tyner, Roseland Cemetery, Berkeley; Paul Williams, Lincoln Park Cemetery, Clinton Township; Son House, Mt. Hazel Cemetery, Detroit; Sippy Wallace, Trinity Cemetery, Detroit; David Ruffin, Woodlawn Cemetery, Detroit; Otis "Lightnin' Slim" Hicks, Oak Hill Cemetery, Pontiac; Jackie Wilson, Westlawn Cemetery, Wayne.

Missouri "Boxcar Willie" Martin, Ozarks Memorial Park, Branson; Bennie Moten,

Highland Cemetery, Kansas City; Louis Jordon, Mount Olive Cemetery, St. Louis; Gene Clark, St. Andrew's Cemetery, Tipton.

Mississippi Mississippi John Hurt, St. James Cemetery, Avalon; Lamar Williams, Biloxi National Cemetery, Biloxi; Mississippi Fred McDowell, Hammond Hill Church Cemetery, Como; Big Joe Williams, Private Property, Crawford; Tommy Johnson, Warm Springs Cemetery, Crystal Springs; Elmore James, Newport Baptist Church, Ebenezer; Lonnie Pitchford, Newport Baptist Church, Ebenezer; Willie Foster, New Jeruselum Churchyard Cemetery, Holly Ridge; Charley Patton, New Jeruselum Churchyard Cemetery, Holly Ridge; Asie Payton, New Jeruselum Churchyard Cemetery, Holly Ridge; Junior Kimbrough, Private Cemetery, Holly Springs; Robert Johnson, Payne's Chapel, Itta Bena; Sonny Boy Nelson Powell, Unnamed, Greenville; Robert Johnson, Little Zion M.B. Church, Greenwood; Ishman Bracey, Willow Park Cemetery, Jackson; Carl Cunningham, New Park Cemetery, Lake Horn; Al Jackson, New Park Cemetery, Lake Horn; Phalon Jones, New Park Cemetery, Lake Horn; Jimmie King, New Park Cemetery, Lake Horn; Rufus Thomas, New Park Cemetery, Lake Horn; Bukka White, New Park Cemetery, Lake Horn; James Son Thomas Bogue Memorial Cemetery, Leland; Jimmie Rodgers, Oak Grove Cemetery, Meridian; J.B. Lenoir, Salem MB Church, near Monticello; Robert Johnson, Mt. Zion Church, Morgan City; Gus Cannon, Oak Grove M.B. Church, Nesbit; Mississippi Joe Callicott, Mount Olive C.M.E. Church Cemetery, Pleasant Hill; Sonny Boy Williamson II, Whitfield Church Cemetery, Tutwiler; Memphis Minnie, Morning Star M.B. Church, Walls.

Nevada Harry James, Eden Vale Memorial Park, Las Vegas; Albert Collins, Paradise Memorial Gardens, Las Vegas.

New Hampshire G.G. Allin, St. Rose Cemetery, Littleton.

New Jersey Danny Rapp, St. Mary's Cemetery, Bellmawa; Sarah Vaughan, Glendale Cemetery, Bloomfield; "Big" Joe Lee Williams, Crigler Cemetery, Crawford; Joey Ramone, Mt. Zion Cemetery, Lyndhurst; Beulah Bryant, George Washington Cemetery, Paramus; Clyde McPhatter, George Washington Cemetery, Paramus; Joe Pass, Resurrection Cemetery, Piscataway; Dudley Moore, Hillside Cemetery,

Scotch Plains; Dave Prater, Holy Sepulchre Cemetery, Totowa.

New York George Gershwin, Westchester Hills Cemetery, Ardsley; Ira Gershwin, Westchester Hills Cemetery, Ardsley; Scott Joplin, St. Michael's Cemetery, Astoria; Irving Berlin, Woodlawn Cemetery, Bronx; George M. Cohen, Woodlawn Cemetery, Bronx; Miles Davis, Woodlawn Cemetery, Bronx; Duke Ellington, Woodlawn Cemetery, Bronx; Lionel Hampton, Woodlawn Cemetery, Bronx; W.C. Handy, Woodlawn Cemetery, Bronx; Coleman Hawkins, Woodlawn Cemetery, Bronx; Victor Herbert, Woodlawn Cemetery, Bronx; Fritz Kreisler, Woodlawn Cemetery, Bronx; Joe King Oliver, Woodlawn Cemetery, Bronx; Felix Pappalardi, Woodlawn Cemetery, Bronx; Charles "Cootie" Williams, Woodlawn Cemetery, Bronx; Henry "Red" Allen, St. Raymond's Cemetery, Bronx; Billie Holiday, St. Raymond's Cemetery, Bronx; Frankie Lymon, St. Raymond's Cemetery, Bronx; Eubie Blake, Cypress Hills Cemetery, Brooklyn; Lester Young, Evergreen Cemetery, Brooklyn; Leonard Bernstein, Green Wood Cemetery, Brooklyn; Zutty Singleton, Long Island National Cemetery, Farmington; John Coltrane, Pinelawn Cemetery, Farmington; Count Basie, Pinelawn Cemetery, Farmington; Freddie Green, Pinelawn Cemetery, Farmington; Guy Lombardo, Pinelawn Cemetery, Farmington; Curtis "King Curtis" Ousley, Pinelawn Cemetery, Farmington; Buddy Tate, Pinelawn Cemetery, Farmington; Louis Armstrong, Flushing Cemetery, Flushing; Dizzy Gillespie; Flushing Cemetery, Flushing; Johnny Hodges, Flushing Cemetery, Flushing; Jerry Nolan, Mount St. Mary's Cemetery, Flushing; Johnny Thunders, Mount St. Mary's Cemetery, Flushing; Aaliyah, Ferncliff Cemetery, Hartsdale; Connie Boswell, Ferncliff Cemetery, Hartsdale; Alan Freed, Ferncliff Cemetery, (former) Hartsdale; Judy Garland, Ferncliff Cemetery, Hartsdale; Jerome Kern, Ferncliff Cemetery, Hartsdale; Jason "Jam Master Jay" Mizell, Ferncliff Cemetery, Hartsdale; Thelonious Monk, Ferncliff Cemetery, Hartsdale; Victoria Spivey, Greenfield Cemetery, Hempstead; Harry Chapin, Huntington Rural Cemetery, Huntington; Jimmy Rushing, Maple Grove Cemetery, Kew Gardens; Kate Smith, St. Agnes Cemetery, Lake Placid; Reverend Gary Davis, Rockville Cemetery, Lynbrook; Eric Carr, Cedar Hill Mausoleum, Middlehope; Tito Puente, St. Anthony's Church Cemetery,

Nanuet; Lillian Brown, Frederick Douglas Memorial Park Cemetery, Staten Island; Rosa Henderson, Frederick Douglas Memorial Park Cemetery, Staten Island; Mamie Smith, Frederick Douglas Memorial Park Cemetery, Staten Island; Tommy Dorsey, Kensico Cemetery, Valhalla; Rachmaninoff, Kensico Cemetery, Valhalla; Rick Danko, Woodstock Cemetery, Woodstock.

North Carolina Blind Boy Fuller, Grove Hill Cemetery, Durham.

Ohio Big Mabel Louise Smith, Evergreen Cemetery, Bedford; John Mills Sr., Bellefontaine Cemetery, Bellefontaine; John Mills Jr., Bellefontaine Cemetery, Bellefontaine: Charles "Cow Cow" Davenport, Evergreen Cemetery, Cleveland; Alan Freed, Rock 'n' Roll Hall of Fame, Cleveland; Benjamin "Bull Moose" Jackson, Lincoln Cemetery, Suitland.

Oklahoma Bob Wills, Memorial Park Cemetery, Tulsa.

Oregon Henry Vestine, Oak Hill Cemetery, Eugene; Johnnie Ray, Hopewell Cemetery, Hopewell; John Fahey, Restlawn Memorial Gardens Cemetery, Salem.

Pennsylvania Grover Washington Jr., West Mt. Laurel Cemetery, Bala-Cynwyd; Jim Croce, Haym Salomon Memorial Park, Frazer; Harold Melvin, Ivy Hill Cemetery, Philadelphia; Stanley Turrentine, Allegheny Cemetery, Pittsburgh; Errol Garner, Homewood Cemetery, Pittsburgh; Bessie Smith, Mount Lawn Cemetery, Sharon Hill; Tammi Terrell, Mount Lawn Cemetery, Sharon Hill; Jimmy Dorsey, Annunciation Cemetery, Shenandoah; Pearl Bailey, Rolling Green Memorial Cemetery, West Chester.

South Carolina Tommy Caldwell, Floyd's Greenlawn Cemetery, Spartanburg; Toy Caldwell, Floyd's Greenlawn Cemetery, Spartanburg.

Tennessee Sleepy John Estes, Elam Baptist Church, Durhamville; Conway Twitty, Sumner Memorial Park, Gallatin; Chris Bell, Memory Hills Gardens, Germantown; Jimmie Lunceford, Elmwood Cemetery, Memphis; Lillian Mae Glover (Ma Rainey #2), Elmwood Cemetery, Memphis; "Memphis Slim" Chatman, Galilee Memorial Gardens, Memphis; Elvis Presley, Graceland, Memphis; Furry Lewis, Hollywood Cemetery, Memphis; Bill Black, Forest Hill Cemetery, Memphis; Charlie Rich, Memorial Park, Memphis; Jack Anglin, Forest Lawn Memorial Garden, Goodlettsville; Cowboy Copas, Forest Lawn Memorial Garden, Goodlettsville; Lefty Frizzell, Forest Lawn Memorial Garden, Goodlettsville; Hawkshaw Hawkins, Forest Lawn Memorial Garden, Goodlettsville; Stringbean, Forest Lawn Memorial Garden, Goodlettsville; Douglas Allen Woody, Hermitage Memorial Gardens, Goodlettsville; Ernst Tubb, Hermitage Memorial Gardens, Goodlettsville; Sonny Boy Williamson I, Blair's Chapel C.M.E. Church, Jackson; Carl Perkins, Ridgeview Cemetery, Jackson; Roy Acuff, Spring Hill Cemetery, Madison; Pete Drake, Spring Hill Cemetery, Madison; Dockey Dean, Manual Spring Hill Cemetery, Madison; Hank Snow, Spring Hill Cemetery, Madison; Keith Whitley, Spring Hill Cemetery, Madison; Eddie Rabbitt, Calvary Cemetery, Nashville; Chet Atkins, Harpth Hills Cemetery, Nashville; Otis Blackwell, Woodlawn Cemetery, Nashville; Red Foley, Woodlawn Cemetery, Nashville; Johnny Paycheck, Woodlawn Cemetery, Nashville; Webb Pierce, Woodlawn Cemetery, Nashville; Marty Robbins, Woodlawn Cemetery, Nashville; Red Sovine, Woodlawn Cemetery, Nashville; J.D. Sumner, Woodlawn Cemetery, Nashville; Tammy Wynette, Woodlawn Cemetery, Nashville; Lester Flatt, Oakwood Memorial Park, Sparta.

Texas Doug Sahm, Sunset Memorial Parks, Alamo Heights; Charlie Christian, Gates Hill Cemetery, Bonham; Jim Reeves, Hwy 79, Carthage; Selena, Seaside Memorial Park, Corpus Cristi; Stevie Ray Vaughan, Laurel Land Cemetery, Dallas; Freddie King, Hillcrest Memorial Park, Dallas; Tex Beneke, Greenwood Memorial Park, Fort Worth; Sam 'Lightnin' Hopkins, Forest Park Cemetery, Houston; Johnny Copeland, Paradise Memorial Cemetery, (South) Houston; Buddy Holly, City of Lubbock Cemetery, Lubbock; Ivory Joe Hunter, Magnolia Springs Cemetery, Magnolia Springs; Texas Alexander, Longstreet Cemetery, New Waverly; J.P. Richardson, Forest Lawn, Port Arthur; Tex Ritter, Oak Bluff Memorial Cemetery, Port Neches; Blind Lemon Jefferson, Wortham Cemetery, Wortham.

Virginia Roy Buchanan, Columbia Cemetery, Arlington; Big Boy Crudup, Local Cemetery, Franktown; Patsy Cline, Shenandoah Memorial Park, Winchester.

Washington Jimi Hendrix, Greenwood Cemetery, Renton.

District of Columbia John Philip Sousa, Congressional Cemetery, Washington D.C.

Wisconsin Bunny Berigan, St. Mary's Cemetery, Fox Lake.

Cremated
Stuart Adamson
Stiv Bators
Victor Borge
Jeff Buckley
Tim Buckley III
Cliff Burton
Eva Maria Cassidy
John Cipollina
Michael Clarke
Kurt Cobain
Brian Connolly
Aaron Copland
Papa John Creach
Robbin Crosby
John Denver
Ian Dury
Billy Eckstine
Gil Evans
Tom Evans
Mickey Finn
Tom Fogerty
Jerry Garcia
Danny Gatton
Marvin Gaye
Lowell George
Stan Getz
Maurice Gibb
Dave Guard
Woody Guthrie
Tim Hardin
Bill Haley
Pete Ham
George Harrison
Michael Hedges
Michael Hutchence

Bob "The Bear" Hite
Will "Dub" Jones
Janis Joplin
Paul Kossoff
John Lennon
Curtis Mayfield
Kirsty MacColl
Henry Mancini
Steve Marriott
Freddie Mercury
Ethel Merman
Roger Miller
Herbert Mills
Charlie Mingus
Country Dick Montana
Keith Moon
Marc Moreland
Sterling Morrison
Notorious B.I.G.
Laura Nyro
Phil Ochs
Benjamin Orr
Cozy Powell
Pee Wee Russell
Tupac Shakur
Del Shannon
Fred "Sonic" Smith
Dusty Springfield
Layne Staley
Billy Strayhorn
Sid Vicious
Fats Waller
Alan "Blind Owl" Wilson
Brian Wilson
Faron Young
Frank Zappa

Body Donated to Science
Bobby Darin

Missing at Sea
Randy California
Glenn Miller
Scott Smith

Photo Credits

t – top; m – middle, b – bottom, l – left, r – right

© Janice Dunn, xxi, xxiii

Courtesy of the Motley Crue website, xxii (t,m,b)

© Scott Stanton, 3, 4b, 5, 7, 8t, 8b, 9, 10b, 12, 13t, 13b, 14t, 14b, 15, 17, 20, 29, 31, 34b, 35, 36, 39, 41, 42b, 43t, 43b, 44b, 45m, 47, 49, 51, 54b, 55, 57, 58b, 60b, 61, 62, 63, 65, 67, 69, 70b, 71, 72t, 72b, 73t, 73b, 76, 77, 78b, 79, 81, 83, 84b, 85, 88, 89m, 94t, 95t, 95b, 97, 106, 109, 112t, 113t, 113m, 117, 119, 123, 127, 129, 130t, 133, 135, 137, 138, 140t, 140b, 145, 146, 147, 149, 151, 153, 154, 156t, 156m, 156b, 159t, 160b, 161, 162, 163t, 163m, 163b, 165t, 165b, 167, 171, 175, 176t, 177t, 177m, 177b, 179, 181, 182b, 183l, 183r, 185, 187, 190b, 191t, 191b, 193, 194, 195, 197, 199, 200t, 200b, 203, 206b, 208t, 211, 212, 213, 215, 216b, 217, 219, 220b, 221, 227, 229, 230b, 231, 232b, 233, 235b, 236, 237, 239t, 239m, 239b, 240b, 241, 244b, 245, 247, 249, 251, 252b, 253, 254t, 258, 261, 262, 263, 266t, 267t, 267m, 271, 273, 275, 277b, 278t, 278b, 281, 282, 284b, 285, 287t, 289t, 290t, 291t, 291m, 291b, 292, 293t, 293m, 293b, 294, 295, 298, 300, 304b, 306t, 306b, 307, 311t, 312, 313t, 313b, 314b, 316b, 318t, 318b, 321, 322b, 323, 324, 325t, 325b, 326t, 328t, 328b, 329t, 329b, 334, 336, 337, 338, 339t, 340, 341t, 341b, 342b, 343, 344, 345t, 347t, 347b, 348, 350t, 350b, 351, 352, 353, 354t, 357t, 358t, 361, 362b, 364t, 364b, 366t, 367b, 368, 372t, 373b, 374t, 374b, 375, 378t, 378b, 381t, 381b, 383t, 385t, 387bl, 388b, 390, 391, 393t, 393b, 395t, 395b, 397b, 398t, 399b, 427

© Robin W. Stanton, 202b, 265; © Michael Carroll, 115, 317t, 322t; © Judy Garland Museum, 86t, 86b; © Alan Freed Estate, 80t, 80b; © Suzanne Gratton, 44t; © Freeborn County Historical Museum, 50t, 50b; © S. Dale Stanton, 27, 100, 101, 103b, 112b, 113b, 159b, 173, 176b, 189, 209t, 209m, 209b, 235t, 243, 255b, 256b, 269, 286, 289b, 301, 310t,

315, 335t, 349, 354b, 363b, 367t, 369b, 377, 382, 387br, 389, 396b; © Harlan McCanne, 103t; © Museum of the Gulf Coast, 111, 139, 216t; © Derek Adams, 24, 25t, 25b, 33, 89t, 168b, 287b, 288t, 288b, 309, 311b, 339b, 366b, 370, 371, 380; © J.P. Sullivan Collection, 4t, 30t, 42t, 45t, 45m, 82, 172, 210, 218, 260, 387t, 396t, 398b; © PromoPhoto Archives, 16, 18, 19, 22, 26, 28, 32, 38b, 40t, 46t, 46b, 54t, 58t, 59, 64, 70t, 74t, 75, 78t, 84t, 90, 92, 94b, 96, 98, 104, 105, 108, 110t, 116b, 118, 120, 122, 124, 126, 132, 134, 136, 142, 144, 148, 150, 152, 158, 160t, 164, 166, 168t, 170, 174, 178, 180, 182t, 186, 188, 190t, 192, 196, 198, 204, 214, 220t, 222, 223, 226, 228, 230t, 232t, 234, 240t, 242, 246, 248, 250, 252t, 256t, 259, 264, 268, 270, 272, 277t, 280, 284t, 304t, 308t, 332b, 333, 342t, 345b, 346, 357b, 359, 369t, 376t, 383b, 388t, 392b, 397t; © Julie Blattberg, 74b, 205, 276t; © Michael P. Smith, 40b, 68, 116t, 202t, 290b, 310b; courtesy of the Georgia Music Hall of Fame, 6, 206t, 207, 317b; courtesy of the Los Angeles, California Police Department; 60t, 91; courtesy of the Louis Armstrong Archives at Queens College, 10t, 11, 13m, 184; © Dick Waterman, 66t; © Jonas Crudup, 66b; © Cindy and Jim Funk, 38; © Hugh J. Moore, Jr., 110b; © Bill Beard, 52t, 52b; © Brett Bonner, 121, 330; © Eddie Wood, 130b, 266b, 276b, 279, 283, 302, 316t, 332t, 335b, 358b, 363t, 384, 385b, 399t; © Joe Baird, 130m, 131t, 131m, 131b, 143, 267b; © John Wing, 169; © Denise Fritze, 208b; © Eric Predoehl, 30b; courtesy of the Saint John Coltrane African Orthodox Church, 56b; © W.A. Williams, 244t; courtesy of Barry Bilicki, 34; © Duane Crosson, 112m, 296; © Randy Farrar, 297b; © Roy Morales, 297t; © Sabrina Feldman, 299; © Bert Dros, 319; © Virginia Michaels, 362t; © Liza Benton, 326b; © Merri Cyr, courtesy of the estate of Lonesome Dave Peverett, 355; © Sean Gordon, 371t; © Timothy Murphy, 373; © Edgar A. Naratil, 376b; © Sheila Stanford, 308, 379; © Doug Bandos, 392t; © Paul Kozar, 45b; © Wade Donaldson, 125.

This is the end . . .

LILLIE MAE GLOVER

aka Ma Rainey #2 of Beale Street
Springhill Cemetery
Memphis, Tennessee